SIXTH EDITION

THE INFORMED ARGUMENT

ROBERT P. YAGELSKI
State University of New York at Albany

ROBERT K. MILLER
University of St. Thomas

with AMY J. CROUSE-POWERS
State University of New York at Oneonta

THOMSON
✳ ™
WADSWORTH

Australia • Canada • Mexico • Singapore • Spain • United Kingdom • United States

THOMSON
WADSWORTH

The Informed Argument, Sixth Edition
Yagelski/Miller

Publisher: *Michael Rosenberg*

Acquisitions Editor: *Dickson Musslewhite*

Senior Development Editor: *Michell Phifer*

Editorial Assistants: *Marita Sermolins, Stephen Marsi*

Senior Production Editor: *Sally Cogliano*

Director of Marketing: *Lisa Kimball*

Marketing Manager: *Carrie Brandon*

Senior Print Buyer: *Mary Beth Hennebury*

Compositor: *ATLIS Graphics & Design*

Project Manager: *Hearthside Publishing Services*

Photography Manager: *Sheri Blaney*

Photo Researcher: *Kathleen Olson*

Cover/Text Designer: *Linda Beaupré/Stone House Art*

Printer: *World Color*

For permission to use material from this text or product contact us:
Tel   1-800-730-2214
Fax   1-800-730-2215
Web   www.thomsonrights.com

ISBN: 0-1550-6983-7
(Sixth Edition with Infotrac® College Edition)

Library of Congress Control Number: 2003111204

Cover Image: © 2003 Getty Images

Inside Front Cover Image: Oil on canvas mural from the U.N. Security Council Chamber, by Per Kogh. UN/DPI Photo.

The Informed Argument, sixth edition, represents a significant revision and redesign of *The Informed Argument,* fifth edition. Like the previous editions, this new edition of *The Informed Argument* grows out of the belief that argumentation can be a powerful vehicle for learning. The book is intended to encourage students to read, reflect, and write arguments about serious issues in an informed way. But although our focus in this new edition is squarely on argumentation, our more ambitious goal is to contribute to the development of students as literate citizens in a complex and changing society.

Accordingly, this new edition builds on an idea that was introduced in the fifth edition: that argumentation should be a means of negotiating differences in an effort to address serious problems that we face as citizens, consumers, and members of various communities and cultures. Our hope is that as students inquire into argumentation, develop an understanding of its complexities, and gain the competence to engage effectively in argumentation, they will also acquire a sense of the possibilities for argument to serve social and ethical purposes.

This new edition of *The Informed Argument* incorporates recent scholarly thinking into a traditional framework for argumentation based on the principles of classical rhetoric. Specifically, our presentation of argument reflects a contemporary understanding of the ways in which cultural context shapes arguments. In addition, our approach to argument draws on recent theories of language and discourse to provide students with a sophisticated lens through which to view the arguments they read and develop their written arguments.

KEY FEATURES OF THIS EDITION

A CONTEMPORARY PERSPECTIVE ON TRADITIONAL ARGUMENTATION

Throughout this book, we present argument as an activity that always occurs within specific contexts and is intended to serve a wide range of social and political purposes. Chapter 1, "The Purposes of Argument," will help students appreciate how argumentation occurs in various situations for a variety of ends. Chapter 3, "The Contexts for Argument," explores the different aspects of context, including culture, influence argumentation. Chapter 4, "The Media for Argument," examines how various media shape argumentation and can be powerful tools for argument in their own right. These chapters all include substantial new material. However, we have retained from the previous edition the discussions of traditional elements of argumentation that will be familiar to writing teachers, especially in Chapter 2, "Strategies for Argument." There you will find treatment of various approaches to logic in argument, including the Toulmin model for argumentation, as well as logical fallacies. You will also find expanded discussions of *ethos* and *pathos* in argument. Similarly, Chapter 5, "Constructing Effective Arguments" includes the same straightforward advice to student writers that has characterized the previous editions of *The Informed Argument.* But it also includes an expanded treatment of the writing process as an integral part of inquiry into the topics about which students compose their arguments. As in previous editions, student essays are included here as examples of effective arguments and as models.

RESEARCH AS AN INTEGRAL PART OF ARGUMENT

Like all previous editions, *The Informed Argument,* sixth edition, includes substantial treatment of research — from exploring a topic to finding and documenting sources. We believe that effective argumentation is informed argumentation; consequently, we present research as an integral part of the process of writing an effective argument. In Chapter 6, "Doing Research" and Chapter 7, "Documenting Your Sources," students will find useful advice for becoming informed about their subjects in ways that will enhance their arguments.

DIVERSE READINGS THAT FOCUS ON NEGOTIATING DIFFERENCES

The reading selections in this edition reflect the book's focus on argumentation as a way to negotiate differences and solve problems. The readings are organized around six main themes, each of which is further divided into three sub-themes, or "clusters." This organizing scheme grows out of our view that arguments that follow familiar pro/con patterns tend to oversimplify important issues and thus work against problem solving. Accordingly, we have resisted presenting examples of arguments that fall easily into pro or con categories. Although each cluster of readings can stand on its own, the three clusters in each chapter are closely related. We believe this organizing scheme will help students appreciate the complexity of the issues addressed in each chapter and offer instructors many more options for grouping readings and fitting the selections easily into their courses.

The themes of these six chapters reflect traditional issues — education, the environment, free enterprise, and so on — that are being transformed by recent social, political, cultural, and technological developments. The writers represent a range of interests, professions, perspectives, and cultural backgrounds. Moreover, the majority of readings are recent, reflecting contemporary points of view; they also reflect a diversity of media: there are selections from traditional print publications, such as the *New York Times,* newer publications such as *Z Magazine,* and online journals. Some classic arguments, such as Martin Luther King, Jr.'s "Letter From a Birmingham Jail," have been retained from previous editions, which helps provide historical context for contemporary arguments and also gives students traditional examples of argumentation.

NEW TO THIS EDITION

The new features of *The Informed Argument,* sixth edition, can be grouped into three main categories: (1) expanded discussion of key elements of argumentation, including new sections on context and media; (2) new and re-organized readings selections; and (3) innovative new pedagogical features — all in a completely redesigned text.

SIGNIFICANTLY EXPANDED TREATMENT OF KEY ELEMENTS OF ARGUMENTATION

- A new chapter on context includes discussion of the role of culture in argumentation.

- A new chapter on the media for argument, which includes in-depth treatment of electronic media such as the Internet.

- Expanded discussion of visual rhetoric, including issues of design and layout.

- Expanded discussion of the uses of evidence in argumentation.

- New student essays that provide models of different approaches to argument.

NEW READING SELECTIONS ORGANIZED AROUND SIX MAIN THEMES AND EIGHTEEN SUBTOPICS

- Three "clusters" of readings on related subtopics in each chapter: ownership, education, environments, national identity, free enterprise, and globalization.

- New reading selections that reflect diverse viewpoints and cultural backgrounds.

- Readings from a variety of traditional and online publications.

- "Con-Texts" that include important documents to provide historical and cultural background and reinforce the importance of understanding argument in context.

INNOVATIVE NEW PEDAGOGICAL FEATURES

- Lively introductions to each cluster to provide background for the cluster topic.

- Four kinds of supplementary boxes for each reading selection to help students better understand the argument and to highlight argumentative strategies:
  - *Gloss:* Information on specific people, events, or concepts in the reading. Glosses are linked to the text with asterisk and dagger symbols.
  - *Context:* Background on issues, ideas, events, or persons in the reading.
  - *Sidebar:* Excerpts from texts referred to in the reading.
  - *Complication:* Information that complicates the argument made in the reading.
  - Context, Sidebar, and Complication boxes are color keyed to the text.

- *Questions for Discussion* for each reading that include three main kinds of questions:
  - Questions to help students understand the argument,
  - Questions that focus attention on argumentative strategies and context, and
  - Questions that encourage students to be self-reflective about their views.

- *Negotiating Differences* assignments at the end of each cluster that engage students in argumentation as way to solve a problem related to the cluster topic.

ACKNOWLEDGMENTS

The debts we have incurred in writing this new edition are too great to repay in words. Many people have helped us put this project together and have seen it through to publication. In particular, several terrific people at Heinle have been instrumental in producing this new edition. Most importantly, Dickson Musslewhite provided guidance, leadership, insight, savvy, and good humor throughout; we are deeply grateful to him and appreciate his efforts and friendship. Michell Phifer was an extremely dependable and consistent editor whose knowledge of the editorial process and attention to detail kept the project moving in the face of many unexpected obstacles; we are sincerely thankful for her good humor and seemingly infinite patience. Also, Steve Marsi deserves our gratitude for putting up with endless requests and complaints in handling paperwork, answering questions, and getting materials where they needed to go. Sally Cogliano offered timely guidance as production editor, and Linda Beaupré expertly created the innovative design of this edition. Laura Horowitz and Karyn Morrison were also instrumental in keeping the project on track. The many other Heinle staff members involved in this project were always professional and efficient and ultimately helped make the work go smoothly and successfully. We are very grateful to all of them.

We owe an enormous debt to Amy Crouse-Powers, of the State University of New York at Oneonta, who served as research assistant and sometime writer for this project. As reliable as she is efficient, Amy's excellent work was crucial for this project, which would never have been completed without her. We cannot thank her enough.

Sincere thanks also go to Cheryl Glenn, of Pennsylvania State University, who offered advice and moral support at key moments in the writing of this edition, and Maria Markiewicz, of the State University of New York at Albany, who never failed to get manuscripts in the mail on time, even when they were dropped on her desk at the last minute.

We also wish to thank Kristen Brubaker, Rachel Guetter, and Kristen Montgomery Szala, all of whom contributed essays to this edition and who displayed patience and commitment throughout the process of responding to our comments on their writing. Their hard work and dependability made our work easier, and their essays have made this a better book.

In addition, we are grateful to the reviewers who examined parts of the manuscript for this edition as we developed it: Brenda Brueggemann, Ohio State University; Jim Crosswhite, University of Oregon; John Fleming, Southern New Hampshire University; Julie Foust, Utah State University; Debbie Hawhee, University of Illinois; Andrea Herrmann, University of Arkansas, Little Rock; Elizabeth Johnston, Indiana University of Pennsylvania; Thomas Mitchell, Texas A&M International University; John Orozco, Los Angeles Community College, Mission; Phil Stucky, Harold Washington College; Theresa Thompson, Valdosta State University; and Mark Wiley, California State University, Long Beach. Their careful and thoughtful comments gave us much needed guidance as well as affirmation for the project. We also wish to thank the many instructors and students who have used earlier editions of this book and helped us to understand what to retain and what to revise.

Finally, special thanks must go to Adam and Aaron Yagelski, and especially to Cheryl Hafich Yagelski, who provided space, support, love, and confidence as this book was being completed.

Bob Yagelski
Robert K. Miller

CONTENTS

Part II
WORKING WITH SOURCES

Part III
NEGOTIATING DIFFERENCES

CHAPTER 13 | GLOBALIZATION 602

PART I

AN INTRODUCTION TO ARGUMENT

Argument is a means of discovering truth, negotiating differences, and solving problems. Although argumentation focuses on problems, argument itself is a solution. You routinely engage in argumentation in all aspects of your life. When you ask your teacher to extend the deadline for an assignment or seek admission to a study-abroad program or a graduate school, you are putting yourself in a position that requires effective argumentation. You might also have occasion to argue seriously about political and ethical concerns. Someone you love might be considering an important step such as opening a business, a large corporation might try to bury its chemical waste on property that adjoins your own, or you might suddenly be deprived of a benefit to which you feel entitled. Such situations require you to organize, articulate, and support your beliefs so that others will take them seriously. In doing so, you are engaging in a social interaction about important matters that can deeply affect your life and the lives of others.

One of the most common misconceptions about argument is that it is about winning. Look again at the examples in the preceding paragraph. Each case involves people trying to address a complicated situation and solve a problem satisfactorily. The need to ask a teacher for a deadline extension, for example, might have arisen from a complicated set of circumstances involving, say, an illness or a schedule conflict. Perhaps you caught the flu a few days before the assignment is due and are therefore unable to complete it on time. Consider some of the many other factors that complicate that apparently simple situation. For one thing, the deadline itself results from your teacher's effort to organize the course, anticipate the time it takes for grading, and perhaps accommodate a school holiday that required a class to be canceled. For another thing, you probably have other responsibilities to fulfill — a work schedule, assignments for other classes, maybe meetings for a club you belong to — all of which are also affected by your illness. All these factors complicate the problem created by your illness. In asking for a deadline extension, you are attempting to solve that problem. So you make an argument to justify an extension.

But the matter doesn't end there, because extending your deadline might create problems for your teacher. She might, for instance, have a tight deadline of her own for reading her students' essays. She might also worry about being fair to other students whose requests she denied or to the students who handed their work in on time. So your argument in this case is not just a matter of convincing your teacher that you need an extension. Rather, your argument is an attempt to solve your problem in a way that also takes into account the potential problems your teacher faces. Ideally, a successful argument in this case would mean that both you and your teacher "win." In this sense, you can think of argumentation as an intellectual effort that is intended to solve a problem by drawing people together.

As this hypothetical example suggests, argument requires you to look beyond the surface. When you address a more difficult or controversial issue, argument might also involve moral or ethical choices. Imagine a situation in which you are trying to decide on a course of medical treatment for a family member who is in a coma. You might feel strongly that your relative would not want to remain on artificial life support systems, and you might even have ethical misgivings about such medical treatments. In trying to articulate your position to your family members, who might wish to continue artificial life support, you will probably address several deeply complicated and difficult moral and ethical issues. For instance, you might believe that artificial life support is unethical if it diminishes the quality of life for both the patient and his or her family. You might argue, too, that the costs — financial and emotional — of such life support outweigh the potential benefits. You might even invoke probability, noting that the doctors cannot guarantee a full recovery for your relative. And you would certainly discuss these matters in the context of your love — and the love of your family members — for your relative, perhaps arguing that your love requires you to make a choice that is best for the patient, no matter how difficult it is for the family. Moreover, you would want to listen carefully to what other members of your family have to say and consider what doctors and nurses have said. You could not argue in a vacuum, as if only your opinion matters. It would be irresponsible to try only to prevail in such a case. Rather, you would want to recognize what others think and try to draw people together. You would use argument to build consensus so that your family will be able to live with its decision.

Fortunately, most argumentation that you will be involved in will not address such weighty matters. But if you consider the many different kinds of arguments you may encounter or make in your daily life, you quickly begin to see that argument is not just an important skill that will serve you well as a college student or as an employee. Argument is also an important part of how you live your life with others. It is a central feature of the way our communities, social networks, and institutions function.

Written argumentation in particular, which can take many forms, is a way for you to work out your ideas and positions on an issue. It is also a way to consider carefully the situation in which you are making your argument and addressing the positions and needs of others involved. Constructing an effective written argument requires you to think clearly about an issue or problem without letting your feelings dominate what you say, which can be difficult at times. It encourages careful inquiry that can lead to a deeper understanding of the issue or problem. In addition, it can be tremendously satisfying to succeed in making other people understand what you mean and to engage with them in a genuine effort to address a problem. You might not always convert others to your point of view, but you can earn their respect and perhaps enhance understanding of an important issue on all sides. This, in the end, is what argument is all about: engaging with others to address problems.

This book is intended to help you learn to solve problems through argument. It rests on the conviction that effective argumentation requires an ability to understand differences, for you cannot solve a problem or resolve a conflict that you don't understand. When writing an argument, you must often give consideration to beliefs that might differ from your own, recognizing what makes those beliefs appealing in a given situation. Indeed, the fact that many arguments involve deeply held beliefs is one reason that argumentation can be so challenging. Becoming familiar with diverse points of view will help you write arguments that address the concerns of people who might disagree with you. In the process, you might learn more about your own beliefs. Ideally, such learning not only will enable you to develop your own thinking and be more persuasive in your arguments, but might also enable you to negotiate differences with others and thus solve problems to everyone's advantage.

The situations we have described so far — and the examples we discuss throughout this book — reflect the complexity of the problems and conflicts that we routinely face in a diverse and increasingly technological world. The more informed you are about such issues, the more effectively you can write about them. But remember that controversial subjects are controversial in part because they are so complex and because so much can be said about them — much more than you might realize at first. You do not need to become an expert on a topic before you can write a thoughtful argument about it, but you do need to be able to support the claims you make, and that requires adequately understanding the issues involved.

As you'll see, arguments that are made without adequate support for their claims can be persuasive in many cases, depending on the issues and the audiences involved. But being persuasive might not actually lead to a solution to the problem you are trying to address in an argument. You might, for example, persuade your teacher that you do need that deadline extension, yet she might decide against granting it because it would create too many problems for her. Or you might persuade your brother to support your wish to end life support for another relative. But if your brother is not truly at ease with the position you persuaded him to adopt, your relationship with him could become troubled. This complexity is part of our view that argument is more than persuasion: Argument seeks to clarify thought, not obscure it; argument relies on evidence or widely accepted truths and does not necessarily dictate any particular course of action. The truly effective argument would have well-supported claims that ultimately lead to a satisfactory resolution of the problem at hand. While such a goal may not be realistic in every situation that calls for argumentation, it is the ideal toward which we hope you will strive when you write an informed argument.

WHAT IS AN ARGUMENT?

That question is not as simple as it might seem, and we can begin to answer it by first examining what is *not* an argument. In the first place, a quarrel is not an argument. Typically, when we use the term *argument* in casual conversation, we mean a quarrel or a disagreement. But there are significant differences between a quarrel and the kind of argument addressed in this book. Quarrels rarely involve any genuine effort to engage in a dialogue for the sake of understanding an issue, and very often quarrels have nothing to do with trying to resolve a conflict. If you find yourself arguing with your roommate over which kind of music to play on your stereo, for instance, you are not likely to be engaged in a reasoned attempt to make a decision on the basis of claims or evidence. Nor are you likely to be very concerned about understanding your roommate's reasons for choosing a particular CD. Rather, you probably want to hear a certain kind of music and are interested primarily in getting your way. It is perhaps conceivable that you will try to persuade your roommate to let you have your way rather than simply insisting on your choice of music, and in doing so, you may actually employ some of the strategies for argument discussed in this book. But even so, the point in such a situation is not to present a convincing argument in order to address the conflict; the point is simply to state your demand and oppose your roommate's choice.

This example might seem trite or even silly, but if you look closely at popular discussions in our culture, you will notice that many such discussions are not too different from arguing with a roommate about music. Consider the following exchange, which was taken from an online discussion forum at the *New York Times* Web site. In this case the participants were discussing an editorial written by columnist Bob Herbert in which

Herbert argued that we must address the problem of global warming very soon if we are to avoid disasters caused by the melting of the polar ice sheets:

"The public is wonderfully tolerant. It forgives everything except genius." — Oscar Wilde

Your most "well reasoned post." Incredible!

Recent reports indicate that the planet Mars is warming up. What a coincidence. Is it possible that something outside the atmosphere is warming both Earth and Mars? No, let's not let any contradictory evidence upset our political agenda.

1. How much will the earth warm up in the next century if we do nothing, Bob?
2. We can build atomic power plants for electricity. Are you for that, Bob?
3. Our caves will keep us cool & cut air conditioning costs.
4. Do you want to compare your use of power & energy annually with my usage Bob? Perhaps you can cut back.

Such an exchange amounts to little more than a quarrel, despite the seemingly sophisticated ideas that several participants present. The first post, which quotes Oscar Wilde, a well-known British playwright from the 19th century, can be read as either a compliment or a criticism of Herbert's editorial, but it makes no argument itself. The second post is a thinly veiled insult directed at the writer who posted the Oscar Wilde quote. The third post is characterized by a sarcasm that reflects that participant's disdain for Herbert's argument (and perhaps for Herbert himself). And although the fourth post does present some potentially effective counterarguments to Herbert's position, it too is marked by sarcasm and doesn't lend itself to reasoned debate. In many ways, then, this exchange might be an "argument" in the popular sense of the term, but it is not an argument of the kind discussed in this book. And notice here that what makes a genuine argument is not the nature of the topic being argued about. Obviously, these participants are discussing a serious matter. But to engage in genuine argument requires an effort to address the issue at hand in a substantive way, not just to criticize or oppose another's position.

Given the adversarial nature of so much public debate today, especially with the proliferation of various kinds of radio and television talk shows, electronic discussion forums on the Internet and e-mail lists, it is easy to mistake such quarreling for argument. Often, in popular media, the primary purpose is to entertain — not to inform, address a problem, or resolve a conflict. As a result, people with deep differences and even intractable positions on controversial issues are selected to participate. Nor surprisingly, their discussions rarely move beyond staking out their positions or criticizing one another. Such discussions are not very different from an argument between two roommates or family members about what kind of music to play on the stereo.

Some scholars believe that genuine argument is not a conflict between adversaries but an effort to find truth (see the sidebar). This notion that arguments involve truth can help

ARE ARGUMENTS ADVERSARIAL?

Although arguments often involve people with divergent and even opposing views, they are not inherently adversarial. In fact, British philosopher Ralph Johnson believes that "the adversarial approach is inimical to argumentation" (*Manifest Rationality*, 2000). Johnson believes that what separates genuine argumentation from quarrels, debates, legal argumentation, and even conflict negotiation, such as in a divorce or a worker's compensation case, is the role of truth. He asserts that a genuine argument invokes truth not only as a way to evaluate claims, but also as a standard by which to judge the effectiveness of an argument. In other words, when we consider an argument, we try to determine whether or not it is true.

us distinguish argument from other kinds of discourse in which participants seek to win or persuade without concern for the truth of their claims or positions. Let's return to our earlier example of a student asking a teacher to extend an assignment deadline. In that case the ideal goal was to solve the problem created by the student's illness to the satisfaction of both student and teacher. That goal assumes good intentions on all sides. But the student cared only about getting the extension to solve *his* problem of not being able to meet the original deadline, and he might make claims without concern for their truth value. He might not have taken the teacher's concerns into account, or if he did, it was only for the purpose of getting the extension. By our definition he would be engaged in something other than genuine argumentation, no matter how persuasive he might be. Genuine argumentation should be an ethical endeavor.

This example reveals how difficult it can be to distinguish between argument as a genuine effort to negotiate differences or solve a problem and argument as a way to get what you want. In some ways two such arguments might seem very much the same — with the same kinds of claims and evidence, even the same strategies. You might even say that the distinction is irrelevant because it emphasizes a kind of argument that is unrealistic in our complicated day-to-day lives. But if argument were only about getting your way — about winning — then it would not be an effective tool for living our complicated lives with each other. In fact, it is precisely because our lives are complicated — and because we must live among others with their own complicated needs and opinions — that a view of argument as a way to solve problems and negotiate differences is so important.

WHY LEARN TO WRITE EFFECTIVE ARGUMENTS?

There are at least two important reasons to learn how to write effective arguments:

1. **To be able to engage with others, through language, to solve problems and negotiate differences satisfactorily.** Your daily life presents you with numerous opportunities to engage in argumentation, and the more effectively you can do so, the more successfully you can fulfill your own responsibilities as a member of the communities to which you belong. You might, for example, find yourself writing a letter to the editor of your local newspaper about a controversial construction project that may affect traffic in your neighborhood. Or you might file a petition with your local school board to oppose a property tax increase. Writing such arguments is an important kind of participation in your community. It is part of the means by which we address issues and solve problems together. Given the increasing diversity of our communities and the way in which media such as the Internet have made our world smaller, learning to argue in these ways may be more important than ever. As citizens, we now encounter diversity perhaps more readily than we did in the past, and diversity and change can lead to conflict. Being able to engage in argument as a way to negotiate differences may be a step toward resolving such conflict.

2. **To succeed as a writer in college as well as in other contexts, such as your workplace or community.** This is perhaps a more practical reason to learn to write effective arguments. Indeed, writing various kinds of arguments is one of

the most common tasks you will be assigned in your college courses. To write effective arguments about important issues within an academic discipline, such as history and economics, is to engage in substantive inquiry about those issues and learn about the central ideas of that discipline. When you write an essay for your history course arguing against, say, the decision by the United States to drop atomic bombs on Japan during World War II, you are not only participating in an ongoing debate about a pivotal moment in history, but also learning about that event — and about history more generally — in a sophisticated way. In this sense, writing arguments is an important kind of thinking.

In addition, we must regularly evaluate arguments made by others to make appropriate decisions about an issue or problem. When someone approaches you asking you to sign a petition opposing, say, the building of a prison in your community, you will almost certainly be presented with an argument to justify the petition. Politicians, of course, not only make arguments in favor of the positions they take on specific issues, such as gun control or tax reform, but also make arguments to persuade you to vote for them. Television, radio, print, and Internet advertisements can be considered arguments whose purpose is to persuade you to purchase an item or service. Your ability to understand what argument is and how arguments work will enable you to evaluate the merits of the argument before deciding how you will act.

There is no better way to understand argument than to write arguments. Writing engages you in an issue or topic as no other intellectual activity can. In addition, writing an argument involves important thinking and language skills that can serve you well in other contexts. In working through an argument, you will have to read critically, think carefully and in sophisticated ways about complex issues, and use language effectively to articulate your position. In short, writing effective arguments can make you a better writer, a more careful thinker, and a more informed person.

1

THE PURPOSES OF ARGUMENT

THE PURPOSES

Almost anything can be argued, but not everything *should* be argued. The decision about what to argue and how to make an argument is not just a practical one (What topic should I argue about for the essay due in my English class next week?) but can also be an ethical one (What position should I take in a debate banning smoking from public places? What are the potential consequences of opposing a local ordinance prohibiting pesticides on private lawns?). To make an argument is to engage in a social activity that can have consequences for you and others, and it's part of your task as a writer to consider those consequences as you decide what to argue, how to do so, and even whether to make an argument. To make such a decision, it is helpful to consider *why* we engage in argument.

OF ARGUMENT

We engage in argumentation in all kinds of circumstances. Consider the following situations:

A local school board has been asked by the parents of a first-grade girl to adopt a policy that would allow their daughter to say a prayer before her lunch each day in school. When the girl tried to pray in school, her teacher stopped her. The teacher subsequently explained to the parents that vocal prayer in school is illegal. At the public school board meeting, debate among school board members focuses on the legal problems and expenses the school district could face if the parents of the girl take the case to court. They are sympathetic to the parents but worried about legal complications. In view of these concerns, the board eventually decides, by a 4–1 vote, on a policy that allows the girl to pray before lunch but not in the presence of her classmates. The school board member who voted against the policy expresses concern after the vote that the new policy will not hold up in court and emphasizes the necessity of maintaining the constitutional separation of church and state. After the meeting, he decides that his concerns should be heard by members of the community who did not attend the board meeting, and he writes an article for the monthly school district newsletter explaining his opposition to the new policy.

A young couple has decided to buy a car, but they disagree on which kind of car to purchase. Both are concerned about the environmental impact of their driving, and both wish to keep expenses low. But one partner will use the car primarily for commuting eleven miles to work on city streets and therefore sees fuel efficiency as a primary concern. This partner advocates buying one of the new hybrid cars, which are very small but have high fuel efficiency. The other partner shares the concern for fuel efficiency but sees a need for more space than the hybrid cars offer, primarily to deliver the vegetables that the couple raise for the local farm market. Neither partner feels knowledgeable about the technical details of the hybrid cars or about the potential environmental impact they have compared to conventional cars. After exploring these issues at local car dealers, reading about them on the Internet, and consulting with knowledgeable friends, the couple decides to write a letter to the editor of their local paper in which they discuss their decision to purchase a new hybrid car and advocate the purchase of these cars as a way to address problems of air pollution, global warming, and dependency on foreign oil.

A state legislator delivers a stinging speech after the legislature has voted against the reform of the state's laws regarding criminal penalties for drug offenses. He attacks his colleagues who voted against the reforms, charging that they care more for their political careers than for the lives of people who have been treated unfairly under the state's drug laws. Although those laws were implemented in the 1980s in an effort to combat large-scale drug dealers, the laws are regularly used to imprison individual drug users for relatively minor offenses. As a result, many citizens and legal experts consider the laws too harsh and unfair. A proposal to reform the laws to ensure that they target drug dealers rather than users moved through the legislature but was opposed by the governor, who feared that it would make the state appear soft on drug-related crimes. At the last minute, legislators in the governor's party have mustered enough votes to defeat the reform bill. The legislator knows that his speech will not change the outcome of the vote, but he delivers an angry attack on his colleagues nevertheless, arguing that they have voted in a way that undermines the principles of fairness and justice on which the legal system rests. His speech, which will later be published in the legislature's proceedings, is carried on television.

For several years a union has been trying to organize workers at a large hospital without success, but recent job cuts at the hospital have made unionization more popular among the workers. One of their complaints involves benefits, including the retirement plan, which the union claims is less lucrative for workers than its own plan would be. As the vote on whether to accept the union draws near, the administrator in charge of retirement benefits is asked by her boss to write a memo describing the potentially negative impact on the hospital's retirement plan if the workers vote in favor of the union. The retirement plan administrator believes that the union has not fairly represented the hospital's retirement plan, but she also believes that the union's plan has some advantages. However, if she describes those advantages in her memo, she could help convince some workers to vote in favor of unionization, which the hospital opposes. In her memo, she explains the advantages of the hospital's retirement plan for workers — advantages that would be lost to the workers if they voted for the union. But she also acknowledges some of the advantages of the union's retirement plan, and she argues in her memo that the hospital should consider altering its plan to include some of the features of the union's plan. Doing so, she believes, would serve the workers' interests without compromising the hospital's budget.

As these four examples show, people engage in argument for many reasons, and the complexity of arguments can make it difficult to categorize different kinds of arguments. Moreover, all arguments contain certain essential elements, such as an identifiable position on a subject, specific claims, and supporting evidence, and many arguments address several purposes at once. But to understand argumentation better, we can identify at least four broad purposes for argument:

- To inquire
- To assert
- To dominate
- To negotiate differences

The preceding examples illustrate each of these purposes, which we will examine in this chapter.

ARGUMENTS TO ASSERT

In the first example the school board member who opposed the district's new policy on school prayer saw a need to publicize his view. He wished to assert his position as part of the ongoing discussions about prayer in his district's schools. You can probably imagine many situations in which your primary goal is to assert a position on an issue about which there may be disagreement or controversy:

- In a class discussion about teaching evolution in science classes in public schools
- In a meeting of a student organization that is deciding whether to boycott products in the school's bookstore that are produced in sweatshops

■ In your place of employment as your coworkers decide how to respond to a new overtime policy

In such situations many voices may be heard, and each one asserts a position on the issue. To do so effectively not only can contribute to resolution of an issue, but can also help you gain credibility as a participant in the discussion of the issue.

In some ways, all arguments are arguments to assert. Even advertisements whose primary purpose is to persuade people to purchase a product often assert a position or perspective (see Figure 1-1). Traditionally, argument has been understood as a formal attempt to state a position on an issue (your thesis), offer acceptable reasons for that position, provide evidence in support of those reasons, and anticipate objections. Indeed, to write an effective argument of any kind requires you to make a clear assertion and support it

FIGURE 1-1

Advertising as Arguing to Assert

This advertisement for a climbing rope manufacturer might be seen as an argument to assert a particular point of view about women. It plays off cultural stereotypes about women as passive and presents a different view of women as aggressive and athletic.

adequately. But what counts as "adequate" evidence isn't always obvious, and different readers can bring different assumptions and expectations to an argument. (We'll address the issue of evidence in Chapter 4.) Moreover, in argument writers are usually dealing with probabilities rather than certainties. So part of the challenge in writing an effective argument is managing probability in a way that readers will find acceptable. In other words, we rarely can know something for sure (Will allowing prayer in schools result in legal problems? Will driving hybrid cars reduce global warming?), so we must proceed as best we can by working with what we do know (the Supreme Court has banned school prayer in the past; all cars emit carbon dioxide, which is a greenhouse gas) and then taking probability into account. Learning how to do so is an important component of writing effective arguments.

ARGUMENT TO INQUIRE

In the second example described previously, the letter written by the couple does argue in favor of a position — that consumers should buy fuel-efficient cars — and their argument might be seen as an effort to convince others to do the same. But its primary purpose is to explore the complexities of their decision as well as its environmental and economic implications. In other words, the couple is just as interested in examining some of the complexities of the issue as they are in asserting their position that purchasing a new hybrid car is an environmentally responsible act (see Figures 1-2 and 1-3). You probably engage in similar kinds of arguments. Perhaps the best example is class discussion. In a sociology class, for instance, you might find yourself discussing welfare reform. As a student in the class, you are not considered an expert on welfare reform, nor do your arguments or your classmates' arguments have consequences outside your class (unlike, say, a

FIGURE 1-2

A Prototype Hybrid Car

The couple in the example on page 10 are making an argument as part of an effort to inquire into the consequences of buying such a car. This photo might also be seen as an argument to assert: It portrays a sleek, almost sporty car that seems to suggest not only fuel efficiency but also sexiness and speed.

FIGURE 1-3

FIGURE 1-3

A Page from the Web Site of the Institute for Lifecycle Energy Analysis (ILEA)

In its mission statement, ILEA states that its goal is to "provide United States consumers with the education and tools necessary to make purchasing and lifestyle choices that work toward a sustainable global economy." This Web page can be seen as an argument to inquire: it is part of ILEA's effort to examine the environmental impact of purchasing a hybrid car as compared to a conventional car.

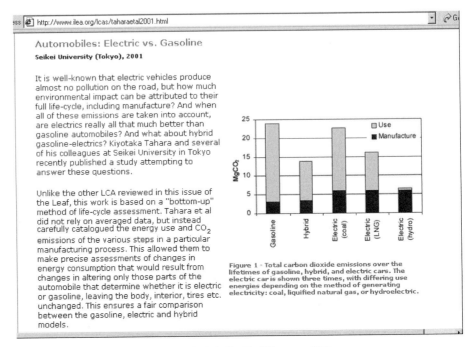

http://www.ilea.org/lcas/taharaetal2001.html

Automobiles: Electric vs. Gasoline
Seikei University (Tokyo), 2001

It is well-known that electric vehicles produce almost no pollution on the road, but how much environmental impact can be attributed to their full life-cycle, including manufacture? And when all of these emissions are taken into account, are electrics really all that much better than gasoline automobiles? And what about hybrid gasoline-electrics? Kiyotaka Tahara and several of his colleagues at Seikei University in Tokyo recently published a study attempting to answer these questions.

Unlike the other LCA reviewed in this issue of the Leaf, this work is based on a "bottom-up" method of life-cycle assessment. Tahara et al did not rely on averaged data, but instead carefully catalogued the energy use and CO_2 emissions of the various steps in a particular manufacturing process. This allowed them to make precise assessments of changes in energy consumption that would result from changes in altering only those parts of the automobile that determine whether it is electric or gasoline, leaving the body, interior, tires etc. unchanged. This ensures a fair comparison between the gasoline, electric and hybrid models.

Figure 1 - Total carbon dioxide emissions over the lifetimes of gasoline, hybrid, and electric cars. The electric car is shown three times, with differing use energies depending on the method of generating electricity: coal, liquified natural gas, or hydroelectric.

SOURCE: ILEA *Leaf*, Institute for Lifecycle Energy Analysis (Seattle, WA), summer 2002. www.ilea.org/lcas/taharaetal2001.html.

social worker's arguments to a family court judge about a specific case). Most important, your arguments in this situation are not necessarily intended to convince your classmates to support or oppose a particular position about welfare reform; rather, in making your arguments and listening to those of your classmates, you are engaged in a collective inquiry into the sociological issues surrounding welfare reform. You are arguing to learn and to understand.

Arguments to inquire imply a special kind of dialogue between writers and readers. Although all arguments to some extent imply a dialogue, in arguments to inquire, the author's goal is to open up an issue for careful inquiry, to convince readers that the issue is worth their attention, and to encourage them to consider the writer's perspective on the issue. Indeed, in such an argument the writer's primary goal might be to persuade readers that a particular kind of problem even exists.

As a college student, you will probably be asked to write arguments to inquire more often than other kinds of arguments. Indeed, much academic writing can be characterized as arguments to inquire. The author will perhaps argue for a position on an issue, but the argument is exploratory and even informative, implicitly inviting readers to join the inquiry into the issue at hand. Consider this excerpt from the opening chapter of *Writing Space*, a book by Jay David Bolter about how new computer technologies are changing the nature of writing. As the following excerpt suggests, Bolter believes that computers are fostering dramatic changes in how and what we write. His position is not universally shared among scholars interested in literacy and technology, however. Bolter knows this, of course. He isn't concerned about convincing other scholars that he's right and they're wrong; rather, he wishes to examine a very complex issue that other scholars want to understand better.

In Victor Hugo's novel *Notre-Dame de Paris, 1482,* the priest remarked "Ceci tuera cela": this book will destroy that building. He meant not only that printing and literacy would undermine the authority of the church but also that "human thought . . . would change its mode of expression, that the principal idea of each generation would no longer write itself with the same material and in the same way, that the book of stone, so solid and durable, would give place to the book made of paper, yet more solid and durable" (p. 199). The medieval cathedral crowded with statues and stained glass was both a symbol of Christian authority and a repository of medieval knowledge (moral knowledge about the world and the human condition). The cathedral was a library to be read by the religious, who walked through its aisles looking up at the scenes of the Bible, the images of saints, allegorical figures of virtue and vice, visions of heaven and hell. . . . Of course, the printed book did not eradicate the encyclopedia in stone; it did not even eradicate the medieval art of writing by hand. People continued to contemplate their religious tradition in cathedrals, and they continued to communicate with pen and paper for many purposes. But printing did displace handwriting: the printed book became the most valued form of handwriting. And printing certainly helped to displace the medieval organization and expression of knowledge. As Elizabeth Eisenstein has shown, the modern printing press has been perhaps the most important tool of the modern scientist. (See *The Printing Press as an Agent of Change* by Elizabeth Eisenstein, 1979, especially vol. 2, pp. 520ff.)

Hugo himself lived in the heyday of printing, when the technology had just developed to allow mass publication of novels, newspapers, and journals. Hugo's own popularity in France (like Dickens' in England) was evidence that printed books were reaching and defining a new mass audience. Today we are living in the late age of print. The evidence of senescence, if not senility, is all around us. And as we look up from our computer keyboards to the books on our shelves, we must ask ourselves whether "this will destroy that." Computer technology (in the form of word processing, databases, electronic bulletin boards and mail) is beginning to displace the printed book. . . .

The printed book, therefore, seems destined to move to the margin of our literate culture. . . . The shift to the computer will make writing more flexible, but it will also threaten the definitions of good writing and careful reading that have been fostered by the technique of printing. The printing press encouraged us to think of a written text as an unchanging artifact, a monument to its author and its age. . . . Electronic writing emphasizes the impermanence and changeability of text, and it tends to reduce the distance between author and reader by turning the reader into an author. It is changing the cultural status of writing as well as the method of producing books. It is changing the relationship of the author to the text and of both the author and text to the reader.

To write an effective argument of inquiry requires researching the topic and examining the issues surrounding it. It might require using evidence, but the evidence might be used as a means to *illustrate* a point rather than to support it. For example, in the excerpt above, Bolter refers to historian Elizabeth Eisenstein to help him develop his point about the important impact of the printing press. He doesn't do this as a way to say, "I'm right," but as a way to lend credibility to his main point about writing and technology.

What is especially noteworthy about an argument to inquire is that your own position might very well change or evolve as you examine the topic and go through the process of planning, writing, and revising your argument. In fact, you might begin the process of writing this kind of argument without a clear position on the topic. Your position will emerge through the process of writing. These arguments, then, are exploratory in two ways: (1) They encourage the writer to explore a topic in order to arrive at a reasonable position, and (2) they invite writers to engage in exploring that topic as well.

ARGUMENTS TO DOMINATE

Perhaps when most people think of formal arguments, they think of arguments whose primary purpose is to dominate. The most common example is an argument made in a legal case. A lawyer might be arguing before a judge to grant bail to her client — let's say a young man accused of stealing a car — so that the client will not have to remain in jail while waiting for the trial to begin. In such a case the lawyer has one main goal: to win. She wishes only to convince the judge that the client should be free on bail. Her opponent, the prosecutor, will try to counter the defense lawyer's argument so that the young man remains imprisoned. In most such cases the arguments tend to be adversarial and the opponents easily identified. The writer of an argument in such a case will try to muster any available evidence and employ any available strategy to win. We encounter other such arguments to dominate — for example, protests against a particular law or corporation (see Figure 1-4).

But as the example of the state legislator suggests, you can make an argument whose purpose is to dominate, even when winning is not likely. The state legislator understood that the vote on the bill would go against his position, yet he argued vigorously for his position anyway. In that instance winning the argument wasn't necessarily the goal. A closer look reveals that the legislator might lose the immediate argument — because the vote goes against reforming the drug laws — but his speech might win the larger battle for public opinion about the state's drug laws. In other words, he can use his defeat in the vote on the reform bill as part of his effort to change the public's attitude about drug laws and perhaps win a later vote to change the drug laws.

We noted above that legal arguments often seem to be concerned only with winning and not with truth. For the lawyer trying to gain a legal victory for her client, getting at the truth of the situation (Did her client in fact steal the car?) is not the goal. She may therefore argue to win even if her client is guilty. But such situations are not always so clear-cut. Consider a different example of a young man pulled over for drunk driving:

A man in his twenties with no criminal record and a clean driving record is driving home late at night from a party celebrating his company's recent increase in sales. On the way home he realizes that he has had too much to drink and that it is dangerous for him to be driving. So he pulls onto the shoulder of the road, puts the car in park, and then falls asleep with the car still idling. Later, a police officer stops to investigate and, realizing that the young man has been drinking, arrests him for drunk driving.

According to the laws in that state, the young man is technically guilty of driving while intoxicated, because he was seated behind the wheel of the car while the car was still running. In the eyes of the law it doesn't matter that the car was parked and not moving at the time the officer found the man. In his summary argument to the jury, the defense lawyer points out that his client is indeed technically guilty but that convicting him would amount to penalizing him for realizing that he shouldn't have been driving; a conviction would punish him for making the safe and responsible decision to stop his car and wait until he sobered up before continuing to drive home. In other words, the lawyer argued that his client did the right thing, even though he was legally guilty of driving while intoxicated. Why, he asked, should this young man, with no prior offenses, be punished for making the right decision?

In this case the lawyer's purpose was to win — to dominate his opponent, the prosecutor, by convincing the jury that they should find the defendant not guilty. And his argument that his client did the "right" thing — if not the legal thing — can be seen as a strategy to win the jury's sympathy and appeal to their sense of justice. But if you consider the argument in the larger context of the state's efforts to impose laws that will reduce drunk driving accidents, then the lawyer is arguing in a way that contributes to that larger purpose. He tries to persuade the jury that what his client did — pulling over his car so that he would avoid an accident — was really what the drunk driving laws are all

SOURCE: www.abolishthebank.org.

about. Punishing the young man for his decision therefore makes no sense. In short, the social and ethical considerations of the case go beyond the immediate goal of winning the argument and the case.

You will at some point very likely find yourself in a situation in which winning an argument is extremely important to you. Understanding arguments to dominate can help you to construct an effective argument in that situation. In the same way, being able to recognize the complexity of such situations will help you identify arguments to dominate so that you can make informed decisions about them. Even then, you might find that your position evolves as you develop and revise your piece.

ARGUMENTS TO NEGOTIATE AND RECONCILE

Glance through your morning newspaper, and you will quickly find examples of situations in which people have seemingly irreconcilable or even intractable differences about an issue or occupy such divergent perspectives that no option seems to exist except for one side defeating or silencing the other. At the same time communications technologies have brought people into more frequent contact with one another, so we now routinely confront all kinds of differences — social, cultural, religious, political, ethnic, regional. Such diversity enriches our lives, but it also challenges us to learn how to live together peacefully. In this sense, one of the main purposes of argument is to confront the complexity that arises from diversity in order to negotiate and, ideally, to reconcile differences. This might be the most difficult kind of argument of all.

In the hospital unionization example on page 11, the administrator of the hospital's retirement plan must consider a number of factors as she drafts her memo. As a hospital administrator she is responsible for managing the retirement plan in a way that serves the hospital's interests as well as the interests of the employees. It isn't hard to see that those interests can diverge. For example, to keep the hospital running efficiently in tough economic times, the hospital might find it necessary to reduce some of the retirement plan benefits, such as how much money the hospital contributes to each employee's retirement account. Reducing that contribution might serve the hospital's financial interests, but it might compromise the employees' financial well-being by giving them less money just when they need it most. Each side seems to be protecting its interests in reasonable ways. So it wouldn't seem wrong for the administrator of the retirement plan to make a strong argument against the union's proposal for the retirement plan. It would make sense, furthermore, for her to argue so that the hospital wins (by encouraging the employees to vote against the union). But it also seems to make sense for the union to argue as aggressively as possible for its own plan, which seems to protect the employees. If both sides proceed in that way, one will win, and presumably, the other will lose.

The administrator of the hospital's retirement plan, however, recognized that both sides could benefit by some changes to the hospital's plan. In a sense, she argued for a win-win outcome: Both the hospital and its employees would gain some benefits, and neither would really lose. Her argument was an effort to negotiate a complicated situation and reconcile the differences between the two sides.

Such an outcome might sound idealistic, but in fact many situations are argued in this way. Return for a moment to our examples of the two legal cases. In such situations it is quite common for defense lawyers and prosecutors to negotiate a plea bargain, which amounts to a compromise in which each side gains something and neither side loses everything. In the case of the young man on trial for drunk driving, the prosecutor and defense lawyer could agree to a lesser charge so that the young man would avoid the harsh consequences of a drunk driving conviction but would still suffer some penalty for having been driving after drinking. In such a situation both sides would argue in front of a judge in a way that would be intended to work out a compromise that is fair and appropriate. Accordingly, the defense lawyer would employ different strategies and make different claims than he did when he argued in front of a jury. The purpose of negotiating the conflict changes what and how he argues.

FIGURE 1-5

Carl Rogers

The ideas of famed psychotherapist Carl Rogers (1902–1987) about empathetic listening have influenced teachers and scholars of argumentation.

Arguing to negotiate differences is sometimes called Rogerian argument, after the influential psychotherapist Carl Rogers, who emphasized the importance of communication as a means to resolve conflicts (see Figure 1-5). Rogers believed that most people are so ready "to judge, to evaluate, to approve or disapprove" that they fail to understand what others think. He urged people to "listen with understanding" and recommended a model for communication in which listeners are required to restate what others have said before offering their own views. This restatement should be done fairly and accurately, without either praise or blame, so that the original speaker is able to confirm, "Yes, that is what I said."

Although this model might seem simple, Rogers cautioned that it takes courage to listen carefully to views that are contrary to one's own, especially in volatile situations or on charged and difficult issues (such as abortion or capital punishment). It is extremely hard to listen when feelings are strong. The greater the conflict, the greater the chance of misinterpreting what others have said. Moreover, it's easy to think of situations in which any kind of listening seems impossible because the people involved are engaged in such deep conflict. Rogers envisioned situations in which individuals are engaged in dialogue, and his commitment to the importance of restating others' ideas (without evaluating them) rests on the assumption that language can be completely neutral — an idea that has been seriously questioned by modern linguists and philosophers. And Rogers's emphasis on the importance of listening may be more helpful to people who are used to speaking than to those who have been silenced. Feminists, for instance, have argued that because public discourse has long been dominated by men, women need to learn how to assert themselves, and men need help in learning to listen. For these reasons, many scholars questioned the extent to which Rogers's ideas can be applied to written

FIGURE 1-6

Nelson Mandela

In helping to reconstruct his country after apartheid was dismantled in 1991, former president of South Africa Nelson Mandela made many speeches that can be considered Rogerian argument.

arguments. (To learn how to organize an argument according to a Rogerian model, see pages 127–128.)

Nevertheless, if you think carefully about the role of argument in resolving conflict and achieving social cooperation, Rogers's perspective on communication can be useful in helping you formulate effective arguments. And the examples we have cited here underscore the advantages of approaching argument in this way when a situation is characterized by a difficult conflict. Indeed, given the scale of the conflicts we face today within our communities, in our cultures, and in the world, a Rogerian perspective might be the most ethical way to approach an argument and might offer the only viable alternative available in certain situations. Think, for example, of the situation faced by Nelson Mandela as the new president of South Africa after the previous apartheid government was dismantled (see Figure 1-6). The long history of oppression and conflict that characterized South Africa and the terrible struggle that Mandela and his supporters endured to defeat apartheid and achieve equality would have made it easy for Mandela to argue for his new government's policies with only the goal of domination and victory in mind. Instead, Mandela recognized that even supporters of the defeated apartheid government were citizens of his country and that it was in everyone's interest to confront and negotiate their differences. As a result, he often argued with the goal of resolution in mind.

The usefulness of an approach to argument that emphasizes negotiating differences extends to much more common situations. For example, neighbors in conflict over a drainage problem on the boundary between their properties might be better served by arguing to their town supervisor for a resolution that fairly addresses the problem on both sides of the boundary rather than for one neighbor to try to force the other to fix the problem by winning the case in court. Or you might find yourself working with other classmates as part of a group project for one of your college courses; if a conflict arises between group members, it's possible that a "victory" by one group member over another could result in a project that is less effective and therefore earns a lower grade for all group members. In short, arguing to negotiate differences rather than to defeat an opponent might best serve your own interests as well as those of the other people involved, and it may be the best way to avoid further conflict.

There is no question that some differences may be irreconcilable. The news headlines about bombings in the Middle East or religious conflict in Europe remind us that no matter how genuinely we engage with one another in arguments, negotiation and resolution might not always be possible. And there are certainly times when winning an argument, rather than negotiating differences, may be ethical. Still, in all but the most extreme situations, genuine engagement in argument as a way to solve a problem, negotiate serious differences, and work toward resolution can offer the best alternative for all concerned. As a writer, you also benefit from writing arguments in this way, in the sense that your engagement in such argumentation may lead to a greater understanding of the situation, which can enrich your perspective on conflict and enhance your ability to engage in future arguments.

2

STRATEGIES FOR ARGUMENT

STRATEGIES

When you write an argument, you might feel confident about what you want to say or about the position you wish to take on an issue. In such a case your primary challenge is to examine the issue carefully so that you can develop the most effective argument. In other situations you might be faced with the prospect of arguing about an issue about which you are unsure or have mixed emotions. In that case writing your argument will involve exploring the issue more fully and perhaps even discovering your own position as you write. In both cases, however, you are engaged in what classical rhetoricians termed *invention,* that is, exploring and developing ideas about a specific topic to make an effective argument about it. Aristotle, whose treatise on rhetoric is still an important work for rhetoricians today, defined *rhetoric* as "the faculty of observing in any given case the available means of persuasion." In other words, rhetoric is finding an effective way to persuade other people to believe or do something. We can usefully think of argumentation in similar terms.

R ARGUMENT

In his *Rhetoric* Aristotle identified three primary modes of persuasion:

- Logical, or arguments based on reason
- Emotional, or arguments that appeal to the emotions
- Ethical, or arguments based on the speaker's character

Obviously, these categories can overlap. You can, for example, make a logical argument that also appeals to your audience's emotions. In practice, most arguments use all three modes of persuasion in some way. But we can use these categories to identify arguments on the basis of the primary strategy the writer (or speaker) employs, and understanding these strategies will help you write effective arguments of your own.

LOGICAL ARGUMENTS

Logic is often associated with objectivity. We tend to think of a logical argument as one that is made objectively on the basis of facts or reason rather than emotion. Consider the following letter written in 2002 by Gerald Gordon to the *New York Times* in response to an editorial by David Plotz. In his editorial Plotz criticized Fairfax County, Virginia, for its policies concerning growth and development. (You can read Plotz's editorial on pages 398–401.) At the time Gerald Gordon was president of the Fairfax County Economic Development Authority:

> I disagree that the county is in crisis. In 2001, my agency helped 164 companies that said they would create more than 11,500 jobs here. Compare that with tech centers like San Jose, California, and Atlanta, which have been shedding jobs by the tens of thousands.
>
> Also, Mr. Plotz says there is only enough "greenery left for a side salad." Funny line, but the county has more than 30,000 acres of dedicated parkland, including a national wildlife refuge established to protect bald eagles and one of the largest urban marshes on the east coast.

Gordon makes his main argument — that Fairfax County is not in crisis — by claiming that the county has plenty of jobs as well as substantial open green spaces. He cites specific figures (the potential creation of 11,500 jobs by 164 companies, 30,000 acres of parks) to support his claim. His position as president of the Fairfax County Economic Development Authority would suggest that Gordon does have an emotional stake in this issue, but he seems to remain objective, using facts to make his case. His argument relies on logic:

Jobs and open spaces are indicators of a healthy county.

Fairfax County has both; therefore, it is a healthy county (it is not in crisis).

His major assumption is that jobs and open spaces are good for a county. If you share that assumption, his argument will probably be persuasive to you; if you don't, then the support he offers becomes meaningless. For example, you might assume that a truly healthy county is one in which the majority of residents are homeowners and have median incomes above the national average. If so, then the existence of jobs alone would not indicate a healthy county, nor would the existence of green space. In other words, the effectiveness of a logical argument depends in large part on whether or not the main assumption — usually called the *main premise* in formal logic — is valid or acceptable.

Arguments rarely rely on logic alone, but the use of logic in an argument can be extremely effective, in part because we tend to think of reason as being superior to emotion when it comes to argumentation. As a result, objective, rational arguments are often considered more valid than openly emotional ones. Of course, the very idea of objectivity can be (and has been) questioned, and since we often engage in argument over complex and important issues that matter deeply to us, avoiding or eliminating emotion is rarely possible and not necessarily even desirable. (Some scholars argue that the distinction between logic and emotion is invalid in the first place.) Nevertheless, logic can be a powerful component of a writer's effort to engage in argumentation, and even when we make arguments that appeal to emotion or character, we will probably incorporate some elements of logic and reason.

Logical arguments can take several different forms. The two most common, which derive from classical rhetoric, are arguments based on *inductive reasoning* and those based on *deductive reasoning*.

REASONING INDUCTIVELY

When we use induction, we are drawing a conclusion based on specific evidence. Our argument rests on a foundation of details that we have accumulated for its support. This is the type of reasoning we use most frequently in daily life. In the morning we look at the sky outside our window, check the outdoor temperature, and perhaps listen to a weather forecast before dressing for the day. If the sun is shining, the temperature is high, and the forecast is favorable, we are drawing a reasonable conclusion if we decide to dress lightly and leave the umbrella at home. We haven't *proved* that the day will be warm and pleasant; we have only *concluded* that it will be. This is all we can usually do in an inductive argument: arrive at a conclusion that seems likely to be true on the basis of our available evidence. Ultimate and positive proof is usually beyond reach. In this sense, induction can be seen as a way for a writer of an argument to deal with probability.

Listen, for example, to literary critic Sven Birkerts as he considers the technological changes he sees around him in the 1990s. Birkerts is concerned that new electronic media, especially those driven by computers, are adversely affecting our lives, in particular how we read and write, without our being very aware of it. "A change is upon us," he asserts, "away from the patterns and habits of the printed page and toward a new world distinguished by its reliance on electronic communication":

> The evidence of the change is all around us, though possibly in the manner of the forest that we cannot see for the trees. The electronic media, while conspicuous in gadgetry, are very nearly invisible in their functioning. They have slipped deeply and irrevocably into our midst, creating sluices and circulating through them. I'm not referring to any one product or function in isolation, such as television or fax machines or the networks that make them possible. I mean the interdependent totality that has arisen from the conjoining of parts — the disk drives hooked to modems, transmissions linked to technologies of reception, duplication, and storage. Numbers and codes and frequencies. Buttons and signals. And this is no longer "the future," except for the poor or the self-consciously atavistic — it is now. Next

to the new technologies, the scheme of things represented by print and the snail-paced linearity of the reading act looks stodgy and dull. Many educators say that our students are less and less able to read, or analyze, or write with clarity and purpose. Who can blame the students? Everything they meet with in the world around them gives them the signal: That was then, and electronic communications are now.

Notice that Birkerts offers a series of observations about the impact of the technological changes he sees in our lives. He cites examples to illustrate the effects that these changes seem to be having on how we communicate. He then concludes that students no longer learn to read and write as they did before the advent of these new technologies. He cannot be certain of this result; no one can. But the evidence around him suggests that such a result is not only possible but perhaps even likely.

This kind of reasoning is common in scientific research. A scientist may have a theory that explains some phenomenon, but she or he must carry out many experiments to prove the theory is valid. These experiments will enable the scientist to eliminate certain variables and gather enough data to justify a generally applicable conclusion. Ideally, a well-researched scientific conclusion will reach a point at which it seems uncontestable. One such example is the warning on cigarette packages. Over the years so much evidence has accumulated to link cigarette smoking to cancer that the warning has evolved from a probability to a veritable certainty. Most writers of arguments cannot hope to reach such certain conclusions through induction. Instead, like Sven Birkerts, they try to draw reasonable conclusions based on their observations and the evidence they present. If a writer is careful and thorough and has gathered sufficient evidence, his or her conclusion will usually seem valid to readers.

REASONING DEDUCTIVELY

When an argument rests on a fundamental truth, right, or value, rather than on available evidence, it employs deductive reasoning. Whereas in inductive reasoning a writer begins with observations or evidence and draws conclusions from those, in deductive reasoning the writer begins with a basic truth or belief and proceeds from there. Evidence is still cited in support of the argument, but evidence is of secondary importance. The writer's first concern is to define a commonly accepted value or belief that will prepare the way for the argument she or he wants to make.

One of the most famous examples of an argument based on deductive reasoning is the Declaration of Independence, written by Thomas Jefferson. (To read the Declaration of Independence, go to page 507.) Although Jefferson cited numerous grievances against England, he rested his argument on the belief that "all men are created equal" and that they have "certain unalienable Rights," which King George III had violated. This was a revolutionary idea in the 18th century, and even today there are people who question it. But if we accept the idea that all people are created equal and have an inherent right to "Life, Liberty, and the pursuit of Happiness," as Jefferson asserted, then certain conclusions follow. The writer's task is to work logically toward those conclusions. Accordingly, Jefferson argued for a specific action — the separation of the colonies from England — based on the basic idea of equality. In other words, having established the fundamental truth of the equality of all people, he reasoned that the king's actions were unacceptable and concluded that the colonies must become independent.

The truth, right, or belief from which a writer deduces an argument is called the *premise*. Often, the main premise of a deductive argument is not immediately obvious, but even when we don't recognize it, it is the crucial element holding together the argument. Let's look at a more current example of an argument based on deductive reasoning, a *New York Times* editorial written in 2002 in response to a controversial court ruling that declared the Pledge of Allegiance unconstitutional:

> Half a century ago, at the height of anti-Communist fervor, Congress added the words "under God" to the Pledge of Allegiance. It was a petty attempt to link patriotism with religious piety, to distinguish us from the godless Soviets. But after millions of repetitions over the years, the phrase has become part of the backdrop of American life, just like the words "In God We Trust" on our coins and "God bless America" uttered by presidents at the end of important speeches.
>
> Yesterday, the United States Court of Appeals for the Ninth Circuit in California ruled 2 to 1 that those words in the pledge violate the First Amendment, which says that "Congress shall make no law respecting an establishment of religion." The majority sided with Michael Newdow, who had complained that his daughter is injured when forced to listen to public school teachers lead students daily in a pledge that includes the assertion that there is a God.
>
> This is a well-meaning ruling, but it lacks common sense. A generic two-word reference to God tucked inside a rote civic exercise is not a prayer. Mr. Newdow's daughter is not required to say either the words "under God" or even the pledge itself, as the Supreme Court made clear in a 1943 case involving Jehovah's Witnesses. In the pantheon of real First Amendment concerns, this one is off the radar screen.
>
> The practical impact of the ruling is inviting a political backlash for a matter that does not rise to a constitutional violation. We wish the words had not been added back in 1954. But just the way removing a well-lodged foreign body from an organism may sometimes be more damaging than letting it stay put, removing those words would cause more harm than leaving them in. By late afternoon yesterday, virtually every politician in Washington was rallying loudly behind the pledge in its current form.
>
> Most important, the ruling trivializes the critical constitutional issue of separation of church and state. There are important battles to be fought virtually every year over issues of prayer in school and use of government funds to support religious activities. Yesterday's decision is almost certain to be overturned on appeal. But the sort of rigid overreaction that characterized it will not make genuine defense of the First Amendment any easier.

Obviously, the editors of the *New York Times* disagree with the court's ruling. They support the idea of the separation of church and state, which is a fundamental principle contained in the U.S. Constitution. Notice that they are not arguing for or against this principle; they accept it as true and good. Their argument proceeds from that principle. But in this case they criticize the ruling not because it violates this principle, but because they see no genuine threat to this principle that would justify the court's decision. According to the editors, the ruling is intended to help maintain the constitutional separation of church and state, which they believe is admirable. But in their view, common sense indicates that the words "under God" in the Pledge of Allegiance do not represent a significant threat to that constitutional principle. So we might articulate the editors' main premise as follows:

> Serious threats to the constitutional separation of church and state should be opposed.

In this instance no serious threat exists in the editors' view; therefore, the ruling makes no sense. They develop their argument by examining what they consider to be some of the negative consequences of the ruling.

This kind of argumentation is quite common. Glance at an editorial page of any newspaper, and you're likely to see one or more examples of an argument based on deductive reasoning. But as the preceding example shows, formulating — or identifying — a good premise can be a challenge. A good premise should satisfy at least two basic requirements:

1. It should be general enough that an audience is likely to accept it, thus establishing a common ground between writer and audience.
2. It should be specific enough to prepare the way for the argument that will follow.

In this example the editors can be confident that most of their readers will understand the idea of the separation of church and state. Certainly, not all of their readers will agree that this principle is a good one that should be maintained, but most readers very likely will agree. So the editors' task is to build an argument that might convince those readers that no threat to that principle exists in this case.

What makes formulating a good premise difficult is that a premise usually refers to or invokes fundamental values or beliefs that we don't often examine consciously. In the case of the Declaration of Independence, Jefferson clearly articulated a fundamental belief in equality, which most of us today understand and accept. The *New York Times* editors invoke a constitutional principle that, while controversial, is nevertheless well known and easily identified. In some cases the premise will be harder to identify. But being able to identify the basic premise of an argument is an important skill that will help you more effectively evaluate arguments you encounter; it will also help you write effective arguments.

The Syllogism　If you look closely at the examples in this section, you'll notice that having a main premise is only part of the writer's task. Deductive reasoning often follows a pattern of what is called a *syllogism,* a three-part argument in which the conclusion rests on two premises, the first of which is the *major premise,* because it is the main assumption on which the argument rests. Here's a simple example of a syllogism:

Major Premise:	All people have hearts.
Minor Premise:	John is a person.
Conclusion:	Therefore, John has a heart.

If both premises are true — as they are in this case — then the conclusion should also be true. Note that the major and minor premises have a term in common (in this example, *people* or *person*). In a written argument the minor premise usually involves a specific case that relates to the more general statement with which the essay began. For instance, we might set up a syllogism based on the *New York Times* editorial on page 27 like this:

Major Premise:	Serious threats to the constitutional separation of church and state should be opposed.
Minor Premise:	The phrase "under God" in the Pledge of Allegiance does not constitute a serious threat to the constitutional separation of church and state.
Conclusion:	Therefore, the Pledge of Allegiance should not be opposed. (That is, the appeals court ruling that the Pledge is unconstitutional is incorrect.)

Notice that the minor premise cites a specific threat, whereas the major premise refers to a more general principle or belief. You can see from this example, however, how quickly syllogistic reasoning can become complicated. You can also see that the major and minor premises are not universally held to be true or valid; many people may disagree with either or both of them. The writers of this editorial surely knew that, and they probably calculated that most of their readers would accept their major premise as true.

The Enthymeme   Because it can be difficult to follow the rules of logic, faulty reasoning is common. Consider another simple example:

Major Premise:	All women like to cook.
Minor Premise:	Elizabeth is a woman.
Conclusion:	Therefore, Elizabeth likes to cook.

Technically, the *form* here is correct. The two premises have a term in common, and if we accept both premises as true, then we also have to accept the conclusion. But the major premise is faulty. Elizabeth, like many women (and men) might *hate* to cook, preferring to go out bowling at night or to read the latest issue of the *Journal of Organic Chemistry.* A syllogism may be valid in terms of its organization, but it can be *untrue* if it rests on a major premise that can easily be disputed. Usually, the major premise is a generalization, as in this example, but some generalizations make sense and will be widely accepted, while others will not. And it is easy to confuse generally accepted truths with privately held beliefs. In this case some people might well believe that all women like to cook, but many will not hold that belief. You can argue in favor of a private belief, but you cannot expect an audience to accept an easily debatable opinion as the foundation for an argument on behalf of yet another opinion.

It is also important to realize that in many arguments a premise might be implied but not stated. You might overhear a conversation like this one:

"I hear you and Elizabeth are getting married."
   "Yes, that's true."
   "Well, now that you've got a woman to cook for you, maybe you could invite me over for dinner sometime."
   "Why do you think that Elizabeth will be doing the cooking?"
   "Because she's a woman."

The first speaker has made a number of possible assumptions. He or she might believe that all women like to cook or perhaps that all women are required to cook whether they like it or not. But these assumptions were not stated. If they were, it would be easy for the other speaker to point out the flaw in the first speaker's reasoning.

This example suggests why many people see formal logic as too rigid for everyday arguments. Although formal logic can help us understand arguments and identify the assumptions we use in argument, rarely do writers of arguments consciously try to follow its rules. However, we do routinely use logic in our day-to-day discussions and arguments, though more informally. We regularly make and support claims, make and evaluate assumptions, and draw or oppose conclusions, and doing so according to the rules of formal logic would be cumbersome and perhaps even silly. Consider the following statement:

"I'd better close the windows, because the sky is getting darker."

If we examined this statement carefully, we could devise a syllogism to reveal the logic inherent in the statement:

Major premise:	A dark sky indicates rain.
Minor Premise:	The sky is getting darker.
Conclusion:	Therefore, it will probably rain (and I should close the windows).

You'll notice that in the original statement the major premise is implicit. Yet the statement is a form of logic nonetheless. Indeed, it would sound quite silly if we spoke in formal syllogisms in such situations. The point is that we need to make claims and provide reasons as we conduct our day-to-day affairs, but we need to do so efficiently. And we can usually assume certain beliefs or knowledge on the part of our listeners without having to state them explicitly.

In fact, for centuries theorists have been exploring the uses of such informal logic in arguments. Aristotle called this kind of informal logic a rhetorical syllogism, or an *enthymeme*. You might think of an enthymeme as a syllogism that consists of only two parts. In the example above, the major premise is missing. But it might be more helpful to think in terms of practical logic. In other words, rather than trying to follow the rigid rules of formal logic when making an argument, you are applying logic where it is most useful to you. Aristotle understood that in most situations such informal uses of logic are not only efficient and practical but effective as well.

There are two important ways in which understanding logic and employing informal logic, such as enthymemes, can be helpful to you: (1) as a reader (or listener) who is trying to make sense of and evaluate an argument and (2) as a writer who is trying to construct an effective argument. As a reader, you are often confronted with arguments — on a newspaper editorial page, in a reading assignment for a college course, in a political flyer you received in the mail. Being able to identify the premises on which an argument is based, especially when they are implicit, enables you to evaluate the argument and perhaps to uncover problems or flaws in the argument. For writers logic can be a powerful way not only to make a persuasive case for a position but also to organize an argument. (See pages 125–144 for a discussion of organizing an argument.)

Cultural Differences in Logical Arguments   It is also important to keep in mind that people from different cultural backgrounds might make different assumptions that they take for granted their audience shares. For example, in making an argument against sweatshops in which U.S. corporations employ young workers in Asian countries, an American writer might assume that her readers share her belief that child labor is a bad thing. Indeed, that would be a safe assumption with an American audience, since child labor has long been illegal in the United States (except under certain circumstances), and Americans generally seem to agree that it should be illegal. However, a reader from a rural community in Bangladesh, for instance, where children routinely work on local farms, might not share that assumption. In such a case the writer's argument would likely have very different effects on these different readers. You can easily think of more dramatic examples of such cultural differences and how they might affect logical argument. The suicide bombings taking place in the struggle between Israelis and Palestinians in the Middle East have been the subject of intense debate, which has revealed deep differences in how the participants view violence, suicide, national identity, and religious belief. In such a charged and difficult context a writer cannot safely assume, for instance, that his or her readers will accept the view that suicide is inherently wrong. You might not often engage in argumentation about such difficult issues, but you will almost certainly encounter the need to understand how cultural difference might influence the way readers will react to your assumptions. (For an example of how culture differences can influence an argument, see "Values Beyond Price" by Vandana Shiva on pages 443–446.)

THE TOULMIN MODEL OF ARGUMENTATION

Formal logic, although it is a powerful framework for argumentation, has its limitations. Most people prefer not to be bound by a predetermined method of structuring an argument and regard the syllogism, in particular, as unnecessarily rigid. Many writers will therefore combine inductive and deductive reasoning in making an argument and often make arguments without the use of formal logic. Partly for these reasons scholars have long explored alternative ways of employing logic so that it becomes more practical and effective in arguments. One of the best-known systems for doing so was developed by a British philosopher named Stephen Toulmin in the 1950s. Emphasizing that logic is concerned with probability more often than with certainty, Toulmin provided a new way of analyzing arguments that focused on the nature of claims.

Toulmin's model includes three main components: the *claim,* the *data* or *reasons,* and the *warrant.* According to Toulmin, the basis of all arguments is the *claim,* which is the writer's (or speaker's) statement of belief — the conclusion or point he or she wishes to prove.

ELEMENTS OF THE TOULMIN SYSTEM OF ARGUMENT	
Claim:	The conclusion or the main point being argued.
Data:	The evidence supporting the claim. Also called the *reasons.*
Warrant:	Basic principle or assumption that connects the data and the claim.

The *data* or reasons are the evidence or information a writer or speaker offers to support the claim. The *warrant* is a general statement that establishes a trustworthy relationship between the data and the claim; it is a fundamental assumption (similar to the major premise in formal logic) on which a claim can be made and supported. In an argument the claim and data will be explicit, but the warrant is often implied, especially if the person making the argument assumes that the audience accepts the warrant. In that case the task is simply to present sufficient evidence to support the claim. However, if the audience disagrees with the warrant or finds it unacceptable, then the writer must defend it to make the claim.

To better understand these terms, let's consider an example adapted from one of Toulmin's examples:

Claim:	Raymond is an American citizen.
Data:	Raymond was born in Puerto Rico.
Warrant:	Anyone born in Puerto Rico is an American citizen.

These three statements might remind you of the three elements in a deductive argument. If arranged as a syllogism, they might look like this:

Major Premise:	Anyone born in Puerto Rico is an American citizen.
Minor Premise:	Raymond was born in Puerto Rico.
Conclusion:	Raymond is an American citizen.

The advantage of Toulmin's model becomes apparent when we realize that the major premise here might not be true. For example, Raymond might have been born to French parents who were vacationing in Puerto Rico, or perhaps he was an American citizen but became a naturalized citizen of another country. Because the rigid logic of the syllogism is designed to lead to a conclusion that is *necessarily* true, Toulmin argued that it is ill suited for working toward a conclusion that is *probably* true. Believing that the syllogism was overemphasized in the study of logic, Toulmin saw a need for a "working logic" that would be easier to apply in the rhetorical situations in which most people find themselves — a kind of logic that would function in the kinds of arguments that people engage in every day. His model therefore easily incorporates *qualifiers* such as "probably," "presumably," and "generally." Here is a revision of the first example, employing Toulmin's model:

Claim:	Raymond is probably an American citizen.
Data:	Raymond was born in Puerto Rico.
Warrant:	Anyone born in Puerto Rico is entitled to American citizenship.

Both the claim and the warrant have been modified. Toulmin's model does not dictate any specific pattern in which these elements must be arranged, which is a great advantage for writers. The claim can be made at the beginning of an argument, or it can just as easily be placed after a discussion of the data and the warrant. Similarly, the warrant may precede the data, it may follow it, or it may be implied, as we already noted.

It is easy to see that claims and warrants can be extremely complicated and controversial, and one advantage of Toulmin's system is that it not only offers writers great flexibility in constructing effective arguments but also provides readers with a way to evaluate arguments carefully. In Chapter 5 we'll explore how Toulmin's model can help you structure your own arguments. For now it's important to examine some of the complexities of claims and warrants.

Understanding Claims and Warrants   There are different kinds of claims: claims supported by facts, claims supported by expert opinion, claims supported by values. For example, if you wanted to argue that the stock market should be subject to greater regulation, you could base your claim primarily on facts: You could define current regulations, report on laws governing markets, cite specific abuses and scandals involving insider trading, and include figures for the money lost to investors as a result of unethical trading practices. You would present these various facts to support your claim that greater regulation is needed. By contrast, another writer might argue in favor of regulating the stock market on the basis of the values of honesty and fair play. Of course, when we argue, we often use several different kinds of claims. For example, if you wanted to argue against capital punishment, your data might consist of facts (such as the numbers of executions performed annually, differences in these figures by state or by race, the number of death row inmates, and so on), the views of criminologists or legal experts regarding the death penalty, and an appeal to moral value (such as the sanctity of human life) that you believe your audience might share. In short, you would present different types of data depending on the nature of the claim you are making.

Warrants are also complex, and the nature of a warrant will differ from one argument to another. Some warrants may be relatively straightforward. For example, law often constitutes a warrant. A lawyer arguing on behalf of someone claiming American citizenship might invoke the Jones Act of 1917, which guarantees U.S. citizenship to citizens of Puerto Rico. That law would become the lawyer's warrant for the claim that a person born in Puerto Rico should be considered a U.S. citizen. But because warrants sometimes reflect assumptions or beliefs, they can be disputable and controversial. If you base a claim that capital punishment should be banned in the United States on a belief that taking any human life is wrong, you should be prepared to defend that warrant, since many people would not accept it. In such a case you would strengthen your argument against capital punishment if you explained and defended your view about the wrongness of taking human life. Simply stating or implying such a controversial warrant would likely result in some readers dismissing your argument altogether.

These examples reflect the challenges that writers — and readers — can often face when they engage in argumentation about difficult or charged issues, and they remind us that no model, including Toulmin's, will always lead to effective arguments. But if our goal is to understand the issues adequately in order to address a problem or negotiate differences that create conflict or discord, then Toulmin's model can be a useful framework for both writers and readers.

Evaluating Claims and Warrants   Being able to make strong claims and support them adequately is a crucial part of what makes an argument effective. It is also a challenge, largely because most claims deal with probability rather than certainty. If you engage in serious argumentation out of a desire to address an important issue or solve a problem, you need to understand how claims function and how to evaluate claims effectively. Toulmin's ideas about claims, data, and warrants can be useful tools in helping us make and evaluate claims.

Let's look at an example of an argument about an issue that became deeply important to Americans after the terrorist attacks on the United States on September 11, 2001: national security. In response to those attacks, the U.S. government began removing information that had previously been available on many of its Web sites. Among the kinds of information removed were environmental statistics, emergency plans, and data on health and safety risks to Americans. A year after the attacks and several months after the government began censoring its Web sites, writer Mary Graham argued in *The Atlantic Monthly* that keeping such information secret in the interest of national security is not only wrong but dangerous. She asserted that "the wholesale censorship of information on Web sites carries insidious costs." To support this central claim, Graham describes how this censorship policy can undermine, rather than increase, national security. She also asserts that this kind of censorship is unfair, and she questions whether secrecy will actually accomplish the goal of enhancing security: "National security is everyone's concern, and the idea that openness can be more effective than secrecy in reducing risks has received too little attention."

Evaluating Graham's argument requires us to examine how these assertions relate to her central claim. We might restate her claim as follows:

Claim: The censorship of information on U.S. government Web sites should end because it is unfair to Americans and does not necessarily increase Americans' security.

Here we see that Graham offers two main reasons for her claim: (1) Censorship is unfair, and (2) secrecy might not enhance security. So far so good. But this claim rests on a basic assumption — her warrant — that isn't as obvious. We might state her warrant as follows:

> Warrant: Americans have a right to information related to their security.

Notice that this warrant invokes a legal principle (a specific legal right that Americans have to information); it also invokes more general ethical values (openness and fairness). Because such a warrant is likely to be acceptable to most readers of the *Atlantic Monthly*, Graham need not defend it and can therefore concentrate on supporting her claim by offering reasons why the government's censorship policy won't achieve its goal of enhancing security. In short, her claim is clear, supported with various reasons, and strengthened by a warrant that is generally acceptable to her intended audience. As a reader, you can disagree with her claim, and no doubt some readers will also disagree with her warrant (believing, for example, that only government officials should have access to the kinds of information that has been censored from government Web sites). But if you accept her warrant, you can evaluate her argument against censorship on the basis of the evidence she presents.

If a claim is based on a warrant that isn't necessarily acceptable to an audience, the writer might have to defend that warrant. Otherwise, the argument for the claim might be less persuasive to the audience. Sometimes, it is the warrant and not the claim that is problematic for an audience. Let's examine an example in which the writer might have misjudged his audience and relied on a warrant that might be questionable for that audience. The following passage was taken from an essay arguing against a national boycott of gasoline — called a "gas out" — that some consumer advocates and environmental groups proposed in 2000, when gas prices were rising quickly in the United States. The writer, Gary Foreman, disagreed with this proposal. He made his claim against the boycott:

> I can pretty much tell you that "Gas Out 2000" won't work. It might draw some media attention. But it won't change the price you pay at the pump by one penny. And if you'll consider the facts you'll understand why.

Let's restate Foreman's claim:

> It's useless to participate in "Gas Outs," because they won't reduce the price of gas.

If we restate his claim in this way, his main reason supporting his claim also becomes clear: The boycott won't reduce gas prices. Most of Foreman's essay is devoted to an explanation of the economics of gasoline production and distribution, which he uses to support his claim. In other words, he relies on facts about the economics of the gasoline market to demonstrate why a boycott cannot reduce prices. But what is his warrant? Later in his essay he writes,

> So if a "Gas Out" won't help, what can you do? One very practical thing. Use less gas. Carpool, take public transportation, combine trips or get your car tuned up. Anything you can do to save gas will put more money in your pocket. And that's the one "statement" that oil producers will notice. More importantly, you'll notice it in your wallet, too.

Here he implicitly conveys his warrant, which we can restate as follows:

> Paying less money for gas is desirable.

Notice that this warrant is likely to be acceptable to many people. But this essay was published in a newsletter called *Simple Living,* which promotes an environmentally sound lifestyle. The readers of that newsletter are likely to be as concerned about the environmental effects of gasoline combustion as they are about gasoline prices. In other words, for such an audience, Foreman could safely use a much more environmentally conscious warrant; he could have made an argument that focused on environmental impact as well as price. Such an argument would likely have resonated with the readers of *Simple Living.* In fact, it is likely that many of those readers would find Foreman's argument *less* persuasive precisely because he focuses on reducing gas prices and ignores the ethical and environmental concerns that those readers probably share. In this case, readers of *Simple Living* might very well accept Foreman's claim that a boycott may not be a good idea while resisting his warrant.

This last example highlights the fact that claims and warrants, like other aspects of argument such as style or tone, must be understood in rhetorical context. No claim is universally valid; no warrant is universally acceptable. The audience, the cultural context, and the rhetorical situation all influence the impact of an argument. It's worth noting here too that because this newsletter was published on the World Wide Web, the writer might have assumed his audience to be much larger than just the subscribers to the newsletter. If so, we can see how the medium can influence an argument's warrant. (See Chapter 4 for a discussion of how media can affect argument.)

FALLACIES

If you look closely at some of the examples in this chapter, you can find problems with the arguments. Any apparently logical argument can reveal serious flaws if you take the trouble to examine it carefully. Here is an excerpt from a letter written by a person opposed to a federal appeals court decision in 2002 ruling that the phrase "under God" in the Pledge of Allegiance is unconstitutional:

> In light of the events of this past September (9/11/01), I think it would be hypocrisy to omit an acknowledgement of a divine being under which the ideals and beliefs of this nation were created. And if you don't think so, ask everyone how many of them prayed to God that day.

This writer suggests that a large number of people praying is evidence of the existence of God. Obviously, whether or not you agree with him that there is a God, you can easily see that the number of people who pray does not necessarily prove God's existence. This flaw in the writer's reasoning is called a *logical fallacy* (specifically *attributing false causes,* which is discussed on page 38). Fallacies are often unintentional. We might think that we are making a strong argument but have actually engaged in flawed reasoning without realizing it, as is likely to have been the case with the writer in this example. Sometimes, however, writers know that their reasoning may be suspect but deliberately use it to win an argument. Some fallacies can in fact be powerful strategies for writers of arguments. But if we are concerned about truth — about addressing a problem or negotiating a conflict — then it makes sense to guard against fallacies so that we do not undermine our efforts to come to a reasonable resolution. And it is important to be able to identify fallacies in the arguments of others. In this section, we discuss some common fallacies.

APPEALING TO PITY

Writers are often justified in appealing to the pity of their readers when the need to inspire this emotion is closely related to whatever they are arguing for and when the entire argument does not rest on this appeal alone. For example, someone who is attempting to convince you to donate one of your kidneys for a medical transplant would probably assure you that you could live with only one kidney and that there is a serious need for the kidney you are being asked to donate. In addition to making these crucial points, the arguer might move you to pity by describing what will otherwise happen to the person who needs the transplant.

When the appeal to pity stands alone, even in charitable appeals in which its use is fundamental, the result is often questionable. Imagine a large billboard advertisement for the American Red Cross. It features a close-up photograph of a distraught (but nevertheless good-looking) man, beneath which, in large letters, runs this caption: PLEASE, MY LITTLE GIRL NEEDS BLOOD. Although we might already believe in the importance of donating blood, we should question the implications of this ad. Can we donate blood and ask that it be reserved for the exclusive use of children? Are the lives of children more valuable than the lives of adults? Few people would donate blood unless they sympathized with those who need transfusions, and it might be unrealistic to expect logic in advertising. But consider how weak an argument becomes when the appeal to pity has little to do with the issue in question. Someone who has seldom attended class and has failed all his examinations but then tries to argue, "I deserve to pass this course because I've had a lot of problems at home," is making a fallacious appeal to pity. The "argument" asks the instructor to overlook relevant evidence and make a decision favorable to the arguer because the instructor has been moved to feel sorry for him. You should be skeptical of any appeal to pity that is irrelevant to the conclusion or that seems designed to distract attention from the other factors you should be considering.

APPEALING TO PREJUDICE

Writers of argument benefit from appealing to their readers' values. Such appeals become fallacious, however, when couched in inflammatory language or when offered as a crowd-pleasing device to distract attention from whether the case at hand is reasonable and well informed. A newspaper that creates a patriotic frenzy through exaggerated reports of enemy "atrocities" is appealing to the prejudices of its readers and is making chances for reasonable discussion less likely. Racist, sexist, classist, and homophobic language can also be used to incite a crowd — something responsible writers should take pains to avoid doing. Appeals to prejudice can also take more subtle forms. Politicians might remind you that they were born and raised in "this great state" and that they love their children and admire their spouses — all of which are factors that are believed to appeal to the average voter but that nevertheless are unlikely to affect performance in office. When candidates linger on what wonderful family life they enjoy, it might be time to ask a question about the economy.

APPEALING TO TRADITION

Although we can learn from the past and often benefit from honoring tradition, we can seldom make decisions based on tradition alone. Appealing to tradition is fallacious when tradition becomes the only reason for justifying a position. "We cannot let women join our club because we've never let women join in the past" is no less problematic that arguing, "We shouldn't buy computers for our schools, because we didn't have computers in the past." The world changes, and new opportunities emerge. What we have done in the past is not necessarily appropriate for the future. If you believe that a traditional practice can guide us in the future, you need to show why this is the case. Do not settle for claiming, "This is the way it always has been, so this is the way it always has to be."

ARGUING BY ANALOGY

An analogy is a comparison that works on more than one level, and it is possible to use analogy effectively when reasoning inductively. You must first be sure that the things you are comparing have several characteristics in common and that these similarities are relevant to the conclusion you intend to draw. For example, you might argue that competition is good for schools, since it is considered to be good for businesses. But the strength of this argument would depend on the degree to which schools are analogous to businesses, so you would need to proceed with care and demonstrate that there are important similarities between the two. When arguing from analogy, it is important to remember that you are speculating. As is the case with any type of inductive reasoning, you can reach a conclusion that is likely to be true but not guaranteed to be true. It is always possible that you have overlooked a significant factor that will cause the analogy to break down.

Unfortunately, analogies are often misused. An argument from analogy that reaches a firm conclusion is likely to be fallacious, and it is certain to be fallacious if the analogy itself is inappropriate. If a congressional candidate asks us to vote for him because of his outstanding record as a football player, he might be able to claim that politics, like football, involves teamwork. But because a successful politician needs many skills and will probably never need to run across a field or knock someone down, it would be foolish to vote on the basis of this questionable analogy. The differences between football and politics outweigh the similarities, and it would be fallacious to pretend otherwise.

ATTACKING THE CHARACTER OF OPPONENTS

If you make personal attacks on opponents while ignoring what they have to say or distracting attention from it, you are using what is often called an *ad hominem* argument (Latin for "to the man"). Although an audience often considers the character of a writer or speaker in deciding whether to trust what he or she has to say, most of us realize that good people can make bad arguments, and even a crook can sometimes tell the truth. It is always better to give a thoughtful response to an opponent's arguments than to ignore those arguments and indulge in personal attacks.

ATTRIBUTING FALSE CAUSES

If you assume that an event is the result of something that merely occurred before it, you have committed the fallacy of false causation. Assumptions of this sort are sometimes called post hoc reasoning, from the Latin phrase *post hoc, ergo propter hoc,* which means "after this, therefore because of this." Superstitious people offer many examples of this type of fallacious thinking. They might tell you, "Everything was going fine until the lunar eclipse last month; *that's* why the economy is in trouble." Or personal misfortune might be traced back to spilling salt, stepping on a sidewalk crack, or walking under a ladder.

This fallacy is often found in the arguments of writers who are determined to prove the existence of various conspiracies. They often seem to amass an impressive amount of "evidence," but their evidence is frequently questionable. Or, to take a comparatively simple example, someone might be suspected of murder simply because he or she was seen near the victim's house a day or two before the crime occurred. This suspicion might lead to the discovery of evidence, but it could just as easily lead to the false arrest of the meter reader from the electric company. Being observed near the scene of a crime proves nothing by itself. A prosecuting attorney who would be foolish enough to base a case on such a flimsy piece of evidence would be guilty of *post hoc, ergo propter hoc* reasoning. Logic should always recognize the distinction between *causes* and what might simply be *coincidences.* Sequence is not a cause because every event is preceded by an infinite number of other events, not all of which can be held responsible for whatever happens today.

This fallacy can be found in more subtle forms in essays on abstract social problems. Writers who blame contemporary problems on such instant explanations as "the rise of violence on television" or "the popularity of computers" are no more convincing than is the parent who argues that all the difficulties of family life can be traced to the rise of rock and roll. It is impossible to understand the present without understanding the past, but don't isolate at random any one event in the past and then try to argue that it explains everything. And be careful not to accidentally imply a cause-and-effect relationship where you did not intend to do so.

ATTRIBUTING GUILT BY ASSOCIATION

This fallacy is frequently apparent in politics, especially toward the end of a close campaign. A candidate who happens to be religious, for example, might be maneuvered by opponents into the false position of being held accountable for the actions of all the men and women who hold to that particular faith. Nothing specific has been argued, but a negative association has been either created or suggested through hints and innuendo.

BEGGING THE QUESTION

In the fallacy known as begging the question, a writer begins with a premise that is acceptable only to anyone who will agree with the conclusion that is subsequently reached — a conclusion that is often very similar to the premise itself. Thus, the argument goes around in a circle (and is sometimes referred to as *circular reasoning*). For instance, someone might begin an essay by claiming, "Required courses like first-year Composition are a waste of time" and end with the conclusion that "first-year Composition should not be a required course." It might indeed be arguable that first-year Composition should not be required, but the author who begins with the premise that first-year Composition is a waste of time has assumed what the argument should be devoted to proving. Because it is much easier to *claim* that something is true than to *prove* it is true, you may be tempted to beg the question you set out to answer. This temptation should always be avoided.

EQUIVOCATING

Someone who equivocates uses vague or ambiguous language to mislead an audience. In argumentation, equivocation often takes the form of using one word in several different senses without acknowledging the change in meaning. It is especially easy to equivocate when using abstract language. Watch out in particular for the abuse of such terms as "right," "society," "freedom," "law," "justice," and "real." When you use words like these, make sure your meaning is clear. And make doubly sure your meaning doesn't shift when you use the term again.

IGNORING THE QUESTION

When someone says, "I'm glad you asked that question!" and then promptly begins to talk about something else, that person is guilty of ignoring the question. Politicians are famous for exploiting this technique when they don't want to be pinned down on a subject. Students (and teachers) sometimes use it too when asked a question that they want to avoid. Ignoring the question is also likely to occur when friends or partners have a fight. In the midst of a quarrel, we might hear remarks like "What about you?" or "Never mind the budget! I'm sick of worrying about money! We need to talk about what's happening to our relationship!"

JUMPING TO CONCLUSIONS

This fallacy is so common that it has become a cliché. It means that the conclusion in question has not been supported by an adequate amount of evidence. Because one green apple is sour, it does not follow that all green apples are sour. Failing one test does not mean that you will necessarily fail the next. An instructor who seems disorganized on the first day of class might eventually prove to be the best teacher you ever had. You should always try to have more than one example to support an argument. Be skeptical of arguments that seem heavy on opinion but weak on evidence.

OPPOSING A STRAW MAN

Because it is easier to demolish a man of straw than to address a live opponent fairly, arguers are sometimes tempted to pretend that they are responding to the views of their opponents when they are only setting up a type of artificial opposition that they can easily refute. The most common form of this fallacy is to exaggerate the views of others or to respond only to an extreme view that does not adequately represent the arguments of one's opponents. If you argue against abolishing Social Security, you should not think that you have effectively defended that program from all criticisms of it. By responding only to an extreme position, you are doing nothing to resolve specific concerns about how Social Security is financed and administered.

PRESENTING A FALSE DILEMMA

A false dilemma is a fallacy in which a speaker or writer poses a choice between two alternatives while overlooking other possibilities and implying that no other possibilities exist. A college freshman who receives low grades at the end of the first semester and then claims, "What's wrong with low grades? Is cheating any better?" is pretending that there is no possibility other than cheating or earning a low grade — such as that of earning higher grades by studying harder, a possibility that is recognized by most students and teachers.

REASONING THAT DOES NOT FOLLOW

Although almost any faulty argument is likely to have gaps in reasoning, this fallacy, sometimes called the *non sequitur* (Latin for "it does not follow"), describes a conclusion that does not follow logically from the explanation given for it.

Gaps of this sort can often be found within specific sentences. The most common type of non sequitur is a complex sentence in which the subordinate clause does not clearly relate to the main clause, especially where causation is involved. An example of this type of non sequitur would be "Because the teacher likes Joe, Joe passed the quiz in calculus." Here a cause-and-effect relationship has been claimed but not explained. It might be that Joe studied harder for his quiz because he believes that his teacher likes him, and that in turn resulted in Joe passing the quiz. But someone reading the sentence as written could not be expected to know this. A non sequitur can also take the form of a compound sentence: "Mr. Blandshaw is young, and so he should be a good teacher." Mr. Blandshaw might indeed be a good teacher but not just because he is young. On the contrary, young Mr. Blandshaw might be inexperienced, anxious, and humorless. He might also give unrealistically large assignments because he lacks a clear sense of how much work most students can handle.

Non sequiturs sometimes form the basis for an entire argument: "William Henderson will make a good governor because he is a friend of working people. He is a friend of working people because he has created hundreds of jobs through his contracting business." Before allowing this argument to go any further, you should realize that you've been asked to swallow two non sequiturs. Being a good governor involves more than being "a friend of working people." Furthermore, there is no reason to assume that Henderson is "a friend of working people" just because he is an employer. He might have acquired his wealth by taking advantage of the men and women who work for him.

SLIDING DOWN A SLIPPERY SLOPE

According to this fallacy, one step will inevitably lead to an undesirable end. An example would be claiming that legalized abortion will lead to euthanasia or that censoring pornography will lead to the end of freedom of the press. Although it is important to consider the probable effects of any step that is being debated, it is fallacious to claim that people will necessarily tumble downhill as the result of any one step. There is always the possibility that we'll be able to keep our feet firmly on the ground even though we've moved them from where they used to be.

EMOTIONAL ARGUMENTS

There is perhaps no more powerful way to construct an argument than to appeal to your readers' emotions. No argument is completely devoid of emotional appeal. But some arguments rely on emotions much more than others do. And because emotional appeals can be so powerful, they carry risk for both writer and reader.

One reason that emotional arguments don't work in all circumstances is that emotion itself is so complex and often poorly understood. Think for a moment about the range of emotions that might figure into an argument about, say, capital punishment: anger, pity, worry, fear, sadness, relief. Trying to anticipate how readers might react emotionally to a specific point about such charged issues can be daunting. You might try to inspire sympathy among your readers by, for instance, invoking a call to patriotism in an argument about measures to be taken against terrorism but find that your argument sparked anger among some readers instead. In fact, it is impossible to know with certainty what emotional responses you might elicit with a particular line of argument; you can only try to anticipate their responses on the basis of your experience, your knowledge of them, and your understanding of the rhetorical context.

Because of this uncertainty and because emotions will very likely be involved in any argument, it is a good idea to think of the use of emotion in argument as an ethical matter. You might suspect that a line of argument may evoke very strong emotions in some readers and, as a result, make those readers more susceptible to that line of argument. In other words, you might be able to "push the buttons" of your readers intentionally to elicit strong emotions. Doing so might enable you to win the argument, but will it truly solve the problem about which you are arguing? Is it the right way to address the issue at hand?

Used carefully and ethically, emotional appeals can be very effective. Let's consider how one writer employs emotion in an argument about the ongoing controversy over gun control. In this case the writer, Jeanne Shields, argues in favor of restricting the sale and ownership of handguns. But she writes from an especially wrenching position: Her own son was murdered by someone using a handgun. Here are the opening paragraphs of her essay:

> If the telephone rings late at night, I always mentally check off where each child is, and at the same time get an awful sinking feeling in the pit of my stomach.
>
> Four years ago, April 16, we had a telephone call very late. As my husband answered, I checked off Pam in Long Beach (California), Nick in San Francisco, David in New Brunswick (New Jersey) and Leslie outside Boston. The less my husband spoke, the tighter the knot got in my stomach. Instinctively, I knew it was bad news, but I wasn't prepared for what he had to tell me. Our eldest son, Nick, 23, had been shot dead on a street in San Francisco.
>
> Nick was murdered at about 9:30 p.m. He and a friend, Jon, had come from lacrosse practice and were on their way home. They stopped to pick up a rug at the

home of a friend. While Jon went in to get the rug, Nick rearranged the lacrosse gear in the back of their borrowed Vega. He was shot three times in the back of the head and died instantly, holding a lacrosse stick.

Nick was the fourteenth victim of what came to be called the "Zebra killers." Between the fall of 1973 and April 16, 1974, they had randomly killed fourteen people and wounded seven others — crippling one for life. Four men were subsequently convicted of murder in a trial that lasted thirteen months.

Shields goes on to describe how she and her husband eventually became involved in efforts to strengthen gun laws in the United States, arguing that current laws were too weak to control the proliferation of handguns like the one that killed her son. In setting up her argument, Shields describes a situation that she knows is likely to evoke strong emotions among her readers. Readers who are parents themselves will surely identify with Shields and her husband, and other readers are likely to feel empathy for them as well. Those feelings can make readers more likely to be open to Shields's support for tougher gun laws, even if those readers are not in favor of gun control in principle. Notice how the opening paragraphs of her essay describe two vivid scenes: two parents receiving a dreaded late-night phone call and an innocent young man shot in cold blood while doing an everyday task. Such a strategy is likely to give many readers pause, since the emotions surrounding these scenes can be deep and powerful.

Shields isn't just tugging at her readers' heartstrings here. Later in her piece, despite her own unequivocal support for stronger gun laws, she discusses both the pros and cons of gun control, and she refers to well-funded lobbies that oppose such laws. In this way she is making a reasoned, logical argument. But she employs emotion as well, appealing to her readers' empathy and perhaps also appealing to their emotional commitment to their own children. In short, her emotional appeal becomes an integral part of the logical argument she makes regarding gun control.

This example illustrates that emotional appeals must be used judiciously and ethically. It is easy to imagine some readers rejecting Shields' argument in favor of gun control and turning her appeal to the opposite position. The same emotions she invokes in favor of gun control can be used in an argument opposing it. For example, a parent whose child was murdered might well take the position that arming oneself with a handgun can help to prevent violent crime and might have saved his or her child. In evaluating positions like these, it is important to sort out the emotional appeals as well as the specific logical arguments each person is making.

Arguments about controversial issues such as gun control are fertile ground for emotional appeals, but emotion can be used in any argument. Here's an excerpt from an essay by Filip Bondy published the day after Brazil's soccer team won the 2002 World Cup:

He cried, he laughed, he scored. Ronaldo put his mark on this special World Cup Sunday with a redemptive samba — two second-half goals in the 2-0 championship victory by Brazil over Germany, and eight goals in seven matches.

Ronaldo's tale is now one for the ages, from the streets of Rio to the Yokohama stadium where he trotted about the field in triumph, hugging everyone, with a Brazil flag draped from his broad shoulders.

The son of a drug-addicted father and a rock-steady mother, Ronaldo had blown off school as a youngster to play street soccer, to become that odd athletic combination of bull and gazelle that made him such a unique talent.

He wouldn't listen to his mother, who wanted him to study hard and to become a doctor. Instead, he aimed for something even more impossible — a career in soccer — and somehow succeeded. The trail, however, was not always as direct as his style.

In this argument celebrating Ronaldo, Bondy appeals not only to his readers' admiration for Ronaldo's achievement, but also to the joy that sports fans so often feel when they witness a victory by a great champion. In addition, in referring to the story of Ronaldo's difficult childhood, Bondy is also likely to stir up positive feelings about family, hard work, and the pursuit of individual dreams. Although he is not writing about something as complex and controversial as gun control, Bondy's appeal to these emotions may help make his argument about Ronaldo's achievement more convincing to his readers, whether they are fans of Brazil's soccer team or not.

This example illustrates that emotional appeals can work on several different levels. Notice, for example, that the idea of a world championship in sports can be used to evoke pride or admiration in readers. A writer like Bondy can try to employ that emotion throughout his or her argument. In other words, the very idea of a championship elicits certain emotions that become integral to the entire argument. By contrast, the brief descriptions in Bondy's essay of Ronaldo's childhood can elicit different emotions, which the writer uses for different purposes — in this case, to help support his point that Ronaldo's achievement is a special one and perhaps to create additional admiration for Ronaldo as an individual. Visual details and individual words or phrases can have the same effect. For example, think about your own reaction to the description of Ronaldo "hugging everyone, with a Brazil flag draped from his broad shoulders" or of Ronaldo's father as "drug-addicted." Certain words have powerful associations; in this case "drug-addicted" might create greater sympathy for Ronaldo. Terms such as *family values, environmentally friendly, freedom of choice,* and *American* are often used precisely because of the emotions they evoke. As a writer you can employ such carefully chosen words as you build your argument. But be mindful of the potential pitfalls of doing so. A single word, such as "drugs," can elicit very different responses in different readers, and it is important to try to understand the associations that a particular word or phrase might carry for readers. It is equally important to recognize how such words might influence you when you encounter them in someone else's argument.

How we use the power of emotion in an argument, of course, depends not only on our ability to assess the impact of a line of reasoning or an emotional appeal on our audience; it depends as well on what we hope to accomplish with an argument. If our purpose is to address a problem or to negotiate differences regarding a difficult or complex issue, then we must take care to employ emotional appeals appropriately and ethically.

CHARACTER-BASED ARGUMENTS

"You can count on her."

"I wouldn't trust a word he says."

How many times have you heard — or spoken — some version of those two statements? Very likely, you have done so often, perhaps without realizing that you were engaging in one of the most basic and long-standing strategies for argument: invoking character. Aristotle identified character, or *ethos,* as one of the most powerful components of persuasion available to a speaker: "We believe good men [and women] more fully and more readily than others," he wrote, adding that a speaker's character "may almost be called the most effective means of persuasion he [or she] possesses" (*Rhetoric*, p. 25). But character is not just a strategy; it is also a quality. Like Aristotle, the famous Roman rhetorician Quintillian believed that the most effective orator is a "good" person. Above all, Quintillian wrote, the effective orator "must possess the quality which . . . is in the very nature of things the greatest and most important, that is, he [or she] must be a good man [or woman]" (*Institutio Oratoria,* Book XII, p. 355). In short, the best way to sound or appear ethical in an argument is to *be* ethical.

We often rely on our sense of someone's character when making decisions in our daily lives. For example, you might seek advice about attending graduate school from a relative or a teacher you trust and whom you know to be careful with advice about such matters. In some cases character might grow out of one's authority and expertise: Your professor's knowledge of universities and education can lead to useful advice about graduate school. You wouldn't necessarily have the same confidence about such advice from, say, a friend who is a chef. From her you might seek suggestions for a good restaurant or recipe. One's authority or expertise is not the same thing as character (a professor can be unethical and untrustworthy, for instance), but it is usually part of one's character and can be a powerful source of appeals in argument.

This kind of appeal is common in advertising. Corporations select celebrities to represent them or their products — for example, basketball star Michael Jordan for Nike shoes. The implicit argument is that if someone like Michael Jordan endorses this product, it must be good. An advertising campaign for the soft drink Sprite even parodied this strategy. In several television ads, professional basketball players, such as Grant Hill, were shown drinking Sprite. The ads seemed to suggest that drinking Sprite would enable anyone to perform the athletic feats of a player like Hill. But at the end of the ad, a person fails to perform such a feat after drinking Sprite. The ads end with the line "Obey your thirst." The suggestion was that you shouldn't trust a celebrity for advice about how to quench your thirst. These ads presented a twist on the common approach to using celebrities to sell products, suggesting how routine that approach has become in American culture.

Character is especially important in the arenas of law and politics. In court, for instance, lawyers will try to establish or undermine the credibility of witnesses as they try to convince a judge or jury about a person's guilt or innocence. Defense lawyers sometimes call "character witnesses" to establish that the defendant was a particular kind of person (usually, of course, a good person). Similarly, when it comes to politics, character often looms large. Consider how often candidates for elected office try to establish their own credibility as trustworthy and dependable. Advertisements showing a candidate's family, for example, are standard fare in U.S. elections. Such advertisements intend to convey that politicians who are married and have children are more reputable than candidates who are single — an old-fashioned idea that has been strangely enduring even though most people these days recognize that there's nothing necessarily odd about being single and that families who smile together are not necessarily happy. Just as common are advertisements attacking an opponent's credibility. Often such "attack ads" will suggest that a candidate is not concerned with issues affecting voters and therefore isn't to be trusted.

A writer can raise questions about someone's credibility to support a particular point or position on an issue. Consider, for instance, the following excerpt from an editorial by *Chicago Tribune* columnist Clarence Page. Page is arguing in favor of a controversial policy at the University of North Carolina requiring all incoming first-year students in 2002 to read a book about the Koran. The purpose was to encourage students to learn and think carefully about an important book that they might not be familiar with. Page is reacting specifically to an appearance by a University of North Carolina professor on *The O'Reilly Factor*, a popular television news talk show hosted by journalist Bill O'Reilly:

> The important thing, as Robert Kirkpatrick, the professor who chose the book, explained on "The O'Reilly Factor" TV show is this: First-year students need to know that "as a member of an academic community they have to learn to think and to read and to write and to defend their opinions."
>
> That's right. Start pushing a book on college freshmen and, who knows? They might try reading another one.
>
> That's what college is supposed to be about. It is not just a time for learning but a time to arouse curiosity in preparation for a lifetime of learning.
>
> That process begins when you learn not only to have opinions but also how to express and defend them.
>
> "And defending the right not to read the book is something that will be very interesting to read," the professor said.
>
> Indeed, it should be at least as interesting as listening to showman-journalist O'Reilly explain why he will not read the book. According to a Fox transcript, he called UNC's assignment "unbelievable," compared it to assigning "Mein Kampf" during World War II and asked why should freshmen be required to study "our enemy's religion."
>
> Yes, there is a lot more to Islam than Osama bin Laden and his violent brethren, but apparently not in O'Reilly's mind.
>
> "I mean, I wouldn't give people a book during World War II on [how] the emperor is God in Japan. Would you?"
>
> "Sure," Kirkpatrick said. "Why not? Wouldn't that have explained kamikaze pilots?"
>
> That's a sensible answer, not that sensibleness gets you anywhere on high-energy cable TV news-talk shows these days or, for that matter, in politics — especially religious politics.

Here, Page supports his own position in favor of the reading requirement by questioning O'Reilly's credibility (and even his common sense) on the issue. He suggests that O'Reilly's interest as a TV talk-show host is not in arriving at a "sensible" answer to the question raised by the University of North Carolina requirement but rather in being a "showman." Such a strategy can be effective when a person advocating a certain position is well known and likely to be considered credible by many people. Because of his television show, Bill O'Reilly was widely known in the United States in 2002, and it is likely that many of his viewers saw him as an important voice on issues such as public education.

By calling O'Reilly's credibility on the issue into question, Page could weaken O'Reilly's position and strengthen his own argument that the reading requirement is justified and sound.

A writer can take the opposite approach in making a character-based argument; that is, the writer can invoke certain positive aspects of someone's character to advance an argument. In the following passage, notice how sports columnist Harvey Araton establishes Pakistani tennis player Qureshi as a committed professional athlete who overlooks political and religious affiliations and focuses on winning at tennis (see Figure 2-1). As you read, keep in mind that Qureshi was harshly criticized by other Pakistanis for agreeing to have an Israeli player as his doubles partner. These criticisms came during the 2002 Wimbledon tennis tournament at the same time that the conflict in the Middle East between Israelis and Palestinians was intensifying and had become especially bloody.

They played together, then sat together, Pakistani and Israeli, Muslim and Jew, and wanted everyone to know it was no big deal. There was no statement made, no cause advanced, other than the bid to go as far they could in the Wimbledon draw. Pragmatism, not peacemaking, made doubles partners of Aisam ul-Haq Qureshi and Amir Hadad.

"We are not here to change anything," said Qureshi, 22, of Lahore, Pakistan. "I don't like to interfere religion or politics into sport."

Hadad, 24, of Ramala, Israel, near Tel Aviv, said: "I know Aisam is very good on grass, good serve, good volley, and also I like him as a person. When he asked me to play, we didn't even think it's going to get so big."

Then they survived the qualifying tournament and won two rounds in the main draw last week. No Pakistani had lasted past this round at Wimbledon, or in any Grand Slam event. What would have been a feel-good story in Pakistan became an inflamed issue when Qureshi, the country's No. 1 player, from a family with a rich tennis history, made a bit of his own history with Hadad — until they were dispatched by the Czechs Martin Damm and Cyril Suk yesterday, 6-1, 7-6 (5), 6-4.

It was, for them, a productive pairing, one they said they might reprise at the United States Open next month, no matter the ominous reports from Pakistan that Qureshi has read on the Internet.

His family, stationed by Court 5 yesterday in the shadow of Center Court, was only interested in what was happening here, saying they had received support from Pakistanis all over London. His mother, Nosheen, formerly No. 1 in Pakistan and still an active player at 41, kissed the Israeli, Hadad, on the cheek and called him a good boy. The father, Ihtsham, a 50-year-old businessman, videotaped the third-round match, right down to the volley his son misplayed on match point. An uncle, Khalid Rashid, dismissed the protests, calling them the work of "Al Qaeda and extremists in the north."

The reports, without subtlety, said otherwise. A former Pakistani champion, Saeed Haid, was quoted in *The Times* of London saying, "The bloodshed in the

Middle East means his pairing with an Israeli is wrong." A director of the country's
official Sports Board, Brig. Saulat Abbas, told Agence France-Presse: "Although he
is playing in his private capacity, we officially condemn his playing with an Israeli
player and an explanation has been sought from him. Since we have no links with
Israel, Qureshi may face a ban."

In the heart of aristocratic-mandated civility, the lawns neatly manicured and
the sportswear lily white, this sounded like hardened geopolitical zealotry bor-
dering on lunacy. A cautious Ihtsham Qureshi said it was his understanding that
the Pakistani news media were supporting his son, and many positive e-mail messages had been received. His wife, whose father was the best player in India before partition in 1947, said, "People with the right perspective don't think like
that."

Within this insular sport, which rears wandering citizens of the world, the players sounded mature and wise as they spoke of a friendship formed along the endless road of small-time events for those on the far periphery of fame. They joked
about how their greatest faith must be in their ability to stay fit and focused in
the pursuit of almighty computer points.

"I don't pray at all, but I practice a lot," Hadad said.

In this editorial Araton is not just establishing the two tennis players as credible and
principled people; he also shows them to be committed to excellence in their sport. He
implies that such a commitment allows them to be open-minded about others who might
have different religious beliefs or political views from their own. Obviously, not all
Araton's readers will agree that such character is a good thing in view of the ongoing conflict between Arabs and Israelis — a conflict in which Qureshi and Hadad are indirectly
involved. But Araton uses the character of these two players to make his larger argument
that we must get beyond our religious differences if we will ever solve this terrible conflict. Here is Araton's final paragraph:

He [Qureshi] said he had played with Israelis before, but on nothing like the world
Wimbledon stage. Here, as Hadad said, the point was to "improve our ranking, make
some money." A Muslim and a Jew partnered and got the job done in a game that
begins with the score at love. If only doubles were that easy in settling conflicts
plagued and prolonged by hate.

If Araton had not established that Qureshi and Hadad have a certain kind of integrity
and commitment to their profession, his argument would not have the same impact.
Araton believes that it is precisely the kind of character possessed by Qureshi and Hadad
that can help us overcome prejudice and cultural conflict. In this regard, he is employing
a character-based argument as a way to try to address a horrible conflict; his is an example of an argument whose ultimate purpose is to negotiate deep religious differences that
seem intractable and that have led to great suffering.

FIGURE 2-1 **Qureshi (left) and Hadad**

SOURCE: AP, July 4, 2002.

The character of the writer himself or herself can also play a powerful role in an argument. In the previous example readers who don't know anything about Harvey Araton can still find his argument, based on the character of the two tennis players, effective. But sometimes it is the writer's character that becomes an important basis for an argument. As we noted above, the advice of a professor about graduate school or of a chef about a recipe carries weight because of who is giving the advice. Similarly, many arguments have force because of the authority or character of the writer. Consider the following letter to the editor of the *Cleveland Plain Dealer,* written in response to an editorial about the promise of medical technology:

The *Plain Dealer's* Aug. 13 editorial "Miracles on demand" was right that emerging medical breakthroughs hold incredible promise in overcoming serious diseases like cancer and heart failure. And it was right that, in our imperfect world, it is impossible to provide an absolute guarantee of the safety of medical technology. But it missed the fact that manufacturers and the Food and Drug Administration are doing an excellent job making sure new tests and treatments are as safe as possible.

. . .

FDA data on product recalls show that the agency's system of pre-market and post-market regulations is working well. Even as the number and complexity of medical technologies has increased, the total number of recalls has remained steady over the last 10 years. The vast majority of recalls are not considered a serious public-health issue and are due to issues like labeling errors that can be easily corrected. Are medical technologies always perfect? Unfortunately, no. But manufacturers and the FDA have maintained an impressive safety record as a result of their mutual commitment to the safest possible products.

The agency itself concludes: "The public's confidence in FDA is well justified." After examining the facts, we wholeheartedly agree.

The letter was signed as follows:

Pamela G. Bailey.
Bailey is president of the Advanced Medical Technology Association, which represents more than 1,100 innovators and manufacturers of medical devices, diagnostic products and medical information systems.

Obviously, Bailey is making a logical argument here about the safety of medical technologies. But her argument might have greater impact on readers who notice that she is president of an organization of medical technology professionals. You might consider whether you assign greater credibility to this argument on the basis of your knowledge of Bailey's position. (Of course, your reaction would depend in part on your opinion of large companies that manufacture medical technologies. For some readers, knowing who Bailey is will undermine her argument.)

The public prominence of a person can work in much the same way in an argument. In the summer of 2002, the *New York Times* published an essay in favor of school vouchers by the famed economist Milton Friedman. After the Supreme Court decision in June 2002 upholding the voucher program in the Cleveland, Ohio, city schools, many editorialists wrote arguments supporting or opposing the Court's ruling. Many of those writers had no authority as either legal experts or educators. In that regard, their character probably did not figure prominently into their arguments — or in readers' reactions to their arguments. Friedman, by contrast, is an internationally known figure who is one of the most influential economists of the 20th century. Consider how this blurb, which was included at the end of his essay, might influence your reaction to his argument:

Milton Friedman, the 1976 recipient of the Nobel Prize in economics, is a senior research fellow at the Hoover Institution.

(You can read Friedman's essay on pages 338–340.)

Writers of arguments need not have such impressive reputations as Friedman's to employ character effectively. Establishing credibility is an important strategy in argumentation that all writers can use. When you refer to your own experiences, for example, as a way to indicate to your readers that you know something about a situation or an issue, you are establishing credibility that can give your argument greater weight. Here is writer Joshua Wolf Shenk addressing the issue of legalizing drugs:

> There's no breeze, only bare, stifling heat, but Kevin can scarcely support his wispy frame. He bobs forward, his eyes slowly closing until he drifts asleep, in a 45-degree hunch. "Kevin?" I say softly. He jerks awake and slowly rubs a hand over his spindly chest. "It's so hot in here I can hardly think," he says. . . .
>
> This July I spent a long, hot day talking to junkies in New York City, in a rundown hotel near Columbia University. Some, like Kevin, were reticent. others spoke freely about their lives and addictions. I sat with Melissa for 20 minutes as she patiently hunted her needle-scarred legs for a vein to take a spike. She had just fixed after a long dry spell. "I was sick," she told me. "I could hardly move. And Pap" — she gestures toward a friend sitting across from her — "he helped me out. He gave me something to make me better. . . ."
>
> Making drugs legally available, with tight regulatory controls, would end the black market, and with it much of the violence, crime, and social pathology we have come to understand as "drug-related." And yet, history shows clearly that lifting prohibition would allow for more drug use, and more abuse and addiction.
>
> I spent that day in New York to face this excruciating dilemma. It's easy to call for an end to prohibition from an office in Washington, D.C. What about when looking into Kevin's dim eyes, or confronting the images of crack babies, shriveled and wincing?

Shenk uses his own experience not only to make his point about the horrors of drug addiction, but also to establish himself as someone who knows about this problem from direct experience. Notice, too, that Shenk's gentle, sympathetic descriptions of the addicts he met help to convey a sense of him as caring and deeply concerned, which might add to his credibility for many readers. (Obviously, there is an emotional appeal here, too.)

There are other ways for a writer to establish credibility as well. Establishing an honest, straightforward voice as a writer can help to convince readers that you are credible and believable and that they can take you seriously. Indeed, the very quality of your writing can help establish your credibility by demonstrating your competence to readers. Acknowledging your own limitations can be an effective strategy for establishing credibility, too. For example, imagine that you wish to contribute to a discussion of standardized testing in your community, an important educational issue that affects all students (including you). In writing a letter to your local school board, for instance, you might concede at the outset that you are not an expert in educational testing but that your own experiences as a student give you insight into the problems associated with testing. Such a statement can gain you credibility by showing that you are not trying to claim expertise that you don't have, yet you are genuinely concerned about the issue at hand. In this sense you are being honest with your readers and thereby communicating to them that they can trust you. You are, in other words, establishing your own character as the writer of an argument.

Sometimes, claiming authority as the writer of an argument can backfire. You have no doubt heard or read statements by someone engaged in argument who claims to know more than someone else about the issue being discussed. For instance, let's return to the example in the previous paragraph. Imagine that your letter to the school board has provoked a response from a school board member who is an expert in educational testing. Imagine further that he explicitly refers to that expertise in his attempt to call your position into question. In effect, he says, "I know what I'm talking about, because I'm an expert in this area. This other person, on the other hand, doesn't know what he's talking about." Even if your purpose is to dominate, such an approach can undermine your credibility, since readers could find you arrogant. The school board member in this example might well have expertise in testing, but residents of the school district might reject his position if they believe that his arrogance gets in the way of the best interests of the students. If your purpose in this argument, by contrast, is to address a problem involving the testing of students in your school district, then perhaps the strategy is inappropriate. Like all appeals, the appeal to character can be complicated and should always be assessed in terms of the specific situation at hand.

3

THE CONTEXTS OF
ARGUMENT

W henever we engage in argumentation, we must do more than examine the topic carefully and construct a sound argument in support of our position. We must also take into account our audience, the specific situation we and they are in, the cultural factors that might affect how an audience responds to a particular argument, even the historical moment we are in as we argue. In short, we always argue within a context — actually, within several contexts simultaneously — and we must address context if we expect to argue effectively.

O F   A R G U M E N T

Let's imagine for a moment that you have been given an assignment in your composition course to take a position on the issue of racial profiling and write an argument justifying your position. Let's assume further that you will be asked to read your essay to your class, which includes students of different racial groups. Obviously, racial profiling is a controversial topic, and you know that your classmates' views about the topic are likely to be varied and strong. After reading a number of articles and essays, you have decided that despite some problems with racial profiling, you believe that it can be an important tool for fighting crime if used carefully. You write an argument in which you acknowledge the serious problems that can occur as a result of racial profiling by law enforcement agencies, but you justify its use on the grounds of security and public safety. In your argument you try to address your teacher as well as your classmates, some of whom have voiced strenuous opposition to profiling. You wish to make an effective argument that your classmates, even those who are opposed to profiling, will take seriously, though you are mindful that some of them might reject what you have to say because of their own passionate engagement with the issue. You also know that your teacher will be assessing your argument and that your classmates' reactions might influence her assessment. So you have gathered some evidence that profiling can reduce some kinds of crime, and you have identified what you consider to be good arguments in support of profiling policies that can protect citizens' privacy and civil rights. But you also know that the charged nature of the topic will make some of these arguments seem less than convincing to some of your classmates. What will you write?

As a writer you might not have faced a situation quite as challenging as the one described here, but if you have engaged in argument, you have had to think about some of the same problems you would encounter in this situation. The answer to the question "What will you write?" in a given situation requires that you consider the context of your argument. No matter what kind of argument you wish to make, no matter what your purpose, there are at least three main contexts you should consider as you construct an argument:

- The rhetorical situation
- The cultural context
- The particular moment in which we are arguing, which we can call the historical context

THE RHETORICAL SITUATION

Rhetoricians have long used the metaphor of a triangle to help define the rhetorical situation (see Figure 3-1). The classical rhetorical triangle reminds us that when we write an argument, we are engaged in an interaction with a particular audience about a particular subject. Both audience and writer have a connection to the subject matter in the form of knowledge about the subject, opinions about it, experience with it, and so on. But the writer and the audience will never have identical connections to that subject. A big part of the challenge, then, is to try to understand your audience and its connection to your subject so that you can address your audience effectively as you construct your argument.

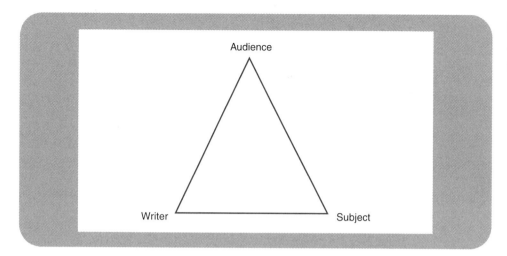

FIGURE 3-1

**The Rhetorical
Situation**

ANALYZING YOUR AUDIENCE

Obviously, the audience for a particular argument can vary dramatically from one situation to another, and as we'll explain in more detail later in this chapter, the specific characteristics of the rhetorical situation (when and where someone is making an argument, for example) can profoundly affect how a writer addresses an audience and how an audience might respond to an argument. But because an argument is very often an attempt to communicate with an audience about a conflict or a problem, and because ideally an argument will effectively address that conflict or resolve the problem, it is essential for writers to try to understand their audience to the extent that they can. And there are some general guidelines for doing so.

First, try to determine what you already know about your intended audience. In some cases, the audience for an argument will be very specific. In our hypothetical example, you would literally know your audience (your teacher and your classmates), and you would have some sense of their knowledge and opinions about your subject (racial profiling). Moreover, because you would have engaged in class discussion about racial profiling, you might even know how some of your classmates (and perhaps your teacher) might react to specific arguments in favor or against racial profiling. You can imagine other situations in which you might know your audience well. For instance, if you were writing a letter to your local school board in support of a proposal for, say, a new swimming pool at the high school, you would know something about the members of the school board and community members who might read your letter. You might even know them personally. If you wrote a letter to the editor of your local newspaper, you would have a good sense of who the readers would be, since they live in your community. A writer can draw on such knowledge to identify effective arguments. In some ways this is almost an ideal situation for a writer, because there would be very little of the uncertainty about the audience that writers usually face in writing an argument. And if the goal is to try to solve a problem, then knowing the audience can lead to a better understanding of their positions and a more genuine engagement with them about the issue.

In most cases, however, writers are likely to have much more general knowledge — or very little knowledge — about their audience. Imagine the difference between writing a letter to the editor of a local newspaper, which is read by a few thousand people, almost all of whom live in the same town, and writing a letter to the editor of a national publication such as *USA Today*, which is read by millions of people from all over the country. The assumptions that you can reasonably make about these audiences can differ dramatically. But it is not really feasible to analyze a general audience, such as the readership of *USA Today*, in depth because that audience is far too diverse for you to know anything about it in detail. At the same time, you can approach such an audience in a way that is likely to engage a majority of readers and address them effectively. In other words, even though there is a limit to what you can really know about an audience (after all, even a close friend can surprise you), you can make some general assumptions about your audience that will help you to argue effectively.

You can begin by assuming an intelligent and fair-minded audience. Assume as well that intelligent and fair-minded people tend to be skeptical about sweeping generalizations and unsupported claims. (Indeed, they might be skeptical about the generalization made in that sentence!) In some cases you might be able to expect your audience to agree with you. For example, if you are the keynote speaker at a political convention, chances are that most people in the audience will share your viewpoint. But if you are attempting to reconcile differences or solve a conflict through argument, you should probably assume that your audience will disagree with you. Some members of your audience might be neutral about the issue you're addressing. But imagining a skeptical audience will enable you to anticipate and respond to opposing views or objections to your position, thus building a stronger case.

IMAGINING YOUR AUDIENCE

In some ways imagining an audience is a creative act. Well-known 20th century scholar Walter Ong wrote a famous article called "The Writer's Audience Is Always a Fiction," in which he argued that when writers write, they must always create a sense of an audience that doesn't necessarily correspond directly to a "real" audience. This act of "fiction," Ong maintained, is necessary because rarely do writers know in detail just whom they are writing to or for. But this imagined audience is always based on a general sense of who might read what we are writing, our experiences with people in general, our experiences as readers of other people's writing, and our knowledge of the conventions of writing. All these figure into our imagined audience. In other words, our imagined audience is based on our real experiences with writing and with other people. When it comes to argument, this act of imagining an audience influences the specific arguments you will make in support of your position on an issue.

Even when imagining a general audience, writers often make specific assumptions about their readers beyond assuming that they are intelligent but skeptical. Consider, for example, the following letter, which was written to the editors of *Newsweek* in response to an essay by columnist Allan Sloan criticizing greed and unethical behavior by large corporations:

> Right on, Allan Sloan! I have long thought that no economic system, certainly not capitalism, can function successfully without the moderating effects of virtuous, ethical behavior on the part of the key players. That said, I'm afraid that we have yet to widely acknowledge that such behavior can never be reliably coerced by endless rounds of civil regulation. In a free society there will always be loopholes to be identified and exploited by those with selfish, greedy attitudes.

Notice that this writer implicitly assumes that his readers are not necessarily those with "selfish, greedy attitudes," nor are they likely to be the "key players" in the capitalist system. In other words, he assumes that his readers are more "average" people who share his basic values regarding ethical behavior. He can further assume that his readers have read Allan Sloan's essay and that they probably have a basic understanding of the principles of capitalism that Sloan discussed. The point is that even a "general" audience can be specific in certain respects. Narrowing an audience in this way can help a writer determine how to cast an argument so that it effectively addresses that general audience.

Sometimes, a writer can define a general audience more directly by explicitly excluding specific kinds of readers. In the following letter, which was also written to the editors of *Newsweek,* the writer is responding to an article about electroshock therapy:

> I was surprised to find no mention of neurofeedback in your article "Healthy Shocks to the Head." Noninvasive, relatively inexpensive and proving to be effective with a long list of central nervous-system disorders, this procedure should be given an opportunity to demonstrate its effectiveness before more invasive procedures are tried. It's too bad the medical community is so enamored with drugs and surgery.

Notice that this writer refers to "the medical community" in a way that excludes members of that community from his audience. In effect, he is addressing everyone outside "the medical community." Of course, this writer probably knows that members of that community are likely to read his letter, too, so indirectly he is also addressing them — as well as criticizing them — and perhaps inspiring an Ong-like fiction: "You're a *good* doctor or nurse, not one of those types I am referring to here." But by referring to them as he does, he defines his intended audience as those readers who are not members of that community, thus narrowing his "general" audience and assuming that they might well share his concerns.

It is worth noting here that if the writer in the preceding example hoped to try to negotiate the apparent conflict that exists among those who advocate noninvasive techniques for treating disorders of the central nervous system, as he does, and those in the medical community who might have a different view, then he would ultimately need to address the medical community directly, too. In other words, a sense of purpose for an argument will shape the writer's sense of audience.

The audience for an argument is also influenced by the specific circumstances in which the argument is being made. In the previous example the writer is addressing a general audience made up of readers of *Newsweek,* and he is doing so in response to a specific article that appeared in that magazine. Imagine if he were making the same argument — in favor of noninvasive techniques for treating disorders of the central nervous system — in a letter written to the *Journal of Mental Health*. In that case the audience would likely include some of the same readers of *Newsweek*, but it would now be composed primarily of mental health professionals who read that journal — that is, members of the "medical community" that he criticized in his original letter. Although his argument might not change, this writer would now be able to use more technical language and would likely have to address his readers differently if he wished them to take him seriously. Imagine further that he is not responding to an article in *Newsweek* but instead is writing about the issue of electroshock therapy in general. In this case he must introduce his topic differently, since he would not be able to refer to a specific article that he could assume his readers had read. But he *could* assume that his audience knew more about these treatments than the readers of *Newsweek* are likely to know, which would affect what information he might include in his argument and how he might present it. The circumstances for his argument would therefore affect several important aspects of his argument even if his basic position is the same.

As these examples suggest, the circumstances within which an audience is being addressed can also have a big impact on how that audience will respond to a specific argument. Obviously, it is impossible for a writer to know about everything that is part of a rhetorical situation, just as it is impossible for a writer to be able to anticipate how every member of the audience will react to a specific word, phrase, tone, fact, or line of argumentation. Human beings are simply too complex. But effective arguments are usually effective only within a specific rhetorical situation. What works in one situation might not work in another. So it is crucial for writers of arguments to examine the rhetorical situation they are in and make their best judgments about how to address their audience in that situation. And although trying to understand an audience in itself takes time and effort, it offers a great reward: knowledge about human nature that can make it easier for you to live and work with others.

CULTURAL CONTEXT

When writers engage a particular audience in argumentation, they never address generic readers, even when they are addressing the kind of general audience discussed in the previous section. Instead, they address human beings, each of whom brings a different set of experiences, knowledge, beliefs, and background to the interaction. In other words, who we are as individuals shapes how we will react to an argument. And who we are is a complex matter that encompasses our racial, ethnic, gender, and cultural identities. In this regard, *culture* will always be part of any rhetorical situation and thus shape any argument.

UNDERSTANDING CULTURE

Culture can be understood in several ways when it comes to argumentation. As was suggested in the preceding paragraph, we can think of culture as our sense of identity as it relates to our racial and ethnic backgrounds, our religious upbringing (if any), our membership in a particular social class (working class, for example), and the region where we live (for example, rural West Virginia versus urban Los Angeles). These aspects of our identity affect how we understand ourselves as individuals in relation to others and as members of various communities. Culture in this sense will shape how we view the world, what we believe and value, and how we experience various aspects of life. We can also think of culture as a setting within which we live and interact with each other, as in the culture of New York or the culture of Japan. These ways of understanding culture overlap, of course, but they provide a sense of the powerful influence that culture will have on individual writers and readers as they engage in argumentation.

Let's return to the example at the opening of this chapter. Consider how classmates with different cultural backgrounds might react to your argument in favor of racial profiling. Obviously, an African American student might be highly sensitive to the subject — and perhaps passionate about it — because the controversy about the subject has directly involved Blacks in many communities. In addition, if that student grew up in an urban neighborhood where relations between residents and police are strained, he or she might have strong feelings related to his or her experience as well as his or her identity as a Black person. Compare that student to, say, an exchange student from Japan, where racial issues have a very different history. A Japanese student might also have a different sense of authority and of the relationship between individuals and the government than Americans students have. To invoke a somewhat different example, what if one of your White classmates was raised in a Quaker household that emphasized a lifestyle based on nonviolence? How might that person react to an argument in favor of racial profiling? All these hypothetical examples indicate the various ways in which culture can influence both the writing and reading of an argument.

These examples tell us something else: that culture is complex. The student who was raised as a Quaker, for example, is White but can legitimately claim a different cultural identity from other White students in your class, even though all of them can claim to be part of American culture. The same can be said of two different Black students: one who might have grown up in a middle-class suburb and another whose parents might be working-class immigrants from the Caribbean. In other words, even if two people have similar cultural backgrounds, they will not have *identical* cultural backgrounds and will not have identical experiences as members of that culture. As a writer of arguments you can't be expected to sort out all these subtle complexities, but you should always be sensitive to culture and assume that culture will play an important role in argumentation. Brian Fay, a philosopher of social science, describes the influence of culture in this way:

My experience has been deeply shaped by the fact that I am male, a (former) Catholic, American, and middle class. Because of these characteristics I look at the world in a certain way, and people treat me in a particular manner. My Catholic upbringing, for example, gave me a view of myself as fallen and as needing to be redeemed by something other than myself or the natural world; it made me think that certain desires and behaviors are bad, and led me to (try to) repress them; even my body was shaped by certain typical Catholic disciplines (kneeling, for instance). Even when in later life I reacted against this upbringing, I was still reacting against my particular Catholic heritage, and in this way this heritage continues to shape me; it will do so until I die.

It seems obviously true that I am in part who and what I am in strong measure because of the groups to which I belong (to which in many cases I had no choice but to belong). If I had been born and raised in New Guinea then I would be quite other than what I am: I would not only describe the world differently, I would experience it differently.

Fay does not use the term *culture* in this passage, but he is referring to aspects of one's background — such as religious upbringing, social class, gender, and national origin — that are usually associated with culture and considered part of one's cultural identity. Think of how these aspects of Fay's cultural identity might affect his reaction to an argument about racial profiling or school voucher programs.

CONSIDERING CULTURE IN ARGUMENT

We can return to another example to examine the role of culture in argument more closely. Earlier, we referred to an essay by Harvey Araton about a tennis doubles team comprising a Muslim player and a Jewish player (see pages 46–48). Araton's essay was published in the *New York Times,* whose readership certainly includes Arabs and Jews, both in the United States and abroad. But that readership is composed primarily of people living in the United States, the great majority of whom are American citizens. Those in that audience who are neither Jewish nor Muslim are likely to react differently to Araton's argument than Jews or Muslims will. In fact, Araton quotes former Pakistani tennis champion Saeed Haid as criticizing Qureshi, the current Pakistani tennis player, for playing with a Jewish partner in view of the bloodshed between Arabs and Jews; Araton quotes the Pakistani sports director as condemning Qureshi as well. Araton suggests that these criticisms amount to zealotry and lunacy, but his argument grows out of a cultural context (that of the United States) in which pluralism and religious diversity are deeply held values. The former Pakistani tennis champion and sports director are arguing out of a different cultural context (that is, an Arab and Muslim nation in Asia) that does not necessarily share those values. In such a context the criticisms of Qureshi would not sound like zealotry at all. As is often the case in situations in which different cultures come into conflict, this situation is not simply a matter of differing opinions or a disagreement about whether or not Qureshi was right to take Hadad as his doubles partner; rather, the different cultural contexts complicate the matter. Araton brings to his argument a different worldview, which grows out of his cultural identity, from that of the Pakistani tennis champion or the sports director. These cultural differences profoundly shape not only how these individuals view the situation with Qureshi and Hadad, but also what kinds of claims or assertions are likely to be persuasive to each.

Culture not only influences how individual readers or writers might react to an argument, but it also can affect how people engage in argumentation. Different cultures might have different values, as we saw in the previous example of the Pakistani tennis player Qureshi, and they might have different ways of engaging in argument as well. For example, in some cultures it is considered impolite or even disrespectful to question another's statements, claims, or credibility. In such cultures people follow certain implicit protocols that govern what they can say to each other. In Japan, for example, if it is raining and you are without an umbrella, it would be impolite to directly ask a person who has an umbrella if you may borrow it. Instead, you would be expected to make a statement such as "It's raining very hard" or "We are likely to get wet," which the other person would know to interpret as a request to borrow the umbrella. Such cultural protocols govern how a writer might structure an argument and how he or she might support his or her position on an issue. A Japanese writer arguing in favor of, say, having American troops leave Okinawa, which is a Japanese-controlled island, might focus his argument on the capabilities of the Japanese security forces to protect Okinawa rather than asserting that Americans have no business occupying that island.

CONSIDERING GENDER

We can also think of culture as encompassing important aspects of our identity such as gender, sexual orientation, and age. It is risky to generalize about such things, and many arguments are directed toward audiences without regard to gender, sexual orientation, age, or other such factors. But it is important to be sensitive to how these factors can influence the way an audience might react to an argument. Moreover, there are times when it is appropriate to take those factors into account in making an argument. Sometimes an argument is intended specifically for an audience of, say, young women or retired men. Sometimes the topic might be one that has different implications for different audiences. An argument in favor of a woman's right to choose an abortion will mean something different to women than it will to men, and it will mean something different to young women than to older women — no matter whether men and women of any age agree with the argument. In such cases writers will make certain assumptions based on these important aspects of their readers' identities and will adjust their claims and appeals accordingly.

Consider the following two examples, both of which are arguments about differences in how men and women are treated. The first is a letter written to the editor of *Health* magazine, which is devoted to health-related and lifestyle issues for women. The writer was responding to an article about changing ideas of beauty:

> Dorothy Foltz-Gray's article "The Changing Face of Beauty" [*Mind*, July/August] is a stunning example of a woman co-opted by our patriarchal society's focus on skin-deep appearance.
>
> She writes that the power of beauty gets you "more than just admiration." And that "it was exhilarating to think I had a little of that power, too."
>
> After 15 years in the corporate world, I have had my fill of women getting ahead because of their looks. Foltz-Gray was careful to assert that she got the "homely" woman's job based upon her own merits, even though she does acknowledge that her looks played a part. She did "feel uncomfortable" with that but accepted the job.
>
> I would have liked to see the article point the finger at the real culprit (men in power) and advocate for change, rather than continuing to accept the status quo. I believe that the media has an obligation to expose abuses of power, especially a magazine devoted to women's total wellness.

This writer is obviously addressing the magazine's editors directly, but she makes it clear that she assumes *Health* to be a magazine for and about women. She also makes an assertion that might be acceptable to most readers of this magazine (most of whom are women) but would certainly be controversial for other audiences: that "men in power" are the reason for women's struggles to advance in the workplace. Given the audience for *Health*, she perhaps doesn't need to worry about alienating male readers. She seems to be saying to her female readers, "C'mon, let's call this problem what it is!" If she were writing for a different audience — say, a more general audience that would include as many men as women or readers of a business-oriented publication such as the *Wall Street Journal* — she would have to assume that her assertion would not be accepted by many in her audience, and she would probably have to defend it.

The second example also addresses the issue of differences in how men and women are treated, but it does so in a less strident way and for a less specific audience. Nevertheless, although the writer, Susan Brownmiller, is addressing a broader audience than the readers of *Health* magazine, she seems to address male and female readers differently. This excerpt is taken from her book *Femininity:*

> We are talking, admittedly, about an exquisite esthetic. Enormous pleasure can be extracted from feminine pursuits as a creative outlet or purely as relaxation; indeed, indulgence for the sake of fun, or art, or attention, is among femininity's great joys. But the chief attraction (and the central paradox, as well) is the competitive edge that femininity seems to promise in the unending struggle to survive, and perhaps to triumph. The world smiles favorably on the feminine woman: it extends little courtesies and minor privilege. Yet the nature of this competitive edge is ironic, at best, for one works at femininity by accepting restrictions, by limiting one's sights, by choosing an indirect route, by scattering concentration and not giving one's all as a man would to his own, certifiably masculine, interests. It does not require a great leap of imagination for a woman to understand the feminine principle as a grand collection of compromises, large and small, that she simply must make in order to render herself a successful woman. If she has difficulty in satisfying femininity's demands, if its illusions go against her grain, or if she is criticized for her shortcomings and imperfections, the more she will see femininity as a desperate strategy of appeasement, a strategy she may not have the wish or the courage to abandon, for failure looms in either direction.

Here Brownmiller is addressing the same basic issue as the previous writer: the potential effect of being a woman on one's success in life. Brownmiller knows that her readers will be both men and women. Yet there seems to be a subtle difference in the way she addresses readers who are men compared to readers who are women. For one thing, she is writing as a woman, and in doing so, she refers to experiences that only women readers will be able to relate to. For example, she describes the "enormous pleasure" of "feminine pursuits." Although she always uses the third person and never speaks of women as "we," these references to the female experience seem to create a bond between her and women readers that cannot exist with male readers because women readers will be able to share these experiences with her. But she makes these references without referring to men in a way that might alienate them (as the previous writer seems to do). No doubt Brownmiller understands that men and women might react very differently to her argument, but she takes advantage of those different reactions in presenting her argument — assuming, it seems, that women will know what she is talking about and perhaps inviting men to try to understand the experience of femininity that she is describing.

CONSIDERING AGE

Look again at the passage written by Susan Brownmiller and imagine that she is writing for an audience composed mostly of older readers — for example, the readers of *Modern Maturity*, a magazine published by the American Association of Retired Persons. She might wish to handle the issue of femininity somewhat differently, since many of those readers would probably experience gender in different ways than younger readers would. In this sense the age of an intended audience can influence how a writer makes an argument. In some cases an argument is intended for readers of a very specific age, and the writer's language, strategies, and even topics will be shaped accordingly. An argument in favor of a particular kind of retirement fund might play well with readers of *Modern Maturity*, but it wouldn't appear in *Seventeen* magazine or in a flyer from a college career development service. Sometimes, the effect of the age of intended readers is more subtle. Consider what assumptions journalist Camille Sweeney makes about the age of her readers in the following passage, taken from the beginning of an article in which Sweeney argues that the appeal of Internet chat rooms for teens has to do with the age-old adolescent struggle to establish an identity:

> "Yo yo yo, what's up what's up?" The lines scroll up my screen. Difference fonts, different colors, the words whiz by, everyone's screen name sounding vaguely pornographic. I'm on America Online, in a chat room for young adults. There are hundreds of such chat rooms on AOL, and it has taken a lot of Net navigating simply to find one that has room enough to let me in.
>
> For all the crowds and clamoring, there's not much being said in this chat room, or rather, not much that's being paid attention to. A 16-year-old girl is talking about her baby due in two months. A grumpy 15-year-old guy reluctantly wishes her well. Another girl, 17, asks, "Are your parents cool with it?" The lines continue to scroll, a word here, a phrase there, live text that reads much like a flow of conversation you might overhear in a crowded high-school hallway or parking lot between classes in old-fashioned meat space (that is, anyplace not in the cyber-world).

Sweeney goes on to tell readers that she spent several months visiting chat rooms in an effort to "determine if there is such a thing as a cyberself," and she ultimately takes the position that what goes on in cyberspace with teens isn't really new: Teens are just trying to discover who they are. It's obvious that Sweeney isn't addressing her essay to teens themselves; she knows that teenagers will make up only a small number of her readers. But older readers might be much less familiar with the cyberworld Sweeney is describing. As a result, she not only must try to give her readers a sense of what happens in chat rooms, but she also must explain some terms (such as "meat space"). Perhaps more important, Sweeney refers to teens as "other" — that is, she discusses teens as if they are different from her readers. In this way she tries to connect with her readers on the basis of age. And that sense of connection — of older readers observing unfamiliar teen social behavior — runs throughout her essay and gives it some of its persuasive impact. To appreciate that impact, imagine how different her opening paragraphs might be if they had been written for readers of *Teen* magazine.

CONSIDERING SEXUAL ORIENTATION

To turn to another kind of cultural context, consider the implications of the simple question "Do you have a family?" When one adult asks it of another in the United States, the question usually means "Are you married with children?" So how is a single gay man to respond? He might cut the conversation short by interpreting it to be a query about marriage and children and simply respond, "No." Or he might take the question literally (or subversively) by saying, "Yes, I have two brothers and several nieces," although this response could trigger annoyance, confusion, or a more direct question about his own household.

What might happen, then, if you use an expression such as "family values" or "our children" in an argument? Strictly speaking, no one is excluded from these words on the basis of sexual orientation. Anyone can create a family, and increasing numbers of same-gender couples are adopting children. Nevertheless, someone who is gay, lesbian, bisexual, or transgendered might associate expressions such as "family values" and "our children" with a heterosexual majority to which they do not belong. The phrase "family values" is especially problematic because it has often been used in rhetoric designed to limit the rights of minorities — as in the campaign that led to the Defense of Marriage Act, a 1996 federal law that excludes same-gender couples from the right to have a civil marriage.

If it can be problematic for writers to assume that all members of their audience are heterosexual, it can be challenging to write about sexual orientation. Words such as "gay" and "queer" are emotionally charged, and occasions for stereotyping abound. For example, a reference to the "gay community" implies that all gay individuals (regardless of religion, race, or social class) socialize together. And it might not be clear whether the "gay community" includes women, since there are women who describe themselves as "gay," while others insist on the use of "lesbian" on the grounds that "gay" was taken over by men. Unless we assume that it is reasonable to write about "the heterosexual community," which would be a very big community indeed, it is better to write about "gay and lesbian communities" instead of lumping diverse people into a single group about which a generalization is going to be made.

In the introduction to *A Queer Geography*, Frank Browning writes,

> As an American, as a white man, as a creature of the late twentieth century, as a male who grew up when the *New York Times, Time, Life, Newsweek,* and all of television and radio regarded homosexuality as either criminal or diseased, I am incapable of experiencing my desires as either a young Neapolitan in Italy or a Sambia tribesman in New Guinea — two places where homosexuality has a rich and ancient history and few make much effort to disguise. The strategies of social and psychological survival I have employed set me apart radically from middle-class Brazilians or Filipinos and even from most of the young men I write about in this book.

In other words, Browning sees his cultural context as being defined by nationality (American) race, (white), gender (male), and age (being no longer young in the late twentieth century) in addition to sexual orientation (homosexual). As you read and write arguments, recognize that sexual orientation is an element of culture but cannot exist separately from other aspects of cultural context. It would be risky to assume that anyone could be either completely defined by sexual orientation or completely understood without some consideration of it.

HISTORICAL CONTEXT

The previous example of Harvey Araton's essay about Qureshi, the Pakistani tennis player (see pages 46–48), points to another crucial kind of context for argumentation: the moment at which an argument is being made. Araton's essay might have had a certain impact because it was published in the midst of intense, terrible fighting between Israelis and Palestinians in the Middle East in 2002. It was also published during the Wimbledon tennis championship, the world's most prestigious tennis tournament. If Araton had written his essay a year earlier (assuming that Qureshi and Hadad were playing as doubles partners at that time), when the conflict in the Middle East was not as intense and when international attention was not focused on that part of the world, his argument might have been less provocative or persuasive for many readers. It might even have had an entirely different significance. Araton's main argument, which focused on achieving a peaceful solution to a long-standing and bloody conflict, was really not about tennis at all, but he used the decision by Qureshi and his tennis partner Hadad — and the controversy surrounding their decision — to give his argument a timeliness and force it might not otherwise have had. In other words, *when* an argument is made can be as important as how it is made.

The ancient Greek rhetoricians used the term *kairos* to describe an opportune moment for making a specific argument or trying to persuade an audience to act in a specific situation. We might think of *kairos* as making the right argument at the right time. Araton's essay is a good example of an author taking advantage of a particular moment to make his argument. Historical context, then, can refer to understanding when to make a particular argument. A particular appeal might be persuasive at one time but not at another. Circumstances change, and that change can affect what a writer chooses to write in an argument as well as how readers respond to that argument. After the horrible events of September 11, 2001, for example, many people thought that certain kinds of statements and criticisms were inappropriate. Comedians refrained from skewering politicians, especially President George W. Bush; editorialists and political commentators did likewise. In such a climate arguments that relied on criticisms of the President would widely be considered not only ineffective but inappropriate and even disrespectful. Indeed, filmmaker and political essayist Michael Moore found himself in this very situation when his publisher hesitated to release Moore's book *Stupid White Men* after the events of September 11. Given the sudden change in the American political climate as a result of September 11, the publisher asked Moore to rewrite the book, which was a humorous but irreverent attack on the Bush presidency. In effect, Moore was asked to change his argument about the Bush administration because the times had changed. Although Moore refused to do so, it took many months before his book was finally made available for sale to the public. Moore's experience is a dramatic but revealing example of how events can profoundly affect what audiences will accept as appropriate in argumentation.

Historical context encompasses more than just making the right argument at the right time, however. The time in which an argument is made can profoundly affect not only how an audience reacts to it but also its very meaning and import. Consider the opening paragraph of the Declaration of Independence, one of the most famous arguments ever written:

> When in the course of human events, it becomes necessary for one people to dissolve the political bands which have connected them with another, and to assume among the powers of the earth, the separate and equal station to which the Laws of Nature and Nature's God entitle them, a decent respect to the opinions of mankind requires that they should declare the causes which impel them to the separation.

Jefferson's well-known words are general, even abstract, but we know that they refer to a specific situation and to specific events that occurred in 1776 and before. But some of the abstract ideas in this passage carry different meanings in 1776 than they do today. For example, the very idea of a colony or state separating from a monarchy such as ruled Great Britain at that time was radical and even unthinkable to many people. Today, such a notion does not seem so radical. Similarly, what Jefferson meant by "Nature" and "Nature's God" is not necessarily what we might mean if we used those terms today. Indeed, the most famous lines from the Declaration of Independence make an argument that most Americans probably accept as universal but which Jefferson knew to be extremely radical in his day:

> We hold these truths to be self-evident, that all men are created equal, that they are endowed by their Creator with certain unalienable Rights, that among these are Life, Liberty and the pursuit of Happiness.

Such "truths" were not widely considered "self-evident," as Jefferson surely knew, which gave his argument a kind of shock value it would not have today. Perhaps an even more revealing illustration of how the historical context can affect the meaning of an assertion is contained in the famous statement that "all men are created equal." Today such a statement might carry a sexist message that it would not have had for readers in 1776. Indeed, today this statement might be interpreted as a negative one because of what we now consider to be sexist language.

We need not look back 200 years for examples of how historical context can alter meanings in this way. Think of the connotations of the contested and often controversial term *patriotism* in the United States. At times — for example, at the height of the anti–Vietnam War protests in the early 1970s — that term carried largely negative connotations for some audiences and positive connotations for others. At other times — during the takeover of the U.S. embassy in Iran in the late 1970s, say — a writer could assume that the term would be interpreted positively by most American readers. Even in cases that are not quite as dramatic as these, historical context is part of any argument and affects how that argument works and what it means. Good writers attend to historical context, and careful readers are attuned to it as well.

Obviously, in composing an argument, you can never address every possible contextual factor, and very likely you will not even be aware of the potential impact of some of those factors. But you will always be making your argument about a specific issue at a specific moment in time in a specific rhetorical situation. The more carefully you consider those factors, the more effective your argument is likely to be.

4

THE MEDIA FOR ARGUMENT

THE MEDIA

George Will is a well-known conservative commentator who appears regularly on television shows devoted to political affairs. Will also writes a syndicated column for newspapers as well as essays for publications such as *Newsweek*. His arguments about political and social issues are conservative; his basic message regarding the limits of government in American social and economic life is constant. But do his arguments change in any way when he is making them on a political affairs television show as compared to his columns or essays? Here's the opening paragraph of a *Newsweek* essay Will wrote in 2002:

> These are the best of times for the worst of people. And for the toxic idea at the core of all the most murderous ideologies of the modern age. That idea is that human nature is, if not a fiction, at least so watery and flimsy that it poses no serious impediment to evil political entities determined to treat people as malleable clay to be molded into creatures at once submissive and violent.

OR ARGUMENT

Will goes on in his essay to pursue this philosophical point about human nature. You will probably agree that even this brief passage reflects a sophisticated writing style and a learned voice. Look at the third sentence, for example; it is complex and sounds scholarly. Do you think Will would use this same kind of language to make this point if he were speaking on a television talk show? Would he write the essay differently if he intended to publish it on the Web? In other words, what role does the medium play in his arguments — or anyone's arguments?

In this chapter we examine the role of the medium in argumentation. As you will see, many elements of argumentation, such as addressing an audience appropriately and using evidence effectively, apply to all medium. So some of what we discuss in relation to print will be important for arguments in any medium. But although print remains an important medium for making arguments, other media, including television, radio, and newer online media such as Internet discussion groups and the World Wide Web, have become increasingly significant as forums for public discourse. To argue effectively in these media requires an understanding of how media might influence or change the way you construct and present an argument.

ANALYZING ARGUMENTS IN PRINT

We live in a culture defined by print — so much so that we take it for granted. We tend to see print as a "natural" medium for literacy and for communication. But print isn't natural. It is a technology — or rather, a set of technologies — for transforming human language into something other than oral speech. Historians tell us that the invention of the printing press in the 15th century changed the way writing and reading were done and the role they played in Western culture. Five hundred years later, print permeates our lives, and we probably engage in written argumentation without ever thinking about the way print can shape arguments. In this section we examine how arguments tend to be made in print so that you can become a more careful reader of written arguments.

READING ARGUMENTS CRITICALLY

Reading is not a passive activity. When you read a newspaper editorial, for example, you are not simply trying to understand the writer's point. You are also engaged in a sophisticated intellectual and social activity in which you try to analyze, evaluate, and react to the argument. The more carefully you do so, the more substantive will be your engagement with the argument and the better will be your understanding of the issue under discussion. Ideally, reading an argument should be as careful and sophisticated an act as writing an argument.

The more you know about the strategies writers use in constructing their arguments, the better able you will be to analyze and evaluate those arguments without falling victim to subtle persuasive techniques that a writer might use. In addition, the more you know about yourself as a reader, the easier it will be for you to identify appeals or lines of reasoning that might be questionable or flawed. But as we have already noted, human beings react in countless ways to their experiences and to each other in various situations. One

FIGURE 4-1

Wooden Screw Printing Press, circa 1450

Gutenberg's technology still influences how written arguments are made.

of the challenges of reading arguments critically, then, is to try to manage the complexity that is inherent in human interactions, especially when it comes to the kinds of difficult issues about which we tend to engage in argument.

Print is often considered the traditional medium for formal argument (even though formal arguments have always been made orally as well, for example, in a courtroom, government hearing, or political rally). And print can influence arguments in other media. For example, arguments delivered as speeches are usually written out first; similarly, radio or television essays are also crafted in written form first. But print is not a monolithic medium for arguments. There are countless varieties of print forums within which people can argue:

- Magazines and newspapers of all kinds
- Flyers and circulars
- Memos, letters, and pamphlets
- Essays written for college classes
- Books

Reading an argument carefully requires you to take into account the specific print forum in which that argument appears, for different forums lend themselves to different kinds of arguments. For example, an editorial in the conservative business newspaper the *Wall Street Journal* will usually differ in tone, style, and content from an essay in the left-leaning magazine *Mother Jones*. Each of these publications has a different purpose and addresses a somewhat different audience. To understand an argument published in each of these print forums requires you to have some sense of those differences.

Let's look at arguments in two very different publications to see how the nature of the publication affects the way each writer approaches his argument. The first example is taken from an essay in *USA Today* by its founder and publisher, Al Neuharth. In the opening paragraphs of his essay, Neuharth introduces the issue of the early starting dates for the school year:

> "Back to School." The three most wonderful words for the ears of most parents.
>
> This year, more classrooms in grades K-12 are opening sooner than ever. August has become back-to-school month. Some will open as early as next week. Many on August 12. Most by August 19.

The audience for *USA Today* is a very general one, and Neuharth knows that. The style of writing on the opinion page of *USA Today*, where this essay appeared, tends to be informal, and the topics tend to be current events or controversies. Notice that although Neuharth implicitly addresses the broad audience of all readers of his newspaper, he also narrows the audience somewhat by referring to parents of school-age children. By attempting to establish this connection with a specific audience, Neuharth might strengthen his argument, appeal to those many readers who share his experience of preparing children for school in August. As a reader, you might want to evaluate the extent to which sharing that experience affects your response to his argument, which rests on the assumption, as he writes, that "most kids get a little bored with fun and games by August." While that might be true — and it might resonate with parents who must deal with their own bored children — it might not address more complex implications associated with starting school earlier in August. For example, businesspeople who rely on summer tourism for their livelihood might point to income that is lost as a result of families not vacationing in August. For such readers, Neuharth's appeal might ring hollow. However, given the nature of *USA Today's* opinion page and its broad audience, Neuharth probably doesn't need to address such specific aspects of the issue. In short, his general argument and his strategy of trying to establish a connection with his readers as parents are appropriate for this publication.

Compare Neuharth's approach to the following excerpt from an essay in *Climbing* magazine, in which editor Duane Raleigh addresses a very specialized topic for a much narrower audience:

> You've seen the ads in this magazine and you've visited the websites. Euro dot.coms selling top-brand merchandise for as much as half what you'd pay for the same gear at your local shop. High-end shoes for $60, ropes for $70, ice tools for less than retailers pay at wholesale. Crazy! These are the prices I used to pay for much, much lower-tech gear back in the 1970s. Something screwy must be going on — what's the catch?
>
> The catch is not simple, and takes a tangled, often convoluted and contradictory path. Mostly, foreign dot.coms, because they typically buy directly from the

manufacturer (usually also European) and sell directly to you, bypass the usual distribution (the importers here in the U.S.) and sales channels (your retail climbing shops). Cutting out these two channels eliminates two U.S.-based markups, which largely explains why their prices are so low.

In this instance Raleigh's audience is obviously composed of people who climb and would therefore be interested in the prices of climbing gear. His magazine has a very specific focus on climbing-related issues, which would perhaps seem esoteric to a more general audience. If you are not a climber, Raleigh's appeal might not have much impact on you; indeed, if you are not a climber, he might not care, since it is unlikely that you buy climbing gear or are concerned about the effect of Internet sales on U.S. climbing retailers. Moreover, nonclimbers would probably not understand the importance of the prices Raleigh quotes in his first paragraph. (In 2002, climbing shoes typically sold in the U.S. for between $100 and $160, ropes for $120 to $180; you need to know this to understand his argument.)

If you look a bit more closely, you can see other ways in which Raleigh's argument is shaped by the nature of the magazine he writes for. For one thing his conversational writing style is typical of *Climbing* magazine. An assertion like "Crazy!" fits here, whereas it might be inappropriate for other publications. In addition, Raleigh refers to the 1970s in a way that establishes his authority as someone who understands the markets for climbing gear as a result of his many years of experience as a climber. That strategy is likely to be persuasive to his readers, since climbers often identify credibility with climbing experience. In these ways, Raleigh's argument is very specifically tuned to his magazine.

In these examples the writers tailor their strategies to the audiences that read their publications. In a sense they write in a way that assumes a kind of community of readers, defined by the publication as a medium. But writers can also intentionally provoke an audience in making their argument. For example, a person who is opposed to teaching evolution in schools and is responding to an editorial in favor of teaching evolution might intentionally criticize advocates of evolution on moral grounds, knowing that such readers would object. Those readers would very likely not be persuaded by an antievolution argument in any case, and the writer's criticisms would play well with supporters of his or her stance. Such a strategy is common in some kinds of publications, such as letters to newspaper editors, but it might be inappropriate for others.

In reading an argument critically, you should try to account for these strategies and be aware of how an argument can be shaped by the specific print publication for which it is written. Some teachers might advise you always to read skeptically, and that can be good advice because it can help you guard against subtle but powerful appeals that can shape your reaction to an argument. In sum, reading critically means looking carefully at the way a writer tries to address a specific audience for a specific publication; it means being aware of how your own perspective, beliefs, and values might influence your reaction to particular arguments.

EVALUATING ETHOS

If writers of arguments try to establish a connection with readers in a print medium, readers also gain a sense of connection to a writer through that same medium. But as a reader you have the option of resisting that connection. In other words, you might not identify with the writer — or with the audience he or she directly addresses — or you might not *wish* to identify with the writer. There can be many reasons to resist such a connection, but one important reason has to do with your sense of the writer's credibility. You are not likely to be persuaded by a writer whose credibility you question, no matter how inclined you might be to agree with his or her argument. In Chapter 2 we examined how ethos — a writer's persona and credibility — can be a powerful strategy for writers of arguments. Here we'd like to explore the control *you* exercise as a reader in analyzing and evaluating a writer's *ethos.*

Writers can establish their ethos in a variety of ways. For example, the following excerpt is the opening paragraph of an essay entitled "The Laments of Commuting" by Daisy Hernandez, which was published in the *New York Times:*

> It's hard to make commuters happy. So much is working against us. Virtually no subway platforms have air conditioning. Express lines suddenly go local. And it's a long-distance hike through the underground pedestrian connection between ACE and the NRQWS1237 trains.

Notice that Hernandez immediately identifies herself as a commuter in her essay. Readers will be more likely to consider her credible because of her knowledge and her experience as a commuter. In addition, her conversational tone suggests that she is reasonable and personable — someone you might find yourself sitting next to on the train as you commute to work. Even though commuting is a serious matter for millions of people, Hernandez adopts a tone that isn't overly serious, and her lighter tone might invite readers — especially those who do not commute — to engage her argument. So in this case Hernandez's experience as a commuter as well as her tone may help establish her credibility with readers. As a reader, you will want to take note of your own reaction to Hernandez's experience and tone and decide whether they do make her a more credible writer in this instance.

Compare Hernandez's approach with that of the following writer, whose letter to the editor of *USA Today* was written in response to an article about actor Mike Myers:

> The sheer stupidity of what many Americans find entertaining never ceases to amaze me. Another tired, hackneyed sequel to the foolish *Austin Powers* series is dragged out for the people who wouldn't get a joke if it didn't include obvious "you're-supposed-to-laugh-now" cuts.
>
> The debate still rages as to who is less funny: Jim Carrey or *Austin Powers'* Mike Myers. Both couldn't act their way out of a wet paper bag, so instead they pump out inane movies with a grade-school humor level. It's as if IQ is unwelcome in movie production these days.
>
> Honestly, who couldn't star in *Austin Powers?* The only difference between Myers' embarrassing himself and any number of fools we've all had to tolerate is that Myers has cultivated an entire career by being gratingly unfunny.
>
> I gave in this past weekend and managed to suffer through about 15 minutes of *the Spy Who Shagged Me,* playing on cable. I want my 15 minutes back, Mr. Myers.

This writer's opening sentence immediately creates a distinction between him and the "many Americans" who find Myers' movies entertaining. That distinction might serve the writer's purpose, since he obviously excludes himself from that category of readers. So he might not be concerned if such readers dismiss his argument. However, consider how the writer's tone might affect his ethos among other readers, who might even agree with his assessment of Myers. This writer criticizes Myers's comedy, but he offers no evidence to support his main contention that Myers's acting ability is poor; instead, he offers simple assertions to that effect. Although readers who share the writer's opinion might nod in agreement, it is worth considering how other readers, who might have no strong opinion one way or the other about Myers, might react to this argument. For such readers this writer might sound arrogant or unreasonable, and his credibility therefore suffers. In this case, then, the writer's ethos might undermine his argument for some readers while enhancing it for others.

Usually, writers of arguments convey their ethos in much more subtle ways. We've already discussed several strategies:

- The writer's tone
- The writer's knowledge and/or experience
- The specific evidence a writer offers to support his or her points

Writers can also invoke values that they assume their readers will share as a way to establish themselves as credible. Here is well-known television news anchor Dan Rather writing about the AIDS epidemic:

Eighty-five million. It's a big number, more than one percent of the total world population. Eight-five million is what the world health experts say will be the total number of cases of HIV/AIDS in eight years, if the epidemic continues its terrible advance.

Twenty-five million — also a big number. By the end of the decade, that's the number of children worldwide that the United Nations believes will be growing up having lost one or more parents to AIDS.

These figures are terrifying, in purely human terms and in view of their larger social implications.

Rather's column appeared in hundreds of newspapers and was therefore read by a large audience, most of whom probably already knew him as a television news anchor. So he already had credibility among many of his readers. But notice that Rather does not rely exclusively on his fame as a news anchor; he does not simply assert that the AIDS epidemic is terrifying, assuming that readers will believe him. Instead, he offers statistics to establish the scale of the epidemic, and then he appeals to his readers' sense of humanity, to their concern for the human suffering that this epidemic will cause. This appeal helps to establish a connection with his readers as caring human beings, but it also helps to reinforce his credibility as someone who shares their concerns and not someone who simply reports the news. Such an ethos might make his argument more persuasive to his readers. Does it do so for you?

Ethos plays a role in all arguments, but in print it is primarily how a writer chooses his or her words that establishes ethos. As a reader you can gain a better sense of the way a writer tries to present himself or herself to an audience by attending carefully to how words are used in an argument. In arguments that are intended to address problems or negotiate differences, ethos becomes even more important, for the credibility of participants in the argument can deeply affect our sense of purpose and motivation in an argument: We are more apt to believe those we trust.

APPRAISING EVIDENCE

One of the most important — and difficult — aspects of making effective arguments is identifying and using appropriate evidence. Being able to appraise evidence is a crucial part of evaluating arguments, but appraising evidence can be challenging. Consider the following examples. The first is a letter to the editors of *Consumer Reports* magazine; in this letter the writer challenges a recommendation the magazine made in a report on how to save money:

> I disagree with your money-saving recommendation to stick with regular gasoline. I own a 2001 *Chrysler Sebring* and a 1996 *Ford Taurus GL,* both of which are supposed to use regular. But I've found that using midgrade 89-octane fuel increases highway mileage by 2 to 5 mpg.

Here's the editors' response:

> It's good to hear that something yields better fuel economy, but we wouldn't credit the fuel. We have found that temperature and climate conditions affect mileage more than octane.

Who is right? Or we might rephrase the question: Whose evidence is more convincing? The writer of the letter provides evidence of good fuel economy using a higher-octane fuel; the magazine editors refer to their own tests as evidence suggesting otherwise. How do we judge the evidence in such a case?

As these examples suggest, almost anything can be used as evidence: statistics, opinions, observations, theories, anecdotes. It is not always easy to decide whether a particular kind of evidence might be appropriate for a specific claim. Moreover, what counts as appropriate and persuasive evidence always depends upon context. Personal experience might be acceptable to readers of a popular consumer magazine but not necessarily for a technical report on fuel economy for a government agency. The rhetorical situation in which an argument is made will help determine not only what kinds of evidence are most appropriate for that argument but also whether that evidence is likely to be persuasive.

With that in mind, let's look at four commonly used kinds of evidence:

1. Facts or statistics
2. Personal experience
3. Authority
4. Values

Facts as Evidence   In the following excerpt from an essay published in the online public interest journal *TomPaine.com,* writer Joan Wile argues against a tax refund that President George W. Bush sponsored in 2001. Wile contends that opposition to the Bush tax policies is important, even a year after the policy was adopted. Writing in 2002, she asserts,

> However, the tax abatement issue is still, if not more, critical today than a year ago. Our needs are even greater but with less revenue to address them — our receding economy; our health care crisis; our worsening environment; our failing education system; the reestablished deficit; our increasing numbers of poor with the

concomitant smaller numbers of rich controlling greater amounts of wealth, as well as the necessity for greater defense (but sane and non-threatening to our civil liberties) measures against terrorism.

Wile tries to establish the importance of the tax abatement issue by presenting evidence that the nation's ongoing "needs" continue to be great. Her evidence consists of references to the problems facing the United States: "our receding economy; our health care crisis; our worsening environment; our failing education system; the reestablished deficit; our increasing numbers of poor." Notice that Wile refers to these problems as facts without necessarily establishing them as such. For example, she refers to the "receding economy" without providing, say, statistics on economic activity or stock market performance to demonstrate that the economy is indeed in recession. She can do so because in September 2002, when her essay was published, the U.S. economy was in recession. So simply referring to the economic situation suffices as evidence in this instance. Similarly, she cites "our worsening environment" and "failing education system" without specific information about them. Given the audience for *TomPaine.com,* Wile can assume that most of her readers will accept these references as adequate evidence, because she knows that those readers are likely to view both the environment and the education system as being in crisis; they will not demand further information to support those "facts." But what if she were writing for a politically conservative journal? In that case she would most likely have to supply additional evidence — perhaps in the form of figures indicating increased air and water pollution or declining scores on standardized educational tests — to persuade readers that such crises do exist. In short, what counts as a fact and what is considered ample evidence depend on context and audience.

Whatever the writer's intended audience, a reader must ultimately decide whether the evidence presented in support of a claim is adequate. In this example Wile's argument that the tax refund was a bad idea rests on her claim that the nation has pressing problems that require tax dollars. She supports that claim by listing those problems. If you agree that the problems she lists are real and pressing, then you will likely accept her claim and find her argument persuasive. If you don't agree that such problems exist, her evidence will not be adequate to persuade you that the tax refund should be opposed. Sometimes, simply referring to something won't suffice. More specific evidence is required. Here is part of an essay by a college president who believes that the problems in U.S. schools will not be solved unless teachers are adequately supported in their work:

> We often marginalize our teachers rather than celebrate and reward their contributions. Recent national data reveal that the average annual earnings of young teachers between the ages of 22 and 28 was 30 percent less than similarly aged professionals in other fields. By the time these teachers reach 50, the salary gap almost doubles — a little more than $45,000 for veteran teachers versus almost $80,000 for non-teachers. Of course, many of these new teachers don't stay in the profession to age 50. We lose 30 percent of our new teachers in their first five years of teaching and more than 40 percent in large metropolitan areas like New York City.

This writer, R. Mark Sullivan, provides statistical data to support his claim that teachers are not celebrated and rewarded for their contributions. His audience is a general one: the readers of a regional newspaper. He can assume that they will be familiar with some of the problems facing schools, but he probably cannot assume that all his readers will accept his claim that teachers are not supported adequately. To establish that point, he cites evidence showing income disparities between teachers and other professionals. For many readers such figures can be very compelling, since income is such an important factor in most people's lives. As a result, many readers will likely see figures demonstrating lower incomes for teachers as very good evidence that teachers are not in fact well supported.

But look carefully at the second set of statistics Sullivan offers: the percentage of new teachers who quit teaching within five years. Does this evidence really support his claim that teachers are not well supported? On the surface it might seem so. One explanation for the seemingly high number of teachers leaving the profession might be their low salaries (which is what Sullivan suggests). Another explanation (which Sullivan does not suggest) might be that teachers' working conditions are difficult. These figures might also suggest that not everyone can be a good teacher, and you might believe that those who quit shouldn't be teaching anyway. If it is true that these young teachers quit because they simply have not been effective teachers, then the figures Sullivan cites might actually work against his claim: They could suggest that the best teachers remain in the classroom, while ineffective ones leave. Moreover, we are never told what the attrition rates are for other professions. How many accountants or engineers quit their jobs within five years, for example? That information could change the significance of the figures that Sullivan cites. If 25 percent of accountants or engineers quit in their first five years, then 30 percent of teachers might not seem so high a number — in which case it would not be very persuasive evidence for Sullivan's claim.

This example suggests the importance of examining evidence carefully to determine whether it actually supports a claim. As a reader, you should pay close attention to *how* a writer is using evidence as well as to *what* evidence is presented. In this example Sullivan uses statistical evidence, which is usually considered valid and can be persuasive for many audiences. But as we noted, it is important to examine just what the statistics might indicate. Even if statistical evidence is accepted as true, it may still be open to interpretation. Think about the ongoing debates about global warming. In these debates participants often point to statistics showing the rising average temperature of the earth. Most scientists seem to agree that the average global temperature has increased in the past century, but they do not agree about what that means. Do rising global temperatures *prove* that humans have caused global warming? Or do they reflect natural cycles of warming and cooling? A statistical fact by itself has no inherent significance. How it is used and in what context it is used make all the difference.

Personal Experience as Evidence   In the previous example writer R. Mark Sullivan's use of statistics can be seen as a savvy strategy because many readers are likely to accept statistical evidence as valid. But Sullivan might have used other kinds of evidence to support his claim that teachers are not adequately rewarded for their work. For example, he might have included statements from people who have left teaching because they didn't feel supported. Or he might have referred to his own experience as a teacher (assuming that he had such experience) or perhaps to the experience of someone he knows well — say, a brother or neighbor — who left teaching for that reason. The readers of a regional newspaper might well find that kind of evidence as compelling as statistical evidence. Consider how the writer of the following passage uses his own experience as evidence; the passage is taken from an essay that argues against the designation of New York's Adirondack Mountains as "wilderness":

The irony is that one actually has a truer "wilderness experience" in Adirondack lands designated "wild forest" than in those designated "wilderness." How can this be? The answer is in the numbers — of people, that is. Without the "status" of wilderness, the lowly wild forest just grows on, with little to no human molestation. While there may be a road or two, it is the road less traveled. There may not be a High Peak to bag, but chances are you'll see real wildlife . . . and some lower elevation vistas that fewer eyes have seen. And amazingly enough, you will probably not see another human. I can say this because I have experienced it.

This writer supports his claim about the wilderness experience in "wild forest" areas by stating that he has had that experience himself. It can be hard to deny the validity of such experience. Think of the weight often given to eye-witness testimony in legal cases: if a person saw something, it must be true. But the extent to which readers will find such first-hand evidence compelling will vary. And we can question this kind of evidence, just as we can question statistical data. For one thing, where exactly did this writer go in the Adirondacks? It's possible that he visited a few very unusual locations that are not representative of most "wild forest" areas. Also, *when* did he go? He would almost certainly encounter fewer (or no) other hikers in February than he would in July. And how often did he visit these places? If he visited them only once or twice, then his experience might not be typical for those areas. If so, that experience becomes much less forceful as evidence for his claim than it would be if he regularly visited these areas throughout the year. As a reader, raising questions like these will help you evaluate personal experience that is used as evidence. It can also keep you alert to questionable evidence and help you spot evidence that simply does not support the claim being made.

Authority as Evidence   Citing experts or authorities as evidence is common in all kinds of arguments, but it is especially important in many academic disciplines. Here is an excerpt from *Ecological Literacy*, in which environmental studies scholar David Orr argues that perpetual economic growth cannot be sustained without irreparable damage to the earth's ecosystems:

> In a notable book in 1977, economist Fred Hirsch described other limits to growth that were inherently social. As the economy grows, the goods and services available to everyone theoretically increase. . . . After basic biological and physical needs are met, an increasing portion of consumption is valued because it raises one's status in society. But, "If everyone in a crowd stands on tiptoe," as Hirsch puts it, "no one sees better." Rising levels of consumption do not necessarily increase one's status.

In this passage Orr draws on the work of a respected economist to support his claim about the dangers of constant economic growth. Notice that Orr underscores the authority of Hirsch's work by describing his book as "notable." Then he presents Hirsch's views about economic growth. Following this passage, Orr summarizes what Hirsch describes as the effects of the desire for more consumption, including such unhappy consequences as "a decline in friendliness, the loss of altruism and mutual obligation, increased time pressures," and so on. Then Orr concludes, "In short, after basic biological needs are met, further growth both 'fails to deliver its full promise' and 'undermines its social foundations.' "

In this case Orr does not offer factual evidence; rather, he cites Hirsch's theories to make the claim that unchecked economic growth is undesirable. In effect, Orr is deferring to Hirsch's expertise as an economist to support this claim. Although what Hirsch offers is essentially an interpretation of economic data and social and economic developments, rather than the data themselves, his status as an expert gives his interpretation weight. Orr relies on that status in using Hirsch's ideas as evidence.

In evaluating an argument like Orr's, you must decide how credible the authority or expert really is. If you know nothing about the work of Fred Hirsch, you have to take Orr's word for it or find Hirsch's book and examine it for yourself. Notice that Orr summarizes Hirsch's key ideas in this passage. He probably assumed that many of his readers would not be familiar with Hirsch's theories. So telling us that Hirsch is an economist who authored a "notable" book helps to establish Hirsch's authority on the subject. Orr's claim depends in large measure on whether his readers accept that authority as credible.

In many cases writers cite a well-known authority or expert in supporting a claim. Using such an authority to support a claim has obvious advantages. Not only will readers be familiar with the authority, but a widely accepted authority can have an established credibility that a writer can rely on. Consider how Martin Luther King, Jr., in this passage from his famous "Letter From a Birmingham Jail," draws on biblical and historical figures to support his claim that being an extremist for freedom is just and right:

> But though I was initially disappointed at being categorized as an extremist, as I continued to think about the matter I gradually gained a measure of satisfaction from the label. Was not Jesus an extremist for love: "Love your enemies, bless them that curse you, do good to them that hate you, and pray for them which despitefully use you, and persecute you." Was not Amos an extremist for justice: "Let justice roll down like waters and righteousness like an overflowing stream." Was not Paul an extremist for the Christian gospel: "I bear in my body the marks of the Lord Jesus." Was not Martin Luther an extremist: "Here I stand; I cannot do otherwise, so help me God." And John Bunyan: "I will stay in jail to the end of my days before I make a butchery of my conscience." And Abraham Lincoln: "This nation cannot survive half slave and half free." And Thomas Jefferson: "We hold these truths to be self-evident, that all men are created equal."

Clearly, King expects these names to have credibility with his readers. The moral weight of the names he cites will give force to the quotations he uses as evidence in this passage.

Values as Evidence   The passage from Martin Luther King's "Letter From a Birmingham Jail" points to a final kind of evidence: values or beliefs. (You can read King's Letter From a Birmingham Jail on pages 508–520.) Although King uses the authority of the names he cites in this passage, he is also invoking deeply held moral values. Elsewhere in his "Letter" he uses these values directly as evidence to support specific claims. For example, in arguing that he and his followers were justified in breaking laws prohibiting Blacks from visiting public places, King cites a moral principle:

> One has not only a legal but a moral responsibility to obey just laws. Conversely, one has a moral responsibility to disobey unjust laws. I would agree with St. Augustine that "an unjust law is no law at all."

In effect, King uses the value of justice as evidence that his disobedience was justified and even necessary. Of course, using values or beliefs as evidence can be tricky. If you invoke a principle or value that your readers do not share, your evidence will not be very per-

FIGURE 4-2   **Presenting Information Visually**

Charts such as these, which include data related to driving and fuel economy, present information efficiently and effectively.

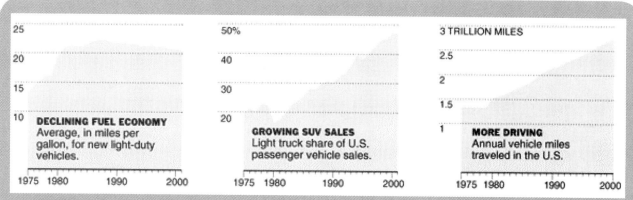

SOURCES: World Resources Institute, Dr. James J. MacKenzie, American Council for an Energy-Efficient Economy, Federal Highway Administration, Environmental Protection Agency

suasive to them, and your argument may be weakened. In addition, values and beliefs can be open to interpretation, just like factual evidence or personal experience. Consider, for example, the ongoing controversies about capital punishment. Both opponents and supporters of capital punishment cite moral values to support their arguments — sometimes, the very same value or principle (for example, "Thou shalt not kill"). In assessing such evidence, be aware of how it might be received by readers.

Presenting Evidence in Visual Form   Evidence, especially factual or statistical evidence, is sometimes presented in visual formats within a written argument. In some cases presenting evidence graphically can be more effective than simply incorporating it into the text.

Imagine that you are writing an essay in which you argue that American driving habits are a prime contributor to environmental destruction and possibly to global warming. The charts in Figure 4-2 present three sets of statistical data:

- Changes in average fuel economy for light-duty vehicles in the United States
- Increasing sales of sport utility vehicles (SUVs)
- Changes in the number of miles driven annually by American drivers

All three charts show data over a twenty-five-year time period, and all three include data that you could use as evidence to support a claim that U.S. driving habits have changed over time in ways that potentially damage the environment.

But notice that each of these charts actually represents a *set* of data, not just a single fact. For example, the first chart reveals that average fuel economy rose dramatically from 1975 to about 1989, from less that 15 miles per gallon to approximately 22 miles per gallon. The same chart shows that fuel economy declined steadily from about 1989 to 2000; the decline was about 2 or 3 miles per gallon, or about 10 percent. The chart also indicates that the steepest rise in fuel efficiency occurred around 1980. All of this information might be relevant as evidence for your claim. You might include several sentences with selected statistical information, much as we have done in this paragraph. Or you can present the chart, which includes all the information we have just described efficiently and in a format that makes it easily accessible to your readers. Indeed, the chart might make your evidence more effective because of the visual impact of the line indicating the decline in fuel efficiency since 1989. Placed next to the other two charts, which present different but related data, the chart becomes a means to convey important evidence efficiently and with a potentially powerful impact on readers. In effect, the format of the chart lets your readers "see" the evidence.

Word processing and desktop publishing computer software, along with the rise of the World Wide Web as a medium with multimedia capabilities, make it easy for writers to incorporate visual elements into their arguments. At the same time these technologies make it even more important for readers to develop the ability to evaluate evidence carefully. Evidence presented visually, as in the charts above, can be appealing and persuasive, but it should be subjected to the same careful scrutiny that you would use to assess any evidence.

ANALYZING ARGUMENTS IN VISUAL MEDIA

Images have power. It is no coincidence that in the months following the terrible events of September 11, 2001, the American flag and the colors red, white, and blue began to appear everywhere: in television and print advertisements, on flyers and posters, on book and magazine covers, on the windows of cars and trucks. At that time the well-known clothing company, Ralph Lauren, was running a series of ads featuring images of attractive models in Ralph Lauren clothing to show "the world of Ralph Lauren." Shortly after September 11, those same ads began to include images of the American flag, including one displayed discreetly but clearly on the final screen of the television commercial.

We take for granted that images are used in this way. We live in an age of multimedia communications, and we are surrounded by images on television, in print, and on the World Wide Web; on signs and billboards; on flyers and pamphlets; from the logos on race cars to the Nike swoosh on golfer Tiger Woods's ever-present baseball cap. Not only advertisers, but politicians, advocates for all kinds of causes, institutions like schools and hospitals, even individuals — all use and manipulate visual elements to communicate an idea or position and to influence a particular audience. They all use *visual rhetoric* to make an argument.

To appreciate the power of images to convey ideas, look at the photograph of President George W. Bush in Figure 4-3, which appeared in August 2002 when the President was trying to generate support for his proposed new Department of Homeland Security. This photo was taken by an Associated Press photographer, but it was certainly set up by the President's staff. For example, the staff would have determined where photographers could stand during the news conference; in that way they set the angle from which photographs of the President could be taken. Those photographs would thus produce the desired effect: to show the President along with the famous faces of past American presidents carved into Mount Rushmore.

FIGURE 4-3   President George W. Bush at a News Conference at Mount Rushmore

What does this photograph communicate about President Bush? What argument does it seem to make?

What does such a photograph communicate about President Bush? How might it influence readers' opinions about him and about his proposal for a Department of Homeland Security? Consider the cultural significance of the Mount Rushmore national monument and what it means to Americans. It not only invokes the idea of patriotism for many Americans, but it also suggests greatness with its gigantic figures of four revered American presidents. The photograph associates President Bush — and, by extension, his proposal — with those ideas of patriotism and greatness. Now consider how different the impact of a photograph of the President might be if the background at his press conference had been a wall at an airport or a dark blue curtain in a hotel conference room rather than the striking and deeply symbolic stone visages of Mount Rushmore.

The effects of visual elements can of course be much more subtle and complex than the photograph in Figure 4-3. Consider the use of the American flag in the Ralph Lauren

FIGURE 4-4   **Patriotic Advertisements**

The use of an American flag in commercials after September 11, 2001, associated companies like Ralph Lauren with patriotism.

television ads (see Figure 4-4). Like many ads, those employed appealing images to convey a positive sense of Ralph Lauren's clothing and of the company in general. The attractive models not only are well dressed, but also appear in appealing poses, doing things we associate with affluence and leisure, such as boating or horseback riding. Those images invite us to imagine ourselves enjoying such a life and suggest that Ralph Lauren's clothing is part of that life. But the addition of the American flag communicates something different, though equally powerful: that this company is an American company, even a patriotic one. It suggests that aspiring to the kind of life portrayed in the ads is patriotic. It may also convey the more serious suggestion that this company is a good citizen, united with the rest of us as Americans. Sometimes companies avoid associations with patriotism for fear of alienating U.S. consumers who might be cynical about politics and about their government. After September 11, 2001, however, when the Ralph Lauren ads appeared, an association with patriotism was likely to evoke positive feelings among Americans.

It would be difficult to communicate all those ideas succinctly in words during a thirty- or sixty-second television advertisement. The image of the American flag does so in ways that words alone might not do. Part of the power of visual elements, then, is their capacity to communicate complex messages efficiently (see Figures 4-5 and 4-6). Recognizing this capacity can enable you to employ visual elements to enhance your own arguments and to understand their impact on you as a reader or viewer.

To an extent, arguments in visual media can be categorized in the same way as arguments in print media: Visual elements used in argumentation can appeal to our emotions, they can make logical appeals, and they can address character. However, it is important to distinguish between argument and persuasion. While we can describe an advertisement like the Ralph Lauren commercial as an argument (for example, in favor of buying American-made clothing, in support of an affluent lifestyle, or even to assert that clothing is an important part of who you are), the primary purpose of such ads is to persuade you to purchase a product. Genuine argumentation, by contrast, seeks to clarify thought in an effort to address an issue or solve a problem; ideally, it aspires to truth. Persuasion of the kind generally used in advertising has no such goal. The appeal to patriotism in advertising like the Ralph Lauren commercials is intended to persuade you to buy that company's products; if that appeal is successful, it is not likely to have been the result of careful, critical evaluation on your part, but rather the result of the strength of your emotional response to that patriotic appeal.

Despite these differences between advertising and genuine argument, examining advertising can help us understand the subtlety and complexity of visual elements in argument. Consider, for example, the advertisement for Evian Natural Spring Water in Figure 4-5. At first glance, the advertisement seems directed exclusively at pregnant women. The use of the second person, as in "If you plan to breast feed, experts say you should drink up to *30% more water* every day," seems to exclude anyone who is *not* planning to breast feed. But although the written text seems to target only a small percentage of potential buyers of imported spring water, the ad as a whole is designed to persuade a much larger group. By associating their product with motherhood, the advertisers have made an appeal to emotion. According to an old adage, mothers are as American as apple pie, so by associating a European product with motherhood, the advertisers are appealing to a widely held American value. Mother figures are revered in many different cultures, however, so the ad has the potential to reach a very large market. The opening line, "Mommy, can I have a drink of water?" perhaps invites readers to assume the role of

ARGUING WITH IMAGES

Consider the ideas conveyed by this graphic, which appeared on the Web site of a political activist group called NoLogo.org. How would you explain in words the argument being made by these images? Do they make a point about strength in numbers? About organizing for power? About individuals versus large and powerful organizations? About all these ideas?

SOURCE: http://nologo.org/ (10/13/02).

FIGURE 4-5

Complexity in Visual Rhetoric

This ad for bottled water suggests how subtle and complex visual elements can be in communicating ideas. What impressions do you take away from this ad? Why?

children. To put this ad's message simply: "Mothers are good. Evian water is good for mothers. If you are a good mother, you should buy some. If you are a good child, you should also buy some."

On closer examination we can see that the persuasive appeal of this ad relies on visual elements that are more subtle than just the image of an expectant mother. For one thing, the woman is wearing a white dress, emphasizing the purity that apparently comes with drinking the product in question. She is thoroughly at ease, reclining, a book in hand. What could be more peaceful? The image suggests the comfort that comes with wealth. After all, for every pregnant woman who can lounge in the French Alps, there are many hundreds who are working for a living. Thus, in addition to being the drink of mothers, Evian water becomes the drink of wealth and privilege; it is presented as the right water for those who are healthy, wealthy, and sophisticated. Obviously, the careful manipulation of visual elements can be very powerful in conveying a message.

DESIGN AND COLOR

Our discussion of the Evian advertisement highlights two important aspects of visual rhetoric: design and color. Notice how your eye is initially drawn to the large photograph placed prominently near the center of this ad. The image of the relaxed and slightly smiling (and attractive) woman is the first thing you focus on, and it sets the tone for the ad. If you look closely, you'll notice that the photo is placed slightly above the exact center of the advertisement. That makes it more prominent. (This is why photographers usually display their photographs slightly above center in the frame, leaving more space below it than above it. Such placement attracts your eye and focuses attention on the image.) Notice, too, the symmetry of the advertisement: It is arranged in a rectangular format that is familiar to the eye, and the text at the bottom is placed in equal proportions around the Evian logo, which appears at the bottom center of the ad. Because such a layout is familiar and proportional, it can evoke feelings of comfort, which reinforce the relaxed image of the woman. Finally, the wavy appearance of the Evian logo not only suggests the flow of water but also contributes to the feeling of relaxation.

The size, style, color, and placement of text also contribute to the effect of the page. In this case the one line of text above the photograph is larger and darker than the text below it. Its size and placement draw your eye before you move to the smaller-sized text below the photograph. The first thing you are likely to read, then, after noticing the larger and stylized word *Evian* at the bottom of the page, is the question "Mommy, can I have a drink of water?" That question, which carries positive associations with childhood, highlights the connection between Evian water and family — another positive association. It also invites us to read the smaller text at the bottom of the ad. Notice as well that the larger, stylized font of the Evian logo draws your eye to it and emphasizes it, connecting the word *Evian* with the appealing photo.

The use of color in this ad also contributes to its persuasive power. We have already noted the white dress of the woman. White has powerful associations with purity and goodness. The colors of the sky and the mountains evoke feelings of relaxation, and the darker color of the text helps to emphasize it for viewers. Even the color of the word *Evian* conveys a positive sense of relaxation.

These design principles can function in much simpler illustrations than the Evian ad. For example, the following passage and illustration are taken from an essay entitled "The Seductive Call of School Supplies," by Michelle Slatalla, in which the author makes an argument about the appeal of increasingly high-tech school supplies to younger students:

> If I had to pinpoint the moment when I went wrong during the back-to-school season last year, I wouldn't necessarily say it was when I took my daughters to a local store so that they could pick out their own school supplies.
>
> I still believe the goal — to make them feel excited instead of nervous about the impending school year — was sound. The shopping trip allowed them to exercise control over their own destiny, or at least over their own three-ring-binder selections. And it's true that my plan seemed at first a success, as they headed off to the first day of class confident in their careful choices of glue (medium-size squeeze bottle) and scissors (purple molded hand grips).
>
>
>
> No, the error I made was more fundamental. Blinded by relief that they had headed back to school (for six blessed hours a day!), I let my guard down. That very night, Ella, who was 10 then but no less wily, announced calmly at supper, "I can't go back to the fifth grade, ever."
>
> The problem revolved around a product she described as the stretchable book cover, an apparently essential item that until that moment I did not know existed. As Ella explained it, the march of progress had trampled those good old-fashioned book covers that we had been cutting from brown paper bags. Instead, she said, everyone in her class had to have elasticized fabric covers.

The small, sepia-toned illustration is the only visual element in this essay, but it contributes to the author's argument in a variety of ways. In this case the rather whimsical character of the illustration reinforces the light tone of the essay. The image of the woman with a laptop helps to underscore a contradiction the author highlights in her essay: the traditional activity of buying school supplies is now focused on modern high-tech items. The sepia tones of the image contribute to this point by suggesting a bit of nostalgia for a bygone era when high-tech school supplies were not the norm. A full-color version of this illustration would not have worked as well for this purpose. Even the simple placement of this illustration at the beginning of the essay — rather than in the middle or near the end — contributes to its persuasive effect by helping to establish the tone of the piece.

Authors who understand these design principles can employ them to enhance the effectiveness of their arguments. Readers who understand these principles will be better able to evaluate those arguments.

TWISTING AN IMAGE TO MAKE A POINT

This ad by a group called Adbusters (http://adbusters.org) makes a statement by altering an image from an advertisement for a popular vodka. The ad uses the same layout and color scheme as the original ad, the same image of the vodka bottle, and even the name of the vodka itself. But here the image of a sagging bottle and the advertising tag line ("Absolut impotence"), which parodies the original tag line, create an association between the vodka and sexual dysfunction. Consider how effectively this ad employs visual elements to make its argument. Would a print advertisement explaining the connection between alcohol and impotence work in the same way?

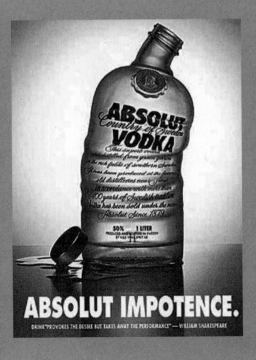

ART AS VISUAL ARGUMENT

You might not associate art with argument, but the design principles discussed in the previous section apply to paintings and other kinds of art as well. You can think of any painting as an argument for the artist's vision. The painting shown in Figure 4-6 was completed in 1816, eight years after Spanish troops had suppressed a revolt in Mexico, which was still part of the Spanish Empire at the time. It is the work of Francisco José de Goya, one of the great European painters of the 19th century. Because he was such a good painter, Goya was frequently commissioned to paint portraits of Spanish royalty and aristocrats, but his sympathies were with people who struggled for freedom. This sympathy is evident in his painting of an execution in Mexico. Most of the painting is dark, symbolizing the darkness of the event. Bright color is reserved for the man who is about to be shot. He is wearing a white shirt, which implies purity, and gold trousers, a warm color that contributes to the sense that he is someone worthy of sympathy. The coloring of the lantern that is illuminating the execution echoes the color of his clothing. Light has positive connotations, especially when surrounded by darkness. So the man in white and gold is in the light created by the white and yellow lantern.

Other aspects of the design direct attention to this man, whose complexion suggests that he is a person of color. His arms are raised in

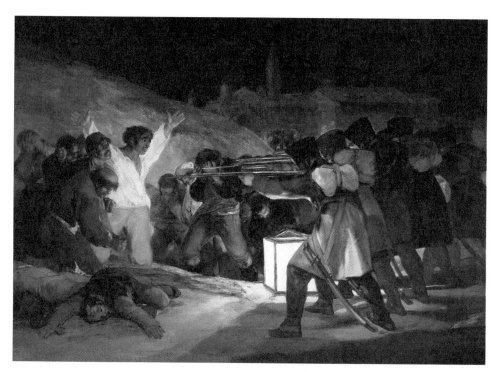

FIGURE 4-6

Painting a Subversive Argument.

Francisco José de Goya's famous 1816 painting of an execution in Mexico might be seen as an argument against government oppression.

PHOTOGRAPHY AS ARGUMENT

This photograph was taken several months after U.S. armed forces defeated the Taliban, a group that had previously imposed a strict Islamic government on Afghanistan. What argument does this photograph make? In answering that question, consider the contrast between the traditional dress of the girls in the photograph, which is intended to hide a woman's physical appearance, and the Western beauty items on the shelf, which are intended to enhance physical beauty. Consider, too, the uncovered face of the girl, placed at the center of the photo, just in front of her companion, whose face remains obscured by the traditional dress. How do these elements help to make a statement?

Kabul, Afghanistan. September 13, 2002. Manizha, 13 (center), and Mina, 16, take in an array of beauty products that were not openly available under Taliban rule.

PAINTING AS ENVIRONMENTAL AWARENESS

The landscape paintings of the famous Hudson Valley School in the 19th century are sometimes described as making a case for environmental conservation. They presented an idealized version of nature as beautiful and sublime, worthy of our admiration and protection, at a time when many people were concerned about the destructive effects of industrialization. Consider what claim Thomas Cole might be making in this painting of a well-known mountain along the Hudson River. How does his depiction of Storm King Mountain make a case for a particular view of nature?

Thomas Cole, *Storm King of the Hudson*, c. 1825–1827.

what could be seen as either a gesture of surrender or an embrace that encompasses the soldiers and anyone viewing the picture. The guns are not only aimed at him; they also visually direct the viewers' eyes to him. Furthermore, the man in the white shirt is one of the few figures with eyes the viewers can see. (The other two are also victims.) The expression in his eyes seems tender rather than fierce, contributing to the sympathy Goya creates for him. Significantly, we cannot see the eyes of any of the soldiers; they are presented as part of a faceless mass.

So what claim does this painting make? Interpretations vary. But the painting clearly conveys sympathy for the victim. It is arguing that the repression of the revolt was brutal, that governments do wicked things under the cover of night, or that the repression of native peoples cannot last forever. It is worth noting, in this respect, that although the soldiers have all the guns, there are more victims than soldiers — a fact that suggests that the imperial authority is outnumbered. (The drama of this painting is reinforced by its size, approximately 6 feet by 8 feet. If you ever have the chance to view the original in Madrid, you will feel as if you are witnessing a life-size event.)

Sometimes art is enlisted directly in an effort to persuade or to put forth a particular position on an issue or situation. A poster designed to advertise the French State Railways (see Figure 4-7) makes more than one visually compelling argument. Train service is associated with *Exactitude,* which is French for "getting things exactly right" or, more precisely, *precision.* The streamlined appearance of the train and the uncluttered look of the platform convey the sense that the technology in question is efficient as well as reliable. The clock positioned above the engineer's head suggests that this train will leave the station at exactly the right time. Addressed to travelers, the poster makes the claim: "You can count on us."

Another argument conveyed by the poster's design emerges when we consider its historical context. The poster was published in 1932, when the economies of Western nations were in deep depression and democratic governments were at risk. In Italy, one of

France's neighbors, Benito Mussolini had won respect for his fascist government by fulfilling his promise "to make the trains run on time." One year after this poster appeared, Hitler would seize power in Germany, bringing fascism to another of France's neighbors. The fascists came to power in part because they offered a message that appealed to people during troubled times. The heart of that message was that strong government, represented by a strong leader, could preserve both capitalism and nationalism by repressing communists and any social group considered a threat to economic growth. It would do so through the imposition of a new order suitable for a new age. So in the early 1930s fascism, like the train, could claim to be modern and efficient.

With this in mind, take another look at the poster. Most of the colors are muted; the boldest color, red, highlights the word *Etat,* which means "State." The train becomes a metaphor for the power of the state. It is long,

FIGURE 4-7

A Poster as Argument

This poster for the French State Railways in the 1930s may be making several arguments. What are they?

PIERRE-FÉLIX FIX-MASSEAU (1905–1994) French
Exactitude, 1932. Poster / color lithograph. Printer: Edita, Paris. Designed as an advertisement for the French State (État) Railways. H: 39¼ in (99.7 cm) x W: 24¼ in (61.6 cm) // 44 in (111.8 cm) x 29½ in (74.9 cm)

massive, and potentially dangerous. We view the train from a position on the platform that is precariously close to the edge. One false step, and we might fall beneath the power of the state. We are, moreover, alone on the platform. Everyone else seems to have already boarded the train. Do we want to be left behind? Do we want to get hurt? So in addition to urging people to travel by train, which continues to be a widely used means of transportation in Europe, this poster argues, "Get on board for the future, or get out of my way. The government is powerful; you are not. It will be dangerous for you to resist." The future is either technology or the power of a strong central government — or both, as is the case when a central government uses technology to increase its power.

The U.S. government also used paintings and sketches during World War II to encourage enlistment in the armed forces, sell war bonds, publicize efforts to conserve items such as gasoline and butter, and generally exhort citizens to support the war effort. We might think of these images in the same way that we think of contemporary print or television advertisements: as propaganda whose purpose was to persuade rather than to engage viewers in serious argumentation. However, if you understand World War II as a moral endeavor to combat the evils of totalitarianism and ethnic extermination, then you might view these posters as part of a larger attempt to engage U.S. citizens in a collective effort to oppose evil. From such a perspective, individual posters can be seen as making an argument for a particular kind of activity associated with the war effort. Each poster might be posing a version of the question "Won't this particular activity help in the war effort?"

For example, the message in the poster in Figure 4-8 seems clear: Buy war bonds to help the U.S. airmen. In a sense the claim made in this poster is that war bonds will help the war effort by keeping U.S. airmen flying; the warrant is that sustaining the war effort is desirable. The image of the airman in the poster, with his eyes looking skyward, his hands holding his combat equipment, a determined expression on his face, is noble and inspiring. The phrase at the top of the poster seems to be a statement this airman would make, and the large, bright words at the bottom of the poster drive the argument home. But notice that this airman is African American. At a point in history (the 1940s) before the Civil Rights Movement and before the landmark U.S. Supreme Court rulings that helped to guarantee those rights to African Americans, this image would have struck many citizens as unusual and even disturbing, since this airman was fighting for a country that did not extend full rights to people of his racial background. Indeed, at that time the U.S. armed forces were still segregated. Yet the poster seems to suggest that *all* Americans are part of the war effort. And it might have spoken especially powerfully to Black Americans, whose experience of racism might have made them hesitant to support the U.S. government's efforts. The airman in this poster might suggest to those citizens that their support is needed and appropriate.

The poster in Figure 4-9 can also be seen as presenting an argument rather than simply trying to persuade. This poster was used in General Motors automobile factories in 1942, when that company was producing vehicles for the war effort. However, even during the war, companies and workers faced many of the same challenges that they face in peacetime, and labor relations were always a potentially difficult matter. In fact, strikes by auto workers in the 1930s had a serious economic and social impact on the country. But a labor conflict — especially a strike — during war time could have been disastrous. In such a context we might see this poster as making an argument about the need for good relations between workers and their employers. The claim might be stated as follows: Avoiding labor conflict will aid the U.S. war effort because it will enable the company to continue production of military vehicles. Again, the warrant is that aiding the war effort is desirable for all Americans. The design of the poster is intended to present that claim effectively. The most noticeable item is the word *together*, which appears in large red letters at the very top of the page. The images of the two fists — both clenched, both exuding strength, both exposed by rolled-up sleeves as if to suggest getting down to work — reinforce the idea of working together. Both are also identical in every respect except for the color of their shirt sleeves, which are used to reinforce their respective positions: blue for the blue-collar workers, white for management. The light yellow background not only highlights the arms by bringing them into relief, but it also conveys a sense of possibility: yellow is associated with the sun, with the idea of a new day. Notice, too, that aside from that background color and the green tank and fighter aircraft, everything else on the

Art in Support of a War Effort

These posters were distributed by the U.S. government during World War II. Their message of support for the U.S. war effort is obvious, but what specific arguments do these posters make?

FIGURE 4-8

FIGURE 4-9

poster is red, white, or blue, colors that are obviously associated with patriotism. Every element of the design thus supports the poster's claim.

INTEGRATING VISUAL ELEMENTS AND TEXT

The examples we have included so far in this chapter reveal that combining text and visual elements can be an extremely effective technique for argumentation. You probably have noticed a trend in television advertising in recent years toward structuring commercials around text. One widely broadcast ad for Nike shoes, for example, included a series of images of world-class athletes in many different sports preparing for their respective

CARTOONS AS ARGUMENT

One of the most common and effective kinds of visual argument is the political cartoon. Consider this cartoon by Jim Morin. What argument does it make about weapons of mass destruction and pollution — two serious concerns in the early 21st century? How effectively does it make its argument? Compare this approach with a conventional editorial. What are the advantages and disadvantages of each?

SOURCE: Jim Morin, *Miami Herald*, September 6, 2002.

events: a sprinter getting ready at the starting blocks, a swimmer stretching at the edge of the pool before the start of the race, an archer drawing her bow. As these images appear in quick succession on the screen, the sound of an orchestra warming up gets louder. As the sound reaches a crescendo and then suddenly stops, the images also disappear, leaving a black screen on which only the words "Just do it," the famous Nike slogan, appear, with the equally famous Nike swoosh logo above them. The words on the screen seem to have greater impact without sound and color.

When you encounter textual arguments that incorporate visual elements, it is important to be aware of the impact that the combination of text and image can have on you as a reader or viewer. Engaging these arguments critically includes assessing visual elements and what they might contribute to the author's claims. Consider, for example, the open letter in Figure 4-10, which was distributed as a newspaper advertisement by St. Lawrence Cement, a company that found itself in an environmental controversy in 2002 when it sought to build a cement plant in upstate New York. In this example the letter includes an extended written argument in which the company presents its claim that its proposed plant will not harm the environment. We might see this argument as an example of an argument to negotiate differences (see pages 18–21): It addresses its audience in a way that is respectful and direct, acknowledging the validity of its opponents' concerns; it presents evidence that supports its central claim that its plant will not cause environmental damage; and it rests this claim on a warrant that seems acceptable to its intended audience (that all residents want and will benefit from a healthy environment).

But the text of the letter in this advertisement is only part of the argument. The ad also includes a photograph along with several graphs that reinforce the claim. Those graphs ostensibly present factual evidence that the company's new plan will significantly reduce its impact on the environment. Note that the visual form of the graphs highlights facts that might otherwise be harder for readers to pick out of the lengthy text. The photograph doesn't present evidence in the way the graphs do, but it reinforces the company's message that it is staffed by concerned and competent professionals. Notice that the four people in the photograph represent racial and gender diversity as well, sending a further positive message about the company to readers. The layout of the ad also contributes to the argument. Because the photo is placed before the first paragraph, readers are likely to view it before reading the text. If they have a positive reaction to that image, they might be agreeable to the company's argument. In addition, the letter discusses environmental

An Open Letter to the Community:

The community plays an important role in shaping the quality of life for the individuals and families who live there. Communities, and all the people who make them up, are concerned with whether a new facility, such as the St. Lawrence Cement Greenport replacement plant, will be good for the environment. They want to know if the project will stimulate the local economy and create new jobs, and whether the company will operate as a responsible community member. Overall, the community wants to be assured that any proposed facility is safe and that it upholds the high environmental standards that many have worked hard to establish.

At St. Lawrence Cement, we believe that this is all as it should be. We regard ourselves as part of this community, both Hudson and Greenport locally as well as New York State. We believe that we should be open with the community and share our plans for the new Greenport facility and its benefits. We also feel compelled to correct misinformation, misleading statements and untruths about the plant. This is especially important when issues begin to drive a wedge between community members. Finally, we are convinced that our proposed project to replace the existing Catskill plant with the new Greenport facility will provide an overall net benefit to the communities and regions in which we operate.

St. Lawrence Cement has been a community member for nearly two decades, operating a cement facility at Catskill since 1984. We are proud of our track record in Catskill, and we hold it up to the community as an indicator of the commitment we have to meet and exceed the most rigorous environmental standards in the country.

Environmental Benefits

While the current Catskill plant is safe and emissions are well under the allowable standards, the Catskill plant is also older and unable to accommodate new environmental control technologies that are now available. Economically, it is not feasible to try to retro-fit the existing plant. This is why St. Lawrence Cement has proposed to build a replacement facility at Greenport—a new plant for a new age.

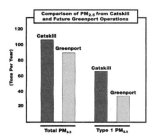

Our proposed Greenport replacement facility will incorporate a unique combination of environmental control technologies, making it one of the most environmentally friendly cement plants in the world. The replacement of Catskill with the new state-of-the-art Greenport plant will allow us to substantially lower those emissions that the public tends to be most concerned about.

Emissions of fine particulates (most commonly referred to as PM 2.5) will be cut by 14%, with the most troublesome combustion-related particulate matter dropping by 40%. Emissions of mercury will be reduced by 95% and lead emissions by 94%. Similarly, the emissions that cause acid rain—

sulfur dioxide and nitrogen oxides emissions—will be reduced by 45%. Studies by the EPA and NYSDEC corroborate these figures, providing credible and expert third-party validation that the environmental benefits we promise are real.

St. Lawrence also recognizes the community's concerns about the impact of plant emissions on historic structures and facades. Emissions from our Catskill plant are already well below allowable limits, and do not accelerate the deterioration of historic buildings and facades. The even lower emissions at Greenport should re-assure the community that St. Lawrence Cement is committed to the community and the preservation of our historic buildings—valuable community assets that enrich our area and attract tourists.

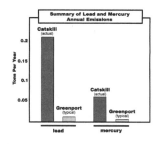

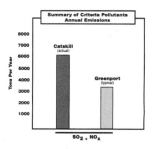

Economic Benefits

The history of this region is grounded in the cement industry. The community recognizes the importance of industry to create a diverse economy, one that takes advantage of tourism while also providing meaningful jobs for the families who live here. The Greenport replacement plant respects this need for balance, and promises to bring economic improvements to the area while preserving and enhancing the community's overall appeal.

The replacement plant, for example, will use a different process for cement production than the Catskill facility. Instead of the current 'wet' process utilized at Catskill, the Greenport plant will employ a dry process. The net benefit here it that the replacement facility will use 99% less Hudson River water and discharge absolutely nothing back into the River. Add to this St. Lawrence's restoration of 3.0 acres of former inter-tidal wetland in South Bay, an area filled over a half-century ago (long before St. Lawrence bought the property) that has been deemed extremely well-suited, if restored, for fish and wildlife habitation.

Of course, the Greenport replacement plant also holds enormous economic promise for the community, Columbia County and upstate New York. In addition to the costs of constructing the new facility (much of which will be spent right here in Greenport), jobs will be both preserved and created, a host of products and services will be required, and local, county and state taxes will be paid. St. Lawrence Cement is committed to the local community, its economy and its future, and we've proposed a project that promises multiple benefits for all of us.

St. Lawrence Cement welcomes this opportunity to provide our community with important facts and information that will help the community better understand the environmental and economic impact of our proposed replacement plant in Greenport. For certain, we want to see a successful conclusion to the process, but we also want our fellow members of the local and regional community to know the facts, recognize the benefits and support the plant.

ST. LAWRENCE CEMENT

USING PHOTOGRAPHY TO ENHANCE AN ARGUMENT

This photograph appears on the title page of *Tigers in the Snow*, a book by Peter Matthiessen about a shrinking population of tigers in a remote part of Siberia, Russia. In his book Matthiessen describes the efforts of U.S. and Russian biologists to study these tigers in order to help prevent them from becoming extinct. Matthiessen clearly supports these efforts. What do you think this photograph suggests? What might it say about the tiger? About the efforts to save it? Why do you think it was placed on the title page with nothing else aside from the title and author's name? How might this use of the photograph figure into the argument Matthiessen makes in his book?

Photograph by Maurice Hornocker

issues before economic ones, which seems to reinforce the company's claim that it is concerned about the environment. The subheadings ("Environmental Benefits," "Economic Benefits") highlight these concerns and make them easier for readers to access. In short, the combination of these visual elements with the text of the letter contributes subtly to the effectiveness of this argument.

This example illustrates both the importance and potential risks of using visual elements in genuine argumentation about controversial issues. If we engage in argument with an honest intent to address difficult problems, then it makes sense to employ whatever strategies and resources we have available to us, including visual elements, to make our argument as effectively as possible. In the case of the St. Lawrence Cement Company it is easy to suspect the company's motives and accuse them of trying to manipulate public opinion. (Of course, the same can be true of the company's opponents.) From such a perspective you might see the use of visual elements as part of an effort to win at any cost, and you might be right. One element in analyzing the argument in a case like this is the company's track record in such disputes. Has the company been unforthcoming about the environmental impact of its plants in the past? Has it engaged in underhanded tactics to manipulate public opinion? If so, you would have reason to be skeptical of the company's motives and you should assess its argument accordingly. You might, for example, view the photograph negatively because you may suspect that the company is trying to soften its image and divert attention from its environmental record.

But it might also be true that many long-time residents of the town work for the company and therefore have a sincere interest in ensuring that the new plant will not harm the local environment. Because those workers live in the community where the plant will be built, their interests will be similar to those of opponents of the plant who also hope to preserve the health of the local environment. From this perspective the argument made by the company — and arguments made by other parties in the conflict — can be seen as negotiating differences among the participants. Visual elements become tools that all participants employ as they seek to resolve the problems created by the company's plans to build the new plant. If it turned out that the company or other parties in the controversy did not have honorable motives, you could still engage their arguments thoughtfully and decide on their merits accordingly. Your attention to the visual elements is an important part of the process by which you make that decision.

ANALYZING ARGUMENTS IN ELECTRONIC MEDIA

Because they offer capabilities that are not available in print forms, electronic media provide a rich context for argumentation that can differ significantly from print media. For example, radio allows speech, music, and other sound effects to be used in arguments in ways that cannot be reproduced in print. Television enables the use of sound in addition to moving images and text. And the computer-based media on the Internet and World Wide Web offer previously unseen configurations of text, image, and sound that can be more interactive than other media. Moreover, the specific characteristics of communication in these new electronic media, especially their speed and availability, might be changing the nature of communication itself.

Because of the rapid development of new technologies (such as multimedia online capabilities, digital video and audio technologies, and high-definition TV), the characteristics of electronic media are changing constantly. No one can anticipate how these media will influence the ways we engage in argumentation about important issues in our lives. (Who could have predicted ten years ago that email and cell phones would become as commonplace as the traditional telephone?) But what we can do is examine some of the important features of these media and begin to explore how they can be used to make effective arguments.

THE INTERNET

It is probably no exaggeration to say that the Internet will eventually have as big an impact on our society as television. And because the Internet has become so important in how we interact and communicate with each other, it is inevitably influencing how arguments are made.

The emergence of the Internet and the World Wide Web as a means of communication and as a forum for public discussion has been touted by some observers as a watershed development for democratic societies, which — in theory at least — are built around the idea that citizens make collective decisions about how they should be governed. Some believe that Internet technologies like email and the multimedia capabilities for transmitting ideas and information on the World Wide Web will eventually enable many more people to participate directly in in the political process than they could have without these technologies. Today, newsgroups, email discussion lists, (such as *listserv*), Web-based bulletin boards, and online chat rooms enable millions of people to join in discussions about current issues that affect their lives. With access to these online forums, you can debate a recent Congressional decision or political election with someone from across the country almost as easily as — indeed, perhaps *more* easily than — you can debate your neighbors or roommate. Moreover, the Internet and World Wide Web enable people with similar interests or concerns to form "virtual communities," in which they can share ideas quickly and easily without having to be in the same place at the same time. Online forums now exist for every imaginable kind of group, from academics to zoologists, from sales to sailing. These forums allow participants to engage in conversations about issues that are important to them, and many professional organizations use online forums for conducting meetings, circulating petitions, voting, and similar activities. In these ways Internet technologies help people to form and maintain communities by providing a ready medium for communication, discussion, and debate.

Chances are that you have participated in one or more of the online forums now available on the Internet or World Wide Web. If so, you might share the enthusiasm expressed by many commentators for these technologies. At the same time you might also have experienced the "flame wars" that frequently occur in newsgroups, mailing lists, and chat rooms. Visit a chat room or skim the messages posted to a mailing list or newsgroup, and you quickly see that much of the discussion that occurs in some of these forums is not argumentation but more like the quarreling you see on television talk shows. This is true even in online forums devoted to serious issues and maintained by professionals such as lawyers or academics. Many critics have expressed skepticism about the possibilities of these forums to enhance public debate about serious issues. They worry about the overwhelming volume of online discussion and of information on the Internet and World Wide Web, and they raise questions about the usefulness of online discussion. Here, for example, is Mark Slouka, a well-known writer specializing in issues related to these new technologies:

> Will virtual communities help us "reclaim democracy, vent our opinions about the OJ trial, and circumvent Op-Ed newspaper editors" etc.? Clearly, there's something very powerful (and potentially very positive) about a technology that allows millions of people to share ideas and allows them to side-step the occasionally ignorant or biased "filters" like magazine Op-Ed editors. My concern (a viable one, to judge from the mass of stuff online) is that the Net will privilege "venting" over debate and knee jerk speed over reflection. There's a very real chance that what the Net will produce is not "tons of useful information," but virtual mountains of babble among which the occasionally useful tidbit of information (the kind not available in the local library) will be as easy to find as a nickel in a landfill.

Slouka expresses two of the main concerns skeptics often cite in their criticism of online forums for public discourse: the questionable nature of much of the discussion that occurs online and the sheer volume of online discussions. A single newsgroup or mailing list can generate hundreds of messages in one day, far too many for any person to sort through carefully. In addition, as Slouka notes, many online discussions are characterized by superficial exchanging of opinions instead of careful, considered debate. Genuine argumentation is often as hard to find online as it is on popular talk radio.

What does all this mean for those who are interested in argument? No one can be sure, despite the enormous amount of discussion among scholars, critics, and policy makers about the role of electronic technologies in public discourse. But the Internet and World Wide Web are not likely to disappear. They will continue to evolve, and they will very likely become more important for communication and argumentation in our society. The capabilities of these technologies seem to promise new ways of engaging in argument for the purpose of solving problems and negotiating differences. But it is also true that these technologies will complicate argumentation in ways that we cannot anticipate. In the meantime you will almost certainly encounter arguments in online forums, and you might well present your own arguments in such forums. In many respects engaging in genuine argumentation online is similar to engaging in argumentation in other forums, and the advice we have offered in this chapter and elsewhere will generally apply to on-line forums as well. But there are some characteristics of online technologies that can shape argumentation, and you should be aware of how these characteristics might affect arguments online.

Not all online forums are alike, and for the purposes of our discussion of them, we will distinguish between online forums that are used primarily for discussion — including email mailing lists, newsgroups or Web-based bulletin boards, and chat rooms — and Web sites, which can advance arguments but do not necessarily involve discussion and which have multimedia capabilities that most discussion forums lack.

WEB SITES

The World Wide Web represents a potentially unprecedented medium for argument. Because of the Web's complexity and because of the rapid pace at which Web technologies are evolving, no one can predict how its role as a medium for argument might grow or change. What we can say is that the Web offers intriguing possibilities for structuring and presenting arguments. In this section we review some of the characteristics of the Web and their implications for argument.

Online Versions of Print Arguments   To begin, it is important to point out that there are different kinds of Web sites. Some Web sites essentially offer online versions of print documents. For example, many newspapers and magazines are available on the Web in more or less the same format as their print versions. If you visit a site such as the *Los Angeles Times* online (**www.latimes.com**), you will find the same articles that appear in the printed newspaper. Although the online versions of these articles might have links to other Web sites and might include graphics that do not appear in the print versions, their content and format are essentially the same as the printed versions. In terms of structure, content, and related matters, therefore, arguments on such Web sites are not very different from arguments in a print medium. An editorial essay in the *Los Angeles Times* is the same essay online and in print. Currently, most arguments on the Web are of this kind. (See Figure 4-11.)

Hypertextual Web Sites   True hypertext is another matter altogether. *Hypertext* refers to the capacity to link documents through *hyperlinks* that a user clicks to move from one document to another. Web sites that are truly hypertextual can differ dramatically from a print document (or an online version of a print document) in the way they are structured. Hypertextual documents need not be organized in a linear fashion, as most print essays are; rather, links can be embedded on Web pages so that users can move from one page to another in the Web site in a variety of ways: hierarchically, in a radial fashion, or randomly. The possibilities for arranging textual and graphical information in a hypertext are

endless. Moreover, hypertexts can be more interactive than print text in the sense that readers select which links they will follow as they move through a document. In a print essay, readers generally move from the opening paragraph to the final paragraph. By contrast, true hypertexts offer countless ways for readers to move through them, so it is possible that no two readers will read a hypertext in exactly the same way.

These features of hypertext offer new possibilities for authors to present their arguments. In addition to enabling authors to incorporate graphics and sound easily into an argument, hypertext allows authors to structure an argument in a variety of ways that affect the impact of the argument. Keeping in mind that arguments in print form tend to be organized in a linear fashion, consider the following example of a hypertextual Web site entitled "Argumentation on the Web," by Tom Formaro. In this hypertext Formaro examines the implications of using hypertext for argumentation, actually demonstrating his argument by presenting it in hypertext. Obviously, Formaro might have made the same argument in a conventional print format. But hypertext offers options for presenting his argument that would not be possible in print.

Figure 4-12 shows the first screen of his hypertext. Notice that this Web page doesn't really introduce Formaro's topic; rather, it gives the reader advice on how to move through, or navigate, his hypertext. Notice, too, the links on the left side of the screen. As you'll see, those links will remain visible no matter which Web page you visit in this hypertext; they help you find your way to specific pages in the document. However, Formaro has also embedded links within each page. Those links function very differently within his argument than the links on the left side of the screen. For example, a few links from this first screen will bring you to the screen in Figure 4-13. Here, Formaro raises questions that are central to his main argument — questions about the meaning of a "beginning" in a text and how the idea of a beginning or introduction can be complicated by hypertext. You can read this paragraph and then click one of the links at the bottom of the screen, which will take you to another screen related to this one — almost like

ARGUMENTATION ON THE World Wide Web

Links

Sections

General Index

Authors Index

Topics Index

Bibliography

Navigation Tips

How to Use This Hypertext

A Caveat

I've chosen to use frames because of the effect frames have on the boundaries of a work. What you'll notice throughout this piece is that when you jump to other sites from links I've provided, you haven't really left this work at all. The Links sidebar and the title remain visible. The boundary between my work and the work of others becomes difficult to discern.

Blurring the boundaries between works is the reason for the frames and illustrates an important point about hypertext on the World Wide Web. I'll discuss this idea formally throughout the work, especially when considering the World Wide Web and texts. If you are not using a frames compatible browser, you will still be able to view the work, but the boundary between this piece and others to which it is linked will be more distinct.

Navigation Tips

Receiving image (0 bytes of 321 bytes, 0 bytes/sec): button.home.gif

FIGURE 4-12

Opening Screen of "Argumentation on the World Wide Web"

ARGUMENTATION ON THE World Wide Web

Links

Sections

General Index

Authors Index

Topics Index

Bibliography

Navigation Tips

What *Is* the Beginning?

Linear designations such as beginning, middle, and end are problemitized by postmodern and hypertext theory. They are also difficult to discern on the Web. Where exactly is the beginning of the Web? Such a question is like asking "where is the beginning of the Interstate highway system in the U.S." Certainly there are many places where you can get on, drive for a while, and get off, but would that constitute the beginning, middle and end of the Interstate system? It does constitute a beginning, middle, and end of a trip, but that's not the same as the system on which the trip took place. So, like a trip, it is possible to have a beginning, middle, and end in a Web *session*; the Web itself, however, does not have such designations.

 What's in a Name? Lineraity and Print
An Introduction?

| Sections | General Index | Authors Index | Topics Index |
| Bibliography | Navigation Tips |

FIGURE 4-13

A "Beginning" Web Page in "Argumentation on the World Wide Web"

FIGURE 4-14

One Link from the
"Beginning"

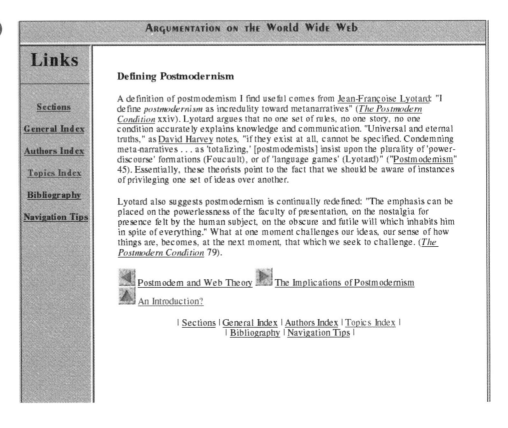

turning a page in a book. But you can also click one of the underlined words in the first sentence to move to a different screen. If you click the word *postmodern,* for instance, you'll see the screen in Figure 4-14.

On this Web page, Formaro defines the term *postmodernism* in a way that serves his purposes in his argument. However, if you clicked the word *hypertext* instead of *postmodern* in the previous screen, you would see the screen in Figure 4-15.

Here Formaro discusses what he sees as the key feature of hypertext for argumentation. Notice the many underlined words on this screen. Each of them is a link that leads to a different screen. As a reader you make choices about which links to follow, and these choices affect how you engage Formaro's argument. Different readers will follow different links, thus reading Formaro's text in different ways, in effect deciding how to organize Formaro's argument. As a writer, Formaro creates these links as transitions to various parts of his argument. In this sense his links are not only a means of moving through his document, but also a way to connect ideas. He can thus use them to help make his claims or provide evidence.

Because we are so used to the conventions of print and its usual linear structure, reading through a complicated argument in a hypertext such as Formaro's can be disconcerting. Hypertext forces us to read differently. It also forces the writer to think differently about how to present an argument. Because the author does not determine the precise order in which each reader will read the various pages in a hypertext, the author cannot think of his or her argument in a linear way, in which every reader moves from point to point in the same way. Instead, the author may think of an argument as a collection of large pieces, each representing a distinct topic, point, or claim. The author must then de-

---

ARGUMENTATION ON THE WORLD WIDE WEB

Links

Sections

General Index

Authors Index

Topics Index

Bibliography

Navigation Tips

Hypertext Theory

The core of hypertext and the Web can be summed up in one word: <u>freedom</u>. Freedom for <u>authors</u>, for <u>readers</u>, for <u>texts</u>, freedom for the <u>argument</u>, and even freedom for the technology (the relationship among each of these elements relates to <u>Burke's</u> concept of <u>container and the thing contained</u>). There are some <u>exceptions</u> to the freedom of hypertext on the World Wide Web. However, together with my conception of <u>privileging</u> as the core of postmodern theory, freedom in hypertext--and particularly on the Web--are the theoretical legs on which my discussion stands.

<u>Freedom and the Author</u>

<u>An Introduction?</u>

| <u>Sections</u> | <u>General Index</u> | <u>Authors Index</u> | <u>Topics Index</u> |
| <u>Bibliography</u> | <u>Navigation Tips</u> |

FIGURE 4-15

A Different Link from the "Beginning"

---

cide how those pieces relate to each other so that the overall argument makes sense to readers, each of whom might experience the argument differently. Should a particular claim or bit of evidence appear on a main page or on a page linked to that main page? Why? What pieces of an argument should *every* reader see? Which pieces can be skipped without weakening the argument? Such questions can encourage a writer — and readers — to reexamine how an argument fits together. And the links themselves represent transitions that can support or enhance an argument. For example, an author can make a claim based on an implied warrant, then create a link to a page that defends that warrant. In a print article such a defense would have to be incorporated into the text (or perhaps included in a footnote or sidebar), which perhaps would interrupt the flow of the author's argument. Hypertext enables authors to decide on alternative ways of presenting claims, evidence, and warrants.

Notice, too, that hypertext enables an author to embed multimedia in a Web site to help support an argument. The Web enables Formaro to use color and design very easily to present and enhance his argument in ways that we discussed earlier in this chapter. If he desired, he could also link video or audio clips to specific points in his argument. These features can become powerful tools in an author's efforts to present his or her argument.

It remains to be seen whether the potential of hypertext to enhance arguments will be realized in a widespread way in the years ahead. Formaro's Web site represents a use of hypertext for argumentation that is still quite rare, despite the rapid growth of the Web. But as his hypertext suggests, the Web offers intriguing new possibilities for people to address complex issues and try to solve problems through argumentation.

Web Sites as Arguments We have been discussing Web sites in which authors make arguments in hypertextual form. But Web sites themselves can also be seen as making arguments in the way that a brochure or a flyer does. Today, advocacy groups, political organizations, government and nongovernmental agencies, institutions, and community groups of all kinds maintain Web sites on which they present themselves to the public. On the surface such Web sites do not seem very different from a flyer or brochure that a group might distribute to publicize itself. But individuals or groups can take advantage of the Web's capabilities to make implicit arguments. Consider the home page of the Web site for the Minnesota Public Radio program *Marketplace*® (Figure 4-16). At first glance, this Web page seems straightforward enough, presenting information about *Marketplace* along with links to additional information and to related sites. But a closer look reveals that this site makes good use of the multimedia capabilities of the Web. For one thing it contains links to audio clips of its programs as well as links to archives of text versions of some segments of its broadcasts. It also employs a sophisticated design with careful use of layout and color, suggesting a professional operation. Notice too, the logos for several large businesses. Not only do these logos convey the information that Fannie Mae, BankOne, and Deloitte & Touche are corporate sponsors of Marketplace, but their inclusion on the front page of the Web site might also be seen as an implicit argument that the program has legitimacy as a source of business information. All three major sponsors are large corporations that are easily recognizable and associated with business success in a way that might well appeal to the Marketplace audience.

The Web site for the Digital Freedom Network, an advocacy group, takes similar advantage of the capabilities of the Web (Figure 4-17). This site presents the Digital Freedom Network overtly as an activist group with a particular view of freedom in the digital age.

Like the *Marketplace* home page, Digital Freedom Network's home page employs principles of design to present itself effectively to its audience. Graphics and color highlight ideas and links to related information. However, as an advocacy group, the Digital Freedom Network uses its Web site to present an overt stance on the issues it is concerned about. The photograph, whose prominent placement in the center of the page draws the eye, makes a powerful statement about the incarceration of activists in China. That photo is also a link to the group's report on that topic. The caption placed above the photo is colored red, which connotes danger and contrasts noticeably with the surrounding colors. In these ways this site combines some of the hypertextual capabilities of the Web with solid design to make a strong statement about its activism. In addition, notice how this site invites a visitor's participation in the group's activities. The caption above the photo

---

FIGURE 4-16

Presenting an Image on the Web

Organizations of all kinds can use the Web to present an image of who they are to the public. The Web site for Minnesota Public Radio's *Marketplace*® is both a source of information about the show and a means of projecting its image to its audience.

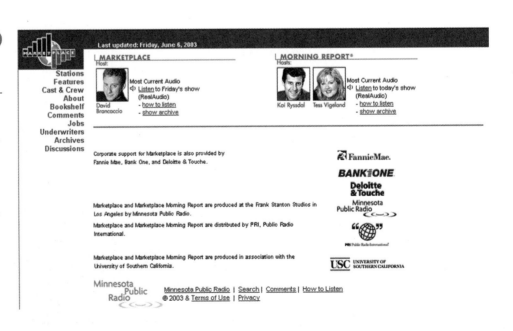

FIGURE 4-17

Advocacy on the Web

The Digital Freedom Network, an advocacy group, uses its Web site to make a political statement.

exhorts readers to "take a stand," and the link with the same words to the right of the photograph provides readers with a way to do so: They can become members of the group, volunteer, or become involved in one of the group's activities. In this regard the site uses the interactive character of the Web to encourage participation in the group's activist work. It also implicitly makes an argument in favor of such activism.

ONLINE DISCUSSION FORUMS

Online discussion forums have proliferated dramatically in the past few years. Today you can find a newsgroup, mailing list, or Web board on any imaginable topic. In addition, college instructors now commonly set up online forums as a component of their courses. (In courses that are offered exclusively online, online forums often replace traditional face-to-face classroom discussion.) A common use of such forums is to foster discussion among students about important course topics. In effect, students often go online to engage in argumentation about course-related issues.

One obvious advantage that an online forum has over a more traditional print medium (such as a newspaper editorial page) is that it is more immediate and opens up the possibility for more voices to enter the conversation. You can post a message to a newsgroup in which you defend a position on an issue, and within a few hours or even minutes several people might have responded to your post. Many more people can join in the conversation in this way than could possibly do so on a newspaper editorial page or in the letters-to-the-editor section of a magazine. In *asynchronous* forums such as mailing lists, newsgroups (in which messages remain available to participants at any time that they log on — the electronic equivalent of a bulletin board containing many messages pinned to it), or Web boards, readers can sort through messages and analyze them before posting a response. In this respect asynchronous forums have an advantage over face-to-face discussion (such as in a classroom or at a public meeting) in that they allow participants time to consider their responses before posting them. Usually, in a face-to-face discussion a response must be made soon after someone has spoken, providing little time for discussants to formulate their responses carefully. If the conversation moves quickly, you might not even get the chance to make your comment before the conversation moves to another point. On a mailing list, newsgroup, or Web board, by contrast, you can write and even revise your response offline before posting it. Of course, it's possible to respond prematurely in an asynchronous forum, just as it is possible to respond rashly in a face-to-face discussion or to damage a relationship by responding to an email in anger.

Here's part of a discussion about plagiarism that occurred on the Usenet newsgroup soc.college.admissions. The discussion began when one participant posted part of a news report about plagiarism in American colleges and universities. Several other people joined in. (The lines preceded by >'s are quoted passages from previous messages.)

> Plagiarism is running rampant on American college campuses, and everyone
> knows that technology is partly to blame. After all, any student with a few
> dollars can go to one of the many Web sites that sell research papers and
> buy the perfect paper for the assignment.

I fail to understand why plagiarism is so hard to define and understand. If every teacher in every class started out on the first day of class to define plagiarism as:

1. submitting ideas or words that are not one's own without properly and accurately attributing them to their true author
2. papers that are copies of papers someone else wrote or which have been previously submitted to another class
3. whatever else the teacher does not want in original works (specifically "cut and paste" items from the Internet) along with examples of what is permitted and what is not permitted, the students would know upfront specifically what is allowed and not allowed.

Each student should then be required to write a brief summary of the rules in his/her own handwriting, sign it., and turn it into the teacher. This can be done even by very young children. Nothing affects understanding so much as having to put it in one's own words (how ironic for a definition of plagiarism). Then if someone is found to have violated the rules, he or she fails the class. And schools must back up the teachers, not be weakened by litigious parents.

Kate

"Kate" wrote in #1
> I fail to understand why plagiarism is so hard to define and understand.
> If every teacher in every class started out on the first day of class to
> define plagiarism as:
> 1. submitting ideas or words that are not one's own without properly and
> accurately attributing them to their true author

This is precisely why it's so hard to define. Most students (or people for that matter) go through entire days without thinking a single original thought. How is a student expected to write an entire paper of almost entirely unoriginal ideas and credit every single 'true author'. I obviously know what your point is, I'm just saying the line isn't that clear. I know that one of the greatest feelings for a teacher is discovering new ideas coming from his students, but can you really expect this from everyone (the C student as well as the B and A students?)

How strict would you propose enforcing your Rule No. 1? Would you like to end up with papers with citations noted after every single sentence? I think plagiarism is awful, I just think its not as clear-cut as you say.

matt

> I think plagiarism is awful, I just think its not as clear-cut as you say.

Hmmm. I find that I agree with a lot of this. How about: 1) I read Joe Expert's book and he lays out a few facts. I think to myself, "(Insert some conclusion from those facts here)" Then, I turn the page and Joe Expert reaches the same conclusion. Do I need to cite that? (I would, to be on the safe side, but I'm not sure I should have to)

Also, how about the line between "common knowledge" and what needs to be cited? Interestingly, Vanderbilt University defines this specifically in their honor code documentation: common knowledge is an idea that appears in 3 or more distinct sources. This is the first time in my life I have seen such a clear cut definition.

Joe

"Joe" wrote in message #3

> How about: 1)I read Joe Expert's book and he lays out a few facts. I think
> to myself, "(Insert some conclusion from those facts here)" Then, I turn
> the page and Joe Expert reaches the same conclusion. Do I need to cite
> that? (I would, to be on the safe side, but I'm not sure I should have to)

It's not plagiarism to use the same idea another person had if you put it into your own words and expand upon it or criticize it positively or negatively. Such as: "Joe Expert says George Bush is the Anti-Christ [cite]. Many people may believe this to be true but I disagree for several reasons." . . .

The problem with plagiarism today is that it is far easier to heist information from the Internet in one's bedroom than it is to crawl through dusty library stacks before computers were everywhere. Perhaps, teachers can require that a certain percentage of citations in a paper must be from real books -- which requires real page numbers; maybe require a few xeroxed book pages in support. Maybe that's all too much.

Kate

"Kate" wrote:

> The problem with plagiarism today is that it is far easier to heist
> information from the Internet in one's bedroom than it is to crawl through
> dusty library stacks before computers were everywhere.

Wait, is this a bad thing . . . ?

> Perhaps, teachers
> can require that a certain percentage of citations in a paper must be from
> real books -- which requires real page numbers; maybe require a few xeroxed
> book pages in support. Maybe that's all too much.

If the information is appropriate for the paper, accurate, and from a credible source, does it matter where it came from? I think it would be unhealthy to search for reasons to cling to real books (especially when the whole world is opting for change.) After all, 'real' (or perhaps not so real) books are now being published over the Net.

This excerpt is a good example of the way argumentation can occur in asynchronous online forums. The participants seem genuinely concerned about plagiarism, and the discussion seems to move toward a loose consensus about how schools might solve the problem. Notice that the participants follow some of the conventions of traditional argument. For example, they present claims (e.g., plagiarism is hard to define), support their claims (e.g., students do not generally work with original ideas, so identifying what is original and what is not can become a problem), and imply warrants (plagiarism is bad). In addition, participants address their audience — indeed, they do so directly by responding to points made by other participants. And they seem to make certain assumptions about that audience and about the larger context of the discussion. For example, the participants all seem familiar with American higher education, and they are responding to recent events involving plagiarism at American universities. In these ways this newsgroup discussion resembles traditional argumentation.

It is easy to see some of the advantages of arguing in such a forum. The medium allows for a great deal of back-and-forth discussion in a way that simply is not possible in traditional print forums. And many people can participate without the discussion becoming overwhelming. The immediacy of the forum allows participants to focus narrowly on specific claims or evidence, as you might in a face-to-face debate but without the pressure of having to respond immediately to someone else's challenge or rebuttal. But notice that argument in this forum tends to be more informal and less rigorous than it can be in print media. Because messages tend to be relatively short, and because active discussions can generate many messages very quickly, claims and evidence need to be presented concisely, without the lengthy explanations and extensive support that might be expected in the formal essays you write for your college courses. For the most part participants understand and accept this fact. But if you engage in discussions in online forums, it is worth remembering that the principles of genuine argumentation don't always apply.

The matter of ethos can also be complicated in online forums. Generally, there is no way of knowing who participants really are, whether they have any legitimate knowledge or experience related to the topic at hand, and whether they are being honest about what they say. As we noted in Chapter 2, determining the credibility of the author of an argument is an important part of analyzing that argument. Participants in online forums can establish their own ethos over time through the messages they post, but you usually have no way to verify what others say in their messages. To an extent one's ethos is always constructed, even in a respected print medium. But writers whose essays appear in a magazine such as the *Atlantic Monthly* or a newspaper such as the *Wall Street Journal* must work with editors and generally have well-established credentials. Just being published in a respected magazine gives them a measure of credibility. By contrast, anyone can log into a newsgroup such as soc.college.admissions and post a message. And a participant can claim to be a college instructor or an admissions officer without having to provide proof. If you know that the person is who he or she claims to be, you are more likely to take that person's arguments seriously. But without a way to verify their claims, you should always view their messages with at least a small measure of skepticism.

It goes without saying that your own ethos can be questioned too. So as a participant in an online discussion you are likely to be more effective in making your arguments if you can establish credibility, just as you would in a print medium. Keep in mind that other participants might take your claims about who you are with a grain of salt. Keep in mind, too, that following the protocols of arguing in online forums is one of the best ways to establish your credibility in such a forum. Posting relatively brief messages that respond to previous messages, keeping your responses to the point, and avoiding criticism or ridicule of other participants (that is, avoiding flame wars) will likely encourage others to take your arguments more seriously.

Synchronous forums, such as chat rooms, instant messaging, or MUDs (multi-user domains), differ from asynchronous forums in that participants post and read messages in "real time." In other words, when you are logged onto a chat room or other kind of synchronous forum, your message appears on the screens of all the other logged-on participants as soon as you write it on your computer; any messages posted by other participants appear on your screen immediately as well. And those messages do not remain available once the conversation has ended; that is, you cannot always retrieve them later, as you can on a newsgroup or mailing list.

The experience of engaging in a synchronous discussion is very much like having a face-to-face conversation, except that you are reading and writing comments rather than speaking or hearing them. As a result, discussions in synchronous forums tend to be somewhat slower than face-to-face discussions. And usually several different topics — or "threads" — occur simultaneously. These characteristics of synchronous forums result in messages that tend to be very short and, ideally, concise as well. Longer messages, even messages of a few sentences, can slow down the discussion and make it harder for participants to keep up with the conversation. Consequently, synchronous forums do not lend themselves to considered debate about complex issues that require participants to present lengthy arguments or cite extensive evidence to support their arguments. If you engage in synchronous discussions, you will be most effective if you can keep your statements short but clear and if you can focus on one claim at a time. Similarly, offer clearly identifiable support for a claim that can be easily digested by other participants.

Although the advice we have offered here applies generally to any kind of online discussion forum, all online forums are not the same. Public newsgroups such as soc.college.admissions tend to be much more freewheeling and informal than specialized newsgroups for professionals, which are often moderated (that is, a moderator reviews messages and decides whether they are appropriate for the forum; the moderator is the equivalent of a newspaper or magazine editor). The protocols governing online behavior can vary widely from one forum to another. Sarcasm and ad hominem attacks that are common on many public newsgroups might result in your removal from a moderated academic mailing list. The audiences for online forums can differ dramatically as well. Participants in a newsgroup such as soc.law may include lawyers and other legal professionals, but participants are just as likely to be people with little or no knowledge of the law. By contrast, a mailing list maintained by the American Bar Association will probably be made up mostly of lawyers. The nature of the audience will affect the kinds of topics discussed in a forum and the ways in which participants engage with each other. Flame wars, for example, are much less common in specialized professional forums than in public newsgroups and chat rooms. The expectations for claims and evidence are likely to be more rigorous in a professional forum as well. Even the length of messages and the conventions for how people identify themselves can be different in these different forums. Because of these differences, to engage effectively in argumentation in any online forum, you need to become familiar with the forum and its protocols. It makes sense to read a newsgroup or mailing list for several days or even weeks before jumping into the discussion. If you do so, you will probably find that online discussions can be fruitful and interesting and can be part of your effort to solve problems and negotiate difference through argument.

RADIO AND TELEVISION

The differences between these two media are obvious; most important, radio is not a visual medium. When television began to come into widespread use in the 1950s, many critics feared that it would mean the end of radio. However, radio has thrived since that time, a fact that suggests that it has characteristics as a medium for communication that television lacks. At the same time radio and television share many characteristics that can escape our notice.

Perhaps the most important feature of radio and television is their reach: They are available to hundreds of millions of people worldwide — many more people than currently have access to the Internet. This reach gives them enormous power for making an argument available to a large audience. Moreover, radio and television are local, national, and international at the same time. Your local talk-radio station might have a host who addresses issues of importance to residents of your region. At the same time the station might be part of a national network, enabling it to broadcast national (and possibly international) shows as well. So someone can direct an argument to a very specific audience or to a much wider national audience on the same station. The same can be said of most television stations. Although it is true that local newspapers and other print forums also print local as well as national and international news, more people listen to radio shows and watch television news programs than read newspapers and newsmagazines. The easy availability of radio and TV seems to matter. And that ease becomes a factor in making an argument in these media.

The immediacy of radio and television is also important. If you are listening to an editorial on radio or on a television news program, you are hearing an electronic version of a speech. In most cases you will not have access to a printed version of the editorial, so you will not be able to rehear it or reread sections of it (unless of course you record it). This characteristic of radio or television arguments requires the speaker to adjust diction, style, and arrangement so that listeners can follow the argument easily. Long, complex sentences can be difficult for an audience to follow in oral arguments, and very complicated reasoning or detailed evidence can be lost on listeners. For these reasons constructing an argument in these media usually means choosing accessible words, crafting relatively simple sentences, perhaps repeating key phrases, and generally being more succinct than you might be in, say, a research paper for a college course or a newspaper editorial.

Sound is a very powerful tool in both television and radio. Listen to any commercial, an announcement for an upcoming program, or a political advertisement, and you will almost certainly hear music or some other sound effect that was specifically chosen for that spot. Political advertisements, for example, are often accompanied by patriotic music or other kinds of music intended to influence listeners positively. Television commercials for sporty cars use contemporary rock music that appeals to younger people who are likely to buy such cars. Similarly, ads for many products now include popular songs from the 1970s that would have positive connotations for viewers who grew up during that decade. As a listener or viewer you might find yourself reacting to such sound effects in ways that might influence how you think about the claim being made on behalf of a political candidate or for a particular car. Would you react to the pitch in the same way if it did not incorporate that favorite song of yours? Would your feelings about the political candidate be different if no music were played during his radio ad? Being aware of the impact of such uses of sound is part of being able to engage public arguments critically.

Earlier in this chapter, we discussed the role of visual elements in argumentation, and we referred to television advertisements and other kinds of television arguments, in which images are so central to their impact. It is worth reemphasizing here that the video and sound capabilities of television make it an enormously powerful medium, and it is important to keep in mind that much of what appears on television is persuasion rather than genuine argumentation. In fact, aside from editorials on news programs, discussions on some public affairs programs (such as *Face the Nation*), and some special documentary programs, very little of what appears on television can be described as genuine argumentation of the kind we have been exploring in this book. At the same time the power of this medium, its ubiquitous nature, and even its seductiveness are compelling reasons for you to be aware of its persuasive qualities and to be able to distinguish between the many kinds of persuasion on television and the few genuine arguments appearing in that medium.

Perhaps the most obvious instance of argumentation on television occurs during political conventions, especially during presidential elections. When the major political parties convene, they take great pains to present themselves in a certain light on the extensive television coverage of those events. The stage and backdrop for speeches, the music, the colors of banners and signs, the camera angles are all carefully arranged to communicate certain messages to voters. When a candidate addresses the convention, his or her appearance on the television screen is as important as the speech itself. Think of your own reaction to a televised political speech. How much was it influenced by your feelings about the appearance of the candidate? By his or her delivery? How much attention did you pay to the words themselves? How closely did you follow the argument, identifying and evaluating claims and evidence? Chances are that for many viewers the messages communicated by the candidate's appearance and presentation overshadow the specific claims made in the speech itself. A candidate's confident and trustworthy appearance might impress the viewer more than his or her specific arguments about, say, tax reform. The power and subtlety of visual messages thus present a challenge to those who wish to engage in genuine argumentation in this important medium.

You might never have an opportunity to make an argument on radio or television, but you will certainly encounter arguments in those media. And many of those arguments will be about important matters in your life, including political elections. Being aware of the way these media are used to communicate and persuade — as well as to argue — will make you a more savvy citizen.

■ ■ ■

The well-known critic Marshall McLuhan once famously asserted that the medium *is* the message. In this chapter we have examined some ways in which McLuhan may have been right. But we have also pointed out that in many ways argument is argument is argument. In other words, the principles of sound argumentation apply in any medium. Moreover, our motives for argument will determine much of what we say and how we make use of a particular medium. If we are genuinely committed to engaging in argumentation to solve problems, then our uses of media can enhance our arguments and contribute powerfully to our efforts to negotiate differences as we address the many complex issues that affect us as we live and work together.

5

CONSTRUCTING
ARGUMENTS

CONSTRUCTIN

An assignment for your cultural anthropology course requires you to write an essay examining the ethical issues faced by Western anthropologists who study nonindustrialized societies in places such as the Amazon basin. In your essay you are to take a position on the ethical guidelines for such research that have been proposed by a professional organization for anthropologists.

■ You have been asked by other residents of your college dormitory to write a letter to the campus director of residential life to urge him not to implement new security measures that the college is considering. These measures include a new policy that would prohibit students from having visitors in their dorms except during specified hours in the early evening. You and your dorm-mates oppose these measures. Your letter to the director of residential life will try to convince him that the proposed measures would significantly restrict students' social activities without enhancing campus security.

■ A local organization that you belong to advocates sustainable community development. A national retail business has requested a permit to build a large store on farmland near a residential neighborhood in your community. Many residents are pleased because they believe that the new store will improve the community's economic status. Others worry about the impact of the new store on surrounding land, especially regarding water runoff into a nearby marsh that is part of a community park and natural area. Your organization has decided to oppose the building of the new store on the proposed site unless certain measures to protect the marsh are required. You are part of a team that will create a new Web site devoted to presenting your organization's perspective on the new store.

ARGUMENTS

How do you proceed?

The answer to that question is the same for each of these situations. It is also different for each of them.

In each of these cases you would try to present and support your claims to your intended audience in a way that is persuasive. To make an effective argument, you must examine the issue carefully so that you understand it well, which might require some research. You must also gather and present evidence to support the claims you will make in your argument. You will want to consider how your intended audience is likely to respond to your claims and warrants in each case. And you must adopt a style — and, in the case of the Web site, a design — that most effectively presents your case.

But each of these situations is different, and arguing effectively means understanding the specific factors involved in each case.

1. *The rhetorical situation.* The audience and circumstances for each of these writing tasks are very different. Your anthropology teacher, for instance, will have different expectations for your paper than the director of residential life will have for your letter. And the audience for the Web site would be an entire community, with complex and perhaps divergent expectations for a persuasive argument.

2. *The goals for argument.* Although we can see each of these arguments as part of an effort to solve a problem, the problems in each instance represent different challenges to you as writer. In your anthropology course you hope to understand the ethical issues of anthropology research sufficiently to make an effective argument to earn you a good grade. Your letter to the residential life director is intended to convince him not to implement new security rules that would have a direct impact on your living situation. And your organization hopes that its Web site will generate support among community residents for environmental restrictions on a very large construction project.

3. *The medium.* The anthropology paper will have to adhere to the conventions of academic writing in the field of anthropology. The letter to the residential life director is also a print document, but one that follows different conventions for writing. And the Web site is an entirely different medium that requires you to consider such matters as layout, color, and hyperlinks.

Adapting to different situations like these is part of making effective arguments. Everything included in the first four chapters of this book is intended to help you understand argumentation in order to construct effective arguments in any situation. The principles we have examined apply to all kinds of arguments. But in this chapter we offer a more focused discussion of how to construct arguments, whatever the situation.

MANAGING THE COMPOSING PROCESS

UNDERSTANDING COMPOSING AS INQUIRY

In some ways composing an argument, whatever the medium, is like any other kind of writing: You must define your topic, develop your ideas, gather sufficient information, organize your material, revise accordingly, and edit so that your writing is accurate, effective, and correct. In other words, you must move through the composing process. Composing arguments can make that process both easier and harder. It can make the process easier in the sense that some of the conventions of argumentation will help you determine what you will say and how you will say it. For example, in an argument you will generally be expected to make your claims clearly and support them with adequate evidence. Knowing that can help you generate ideas and organize the information more easily. But as we have seen throughout this book, argumentation involves confronting the complexities of human beliefs and opinions. Part of your challenge in composing your argument is managing that complexity and showing that you are knowledgeable and fair-minded. For example, the essay for your anthropology course will probably address issues of racial diversity, and you will have to consider how the controversial nature of race relations might figure into your argument. In addition, if your goal is to address a serious issue and try to solve a problem through argumentation, you will always be concerned about arguing ethically and honestly. In other words, your goal isn't to win but to engage with others in order to work through a difficult problem. That goal requires you to consider the implications of your argument and the potential effects of your claims on your audience.

Of course, you can't hope to do everything at once. Think of the process of composing an argument as an ongoing process of inquiry. By composing an argument, you are carefully exploring an issue, learning about that issue and about yourself and others as well. That learning might require you to rethink your claims or your position on the issue at hand. For instance, you might begin your essay for your anthropology course believing that strict ethical guidelines for anthropology research are not necessary, but you might find as you compose your essay that the issue is more complicated than you initially thought. That process of inquiry might therefore lead you to revise your original position.

If you approach the writing of an argument in this way — as a process of inquiry — you are more likely to construct effective arguments. Moreover, you might gain a deeper understanding of the issue at hand and perhaps address the problem more effectively as well.

DEFINING YOUR TOPIC

In the scenarios at the beginning of this chapter the topic for argument in each case may seem clear. But it is important to distinguish between a *subject* and a *topic*. That distinction is even more important if you are faced with a situation in which you are asked to write an argument about anything you want (which is not uncommon in a college writing class). In the case of the anthropology essay, for example, the subject is anthropology, or more specifically, *anthropology research;* we might define the topic as *the ethical problems facing anthropologists who study other cultures.* We can narrow that topic even further: *the specific ethical problem of the relationship between the anthropologist and the people he or she is studying.* Because issues like this are so complex, narrowing the topic will enable you to address it adequately in your essay. It would be impossible to write anything but a very superficial five-page essay about an issue as big as the ethics of anthropological research. Entire books have been written about that issue. But you can feasibly write a five-page essay arguing for specific ethical guidelines relating to the personal relationship between an anthropologist and the people being studied.

If you are given the flexibility to write an argument on any topic, part of your challenge is to select a suitable topic worth arguing about. The best topics are those that are complex: They are about issues that matter to people; they generate controversy; and usually there is a variety of views about them. The topics in the scenarios at the beginning of this chapter are good topics for those reasons. But it is important that the topic you choose matter to *you*. Composing an effective argument is an intellectually rigorous process. There is no point in carefully examining an issue that you're not interested in or concerned about.

Almost all intelligent arguments involve *opinions,* but not all opinions lead to good arguments. Simply having an opinion about something is not the same thing as being able to make a considered argument about it. And some opinions are just not worth arguing. What would be the point of making an argument that golden retrievers are more handsome dogs than poodles? You might love golden retrievers, but will such a topic generate much interest among your classmates? Probably not. It would be better to choose a topic that will matter to others.

Be careful to distinguish between opinions that are a matter of taste and those that are a question of judgment. Some things — broccoli, for example — are a matter of personal preference. You might be able to write an amusing essay about broccoli, but no matter how hard you try, you will not convince someone who hates green vegetables to rush to the produce department of the nearest supermarket. And why would you want to? Questions of judgment, on the other hand, are more substantial. Our judgments are determined by our beliefs, which in turn grow out of basic principles to which we try to remain consistent. These principles ultimately lead us to decide that some judgments are correct and others are not. Should a university require first-year students to live in dormitories? Should it restrict their social activities? Does the state have a right to execute criminals? Should couples live together before getting married? All these are to a great extent questions of judgment.

Questions like these provide rich topics for argumentation because they are complex and offer many avenues to explore. But the very richness of these topics can also be challenging when you are composing an argument. Arguments written about these topics can take many directions. Trying to explore too many directions at once can lead to confusing and ineffective arguments. For this reason defining your topic is only one step in the process of composing an argument. As we noted earlier, composing an argument amounts to engaging in inquiry — that is, exploring your topic fully, and perhaps changing it along the way. In some cases you might have a clearly defined topic even before you begin to write. The letter to the director of residential life in our example at the beginning of this chapter is one such instance. But often you will find that your specific topic will change as you explore the issue you are writing about.

Whatever your topic, the following questions can help you define it carefully and begin to explore it:

- Do I know what my specific topic is?
- Is the topic suitable for the assignment or situation for which I am writing?
- Do I have an opinion about this topic? What is that opinion based on?
- On what grounds might anyone disagree with my opinion?
- Can I hope to persuade others to agree with my opinion?
- Can I support my opinion with evidence?

CONSIDERING AUDIENCE

The questions above remind us that an argument is always made with an audience in mind. That audience will shape an argument from the very beginning of the composing process. So carefully considering your audience is an important part of the process of exploring your topic and developing your argument. In Chapter 3 we examined the rhetorical context of argument and discussed the role of audience in argumentation. As you prepare to compose your argument, it is a good idea to review that chapter. Here we will focus on how audience considerations will affect the *composing* of your argument.

Identifying Your Audience   In some situations your audience is already well-defined. That letter in which you argue against new dormitory restrictions has a very specific audience: the director of residential life. Your essay about the ethical problems facing anthropologists also has a specific audience — your teacher, though your teacher will probably expect you to assume a larger audience (for example, people interested in anthropology). The Web site about the new store proposed for your town has a more general audience, though even this audience is relatively specific (residents of your community). As you work through the process of composing your argument, try to identify what you know about your audience's interests, views, and knowledge of the topic you are addressing. Your sense of what your audience knows or believes can help you define your topic in a way that will connect with that audience; it can also help you explore that topic so that you can develop ideas for making your argument. For example, in writing the letter to the director of residential life at your college, you can assume that your audience (the director) has detailed knowledge of the problems associated with security in campus housing. He most likely feels a great sense of responsibility for the security of students living on campus. And he probably wants students not only to feel secure on campus, but to enjoy their living arrangements as well. As you develop your argument against new restrictions on dormitory visitors, you can use these assumptions to identify claims and warrants that are likely to be acceptable to the director, and you can more easily identify common ground. For example, you might point out that you and the other students in your dorm share his concerns about safety in the dorms. You can research problems with security on your campus and use that information to support your contention that the new visitor restrictions will not likely enhance security. In short, your understanding of your audience can help to generate specific ideas for your argument and

A METHOD FOR EXPLORING YOUR IDEAS AND YOUR AUDIENCE IN ARGUMENT

Whenever you are making any argument, it can be useful to make a list of the reasons why you believe as you do about the issue. You will probably not be able to discuss, in a short essay, all the points you have listed about the issue, and it is likely that as you compose and revise your argument, you will generate even more ideas — ideas that might prove to be even more important than those on your list. But you can benefit from identifying the reasons for your position, ranking them in order of their importance, and considering the impact they might have on your intended audience. In the case of an essay opposing capital punishment, you might list as one of your reasons "Killing is always morally wrong." If you think about how readers who support the death penalty might react to such a statement, you can begin to anticipate their objections (for example, that killing can be justified in certain cases) or even discover common ground (the idea that human life is sacred).

You can also benefit from making another list: reasons why people might disagree with your position. Then, having explored opposing points of view, you can ask yourself why you have not been persuaded by those reasons. Are there flaws in those reasons? Do you hold beliefs that make it impossible for you to accept those reasons? Adding a brief response to each of these reasons can help you anticipate objections to your position and generate ideas for presenting and supporting your claims. And you are likely to discover that those who hold views opposed to yours have at least one good argument that you cannot answer.

formulate those ideas in ways that might resonate with that audience. Moreover, if you approach argumentation as problem solving, you will tend to see your audience not as an opponent but as a partner in your effort to address the issue at hand. You and your dormmates might have different priorities than the residential life director, and obviously your responsibilities are different. But all of you care about safety, and all of you hope for a pleasant and enjoyable campus lifestyle. Understanding that shared ground can lead you to formulate an argument that works toward a solution rather than a victory. The same can be true even when your audience is more general.

At times, you and your audience might hold very different views on an issue, and your respective positions can seem irreconcilable. In fact, because arguments are so often made about controversial matters, it is quite likely that you will find yourself constructing an argument for an audience that might be passionately opposed to your point of view. Just skim the newspaper on any morning, and you'll quickly find such issues: capital punishment, sustainable development, tax increases, school funding, religious freedom. Because such issues are so important to people, they can make the process of considering your audience more complicated, and they require that you take greater care in understanding your audience.

Imagine, for instance, that you are making an argument to a general audience — say, in an article for your local newspaper — about an issue as emotional and complicated as capital punishment. You can be certain that some members of that audience will hold views that are opposed to your own. As you develop your argument, assume that such readers will be skeptical. But don't dismiss their views; rather, consider their reasons for opposing your viewpoint, and try to address their concerns as you build your own case. Doing so not only will help you make a more convincing argument, but might also enable you to find common ground with those readers.

Making Concessions   Often, especially when we are addressing complex and controversial issues such as capital punishment, we can find ourselves believing that our position is right and those who believe otherwise are simply ignorant or harbor dubious motives. But serious controversies almost always continue because each side of the issue has valid concerns that cannot be dismissed. Identifying these concerns enables you to understand the issue better and to construct an argument that might be not only more convincing but also more useful. This might mean conceding a point or two to those who oppose your position. If you have no rebuttal to a particular point and recognize that your opponents' case has some merit, be honest and generous enough to say so. Making such a concession should not be considered simply a strategic move on your part. Rather, it also signals your willingness to take your audience seriously, even when they disagree with you, and it reflects your genuine interest in addressing the problem at hand effectively and ethically. In this way you might bridge the gap between you and members of your audience who oppose your position, making it easier to reach a more substantial agreement. Insisting in a belligerent way that your opponents are completely wrong will hardly convince them to take you seriously. Life is seldom so simple that one side is unequivocally right and the other wrong.

Having a good sense of your audience will help you decide what concessions to make. Different audiences will have different expectations. Some might want to hear concessions before listening to opposing views. Some might expect lengthy discussions of conceded points; others might not. When making concessions, address what you think are your audience's most pressing concerns. Doing so can help you develop important points in your argument and organize them more effectively.

Understanding Audience Expectations Having a good sense of audience can also help you decide on the examples and evidence that will best illustrate and support your claims. You will want to use examples that your audience will understand, and you will want evidence that will be convincing to them. Examples of actual cases in an argument opposing capital punishment can be persuasive for a general audience, such as readers of your local newspaper. For a college course in legal theory, however, you will probably need to use a court's formal opinion or statistical data if you wish to be persuasive.

There is a great difference, however, between responding to the interests of your audience by discussing what it wants to know and twisting what you say to please an audience with what it wants to hear. A writer should try to tell the truth as he or she sees it. What we mean by "truth" can have many dimensions. When limited space forces us to be selective, it is wise to focus on the facets of a topic that will be most effective with the audience we are hoping to convince. But it is one thing to focus and quite another to mislead. Never present anything to one audience that you would be compelled to deny to another. Doing so not only damages your credibility, but also undermines any legitimate effort to solve problems through argumentation.

You should bear in mind, too, that all of our advice about considering audience can be profoundly influenced by culture. The very idea of truth, for example, can vary from one culture to another or between two people who follow different religious practices. Even the idea of "factual evidence" can be shaped by cultural background. Western societies such as the United States place a high value on scientific evidence, but some cultures do not share that faith in science. Indeed, even in the United States there are communities that, because of religious beliefs or ideological leanings, harbor a deep mistrust of science. You might never have to address such audiences in an argument, but it is always important to remember that whenever you make an argument to an audience, you do so in a cultural context.

How One Student Addresses Her Audience The following essay, which was originally published as an editorial in a college newspaper, illustrates the importance of taking audience into account in argumentation.

To Skip or Not to Skip: A Student Dilemma

This is college, right? The four-year deal offering growth, maturity, experience, and knowledge? A place to be truly independent?

Because sometimes I can't tell. Sometimes this place downright reeks of paternal instincts. Just ask the freshmen and sophomores, who are by class rank alone guaranteed two full years of twenty-four-hour supervision, orchestrated activities, and group showers.

But the forced dorm migration of underclassmen has been bitched about before, to no avail. University policy is, it seems, set in stone. It ranks right up there with ingrown toe nails for sheer evasion and longevity.

But there's another university policy that has no merit as a policy and no place in a university. Mandatory Attendance Policy: wherein faculty members attempt the high school hall monitor–college instructor maneuver. It's a difficult trick to justify as professors place the attendance percentage of their choice above a student's proven abilities on graded material.

Profs rationalize out a lot of arguments to support the policy. Participation is a popular one. I had a professor whose methods for lowering grades so irritated me I used to skip on purpose. He said, "Classroom participation is a very important part of this introductory course. Obviously, if you are not present, you cannot be participating."

Equally obvious, though not stated by the prof, is the fact that one can be perpetually present but participate as little as one who is absent. So who's the better student — the one who makes a meaningless appearance or the one who is busy with something else? And who gets the points docked?

The rest of his policy was characteristically vague, mentioning that absences "could" result in a lower grade. Constant ambiguity is the second big problem with formal policies. It's tough for teachers to figure out just how much to let attendance affect grade point. So they doubletalk.

According to the UWSP catalog, faculty are to provide "clear explanation" of attendance policy. Right. Based on the language actually used, ninety-five percent of UWSP faculty are functionally incapable of uttering a single binding statement. In an effort to offend no one while retaining all power of action, profs write things like (these are actual policies): "I trust students to make their own judgments and choices about coming, or not coming, to class." But then continues: "Habitual and excessive absence is grounds for failure." What happened to trust? What good are the choices?

Or this: "More than three absences may negatively affect your grade." Then again, they may not. Who knows? And this one: "I consider every one of you in here to be mature adults. However, I reserve the right to alter grades based on attendance."

You reserve the right? By virtue of your saying so? Is that like calling the front seat? Another argument that profs cling to goes something like, "Future employers, by God, aren't going to put up with absenteeism." Well, let's take a reality pill. I think most students can grasp the difference between cutting an occasional class, which they paid for, and cutting at work, when they're the ones on salary. See, college students are capable of bi-level thought control, nowadays. (It's all those computers.)

In summary, mandatory attendance should be abolished because:

1. It is irrelevant. Roughly the same number of students will either skip or attend, regardless of what a piece of paper says. If the course is worth anything.

2. It is ineffective. It automatically measures neither participation, ability, or gained knowledge. That's what tests are for. Grades are what you end up knowing, not how many times you sat there to figure it out.

3. It is insulting. A college student is capable of determining a personal schedule, one that may or may not always meet with faculty wishes. An institution committed to the fostering of personal growth cannot operate under rules that patronize or minimize the role an adult should claim for himself.

4. It is arbitrary. A prof has no right and no ability to factor in an unrealistic measure of performance. A student should be penalized no more than what the natural consequence of an absence is — the missing of one day's direct delivery of material.

5. It abolishes free choice. By the addition of a factor that cannot be fought. We are not at a university to learn conformity. As adults, we reserve the right to choose as we see fit, even if we choose badly.

Finally, I would ask the faculty to consider this: We have for some time upheld in this nation the sacred principle of separation of church and state; i.e., You are not God.

Karen Rivedal

Editor

In this essay Karen chose a topic that would certainly interest many college students, the audience for whom she saw herself writing. Her thesis is clear: Mandatory class attendance should not be required of college students. And her writing is lively enough to hold the attention of many readers. All this is good.

But Karen's argument also has some weaknesses. In her sixth paragraph she offers what logicians call a *false dilemma:* offering a choice between only two alternatives when others exist (see page 40). By asking, "So who's the better student — the one who makes a meaningless appearance or the one who is busy with something else?," she has ignored at least two other possibilities. Appearance in class is likely to be meaningful to at least some students, and cutting class may be meaningless if the "something else" occupying a student's attention is a waste of time. The comparison in the tenth paragraph between reserving the right to lower grades because of poor attendance and "calling the front seat" is confusing. In the twelfth paragraph Karen claims, "Roughly the same number of students will either skip or attend, regardless of what a piece of paper says," but she offers no evidence to support this claim, which is really no more than guesswork. And because Karen herself admits that many students skip class despite mandatory attendance policies, her claim in the sixteenth paragraph that required attendance "abolishes free choice" does not hold up.

These lapses in logic aside, the major problem with Karen's argument is that she misjudged her audience. She forgot that professors, as well as students, read the school newspaper. Students cannot change the policies of their professors, but the professors themselves usually can, so she has overlooked the very audience that she most needs to reach. Moreover, not only has she failed to include professors within her audience, but she has actually insulted them. Although her criticisms of professors will strike some students as funny, a professor who is told that she or he is "functionally incapable of uttering a single binding statement" (paragraph 8) is unlikely to feel motivated to change. Only in the very last paragraph does Karen specifically address the faculty, and this proves to be simply the occasion for a final insult. There may be professors who take themselves too seriously, but are there really that many who believe that they are divine?

Although it might be easy to poke holes in this argument, Karen deserves credit for boldly calling attention to policies that might indeed be wrong. Recognizing that her original argument could be stronger but still firmly believing that mandatory class attendance is inappropriate for college students, Karen decided to rewrite her editorial as an essay. Here is her revision:

Absent at What Price?

Karen Rivedal

This is college, right? A place to break old ties, solve problems, and make decisions? Higher education is, I always thought, the pursuit of knowledge in a way that's a step beyond the paternal hand-holding of high school. It's the act of learning performed in a more dynamic atmosphere, rich with individual freedom, discourse, and debate.

But sometimes I can't tell. Some university traditions cloud the full intent of higher education. Take mandatory attendance policies, wherein faculty members attempt the high school hall monitor–college instructor maneuver. It's a difficult trick to justify as professors place the attendance percentage of their choice above a student's proven abilities on graded material.

This isn't to say that the idea of attendance itself is unsound. Clearly, personal interaction between teacher and students is preferable to textbook teaching alone. It's the *mandatory* attendance policy, within an academic community committed to the higher education of adults, that worries me.

Professors offer several arguments to support the practice. Participation is a popular one. I had a professor whose methods for lowering grades so irritated me that I used to skip class out of spite. He said, "Classroom participation is a very important part of this introductory course. Obviously, if you are not present, you cannot be participating."

Equally obvious, though, is the fact that one can be perpetually present, but participate as little as one who is absent. Participation lacks an adequate definition. There's no way of knowing, on the face of it, if a silent student is necessarily a learning student. Similarly, an instructor has no way of knowing for what purpose or advantage a student may miss a class and therefore no ability to determine its relative validity.

As a learning indicator, then, mandatory attendance policy is flawed. It automatically measures neither participation nor ability. That's what tests are for. A final grade should reflect what a student ends up knowing rather than the artificial consequences of demerit points.

Some faculty recognize the shortcomings of a no-exceptions mandatory attendance policy and respond with partial policies. Constant ambiguity is characteristic of this approach and troublesome for the student who wants to know just where he or she stands. It's tough for teachers to figure out just how much to let attendance affect grade point. So they double-talk.

This, for example, is taken from an actual policy: "I trust students to make their own judgments and choices about coming, or not coming, to class." It then continues: "Habitual and excessive absence is grounds for failure." What happened to trust? What good are the choices?

Or this: "More than three absences may negatively affect your grade." Then again, they may not. Who knows? And this one: "I consider every one of you in here to be mature adults. However, I reserve the right to alter grades based on attendance."

This seems to say, what you can prove you have learned from this class takes a back seat to how much I think you should know based on your attendance. What the teacher says goes — just like in high school.

Professors who set up attendance policies like these believe, with good reason, that they are helping students to learn by ensuring their attendance. But the securing of this end by requirement eliminates an important element of learning. Removing the freedom to make the decision is removing the need to think. An institution committed to fostering personal growth cannot operate under rules that patronize or minimize the role an adult should claim for himself or herself.

A grading policy that relies on the student's proven abilities certainly takes the guess work out of grade assigning for teachers. This take-no-prisoners method, however, also demands a high, some say unfairly high, level of personal student maturity. Younger students especially may need, they say, the extra structuring that a policy provides.

But forfeiting an attendance policy doesn't mean that a teacher has to resign his humanity, too. Teachers who care to can still take five minutes to warn an often-absent student about the possible consequences, or let the first test score tell the story. As much as dedicated teachers want students to learn, learning is still a personal choice. Students must want to.

A "real-world" argument that professors often use goes something like "Future employers aren't going to put up with absenteeism, so get used to it now." Well, let's take a reality pill. I think most students can differentiate between cutting an occasional class, which they paid for, and missing at work, when they're the ones on salary.

Students who intelligently protest an institution's policies, such as mandatory attendance requirements, are proof-in-action that college is working. These students are thinking; and learning to think and question is the underlying goal of all education. College is more than its rules, more than memorized facts. Rightly, college is knowledge, the testing of limits. To be valid, learning must include choice and the freedom to make mistakes. To rely on mandatory attendance for learning is to subvert the fullest aims of that education.

In revising her essay, Karen has retained both her thesis and her own distinctive voice. Such phrases as "the high school hall monitor–college instructor maneuver," the "take-no-prisoners method," and "let's take a reality pill" are still recognizably her own. But her argument is now more compelling. In addition to eliminating the fallacies that marred her original version, Karen included new material that strengthens her case. The third paragraph offers a much needed clarification, reassuring readers that an argument against a mandatory attendance policy is not the same as an argument against attending class. The seventh paragraph begins with a fairly sympathetic reference to professors, and the eleventh paragraph opens with a clear attempt to anticipate opposition. The twelfth paragraph includes another attempt to anticipate opposition, and the thirteenth paragraph, with its reference to "dedicated teachers," is much more likely to appeal to the professors in Karen's audience than any statements in the original version did. She still makes a hard-nosed argument, but she doesn't lapse into insults. Finally, the conclusion of this essay is much improved. It successfully links the question of mandatory attendance policies with the purpose of higher education as defined in the opening paragraph.

You might think that Karen's revision has suppressed the strong, critical voice of her original version. As a result, you might feel that her revised essay will not resonate as well with students. However, consider this: If we think of Karen's essay as an effort to address a legitimate concern for both students *and* faculty, is her revised version a more effective attempt to solve the problem of cutting classes?

DEFINING YOUR TERMS

To make sure that your ideas are understandable in an argument, it is important to clarify any terms that are essential to your argument. Unfortunately, many writers of argument fail to define the words they use. It is not unusual, for example, to find writers advocating (or opposing) gun control without defining exactly what they mean by *gun control*. Many arguments use words such as *censorship, society, legitimate,* and *moral* so loosely that it is impossible to decide exactly what the writer means. When this happens, the entire argument can break down.

Don't feel that you need to define every word you use, but you should define any important term that your audience might misunderstand. Avoid defining a word by using the same term or another term that is equally complex. For example, if you are opposed to the sale of pornography, you should be prepared to define what you mean by *pornography.* It would not be helpful to tell your audience that pornography is "printed or visual material that is obscene" because this only raises the question: What is *obscene?* In an important ruling, the U.S. Supreme Court defined *obscene* as material that "the average person, applying community standards, would find . . . as a whole, appeals to the prurient interest," but even if you happened to have this definition at hand, you should ask yourself whether "the average person" understands what *prurient* means — not to mention what the Court might have meant by *community standards.* Unless you define your terms carefully, avoiding unnecessarily abstract language, you can end up writing an endless chain of definitions that require further explanation.

USING A DICTIONARY

If you consult a dictionary to help you define a term, remember that dictionaries are not all the same. For daily use, most writers usually refer to a good desk dictionary such as *The American Heritage Dictionary, The Random House Dictionary,* or *Merriam Webster's Collegiate Dictionary.* A good general dictionary of this sort will usually provide you with an adequate working definition. You might also want to consider consulting the multivolume *Oxford English Dictionary,* which is available in most college libraries and is especially useful in showing how the usage of a word has changed over the years. Your audience might also appreciate the detailed information that specialized dictionaries in various subject areas can provide. Many such dictionaries are likely to be available in your college library. For example, if you are working on an English literature paper, you might consult *A Concise Dictionary of Literary Terms* or *The Princeton Handbook of Poetic Terms.* For a paper in psychology, you might turn to *The Encyclopedic Dictionary of Psychology,* or for a paper on a musical topic, you could consult *The New Grove's Dictionary of Music and Musicians.* There are also dictionaries for medical, legal, philosophical, and theoretical terms as well as for each of the natural sciences. When using specialized dictionaries, you will often find valuable information, but remember that the definition that appears in your paper should not be more difficult than the word or phrase you originally set out to define.

Dictionaries can be helpful when you're defining your terms. But often the important terms in an argument cannot be satisfactorily defined with a dictionary. Consider the term *sustainability,* which is sometimes used in arguments about environmental issues. Such a term has specific and specialized meanings in environmental debates, and it would not suffice to supply only a dictionary definition. So instead of relying exclusively on dictionaries, try to define such key terms in your words. You can choose from among several strategies:

- Give synonyms.
- Compare the term with other words with which it is likely to be confused, and show how your term differs.
- Define a word by showing what it is *not.*
- Provide examples.

Writers frequently use several of these strategies to create a single definition. Sometimes an entire essay is devoted to defining one term; in doing so, the writer makes an argument in which that term is central. For example, a writer can focus an essay on defining *free speech,* in the process making an argument for a particular conception of that term.

When writing an argument, you will usually need to define your terms within a paragraph or two. In addition to achieving clarity, definition helps to control an argument by eliminating misunderstandings that can cause an audience to be inappropriately hostile or to jump to a conclusion that is different from your own. By carefully defining your terms, you limit a discussion to what you want to discuss. This increases the likelihood of your gaining a fair hearing for your views.

STRUCTURING AN ARGUMENT

One of the biggest challenges in composing an argument is structuring it. Once you have explored your topic and developed your ideas, you will need to consider the following questions:

- How should I begin my argument?
- In what order should I arrange the points I want to make?
- How can I most efficiently respond to opposing arguments?
- How should I conclude?

The answers to these questions will vary from one essay to another and from one kind of argument (such as a newspaper editorial) to another (a Web page). Even if no single plan will work for all arguments, you can benefit from being familiar with some basic principles of argumentation that may help you organize your argument effectively. Here we will discuss three traditional ways of structuring an argument:

- Classical arrangement
- Rogerian argument
- Logical arrangements

CLASSICAL ARRANGEMENT

Because classical theories of rhetoric developed at a time when most arguments were oral, the great works of classical rhetoric recommended strategies that could be easily understood by listeners. If speakers adhered to essentially the same plan, listeners were able to follow long, complex arguments because the main components were easily recognizable and the order in which they appeared signaled what was likely to follow.

The common plan for organizing an argument along classical lines included six main components: introduction, statement of background, proposition, proof, refutation, and conclusion, as follows.

Introduction (*Exordium*)	In the introduction you urge your audience to consider the case that you are about to present. This is the time to capture your readers' attention and introduce your issue.
Statement of Background (*Narratio*)	In the statement of background you narrate, or tell, the key events in the story behind your case. This is the time to provide information so that your audience will understand the nature of the facts in the case at hand.
Proposition (*Partitio*)	This component divides (or partitions) the part of the argument focused on information from the part focused on reasoning, and it outlines the major points that will follow. You must state the position you are taking, based on the information you have presented, and then indicate the lines the rest of your argument will follow.
Proof (*Confirmatio*)	Adhering carefully to your outline, you now present the heart of your argument: You make (or confirm) your case. You must discuss the reasons why you have taken your position and cite evidence to support each of those reasons.
Refutation (*Refutatio*)	In this key section you anticipate and refute opposing views. By showing what is wrong with the reasoning of your opponents, you demonstrate that you have studied the issue thoroughly and have reached the only conclusion that is acceptable in this case.
Conclusion (*Peroratio*)	The concluding paragraph(s) should summarize your most important points. In addition, you can make a final appeal to values and feelings that are likely to leave your audience favorably disposed toward your case.

Classical rhetoricians allowed variations on this plan, depending on, as the great Roman orator and scholar Cicero wrote, "the weight of the matter and the judgment of the speaker" (*De Oratore* I, 31). For example, a speaker was encouraged to begin with refutation when an audience was already strongly committed to an opposing point of view. But because this basic plan remains strong and clear, it can still help writers organize their thoughts.

One advantage of this method of arrangement is that it helps writers generate ideas for their arguments. If you follow the common classical plan for organizing your argument, you will have to generate ideas for each of the main parts. For example, you will have to provide background information about the issue at hand and include arguments to refute opposing points. As a result, your argument will tend to be thorough.

Much of classical rhetoric focused on political discourse, in which speakers publicly debated issues that required action by elected officials or legislatures. Because of this, classical arrangement can be especially useful when you feel strongly about an issue and you are trying to convince an audience to undertake a proposed course of action. Since classical rhetoric tends to assume that an audience can be persuaded when it is presented with solid evidence and a clear explanation of the flaws in opponents' reasoning, this plan for arranging an argument might be most effective when you are writing for people who share your basic values.

ROGERIAN ARGUMENT

In Chapter 1 we briefly discussed how the ideas of psychotherapist Carl Rogers have influenced scholars interested in argumentation. Rogers focused on listening with understanding in order to avoid miscommunication that can too often accompany serious conflicts. For Rogers the key to resolving conflict is to try honestly to understand what others mean.

Despite questions raised by some scholars about the extent to which Rogers's ideas can be applied to written arguments, you can benefit from viewing persuasion as a means to resolve conflict and achieve social cooperation instead of thinking that the point of an argument is to defeat your opponents. Accordingly, planning a Rogerian argument means emphasizing concessions rather than refutations and placing concessions early in your essay. Like classically arranged arguments, Rogerian arguments have six identifiable parts, as follows.

Introduction	State the problem that you hope to resolve. By presenting your issue as a problem in need of a solution, you raise the possibility of positive change. This strategy can interest readers who would not be drawn to an argument that seems devoted to tearing something down.
Summary of Opposing Views	As accurately and neutrally as possible, state the views of people with whom you disagree. By doing so, you show that you are capable of listening without judging and that you have given a fair hearing to people who think differently from you — the people you most need to reach.
Statement of Understanding	Having summarized views different from your own, you now show that you understand that there are situations in which these views are valid. In other words, you are offering a kind of concession. You are not conceding that these views are always right, but you are recognizing that there are conditions under which you would share the views of your opponents.
Statement of Your Position	Having won the attention of both your opponents and those readers who do not have a position on your issue, you have secured a hearing from an audience that is in

need of or is open to persuasion. Now that these readers know that you've given fair consideration to views other than your own, they should be prepared to listen fairly to your views.

Statement of Contexts

Similar to the statement of understanding, in which you have described situations where you would be inclined to share the views of your opponents, the statement of contexts describes situations in which you hope your own views would be honored. By showing that your position has merit in a specific context or contexts, you establish that you don't expect everyone to agree with you all the time. The limitations you recognize increase the likelihood that your opponents will agree with you at least in part.

Statement of Benefits

You conclude your argument by appealing to the self-interest of people who do not already share your views but are beginning to respect them because of your presentation. When you conclude by showing how such readers would benefit from accepting your position, your essay's ending is positive and hopeful.

(Adapted from Richard Coe, *Form and Substance.* New York: Wiley, 1981.)

Depending on the complexity of the issue, the extent to which people are divided about it, and the points you want to argue, any part of a Rogerian argument can be expanded. It is not necessary to devote precisely the same amount of space to each part. You should try to make your case as balanced as possible, however. If you seem to give only superficial consideration to the views of others and then linger at length on your own, you are defeating the purpose of a Rogerian argument.

Throughout this book we have advocated an approach to argumentation that draws on some of the principles of Rogerian argument, especially the importance of working toward solutions to conflicts. Any style of arrangement — classical, Rogerian, or otherwise — can strive toward the goal of solving problems through argumentation. But a Rogerian argument might be most effective in situations in which people are deeply divided as a result of different values or perceptions. It is especially useful when you are trying to reconcile conflicting parties and achieve a compromise. However, there will be situations in which such an approach might not be the most effective one. If you hold very strong views about a particular issue, for instance, you might find that it is better to consider other ways of organizing your argument. In some situations presenting a strong argument for a specific course of action or viewpoint might be the most ethical way to proceed, even if the ultimate goal is to resolve a conflict. The point is that planning and organizing your argument should be thought of in the larger context of your purposes for engaging in argument.

Here is a student essay about a very complicated and controversial issue: gay adoption. As you'll see, Rachel uses the principles of Rogerian argument to make her case in favor of a national policy for adoption by same-sex couples:

A Reasonable Approach to Gay Adoption

by Rachel Guetter

Adoption by gay parents recently became an open topic with the help of talk show host Rosie O'Donnell. O'Donnell, who went public with her sexuality in 2001, has adopted several children and is a foster mother (Huff and Gest 2). She is currently taking on a Florida law that bans homosexuals from adopting. In doing so, she is prompting everyone to address a situation that is likely to become more common: gay couples seeking to adopt children.

Currently, there is no national policy regarding gay adoptions, and state laws offer a mixed bag of approaches and restriction. For example, Florida is the only state that has enacted a law explicitly banning gay adoptions. In the states that do not have prohibitory laws, gays and lesbians can file for adoption in court (Maxwell, et al.). It is then up to each court to decide whether a petition for adoption meets the state's adoption policies. Many homosexuals have children from previous marriages, or they become parents by donating their own sperm or egg. Only California, Connecticut, and Vermont have legislation that would allow gays and lesbians to adopt their partner's child (Berman). The forty-six other states must rely on their individual judges to consider the petition. One would hope that a judge would not let personal preference get in the way of a fair ruling, but unfortunately this does not always happen.

The many different state laws may reflect the resistance of many Americans to the idea of gay adoption. Those who feel that children should not be brought up in homosexual households state that their concerns are not the product of homophobia, but are the product of what they find to be in the best interest of the children. These people believe that the best way for a child to be raised is in a family with married mother and father. Also, some opponents of gay adoption argue that children who grow up with same-sex parents are not provided with the same legal benefits and securities as those who are raised in heterosexual, married households.

One reason for this resistance is that America is still dealing with the lack of acceptance for and recognition of homosexuals. Until homosexuality is more widely received, children with gay and lesbian parents will have to deal with the fact that their family is viewed as pejoratively different. Glenn Stanton, senior research analyst for Focus on the Family, says, "While there may be very nice people who are raising kids in homosexual situations, the best model for kids is to grow up with mom and dad" (Stanton). It seems reasonable to believe that having both a mother and father benefits children. Women and men have different parenting traits that give a strong balance for the development of a child. Stanton also states, "Fathers encourage children to take chances ... mothers protect and are more cautious." There exist in parents different disciplining, communication, and playing styles that can be advantages in raising a child. Sandy Rios, president of Concerned Women for America, agrees, "As the single mother of a son, I can see quite clearly that having a mother and father together would be far better for my son" ("Pediatrics").

Another problem is that children who have gay and lesbian parents are not necessarily given the same benefits as children from two-parent, heterosexual families. Often, one person in a same-sex relationship is the biological parent and the other will help raise the child as his or her own. According to the American Academy of Pediatrics (AAP), children in this situation lose "survivor benefits if a parent dies and legal rights if the parents break up" (Berman 1). Both situations leave a dramatic impact on the child, who then is caught in the middle of legal battles. Another benefit that the child would not be given is health insurance from both parents. In all of these cases, the child is not given the same economic stability as one who has a married mother and father.

Many gays and lesbians are like any other people who dream of one day having a family. But they face great obstacles. Often, one parent in a same-sex family is not given the same rights as the other when one partner has a biological child. Sometimes neither partner in a same-sex family is able to obtain a child through adoption. Despite such obstacles, it cannot be denied that homosexual families exist. Depending on which study you consult, there are anywhere from 1.5 to 5 million children being raised in gay and lesbian families (Maxwell, et al.). The children, however, are the ones who are being hurt by the lack of legality of the situation that they are in. We owe it to these children — and to the same-sex couples who are committed to raising them — to address this problem in a way that is satisfactory for all concerned.

This issue needs to be examined from a national point of view for two reasons. First of all, people who wish to adopt a child are not restricted to adopting within their own states. Often, the demand for certain children requires couples to look in another state. Secondly, people tend to move from state to state. A couple may adopt a child in one state and later decide to move to another with different laws governing parenthood. The adoption needs to be legally recognized in all states, so if a couple adopts in one state, they can move to another and still be protected by law as legal parents. Instead of allowing each state to make its own decision concerning this matter, federal legislation needs to be enacted that would not only permit homosexuals to adopt their partner's child, but also allow gay couples to adopt children together. Obviously, such legislation would make it easier for same-sex families to raise their children in safe and happy homes. But it might also address the problem of children who need to be adopted. If homosexuals are legally permitted to adopt, more children waiting to be adopted can be given homes and the homosexual families that currently exist will become legally recognized.

There are children who are constantly being shifted from one foster home to another and deservingly need to be placed in a permanent and stable environment. There are currently not enough homes that children can be adopted into. In 1999, about 581,000 children were a part of the U.S. foster care system. Of those, 22 percent were available for adoption ("Foster Care Facts"). A report by the Vera Institute of Justice states that children raised without a permanent home are more likely to exhibit emotional and behavioral problems and be involved with the juvenile justice system ("Safe and Smart"). This is not to say that the foster care system is bad, but it suggests how important a permanent home and family are for children. Same-sex couples could provide such a home for many of these children.

Florida, the state that bans homosexuals from adopting, nevertheless allows homosexuals to become foster parents (Pertman). It is interesting to think that someone could be allowed to clothe, feed, discipline, and love a child yet not be allowed to call that child their own. By allowing a couple to be foster parents, the state has made a statement about what kind of people those foster parents are: responsible and caring and able to provide a good home and family environment. Why should they not be allowed to become legal parents of their own adopted children?

Both sides agree that children need to be raised in loving and caring families. It is wrong to think that a gay couple cannot provide that. A study in Minnesota shows that "in general, gay/lesbian families tended to score the most consistently as the healthiest and strongest of the family structures" (Maxwell, et al.). Married couples placed a strong second, and unmarried heterosexual couples were found to be the least healthy and least strong, especially when children were a part of the family (Maxwell, et al.). The study done by the courts discloses that homosexual couples deliberately plan to have children and arrange their lives so that both parents are significantly involved with raising the child (Maxwell, et al.). Opponents say that it takes more than just a loving environment; it takes both a mom and dad. As the Minnesota study proved, though, perhaps mother-father households are not as stable as once thought. Gays and lesbians have to make extensive plans in order to obtain or even conceive a child, so the likelihood that a child was an "accident" or unwanted is rare.

In February 2002, AAP issued a new statement titled, "Coparent or Second-Parent Adoption by Same-Sex Parents." It explains the AAP's stance on what is in the best interest of children being raised in same-sex families. Dr. Steven Berman offers a summary: "The AAP concluded that legalizing second-parent adoptions is in the best interest of the children" (Berman). Also in this statement is the reassurance that children are not more inclined to become homosexual or to possess homosexual tendencies from being raised by homosexual parents. Although the AAP does not endorse or condemn homosexuality, they, like the rest of the U.S., cannot ignore the growing number of same-sex families and must deal with what truly would be in the best interest of the children who are caught in the middle.

Whether the stance is for or against gay and lesbian adoption, both sides base their reasoning on what is in the best interest for the children. It would be safe to say that most would agree that having a child brought up in a loving, same-sex family is better than having a child moved from foster home to foster home or raised in an abusive home. Being homosexual does not mean that one loses the right to raise a child. Being an unwanted child does not mean that one loses the right to find a loving home, whether that home is single parent, married, heterosexual or even homosexual.

Works Cited

Berman, Steven. "Homosexuals and Adoption." *Rocky Mountain News* 23 Feb. 2002:1, final ed.: 1 W.

"Foster Care Facts." The Evan B. Donaldson Adoption Institute. 10 Apr. 2002
   <http://www.adoptioninstitute.org/FactOverview/foster.html>.

Huff, Richard, and Emily Gest. "Rosie Takes on Prez About Gay Adoption." *New York Daily News* 14 Mar. 2002, final ed.: 2.

Maxwell, Nancy G., Astrid A.M. Mattijssen, and Charlene Smith. "Legal Protection for All the Children: Dutch-American Comparison of Lesbian and Gay Parent Adoptions." *Electronic Journal of Comparative Law* 3.1 (August 1999) 20 Sept. 2002 <http://www.ejcl.org/ejcl/31/art31-2.html>.

"Pediatrics Academy's Endorsement of Homosexual Adoption." *US Newswire* 04 Feb. 2002.

Pertman, Adam. "Break Down Barriers to Homosexual Adoption." *The Baltimore Sun* 20 Mar. 2002, final ed., sec. A: 23.

"Safe and Smart." Vera Institute of Justice. 10 Apr. 2002

    <http://www.vera.org/project/project1_1.asp?section_id=6&project_id=5>.

Stanton, Glenn T. "Why Children Need a Male and Female Parent." Focus on the Family. 13 May 2002

    <http://www.family.org/cforum/tempforum/A0020006.html>.

Notice that Rachel follows the general Rogerian structure described on page 127. After her introduction she presents the views of those who oppose gay adoptions, and she does so without criticism. She offers a statement of understanding, conceding that the concerns of opponents are valid. But she also offers her own concerns, which are based on the same basic goal of protecting children that opponents of gay adoptions hold. This is the common ground that enables her to present her proposal for national legislation regarding gay adoptions — legislation that she believes will protect children in such situation as well as foster children waiting to be adopted. She clearly lays out the benefits of such legilsation.

Although you do not need to follow the Rogerian structure, you can see that it might help you organize your argument in a way that is likely to connect with your opponents — which is one of the goals of Rogerian argument. As in the case of Rachel's essay, an argument structured according to a Rogerian approach structure places your opponents' concerns first. Notice, too, that Rachel's tone is measured, respectful, and concerned throughout her essay, another indication of her desire to seek common ground and find a solution to the problem she is writing about.

LOGICAL ARRANGEMENTS

Arguments can also be shaped by the kind of reasoning a writer employs. In Chapter 2 we discussed the two basic kinds of logic: *inductive reasoning* and *deductive reasoning*. We also discussed informal logic, in particular the Toulmin model. These kinds of logic represent strategies that writers can use to make their arguments, and like the classical and Rogerian approaches, they can be helpful in deciding how to structure an argument.

Inductive Reasoning When you base an argument on inductive reasoning, you are drawing a conclusion based on evidence that you present. For example, let's say you are making an argument for more stringent enforcement of driving laws in your state. In doing so, you might present a variety of relevant information:

- Experiences you've had with speeding drivers
- Anecdotes about friends or family members who have been in accidents that resulted from reckless driving
- Statistics from the U.S. Department of Transportation about automobile accidents and their relationship to speed limits
- Quotations from law enforcement officials or experts who advocate lower speed limits but admit that posted speed limits are often not vigorously enforced.

From all this evidence you draw the conclusion that higher speed limits are dangerous and that drivers would be safer if laws were enforced more rigorously. Such an argument would be based on inductive reasoning.

In making an argument based on inductive reasoning, keep the following considerations in mind:

- *Try to arrange your evidence so that it leads your readers to the same conclusion you have reached.* Obviously, you need to introduce the issue and demonstrate to your readers that it is a problem worthy of attention. But the primary challenge will be to decide which evidence to present first and in what order the remaining evidence will be presented. Consider, too, how best to begin. You might, for example, cite a particular observation that strikes you as especially important. Or you might begin with an anecdote. Whatever approach you use, your introduction should address your particular audience so that they will want to continue reading. A well-structured inductive essay would then gradually expand as the evidence accumulates so that the conclusion is supported by numerous details.

- *Consider how specific kinds of evidence you have gathered will affect your readers.* Will some kinds of evidence likely be more compelling to them than others? If so, will it be more effective to present such evidence earlier or later in the argument? Answering those questions not only can help you decide how best to organize your essay, but also can generate additional ideas for evidence that will make your conclusion as persuasive to your audience as possible.

- *Decide how much evidence is enough.* Eventually, you will reach a point at which you decide that you have offered enough evidence to support your thesis. You might reach this point sooner in some contexts than others. For example, in an essay for your college writing class, you are not likely to cite as much evidence as you might be expected to include in a research report for a course in freshwater ecology; an essay in a respected political journal such as *Foreign Affairs* will include more extensive evidence than an editorial in your local newspaper. But whatever the context, the process is essentially the same.

- *Interpret and analyze your evidence for your audience.* When you stop citing evidence and move to your conclusion, you have made what is known as an *inductive leap.* In an inductive essay you must always offer interpretation or analysis of the evidence you present. For example, if you use an anecdote about an accident involving a speeding driver in an essay on the enforcement of driving laws, you will have to explain the significance of that anecdote — what it means for your argument. There will always be a gap between your evidence and your conclusion. It is over this gap that the writer must leap; the trick is to do it agilely. Good writers know that their evidence must be in proportion to their conclusion: The bolder the conclusion, the more evidence is needed to back it up. Remember the old adage about "jumping to conclusions," and realize that you'll need the momentum of a running start to make more than a moderate leap at any one time.

The advice we offer here suggests that organizing an argument inductively offers you a great deal of flexibility. As always, the decisions you make will reflect your purpose and your sense of how best to address your audience.

Deductive Reasoning   Deductive reasoning begins with a generalization and works to a conclusion that follows from that generalization. In that respect it can be thought of as the opposite of inductive reasoning, which begins with specific observations and ends with a conclusion that goes beyond those observations. The generalization you start with in a deductively arranged argument is called a *premise* and is the foundation for your argument. As we saw in Chapter 2, it takes much careful thought to formulate a good premise. Nevertheless, because so many arguments employ this kind of logic, deductive reasoning can be a powerful way to construct an effective argument.

The process of reasoning deductively might be difficult to grasp in the abstract, but you can follow some general steps that will help you explore your topic and generate an outline for your argument. In effect, you work backward from the conclusion you wish to reach.

> ## A METHOD FOR REASONING DEDUCTIVELY
>
> Because it can be difficult to formulate a good premise, it is often useful to work backward when you are planning a deductive argument. If you know the conclusion you want to reach, write it down, and number it as statement 3. Now ask yourself why you believe statement 3. That question should prompt a number of reasons; group them together as statement 2. Now that you can see your conclusion as well as some reasons that seem to justify it, ask yourself whether you've left anything out — something basic that you skipped over, assuming that everyone would already agree with it. When you can think back successfully to what this assumption is, knowing that it will vary from argument to argument, you have your premise, at least in rough form.

1. *Identifying Your Conclusion.* Suppose that you have become concerned about the consequences of eating meat. Because of worries about your own health, you have reconsidered eating meat, and you have begun to adopt a plant-based, or vegetarian, diet. But in exploring a vegetarian diet, you have also learned that meat production has potentially harmful environmental consequences. In particular, you are concerned about the destruction of forests that are cut down to allow cattle to graze. You believe that if eating meat leads to such environmental damage, it should be stopped.

   Obviously, given how prevalent meat consumption is and its prominent place in the American diet, you can't reasonably argue for eating meat to be made illegal or restricted by law in some way. But you can argue that it be discouraged — perhaps in the same way that smoking is discouraged. Most important, you believe that people should at least eat much less meat than they currently do.

   So your conclusion is clear: People should eat less meat. Now you begin to write down your outline in reverse:

   3. Americans should not consume so much meat.

   2. Consuming meat can be unhealthy, and meat production damages the environment.

2. *Examining Your Reasons Carefully.* Before going any further, you realize that not all of your reasons for opposing meat consumption can be taken with equal degrees of seriousness. For one thing, diet can be a personal choice, and your concerns about your own health are not sufficient grounds to argue against other people eating meat. So you need to make sure that your point about the health risks of eating meat does not sound self-serving but has validity for others as well. Your own research has shown that eating meat involves a number of health risks.

You also know that a vegetarian diet has health benefits. You will want to discuss these risks and benefits in a way that makes them relevant to people in general so that you are not simply discussing your own health choices.

Your greater concern is the possible environmental damage associated with meat production. Here, too, it might be difficult to convince people who enjoy eating meat that the loss of forests thousands of miles away from their backyard grill should concern them. So it will be important for you to establish not just that meat production leads to the loss of forest, but also that there might also be other environmental consequences closer to home. For example, most livestock in the United States is fed grain, and the production of feed grain not only uses up vast amounts of farmland, but also contributes to pollution through agricultural runoff. Furthermore, the raising of livestock generates pollution in the form of animal waste. There is, as well, the problem of the chemicals and drugs that are used on livestock, which you have heard can be risky for humans who eat meat. All these reasons can be compelling to others who might enjoy eating meat but might be unaware of the problems that can be caused by meat production.

3. *Formulate Your Premise.* You should now be ready to formulate your premise. Your conclusion is that eating meat should be curtailed, and you will urge others to stop or reduce their meat consumption and adopt an alternative diet. So near the beginning of your argument, you need to establish the principle that supports this conclusion. In this case you believe that it is wrong for people to engage in a practice that is ultimately destructive of the environment, especially when there is an alternative to that practice. In effect, you are suggesting that if what we do has damaging consequences (in this case eating meat has negative consequences for the environment and our health), then it is unethical to continue doing it when we have other options. This is your main premise.

A premise can be a single sentence, a full paragraph, or more, depending on the length and complexity of the argument. The function of a premise is to establish a widely accepted value that even your opponents should be able to share. You would probably be wise, therefore, to make a fairly general statement early in your argument — something like this:

> It is unethical to continue engaging in an activity that is harmful and environmentally destructive.

Obviously, such a statement needs to be developed, and you will do so not only by showing how destructive meat production and consumption can be, but also by offering alternatives to eating meat. You will want to suggest that our individual choices about things like diet can affect others. That makes those choices ethical ones. Now you have the foundation for a logical argument:

> If engaging in a practice or activity is harmful to people and their environment, then it should be stopped. Eating meat is such an activity; therefore, we should avoid eating meat and instead adopt an alternative diet.

This example can help you see the utility of structuring an argument deductively. You can see, too, that generating an argument in this way can deepen your engagement with your topic and eventually lead to a more substantive and persuasive essay. The following student essay by Kristen Montgomery, in which she argues against eating meat, is one example of an argument structured in this way. Notice that Kristen presents her main premise — that doing something harmful and environmentally destructive is unethical — implicitly in her second paragraph, after introducing her topic. In this case Kristen's question, "Do we have the right to support eating habits that have such negative consequences, especially when these habits are unnecessary?," implies her main premise. Often in a deductive argument, the main premise is explicitly stated at the beginning. Kristen chose a slightly different strategy. But it is clear that she will argue from this basic principle that we have no right to engage in harmful practices when alternatives to those practices exist. Kristen could have stated her premise explicitly in her opening paragraph and then proceeded to her specific evidence. Either approach is acceptable for an argument that is structured deductively. The important point is to establish the main premise early in the essay and then argue on the basis of that premise, which Kristen does.

Carnivorous Concerns

by Kristen M. Montgomery

Baseball? Apple pie? Shopping? Most Americans love these things, but there is perhaps nothing more American than eating meat. Birthdays, ballgames, and the most American of holidays, the Fourth of July, are all celebrated with barbeques and cookouts featuring burgers, dogs, and steaks. A burger and fries may be the most American meal of all. Each day, Americans eat 46 million pounds. And each year, the average American eats two times his or her weight in meat.

But what if this all-American meal is actually damaging health and home? Is it right to engage in a practice that is not only harmful to our physical health but also destructive to our environment? Do we have the right to support eating habits that have such negative consequences, especially when these habits are unnecessary? Many people oppose eating meat on the grounds that meat production is cruel to animals. And it is. But the consequences for the human population are arguably as bad. And it simply unethical to engage in a practice that is so damaging to the earth and its inhabitants.

A careful look at meat production shows why eating meat contributes to human illness. The animals we eat are pumped full of chemicals that are often unhealthy to them and to humans; they are also neglected and tortured. Meanwhile, their living conditions are feces-ridden and disease-infested. The animals live in their own excrement next to others that are themselves full of disease. It is only reasonable to expect that these conditions contribute to human illness. In fact, the USDA estimates that salmonella, a dangerous pathogen that can cause serious illness and even death in humans, is present in 35 percent of turkeys, 11 percent of chickens and 6 percent of ground beef. Each year, food-borne pathogens cause 76 million illnesses and 5,000 deaths, according to the Centers for Disease Control. And it is alarming to note that certain bacteria in meat have shown evolutionary changes into more dangerous substances. For example, O157:H7 is a mutant strand of E. coli, which is very hard to treat because of its evasiveness in medical tests. Ultimately, for those who eat meat contaminated with O157:H7, organ failure is the cause of death. It is reasonable to assume that this strand of E. coli is not the only bacterium which may have developed strengths against human antibodies. There are likely more out there and more to come.

Exposing ourselves to such illnesses is unnecessary. We have healthier alternatives to meat as a food source. Although many people view a plant-based diet as unthinkable because of their love of meat, a plant-based diet, with a little bit of research and practice, can have more variety and is much healthier than a meat-based diet. Meat is deficient in carbohydrates and vitamins. Not only is meat lacking important nutrients for proper health, but it is also abundant in harmful substances, such as calories and saturated fat. When cooked, most meats produce a variety of benzenes, among other carcinogenic compounds. Benzene is commonly found in paints, cleaners, and cigarettes, and it is poisonous to humans. In addition, the average American gets five times the amount of needed protein in his or her diet, which strains the kidneys with luric acid and can actually cause nephritis.

By contrast, a plant-based diet enables us to avoid such potentially serious problems. And contrary to popular opinion, there is no nutrient necessary for good health that cannot be obtained from a plant-based diet. That is why mom always made us eat our vegetables. High fruit and vegetable consumption has been associated with a lowered risk for heart disease, several types of cancers, and other chronic illnesses. Also, there is a growing body of medical evidence that eating such things as beans, peanuts, lentils, and peas, which contain a variety of beneficial ingredients, may protect against disease. For example, according to the Journal of American Dietetic Association, soybean consumption is linked with a decreased risk of prostate cancer and increased bone density in post-menopausal women. These facts are just the beginning. If we look at the overall benefits of eating a plant-based diet, it doesn't make sense to risk our health by eating meat.

But if eating meat is unhealthy for our bodies, it may be even worse for our planet. And this alone should make us reconsider our reliance on meat as a food source. Some people worry about big business eating away at rural and suburban land, but urban sprawl is not the leading cause of deforestation. Meat production is to blame: "For every acre of forest land consumed by urban development, seven acres are devoured by the meat industry, for grazing and growing feed. If water used by the meat industry were not subsidized by U.S. taxpayers, a hamburger would cost $35." And 125,000 square miles of rain forests are destroyed each year for the purpose of producing meat. For each quarter-pounder fast-food burger made of beef that is raised on land that was once rain forest, fifty-five square feet of land is used. Every second, 2.4 acres of forest is turned into grazing land. Moreover, this use of the land is incredibly inefficient. For example, an acre of land can produce approximately 20,000 pounds of potatoes but only 165 pounds of beef. Large amounts of grain are grown to feed the animals that we butcher for food. In fact, eighty-seven percent of all agricultural land in America is used to raise the animals we eat. Instead of feeding the grain to humans, we feed it to cows and chickens. It takes twice the amount of grain to produce beef and four times the amount of grain for poultry production than to feed this grain to humans.

Not only does raising animals for food require a large amount of land, but it also requires a large amount of energy. Consider for a moment that it takes the water from 17 showers to produce a single hamburger. Or instead of driving a small car for 20 miles, consider using the same amount of energy to make that one hamburger patty. That's how much energy is needed to produce the beef for that burger. In the 1980s, one-half of the world's grain harvest was fed not to people, but to livestock. With world starvation rates as they are, this approach to food production doesn't make sense. What's more, it's unethical.

All of this resource depletion also leads to pollution. On the large portion of land on which we raise animals and the grain to feed them, raw waste is produced. Excrement is produced at a rate of 130 times more than what is produced by the entire human population. It must go somewhere, and where it goes is everywhere, sometimes in nearby waterways. According to *Scientific American,* this waste has increased the pathogenic organisms in the water, which has poisoned humans as well as millions of fish, which serve to maintain the delicate balance of the oceanic ecosystem. Not only are the feces poisoning the soil and waterways, but some people living near these areas must actually wear face masks because of the overwhelming stench. In addition to water and land pollution, the EPA estimates that the world's animal population is responsible for 25 percent of anthropogenic emissions of methane gas, which contribute to the greenhouse effect. Therefore, meat production also contributes to air pollution. These facts are compounded by the fact that since the 1950s, the livestock population has increased more rapidly than the human population. So as our consumption of meat increases, so does the damage we are doing to our earth.

Eating meat is enjoyable for many people, but it is an impractical approach to food production that cannot be sustained. We may neglect to see the consequences of depleting our resources and letting our planet become overburdened with animal waste, because the consequences are not immediate and we are a society where immediate is considered best. Few of us see the dramatic effects described above. But we all must seriously consider what our heavy meat consumption means for our future. The slaughtering of animals to satisfy our hunger contributes to the depletion of our world's valuable resources, results in pollution, and causes human disease. The consequences of our murderous appetite may eventually be as deadly for us as for the animals we kill to satisfy this appetite. Perhaps knowing this may curb our appetite for meat. It's time we adopted more sustainable and ethical eating habits, before we eat ourselves — and our world — to death.

Using the Toulmin Model   Even when you are using logical arrangement to organize your argument, you will rarely follow the rules of logic rigidly. Because most people use logic informally in arguments, the Toulmin model (see pages 31–35) can be extremely useful in helping you construct your argument. The Toulmin model focuses on the *claim* you want to make — that is, the conclusion you are trying to reach or the assertion you hope to prove. Your task, simply put, is to state your claim clearly and offer persuasive reasons (what Toulmin calls *data*) for that claim. The third element in the Toulmin system is the *warrant,* which is the assumption that connects the claim and the data. As we noted in Chapter 2, the warrant is usually a fundamental value or belief that, ideally, is shared by writer and audience (like the premise we discussed in the section above on deductive reasoning).

This model dictates no specified pattern for organizing an argument, so the challenge is to determine how best to present your claim to your intended audience and then to offer adequate reasons for your claim. But the value of this model for constructing an argument lies in the way it requires you to articulate your claim precisely and to pay close attention to the adequacy of your reasons and your evidence, without having to follow the rigid rules of formal logic. In this way the Toulmin model can help you refine your claim and develop convincing support for it. This model also encourages you to think through the often unstated assumptions that lie behind your claim: the warrants. Identifying your warrant can lead to a much more effective argument because it can help you see points of possible contention between you and your audience.

Let's imagine that you live in a small town where a businessperson wishes to build a large meat-processing facility. This person has recently applied to the town board for a permit to begin construction of the plant. As a resident who values the quiet lifestyle of your town as well as its clean and safe environment, you worry about the social and environmental damage the plant might cause. So you decide to write to the town supervisor to express your concerns and urge him to reject the permit for the plant.

Using the Toulmin model for your letter, your first step would be to try to articulate your central claim clearly. You might state your claim as follows:

We should not allow a meat-processing facility to be built in our town.

Before moving to your reasons for your claim, you should consider carefully whether that statement accurately represents the position you want to take. Can you be more specific? Can you focus the claim even more narrowly? In thinking about these questions, you might amend your claim as follows:

Building a meat-packing facility would damage the quality of life and the environment of our town.

Notice that although this version of your this claim is related to the first version, it is a bit narrower and more precise. It also points directly to the kinds of data or the reasons you can offer to support the claim. Being clear about your claim is crucial because your reasons must fit that claim closely in order to be persuasive. Now you can begin exploring your reasons.

At this point it is a good idea to brainstorm, listing the main reasons for your belief that the plant should not be built in your town. You have many reasons: the possible damage to local streams from the waste and runoff from the plant, the increased traffic to and from the plant, the odor, the negative impact of a large plant on the quality of life in a small town. You should examine these reasons and try to identify those that are most compelling. So now you have your claim and main reasons for it:

Claim: Building a meat-packing facility would damage the quality of life and the environment of our town.

Reasons: Meat-packing facilities can cause pollution, endanger the health of local residents, and increase truck traffic on local roads.

Before you begin to develop evidence to support these reasons for your claim, you should think about your warrant — the assumptions that lie behind the claim and connect your reason and claim. This is a crucial step in using the Toulmin model because it helps you identify the assumptions behind your claim or the principles on which you base your claim. In Toulmin's model, the warrant is what provides the basis for a claim.

Without an acceptable warrant the claim becomes weak or even invalid. In this case you might state your warrant as follows:

Warrant: We all have a right to live in clean, safe environments.

You can probably be confident that your audience — the town supervisor — would accept this warrant, so you probably don't need to defend it. However, you might decide to state it in your letter, and you might even defend it in order to drive it home. The point is that you have identified a basic value or belief that you assume others share and without which your claim has no foundation.

Now you can begin developing specific evidence to support your claim and your reasons. The reasons stated above suggest the kinds of evidence you might gather. For example, to support the assertion that meat-processing facilities damage the environment, you might find reports of increased pollution in streams near existing meat-packing plants. You can perhaps find similar reports about the impact of truck traffic around such plants. Evidence to support the assertion that your town's lifestyle would be adversely affected might be trickier. First, you will want to establish the character of the town as it is. That might mean providing facts about the number of residences as compared to businesses, the size and use of roads, and so on. The point is to identify specific and persuasive evidence that fits your reasons for your claim — and to gather evidence that will be acceptable and convincing to your audience.

Here's a letter by a student that takes up this issue. In this letter Kristen Brubaker is writing to the supervisor of her small town in rural Pennsylvania. She expresses concern about a resident's request to build a factory hog farm in the town.

Dear Mr. Smithson:

As township supervisor of Wayne Township, you have had a great impact on our community for the past several years. In the coming months, your service will be needed more than ever. Jack Connolly, a resident of our township, has put forth a plan to build a factory hog farm, called a CAFO. His proposed facility will house 5,600 breeding sows, 100,000 piglets, and will cover nearly five acres of buildings (Weist). I am aware that you support this project, but I think there are some points you may be overlooking. We need to work together to ensure that our basic rights as property owners and citizens are not infringed upon and to protect the quality of life in our community.

I know we share similar values when it comes to the protection of our environment. In fact, you are one of the people who helped to shape my view of the environment. When I was younger, I attended the Dauphin County Conservation Camp that you helped to sponsor. I remember several of our activities, including the stream improvement project we completed and the stocking of trout in Powells Creek. Because of these experiences, I was surprised to find out you did not strongly oppose this project. Were you aware that CAFOs have caused extensive damage to trout streams in many states? I hope we don't have to face the destruction of our creek and surrounding valley before we realize that we made a mistake.

Although the risks to our environment are numerous, the first problem most people associate with CAFOs is the smell. In Powells Valley, we have traditionally been an agricultural community, so we're not afraid of the natural, inevitable odor of farms. Although factory farmers argue that the odor of animal waste is simply part of living in a rural, agricultural area, the air pollution caused by CAFOs is often more than a minor inconvenience. Imagine being unable to hang your clothes out to dry because of a thick, permeating smell that saturates everything it touches. The smell is not harmless either. CAFOs produce dangerous levels of ammonia and methane, gases suspected of causing nausea, flu-like symptoms, and respiratory illness, especially in children or the elderly. These chemicals also return to the ground as rain, polluting our water (Satchell). Another potentially harmful gas produced is hydrogen sulfide. In as small a concentration as 10 parts per million, it causes eye irritation. At 50 parts per million, it causes vomiting, nausea, and diarrhea. At 500 parts per million, hydrogen sulfide causes rapid death (Weist).

Another problem with the proposed location of this facility is its close proximity to houses and the small size of the valley. More than 35 houses are located within a half-mile radius of the proposed operation. Our valley is only a mile wide, so there will be nowhere for the odor to go. It will sit in our valley on hot summer days, saturating the air and everything in it. If this facility must be built, why can't it go somewhere less densely populated or somewhere that would handle odors more effectively?

But the most frightening aspect of having a CAFO in our valley is the strong possibility that we would face severe water pollution. Because of the immense scale of CAFOs, they often produce much more manure than the surrounding land can handle effectively. In cases where overspreading occurs, excess nutrients can run into the streams, disrupting the ecological balance and killing fish. Powells Creek, like most small creeks, sits in a very delicate balance and a small increase of nutrients can seriously alter the habitat of the stream. Nutrients contribute to increased plant and algae life, which can clog waterways and rob them of oxygen. Excess nutrients can also seep into the ground water, creating a problem with illness-causing pathogens such as salmonella (Satchell).

Another cause of water pollution among CAFOs is the waste lagoons used to store manure. Because fields may be spread only certain times of the year, there is a need for immense storage facilities. Most farms use lagoons that can be several acres long, sometimes holding up to 25 million gallons of waste. In North Carolina, waste lagoons are being blamed for the catastrophic fish kills and pollution of the coastal waters that took place in 1996 (Satchell). In the recent flooding in North Carolina due to Hurricane Floyd, over 50 lagoons overflowed, and one burst. Although it is not yet known how these recent spills will affect the environment, more fish kills and contaminated drinking water supplies are virtually guaranteed (Wright).

There are many other problems Powells Valley could face as a result of this facility. The operation that Mr. Connolly is proposing would produce 12 million gallons of waste per year. This waste is going to be spread throughout three townships in our valley. This is a lot of waste for one small stream, yet this is the best-case scenario. Can you imagine what would happen in the case of a leak or spill. Powells Creek is located about 350 feet downhill from these proposed facilities. In the case of an overflow, flood, or leak, the waste would go directly into the creek. To make matters worse, this operation is going to be located in an area that has frequent problems with flooding. In 1996, a small flood destroyed the bridge that crosses Powells Creek just below the proposed operation. If a spill or leak were to occur, the creek's aquatic life would be destroyed. If this facility is approved, we may not have to worry about stocking Powells Creek anymore.

The local increase in traffic is another issue that must be addressed. If this facility goes into operation, there would be approximately 1,750 truck trips per year delivering feed and supplies and transporting the 100,000 piglets to finishing operations. In addition to this, there will be an estimated 3,500 trailer truck trips needed to transport the 12 million gallons of waste (Weist). The roads in our area are not equipped for this kind of traffic. It would put a much greater burden on Wayne Township for the upkeep of its roads. The Carsonville Fire Company, which would be charged with the responsibility of handling any accidents, is dangerously underequipped to handle a large spill. Additionally, the roads entering the area of the proposed operation are small, curvy, and unsafe for large trucks. There are school busses from two school districts traveling these roads. The risk of having a serious accident is simply too high to justify this operation.

One of the key factors that allows these problems to exist largely unchallenged is the lack of regulation for these factory farms. If someone were to build a factory producing the same amount of contaminating waste, they would face numerous regulations. Human waste treatment plants also follow strict environmental controls that ensure that they do not pollute. Because CAFOs are technically agriculture, and not industry, they face virtually no regulations. They are also protected by the "Right to Farm Act," which was originally passed to protect family farms from harassment and lawsuits by developers. This law is making us defenseless because it will back any lawsuit we could make against the owner of the CAFO. Although nutrient management plans are required for a large operation, such a requirement is not enough protection.

As expected, Jack Connolly's plans have not been stifled by the protests of over 100 citizens. His nutrient management plan was recently rejected by the Dauphin County Conservation District, but he continues to build. He realizes that although many people in the community are afraid of his plans, just as many are unwilling to interfere with his right to do what he wants with his property. We don't like being told what we can and cannot do with our land, and when we give up those rights, we feel it starts a dangerous trend. At the same time, we must think of the property rights of those who have inhabited this valley their whole lives. Operations like this can seriously lower property values. People who can't stand the smell would have two choices. They could sell their homes, their sole investments, for a fraction of their worth or live with the smell.

There are some possible benefits to having this operation in our valley. For one, the factory is expected to create between 20 and 30 local jobs. We don't have a problem with unemployment in our valley, though, so it's likely that these jobs will be filled with outsiders. Also, they aren't going to be the high-quality jobs that most of us would want. Another possible benefit, one I'm sure you're aware of, is the possibility of cheap fertilizer. I noticed on the nutrient plan that you were listed among the recipients. Are you aware that if there is an accident with the waste on your land, you are responsible, not Mr. Connolly? If you still decide that this plan is in the best interests of everyone it will affect, do some research of your own to ensure you're not part of the problem by accepting more manure than your land can safely handle. Also, make sure Mr. Connolly hasn't increased your projected amount without your knowledge in order to satisfy his nutrient management plan.

If you agree that his CAFO is not good for our community, there are steps you should take to postpone, or even reject, this proposal. First, you, as township supervisor, can reject his building permits until he gets the necessary approval from the county and state. These agencies will be more likely to approve his plan if he already has a multi-million dollar complex built to house it. You could also pass ordinances to prevent the growth of this "farm." A common scenario is that after the nearby property values are sufficiently lowered due to the offensive smell, a factory farm owner will buy the surrounding land and build more operations. It only makes sense when you consider that the operation Mr. Connolly has proposed is a breeding facility. This means that the piglets will need to be transported to a finishing facility. Wouldn't it be cheaper and more cost effective to build a near-by facility that could house the hogs as they were prepared for slaughter? After that, why not just build a slaughtering facility as well. It's happened before, and it could happen in our valley. Although people tend to be against zoning in rural communities such as ours, sometimes it is imperative to prevent negative changes.

Please think about the possible effects this will have on our valley. As a life-long resident, you must value its beauty. I also assume that you value the right of every person in this community to live in a safe and clean environment. Imagine a day when you couldn't sit on your porch to eat breakfast because of the overwhelming odor that permeates everything it touches. Imagine your grandchildren getting ill because of water-borne bacteria caused by this CAFO. Imagine the day when you can no longer fish in the creek you helped improve. This day could be upon us if we don't take action now. You're a vital part of this equation, and I trust that we can count on you to help us maintain the land that raised us.

Sincerely,

Kristen Brubaker

References

Cauchon, Dennis. "N.C. Farmers, Scientists Begin Taking The Toll." *USA Today* 27 Sept. 1999: 6A.

"Hog Factories vs. Family Farms and Rural Communities." Powells Balley Conservation Association. 8 Oct. 1999. Pennsylvania Department of Environmental Protection. 15 Oct. 1999 <www.dep.state.pa.us>.

Satchell, Michael. "Hog Heaven — and Hell." *U. S. News and World Report* 22 Jan. 1996: 57.

Weist, Kurt, "Petition to Intervene of the Powell's Valley Conservation Association, Inc." Powell's Valley Conservation Association, Inc. 1999.

Wright, Andrew G. "A Foul Mess." *Engineering News Record* 4 Oct. 1999: 26.

Notice that Kristen's claim is implicit in her first paragraph, in which she indicates concern about the hog farm, but she doesn't explicitly state that the permit should be denied until the second-to-last paragraph. Notice, too, that she states her warrant in her second paragraph and then reinforces it in her final paragraph. The Toulmin model does not require that the essay be structured in this way. Kristen might just as easily have begun by stating her claim explicitly and proceeded from there; similarly, she might have left her warrant unstated or waited until the final paragraph to state it. Those choices are up to the writer. But using the Toulmin model can help to identify these elements so that you can work with them in constructing an argument.

We should also point out that Kristen has chosen to document her evidence with a list of references, an unusual step in a letter. However, that decision can make her letter more persuasive, since it indicates to the town supervisor not only that Kristen has taken the time to research this issue thoroughly, but also that her facts and figures have been taken from reputable sources.

In considering these different models for arranging an argument, you should understand that they are not mutually exclusive. In a classically arranged argument, for example, the statement of background can be done in the kind of nonjudgmental language emphasized in Rogerian argument. Similarly, the summary of opposing views in a Rogerian argument requires the kind of understanding that a writer following a classical arrangement would need to have before engaging in refutation. In both cases, the writers need to be well informed and fair-minded. And both classical arrangement and Rogerian argument encourage the use of concessions. The difference between the two is best understood in terms of purpose. Although any argument is designed to be persuasive, the purpose of that persuasion varies from one situation to another (see Chapter 1). You might be writing to assert a position or to inquire into a complex issue. Your plan should fit your purpose.

It is also worth remembering that contemporary arguments rarely follow rigid guidelines, except in certain academic courses or in specialized documents, such as legal briefs, or situations like formal debates. For that reason many teachers today advocate the Toulmin model, emphasizing its flexibility in adapting an argument to a specific situation. Moreover, different media represent different opportunities and challenges for how to present an argument (see Chapter 4). All of this means that you have many options for structuring your argument. The more familiar you are with the principles of organization in argumentation, the more likely it is that you will be able to structure your argument effectively.

SUPPORTING CLAIMS AND PRESENTING EVIDENCE

The letter by Kristen Brubaker (page 140) highlights the importance of presenting good evidence to support your argument. Without compelling evidence even the most carefully articulated claim won't be persuasive. But as we noted in Chapter 4 (pp. 76–82), what counts as good evidence will vary from one context to another. So an important part of generating evidence for your argument is considering your audience and its expectations for evidence as well as the rhetorical situation in which you are making your argument. In Kristen's case the audience is very specific: her town supervisor. And she offers evidence that directly addresses a number of issues regarding quality of life that would concern a person in his position. Indeed, one of the strengths of Kristen's argument is that her evidence fits her audience. Another strength is the amount of evidence she provides. She includes statistics and other facts to support her assertions about pollution, road use, odor, and health problems. She also uses values as evidence, appealing to the supervisor's sense of the importance of private property and community well-being (see page 140). Moreover, the amount of evidence suggests that Kristen has done her homework. By presenting so much appropriate evidence so carefully, she helps to establish her credibility. And although she is writing specifically to one person, Kristen's evidence would probably resonate with a broader audience — say, readers of the local newspaper — if Kristen were addressing such an audience. Implicitly addressing a broader audience might strengthen her argument as well, since the supervisor will probably be sensitive to the views of other people in the community.

Your audience can affect not just the kind of evidence you use, but also whether you need evidence for a particular point. For example, if you are confident that your readers will accept your warrant, then you might decide that you don't need to support it. If it is likely that your audience will disagree with your warrant, then you will need evidence to back it up. Imagine, for instance, if Kristen were writing for a much broader audience — let's say she was making an argument against CAFOs for a newspaper like *USA Today.* Some of her readers might be willing to give up some of the characteristics of a small town for greater economic development. For such readers Kristen might want to defend her warrant about a clean environment, perhaps showing that economic development doesn't have to mean damaging the environment. The point is that your sense of audience and its expectations will affect what you decide to present as evidence and even *whether* some kinds of evidence should be included in your essay.

As you construct your argument and develop your supporting evidence, then, consider the following questions:

- What specific claims and/or warrants am I making that will need supporting evidence?
- What kinds of evidence are available for those claims or warrants?
- Where can I find such evidence?
- What expectations will my audience have for the evidence I present?
- Have I included sufficient evidence for my audience?
- Does the kind of evidence I have included (factual, firsthand experience, philosophical reasoning, expert testimony) make sense for the claims I am making?

USING LANGUAGE EFFECTIVELY

In his famous *Rhetoric,* Aristotle wrote that "the way in which a thing is said affects its intelligibility" (*Rhetoric* 165). We might add that the way in which something is stated also affects its impact and, potentially, its persuasive force. Style matters. It matters because it is sometimes a reflection of the fact that you have followed the appropriate conventions for a particular argument — for example, you have used the right legal terminology in a letter to your insurance company about a pending lawsuit. And it matters because the way an idea or opinion is presented can profoundly affect how an audience reacts to it. In constructing an effective argument, you should attend to how you employ the power of language — how you use diction, sentence structure, tone, rhythm, and figures of speech. Usually, these are matters you can focus on once you have defined your topic, developed your claims and supporting evidence, and arranged your argument appropriately. But how you use language can be an important consideration in constructing an argument, even from the very beginning.

As always, audience is a primary consideration as you decide upon an appropriate style for your argument. Different audiences will have different expectations for what is acceptable — and persuasive — when it comes to your use of language in an argument. You will want to use much more formal language in a cover letter to a potential employer (which is a very common kind of argument) than you might in a letter to the editor of your school's newspaper. Similarly, an essay advocating a specific research method in a biology class will require a different kind of language than an argument in favor of decriminalizing marijuana laws for the campus newsletter of a student advocacy organization. The specific medium in which you are presenting your argument will also influence your decisions about language. *Wired* magazine publishes writing that is noticeably different in style and tone from those of the essays that appear in public affairs magazines such as *Commentary*. The audiences for each magazine are different, but so is each magazine's sense of purpose. *Wired* sees itself as techy, edgy, and hip, and the language its writers use reflects that sense of itself. By contrast, *Commentary* is a more erudite, staid publication, and the writing style reflects its seriousness. As you work through your argument, think carefully about what kind of language will be most effective for the specific audience, rhetorical situation, and medium you are encountering.

Even within a specific rhetorical situation you have a great deal of latitude in deciding on the style and tone you will adopt for your argument. Consider the following excerpts from an essay that appeared on *Commondreams.org*, a Web site that publishes essays and news with alternative views about important social and political issues. In the essay from which the following excerpts were taken, the writer, John Borowski, a science teacher from Oregon, harshly criticizes efforts by interest groups to ban school science books that present an environmentalist perspective, and he argues for parents and others to oppose such efforts:

> Remember this phrase: "Texas is clearly one of the most dominant states in setting textbook adoption standards," according to Stephen Driesler, executive director of the American Association of Publisher's school division. And this November the Texas school board inflamed by the anti-environmental science rhetoric by the likes of Texas Citizens for a Sound Economy and Texas Public Policy Foundation (TPPF) may bring Ray Bradbury's "Fahrenheit 451" to life. Recall that "Fahrenheit 451" (the temperature at which paper bursts into flames) depicts a society where independent thought is discouraged, wall-to-wall television and drugs sedate a numb population and "firemen" burn books.
>
> This past fall "book nazis" at the TPPF, led by Republican Senator Phil Gramm's wife (Wendy) and Peggy Venable, director of the 48,000 member Texas Citizens for a Sound Economy, put several environmental textbooks in their "crosshairs." *Environmental Science: Toward a Sustainable Future* published by Massachusetts-based publisher Jones and Bartlett was canned due to political "incorrectness."

> We as parents, defenders of the constitution and the vigilant flame-keepers of the light of democracy must rise to meet the challenge.

There is no doubt about how Borowski feels about groups like TPPF. Nor is there any doubt about his goal: to exhort people who share his concerns to action against such efforts to ban books from schools. You might find Borowski's language inflammatory. There is a good chance that he intended it to be so. He certainly knew that the audience for *Commondreams.org* would not likely include many people from organizations such as TPPF. Rather, it would be composed mostly of people who share his political perspective and are likely to be as appalled as he is about these efforts to ban textbooks. Nevertheless, we can ask how those sympathetic readers might react to the strong and very critical language Borowski employs. Will such language be more likely to convince those readers that Borowski is right than a more measured style and a less derogatory tone might be? How does it affect his credibility with his readers? Sometimes, provocative language may be warranted. Is this one of those times?

Posing such questions about your own use of language in constructing your argument can lead to a more effective argument. The rhetorical situation and the issue being addressed will help to determine your approach to using language from the outset. In this case Borowski might well have been angry and concerned enough to have decided, even before he began writing his essay, to adopt a harsh and sarcastic tone. Sometimes, however, you might not have a clear sense of the most appropriate tone or style until after you have completed a draft. And often you will have much less flexibility in adopting a tone or style. (A science report or legal brief, for example, has very strict conventions for such matters.) And bear in mind that at times the choice of a single word can make a great difference in the impact a statement will have on an audience. For example, consider how different this sentence of Borowski's might be if the verb *canned* were replaced by *removed*: *Environmental Science: Toward a Sustainable Future* published by Massachusetts-based publisher Jones and Bartlett was canned due to political "incorrectness."

The passage from Borowski's essay illustrates another set of concerns about language in argument: the use of figurative language. At one point Borowski writes that "the vigilant flame-keepers of the light of democracy must rise to meet the challenge." Here he invokes the common metaphors of light and dark to suggest good opposed to evil, right against wrong. Those who share his concerns are "flame-keepers of the light of democracy," a figurative phrase that is clearly intended not only to address his audience in a positive way, but also to stir them to action. Borowski's is a rather extreme example of the use of figurative language, and it suggests the power such uses of language can have in efforts to move an audience. But figurative language can also have a more subtle but no less important impact in helping to clarify an important point or emphasizing an idea. Here, for example, is *USA Today* sports columnist Mike Lopresti in an essay about the significance of a loss by an American basketball team to Yugoslavia in the 2002 World Championships:

> But the big issue is the big picture. The years, the Olympiads, and the World Championships ahead. Because American basketball is like an empty soda cup on the field house floor.

Lopresti's use of a simile — in which he compares the international status of American basketball to an empty soda cup — vividly drives home his point with an appropriate

FIGURATIVE LANGUAGE

For an example of the use of metaphor in an argument, see Gregory Cizek's essay, "Unintended Consequences of High Stakes Testing," on page 316. Cizek uses religion as a metaphor for the debates about standardized tests.

image that readers who follow sports will quickly recognize. (Notice, too, the informal style of his writing, which is typical of many sports columnists.)

Writers can also make references to myths, literature, or legends that will have significance for readers. Henry David Thoreau, for example, in criticizing what he believed was the wasteful and wasting lifestyle of his fellow citizens, wrote,

> The twelve labors of Hercules were trifling in comparison to those which my neighbors have undertaken.

The reference to the well-known Greek myth would have driven home his point to his readers. And his use of farm labor as metaphor for life in the following sentence not only emphasized his primary claim but did so elegantly:

> The better part of the man is soon ploughed into soil for compost.

As these examples show, a few carefully chosen words can do a great deal of work as you build your argument.

When you are constructing your own argument, pay close to attention to your tone and style. Asking yourself the following questions can help you determine whether your style and tone are appropriate for your purpose, your audience, and the situation about which you are arguing:

- Is my overall tone likely to offend my intended audience? If so, what specifically about my tone might be offensive to my audience? How can I revise to avoid that problem?
- Have I used appropriate words and phrases? Will my audience understand the key terms I have used? Will my audience expect me to use any special language that I have not used?
- Can I use figurative language in any way to enhance my argument?

PART II

WORKING WITH SOURCES

6

DOING RESEARCH

W riting effective arguments requires being able to locate and
draw on information that will help
you develop and support your ideas. Often,
writers discover that they must look beyond
themselves to gather the necessary information — They must engage in research.

ESEARCH

You might think of research as what you do when you are assigned long papers that are due at the end of a semester, but there are many other occasions when you engage in research. Any time you look for information before making a decision, you are doing research. If you are trying to decide whether to buy a particular car, for example, you might talk to people who already own the same model, read magazine articles about the car, search the Internet for other drivers' opinions about the car, and take a dealer's vehicle out for a test drive. In other words, you interview people with expertise on your topic, you conduct a periodical search, you search electronic resources, and you undertake trial testing. Academic research requires all of these activities and more, although the degree to which you need to pursue a specific research activity is likely to vary as you move from one project to another. Academic research also requires that you follow specific conventions by using sources responsibly and documenting where your information comes from. But the prospect of doing research shouldn't be intimidating. The key to successful research is simple: Be curious enough about your topic to look in different places until you find what you need.

Traditionally, academic researchers distinguish between primary and secondary research:

1. *Primary research* requires firsthand experimentation or analysis. This is the sort of research that is done in laboratories, in field locations, or in libraries or archives that house original manuscripts. If you interview someone, design and distribute a survey, conduct an experiment, or analyze data that have not been previously published, you are conducting primary research.

2. *Secondary research* involves investigating what other people have already published on a given subject — in other words, finding information about your topic in books, magazine or journal articles, Web sites, and similar sources. College students are usually expected to be proficient at secondary research.

Writing arguments often requires secondary research, and to do such research efficiently, you must know how to develop a search strategy. Different projects will require different strategies. The strategy outlined in this part of the book assumes that you will be writing arguments using material from Part III of *The Informed Argument* and that you will supplement this material with additional information you find elsewhere. As your research needs change from one assignment to another, you will probably use different sources. But the illustrations in this chapter will provide you with sufficient information to help you proceed efficiently when you decide to move beyond the articles gathered in Part III of this book.

READING CRITICALLY

Secondary research obviously involves reading, but it requires a kind of reading that might differ from the way you read the morning paper or an article about your favorite musician on a Web site. The kind of critical reading that is required for good research is active and engaged; it involves careful thinking about what you are reading. Critical reading is going beyond the obvious meaning of a text to gain a more sophisticated understanding of it. Gaining this understanding involves being able to identify key points, such as an author's thesis, and any points that you find difficult to understand. But beyond understanding the material itself, you should also be prepared to *evaluate* it. As a student, you will sometimes be confronted with more information than you can digest with ease. You will also find that different writers might make contradictory statements. Being able to recognize what material deserves the closest reading and what sources are the most reliable is essential to coping successfully with the many academic demands made on your time. By learning to read critically, you will acquire a skill that will help you in any college course. And you will be developing an ability that will enable you to write more effective arguments.

You can learn to read critically by engaging in four related activities:

- Previewing
- Annotating
- Summarizing
- Synthesizing

PREVIEWING

Even before you begin to read, you can take steps to help you better understand the reading you are about to undertake and to place it in rhetorical context (see pages 54–58). A quick preview or survey of a written text should give you an idea of how long it will take to read, what the reading will probably reveal, and how useful the reading is likely to be. When you glance through a newspaper to identify which stories you want to read and which you want to skip over, you are practicing a simple type of preview, one that is often guided primarily by your level of interest in various issues. But when previewing reading material in college, it is usually wise to ask yourself some questions that go beyond whether you happen to find a topic appealing:

- *How long is this work?* By checking the length of a work before you begin to read, you can estimate how much reading time the material will demand, based on the speed and ease with which you normally read. The length might also be a clue in determining how useful a text may be. Although quantity is no sure guide to quality, a long work might contain more information that is useful for your topic than a short work. And when doing research, you can usually learn the length of a work before you even hold it in your hand. This information is included in periodical indexes, book catalogs, and many Web sites. (See the illustrations on pages 170–172 and 174.)

- *What can I learn from the title?* Although some titles are too general to convey adequately the content of an article or book, a title often reveals an author's focus. Obviously, an article called "Drugs and the Modern Athlete" will differ in focus from one called "Drug Testing and Corporate Responsibility." Moreover, a title can often indicate the author's point of view. For example, an essay entitled "Keep the Borders Open" tells you quite clearly what the author's position on immigration will be. Be aware, however, that titles can sometimes be misleading.

- *Do I know anything about the author?* Recognizing the names of established authorities in a field becomes easier as you do more reading, but many written sources offer information that can help you estimate an author's credibility even when that author is unfamiliar to you. A magazine article might identify the author at the beginning or the end of the piece or on a separate page (often called "Notes on Contributors" and listed in the table of contents). A biographical sketch of the author can usually be found on a book jacket, and a list of his or her other published works sometimes appears at the front or the back of the book. Anthologies often include introductory headnotes describing the various writers whose work has been selected.

■ *What do I know about the publisher?* An important work can be published by an obscure publisher, and a small magazine might be the first to publish an author who is destined to win a Pulitzer Prize. The publisher's reputation is not an automatic guide to the reliability of a source, but there are a few factors that can help you determine whether a source is likely to be worthwhile. University presses tend to expect a high degree of scholarship, and academic journals usually publish articles only after they have been examined by two or three other experts in that field. If you read widely in periodicals, you will eventually find that some magazines and newspapers consistently reflect political positions that might be characterized as either liberal or conservative. Once you get a sense of the general orientation of such publications, you can usually anticipate what kind of stand will be taken by authors whose articles appear in one of these periodicals. This will help you to be sensitive to any bias that the author might hold on the topic at hand. Once again, remember that you are only making a preliminary estimate when previewing. The best way to judge a work is to read it carefully.

■ *Is there anything else I can discover by skimming through the material?* A quick examination of the text can identify a number of other features that can help you orient yourself to what you are about to read:

1. *Average paragraph length.* Long paragraphs might indicate a densely written text that you will need to read slowly.
2. *Special features.* Tables, figures, or illustrations can provide visual aids for the content.
3. *Subtitles.* Subtitles can provide you with a rough outline of the work and the main topics it addresses.
4. *Abstracts.* In some cases, a writer will provide you with a summary. Articles from scholarly journals are often preceded by an *abstract* (or summary) that can help you understand the article and determine whether it will be useful to you. Many magazines include brief summaries with each article, usually at the beginning of the text. Often, checking the first few and last few paragraphs can give you a good sense of what the article is about and the stance the writer has taken on the topic.
5. *Bibliography.* Finally, check to see whether the work includes a reference list. Scanning a bibliography, noting both how current the research seems and how extensive it is, can help you appraise a writer's scholarship and alert you to other sources that you may want to read on your own.

ANNOTATING

Marking a text with notes, or *annotating* it, can be a great help when you are trying to understand your reading. Annotation can also help you to discover points that you might want to question when you evaluate this work. One of the advantages of owning a book or having your own photocopy of an excerpt from a book or magazine is that you can mark it as much as you wish. When you are annotating a text that is important to you, you will usually benefit from reading that text more than once and adding new annotations with each reading.

When you are able to spend more time with a text and want to be sure that you understand not only its content but also its strengths and weaknesses, then additional annotations are in order:

- Use the margins to define new words and identify unfamiliar allusions.
- Write comments that will remind you of what is discussed in various paragraphs.
- Jot down questions that you might subsequently raise in class or explore in a paper.
- Make cross-references to remind yourself of how various components of the work fit together and also identify apparent contradictions within the work.
- Write down your own response to an important point in the text before you lose the thought. An annotation of this sort can be useful when you are reviewing material before an exam, and it might very well be the seed from which a paper will later grow.

HIGHLIGHTING VERSUS SIMPLE ANNOTATING

Many students use colored highlighter pens to mark passages that seem important to their research. Highlighting makes these passages easy to find if you need to return to them for specific information or quotations. But highlighters can be hard to write with. So consider reading with a pen or pencil, too. As you read, you can make notes or marks in the margins:

- a **check** when a line seems important
- an **exclamation point** when you find surprising information or an unusually bold claim
- a **question mark** when you have trouble understanding a particular passage or find yourself disagreeing with what it says

This simple form of annotation can be done very easily, and if you use a pencil, you will be able to erase any marks that you later find distracting.

Figure 6-1 shows an annotated excerpt from the Declaration of Independence. As you examine it, remember that different readers annotate a text in different ways. Some annotations are more thorough and reflective than others, but there are no "correct" responses against which your own annotations must be measured. You might notice different aspects of a text each time you reread it, so your annotations are likely to accumulate in layers.

SUMMARIZING

On many occasions, you will be required to summarize what others have said or written — or even what you yourself have said or written. This skill is especially important in argumentation. You will have to be able to summarize the main arguments of your opponents if you want to write a convincing argument of your own. And researched papers will become long, obscure, and unwieldy if you lack the ability to summarize your reading.

There is no clear rule to determine which passages are more significant than others. The first sentence of a paragraph might be important if it introduces a new idea, but sometimes it is simply a transitional sentence, linking the new paragraph with whatever has preceded it. Often, a paragraph will have a *topic sentence,* which may appear anywhere in the paragraph, that states the key idea or point of the paragraph.

When writing a summary, be prepared to *paraphrase* — to restate in your own words something you've read or heard. There are many different reasons for paraphrasing, and

FIGURE 6-1

An Annotated Text

1776 | When in the Course of human events, it becomes nec-
essary for one people to dissolve the political bands *such as Americans*
which have connected them with another, and to as- *such as English*
sume among the powers of the earth, the separate and
equal station to which the Laws of Nature and of Na- *Is "Nature's God" different*
ture's God entitle them, a decent respect to the opin- *from "God"?*
ions of mankind requires that they should declare the
causes which impel them to the separation.

Why should nations have "equal station" when some are more powerful than others?

We hold these truths to be self-evident, that all *Why "self-evident"?*
men are created equal, that they are endowed by their
Creator with certain unalienable Rights, that among *Couldn't he prove them?*
these are Life, Liberty and the pursuit of Happiness. *Permanent, "not to be separated"*
That to secure these rights, Governments are insti-
tuted among Men, deriving their just powers from the
consent of the governed. That whenever any Form of
Government becomes destructive of these ends it is *So the Civil War was ok?*
the Right of the People to alter or to abolish it, and to
institute new Government, laying its foundation on
such principles and organizing its powers in such
form, as to them shall seem most likely to effect their
Safety and Happiness. Prudence, indeed, will dictate
that Governments long established should not be
changed for light and transient causes; and accordingly
all experience has shewn, that mankind are more disposed to suffer, while evils are sufferable, than to right
themselves by abolishing the forms to which they are
accustomed. But when a long train of abuses and
usurpations, pursuing invariably the same Object *What's the difference between a "right" and a "duty"?*
evinces a design to reduce them under absolute
Despotism, it is their right, it is their duty, to throw
off such Government, and to provide new Guards for
their future security. Such has been the patient sufferance of these Colonies; and such is now the necessity
which constrains them to alter their former Systems of
Government. The history of the present King of Great *George III (ruled from 1760 to 1820)*
Britain is a history of repeated injuries and usurpa-
tions, all having in direct object the establishment of
an absolute Tyranny over these States. To prove this,
impartial | let Facts be submitted to a candid world.

Does this include women???

If the rights to life & liberty are "unalienable" how come we have capital punishment and prisons?

wrongful seizure

Why is the capitalization so weird?

you've probably been practicing this skill for a long time —
for example, paraphrasing the words of others to soften
an unpleasant fact. But in writing a summary, you
should paraphrase only to make complex ideas more easily
understandable.

Summarizing requires good editorial judgment. A writer
has to be able to distinguish what is essential from what is
not. If the material being summarized has a particular bias,
a good summary should indicate that the bias is part of the
work in question. *But writers should not interject their own
opinions into a summary of someone else's work.* The tone of
a summary should be neutral. You might choose to summarize someone's work so that you can criticize it later, but
do not confuse summary with criticism. When summarizing, you are taking the role of helping other writers to
speak for themselves. Don't let your own ideas get in the
way.

Summaries vary in length, depending on the length and
complexity of the original material and on how much time or
space is available for summarizing it. When summary is being
used as a preliminary to some other type of work, such as argument or analysis, it is especially important to be concise.
For example, if you are summarizing an argument before offering a counterargument of your own, you may be limited to
a single paragraph. The general rule to follow is this: Try to do
justice to whatever you are summarizing in as few words as possible, and make sure that
you have a legitimate reason for writing any summary that goes on for more than a page
or two.

Experienced writers know that summary is a skill worth practicing. If you find summary difficult, try the method described in the sidebar on page 158.

SUMMARY VERSUS PARAPHRASE

The distinction between summary and paraphrase can be
subtle and sometimes confusing, but it is important to
understand. A *summary* is a brief statement, usually no
more than a paragraph or two, summing up the main
points or ideas of a text. A summary may include direct
quotations from the original text, and it will often include
paraphrase.

A *paraphrase*, by contrast, is a restatement — a re-
phrasing — in your own words of something you've read.
A paraphrase can be as long as the original material; under some circumstances it can even be longer.

A paraphrase of a text is *not* a summary of it. In a paraphrase you restate a specific quotation or passage from
a book or article in your own words; you don't necessarily
sum up the entire book or article, as you would in a
summary.

Summary is important in research in part because it
enables you to make the ideas in a long work manageable and accessible in your own essay. Paraphrase is important because it helps you understand what you have
read and avoid plagiarizing (see page 161).

SYNTHESIZING

Synthesizing ideas from two or more different sources is an essential skill in constructing effective arguments. Synthesis requires identifying related material in two or more
works and tying them together smoothly. Synthesis is often an extension of summary
because writers may need to summarize various sources before they can relate these
sources to one another. However, synthesis does not necessarily require you to cover *all*
the major points of the individual sources. You might go through an entire article or
book and identify only one point that relates to another work you have read. And the
relationships involved in your synthesis may be of various kinds. For example, two different authors might have made the same claim, or one might provide specific information that supports a generalization made by the other. On the other hand, one
author might provide information that makes another author's generalization seem inadequate or even wrong.

For a good example of how
summary can be used effectively in an argument, see
"America: Idea or Nation?" by
Wilfred M. McClay (pages
486–496). McClay's summary
of *Making Patriots*, by Walter
Berns, is a key component of
his argument.

When reading material that you need to synthesize, ask yourself, "How does this material relate to whatever else I have already read on this topic?" If you are unable to answer this question, consider a few more specific questions:

- Does the second of two works offer support for the first, or does it reflect an entirely different thesis?
- If the two sources share a similar position, do they arrive at a similar conclusion by entirely different means or do they overlap at any points?
- Would it be easier to compare the two works or to contrast them?

This process of identifying similarities and differences is essentially what synthesis is all about.

When you have determined the points that link your various sources to one another, you are ready to write a synthesis. One challenge in writing a synthesis is organizing it. For example, suppose you have read four articles on the subject of AIDS written, respectively, by a scientist, a clergyman, a gay activist, and a government official. You were struck by how differently these four writers responded to the AIDS epidemic. Although they all agreed that AIDS is a serious problem, each writer advanced a different proposal for fighting the disease. Your synthesis might begin with an introductory paragraph that includes a thesis statement such as "Although there is widespread agreement that AIDS is a serious problem, there is no consensus about how this problem can be solved." Each of the next four paragraphs could then be devoted to a brief summary of one of the different points of view. A final paragraph might emphasize the relationship that exists among the several

A METHOD FOR SUMMARIZING

A summary should be clear, concise, and easy to read. There is no right way to summarize a text, but here is a general method for summarizing that is straightforward and useful:

1. Identify the topic sentences of the paragraphs you are summarizing, and mark any important supporting details. Limit yourself to marking no more than one or two sentences per paragraph.

2. Copy the material you have noted onto a separate sheet of paper. What you now have are the notes for a summary: a collection of short quotations that are unlikely to flow smoothly together.

3. Read over the quotations you have compiled, and look for lines that seem too long and ideas that seem unnecessarily complicated. Paraphrase these lines. As you do, you might also be able to include important details that appeared elsewhere in the paragraph. Keep in mind that you should not have to restate everything that someone else has written. A summary can include direct quotations, as long as the quotations are relatively short and have a clarity that you yourself cannot surpass.

4. Reread your paraphrasing and any quotations that you have included. Look for gaps between sentences, where the writing seems awkward or choppy. Eliminate all repetition, and subordinate any ideas that do not need to stand alone as separate sentences.

5. Check to be sure that any direct quotations are placed within quotation marks.

6. Rearrange any sentences that would flow better in a different sequence, and add transitional phrases wherever they can help smooth the way from one idea to the next.

7. Make sure that your sentences follow in a clear and readable sequence, and correct any errors in grammar, spelling, or syntax.

8. Read over your summary one more time, making sure that the content accurately reflects the nature of the text you are summarizing.

sources, either by reviewing the major points of disagreement among them or by empha-sizing one or two points about which everyone agreed. Your outline for this type of syn-thesis would be as follows:

PARAGRAPH ONE: Introduction
PARAGRAPH TWO: Summary of first writer (scientist)
PARAGRAPH THREE: Summary of second writer (clergyman)
PARAGRAPH FOUR: Summary of third writer (gay activist)
PARAGRAPH FIVE: Summary of fourth writer (government official)
PARAGRAPH SIX: Conclusion

Any good outline allows for some flexibility. Depending on the material and what you want to say, your synthesis might have fewer than or more than six paragraphs. For ex-ample, if two of your sources were especially long and complex, there is no reason why you couldn't devote two paragraphs to each of them, even though you were able to sum-marize your other two sources within single paragraphs.

An alternative method for organizing a synthesis involves linking two or more writers within paragraphs that focus on specific issues or points. This type of organization is es-pecially useful when you have detected a number of similarities that you want to empha-size. Suppose that you have read six essays about increasing the minimum age for obtaining a driver's license. Three writers favored increasing the minimum age, at least to 20, for much the same reasons; three writers opposing such an increase offered arguments that they shared in common. Your assignment is to identify the arguments most used by people who favor increasing the minimum driving age and those most used by people who oppose it. Your outline for synthesizing this material might be organized like this:

PARAGRAPH ONE: Introduction
PARAGRAPH TWO: One argument in favor of increasing the minimum
                         driving age that was made by different writers
PARAGRAPH THREE: A second argument in favor of increasing the mini-
                         mum driving age that was made by different writers
PARAGRAPH FOUR: One argument against increasing the minimum driv-
                         ing age that was made by different writers
PARAGRAPH FIVE: A second argument against increasing the minimum
                         driving age that was made by different writers
PARAGRAPH SIX: Conclusion

There are other ways of organizing a passage of synthesis in your argument, but how-ever you do so, the key is to present the ideas of the other writers clearly and draw con-nections among them in a way that will support your argument.

TAKING NOTES

Note taking is essential to research. Unfortunately, few researchers can tell in advance ex-actly what material they will want to include in their final paper. Especially during the early stages of your research, you might record information that will seem unnecessary when you have become more expert on your topic and have a clear thesis. So you will probably have to discard some of your notes when you are ready to write your paper.

It is important to distinguish between *note taking* and *annotating,* which we discussed on page 154. Annotating involves making notes about a specific text; note taking involves keeping notes on all your sources, ideas, and information for a single essay or project.

Some writers simply make notes in notebooks, on looseleaf, or on legal pads. Many writers now make their notes using a word processing program such as Microsoft Word. Such programs make it easy to keep separate files for different kinds of notes. (There are also specialized computer programs that are designed to help researchers organize their notes.) Unless you have a laptop computer, however, using a word processing program might not be practical if you must take notes in a library or somewhere else outside your home. Newer technologies called *personal digital assistants* are small but powerful alternatives to computers; many of them allow users to make notes.

A more traditional note card system can also be an effective means of taking notes. Such a system allows for flexibility when you are ready to move from research to composition. By spreading out your note cards on a desk or table, you can study how they best fit together. You can arrange and rearrange the cards until you have them in a meaningful sequence. This system works, however, only when you have the self-restraint to limit yourself to recording one fact, one idea, or one quotation on each card, as shown in Figure 6-2. Whether you use a note card system, a word processing program, or some other system of note taking, sorting your notes is one of the easiest ways to determine whether you have enough material to write a good paper.

FIGURE 6-2

A Sample Note Card

This note card includes a quotation from the writer's source. Notice that the topic and source information are included at the top of the card.

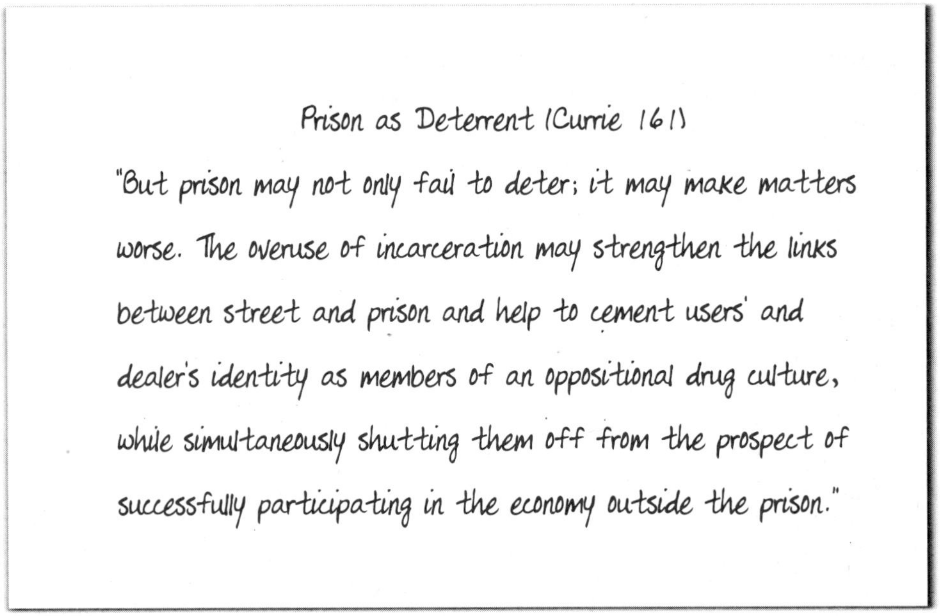

Prison as Deterrent (Currie 161)

"But prison may not only fail to deter; it may make matters worse. The overuse of incarceration may strengthen the links between street and prison and help to cement users' and dealer's identity as members of an oppositional drug culture, while simultaneously shutting them off from the prospect of successfully participating in the economy outside the prison."

AVOIDING PLAGIARISM

Plagiarism is a legitimate concern for anyone engaged in research. To plagiarize (from *pla-giarius,* the Latin word for "kidnapper") is to steal — to be guilty of what the Modern Language Association calls "intellectual theft." Plagiarism is also a form of cheating; some-one who plagiarizes a paper is losing out on an opportunity for learning in addition to running a serious risk. In the workplace intellectual theft (of an essay, a song, or a pro-posal) can lead to lawsuits and heavy financial penalties. In a college or university students who commit intellectual theft face penalties ranging from a failing grade on a paper to ex-pulsion from the school. They are not the only ones who are hurt, however. In addition to hurting themselves, plagiarists injure the people they steal from; the professors who take the time to read and respond to the work of writers who are not their own students; classmates, whose grades might suffer from comparison if a clever plagiarism goes unde-tected; and the social fabric of the academic community, which becomes torn when val-ues such as honesty and mutual respect are no longer cherished.

The grossest form of plagiarism involves submitting someone else's paper as your own. Services that sell papers advertise on many college campuses, and obliging friends or roommates can sometimes be persuaded to hand over one of their own papers for resub-mission. In cyberspace the World Wide Web provides ample opportunities for down-loading a paper written by someone else. Those who are electronically sophisticated can also piece a paper together by lifting paragraphs from a number of sources on the Internet. No one engages in such overt plagiarism accidentally.

On the other hand, it is also possible to plagiarize without meaning to do so. Students sometimes plagiarize by drawing too heavily on their sources. They might forget to put quotation marks around lines that they have taken word for word from another source, or they might think they don't need to quote if they have changed a few words. The im-portant point to keep in mind is that you must give credit for the *ideas* of others, as well as for their *words,* when you are using sources in your writing. If you take most of the in-formation another writer has provided and repeat it in essentially the same pattern, you are only a half-step away from copying the material, even if you have changed the exact wording.

Here is an example:

Original Source

Hawthorne's political ordeal, the death of his mother — and whatever guilt he may have harbored on either score — af-forded him an understanding of the secret psychological springs of guilt. *The Scarlet Letter* is the book of a changed man. Its deeper insights have nothing to do with orthodox morality or religion — or the universal or allegorical applica-tions of a moral. The greatness of the book is related to its sometimes fitful characterizations of human nature and the author's almost uncanny intuitions: his realization of the bond between psychological malaise and physical illness, the nearly perfect, if sinister, outlining of the psychological techniques Chillingworth deployed against his victim.

Plagiarism

Nathaniel Hawthorne understood the psychological sources of guilt. His experience in politics and the death of his mother brought him deep insights that don't have anything to do with formal religion or morality. The greatness of *The Scarlet Letter* comes from its characters and the author's brilliant intuitions: Hawthorne's perception of the link between psychological and physical illness and his almost perfect description of the way Roger Chillingworth persecuted his victim.

This student has simplified the original material, changing some of its wording. But he is still guilty of plagiarism. Pretending to offer his own analysis of *The Scarlet Letter,* he in fact owes all of his ideas to another writer, who is unacknowledged. Even the organization of the passage has been followed. This "paraphrase" would still be considered plagiarism even if it ended with a reference to the original source (page 307 of *Nathaniel Hawthorne in His Times,* by James R. Mellow). A reference or footnote would not reveal the full extent to which this student is indebted to his source.

Here is an acceptable version:

Paraphrase

As James R. Mellow has argued, *The Scarlet Letter* reveals a profound understanding of guilt. It is a great novel because of its insight into human nature — not because of some moral about adultery. The most interesting character is probably Roger Chillingworth because of the way he was able to make Rev. Dimmesdale suffer (307).

This student has not only made a better effort to paraphrase the original material, but has also introduced it with a reference to the original writer. The introductory reference to Mellow, coupled with the subsequent page reference, clearly shows us that Mellow deserves the credit for the ideas in this passage. Additional bibliographical information about this source is provided by the list of works cited at the end of the paper:

Mellow, James. *Nathaniel Hawthorne in His Times.* Boston: Houghton, 1980.

One final caution: It is possible to subconsciously remember a piece of someone else's phrasing and inadvertently repeat it. You would be guilty of plagiarism if the words in question embodied a critically important idea or reflect a distinctive style or turn of phrase. When you revise your draft, look for such unintended quotations. If you use them, show who deserves the credit for them, and *remember to put quoted material within quotation marks.*

FINDING RELEVANT MATERIAL

Up to this point in the chapter we have been discussing how to read and use sources. Obviously, you must have relevant sources before you can read them critically and use them effectively in your argument. Finding those relevant sources encompasses an important set of research skills.

GETTING STARTED

One of the first goals of any researcher is to decide where to focus. The more specific your search, the greater is your chance for efficiently locating the material you need and then writing a well-supported paper. When you know what you are looking for, you can gauge what you should read and what you can probably afford to pass over — a great advantage when you are confronted by the staggering amount of information that a good college library, or the Internet, makes available.

In many cases you will begin your research with your topic already identified. For instance, you might be assigned to write about a specific issue. Or your class might have discussed an issue that interests you enough to want to write an argument about it. Or you might be addressing a problem for which you are seeking a solution, such as a controversy on campus involving a dorm policy or an inflammatory editorial in the student newspaper. In such cases you have a good starting point for your research.

But sometimes you might find yourself in a situation in which you have no clear topic. In such a situation you can take steps to identify a workable topic for your argument. Sometimes, for example, a specific topic will emerge as you scan information on your subject area periodical indexes, online databases, and search engines for navigating the Internet. By beginning with a general idea of what you plan to write about and then using key words to check different sources, you can refine your topic or even discover topics that have generated recent interest — topics that will interest you as well. You can judge, at this point, which topics would be the most manageable ones to research. As you proceed, keep two general rules in mind:

1. If you are overwhelmed by the number of citations you find in your research area, you probably need to *narrow your topic.*
2. If you have difficulty finding material, you might need to *broaden your search.*

If you're unsure about your topic, consider discussing it with other people — in particular, your instructor. (For additional information on choosing a topic, see pages 115–116.)

AVOIDING SELECTIVE RESEARCH

Although you might have a tentative thesis in mind when you begin your search, it's often a good idea to delay formulating your final thesis until your research is complete. Think of your search strategy as an attempt to answer a question. For instance, suppose you are writing an argument about drug-related crime. You can proceed as if you are addressing the following question: "What can be done to reduce drug-related crime?" This is very different from starting your research with your thesis predetermined. If you begin already convinced that the way to reduce drug-related crime is to legalize drugs, you might be tempted to take notes only from sources that advocate this position, rejecting as irrelevant any source that discusses problems with this approach. In this case research is not leading to greater knowledge or understanding. On the contrary, it is being used to reinforce personal beliefs that might border on prejudice. Even if you feel strongly about the issue at hand, keeping an open mind during your research can often lead to a better understanding of that issue — and a more effective argument.

We have seen that anticipating the opposition (see sidebar on page 117) is important even in short arguments. It is no less important in a researched paper. Almost any topic worth investigating will yield facts and ideas that could support different conclusions. It is possible to take significantly different positions on issues such as immigration law, environmental protection, and education. These are extremely complex issues, and it is important to remember that fact as you conduct your research. Your own research might ultimately support a belief that you already hold, but if you proceed as if you are genuinely trying to solve a problem or answer a question, your research might deepen your understanding of the issue and lead you to realize that you were previously misinformed. For this reason, try not to overlook relevant material just because you don't agree with it. Ultimately, your argument will be stronger if you recognize that disagreement about your topic exists and then demonstrate why you favor one position over another or show how different positions can be reconciled.

With this advice in mind you can more effectively make use of the many resources now available to you as you research your topic. In addition to more traditional sources such as books and articles in magazines, journals, and newspapers, you have access to an astonishing amount of information on the Internet. In the remainder of this chapter we will discuss how best to use these resources.

USING THE INTERNET

The kind of information that can be found on the Internet is incredibly diverse; it includes library catalogs, government documents and data, newspaper and magazine articles, excerpts from books and even entire books, and all kinds of information and material published by commercial organizations, special interest groups, and even individuals who wish to make contact with others who share their concerns.

Today, most of us access all this information through the World Wide Web, which is a graphical interface for navigating the Internet. Current software, such as Internet Explorer or Netscape Navigator, makes it very easy to browse the Web. But the enormous scale of the Web can also make it difficult to find relevant information easily. The very richness of the Web can be its drawback, and searching for the right information can be time consuming and sometimes frustrating. You might find yourself scrolling through an endless series of documents and losing sight of your main objective while pursuing an elusive loose end. For this reason it's important to understand some basic principles for searching the Web.

You should also be aware of a key difference between much of the material published on the Internet and material published in print. Writers who publish in print receive professional editorial support. Editors decide what material is worth printing and then assist writers in preparing work for publication. Most of the Internet operates without editors, however. Anyone with a little knowledge of computers can publish whatever comes to mind. In a sense the Internet is wonderfully democratic, and many people have enjoyed activities such as creating a Web site for their cat and connecting with other cat fanciers. On the other hand, the Internet also carries a great deal of misinformation, hate speech, and crank editorials. When searching the Internet, you must carefully evaluate the material you locate and recognize that this material can range from first-rate scholarship to utter trash.

Despite these potential problems, the Internet is an increasingly important resource for research. The challenge is finding your way through the huge amount of material that is floating around in cyberspace. Computer experts have developed systems called *search engines* that work as indexing services for the World Wide Web. Among the most commonly used today are Google, Yahoo!, Alta Vista, Infoseek, and Lycos. Once you learn how to use one of these systems, you can easily learn how to adapt to the others. No search engine provides a complete, error-free index to electronic documents, so you might have to use more than one system, just as you would use more than one periodical index when looking for information in your library.

Search engines require you to identify your research topic by typing key words or phrases into an entry box. After you have entered your search terms, you will be given a list of Web sites that match your request. Each of these sites can, in turn, lead you to others. Many search engines also enable you to refine your search by entering more specific information, such as dates or kinds of publications (see Figure 6-3). And Internet directories allow you to browse through broad subject categories to find subtopics that you might be looking for (see Figure 6-4). Like other electronic resources, search engines provide help screens with

LEARNING TO SEARCH THE WEB

To learn more about efficiently searching the World Wide Web, check to see whether your library or academic computing office provides workshops or similar services. These workshops can help you learn about various search engines available on the Web as well as sophisticated strategies for searching the Web.

EVALUATING INTERNET RESOURCES

The advice we provided earlier about reading critically (see page 152) applies to Internet resources as well. But because of the dizzying variety of material on the Internet and the fact that anyone can publish anything on a Web site, you might have to take special care in evaluating the reliability of information you find on the Web. Most libraries have information on their own Web sites about evaluating Internet resources. Here are a few very good ones:

■ *Evaluating Web Resources*, Wolfgram Memorial Library, Widener University: http://www2.widener.edu/Wolfgram-Memorial-Library/webevaluation/webeval.htm
■ *Evaluating Web Resources*, Cornell University Library: http://campusgw.library.cornell.edu/t/help/res_strategy/evaluating/evaluate.html
■ *Thinking Critically About World Wide Web Resources*, UCLA College Library: http://www.library.ucla.edu/libraries/college/help/critical/index.htm.

FIGURE 6-3

Google's Advanced Search Screen

The advanced search screen enables you to refine your search, making it more efficient.

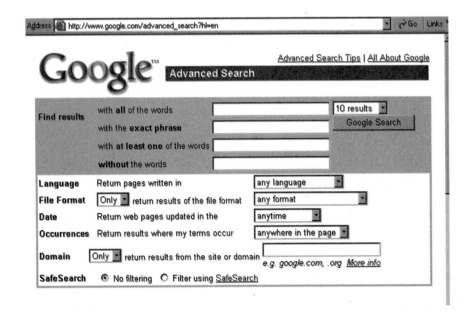

FIGURE 6-4

The Introductory Screen for the Google Web Directory

One of the most popular search engines, Google is easy to use and can be a powerful tool for research on the Web.

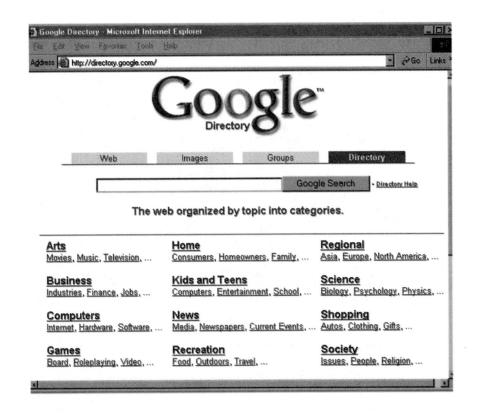

instructions on the best ways to search. These instructions change as the technology changes, and it
is wise to review them whenever you are in doubt
about how to proceed.

Remember that the Internet is constantly changing. New sites are launched on the Web constantly
— literally every minute. And new search systems
are always being developed; hundreds now exist.
Because the Internet contains so much information,
some researchers make the mistake of thinking that
anything they need to find must be available electronically. Not every scholar chooses to make completed work available electronically, so you can miss
important material if you try to do all your research
on the Internet.

At the same time many resources that have traditionally been available only in print form are becoming available on the Internet. Many journals,
newspapers, and magazines now offer full-text articles online, which means that you don't always
have to go to your library to get a copy of an article you might need for your research. In addition,
some publications appear only online. For example, *Slate* magazine and *Salon.com* are two respected publications that do not appear in print
form; you can access their articles only through the Internet. And organizations of all
types sponsor online archives and other sources related to their areas of interest. For
example, you can visit the Web site of the U.S. Department of Health and Human
Services to find a great deal of information on a range of topics related to health issues
(see Figure 6-5). Thousands of such sites exist on the Web. Once you learn to navigate
the Web efficiently and to evaluate Internet sources carefully, the wealth of information that is available online can enrich your research.

TIPS FOR EFFICIENT WEB SEARCHING

Doing research on the Web is more than visiting a popular search
engine such as Google and typing in your topic. Here are a few
suggestions for making your Web searching more efficient and
successful:

- Visit your library's Web site to see whether it has information
  about searching the Web. Many libraries offer excellent advice for using the Web effectively.
- Read the search tips that are usually available on the Web
  sites of search engines. These tips can help you learn to use
  specific search engines more efficiently.
- Learn how to use *Boolean operators* in your searches. Most
  search tools support Boolean, or logical, operators, such as
  and, or, and *not.* These terms help you narrow your search so
  that the search tools will return the most relevant documents. Most search engines include basic instructions for using Boolean terms.
- Learn to recognize Internet *domains* in Web addresses, such
  as .com, .edu., .gov, and .org. Understanding what these domains mean can help you decide whether to visit specific
  Web sites that you find with a search engine.

SEARCHING FOR MAGAZINE AND JOURNAL ARTICLES

Magazines, bulletins, and scholarly journals are all called *periodicals* because they are published on a regular schedule — once a week, once a month, and so on. Although researchers can seldom afford to rely exclusively on periodicals for information, the indexes
and abstracting services that enable them to locate relevant periodical articles are essential
in most searches. Periodicals often include the most current information about a research
area, and they can alert you to other important sources through book reviews as well as
through the citations that support individual articles. In addition, as we noted in the previous section, many periodicals are now available on the Internet, which makes them easily accessible to researchers.

The best-known periodical index is the *Readers' Guide to Periodical Literature,* which is
now available online through OLLC FirstSearch (a service that provides access to over

FIGURE 6-5

Web Site of the U.S. Department of Health and Human Services

Fact sheets available at this Web site contain easily accessible health-related information.

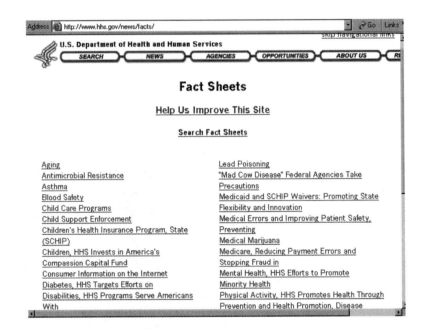

forty electronic indexes), in addition to being published in the familiar book form available in your library. The *Readers' Guide* covers hundreds of magazines; material is indexed by subject and by author. Because it indexes popular mass-circulation periodicals, it can lead you to articles that are relatively short and accessible. InfoTrac, another computerized index for periodicals in general circulation, offers a similar advantage.

Most college libraries have a variety of other indexes that will point you toward more specialized material, and you should be prepared to move beyond the *Readers' Guide* in any serious search. Almost every academic field has its own index available in regularly printed volumes, and most electronic versions of these indexes are now including *abstracts* (short summaries of the articles indexed).

If you have difficulty finding material or if you are in difficulty because you have found too much, you can broaden or narrow an online search by using *Boolean operators* — words that instruct a database to narrow a search or to broaden it. For example, searching for *drugs* in a database would yield an unwieldy amount of material, much of which might be irrelevant to your topic. If you were interested in, say, the relationship between drug use and violent crime, you might enter *drugs and crime* as your search terms. In that case your search would yield only articles that mention both drugs and crime. To narrow your search further, you could enter

SPECIALIZED INDEXES

The following indexes can be useful if you're searching for information specific to an academic discipline or a profession. Your college library will probably have several or all of these.

Applied Science and Technology Index	Business Periodicals Index
Index to Legal Periodicals	Philosopher's Index
Art Index	Education Index
Index Medicus (for medicine)	Science Citation Index
Biological and Agricultural Index	Humanities Index
Music Index	Social Sciences Index
MLA International Bibliography	Essay and General Literature Index

additional search terms, such as *gender,* which would limit the search to articles about gender in drug use and crime. Adding *women,* or *youth,* on the other hand, would identify articles mentioning both drugs and crime and either women or youth. By playing with terms in this way and discovering how much material is available on any given combination, you can find a specific topic for a researched paper within a larger subject area.

The advantage of consulting the *Readers' Guide* online is readily apparent from the accompanying illustrations. After instructing the computer to search for the subject *globalization,* the person conducting this online search in 2002 discovered 1,621 articles, many of them published just a few weeks or months earlier, citations that would not be available in the print version of the *Readers' Guide* (see Figure 6-6). To discover additional articles through printed volumes would require consulting other volumes and following up on a range of cross-references. A computer can do that task within seconds.

USING BOOLEAN OPERATORS

Boolean, or logical, operators are words that command a search engine to define a search in a specific way. The most common Boolean operators are *AND, OR,* and *NOT.* Understanding how they work can help you search the Internet and databases more efficiently:

- *AND* tells the search engine to find only sources that contain both words in your search. For example, if you entered *sports AND steroids,* your search would yield sources that deal with steroids in sports and would not necessarily return sources that deal with steroids or sports in general.
- *OR* broadens a search by telling the search engine to return sources for either term in your search. Entering *sports OR steroids,* for instance, would yield sources on either of those topics.
- *NOT* can narrow a search by telling the search engine to exclude sources containing a specific keyword. For example, entering *steroids NOT sports* would yield sources on steroids but not sources that deal with steroids in sports.

In addition, keep these tips in mind:

- You can use parentheses for complex searches: *(sports AND steroids)* NOT *(medicine OR law);* this entry would narrow the search to specific kinds of sources about sports and steroids that did not include medical or legal matters.
- With most search engines you can use quotation marks to find a specific phrase. For example, "steroid use in sports" would return sources that included that exact phrase.
- Generally, you should capitalize Boolean operators.

Be aware, however, that the *Readers' Guide* will usually locate sources that many college professors are likely to consider inappropriate for academic assignments, such as *People* or *Time.* If you have access to the *Readers' Guide* through FirstSearch, you should also have access to other databases that can help you locate the kind of material you would locate through the *Readers' Guide* as well as much more scholarly work.

Although there is some overlapping from one index to another, each index covers different periodicals. The records that you find in one will usually vary from the records that you find in another. This is worth remembering, for two reasons:

1. If you cannot locate any material in the past few years of one index, you can try another index that seems as if it might include records on your subject.
2. Many subjects of general interest will be found in more than one index. If you consult more than one index, you are increasing the likelihood of being exposed to different points of view.

Let's say you're searching for material on drugs and crime. Of the various specialized indexes that can lead you exclusively to material in professional journals, the *Social Sciences Index* is especially useful for locating information on such topics, since it indexes

literature in sociology, psychology, and political science. Like the *Readers' Guide,* it can be consulted in bound volumes or online, with the online service providing abstracts as well as citations.

Figure 6-7 shows the results of a search of *Social Science Abstracts* on FirstSearch. The screen displays the first four of 515 citations located in a search for articles on the relationship between drug use and crime. The first article listed is from the *Journal of the American Academy of Child and Adolescent Psychiatry,* a scholarly publication that would not be indexed by the *Readers' Guide.* A journal like this is likely to provide more credible data on this topic than an issue of a magazine like *People* for an academic assignment. Figure 6-8 shows the abstract from this article, which can easily be accessed from the main list of articles shown in Figure 6-7.

Very often, if you are using a database such as FirstSearch through your library's Web site, the search results will indicate whether your library has the articles you are interested in — a great convenience when you're doing research.

SEARCHING FOR NEWSPAPER ARTICLES

You can also access many newspaper articles by using a database such as FirstSearch, or you can use an Internet search engine to find archives of articles that are now maintained online by many newspapers. The *Readers' Guide* will also lead you to some newspaper articles. For a serious electronic search of newspaper articles on a research topic involving a public policy issue, use Lexis-Nexis, a powerful database that searches for news articles and legal documents worldwide, often locating material only a day or two after its

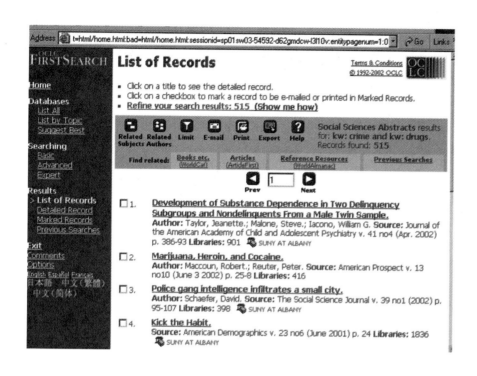

FIGURE 6-7

Results of a Search of *Social Sciences Abstracts* on FirstSearch

This screen shows the first four of 515 articles on drug-related crime located with FirstSearch.

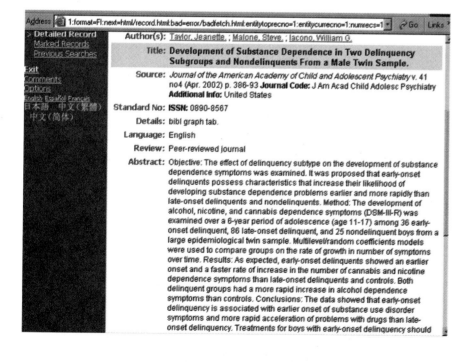

FIGURE 6-8

Sample Abstract from *Social Sciences Abstracts*

This screen shows the abstract from one of the articles listed in Figure 6-7.

FIGURE 6-9

**Search Screen in the
Lexis-Nexis Academic
Database**

The Lexis-Nexis database indexes many newspapers and
magazines that are not listed in
other databases.

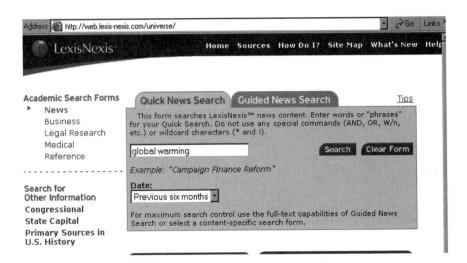

publication. Lexis-Nexis now organizes its vast databases into several subdatabases, such
as Lexis-Nexis Congressional and Lexis-Nexis Academic. Figure 6-9 shows an introductory screen for the Lexis-Nexis academic database, which, as you can see, is broken down
into additional categories (news, business, etc. — visible on the left side of the screen).
From this screen you can narrow or expand your search by limiting yourself to articles
from today, a week ago, or two years ago. If you were writing an argument on global
warming, for example, you could enter those terms. Figure 6-10 shows the results of that

FIGURE 6-10

**The Results of a
Search on Lexis-Nexis**

This search of Lexis-Nexis found
700 articles on global warming.

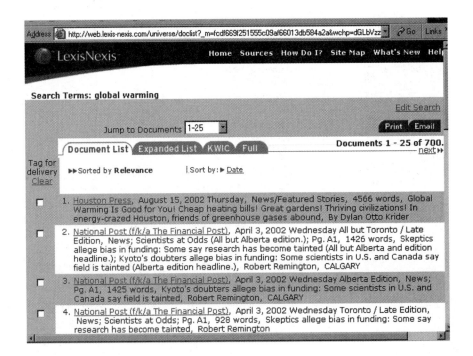

search, limited to the previous six months. By clicking on the tabs above the list, you can choose whether to view citations only, citations with summaries, and — when you find something that seems especially promising — the full text of the article, which you might then be able to print out, depending on the nature of the service your library provides. (Note: Not all libraries have access to Lexis-Nexis, and some that do have it charge for this service.)

Your college or community library might also provide you with the equipment to search online for articles in a local paper. If you are unable to search for newspapers online, look for printed volumes of the *New York Times Index,* which has been published annually since 1913 and is updated frequently throughout the current year.

USING ABSTRACTING SERVICES

Although many electronic indexing services such as *Readers' Guide Abstracts* and *Social Science Abstracts* are now offering summaries of current articles along with the citations a search identifies, they do not consistently provide abstracts for all of the material they index. There are other services that specialize in abstracts. Important abstracting services in printed volumes include the following:

Abstracts in Anthropology	*Biological Abstracts*
Historical Abstracts	*Psychological Abstracts*
Academic Abstracts	*Chemical Abstracts*
Physics Abstracts	*Sociological Abstracts*

These abstracts are organized in different ways, and you might need to consult one volume for the index and another volume for the matching abstracts. When using bound volumes, consult the instructions that can be found within them. However, there is no reason to consult printed volumes of abstracts unless you do not have access to electronic databases. Almost all college libraries provide access to at least a few electronic databases. Ask your reference librarian whether there are electronic resources in your library that are appropriate to your research.

Because it can be hard to tell from a title whether an article will be useful, abstracts offer an advantage over simple bibliographical citations. The summary provided by an abstracting service can help you to decide whether you want to read the entire article. Keep in mind that an abstract written in English does not mean that the article itself is also in English; be alert for notations such as *(Chin), (Germ),* or *(Span),* which indicate when an article is published in another language. Also, remember that good researchers never pretend to have read an entire article when they have read only an abstract of it. Use abstracts as a tool for locating material to read, not as a substitute for a full-length reading.

LOOKING FOR BOOKS

The convenience of the Internet and online databases can tempt you to avoid looking for books on a subject. Yet books remain essential to research. Although the books you locate in your library might vary in quality, they often represent the final and most prestigious result of someone else's research. It is common, for example, for a scholar to publish several journal articles in the process of writing a book. Much of the best information you can find appears somewhere in a book, and you should not assume that your research subject is so new or so specialized that your library will not have books on it. A topic that seems new to you is not necessarily new to others.

Because books take time to read, some researchers look for books at the beginning of their search. Others turn to books after they have investigated the periodical literature to focus their interests and identify the most influential works in their field. Whenever you choose to look for books on your topic, be sure that you do so well before your paper is due. A book full of important information will be of little help if you haven't left yourself time to read it.

Although some libraries still use catalogs consisting of alphabetically arranged cards in multiple drawers, most college libraries now have electronic card catalogs, which are usually accessible both within the library and via the Internet. This accessibility makes it convenient to search the library catalog without having to go to the library itself. Computerized catalogs enable users to search for books by author, title, or subject. Most of these catalogs also permit a search for material via a call number or a *key word* — a word that is likely to appear somewhere in the title or description. In addition to providing all of the information about a book that could be obtained from a card catalog, computerized catalogs are usually designed to report whether the book is currently available.

Figure 6-11 shows the catalog entry for a book entitled *Urban Sprawl*. It contains information about the author, when and where the book was published, and whether it is available in the library. Every library has its own system for displaying information about the books it holds. As you do research, you should expect to find variations on this example. The precise format of a computerized entry depends on the program employed by

FIGURE 6-11

Online Library Catalog

This screen shows an entry for a book that was found by searching this library's online catalog.

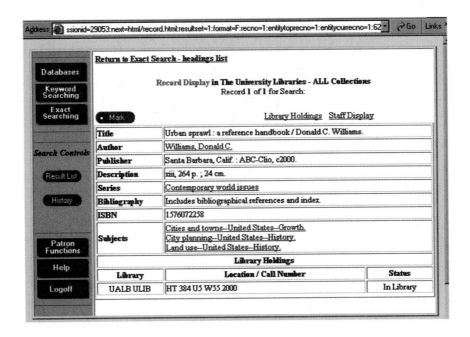

the library you are using. (If your library still uses index cards in a card catalog, you will find the same basic information displayed on those cards.)

There is no foolproof method for determining the quality or usefulness of a book from a catalog entry. The best way to judge a book's usefulness is to read it. But a catalog listing can reveal some useful clues if you know how to find them:

- *The date of publication.* There is no reason to assume that new books are always better than old books, but unless you are researching a historical or literary topic, you should be careful not to rely heavily on material that may be out of date.
- *The length of the book.* A book with 300 pages is likely to provide more information than a book half that size. A book with a bibliography might help you to find more material.
- *The reputation of the publisher.* Academic publishers generally publish books that have gone through rigorous review, which is not always the case with some commercial publishers.

USING OTHER LIBRARY RESOURCES

Because of the great amount of material being published, libraries save space in several ways, most commonly by using microform, digital technology, and interlibrary loan. In doing research, you might need to use one or more of these resources.

Microform is printed material that has been reduced in size through microphotography. Libraries that use microform provide users with special devices to read the material, whether it is available on microfilm or microfiche (which is a flat sheet of microfilm).

Digital technology, in the form of CD-ROMs or online media, makes articles and other resources available to users electronically rather than in print form. Sometimes, you must read these resources at a computer terminal.

Interlibrary loan enables libraries to give their users access to books held at other libraries. You can usually request articles as well as books through this service, and today many libraries enable you to make your requests online. Keep in mind, however, that in can take several days or weeks for requested materials to arrive.

CONDUCTING INTERVIEWS AND SURVEYS

In some cases you might want to conduct original research on your topic. For example, if you are writing an argument about a campus controversy over new parking fees, you can gather useful information by talking to people on campus (such as the person in charge of parking) or soliciting opinions by those affected by the new fees. There are many kinds of original research, but two of the most common are interviews and surveys.

Interviews might be inappropriate for some kinds of papers (for example, science reports), but they can often be useful sources of information. If you are writing a paper on identity theft, for example, you might interview someone working in law enforcement, such as a police officer or a public defender. You might also interview someone who might have had their identity stolen or talk to professionals at a bank or credit card company who deal with identity theft. Whom you interview will depend in large measure on your topic, but you should always evaluate the credibility of anyone you interview. Here are some other tips for interviewing:

- *Plan ahead for your interviews.* It's a good idea to prepare a list of questions before you go. It also helps to learn something about the person or persons you will interview so that you can ask appropriate questions and avoid inappropriate ones.

- *Ask good questions.* Try to compose questions that will take several sentences to answer rather than questions that might be answered with a single word. Good questions usually elicit more useful responses for your research.

- *Be flexible.* Don't necessarily adhere rigidly to the questions you prepare in advance. A good interviewer knows how to ask a follow-up question that is inspired by a provocative response to an earlier question. However, try not to get so caught up in the interview that you forget to take careful notes.

- *Consider using a tape recorder.* A tape recorder will usually preserve more of the interview than you can preserve in your notes, and it will enable you to take notes on important points without having to write everything down. If you want to use a tape recorder, ask permission to do so when you arrange for the interview. Also, make sure that the recorder is working properly before you begin the interview, and check your batteries.

- *Record the date of the interview and the full name and credentials or position of the person you interviewed.* You will need to include this information in your bibliography.

When you ask the same questions of a number of different people, you are conducting a *survey.* When a survey is long, complex, and administered to a large sample group, researchers seeking to analyze the data they have gathered will benefit from having a working knowledge of statistics. But for many undergraduate research projects, a relatively simple survey can produce interesting and useful data. The earlier hypothetical example of a campus controversy about new parking fees illustrates the usefulness of a survey. If you were writing an argument about that controversy, you could gather information about students' attitudes toward the new fees. Such information can be important and potentially persuasive support for your position on the controversy.

Here are some things to consider if you want to use a survey:

- *Carefully compose a list of relevant questions.* Each question should be designed to elicit a clear answer that is directly related to the purpose of the survey. This is more complicated than it might seem, since the kind of questions you ask will determine what results you get. For example, if you ask students whether they agree with the parking fees, you will get a basic yes-or-no response. However, if you ask students whether they would pay higher fees if they were guaranteed a parking space, you might get different results.

- *Decide whether you want to administer the survey orally or distribute it in a written form.* One advantage of an oral survey is that you get your results immediately; with a written survey, weeks can pass before you discover how many people responded to your request for information. On the other hand, written surveys give you clear records to work from. A good rule to follow when conducting a written survey is to distribute at least twice as many copies as you really need to have returned to you.

- *Decide how many people you will need to survey to have a credible sample of the population that concerns you.* For example, in the case of the campus parking fees, let's say there are 4,000 students at your school but only 1,000 drive to campus. You might want to survey both drivers and nondrivers to see whether you get different results. In that case, if you surveyed 100 students, you might want to make sure that twenty-five of them are drivers (which would match the 25 percent of student drivers on your campus).

■ *Consider whether it would be useful to analyze your results in terms of such differences as gender, race, age, income, or religion.* If so, you must design a questionnaire that will provide this information. In the campus parking controversy it might be that older students are most affected, so you would want to account for the age of your respondents.

■ *Take steps to protect the privacy of your respondents.* Ask for no more information than you need, and ask respectfully for that information. Give respondents the option of refusing to answer any question that makes them uncomfortable, and honor any promises you make about how you will use the data you gather.

As this chapter reveals, there are many aspects to doing research and many kinds of resources for the information you need. Which resources you consult and how you search for them will depend on your topic and the specifics of your assignment, such as your deadline and the length of the argument you are writing. But whether you will engage in extensive research or simply look for a few essays about your topic, the general principles guiding research are the same. And the more effective you are as a researcher, the more likely you will be to find the information you need to write an effective argument.

7

DOCUMENTING
YOUR SOURCES

DOCUMENTING

I n Chapter 6 we discussed many of the strategies that you can use to conduct research for an argument. Doing such research, in our view, is part of the process of inquiry that you engage in when you make an argument. By researching an issue or controversy carefully, you can gain a better understanding of that issue or controversy and construct a more effective argument that may lead to a satisfactory resolution. That's the goal. But the process entails some practical challenges, including organizing your paper effectively and properly documenting your sources. We take up those topics in this chapter.

YOUR SOURCES

COMPILING A PRELIMINARY BIBLIOGRAPHY

As you use the strategies that we discussed in Chapter 6 to begin locating sources of possible value for your paper, it is important to record certain essential information about the books and articles you have discovered. You will need this information to compile a preliminary bibliography. Here are some things to keep in mind as you work with your sources:

- For books, record the full title, the full name of the author or authors, the city of publication, the publisher, and the date of publication.
- If you are using a particular part of a book, be sure to record the pages in question.
- When you have located articles in periodicals, record the author(s) of the article, the title of the article, the title of the journal in which it was published, the volume number, the issue number (if there is one), the date of the issue, and the pages between which the article can be found.
- If you are using an article or a story from an anthology that is edited by someone other than the author of the material you are using, make the distinction between the author and title of the selection and the editor and title of the volume.
- For electronic resources, such as Web sites, be sure to record the Internet address, or URL, accurately and make a note of the date you accessed the site.

Today, researchers often use a computer program to keep track of sources. You can easily use certain features of a word processing program such as Microsoft Word to maintain your preliminary bibliography, and you can also use specialized software such as EndNote that is designed specifically for constructing bibliographies. Whatever method you use, be sure to keep accurate records. It can be frustrating to discover that you neglected to record an important reference, especially if this discovery comes after the paper is written and shortly before it is handed in.

ORGANIZING A RESEARCH PAPER

Many students think of outlines as extra work. But in fact using an outline can save you time and help you write a more effective source-based argument. It can help you keep track of your main ideas and make sure that the important parts of your argument fit together effectively. It can also help you identify areas in which you may need to do more research.

Depending on your writing process, you can outline before attempting to write or after you have completed a first draft. If you create an outline before you begin writing, the patterns discussed in Chapter 5 for classical arrangement and Rogerian argument (pages 126–128), which can be adopted for researched papers of almost any length, may be useful to you. You can also use a standard formal outline:

    I. Major idea
       A. Supporting idea
          1. Minor idea
             a. Supporting detail
             b. Supporting detail
          2. Minor idea
             a. Supporting detail
             b. Supporting detail
       B. Supporting idea
   II. Major idea

And so forth. Subdivisions make sense only when there are at least two categories; otherwise, there would be no need to subdivide. Roman numeral I usually implies the existence of Roman numeral II, and supporting idea A implies the existence of supporting idea B. Formal outlines are usually parallel, each part being in balance with the others.

Many writers prefer to work with less formal outlines. Two widely used alternatives to a formal outline are *listing* and *mapping*. When organizing a paper by listing, writers simply make a list of the various points they want to make without worrying about Roman numerals or indention. They then number the points on the list in the order in which they plan to discuss them. When mapping, you can create circles or blocks on a page, starting with a main idea. Each different idea is noted in a separate circle or block, and then lines are drawn to connect ideas that are related.

There is no single method that works equally well for all writers. Unless you are specifically instructed to complete a certain type of outline, practice whatever kind of outlining works best for you. And keep in mind that an outline is not an end in itself; it is only a tool to help you write a good paper. You can rewrite an outline much more easily than you can rewrite a paper, so be prepared to rework any outline that does not help you to write better.

PLANNING AHEAD

When planning a researched paper, allow ample time for drafting and revising. As we noted in Chapter 5, ideas often evolve during the writing process. Even if you have extensive notes, you might discover that you lack information to support a claim that occurred to you when you sat down to write. You would then need to do more research or modify your claim. The first draft might also include material that on rereading, you decide does not relate to the focus of your paper and should therefore be removed. Cutting and adding are a normal part of the writing process, so expect to make changes.

INTEGRATING SOURCE MATERIAL INTO YOUR PAPER

One of the challenges of writing an argument involving research is integrating source material effectively into a work that remains distinctively your own. The most effective source-based arguments include source material that is woven smoothly into the paper with well-chosen quotations that are clearly introduced and properly documented. Papers with too many long quotations or quotations that seem arbitrarily placed are weaker; they lack the student's voice and might lead an instructor to be suspicious about how much of the paper is the student's own. You can avoid such problems if you work with your source material to support your own position in an argument and if you follow some basic advice for quoting and citing source material.

First, make sure that any quotations you use fit smoothly into your essay as a whole. Provide transitions that link quotations to whatever has come before them. As a general rule, anything worth quoting at length requires some discussion. After you have quoted someone, you should usually include some analysis or commentary that will make the significance of the quotation clear. Notice how Rachel Guetter, whose essay appears on pages 129–132, follows this advice to weave a quote from one of her sources effectively into her discussion of problems facing gay parents:

> Often, one person in a same-sex relationship is the biological parent and the other will help raise the child as his or her own. According to the American Academy of Pediatrics (AAP), children in this situation lose "survivor benefits if a parent dies and legal rights if the parents break up" (Berman 1). Both situations leave a dramatic impact on the child, who then is caught in the middle of legal battles.

To help keep your paper your own, try to avoid using long quotations. Quote only what you need most, and edit long quotations whenever possible. Use the ellipsis (. . .) to indicate that you have omitted a word or phrase within a sentence, leaving a space before and after each period. (When the ellipsis follows a completed sentence, include the sentence's period before the ellipsis.) When editing quotations in this way, make sure that they remain clear and grammatically correct. If the addition of an extra word or two would help to make the quotation more easily understandable, you should enclose the inserted material within square brackets [ ] to let your readers know what had been added to the quotation. Here is another passage from Rachel Guetter's essay illustrating these points:

> Until homosexuality is more widely received, children with gay and lesbian parents will have to deal with the fact that their family is viewed as pejoratively different. Glenn Stanton, senior research analyst for Focus on the Family, says, "While there may be very nice people who are raising kids in homosexual situations, the best model for kids is to grow up with mom and dad" (Stanton). It seems reasonable to believe that having both a mother and father benefits children. Women and men have different parenting traits that give a strong balance for the development of a child. Stanton also states, "Fathers encourage children to take chances . . . mothers protect and are more cautious." There exist in parents different disciplining, communication, and playing styles that can be advantages in raising a child.

Remember also that sources do not need to be quoted to be cited. As we noted in Chapter 6 (pages 155–157), paraphrasing and summarizing are important writing skills. They can help you avoid writing a paper that sounds like nothing more than one quotation after another or using quotations that are so heavily edited that readers start wondering about what you have cut out. When you put another writer's ideas into your own words (being careful, of course, to provide proper documentation), you are demonstrating that you have control over your material, and by doing so, you can often make your paper more readable.

Above all, remember that you are the writer of your argument. You are using the sources you have found to support your position or to enhance your own ideas.

CITING SOURCES

Any time you use material from another source, you must cite it properly. Citing your sources simply means revealing the source of any information you report. When you cite your sources, you are providing your readers with information to help them evaluate the credibility of your sources, to credit the authors whose work you are citing, and to make it possible for readers to find your sources for themselves. In general, you must provide documentation for the following:

- Any direct quotation
- Any idea that has come from someone else's work
- Any fact or statistic that is not widely known

There are several different styles for documenting your sources; these styles are usually associated with different disciplines or professions. Writers in the humanities usually follow the form of the Modern Language Association (MLA). In the social sciences writers are often expected to follow the format of the American Psychological Association (APA). MLA and APA are the two most widely used systems for documenting sources, and chances are that you will be asked to use one of them for papers you write for your college courses. *The Chicago Manual of Style* (CMS) is another widely used system, though college instructors are less likely to use that system than MLA or APA. When you are writing a source-based paper, check with your instructor to see which system you should use. (If you are writing a source-based argument for publication, check with the editor about that publication's preferred system for documenting sources.)

Whichever system you use to document your sources, remember that the purpose of all these systems is the same: to provide appropriate information about your sources. And be sure to understand the relationship between the parenthetical, or in-text, citations and the bibliography, Works Cited, or References page, of your essay. When you cite a source in the body of your essay, you are telling your readers where you obtained the quotation or information you are using; your readers can then go to your bibliography for more information about that source. For example, in this passage from her essay (see pages 129–132) Rachel uses MLA style to cite the source of the quotation she is using:

According to the American Academy of Pediatrics (AAP), children in this situation lose "survivor benefits if a parent dies and legal rights if the parents break up" (Berman A1).

The information in the parentheses includes the author's last name and the page (or pages) on which the quotation appears in that author's work. Readers can then use the author's last name to find the full citation in the bibliography at the end of Rachel's essay, which looks like this:

Berman, Steven. "Homosexuals and Adoption." <u>Rocky Mountain News</u> 23 Feb.

2002: A1.

Here's how the same quotation would be documented in Rachel's essay if she were using APA format:

According to the American Academy of Pediatrics (AAP), children in this situation lose "survivor benefits if a parent dies and legal rights if the parents break up" (Berman, 2002, p. A1).

The citation would appear in her bibliography as follows:

Berman, S. (2002, February 23). Homosexuals and adoption. *Rocky Mountain News,*

p. A1.

Notice that the same basic information is provided, no matter which documentation system is used. But the format for providing that information is different in each system. For example, MLA style requires the use of quotation marks around the title of the article, and the title is capitalized; APA style requires no quotation marks and uses lowercase letters for the title.

In the remainder of this chapter we explain the basic features of the MLA and APA systems of documentation and provide model entries for the most frequently used sources. However, a detailed discussion of these systems is beyond the range of this chapter. If you need more information about either MLA or APA format, consult the official sources for each (see sidebar on this page).

MLA AND APA SOURCES

You can find more extensive information about the MLA and APA documentation systems by consulting the official publications for each system. Notice that the following citations are the appropriate format for each system:

Gibaldi, Joseph. MLA Style Manual and Guide to Scholarly Publishing. 2nd ed. New York: MLA, 1998.

Gibaldi, Joseph. MLA Handbook for Writers of Research Papers. 6th ed. New York: MLA, 2003.

American Psychological Association. (2001). *Publication manual of the American Psychological Association* (5th ed.). Washington, DC: Author.

You can also visit their Web sites: www.mla.org or www.apastyle.org.

FOOTNOTES AND CONTENT NOTES

Traditionally, footnotes were used to document sources. Strictly speaking, a "footnote" appears at the foot of the page, and an "endnote" appears at the end of the paper. However, both MLA and APA now recommend that writers use parenthetical, or in-text, citations of the kind we have been describing here; traditional footnotes are not used for documenting sources. Instead, numbered notes are reserved for additional explanation or discussion that is important but cannot be included within the actual text without a loss of focus. Such notes are called *content notes* (though APA discourages the use of such notes unless they are essential to the discussion).

If you are using MLA style, use footnotes or endnotes to provide additional information about sources or topics discussed in your essay. For example, let's return again to the passage from Rachel Guetter's essay. Let's imagine that Rachel has information about gender roles that relates to her point but is not important enough to include in her argument. In such a case by using a note, Rachel could di-

COMMONLY USED STYLE MANUALS

MLA and APA are the two most popular style guides, but there are other manuals that you may need to consult. Here is a list of other commonly used manuals:

The Chicago Manual of Style, 14th ed. (Chicago: University of Chicago Press, 1993).

Huth, Edward J. *Scientific Style and Format: The CBE Manual for Authors, Editors, and Publishers.* 6th ed. New York: Cambridge University Press, 1994.

Dodd, Janet S., ed. *The ACS Style Guide: A Manual for Authors and Editors,* 2nd edition. New York: Oxford UP, 1997.

American Institute of Physics. *AIP Style Manual.* 4th ed. New York: Amer. Inst. of Physics, 1990.

Iverson, Cheryl, ed. *American Medical Association Manual of Style: A Guide for Authors and Editors.* 9th ed. Baltimore: Williams, 1998.

Harvard Law Review Association. *The Bluebook: A Uniform System of Citation.* 17th ed. Cambridge: Harvard Law Review Assn., 2000.

rect her readers' attention to another useful source that she does not cite directly in this passage. First, using MLA format, she would use a superscript number at the end of the relevant passage as follows:

> It seems reasonable to believe that having both a mother and father benefits children. Women and men have different parenting traits that give a strong balance for the development of a child.[1]

Her note (either a footnote at the bottom of the page or an endnote at the end of her essay) would look like this:

> [1] Many researchers and scholars have examined differences between men and women. For example, see Pease and Pease.

Rachel would then include the full citation for Pease and Pease in her bibliography:

> Pease, Barbara, and Allan Pease. <u>Why Men Don't Listen and Women Can't Read Maps: How We're Different and What to Do about It</u>. New York: Broadway Books, 2001.

If she were using APA format, Rachel would follow the same procedure, but she would use APA style for the citation in her bibliography:

> Pease, B., & Pease, A. (2001). *Why men don't listen and women can't read maps: How we're different and what to do about it.* New York: Broadway Books.

Also, APA format requires that content notes be placed on a separate page at the end of the essay (rather than at the bottom of the page as footnotes).

PARENTHETICAL (IN-TEXT) DOCUMENTATION

As we noted earlier in this chapter, the two most common systems for documenting sources, MLA and APA, both recommend the use of parenthetical, or in-text, citations to cite sources. The basic principle for using these parenthetical citations is the same for both MLA and APA styles: You are providing readers with information about a source that is included in your bibliography. However, there are differences between the two systems. These differences reflect conventions within academic fields regarding which information about a source is most important:

- *MLA style,* which tends to reflect the conventions of the humanities (including the arts, literature, history, and philosophy), emphasizes the author and the author's work and places less emphasis on the date of publication.
- *APA style* emphasizes the author and the date of publication, which is more important in the social science disciplines (for example, psychology, sociology, education, and anthropology).

If you understand these basic differences, you might find it easier to become familiar with the specific differences in the formats used by each documentation system.

In the following sections we describe how to use parenthetical citations in the MLA and APA systems.

The MLA Author/Work Style   In a parenthetical (or in-text) citation in MLA form, the author's last name is followed by a page reference; in some cases a brief title should be included after the author's name. It is not necessary to repeat within the parentheses information that is already provided in the text.

A.   WORK BY A SINGLE AUTHOR

If you were citing page 133 of a book called *Ecological Literacy* by David W. Orr, the parenthetical citation would look like this:

> The idea of environmental sustainability can become the centerpiece of a college curriculum (Orr 133).

Alternatively, you could use Orr's name in your sentence, in which case the citation would include only the page reference:

> David Orr has argued persuasively that that the idea of environmental sustainability should be the centerpiece of a college curriculum (133).

There is no punctuation between the author's name and the page reference when both are cited parenthetically. Note also that the abbreviation "p." or "pp." is not used before the page reference.

B.   WORK WITH MORE THAN ONE AUTHOR

If the work you are citing has two or three authors, use the complete names of all of them in your sentence or include their last names in the parentheses:

> Cleanth Brooks and Robert Penn Warren have argued that "indirection is an essential part of the method of poetry" (573).

or

> Although this sonnet may seem obscure, its meaning becomes clearer when we realize "indirection is an essential part of the method of poetry" (Brooks and Warren 573).

Note that when a sentence ends with a quotation, the parenthetical reference comes before the final punctuation mark. Note also that the ampersand (&) is not used in MLA style.

If you are referring to a work by more than three authors, you can list only the first author's name followed by "et al." (Latin for "and others"):

> These works "derive from a profound disillusionment with modern life" (Baym et al. 910).

C.   WORK WITH A CORPORATE AUTHOR

When a corporate author has a long name, you should include it within the text rather than within parentheses. For example, if you were citing a study by the Council on Environmental Quality called "Ground Water Contamination in the United States," you would do so as follows:

> The Council on Environmental Quality has reported that there is growing evidence of ground water contamination throughout the United States (81).

You could also include the corporate author in the parentheses; omit any initial article:

> There is growing evidence of ground water contamination throughout the United States (Council on Environmental Quality 81).

Although both of these forms are technically correct, the first is preferred because it is easier to read.

D.   WORK WITH MORE THAN ONE VOLUME

When you wish to cite a specific part of a multivolume work, include the volume number between the author and the page reference. In this example we are quoting a passage from the second volume of a two-volume book by Jacques Barzun:

> As Jacques Barzun has argued, "The only hope of true culture is to make classifications broad and criticism particular" (2: 340).

Note that the volume number is given an arabic numeral, and a space separates the colon and the page reference. The abbreviation "vol." is not used unless you wish to cite the entire volume: (Barzun, vol. 2).

E.   MORE THAN ONE WORK BY THE SAME AUTHOR

If you cite more than one work by the same author, you need to make your references distinct so that readers will know exactly which work you are citing. You can do so by putting a comma after the author's name and then adding a shortened form of the title. For example, if you are discussing two novels by Toni Morrison, *Song of Solomon* and *The Bluest Eye,* your citations might look like this.

> Toni Morrison's work is always concerned with the complexities of racial identity. This theme is perhaps explored most painfully in the character of Pecola Breedlove (Morrison, <u>Bluest</u>). But even a crowd of unnamed characters gathered near a hospital, listening to a woman break spontaneously into song and wondering "if one of those things that racial-uplift groups were always organizing was taking place," can become a reminder that race is always part of the picture (Morrison, <u>Song</u> 6).

If it is clear from the context that the quotation is from a work by Morrison, there is no need to include her name in the parentheses. If you're not sure, however, include it. In this example we could have left Morrison's name out of the parentheses because it is clear that we are citing her works.

F.   A QUOTATION WITHIN A CITED WORK

If you want to use a quotation that you have discovered in another book, your reference must show that you acquired this material secondhand and that you have not consulted the original source. Use the abbreviation "qtd. in" (for "quoted in") to make the distinction between the author of the passage being quoted and the author of the work in which you found this passage.

For example, let's say you were reading a book called *The Abstract Wild* by Jack Turner and you came across a quotation by the naturalist William Kittredge that you wanted to use in your argument. You would cite the Kittredge quotation as follows:

> Many people misquote Henry David Thoreau's famous line about wilderness and the preservation of the world. William Kittredge has admitted to making this very

mistake: "For years I misread Thoreau. I assumed he was saying wilderness. . . .
Maybe I didn't want Thoreau to have said wildness, I couldn't figure out what he
meant" (qtd. in Turner 81).

G.   WORK WITHOUT AN AUTHOR LISTED

Sometimes a newspaper or magazine article does not include the name of an author. In
such a case, include a brief version of the title in parentheses. For example, let's say you
wanted to cite an article from *Consumer Reports* entitled "Dry-Cleaning Alternatives" that
listed no author:

> Conventional dry-cleaning, which requires the use of dangerous solvents, can result in
> both air and water pollution. However, if you are concerned about potential environ-
> mental damage caused by dry-cleaning your garments, you have several environmen-
> tally-friendly options, including methods using carbon dioxide and silicone-based
> methods ("Dry-Cleaning" 10).

H.   ELECTRONIC SOURCES

When citing electronic sources, you should follow the same principles you would use
when citing other sources. If you are citing an article from an online journal or newspaper, cite it as you would any print article, using the author's last name or, if you don't
know the author, a brief version of the title of the article. However, there are many different kinds of electronic sources, and you might not have access to the same kinds of information as are available for a published book or journal article. For example, Web sites
don't usually have page numbers, and you might not be able to determine the author of
an online source. In such cases incorporate sufficient information about the source into
your sentence so that readers can easily find the citation in your bibliography:

> On its Web site, the Sustainability Institute maintains information about global climate
> change ("Research").

In this case the author of the Web page being cited is unknown, so a brief version of the
title of the Web page, "Research at the Sustainability Institute," is included in parentheses. Notice that the title of a Web site is enclosed in quotation marks, just like titles of articles in periodicals.

The APA Author/Year Style   The American Psychological Association (APA) requires
that in-text documentation identify the author of the work and the year in which the
work was published; where appropriate, page numbers are also included, preceded by the
abbreviation "p." or "pp." This information should be provided parenthetically; it is not
necessary to repeat any information that has already been provided directly in the
sentence.

A.   ONE WORK BY A SINGLE AUTHOR

If you wished to cite a book by Alan Peshkin titled *Places of Memory,* published in 1997,
you might do so as follows:

> Native American students face the challenge of trying to maintain their cultural
> heritage while assimilating into mainstream American culture (Peshkin, 1997).

or

> Peshkin (1997) has argued that the pressures on Native American students to assimilate into mainstream American culture can contribute to poor academic performance.

If the reference is to a specific chapter or page, that information should also be included. For example:

> Peshkin's (1997) study focuses on what he calls the "dual-world character of the students' lives" (p. 5).

Note that the date of publication (in parentheses) follows the author's name; the page reference (also in parentheses) is placed at the end of the sentence. If the author's name is not included in the sentence, it should be included in the parentheses:

> The "dual-world character" of the lives of many Native American students can create obstacles to their academic success (Peshkin, 1997, p. 5).

B.   WORK WITH TWO OR MORE AUTHORS

If a work has two authors, you should mention the names of both authors every time a reference is made to their work:

> A recent study of industry (Cole & Walker, 1997) argued that . . .

or

> More recently, Cole and Walker (1997) have argued that . . .

Note that the ampersand (&) is used only within parentheses.

Scientific papers often have multiple authors because of the amount of research involved. In the first reference to a work with three to five authors, you should identify each of the authors:

> Hodges, McKnew, Cytryn, Stern, and Kline (1982) have shown . . .

Subsequent references to the same work should use an abbreviated form:

> This method was also used in an earlier study (Hodges et al., 1982).

If a work has six authors (or more), this abbreviated form should be used even for the first reference. If confusion is possible because you must refer to more than one work by the first author, list as many coauthors as necessary to distinguish between the two works.

C.   WORK WITH A CORPORATE AUTHOR

When a work has a corporate author, your first reference should include the full name of the corporation, committee, agency, or institution involved. For example, if you were citing the *Buying Guide 2002,* published by Consumer Reports, you might do so like this:

> There are several strategies you can use to protect yourself when ordering merchandise online (Consumer Reports, 2002, pp. 11–12).

If the corporate name is long, you can abbreviate subsequent references to the same source. If you were citing a report from the Fund for the Improvement of Postsecondary Education (FIPSE), for example, you would use the full name when you first cited it, then use FIPSE for any subsequent references.

D. REFERENCE TO MORE THAN ONE WORK

When the same citation refers to two or more sources, the works should be listed alphabetically according to the first author's surname and separated with semicolons:

> Several studies have examined the social nature of literacy (Finders, 1997; Heath, 1983; Street, 1984; Young, 1994).

If you are referring to more than one work by the same author(s), list the works in the order in which they were published.

> The validity of this type of testing is now well established (Collins, 1988, 1994).

If you refer to more than one work by the same author published in the same year, distinguish individual works by identifying them as "a," "b," "c," and so on:

> These findings have been questioned by Scheiber (1997a, 1997b).

ORGANIZING A BIBLIOGRAPHY

A bibliography is an essential component of any essay or report that includes references to sources. The bibliography, also called a Works Cited or References page, lists all the sources that you have cited in your essay or report. The purpose of a bibliography is to provide information about your sources for your readers.

MLA and APA styles for formatting the entries in your bibliography are described in this chapter. As you'll see, there are some differences between MLA and APA styles. However, no matter which style you use, your bibliography provides the same basic information about your sources:

ITALICS OR UNDERLINES

Traditionally, both APA and MLA recommended underlining titles of books, journals, magazines, and newspapers. However, with the widespread use of word processing, it is now as easy to use italics as it is to underline, and either is generally acceptable. Nevertheless, MLA still recommends the use of underlining to avoid ambiguity; it suggests that students who wish to use italics check with their instructors first.

- The author's name
- The title of the work
- The date of publication

In addition, entries in your bibliography will provide the name of the magazine, newspaper, or journal for any articles you cite as well as page numbers (unless you are citing an electronic source without page numbers, such as a Web page).

Works Cited in MLA Style   In an MLA-style bibliography the works cited are arranged in alphabetical order by the author's last name. Here are the main things to remember when you are creating a bibliography in MLA style:

- Provide the author's first and last name for each entry.
- Capitalize every important word in the titles of books, articles, and journals.
- Underline (or italicize) the titles of books, journals, and newspapers.
- Place the titles of articles, stories, and poems in quotation marks.
- Indent the second and any subsequent lines one-half inch (or five spaces).

Here's how a typical entry for a single-authored book appears in an MLA-style bibliography:

Abram, David. <u>The Spell of the Sensuous</u>. New York: Random, 1996.

Here are the important parts of the entry:

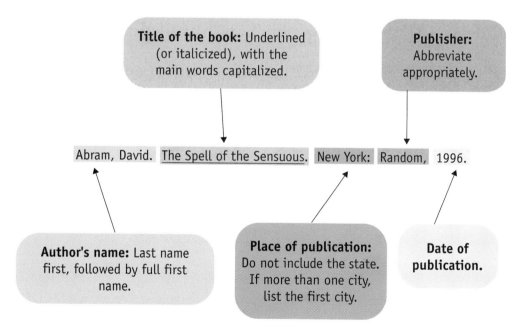

Title of the book: Underlined (or italicized), with the main words capitalized.

Publisher: Abbreviate appropriately.

Abram, David.   <u>The Spell of the Sensuous.</u>   New York: Random,   1996.

Author's name: Last name first, followed by full first name.

Place of publication: Do not include the state. If more than one city, list the first city.

Date of publication.

Notice that there are no page numbers for this entry.

If the work you are citing is a journal article, the entry would look like this:

George, Diana. "From Analysis to Design: Visual Communication in the Teaching of

Writing." <u>College Composition and Communication</u> 54.1 (2002): 11–39.

Here are the parts of this entry:

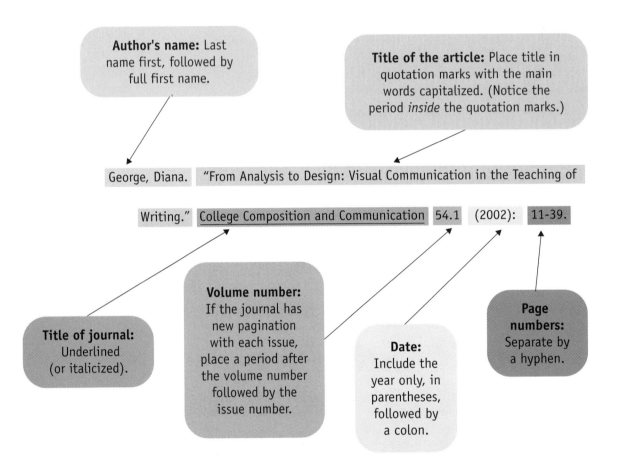

For online sources, you must include the Internet address, or URL, along with two dates: the publication date (if available) and the date you accessed the site. Here's an entry for an online journal article:

Luebke, Steven R. "Using Linked Courses in the General Education Curriculum."

Academic Writing 3 (2002). 16 Dec. 2002 <http://aw.colostate.edu/articles/

luebke_2002.htm>.

Notice where the dates and URL are placed in this entry:

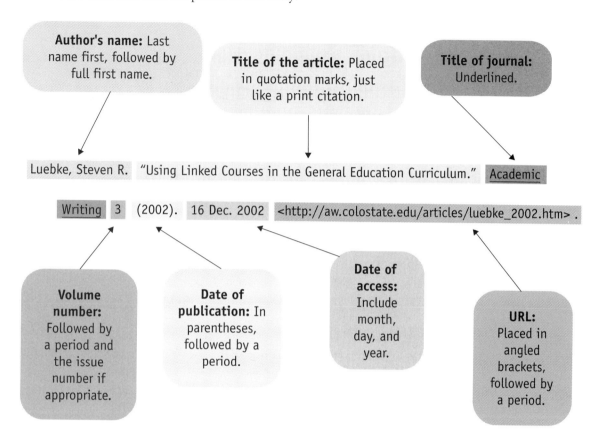

Author's name: Last name first, followed by full first name.

Title of the article: Placed in quotation marks, just like a print citation.

Title of journal: Underlined.

Luebke, Steven R. "Using Linked Courses in the General Education Curriculum." Academic

Writing 3 (2002). 16 Dec. 2002 <http://aw.colostate.edu/articles/luebke_2002.htm> .

Volume number: Followed by a period and the issue number if appropriate.

Date of publication: In parentheses, followed by a period.

Date of access: Include month, day, and year.

URL: Placed in angled brackets, followed by a period.

All entries in MLA format follow these basic principles, but each entry will contain slightly different information, depending on the kind of source that was cited. Keep that in mind as you look for the correct format for the sources you are citing in your bibliography.

A. BOOK WITH ONE AUTHOR

Abram, David. The Spell of the Sensuous. New York: Random, 1996.

B. BOOK WITH TWO OR THREE AUTHORS

Gilbert, Sandra M., and Susan Gubar. The Madwoman in the Attic: The Woman Writer

and the Nineteenth-Century Literary Imagination. New Haven: Yale UP, 1979.

Note that the subtitle is included, set off from the main title by a colon. The second author's name is not inverted, and abbreviations are used for "University Press" to provide a shortened form of the publisher's name. For books with three authors, put commas after the names of the first two authors (invert the name of the first author); separate the second two authors with a comma followed by "and."

C. EDITED BOOK

Glazer, Steven, ed. <u>The Heart of Learning: Spirituality in Education</u>. New York:

Tarcher-Putnam, 1999.

D. BOOK WITH MORE THAN THREE AUTHORS OR EDITORS

Black, Laurel, et al., eds. <u>New Directions in Portfolio Assessment: Practice, Critical

Theory, and Large-Scale Scoring</u>. Portsmouth: Boynton, 1994.

Give the name of the first author or editor only, and add the abbreviation "et al."

E. EDITION AFTER THE FIRST

Tate, Gary, Edward P. J. Corbett, and Nancy Myers, eds. <u>The Writing Teacher's

Sourcebook</u>. 3rd ed. New York: Oxford UP, 1994.

F. WORK IN AN ANTHOLOGY

Owens, Derek. "Sustainable Composition." <u>Ecocomposition: Theoretical and

Pedagogical Approaches</u>. Eds. Christian R. Weisser and Sidney I. Dobrin. Albany:

State U of New York P, 2001. 27–38.

Note that a period comes after the title of the selection but before the second quotation marks. A period is also used to separate the date of publication from the page reference, which is followed by a period.

G. TRANSLATED BOOK

Eco, Umberto. <u>The Aesthetics of Thomas Aquinas</u>. Trans. Hugh Bredin. Cambridge:

Harvard UP, 1988.

H. WORK IN MORE THAN ONE VOLUME

Leckie, Robert. <u>The Wars of America</u>. 2 vols. New York: Harper, 1992.

I. INTRODUCTION, PREFACE, FOREWORD, OR AFTERWORD

Dove, Rita. Foreword. <u>Jonah's Gourd Vine</u>. By Zora Neale Hurston. New York: Harper,

1990. vii–xv.

J. ARTICLE IN AN ENCYCLOPEDIA

Hunt, Roberta M. "Child Welfare." <u>The Encyclopedia Americana</u>. 1993 ed.

In citing material from well-known encyclopedias, give the author's name first, then the article title. If material is arranged alphabetically within the source, which is usually the case, there is no need to include volume and page numbers. You should give the full title of the encyclopedia, the edition (if it is stated), and the year of publication (e.g., 11th ed. 1996). When no edition number is stated, identify the edition by the year of publication (e.g., 1996 ed.). If the author of the article is identified only by initials, look elsewhere within the encyclopedia for a list identifying the names these initials stand for. If the article is unsigned, give the title first. (Note: This same form can be used for other reference books, such as dictionaries and the various editions of *Who's Who*.) For an example of how to cite an electronic encyclopedia, see **T**.

K. GOVERNMENT PUBLICATION

United States. Federal Bureau of Investigation. Handbook of Forensic Science.

Washington: GPO, 1994.

For many government publications the author is unknown. When this is the case, the agency that issued the publication should be listed as the author. State the name of the government (e.g., "United States," "Florida," "United Nations") followed by a period. Then give the name of the agency that issued the work, using abbreviations only if you can do so clearly (e.g., "Bureau of the Census," "National Institute on Drug Abuse," "Dept. of Labor") followed by a period. The underlined title of the work comes next, followed by another period. Then give the place of publication, publisher, and date. Most federal publications are printed in Washington by the Government Printing Office (GPO), but you should be alert for exceptions. (Note: Treat a government pamphlet just as you would a book.)

L. JOURNAL ARTICLE WITH ONE AUTHOR

Hesse, Douglas. "The Place of Creative Nonfiction." College English 65 (2003):

237–241.

The volume number comes after the journal title without any intervening punctuation. The year of publication is included within parentheses after the volume number. A colon separates the year of publication and the page reference. Leave one space after the volume number and one space after the colon.

M. JOURNAL ARTICLE PAGINATED ANEW IN EACH ISSUE

Williams, Jeffrey. "The Life of the Mind and the Academic Situation." College Literature

23.3 (1996): 128–146.

In this case the issue number is included immediately after the volume number, and the two are separated by a period without any intervening space.

N. ARTICLE FROM A MAGAZINE PUBLISHED MONTHLY

Brownlee, Shannon. "The Overtreated American." Atlantic Monthly Jan. 2003:

89–91.

Instead of citing the volume number, give the month and year of the issue. Abbreviate the month when it has more than four letters. (May, June, and July are spelled out.) For an example of how to list an article from a magazine published monthly that was obtained through a computer database, see **R**.

O. ARTICLE FROM A MAGAZINE ISSUED WEEKLY

Kalb, Claudia. "Get Up and Get Moving." <u>Newsweek</u> 20 Jan. 2003: 59–64.

The form is the same as for an article in a magazine that is issued monthly, but you add the day immediately before the month. Note that a hyphen between page numbers indicates consecutive pages. When an article is printed on nonconsecutive pages — beginning on page 34, for example, and continuing on page 78 — give only the first page number and a plus sign: 34+.

P. ARTICLE FROM A DAILY NEWSPAPER

Reich, Howard. "Limited Ambition." <u>Chicago Tribune</u> 9 Feb. 1997, final ed., sec. 7: 13.

If more than one edition is available on the date in question, specify the edition immediately after the date. If the city of publication is not part of a locally published newspaper's name, identify the city in brackets after the newspaper title. Because newspapers often consist of separate sections, you should cite the section number if each section has separate pagination. If a newspaper consists of only one section or if the pagination is continuous from one section to the next, then you do not need to include the section number. If separately paginated sections are identified by letters, omit the section reference (sec.) but include the letter of the section with the page number (e.g., B7 or D19). If the article is unsigned, begin the entry with the title of the article; alphabetize the article under its title, passing over small words such as "a" and "the." For an example of how to cite a newspaper article accessed through a subscription service such as FirstSearch or Lexis-Nexis, see **U**.

Q. EDITORIAL

Terzian, Philip. "Armed Forces Work Just Fine without Draft." Editorial. <u>Albany Times</u>
<u>Union</u> 14 Jan. 2003: A14.

Editorials are identified as such between the title of the article and the title of the newspaper or magazine.

R. PRINTED MATERIAL ACCESSED FROM A PERIODICALLY PUBLISHED DATABASE ON CD-ROM

Many periodicals and reference works such as bibliographies are now available on CD-ROMs, which are sometimes updated. Here's an example of a print article from a journal called *Managing Office Technology* that was found on a CD-ROM issued by UMI-ProQuest:

Holtzman, Henry. "Team Management: Its Time Has Come . . . Again." <u>Managing</u>
<u>Office Technology</u> Feb. 1994: 8. <u>ABI/Inform</u>. CD-ROM. UMI-ProQuest. Oct.
1994.

Notice that this entry includes the same information that would be provided for a magazine or journal article: author (if known), article title, journal title, date of print publication, and page reference. In addition, cite the database you used (in this case, ABI/Inform), the medium through which you accessed it (CD-ROM), and, if available, the vendor that made this medium available (here, UMI-ProQuest). Conclude with the date of electronic publication.

S.   EXCLUSIVELY ELECTRONIC MATERIAL ACCESSED FROM A PERIODICALLY PUBLISHED DATABASE

Many reference works today are published exclusively in electronic form on media such as CD-ROM and computer diskettes.

> African Development Bank. "1995 AFDB Indicative Learning Program." National Trade
>
> Data Bank. CD-ROM. U.S. Commercial Service. Mar. 1996.

Give the author's name (a corporate author in this case), the title of the material in quotation marks, the title of the database (here, *National Trade Data Bank*), the publication medium (in this case, CD-ROM), the vendor (here, U.S. Commercial Service), and the date it was published electronically. Note that the title of the database is underlined.

T.   NONPERIODICAL PUBLICATION ON CD-ROM

Encyclopedias and similar nonperiodical reference works are now regularly available on CD-ROM. Here is an entry for an article from *The Academic American Encyclopedia* on CD-ROM:

> Hogan, Robert. "Abbey Theater." The Academic American Encyclopedia. CD-ROM.
>
> Danbury: Grolier, 1995.

If no author is identified, begin with the work's title; if no author or title is available, begin with the title of the product consulted.

If you are citing an article from an encyclopedia that is available online, use the format for an article accessed through an online database (see **U**).

U.   PRINTED PUBLICATION ACCESSED THROUGH A DATABASE SUBSCRIPTION SERVICE

> Jeffers, Thomas L. "Plagiarism High and Low." Commentary 114.3 (2002): 54–61.
>
> Lexis-Nexis. State U of New York-Albany Lib. 28 Dec. 2002.

Follow the same pattern you would for the print equivalent (in this case, a magazine article), then add the underlined title of the database (if known), the name of the service (in this case, Lexis-Nexis), and how you accessed it (in this example, through the SUNY-Albany Libraries). Then include the date you accessed the article, followed by the URL of the service's home page (if known) in angled brackets < >.

V.   ARTICLE FROM AN ONLINE PERIODICAL

> Sands, Peter. "Pushing and Pulling Toward the Middle." Kairos 7.3 (2002).
>
> 15 Oct. 2002 <http://english.ttu.edu/kairos/7.3/
>
> binder2.html?coverweb.html#de>.

Cite the article as you would for a print article, but add the date you accessed the article just after the publication date (which is in parentheses followed by a period). Then add the URL in angled brackets. Remember to place a period at the end of the entry.

Follow this same pattern for articles from any online periodicals, whether they are from newspapers, popular magazines, or scholarly journals: Cite the article as you would a print article, then add the date you accessed it and the URL. The same patterns holds for on-line books.

W. THESIS PUBLISHED ONLINE

Increasingly, authors make their work available on Web sites. Citing these Web sites can be tricky because you do not always have access to all the publication information. Here's an entry for a thesis that the author published on a Web site:

Formaro, Tom. "Argumentation on the World Wide Web." MA thesis. <u>Some Random</u>

<u>Stuff (and a Thesis)</u>. 9 May 2001. 17 Nov. 2002 <http://users.rcn.com/mackey/

thesis/thesis.html>.

Notice that this entry follows the same pattern as an online periodical (see **V**): the author's name first, followed by the title of the work and of the Web site and date of publication; then add the date you accessed the text and the URL (in angled brackets). If there is no date of publication, use "n.d." for "no date."

X. ARTICLE ON A WEB SITE

There are many different kinds of Web sites where you can find useful information about a topic. Many sites are maintained by advocacy groups, government or nongovernment organizations, and educational institutions. If you are using information from such a Web site, follow the same basic principles for citing the source that you would follow for more conventional print sources. Here's an entry for an article found on the Web site for an advocacy group called the Center for a New American Dream:

"In the Market? Think Green: The Center for a New American Dream's Guide to

Environmentally Preferable Purchasing." <u>Center for a New American Dream</u>. 8

Aug. 2001 <http://www.newdream.org/buygreen/index.html>.

Notice that since there is no author listed on the site, the title of the article is listed first, in quotation marks. The organization hosting the Web site is listed next, followed by the date of access and the URL of the article being referenced.

Y. PERSONAL HOME PAGE

White, Crystal. Home page. 13 Jan. 2003. 22 June 2003

<http://www.geocities.com/lfnxphile/>.

Z. INTERVIEW

Nelson, Veronica. Personal interview. 16 Aug. 1997.

If you interview someone, alphabetize the interview under the surname of the person interviewed. Indicate whether it was a personal interview, telephone interview, or e-mail
interview.

AA. NEWSGROUP, MAILING LIST OR DISCUSSION BOARD POSTING

There are several different kinds of online discussion forums, including mailing lists and
newsgroups. This example is from a Web-based discussion board:

> Mountainman72. "Re: Avalanche Question." Online posting. 10 Jan. 2003. NEice Talk.
>
> 12 Jan. 2003 <http://www.neice.com/cgi-bin/ultimatebb.cgi?ubb=forum&f=1>.

Notice that the author's name (or pseudonym) is first, followed by the title of the posting, the description *Online posting*, the date of the posting, the name of the forum (if
known), the date of access, and the URL.

For a mailing list or newsgroup posting, include the name of the mailing list or newsgroup after the date of the posting, as follows:

> Fleischer, Cathy. "Colearn Logins." Online posting. 9 Dec. 2002. CoLEARN Research
>
> Team Discussion List. 5 Jan. 2003 <researchteam@serv1.ncte.org>.

References in APA Style   In APA style, the bibliography is arranged alphabetically by
the author's last name. The date of publication is emphasized by placing it within parentheses immediately after the author's name. In APA style, the bibliography is arranged alphabetically by the author's last name. The date of publication is emphasized by placing
it within parentheses immediately after the author's name. The APA *Publication Manual*
(5th ed.) recommends a hanging indent style of a half-inch, or five spaces, which is what
is shown in the following illustrations.

Here are the main things to keep in mind when preparing a bibliography in APA
style:

- Provide the author's surname, followed by an initial for the first name.
- Place the date in parentheses and follow it with a period; the date should always
  be the second element in an entry.
- Capitalize only the first word and any proper nouns of any title and subtitle (if
  there is one) in the entry.
- Italicize titles of books, journals, magazines, and newspapers.
- Do *not* place quotation marks around the titles of articles or chapters and do *not*
  italicize or underline them.

In APA style, a typical entry for a single-authored book looks like this:

> Geertz, C. (2000). *Available light: Anthropological reflections on philosophical topics.*
>
> Princeton, NJ: Princeton University Press.

Here are the important parts of the entry:

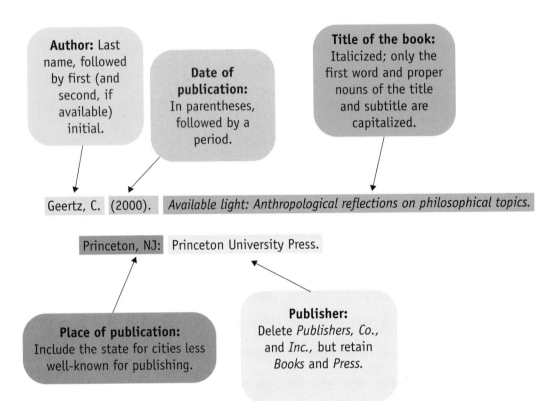

Author: Last name, followed by first (and second, if available) initial.

Date of publication: In parentheses, followed by a period.

Title of the book: Italicized; only the first word and proper nouns of the title and subtitle are capitalized.

Geertz, C. (2000). *Available light: Anthropological reflections on philosophical topics.*

Princeton, NJ: Princeton University Press.

Place of publication: Include the state for cities less well-known for publishing.

Publisher: Delete *Publishers, Co.,* and *Inc.,* but retain *Books* and *Press.*

Here is an entry for a journal article:

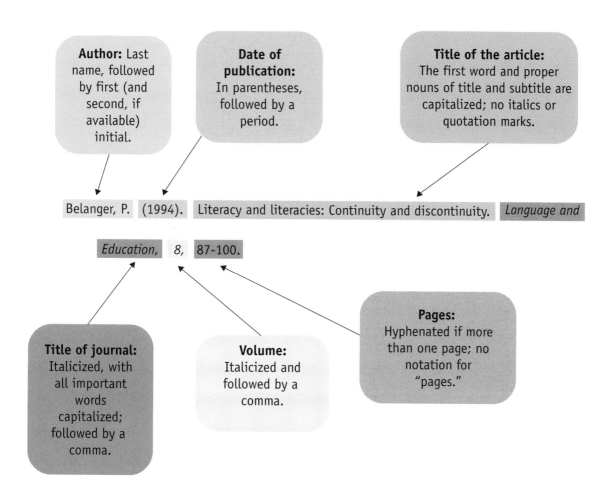

Notice the differences between the entry for a journal article and the following example of an entry for a newspaper article:

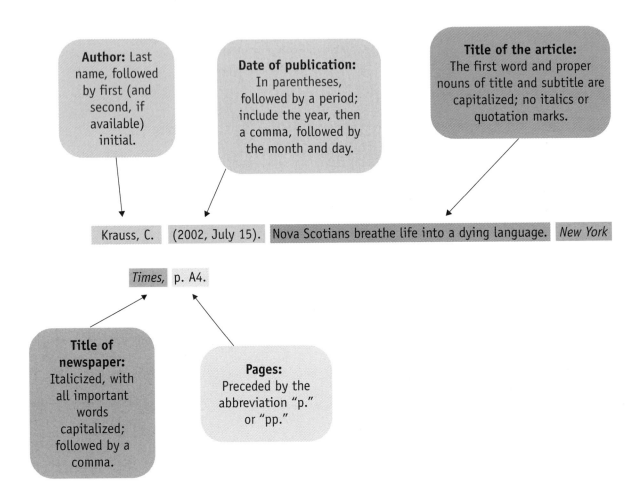

Notice that for newspaper articles the date includes the month and day, along with the year, in parentheses; for monthly magazines, include only the year and month. Notice, too, that the page numbers are preceded by an abbreviation, unlike the entry for a journal article.

If you were citing a newspaper article that you retrieved from a database subscription service, your entry would look like this:

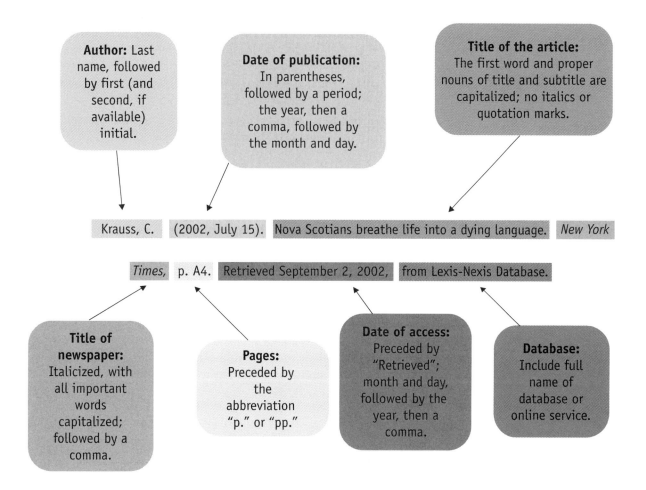

Author: Last name, followed by first (and second, if available) initial.

Date of publication: In parentheses, followed by a period; the year, then a comma, followed by the month and day.

Title of the article: The first word and proper nouns of title and subtitle are capitalized; no italics or quotation marks.

Krauss, C. (2002, July 15). Nova Scotians breathe life into a dying language. *New York Times,* p. A4. Retrieved September 2, 2002, from Lexis-Nexis Database.

Title of newspaper: Italicized, with all important words capitalized; followed by a comma.

Pages: Preceded by the abbreviation "p." or "pp."

Date of access: Preceded by "Retrieved"; month and day, followed by the year, then a comma.

Database: Include full name of database or online service.

A. BOOK WITH ONE AUTHOR

Loy, D. (1998). *Nonduality: A study in comparative philosophy.* Amherst, NY: Humanity

Books.

Note that the author's first name is indicated only by an initial. Capital letters are used only for the first word of the title and the first word of the subtitle if there is one. (But when a proper name appears within a title, it retains the capitalization it would normally receive; for example: *A history of ideas in Brazil.*) The name of the publisher, Humanity Books, is given in its entirety. A period comes after the parentheses surrounding the date of publication and also after the title and the publisher.

B. BOOK WITH TWO OR MORE AUTHORS

Blitz, M., & Hurlbert, C. M. (1998). *Letters for the living: Teaching writing in a violent*

age. Urbana, IL: National Council for Teachers of English.

An ampersand (&) is used to separate the names of two authors. When there are three or more authors, separate their names with commas, keeping each name reversed, and put an ampersand immediately before the last author's name.

C. EDITED BOOK

Street, B. V. (Ed.). (2001). *Literacy and development: Ethnographic perspectives.*

New York: Routledge.

The abbreviation for editor is "Ed."; it should be capitalized and included within parentheses between the name of the editor and the date of publication. The abbreviation for editors is "Eds." Give the names of all editors, no matter how many there are.

D. ARTICLE OR CHAPTER IN AN EDITED BOOK

Faigley, L. (1999). Beyond imagination: The internet and global digital literacy. In G. E.

Hawisher & C. L. Selfe (Eds.), *Passions, pedagogies, and 21st-century technolo-*

gies (pp. 129–139). Logan, UT: Utah State University Press.

Notice that the editor's name is not inverted when it is not in the author's position. Notice, too, that the title of the article or chapter is *not* placed in quotation marks. Use a comma to separate the editor from the title of the edited book. The pages between which the material can be found appear within parentheses immediately after the book title. Use "p." for page and "pp." for pages.

E. TRANSLATED BOOK

Calasso, R. (1993). *The marriage of Cadmus and Harmony* (T. Parks, Trans.). New

York: Random. (Original work published 1988).

Within parentheses immediately after the book title, give the translator's name followed by a comma and the abbreviation "Trans." If the original work was published earlier, include this information at the end.

F. SUBSEQUENT EDITIONS OF A BOOK

Hopkins, B. R. (1993). *A legal guide to starting and managing a nonprofit organization*

(2nd ed.). New York: Wiley.

The edition is identified immediately after the title. Note that edition is abbreviated "ed." — with a lowercase "e" — and should not be confused with "Ed." for editor; it is also placed in parentheses.

G. BOOK WITH A CORPORATE AUTHOR

American Red Cross. (1993). *Standard first aid.* St. Louis, MO: Mosby.

H.   MULTIVOLUME WORK

Eisenstein, E. (1979). *The printing press as an agent of change: Communications and*

cultural transformations in early-modern Europe (Vol. 2). Cambridge, England:

Cambridge University Press.

The volume number is included within parentheses immediately after the title.

I.   JOURNAL ARTICLE WITH ONE AUTHOR

Butler, A. C. (1996). The effect of welfare benefit levels on poverty among single-

parent families. *Social Problems, 43,* 94–115.

Do not use quotation marks around the article title. Capitalize all important words in the journal title and italicize. Put a comma after the journal title and then give the volume and page numbers. Abbreviations are not used for "volume" and "page." To distinguish between the numbers, italicize the volume number and put a comma between it and the page numbers.

J.   JOURNAL ARTICLE WITH MORE THAN ONE AUTHOR

Nugent, J. K., Lester, B. M., Greene, S. M., Wieczorek-Deering, D., & O'Mahoney, P.

(1996). The effects of maternal alcohol consumption and cigarette smoking dur-

ing pregnancy on acoustic cry analysis. *Child Development, 67,* 1806–1815.

Note that all authors' names are listed in the same format: last name followed by a comma and then the first (and second, if available) initial; commas separate all the names.

K.   JOURNAL ARTICLE PAGINATED ANEW IN EACH ISSUE

Major, B. (1993). Gender, entitlement, and the distribution of family labor. *Journal of*

Social Issues, 49(3), 141–159.

When each issue of a journal begins with page 1, include the issue number in parentheses immediately after the italicized volume number. Do not italicize the issue number.

L.   ARTICLE FROM A MAGAZINE ISSUED MONTHLY

Baker, K. (1997, February). Searching the window into nature's soul. *Smithsonian, 745,*

94–104.

Include the month of issue after the year of publication in parentheses immediately after the author's name. Include the volume number. Follow the same form for an article in a weekly magazine issued on a specific day, but add the day after the month:

Hazen, R. M. (1991, February 25). Why my kids hate science. *Newsweek, 331,* 7.

M.   ARTICLE FROM A DAILY NEWSPAPER

Bishop, J. E. (1996, November 13). Heart disease may actually be rising. *The Wall*

Street Journal, p. B6.

Place the exact date of issue within parentheses immediately after the author. After the newspaper title, specify the page number(s). Include *The* if it is part of the newspaper title.

N. GOVERNMENT DOCUMENT

> U.S. Department of Labor. (1993). *Teaching the SCANS competencies.* Washington,
>
> DC: U.S. Government Printing Office.

List the agency that produced the document as the author if no author is identified. Within parentheses immediately after the document title, give the publication number (which is assigned to the document by the government), if available.

O. ANONYMOUS WORK

> A breath of fresh air. (1991, April 29). *Time, 187,* 49.

Alphabetize the work under the first important word in the title, and follow the form for the type of publication in question (in this case a magazine published weekly).

P. JOURNAL ARTICLE RETRIEVED ONLINE

If the article you are citing is from a print journal that also appears online, then cite the article as you normally would but indicate that you viewed the electronic version as follows:

> Smith, K. (2001). Critical conversations in difficult times [Electronic version].
>
> *English Education, 33*(2), 153–165.

However, if the article you are citing might be different online (for instance, it includes additional text or charts) or if it has no page numbers, then indicate when you accessed it and include the URL:

> Smith, K. (2001). Critical conversations in difficult times. *English Education, 33*(2),
>
> 153–165. Retrieved December 12, 2002, from http://www.ncte.org/pdfs/
>
> subscribers-only/ee/0332-jan01/EE0332Critical.pdf

Q. ONLINE JOURNAL ARTICLE

For an article from a journal that appears only online (and not in print form), include the date of access and the URL of the site where the article was located:

> Lassonde, C. A. (2002). Learning from others: Literacy perspectives of
>
> middle-school English teachers. *Networks, 5*(3). Retrieved January 15, 2003,
>
> from http://www.oise.utoronto.ca/~ctd/networks/journal/Vol%205(3).2002dec/
>
> Lassonde.html

Notice that there is no period after the URL.

R. INTERVIEW

Interviews are not considered recoverable data and should not be included in the References.

A Checklist for Documentation

1. Remember to document any direct quotation, any idea that has come from someone else's work, and any fact or statistic that is not widely known. **2.** Be sure to enclose all quotations in quotation marks. **3.** Make sure that paraphrases are in your own words but still accurately reflect the content of the original material. **4.** Remember that every source cited in your text should have a corresponding entry in the bibliography. **5.** Try to vary the introductions you use for quotations and paraphrases. **6.** When you mention authorities by name, try to identify who they are so that your audience can evaluate the source. (For example, "According to Ira Glasser, Executive Director of the American Civil Liberties Union, recent congressional legislation violates . . . .") However, you need not identify well-known figures. **7.** If in doubt about whether to document a source, you would probably be wise to document it. But be careful not to overdocument your paper.

PREPARING YOUR FINAL DRAFT

After investing considerable time in researching, drafting, and revising your paper, be sure to allow sufficient time for editing your final draft. If you rush this stage of the process, the work that you submit for evaluation might not adequately reflect the investment of time you gave to the project as a whole. Unless instructed otherwise, you should be guided by the rules in the following checklist.

A Checklist for Manuscript Form

1. Papers should be typed or word processed. Use nonerasable 8 1/2-by-11-inch white paper. Type on one side of each page. Double-space all lines, leaving a margin of one inch on all sides. **2.** In the upper left corner of page 1 or on a separate title page, include the following information: your name, your instructor's name, the course and section number, and the date the essay is submitted. **3.** Number each page in the upper right corner, 1.2 inches from the top. If using MLA-style documentation, type your last name immediately before the page number. If using APA-style documentation, type a shortened version of the title (one or two words) before the number. **4.** Make sure that you consistently follow a documentation style that is acceptable to your instructor. **5.** Any quotation of more than four lines in an MLA-style paper or more than forty words in an APA-style paper should be set off from the rest of the text. Begin a new line, indenting one inch (or ten spaces) to form the left margin of the quotation. The indention means that you are quoting, so additional quotation marks are unnecessary in this case (except for quotations within the quotation). **6.** Proofread your paper carefully. If your instructor allows ink corrections, make them as neatly as you can. Redo any page that has numerous or lengthy corrections. **7.** If you have used a word processor for your paper, be sure to separate pages that have been printed on a continuous sheet. Use a paper clip or staple to bind the pages together.

PART III

NEGOTIATING DIFFERENCES

8

OWNERSHIP

SHIP

WHO OWNS WORDS

AND IDEAS?

For students, plagiarism is usually a straightforward matter: If you present someone else's words or ideas as your own, you have plagiarized. In most schools, if you are caught doing so, the consequences can be severe, including even dismissal from school. The whole matter of plagiarism rests on an assumption that each of us has our own ideas and is responsible for our own words. In this sense, we "own" those words and ideas; we "own" our intellectual work. And we're not allowed to "steal" others' words or ideas. But the ownership of intellectual work — the matter of intellectual property — is not as straightforward as it might seem. It's easy to see plagiarism when a student hands in a paper that was written by someone else; in effect, that student is submitting as his or her own someone else's intellectual property. But what if you asked a roommate or a relative for help with an essay you are writing for one of your classes? What if that person suggested a way for you to reword a few sentences or a paragraph? Or let's say that person advised you to reorganize your essay to make it more coherent and effective. If you did so and then submitted your essay to your teacher, is that essay "yours"? Or does it belong partly to the roommate or relative who helped you? Who "owns" the ideas and words in that essay? ■ This example suggests how difficult it can be to determine the source — or "owner" — of an idea or a phrase. It also suggests how little of what we tend to think of as our own intellectual work really is the result of an exclusively individual effort. It's common to ask a friend how a sentence sounds when you are writing an essay or a letter. It's also common for students to work together on projects or problems or laboratory experiments. And if it's common for students to do so, it's even more so for professionals in many fields. Scientists rarely work alone, and even those who do usually draw on the previous experiments of other scientists. The same is true of professionals in every kind of field or business. Collaboration is the norm in many settings. And when we collaborate, the matter of whose intellectual property results becomes complicated. ■ Moreover, the ideas that are available to us often come from somewhere else altogether. For example, if you are writing a poem about an ill-fated romantic relationship, where did the idea for that poem come from? From your own experience? From your own imagination? From a movie you happened to see? From a story a friend told you? Are you "stealing" someone else's intellectual property because you have read dozens of love poems written by others? And if you write that poem in an established poetic format, such as a sonnet, are you stealing that format because you didn't create it yourself? ■ Intellectual property, of course, is not just an ethical matter; it is a legal and economic matter as well. The U.S. Constitution provides for the establishment of copyright laws to protect the creators of intellectual property. Copyright laws have existed since 1790, when Congress first passed a law decreeing that an author or artist "owned" a work he or she created for fourteen years. But even when intellectual property is defined legally, questions inevitably arise about who owns specific words or ideas and who has the right to use them (see Con-Text on page 213). The idea of the "fair use" of copyrighted materials, for example, provides for exceptions to protected works. But even when such a principle is spelled out in the legal code, it can never answer all the questions that might arise when we try to determine who owns specific words or a specific idea. ■ Despite these difficulties, the fact that we live in a culture based on private property often means that we have to try to determine the ownership of intellectual property. The authors of the essays in this section all address this need as it emerges in schools and in the commercial culture. They examine questions of the ownership of words and ideas in ways that may help you to appreciate the complexity of intellectual property and consider the many interests that people have in trying to determine who owns words and ideas. As a group, these essays also raise a broader question about intellectual property: Is it really possible for anyone to "own" words or ideas?

CON-TEXT: What Is Fair Use?

1 Congress favored nonprofit educational uses over commercial uses. Copies used in education, but made or sold at monetary profit, may not be favored. Courts also favor uses that are "transformative" or that are not mere reproductions. Fair use is more likely when the copyrighted work is "transformed" into something new or of new utility, such as quotations incorporated into a paper, and perhaps pieces of a work mixed into a multimedia product for your own teaching needs or included in commentary or criticism of the original. For teaching purposes, however, multiple copies of some works are specifically allowed, even if not "transformative." The Supreme Court underscored that conclusion by focusing on these key words in the statute: "including multiple copies for classroom use." . . .

Many characteristics of a work can affect the application of fair use. For example, several recent court decisions have concluded that the unpublished "nature" of histori-cal correspondence can weigh against fair use. The courts reasoned that copyright owners should have the right to determine the circumstances of "first publication." The authorities are split, however, on whether a published work that is currently out of print should receive special treatment. Courts more readily favor the fair use of nonfiction rather than fiction.

SOURCE: "What is 'Fair Use'?" The Consortium of Educational Technology in University Systems.

① JAY MATHEWS, "Standing Up for the Power of Learning"

In the fall of 2001, a student at the Georgia Institute of Technology was accused of cheating because he had discussed an assignment in his computer science course with a friend. By talking about the assignment, the student violated an honor code in that computer science course that prohibits collaboration among students. According to that honor code, "at no time is it acceptable for you to share your solutions to the homework assignments with other students, whether these solutions are complete or partial, nor is it acceptable to compare your solutions with other students." On the surface, such a stipulation might seem reasonable, since students are usually graded on their own ability to do the required work in a course. But as Jay Mathews suggests in the following essay, a closer look at this case raises some tricky questions. For one thing, is it cheating if a student learns by working together with a classmate? Do students always learn by themselves? And if a student learns by getting help from someone else, does that mean that the work that student submits to a teacher — such as the solution to a problem in computer science — does not "belong" to that student? In writing about the incident at Georgia Tech, and in praising that university's willingness to change its policy as a result of the incident, Mathews argues for a position on cheating that tries to hold students accountable for doing their own work but at the same time acknowledges the reality that learning is often not an exclusively individual activity. As you read, consider whether Mathews's position on this issue is realistic. Is it possible to distinguish between collaboration and cheating in the way he suggests? Do schools have any choice but to do so? Mathews reports on education for the *Washington Post* and is the author of *Class Struggles: What's Right (and Wrong) with America's Best Public Schools* (1998). This essay appeared in his column in the *Washington Post* in 2002.

Standing Up for the Power of Learning
JAY MATHEWS

1 I am barely capable of booting up my office computer in the morning. One of those neighborhood computer consultants just paid a house call because I can't get my new CD burner even to acknowledge my existence. But that did not stop me from telling Georgia Tech in a recent column how to monitor homework in its freshman course, Computer Studies 1321.*

I had help from one of the students in the course, a graduate of one of the Washington area's best high schools, who had the disagreeable experience of finding this e-mail addressed to him just before he was to leave on a family skiing vacation last December: "Your name has been turned into the Associate Dean of Students, Karen Boyd, for suspicion of academic misconduct."

A computer check designed to catch cheaters had found similarity between his answers and that of a classmate with whom he had discussed a CS 1321 homework assignment. He had worked hard to earn a B in a course that had started disastrously for him. He could have punted the assignment. It was only 2 percent of his grade. But he wanted to get ready for the final exam. He was eager to learn, which was his big mistake.

The CS 1321 honor code said "at no time is it acceptable for you to share your solutions to the homework assignments with other students, whether these solutions are complete or partial, nor is it acceptable to compare your solutions with other students." Students complained of the reign of terror atmosphere the rule encouraged — don't say anything to anybody because if your approach pops up on their homework, you're screwed.

5 My informant thought it made no sense for the course to prohibit students from working together and from consulting outside materials when dealing with difficult homework assignments. He thought his discussion with a classmate was useful discourse that could only make them better students. And now, it turns out, he was

right. Acting like the great university it is, Georgia Tech ordered a study of the course. With astonishing speed, it announced Thursday that it was changing the rules in just the way the freshman told me they ought to be changed.

News stories on the university's announcement missed the importance of this. They emphasized that three fourths of the 187 Georgia Tech students accused of cheating on CS 1321 homework last fall were found guilty and punished with everything from a zero on the assignment to suspension. Everybody knew weeks ago that was going to happen. Many freshmen, like my informant, accepted the university's strong recommendation that they swallow their punishment, in his case a C in the course, and move on, even though they felt they had done nothing wrong.

Other universities, such as MIT, do not prohibit students from working together on difficult assignments. They are simply required to mark the places where they collaborated. That makes sense to me.

*Computer Science 1321, Introduction to Computers, is described in the Georgia Tech catalog as follows: "Foundations of computing with an emphasis on the design, construction, and analysis of algorithms. Laboratory-based instruction to computers and software tools."

COLLABORATIVE LEARNING

Also referred to as "cooperative learning," collaborative learning has been extensively studied by education researchers. Although there are different kinds of collaborative learning and there is disagreement among scholars on some of the specifics of such learning, most agree that collaborative learning benefits students. Many studies show positive results — including higher academic achievement — when students work together. According to Roger T. Johnson and David Johnson, researchers who have studied cooperative learning, "The fact that working together to achieve a common goal produces higher achievement and greater productivity than does working alone is so well confirmed by so much research that it stands as one of the strongest principles of social and organizational psychology. Cooperative learning is indicated whenever learning goals are highly important, mastery and retention are important, a task is complex or conceptual, problem solving is desired, divergent thinking or creativity is desired, quality of performance is expected, and higher-level reasoning strategies and critical thinking are needed" ("Cooperative Learning: An Overview").

Every successful educational enterprise I know encourages student discussion and cooperation. The anti-collaboration rule was even unusual for Georgia Tech, and only found in that freshman course. I suggested the computerized copying checks be reserved for tests, the proper place to determine what a student has learned. Forcing undergraduates to watch what they say to friends about their homework sounded too much like the rules for discourse in the Chinese universities I used to visit.

The column produced an extraordinary volume of e-mail. That was another sign of my ignorance. I had no idea there were so many people interested in this stuff. (Some messages also discussed my peculiar views on cheating, a separate issue which I will take up in a future column.)

Interestingly, the students, teachers and experts who sent the e-mails were split evenly on the no-collaboration and no-outside-materials rules. Stephen Miller, a senior technical specialist for FleetBoston Financial, said, "Restricting student access to resources in their effort to maximize their learning potential is simply unbelievable. Decreeing that the only valid resources are Georgia Tech staff or course materials is the height of arrogance. To forbid Computer Science students from seeking any help from other students on their homework is to remove one of the prime and fundamental learning tools. Collaboration and cooperation, especially in the computer science field, is one of the tried and true ways of advancement and improvement."

10 But Meredith Skeels, an undergraduate at the University of Washington, said it was vitally important to struggle through your coding assignments on your own, at least while you are learning. "Programming is all about problem solving," she

said. "I will be the first to say that it can be very frustrating when you just cannot get the code to work. It drives you crazy. You walk to class thinking about it and you wake up in the morning thinking of some new way to fix it. That is part of the process that makes you a good programmer."

I had expected Georgia Tech to appoint a committee, give it several months to work up some recommendations, and then stick the results in a drawer until the dean in charge pulled them out to read during a vacation as an excuse to limit conversation with his mother-in-law. That is the way such matters would be handled by some of our better known liberal arts universities, the ones thick with Georgian architecture and administrators who used to be lawyers, economists or English professors. I figured it would be a year before any decisions were made, long after most people had forgotten the cheating charges of 2001.

Imagine my shock to learn Thursday that Georgia Tech's task force on introductory computer science courses had already made its recommendations, and many had been implemented immediately. It must be nice to have engineers in charge. They seem more interested in getting things done than making certain all the bureaucratic niceties are observed.

In its report, the task force acknowledged that "individual programming skills are the foundation upon which successful group programming projects are based" but "we also know that collaboration supports learning." The nine-member group said "many of us have had the experience of having a 'bug' in our program, explaining the program to another person in hopes that he or she might tell us what is wrong, and in the process of explaining, suddenly understanding why the program does not work!"

The most feasible way to check on student programming skills, the report said, was interactive testing in a computer lab. As for homework in CS 1321, it recommended that "any and all kinds of collaboration be allowed . . . including sharing portions of others' programs if that is what is needed for a student to learn to develop a working solution to the assignment." Using such help, as well as outside sources, would be fine "so long as attribution is made."

15 And that, said Bob McMath, a member of the task force and the vice-provost for undergraduate studies, is the way it is going to be, starting right now. "This incident has caused the Georgia Tech community to look closely at the way we teach and the way we hold each other accountable for our actions," he said in a statement. "Because of the serious and thoughtful efforts of many people, I believe that we are coming out of this experience a stronger and better university."

The freshman who told me his story still declines to be identified and is not happy that the university has not wiped clean the records of the many students who, he feels, were punished for doing the best job they could under rules that made no sense.

"I do not like the idea that for the rest of my academic career I will have to explain what happened to me," he said. He is so sour on Georgia Tech that he is transferring to another school, but he said he is "glad that the policy is changed for all of the students that are now going to take the computer science courses."

CONTEXT

As of fall 2002, the collaboration policy in Computer Science 1321 at Georgia Tech stated, "Because homework assignments are now not used for assessment, we can now greatly relax the constraints on collaboration with respect to these assignments. Effective this semester, any and all forms of collaboration between students in CS 1321 are permitted, including the sharing of solutions if that is what is needed for a student to learn to develop a working solution to a given homework problem. . . . As has always been the case, however, plagiarism is not allowed. If you use sources other than those provided for everyone in the course (i.e., instructors, teaching assistants, the textbook, the course web site, the course newsgroups, the lectures, or the recitations), you must give appropriate credit to those sources. Note that so long as you give credit where credit is due, your grade will not be affected nor will you be charged with academic misconduct. On the other hand, a failure to give appropriate credit to sources of help (other than course materials or personnel as noted above) will be treated as plagiarism, a violation of Georgia Tech's Student Conduct Code."

I think the freshman, and the many parents, students, teachers and alumni who protested the non-collaboration rule, should be proud of standing up for the power of learning from one's peers. And I can think of several other universities who might benefit from studying how Georgia Tech handled this. Its adminis- trators wasted no time in disassembling the trouble-prone course, examining each of its parts, and putting it back together in a way that will help young people come to understand the mysteries of the digital world with a minimum of confu- sion and trauma.

Questions for Discussion

1. Why do you think Mathews begins this essay by admitting that he hired a consultant to help him with his computer? How does that anecdote relate to his overall argument? **2.** Mathews includes quotations from two email messages he received from readers of his column. What purpose do these messages serve in his argument? Assess the effectiveness of these email messages as evidence. (In answering this question, you might refer to "Appraising Evidence" on pages 76–82.) **3.** Why is Mathews "shocked" when he learns that Georgia Tech quickly addressed the issue of collaboration raised by this incident? What does his reaction suggest about his opinion of universities? Do you agree with him? Why or why not? **4.** Consider your own experiences with collaborative learning, either in school or in some other setting where you worked with oth- ers. Have those experiences been beneficial to you? Explain. How might those experiences influence the way you respond to Mathews's views about collaboration? What pros and cons can you see in collaborative learning? **5.** Do you think the collaboration policy for Computer Science 1321 at Georgia Tech is a fair and reasonable one? Why or why not? Do you think students should always work individually? Is that possible, in your view? If so, how should that be enforced? If not, how might universities deal with cheating?

② WENDY KAMINER, "Heavy Lifting"

The idea of plagiarism rests on another idea: originality. Plagiarism means stealing someone else's words or ideas, which assumes that those words or ideas are original to that person. But are they? Wendy Kaminer thinks so. In the following essay, she discusses a sensational case of plagiarism that occurred in 2002 when the best-selling historian Stephen Ambrose was accused of using passages from other books without properly acknowledging that he was doing so. Kaminer concedes that borrowing from other authors is a common practice, and she even admits to borrowing passages from an encyclopedia for her own school reports when she was a student. But she also points out that writers like Ambrose profit handsomely from their work, and that fact, she believes, makes plagiarism more than just intellectual dishonesty. You might not agree with her that when money is involved, plagiarism takes on added seriousness. But her essay invites us to think about what plagiarism really is. To what extent do writers create truly original works? Ambrose claimed that his error was not in stealing another writer's words but in failing to use quotation marks properly, just as student writers sometimes fail to do. But even if a writer does acknowledge a source properly, is his or her writing really original? Kaminer's essay might help you answer such questions. A lawyer and author of numerous books on social issues, Wendy Kaminer is a contributing editor to the *Atlantic Monthly* and a senior correspondent for *The American Prospect*, which published this essay in 2002.

Heavy Lifting
WENDY KAMINER

1 Plagiarism charges against pop historian Stephen Ambrose are mounting; as I write this column, as many as six of his books have been found to include passages lifted from other writers without attribution. Scandals like this erupt periodically: Gail Sheehy ceded 10 percent of her royalties from the 1976 best-seller *Passages* to UCLA psychiatrist Roger Gould, who sued her for copyright infringement. (She also borrowed liberally from the work of the late Yale psychologist Daniel Levinson.) Joe McGinnis was exposed as a plagiarist when his 1993 biography of Edward Kennedy was found to include passages from books by William Manchester and Doris Kearns Goodwin* (see page 221). But Goodwin, who was rather unforgiving of McGinnis, had previously committed a similar offense (as *The Weekly Standard* recently revealed): She took passages from Lynne McTaggart's 1983 book about Kathleen Kennedy for her 1987 book *The Fitzgeralds and the Kennedys* — the same book she accused McGinnis of appropriat-

CONTEXT

Accusations of plagiarism against historian Stephen Ambrose came to light in an article by Fred Barnes in *The Weekly Standard* in January 2002. Barnes reproduced passages from Ambrose's book *The Wild Blue*, published in 2001, which resembled passages from a 1995 book by historian Thomas Childers titled *Wings of Morning*. In his article, "Stephen Ambrose, Copycat," Barnes wrote,

The two books are similar in more than just subject. Whole passages in "The Wild Blue" are barely distinguishable from those in "Wings of Morning." Sentences in Ambrose's book are identical to sentences in Childers's. Key phrases from "Wings of Morning," such as "glittering like mica" and "up, up, up," are repeated verbatim in "The Wild Blue." None of these — the passages, sentences, phrases — is put in quotation marks and ascribed to Childers. The only attribution Childers gets in "The Wild Blue" is a mention in the bibliography and four footnotes. And the footnotes give no indication that an entire passage has been lifted with only a few alterations from "Wings of Morning" or that a Childers sentence has been copied word-for-word.

In interviews and in essays he subsequently published, Ambrose acknowledged that he used Childers's book as a source, but he denied plagiarizing. In one essay, he defended himself by asserting, "I always thought plagiarism meant using other people's words and ideas, pretending they were your own and profiting from it. I do not do that, have never done that and never will."

ing. Literary copycats include genuine moral exemplars as well as amateurs and hacks: Martin Luther King's doctoral dissertation was not exactly original.

But originality is not much valued in our consumer culture, which is fueled by the urge to conform. Social trends reflect, in part, the impulse to look, act, or think alike; your status, or fame, reflects your success in acquiring what everyone else wants to acquire or being what everyone else wants to be. (Britney Spears is a star partly because there's nothing unfamiliar about her.) Media moguls profit from our attraction to the familiar. In any given year, there are fashions in sit-coms, movies, music, and self-help books, just as there are in politics, not to mention clothes.

Of course, creativity can prosper in this culture, thanks partly to copyright laws that protect against the most blatant acts of plagiarism and give creators some right to control and profit from their work. (You can't copyright an idea; you can copyright the words or images you use to express it.) But what protects creators more than law is recognition in the marketplace. Plagiarists hardly claim credit for work that is publicly identified with someone else. The difference between ripping off an obscure writer and ripping off a famous one is the difference between plagiarism and homage.

Ambrose seems clearly guilty of the former, but while charges of plagiarism are embarrassing, for popular writers they're not devastating professionally. (In the acad-

emy, they do more harm.) It's clear that Ambrose expects to get away with it. When a *Weekly Standard* cover story revealed that his current best-seller *The Wild Blue* appropriated paragraphs from Thomas Childers's book *The Wings of Morning,* Ambrose promptly apologized — sort of: He acknowledged that the work for which he had taken credit was, in part, created by Childers. But he characterized his apparent plagiarism as an innocent mistake — an oversight, hardly more grievous than a typo. "I wish I had put quotation marks in but I didn't," he explained.

5 Ambrose's publisher is standing by its moneymaking "author," expressing impatience with people who question his integrity. Simon and Schuster publisher

David Rosenthal denied that Ambrose's borrowing constitutes plagiarism: "There is no effort to deceive," he told *The New York Times*. "The material has been appropriately footnoted, and if there have been omissions it appears to be in the methods of citing as opposed to the citation itself," he added unintelligibly. Rosenthal is equally protective of Goodwin, another Simon and Schuster moneymaker, who has denied being a plagiarist. Her borrowings were "inadvertent," he said; ". . . some papers got shuffled."

Ambrose offered his own incoherent defense of his work: "I am not out there stealing other people's writings," he said, ignoring all the evidence. "If I am writing up a passage and it is a story I want to tell and this story fits and a part of it is from other people's writings, I just type it up that way and put it in a footnote." Or, as his defenders explain, Ambrose churns out a lot of books; he can't be expected to keep track of all his borrowings. Some quotation marks are bound to be omitted. But this defense of Ambrose simply underscores his underlying offense: He doesn't author books, it seems, so much as he assembles them, relying on an army of re-searchers and other, less prominent historians. Given the number of books he's produced and the number of unknown works available to plagiarists, we may never know the extent of his borrowings.

"So what," fans of Ambrose will probably say. Some may remember copying grade-school reports from *The World Book Encyclopedia* years ago (as I did). Some will think that I'm nitpicking. They simply won't see the harm in appropriating the words of other writers. Politicians do it all the time; indeed, presidents become famous for the eloquence of their speechwriters. Writers should be flattered when someone borrows their words, people say.

I doubt, however, that workers in the corporate world are flattered when colleagues profit from stealing their ideas or their résumés. Ambrose appears to have built a $3-million-a-year career partly on the toils of other historians. Why does the money matter morally? It measures the number of books he's sold and the number of times he's passed himself off as another. Writing, after all, is self-expression (for people who think and write with some originality). Plagiarism is a kind of identity theft.

*Doris Kearns Goodwin, a well-known political commentator and historian, was publicly accused of plagiarism in 2002. After admitting that she had borrowed from other works for her 1987 book *The Fitzgeralds and the Kennedys*, Goodwin stepped down as a judge for the Pulitzer Prize.

Questions for Discussion

1. Kaminer states that a writer is protected more by recognition in the marketplace than by copyright law. What does she mean by that statement? Why is that point important to her main argument about what she considers to be the plagiarism that Stephen Ambrose committed? Do you think she is right? Explain.

2. Kaminer asserts that originality is not valued in American culture. What do you think she means by "originality"? Why is the idea of originality important to her? Do you agree with her? Why or why not? **3.** *The American Prospect,* in which Kaminer's essay was published, claims to be written for a "broadly educated reader" (see *Con-Text* on page 221). In what ways do you think Kaminer's essay meets this goal? Cite specific passages from the essay to support your answer. **4.** How would you describe Kaminer's tone in this essay? Do you think her tone is appropriate to her subject? Do you find it effective? Explain.

③ RALPH CAPLAN, "What's Yours? (Ownership of Intellectual Property)"

"It isn't always so easy to know what belongs to us." So writes Ralph Caplan in the following essay. Caplan, an expert in architectural design, is referring to ideas. More specifically, he wonders how we can determine when someone owns an idea for the design of a building or a mechanical device. In raising this question, Caplan helps us see that arguments about intellectual property are not limited to words, music, or images, which are often the focus of copyright lawsuits. Here, Caplan explores how abstract ideas for something like the design of a building can also be "owned" through copyright and patent laws. As is often the case in disputes about intellectual property, patents for designs involve money. But Caplan asks us to consider whether questions about the ownership of such ideas go beyond the matter of who gets paid for them. In this sense, his essay, which was published in 1998 in *Print* magazine, suggests that arguments about intellectual property are really about the fundamental value of fairness and about how we wish to share our ideas and our abilities with one another. Caplan is the author of *By Design: Why There Are No Locks on the Bathroom Doors of the Hotel Louis XIV and Other Object Lessons* (1982).

What's Yours? (Ownership of Intellectual Property)
RALPH CAPLAN

1 Victor Papanek was our most fervent practitioner and preacher of alternative design. By the time of his death earlier this year, he had seen many of his most hotly disputed ideas become accepted design wisdom, if not design practice. One of them, however, remains fiercely controversial. Believing that "there is something basically wrong with the whole concept of patents and copyrights," Papanek declined to patent his designs. His critics scoffed that no one would bother stealing them anyway. Actually, they were ripped off in large numbers, for personal use as well as for profit. "If I design a toy that provides therapeutic exercise for handicapped children, then I think it is unjust to delay the release of the design by a year and a half, going through a patent application," Papanek wrote. "I feel that ideas are plentiful and cheap, and it is wrong to make money off the needs of others."

I don't know how money is ever made except off the needs (real or imagined) of others, but the issue here is not money but the rights to what it can't entirely buy.

VICTOR PAPANEK

Victor Papanek (1926–1998) was a renowned and sometimes controversial expert in architectural design. In his groundbreaking book *Design for the Real World: Human Ecology and Social Change* (1971), he questioned conventional beliefs about industrial and architectural design and argued for an approach to design that focused on making the world a better place. His proposals for design were based on his study of indigenous peoples and their relationship to their environments. His last book, *The Green Imperative: Natural Design for the Real World* (1995), was an ardent call to designers and architects to become more environmentally conscious and for people to live in more ecologically and socially responsible ways.

The late Dr. Gerald Fagan, a resident psychiatrist at a boys' school, relieved the guilt of students who masturbated by reminding them: "It's yours, isn't it?"

But it isn't always so easy to know what belongs to us. The protection, and even the identification, of what's yours has been vastly complicated by technology. As media for distributing ideas are multiplied, amplified, and reduced in price, ownership of so-called intellectual property becomes increasingly ambiguous. Even the ownership of hard goods has been softly defined for generations. In Arthur Miller's *Death of a Salesman*, Willie Loman's refrigerator and car are falling apart at the same time as he is. "Once in my life I would like to own something outright before it's broken!" Willie cries. "They time those things. They time them so when you finally paid for them, they're used up." In the audience we smile and nod in recognition, for we are an audience and a society of renters.

The rights to what we do own are subject to interpretation. When film mavens objected to Ted Turner's colorizing black-and-white movie classics, he replied, "The last time I looked, I owned them" — his way of saying he was entitled to make them all mauve if he wished, or keep anyone else from seeing them.

5 Are there public rights to private property? The nadir of my adolescence was not acne, or being turned down by May Allen for the senior prom, or even being suspended from high school. It was a strike by ASCAP — the American Society of Composers, Authors and Publishers — and until it was settled radio stations were prohibited from broadcasting music or lyrics produced by its members. I don't remember exactly how long it lasted, but for what seemed like forever the only songs we heard were in the public domain, usually by Stephen Foster. We understood dimly that the rights of creators to the material they

had created were at stake, but we wanted the music back. If the concept of intellectual property was in legal vogue then, none of us would have thought it applied to "Darn That Dream" or "Flat Foot Floogie with the Floy Floy."

The inheritance of intellectual property is more problematic. The son of a vaudeville comedian, having been given his father's name at birth and taken over his father's act when the old man died, proudly advertised in the trade papers: "This act is not a copy. It is a legacy." Today, Dickensian court battles rage over whether families own in perpetuity the images of their celebrity ancestors. I love a Gershwin tune, but if I can't play one without paying, whom do I pay? Not George and Ira, who have no further use for royalties. The Gershwin Family Trust? Well, why not? If families can inherit money, why shouldn't they inherit cultural resources that can be turned into money?

One reason is that cultural resources not only enrich us but enrich each other through us. Our copyright laws have always acknowledged this by providing only temporary coverage, after which the private holdings become public domain.* But temporary anything has a way of becoming at least semi-permanent. Copyright law has been extended over the years, and there is a good chance it will now be extended for another two decades. (Had that been in effect during the ASCAP revolt of my youth, nothing but Baroque would have been public domain.) A Gershwin trustee warned that without

such protection, "someone could turn Porgy and Bess, into rap music." A dreadful prospect, I guess, but folklorist Steve Zeitlin, noting that Gershwin's opera itself drew on African-American musical traditions, asks, "What could be more appropriate?" Zeitlin finds it similarly ironic that Disney, having used "Snow White" and other public domain materials for major productions, anxiously seeks to protect forever the sanctity of Mickey Mouse, which strikes some people as a Mickey Mouse idea.

Designers know the danger of letting work go unprotected — the danger not only of theft by competitors but of erosion through the negligence of managers who can't see, don't care, or have designs (and designers) of their own. The elaborate graphics standards manuals, devised as security systems, have often been ineffective because the people who understood them were not in control of their implementation.

Intellectual property implies the commodification of what cannot be commodified. If we protect it, why not protect emotional property as well? When William Styron wrote about the Nat Turner uprising, blacks challenged his right to write about the slave experience, on the grounds that it belonged to them collectively and exclusively. A comparable possessiveness attaches to the Holocaust as a phenomenon uniquely applicable to Jews but not to the Gypsies and gays who were also sent to Nazi death camps, or to the Armenians and Rwandans slaughtered at other times under other

*The term *public domain* refers to the status of a creative work or invention that is not protected by copyright or patent law and is freely available to anyone to use or copy. A work is considered to be "in the public domain" if the creator or inventor does not properly register it for copyright or patent protection or if that protection expires.

character in a Thurber story steals another man's dream. Another character in a Thurber cartoon has a friend accompany him to the doctor's office, where he registers the unprecedented medical complaint, "I've got Bright's disease and he's got mine."

"What's mine is yours" is the posture of a saint. "What's yours is mine" is the ideology of a mugger. Frankly, I do not know how to reconcile them. I think I understand rights and privileges in respect to owning things — whether one-of or mass produced. If I find a rock, it's mine. If I fashion it into a tool, it is more decisively mine, because my hands shaped it and my imagination told them how. If it is mine, then, because I am no saint, it is not yours. You therefore have been served with a moral injunction not to covet my rock and a criminal code forbidding you to take it if you do covet it. However, if I give it to you or leave it to you, the rock is yours, with all the rights and privileges pertaining thereto.

Thereto is the rub. What rights and privileges pertain to the rocks in your head? And where do they go when your head is gone? Some things that are yours are part of you. No one can take them from you, but it hurts when they try. To be plagiarized is, as Steve Heller indicated recently in *PRINT,* to be "violated." This can be accomplished with dazzling chutzpah, as when someone overseas used a couple of pages from an article of mine without attribution, then quoted an additional paragraph from the same article, as if I had written it, which of course I had. Thus he put me in the curious position of agreeing with myself.

auspices. When David Leavitt based a novel on the homoerotic autobiographical writing of Stephen Spender, the elderly poet sued, telling Leavitt to get his own sex life instead of appropriating someone else's old one.

10 But Leavitt was writing fiction, in which personal experience may be transferable. In Charles Williams's *Descent into Hell,* Pauline tells Peter about a recurring event that terrifies her. He can't do anything about the recurring event, but he offers to carry the fear for her, just as he would carry a parcel or her books. It's still her fear, he explains, but with him as designated schlepper, she won't have to do the fearing.

No one has yet copyrighted an idiosyncrasy or patented a neurosis, but James Thurber has shown us the way: A

Sometimes what looks like plagiarism is simply coincidence. But not all coincidence is entirely coincidental. After driving to Wesleyan University to hear the brilliant Suzanne Langer* lecture on signs and symbols, I was disappointed to find that she really had nothing more to say on the subject than I had already said in a lecture of my own. Driving home, I figured out why. My ideas were as good as hers because they were hers to start with! I had absorbed them from reading her books.

*American philosopher Suzanne Langer (1895–1985) was well known for her ideas about aesthetics and, in particular, for her writings about language and music. She believed that music was a form of expression of human feelings that cannot adequately be expressed in language.

Questions for Discussion

1. Caplan argues that music and stage acts are cultural resources that should be available to the public. What support does he offer for this point? How persuasive do you think Caplan is on this point? **2.** Caplan writes, "Intellectual property implies the commodification of what cannot be commodified." What does he mean by that statement? In what way is that statement important to his main argument? **3.** What examples does Caplan offer as evidence of the ambiguity of determining the ownership of intellectual property? How effective do you think these examples are in illustrating his point? **4.** Summarize Caplan's main point in this essay. How does his anecdote of attending a lecture by Suzanne Langer reinforce this main point? Do you agree with Caplan? Why or why not? What counterarguments could you offer in response to his position? **5.** Caplan's essay might be seen as an example of an argument to inquire (see pages 13–16). Evaluate its effectiveness as such an argument. Does his argument help to clarify the issues related to intellectual property rights that he addresses? Explain.

④ NICK GILLESPIE, "Let's Roll: You Can Trademark Words but Not Meaning"

Slogans and catchphrases seem to be everywhere in American culture, from the many slogans that businesses use to sell their products (such as Nike's "Just do it" or Chevy Truck's "Like a Rock") to political campaign slogans (such as Ronald Reagan's "Morning in America") to the captions on state automobile license plates (such as Wisconsin's "America's Dairyland" or Florida's "The Sunshine State"). Any business, organization, or even private citizen can acquire a trademark for a slogan or a symbol; the trademark protects the owner from the possibility that someone else will use that slogan or symbol without permission. Trademark law in effect enables one to "own" a phrase or symbol. But what exactly does it mean to "own" a phrase? Nick Gillespie addresses that question in the following essay, focusing on the words "let's roll," which were spoken by a passenger on one of the commercial jets that were hijacked by terrorists on September 11, 2001. Gillespie examines how that phrase has been used in the years since September 11, 2001, and he points out that while laws may empower one to own a phrase like "let's roll" and even profit from it, no one can control what such a phrase means. In this way, Gillespie's essay, which appeared in *Reason Online* in 2002, implicitly asks us to think about how words and ideas acquire significance and meaning — and to wonder who really "owns" them. Nick Gillespie is editor-in-chief of *Reason Online,* a journal devoted to politics and culture that reflects a libertarian viewpoint.

Let's Roll: You Can Trademark Words but Not Meaning
NICK GILLESPIE

*United Airlines Flight 93, en route from New Jersey to San Francisco, was one of the four American commercial flights hijacked by terrorists on September 11th, 2001. Flight 93 crashed in rural western Pennsylvania after passengers overpowered the hijackers and tried to retake control of the plane.

1 In a country that has long been cuckoo for catch phrases — from "Give me liberty or give me death" to "I want my Maypo" to "Whassuupp" — it's hardly surprising that 9/11 would generate a quasi-official slogan. Or that it would be "Let's roll!," the last known words of Todd Beamer, the most widely recognized hero-victim of the terrorist attacks.

Despite its relative inscrutability, "Let's roll!" — Beamer's signature phrase, heard by a GTE phone operator who'd been in contact with him during the doomed flight — somehow summed up the courage of the brave souls who mounted a revolt against the hijackers on United Flight 93.* By causing the plane to crash in a field in western Pennsylvania rather than some likely target in Washington, D.C., Beamer and his fellow passengers saved dozens or hundreds of lives even as they gave up their own.

Yet as soon as a phrase — especially a heartfelt and serious one — is uttered, it immediately starts morphing into something else, typically a parodic version of itself. When's the last time anyone uttered "Ich bin ein Berliner," "I am not a crook," or "I've fallen and I can't get up"[†] as something other than a punch line? "Let's roll!" is itself taking on an increasingly curious afterlife as the specifics of 9/11 recede from public memory.

Ironically, it's the phrase's official guardians who are transforming "Let's roll!" into a generalized "lifestyle" statement. Earlier this year, the Todd M. Beamer Foundation, a nonprofit founded by Beamer's widow, raised eyebrows when it trademarked[‡] the slogan, both to control its usage and to raise money for programs that "seek . . . to equip children experiencing family trauma to make heroic choices every day." But the foundation has done more than just sell its own "Let's roll!" paraphernalia as a fund raising tool. It's pursued a series of odd licensing choices that strain the credulity of even the least cynical observers.

5 In June, for instance, the foundation let Wal-Mart use the phrase as an employee motivation slogan and as a theme for its annual shareholder meeting. "It's an inspirational use of 'Let's Roll,'" Beamer Foundation CEO Douglas A. MacMillan suggested to the *Arkansas Democrat-Gazette,* reiterating that the words are "a call to action."

In August the foundation gave its blessing to Florida State University's football team, which has slapped "Let's roll!" on T-shirts, baseball caps, and other items. Each year legendary coach Bobby Bowden selects a theme for the season. "We are going to go with 'Let's roll,' based on the airplane guy making

that remark," Bowden churlishly explained on the FSU Web site (in Bowden's defense, one of the things he is legendary for is forgetting names). "Not only for that but the season is here, the challenges are here, let's roll."

Rather than distancing the Beamer Foundation from a tasteless equation of the struggle on Flight 93 with college football, MacMillan embraced it. "By picking that phrase, Coach Bowden is carrying on Todd's legacy," he said, adding, "Todd was a huge sports fan. I'm sure he's thrilled."

Maybe, maybe not. He's probably more excited by the latest product to prominently feature the slogan: the book *Let's Roll!: Ordinary People, Extraordinary Courage* (Tyndale), by his widow, Lisa Beamer, and Ken Abraham. Despite many truly odd touches — Abraham is identified on the jacket as a "professional writer with world-class credentials" and the coauthor of a biography of golfer Payne Stewart, who also died in an airplane crash — *Let's Roll!* is mostly a touching memoir, especially the section that uses multiple sources to reconstruct the grim struggle aboard Flight 93. Yet the book is at its weakest precisely when it invokes its vague and overused catch phrase — " 'Let's roll!' is not a slogan, a book, or a song; it's a lifestyle," insists Beamer at one point — rather than poignant human details.

Exactly what "Let's roll!" will come to mean over the years is anyone's guess, though we can safely assume its final iteration will be an odd subversion of its original referent. "Remember the Alamo!," despite its imperative demand for historical consciousness, actually started out as but half of a slogan urging Texans in their war with Mexico to "Remember Goliad!," another infamous massacre. "In like Flynn," now a generic

[†] "I've fallen and I can't get up" was a line uttered in a 1985 television commercial in which an elderly woman calls for aid using a Medic Alert button. Although not intended to be humorous, the strangely comical line found its way into everyday slang.

[‡] The U.S. Patent and Trademark Office defines a trademark as "a word, phrase, symbol or design, or a combination of words, phrases, symbols or designs, that identifies and distinguishes the source of the goods of one party from those of others."

TODD M. BEAMER FOUNDATION

According to its mission statement, the Todd M. Beamer Foundation "is a non-profit public charity created to equip children experiencing family trauma to make heroic choices every day. In honor of Todd Beamer, and the other heroes of United Flight 93, Todd's family and friends established The Foundation to carry on his legacy of character, faith and courage to a new generation of young people. . . . The Foundation focuses on helping not just the children who lost a parent on September 11. The broader vision of The Foundation is to reach many children across the nation who have been affected by family trauma."

term for ease of entry, originated among G.I.s wryly referencing the screen legend Errol Flynn's 1942 trial for statutory rape. 10 "Let's roll!" may well go down as Florida State's great rallying cry, or a mantra mumbled by especially motivated Wal-Mart sales associates. That won't be so bad, assuming that we remember the heroes on Flight 93 for what they did, not just what they said.

NEGOTIATING DIFFERENCES

The essays in this section indicate that "intellectual property" is a broad and complex category encompassing words, ideas, and symbols, among other things. Moreover, they raise the tricky question of who *should* own an idea or a phrase. As a student, you must sometimes confront questions about the ownership of words or ideas when you are completing school assignments that require you to draw on sources. And if you have used the Internet to find information, as most of us do today, then you may have encountered additional uncertainties, since much of the information on the Internet is questionable and its origin unknown. If you have ever been tempted to use a sentence or phrase or idea that you found on an obscure Web page without acknowledging that source, then you know how easy it can be to violate intellectual property standards.

With this in mind, review the policies of your college or university regarding academic dishonesty and intellectual property. (Most schools post such policies on their Web sites, but you can usually also find them in the school's library.) Examine these policies to see

Questions for Discussion

1. What is Gillespie's main point about slogans and other catchphrases that become popular in the culture? Is he in favor of protecting such language through the use of trademarks? Cite specific passages from his essay to support your answer. **2.** How would you describe Gillespie's tone in this essay? What does his tone reveal about his attitude toward the use of slogans like "Let's roll"? Do you think Gillespie's tone is appropriate for this argument? Explain. In what ways might the tone enhance the argument? In what ways might it weaken the argument? **3.** When the Todd M. Beamer Foundation filed an application to trademark the phrase "Let's Roll!" in 2002, many people objected, suggesting that to trademark that phrase was disrespectful to the victims and survivors of the terrorist attacks of September 11, 2001. Do you agree with that criticism? Explain. What counterarguments can you present to Gillespie's position on this issue? What might your counterarguments reveal about your own views regarding intellectual property? **4.** This essay was published in *Reason Online,* which describes itself as a magazine of "free minds and free markets . . . [which] provides a refreshing alternative to right-wing and left-wing opinion magazines by making a principled case for liberty and individual choice in all areas of human activity." Do you think Gillespie's argument reflects that editorial philosophy? Explain, citing specific passages in his essay to support your answer.

what standards for the ownership of words and ideas your school applies to student work. Then write an essay in which you either argue in favor of these policies or question them. In your essay, be sure to summarize the main points of your school's policies regarding intellectual property and academic dishonesty, then explain why you agree or disagree them. Try to identify the principles of fairness and ownership that you hold as a basis for your argument. And try to address the matter of the consequences that students suffer when they are found to have violated your school's poli-cies: What are those consequences? Are they fair? If not, why not? And what alternatives would you provide? Try also to account for new technologies, like those associated with the Internet, and how they might affect intellectual property.

If your teacher allows it, consider working together with several classmates to review your school's policies and collaboratively draft your essay.

CLUSTER 2

WHO OWNS THE BODY?

I n 1976, a lawyer named Noel Keane helped a childless couple arrange to have a baby using a surrogate mother (see Con-Text on next page). The man's sperm was used to inseminate a woman who agreed to carry the baby to term and then turn it over to the couple once it was born. Keane devoted the rest of his career to helping couples find surrogate mothers to bear their children. Ten years later, a case of surrogate parenting known as the "Baby M" case became an international sensation when the surrogate mother filed suit in court to keep the baby. The suit in effect required the court to decide who would be Baby M's legal (as distinct from biological) parents. Eventually, the court ruled against the surrogate mother and awarded legal custody of the child to the couple who had contracted to have the baby through the surrogate mother. The case raised difficult questions about the ethical complexities of such arrangements, which were made possible by advancements in medical science. In the years since then, those questions have become even more complicated, as technology has given us new possibilities that were once unimaginable. ■ For example, women can now become surrogate mothers without having to be artificially inseminated, as Baby M's mother was. Instead, a woman's egg can be fertilized by a man's sperm *in vitro* — that is, in a laboratory procedure — and then the fertilized egg can be implanted in another woman, who carries the baby, which is not biologically "hers," to term. In effect, this surrogate mother "rents" her body to another couple for the purpose of giving birth to their baby. In such a situation, whose baby then is born? The woman whose egg was fertilized in a laboratory? The man whose sperm fertilized that egg? Or the woman who carries the fertilized egg to term and gives birth to the baby? Several court cases have been brought to try to answer those questions, but no clear solutions have been found. ■ Meanwhile, other advances in medical science give rise to similar dilemmas. Sophisticated testing now enables a couple to determine whether their baby carries genes for several terrible congenital diseases. But what should a couple do with the knowledge gained through such testing? If they learn that their baby might possibly develop such a disease, do they have the right to terminate the fetus? And who owns those test results? Is that knowledge private property? For example, if you were able to learn through genetic testing that you carry the gene for a serious medical condition, such as Alzheimer's disease, and that you are likely to develop the disease later in your life, do you "own" that knowledge? Can you protect that knowledge from, say, an insurance company, which may not want to issue you a life or medical insurance policy because you might develop a terrible disease that will lead to great medical expense? ■ Such questions, as difficult as they can be to answer, are likely to become even more challenging as our capacity to gain knowledge increases. The essays in this chapter examine the complexities associated with our often astonishing capabilities to learn about, manipulate, and use our bodies. The authors all ask different versions of the same question, Who owns our bodies? And they challenge us to think more broadly about what can be owned and by whom. Living as we do in a time of great technological and social change, we cannot easily avoid confronting these questions — nor should we.

CON-TEXT: The Father of Surrogate Parenting

1 It was the strangest of requests, even to a lawyer. The couple in Noel Keane's office wanted a child. The woman was not able to bear one herself, but a woman had been found who was prepared to be impregnated with the man's sperm and to hand over the baby as soon as it was born. Mr. Keane was asked to prepare a document to safeguard the interests of all parties. This, as far as is known, was the first formal contract for surrogate motherhood.

Mr. Keane devoted the rest of his life to this specialty: not simply looking after the legal side, but starting what he called ``infertility centres'' throughout the United States where couples could meet women willing to bear their child. These days there are numerous agencies offering to arrange surrogate parenting, but in 1976 Mr. Keane, for better or worse, seems to have been the innovator. . . .

One of the charms claimed for surrogacy is that a baby can be partially designed to order. So a white, fair-haired infant may eventually grace the nursery, if that is what the couple wants. The surrogate baby is formally turned over to its biological father whose wife can then adopt it. But what if the surrogate mother is so attached to the child that she refuses to hand it over? This is what happened in 1986 in the celebrated ``Baby M'' case arising out of a surrogacy arranged by Mr. Keane.

SOURCE: "A Modern Solomon," *The Economist*, 1997.

① RAYNA RAPP AND FAYE GINSBURG, "Standing at the Crossroads of Genetic Testing: New Eugenics, Disability Consciousness, and Women's Work"

In the past, a couple could not know whether their child would develop a serious condition such as Down syndrome until after the child's birth. Today, through prenatal testing, a couple can learn while the child is still in the mother's womb whether the child is likely to develop such a condition. For many parents, this knowledge is invaluable, because it enables them to address the baby's condition even before the child's birth. But as Rayna Rapp and Faye Ginsburg point out in the following essay, such knowledge can also create wrenching dilemmas for parents — especially for women. Should a couple have a child who they know is likely to develop a serious and potentially deadly medical condition? If they choose to have the child, what are the chances that it will develop such a condition? And if it does, will they be able to afford to care for it? And who has a right to this knowledge? Should they inform their insurance company about the prenatal test results? These are ethical and well as legal questions that require parents to make sometimes painful decisions. But Rapp and Rayna argue that such decisions are not exclusively individual ones; rather, they believe that society as a whole has a stake in such decisions. Their argument raises questions not just about how such decisions can be made but about *who* makes them — and who owns the crucial knowledge that is produced as a result of advanced medical techniques such as prenatal testing. As you read their detailed examination of these issues, consider what you would do in the situations they describe. And how would you justify your decision? Rayna Rapp and Faye Ginsburg are professors of anthropology at New York University. Their essay was published in *Gene Watch* in 2002.

Standing at the Crossroads of Genetic Testing: New Eugenics, Disability Consciousness, and Woman's Work
RAYNA RAPP AND FAYE GINSBURG

Neo-Eugenics Meets Disability Activism

1 Genetic knowledge permeates public culture in America; what are the ideas and vested interests that shape everyday understandings of this "brave new world?" Contemporary biomedicine holds the potential to both screen out imperfect lives and to enable people with significant disabilities to survive and flourish. On the one hand, fantasies of genetic perfectibility are a longstanding

part of our culture; the "genome revolution" has made such fantasies seem more possible with promises of designer babies and personalized genetic medicine and other life-extending biotechnologies. Such "soft eugenics" inform the musings of hi-tech gurus in magazines such as *Wired*. They color the comments of pundits on nightly television news and in feature articles in *Time* and *Newsweek*. Most tellingly, hype about genetic futures appears regularly in the *Wall Street Journal* and the business sections of most major newspapers.

On the other hand, disability rights activists have begun to alter the social landscape in an entirely different way. Rather than imagining perfectibility, they insist on the expansion of democratic rights to all citizens, and raise questions about the growing use of prenatal screening to prevent the birth of disabled children. Such concerns are on a continuum with ongoing efforts by many groups to normalize the presence of people with disabilities in everyday life. In part this is accomplished through the integration of visibly disabled people in popular media: we see kids with Down Syndrome and wheelchair users on *Sesame Street;* movies about jazz musicians with Tourette's Syndrome; and even fashion spreads in the *New York Times Sunday Magazine* featuring kids with scoliosis, spinal chord injury, and cardiovascular problems in hip clothes, posed with their personal heroes.

Clearly, these two cultural domains — "soft eugenics" and the democratization of disability — are increasingly part of public life in 21st century America (and elsewhere). They provide contradictory perspectives about the place of genetic knowledge in society: these tensions are particularly evident when families face choices engendered by new biomedical —

and especially reproductive — technologies. Without clear cultural guidelines to follow, these families are placed, sometimes reluctantly, in the position of becoming moral pioneers on an unmapped genetic frontier. That new territory is most commonly encountered in the arena of prenatal diagnosis,* an increasingly routine part of pregnancy care which includes a range of tests intended to identify fetal disabilities: sonograms, amniocentesis, and blood screens such as MSAFP. Readers of *GeneWatch* are aware of the neo-eugenic potentialities of such tests, although in actuality, decision-making is always more complex. However, the very existence of prenatal tests assumes that parents will want to select against anomalous results. This is hardly surprising in a healthcare market dominated by the insurance industry. Cost-benefit analyses are central to the availability (and unavailability) of consumer choices: insurance companies measure the expense of amniocentesis against the potential economic burden of treating a child with atypical and possibly intensive medical needs.

Genetic Decision Making and Economies of Caretaking

The increasingly market-driven health care system is not the only determinant of how families from diverse backgrounds decide to use or forgo these technologies. Our recent research reveals that women come to their decisions regarding their amniocentesis in complex ways. What counts as a disability "worth" an abortion for one pregnant woman and her supporters may be an acceptable condition to another. Some conditions that are now diagnosable prenatally — such as Down syndrome or spina bifida — are feared by families on the basis of very little knowledge (and, sadly,

*Prenatal diagnosis refers to medical testing that is performed on a pregnant woman to determine whether the fetus has or is likely to develop certain genetic disorders, such as Down syndrome or cystic fibrosis. Amniocentesis is one such test, in which amniotic fluid is removed from the womb and tested for various disorders. Another test is the maternal-serum-alpha-fetoprotein test, or MSAFP, a blood test for a protein that is produced by the liver of the fetus; abnormal levels of this protein are associated with some genetic disorders and birth defects.

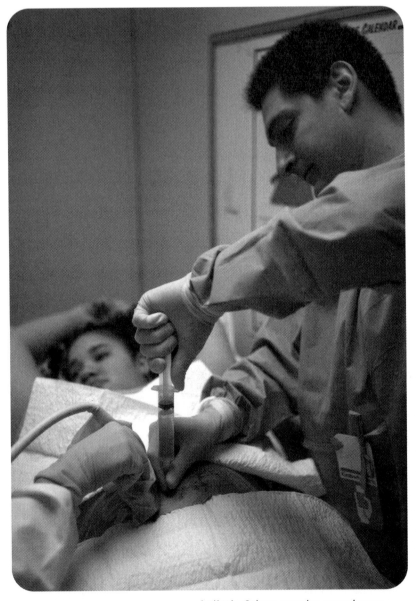

*See Americans with
Disabilities Act on
page 251.

healthcare choices and attitudes toward disability.

5 Reproductive decisions are not only shaped simply by "cultural values," but also by the way that larger social transformations affect household resources, networks of support, and family aspirations. These in turn influence how people understand and act on the offer of prenatal diagnostic testing. Pregnant women's encounters with genetic testing fuse a potent mixture of prior ideologies and realistic assessments of the labor demands on them as mothers and household managers. Women are increasingly in the workforce for longer stretches of their lives and less likely to take significant time off when caring for infants and young children. They also tend to live at a distance from the support systems of extended family and are more likely to be or become single heads of households. Thus, the balance between parenting and paid work becomes increasingly delicate, and the real or imagined responsibilities of caring for a child with disabilities takes on new meaning, especially when ending a pregnancy is still an option.

At the same time, due to the successes of modern medicine and recent disability activism, many more young people with chronic conditions are surviving and are raised at home with their families. A generation ago, middle-class Americans were encouraged to institutionalize children with the kinds of challenges now routinely reported in the pages of mainstream media and seen on TV sitcoms. Clearly, these are gains. However, the labor of caretaking still falls on "the invisible heart" of families, and disproportionately on women. Despite the Americans with Disabilities Act* and other legal provisions for inclusion, it is a constant struggle to make the world accommodate those who are

prejudice). Others may be so unknown — unbalanced chromosome translocations, for example — that pregnant women decide to "take their chances" in accepting a diagnosed fetus into their lives, gambling that "everything will be all right." It is clear that a range of factors — religious, class, racial-ethnic, national backgrounds — play a strong role in

not typical. It is families, and especially mothers, who take up the slack between the realities of everyday life and the promissory notes of a society "beyond ramps." (Of course, fathers frequently have been deeply involved and committed to this kind of labor, and have played exemplary public roles as well.)

These dilemmas raise important questions at the moment of genetic decision-making. Clearly, judgments about the capacity of families to care for disabled children are to be respected. While these are experienced as private, family matters, they cannot be contained within domestic domains. Who determines the social location of care? Caretaking is conventionally attached to the unpaid labor of women in the home. As a result, it is not necessarily the fear of an unknown disability that shapes genetic decision-making, but the fear of being "always on call," as Carol Levine argues in her book of that title.

These circumstances have made caretaking a politicized arena in the US's privatizing economy. If paid, the labor of family caregivers would cost about $200 billion a year. Nevertheless, while health insurance increasingly covers the routinization of new reproductive technologies and the costs of neonatal intensive care units, most home-based personal assistance — a need estimated at 21 billion hours yearly — goes unpaid by public funds, despite the demonstrable bodily, emotional, and economic benefits of deinstitutionalizing support. This is a skeletal sketch of the political economy of health care and assisted living "choices" that affects all Americans. Yet it is a barely visible landscape to most people unless and until their own or a family member's disability reveals its limitations on a practical, daily level. This underfunded dimension of health care

needs haunts reproductive decision-making when women and their families assess what they can handle.

Increasingly, however, challenges to this situation are emerging as a result of the expanding needs of caretaking over the life cycle. Advocacy groups, such as the growing Movement for Independent Living, seek public support for personal assistance, a policy which, Marca Bistro, head of the National Council on Disability, argues, "would relieve an enormous amount of stress on families and, over time . . . would begin to alter the public perception toward significantly disabled people and the people who relate to them." People with disabilities and their families have become activists for radical improvements in home-based health care and personal assistance that would enable people with disabilities to be less dependent on family members. Many of these same activists support genetic research that might lead both to prenatal tests and to ameliorative therapies. Indeed the work of caretaking and the lack of social support for it transform many parents (and children) into

INDEPENDENT LIVING

According to the Access Center for Independent Living, an organization dedicated to helping people with disabilities gain full access to their communities, the Movement for Independent Living is related to the Civil Rights Movement of the 1950s and 1960s. The Movement for Independent Living rests on a belief that "people with disabilities should have the same civil rights, options, and control over choices in their own lives as do people without disabilities." In the late 1970s, disabilities activists organized protests and lobbying efforts that eventually led to federal regulations requiring lifts on public buses to accommodate people in wheelchairs and similarly disabled people. The passage of the Americans with Disabilities Act (ADA) in 1990 encouraged activists to address other areas of discrimination against people with disabilities, including acquiring publicly funded services such as housing and ending the practice of institutionalizing people with certain kinds of disabilities.

activists, pushing for new research and medical services.

Rethinking Genetic Testing in the Context of Caretaking

10 In the world of those who live with genetic disease, prenatal testing for their condition and support for those living with it are not necessarily in contradiction. Indeed they may be part of the same agenda. The activism of families with Familial Dysautonomia (FD) is a case in point. FD is a very rare autosomal recessive degenerative genetic disease that destabilizes the autonomic nervous system. Two generations ago, most children with this disorder did not survive past their fifth birthday. Now, a population of young adults is testimony to the success of complex intensive medical care — gastrostomy tubes and feeding pumps, daily cocktails of drugs to regulate the autonomic system, and therapeutic surgeries. Daily care is provided by those with FD, their family members, and some home-based medical support.

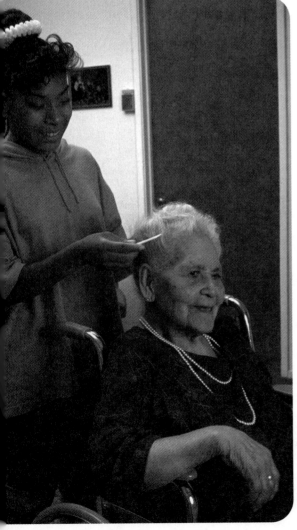

The Dysautonomia Foundation, founded by affected families in the late 1950s, is one of the oldest genetic support groups in the US. In the early 1990s it was among a handful of voluntary health organizations, associated with "orphan diseases,"

to raise substantial private funding to catalyze research at a cutting-edge genetics lab to find the "FD gene." After almost a decade, the gene was located in March 2001 and a prenatal test was quickly made available. The goals for this project were multiple. Many families wanted tests in order to avoid the birth of a second child with this severely disabling condition; among their concerns was their capacity to continue to meet the intensive care demands for the first child. For those opposed to abortion, pre-marital testing is available to avoid matches in which both partners carry the gene. Finding the gene was also intended to spur rapid progress for more effective biomedical intervention that would enable those with FD to live more medically stable lives. Once a gene is found, its underlying mechanisms can be understood and new more targeted therapies can be tested. (While most scientists agree that effective gene therapies are a long way off, some drugs based on molecular inter-

CONTEXT

According to its Web site, the Council for Responsible Genetics (CRG) "fosters public debate about the social, ethical and environmental implications of genetic technologies. CRG works through the media and concerned citizens to distribute accurate information and represent the public interest on emerging issues in biotechnology." Among CRG's core principles are the following: "New technologies must meet social needs. Problems rooted in poverty, racism, and other forms of inequality cannot be remedied by technology alone." CRG publishes *Gene Watch*, which describes itself as "America's first and only magazine dedicated to monitoring biotechnology's social and environmental consequences." To what extent does this essay reflect the principles of CRG?

ventions are becoming a reality in contemporary medicine.)

We offer this example to complicate the polarized frames set out in our introduction that too often structure debates about genetic testing in the abstract world of "ethics." These debates do not always take into account the real-world experiences of those on the front lines of genetic difference. We underscore the significance of caretaking (and its gendered nature) in shaping how decisions are made, how research is increasingly mobilized, and how genetic knowledge will be used. When those affected by genetic disorders participate in setting the research agendas that intimately affect their community and its future, we see a possible model in which both genetic testing and activism supporting those with disabilities and their caretakers need not be on a collision course.

Questions for Discussion

1. Early in their essay, Rapp and Ginsburg discuss "two cultural domains": (1) "soft eugenics," or the ability to manipulate human genetic material to avoid certain medical conditions or to produce desired traits in a child (such as intelligence), and (2) "the democratization of disability," which refers to the efforts of people with disabilities to achieve equal rights with others. What significance do Rapp and Ginsburg see in these two domains? What do these domains have to do with prenatal testing? How do Rapp and Ginsburg use these two domains to build their argument about prenatal testing? **2.** What factors influence a woman's reproductive decisions, according to Rapp and Ginsburg? Why is it important to take these factors into account, in their view? What do these factors indicate about the challenges that prenatal testing creates for society? **3.** In what sense are individual decisions about having a child with a disability also social decisions, according to Rapp and Ginsburg? What support do the authors provide for this position? Do you agree with them? Why or why not? **4.** Rapp and Ginsburg devote a significant portion of their essay to the example of familial dysautonomia (FD). What points do they use this example to make? Evaluate the effectiveness of this example as a way to make these points. **5.** What do Rapp and Ginsburg hope to accomplish through their argument? Do you think their essay is successful in helping them accomplish their goals? Explain. **6.** Which of the four kinds of arguments described in Chapter 1 do you think best describes this essay? Justify your answer by citing specific passages from the essay.

② MAUREEN FREELY, "Designer Babies and Other Fairy Tales"

Because matters of human reproduction are both complex and, to many people, sacred, arguments about reproductive issues can become especially intense. They can encompass medical, economic, ethical, legal, as well as moral considerations. For example, a couple faced with the prospect of having a baby with a serious genetic disorder must confront the economic question of who will pay the enormous costs of caring for the child once it is born. Physicians may face legal questions if they advise the couple to perform a risky medical procedure on the unborn baby. Others may question the morality of such procedures. Writer Maureen Freely appreciates the complexity of such issues. In fact, she argues that the many different kinds of arguments made about such situations complicate the already difficult decisions facing parents and others who may be involved. Drawing on a reproductive case that caused a sensation in Great Britain in 2002, Freely sorts through the many different voices in debates about reproductive medicine, and she asks us to focus on *how* the issues are being debated. She encourages us to think of these issues as social issues that we all have a stake in — whether we will ever face reproductive decisions ourselves. And because these are social rather than private matters, they should properly be debated — and decided — publicly in democratic fashion. As you read, consider how Freely compares the way these issues are addressed in Great Britain to the way they are addressed in the United States. Her essay appeared in the British magazine the *New Statesman* in 2002.

Designer Babies and Other Fairy Tales
MAUREEN FREELY

1 Meet Raj and Shahana Hashmi. Their gorgeous three-year-old son, Zain, has a serious blood disorder. He needs a cell transplant, and if they do not find a suitable donor he could die. On 22 February, the Human Fertilisation and Embryology Authority (HFEA)* gave the Hashmis permission to try to create that donor. Shahana is to have IVF (in vitro fertilization)† (see page 241) treatment. Any embryos that result will be subjected to genetic diagnosis. The hope is that the couple will find an embryo that could become the child with the bone marrow that will save Zain's life.

How strange it must be for them to open the paper and read that they are symbols of moral decay. No one is quite ready to condemn them outright. No one who wants to avoid a writ, anyway. No,

*The Human Fertilisation and Embryology Authority, established in 1990, regulates reproductive research and therapies in Great Britain.

almost everyone is sure that the Hashmis will love any second child just as much as they love their first. Some have gone on the record to say we can count on this even if something goes amiss and their second born turns out not to be Zain's saviour. But what about the six other couples who have already announced they will be following in the Hashmis' footsteps? What about all the faceless others who are bound to follow them? What if the rules get looser still and this sort of thing becomes standard practice? When we work ourselves up into a moralistic froth about reproductive technology, what exactly are we talking about?

The odds are not in their favour. The success rate for a single course of IVF treatment is less than one in three. The likelihood of Shahana Hashmi creating a genetically suitable embryo is one in 16.

So she and her husband must have a hard time understanding why so many people think they're playing God. If only, they must be thinking. All they want is to take this one-in-about-50 chance to keep their son alive.

The short answer is that we are talking about too many things at once, and in a very muddled way. The dirge gets played out on the lowest keys on the piano. Many of the fears it evokes are, however, worthy of attention. There is, for example, the entirely legitimate fear of the new — or of the social havoc that can result when new technology makes false claims, or gives people more power than they know how to use, or changes the rules by which we procreate. There is religious fear — about hubris, damnation, sacrilege and playing God. There is the fear of eugenics trying to "get in

†In vitro fertilization is a process by which eggs are removed from a woman, fertilized with male sperm in a laboratory, and implanted in the woman's uterus, where they can potentially develop into human embryos. The first "test-tube baby" was born as a result of this technique in 1978 in England. Although the procedure is now common and used by women who have not been able to conceive a child by other means, typically fewer than one third of the women who undergo the procedure actually become pregnant.

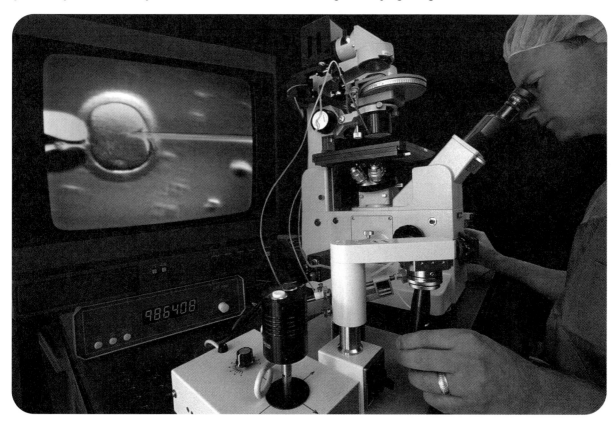

through the back door". There is the free-floating fear of the wrong people being in control. We are afraid of doctors taking control of our bodies to create a master race, of parents buying into the fantasy of perfection, of babies being turned into consumer products. And what if something goes wrong? What if, instead of creating the perfect baby, the scientists accidentally create a monster?

5 One of the most interesting things about the debate on reproductive medicine is its heavy reliance on the language of fairy tales. There are spectres, monsters and bogeymen, wishes and dreams and magic cures. Babies are not just babies, but potent symbols of our cultural future — what we want to pass on, what we stand to lose if the story goes the wrong way. When people talk about designer babies, they're not just talking about the manipulation of genes. They are talking about the next generation and who gets to shape it.

If they sometimes forget that they are talking in symbols and fall too easily into magical thinking, if their ideas about "suitable candidates for treatment" are arch-conservative, and even racist, it is also true that they are asking important questions. A society is not a society unless it can reproduce itself. The social regulation of fertility, the system of controls and supports that decides who gets to have

children, and who does not, is what makes a society what it is. Every time a society changes its system, everyone and everything in that society feels the effects. The faster the change, the bigger the disruption.

In the past generation, we have seen one of the most dramatic changes ever. The regulation of fertility is less and less a private matter: increasingly, it is decided in the public domain. When fertility goes public, the game changes utterly.

Let me give a very obvious example — I cannot live as a free woman, in control of my body, in charge of my choices, unless I live in a society which supports that freedom with affordable, accessible contraception. I depend on the state to make sure that the services I use are regulated and staffed with real doctors. I need to have the right to complain if I find the service poor. I need to know that I can campaign for changes in legislation as and when they seem necessary. I need to bear in mind that other parties are free to do the same, which is why my right to birth control is something I should never take for granted.

As with birth control, so with birth. I need to bear in mind that my right to have a child at all is also subject to political control. If I live in a democratic society, I can fight my corner. If I happen to be in China in the time of the one-child policy, I cannot. If I live in any of the countries that condone the use of sex selection technologies to favour boys and weed out girls, my ability to protest against that policy will depend on the political system within which I am operating.

10 If reproductive medicine is properly regulated and democratically debated, if the use of new technology is overseen by a regulatory agency with a clear ethical framework, it does not lead inexorably to the same place. Our own HFEA is far from

perfect, but you have only to look at the chaotic, under-regulated United States to see how lucky we are. In Britain, at least, we have rules and principles. We can harness change, make sure it is not open to abuse, or slow it down so that we have time to think about it.

Wherever I am, whatever aspect of reproductive medicine I am talking about, the questions are the same. Who decides? And what ideological agenda are those people serving? Thus, Nazi eugenics was evil because it served Nazi ideals. It was dangerous because it was backed up by a fascist state.

The HFEA's slow but steady move to a stance in favour of "eugenics for sound medical reasons" is a case in point. Most experts in the field predict that public attitudes will follow suit. But that is only a tiny part of the picture. The larger, cultural implications of reproductive technology will continue to trouble. Every new technique will challenge power relations within families and kinship networks, and therefore the way we bring up children. Wherever the family loses power over an individual's right to become a parent, the advantage goes not just to the individual but to the medical profession, big business and the state. Is this what we want? If we do not, we are going to have to fight it out politically. But first, we need a more rational debate.

CHINA'S ONE-CHILD POLICY

Established in 1979, the one-child policy of the government of the People's Republic of China restricts most Chinese couples to having one child. The policy, which was adopted as a measure to control China's rapidly growing population, has been controversial in the decades since it was first implemented. Some human rights observers have charged that the Chinese government has subjected women to forced sterilizations and abortions in carrying out the policy. As a result of the policy, the ratio of males to females in China is 118 to 100 (compared to the average ratio of 105 males to 100 females). In 2003, the Chinese government announced plans to relax the policy.

Questions for Discussion

1. Freely asserts that the public debates about reproductive situations like that of the Hashmi's get "muddled" because people "are talking about too many things at once." What exactly does she mean by that statement? How does that point relate to the main argument of her essay? **2.** Freely concedes that many of the concerns expressed by people on various sides of the reproductive controversy involving the Hashmi's are valid concerns. She even concedes that people who have racist ideas are asking important questions about this controversy. Why do you think Freely makes these concessions? In what ways might these concessions strengthen her main argument? **3.** A central point that Freely makes in this essay is that "the regulation of fertility" — and reproductive issues in general — are increasingly public, rather than private, issues. What counterarguments could you offer to that point? **4.** A British writer, Freely writes, "You have only to look at the chaotic, under-regulated United States to see how lucky we are. In Britain, at least, we have rules and principles. We can harness change, make sure it is not open to abuse, or slow it down so that we have time to think about it." She favors deliberate regulation of the technology based on "rules and principles." What purpose does this comparison to the United States serve? Do you think such a comparison is effective, given her audience? (Remember that Freely was writing this essay for a British magazine.) How did you react to this comparison? Does your reaction reflect your own nationality or ethnicity in any way? Explain. **5.** Freely ends her essay by stating that "we need a more rational debate" about reproductive issues. On the basis of her essay, what do you think she means by a "rational debate"? Do you think her essay is an example of an argument that would be part of such a debate? Explain, citing specific examples from her essay to support your answer.

③ **R O B I N   M A R A N T Z   H E N I G , "Adapting to Our Own Engineering"**

In late 2002, a little-known group called the Raelians caused a sensation by announcing the birth of a child who they claim was a human clone. The group would not identify the child and otherwise provided no evidence for their claim. But the stir caused by their announcement reflected the intensity of the ongoing interest in — and anxiety about — cloning. Ever since Scottish scientists were able to clone a sheep (nicknamed Dolly) in 1997, cloning has been the topic of heated debate. Many people, of course, worry about unforeseen consequences of human cloning, and moral arguments are often made against cloning as well. But some proponents argue that research into cloning can lead to beneficial medical advances. For instance, cloning might provide proteins to treat some diseases and genetic disorders; human skin might be cloned to treat burn victims. Yet it is precisely such scenarios that frighten many people, who wonder whether we are prepared for the unexpected dilemmas that such uses of cloning might present. Writer Robin Marantz Henig has monitored these debates and believes that they sound familiar. In her essay, which was published in the *New York Times* in 2002, she reminds us of other medical and technological advancements, such as in vitro fertilization, that once caused great concern but now seem commonplace. Her argument might help you to sort through some of the warnings and accusations that sometimes characterize public discussions about these issues. It might also lead you to wonder about the control — and ownership — we have over our bodies and the genetic material that make them what they are. Henig is the author of many books about science and health issues, including The *Monk in the Garden: The Lost and Found Genius of Gregor Mendel* (2000).

Adapting to Our Own Engineering
ROBIN MARANTZ HENIG

1 In the past few weeks, we've been treated to a familiar spectacle: scientists trying to nudge one another out of the way as they race toward something the rest of society considers beyond the pale. In this case, they're racing to produce the world's first human clone. A few years ago, such a contest would have seemed preposterous. But now, three different groups say they have clones in the making.

Severino Antinori, an Italian fertility doctor, says his clone will be born first. Dr. Antinori, who became famous in 1994 for helping a 62-year-old woman become pregnant by implanting a donor's fertil-ized egg in her uterus, says he has a clone pregnancy under way in an undis-closed country. The clone, he says, is a boy, due in early January.

Panayiotis Michael Zavos in Kentucky, Dr. Antinori's onetime partner and now his bitter enemy, says he does not be-lieve Dr. Antinori, and anyway he is working on something even better. Dr. Zavos, an embryologist, says he has col-lected cells from seven people who want to be cloned, and in the first two weeks of January he will insert the cells' nuclei into donated human eggs from which nu-clei have been removed. He promises that, unlike his rival, he will offer DNA evidence that each of the babies born of this adventure is an exact genetic replica of its parent.

And to add a little spice, there are the Raelians, members of a religious cult who believe the first humans were cloned by space aliens 25,000 years ago and who have taken on human cloning as a sacred mission. According to their chief scien-tist, Brigitte Boisselier, the Raelians now have five clone pregnancies under way, the first of which is to be delivered by the end of this month.

5 These claims, of course, raise all sorts of ethical, moral, religious and societal questions about whether we dare allow such a step. So it might help us to real-ize that we have been here before.

One of the first steps on the slippery slope that got us here was the one we took a generation ago, when scientists developed the technique of in-vitro fer-tilization.* Opponents warned then that in-vitro fertilization would lead to cloning — that without the ability to fertilize human eggs in a petri dish, and to culture them to the stage at which they are ready to implant into a womb, cloning would not be possible. So this is the development we were warned about

30 years ago, and it seems to be about to come to pass.

One crucial difference between then and now is what we are most afraid of. In the 1970's, the biggest fear was that in-vitro fertilization could fail, leading to heartache and, possibly, to grotesquely abnormal babies. Today, the biggest fear about cloning may be that it could succeed.

Still, it's eerie how many of the argu-ments made today against cloning echo the arguments that were made against in-vitro fertilization: that the child's un-natural start would lead to genetic com-plications we couldn't even imagine. That making a barren couple fertile in this ar-tificial way was an act of hubris for which the couple, the scientists and soci-ety would have to pay. That in animals, hundreds of attempts were needed before the first success, so any human investi-gation would require hundreds of failures and hundreds of potential embryos tossed down the laboratory sink. That the exper-imental animals born this way suffered a chromosomal abnormality or aged prema-turely or contracted cancer, even if they seemed normal at birth. That it would be a dreadful burden for children to be born with all the expectations parents bring to a high-tech pregnancy — and to be born, too, with the inevitable sense that there is something bizarre, abnormal or shame-ful about the way they came to be.

Some of these arguments had validity: There were many failures before successes — in humans, as there had been in ani-mals. But most predictions just didn't pan out. Being a test-tube baby never seemed to be much of a psychological burden for a child, not after Louise Brown was welcomed with such delight in July 1978. And animal experiments turned out to predict little about human experience, since mammalian reproduction varies significantly from one species to

*See in vitro fertiliza-tion on page 241.

another. (Rabbit sperm, for example, needs to be activated by a special laboratory treatment before it can fertilize rabbit eggs, but human sperm needs no such prodding.) Perhaps, then, animal cloning experiences like that of Dolly,[†] the cloned sheep who seems to be aging abnormally, can't tell us what we need to know about the safety of cloning humans.

10 The moral and religious arguments against cloning also evoke what some people were saying about in-vitro fertilization 30 years ago. Some of the earliest critics of in-vitro fertilization believed it threatened the very fabric of civilization: marriage, fidelity, the essence of family; our sense of who we are and where we're headed; what it means to be human, connected, normal, acceptable; ideas about love, sex and nurturing; the willingness to yield to the inscrutable, marvelous mystery of it all. If in-vitro fertilization were allowed to continue, some said, all these threads would unravel.

They didn't unravel, we can now see — or, to the extent that they did, it wasn't because of this fertilization method.

Still, these are some of the very same ethical arguments being made today against cloning.

The analogy is imperfect, of course, as most analogies are. In-vitro fertilization was a way to give Mother Nature a hand when it came to conception, while cloning turns Mother Nature on her head. With in-vitro fertilization, nature is imitated, not subverted. The only thing that changes is the place where the egg and sperm unite. After that, things pretty much proceed the way they normally do.

Cloning is a bigger deal. It renders the whole point of sexual reproduction — the blending of the heritage of one mother and one father into a splendid and unique new life — essentially beside the point.

In 2002, after the birth of nearly half a million normal, much-loved test-tube babies around the world, we can see the relative harmlessness of in-vitro fertilization.

[†]In 2002, the scientists who had cloned Dolly reported that she had developed arthritis. At the time, Dolly was five years old, an unusually young age for sheep, whose life expectancy is twelve to fourteen years, to develop arthritis. The scientists acknowledged that the onset of the disease might have been related to the fact that Dolly had been cloned, but they could not be sure. Dolly was created by scientists at the Roslin Institute, which conducts research on animal biotechnology (see http://www.roslin.ac.uk/). She died in 2003.

WHAT EXACTLY IS CLONING?

The term *cloning* refers to several scientific procedures for copying genetic material. The celebrated case of Dolly, the cloned sheep, represents one form of cloning, in which a technique called *somatic cell nuclear transfer* is used to create an embryo whose genetic material (specifically, its DNA) is identical to that of its mother. *Blastomere separation* is another cloning technique by which a developing embryo is split into two, which creates two exact copies of the same organism (much like naturally occurring identical twins). Much of the debate about cloning in the United States in 2001 and 2002 focused on less dramatic techniques by which research scientists create copies of chromosomes and other genetic material for the purposes of studying disease or human development or to create proteins or substances like insulin. Such techniques do not produce complete organisms but "pieces" of organisms by copying parts of their genetic material. According to the U.S. Human Genome Project, cloning can eventually be used for "adding genes (such as those for human proteins) to create drug-producing animals as well as inactivating genes to study the effects and possibly create animal models of human diseases. Cloning technology also might someday be used in humans to produce whole organs from single cells or to raise animals having genetically altered organs suitable for transplanting to humans." (See http://www.ornl.gov/hgmis/elsi/cloning.html.)

But it didn't seem harmless in the 1970's, when we didn't know that the story would have a happy ending.

15 We don't really know, in 2002, what the end of the story will be for human cloning — for the clones or for the rest of us. But just as our collective attitude about in-vitro fertilization took a 180-degree turn after the first few test-tube babies turned out to be normal, there may be an analogous evolution in our attitude toward the genetic and reproductive technologies that today seem most outlandish — not just cloning but manipulating our genetic destinies by altering our cells to make our kids taller or prettier, for example, or swapping genes with other animals.

At least some of this new century's most far-fetched techniques may eventually become so commonplace as to offer no apparent need for deliberation or debate. Ultimately, some of this genetic gerrymandering may become, as with in-vitro fertilization, just another part of the landscape in the strange terrain of genomes, genes and generation.

> **CONTEXT**
>
> One of the most respected and widely recognized newspapers in the world, the *New York Times* is distributed to a large international audience. Although it publishes essays by columnists and writers of many different political viewpoints, it is sometimes criticized for being too liberal. In what sense might Henig's essay be described as reflecting a liberal viewpoint? In what ways does it seem intended for a very broad audience?

Questions for Discussion

1. How would you summarize Henig's main argument in this essay? What assumptions about technology and medical science do you think Henig makes in her argument? Do you agree that these assumptions are valid? Why or why not? **2.** Henig argues that current debates about cloning are similar to the debates about in vitro fertilization that occurred in the late 1970s, when that technique was being pioneered. What evidence does she offer to support this point? How does this point help her make her main argument about cloning? **3.** In paragraph 8, Henig lists a number of arguments that were made against in vitro fertilization in the 1970s. What do you think is the effect of this list of arguments? How might this list help Henig make her main argument? **4.** Henig acknowledges that the analogy she draws between arguments against in vitro fertilization and arguments against cloning is imperfect. What do you think Henig accomplishes by making this acknowledgement? In what ways might it enhance or weaken her main argument? **5.** Henig writes that cloning is "a bigger deal" than in vitro fertilization, because "it renders the whole point of sexual reproduction — the blending of the heritage of one mother and one father into a splendid and unique new life — essentially beside the point." How would you describe Henig's tone here? What might her tone reveal about her position on cloning? Do you find her tone effective? Why or why not?

④ **WENDY McELROY, "Victims from Birth"**

The capability to "engineer" a baby through certain medical reproductive techniques is often described by proponents as a way to avoid serious birth defects and to ensure that a child will be born healthy. But what if a couple wishes their child to be born with what most people consider to be a disability? Do those parents have the right to "engineer" such a child? Do they "own" that child's physical identity to the extent that they can use medical science to give that child certain characteristics that others find undesirable? In the following essay, feminist activist Wendy McElroy says no. She discusses an unusual case involving two women who used reproductive techniques to make it more likely that the child they would have would be deaf, just like the two of them. As McElroy notes in her essay, these parents believe that deafness is not a disability but a culture, and they wished their child to be part of that culture. But McElroy wonders whether the child himself would have chosen to be deaf — if he had had such a choice. She argues that the choice should have been his. Despite her unequivocal position on this case, McElroy complicates the already difficult questions surrounding genetics and reproductive issues. In a sense, she asks us to consider who owns our physical identities in an age when medical science makes it possible to alter and even to determine those identities. Wendy McElroy writes a column for FoxNews.com and has authored many books and articles, including most recently *Individualist Feminist and the Nineteenth Century* (2001) and *Liberty for Women: Freedom and Feminism in the 21st Century* (2002). She is a research fellow at the Independent Institute, a public policy think tank.

Victims from Birth
WENDY McELROY

1 When Sharon Duchesneau gave birth on Thanksgiving Day to a deaf son, she was delighted.

Duchesneau and her lesbian partner, Candace McCullough, had done everything they could to ensure that Gauvin would be born without hearing. The two deaf women selected their sperm donor on the basis of his family history of deafness in order, as McCullough explained, "to increase our chances of having a baby who is deaf."

So they consciously attempted to create a major sensory defect in their child.

Scientists and philosophers have been debating the morality of new reproductive technologies that may allow us to design "perfect" human beings.

Adolf Hitler's infamous ideas about a "master race" were based in part on a belief that a tribe of Indo-Europeans called Aryans invaded and subdued the Indian subcontinent around 1700 B.C. These Aryans were thought to be Nordic in appearance, which contributed to Hitler's belief that Germans were descended from this tribe. Historians and anthropologists generally dismiss the notion that Aryans existed or that any such tribe conquered parts of Eurasia.

Advocates dream of eliminating conditions such as spina bifida; critics invoke images of Nazis creating an Aryan race.*

5 But what of prospective parents who deliberately engineer a genetic defect into their offspring?

Why? Duchesneau illustrates one motive.

She believes deafness is a culture, not a disability. A deaf lifestyle is a choice she wishes to make for her son and his older sister Jehanne. McCullough said she and her partner are merely expressing the natural tendency to want children "like them."

"You know, black people have harder lives," she said. "Why shouldn't parents be able to go ahead and pick a black donor if that's what they want?"

Passing over the problem of equating race with a genetic defect, McCullough seems to be saying that deafness is a minority birthright to be passed on proudly from parent to child. By implication, those appalled by their choice are compared to bigots.

10 Some in the media have implicitly endorsed their view.

On March 31st, the *Washington Post Magazine* ran a sympathetic cover story entitled "A World of Their Own" with the subtitle, "In the eyes of his parents, if Gauvin Hughes McCullough turns out to be deaf, that will be just perfect." The article features Gauvin's birth and ends with the two women taking him home. There they tell family and friends that, "He is not as profoundly deaf as Jehanne, but he is quite deaf. Deaf enough." The article does not comment critically on the parents' decision not to fit Gauvin with a hearing aid and develop whatever hearing ability exists.

The Duchesneau case is particularly troubling to advocates of parental rights against governmental intrusion. The moral outrage it elicits easily can lead to bad law — laws that may hinder responsible parents from using genetic techniques to remedy conditions such as cystic fibrosis in embryos. Selective breeding, after all, is a form of genetic engineering. The Duchesneau case, then, brings all other forms of genetic engineering into question.

The championing of deafness as a cultural "good" owes much to political correctness or the politics of victimhood, which view group identity as the foundation of all political and cultural analysis.

Disabled people used to announce, "I am not my disability." They demanded that society look beyond the withered arm, a clubbed-foot, or a wheel chair and see the human being, a human who was essentially identical to everyone else.

15 Now, for some, the announcement has become, "I am my deafness. That is what is special about me."

Society is brutal to those who are different. I know. As a result of my grandmother contracting German measles, my mother was born with a severely deformed arm. She concealed her arm beneath sweaters with sleeves that dangled loosely, even in sweltering weather. She hid.

Embracing a physical defect, as Duchesneau and McCullough have done, may be a more healthy personal response. Certainly they should be applauded for moving beyond the painful deaf childhoods they describe.

However, I remember my mother telling me that the birth of her children

---

COMPLICATION

"In the case of Duchesneau and McCullough, there is no ethical issue — the couple have the right to procreate with whomever they want. And many couples with a family history of deafness or disability seek to have a child without that disability. But some deaf couples have expressed the desire to use prenatal genetic testing of their fetus or in vitro fertilisation and preimplantation genetic diagnosis to select a deaf child. These choices are not unique to deafness. Dwarves may wish to have a dwarf child. People with intellectual disability may wish to have a child like them. Couples of mixed race may wish to have a light skinned child (or a dark skinned child, if they are mindful of reducing the risk of skin cancer in countries like Australia)." Source: Julian Savulescu, "Deaf Babies, 'Designer Disability,' and the Future of Medicine." *British Medical Journal* (October 2002).

CONTEXT

McElroy's essay was published in 2002 on a Web site called iFeminists.com, which describes itself as "an all-inclusive online center where people looking for a new way to approach feminism can gather online, learn, and access a wealth of information. iFeminists.com offers in-depth resources and portal-like tools for everyone: activists and scholars, experts and beginners, women and men." "iFeminism," according to the site, refers to "independent feminism," which "calls for freedom, choice, and personal responsibility." iFeminists believe that "freedom and diversity benefit women, whether or not the choices that particular women make are politically correct. They respect all sexual choices, from motherhood to porn. As the cost of freedom, iFeminists accept personal responsibility for their own lives. They do not look to government for privileges any more than they would accept government abuse." In what sense does McElroy's argument in this essay reflect an iFeminist philosophy?

— both healthy and physically unremarkable — were the two happiest moments of her life. I contrast this with Duchesneau who, knowing the pain of growing up deaf, did what she could to impose deafness upon her son.

Deafness is not fundamentally a cultural choice, although a culture has sprung up around it. If it were, deafness would not be included in the Americans with Disabilities Act[†] — a source of protection and funding that deaf-culture zealots do not rush to renounce.

20 But if deafness is to be considered a cultural choice, let it be the choice of the child, not the parents. Let a child with all five senses decide to renounce or relinquish one of them in order to embrace what may be a richer life. If a child is rendered incapable of deciding "yes" or "no," then in what manner is it a choice?

[†]According to the U.S. Department of Justice, the Americans with Disabilities Act (ADA), passed in 1990, "gives civil rights protections to individuals with disabilities similar to those provided to individuals on the basis of race, color, sex, national origin, age, and religion. It guarantees equal opportunity for individuals with disabilities in public accommodations, employment, transportation, State and local government services, and telecommunications."

Questions for Discussion

1. On what grounds does McElroy criticize Duchesneau and McCullough's efforts to have a deaf child?

2. Why does McElroy reject the view that deafness is a culture? How convincing is her argument against that view? **3.** Why is this case troubling for advocates of parental rights who resist government intrusion on parenting decisions, according to McElroy? In what sense is this point important to McElroy's main argument about this case? **4.** In making a point about how difficult it is to be different in our society, McElroy refers to her mother's disability. Evaluate the effectiveness of this use of personal experience. Is McElroy's analogy between her mother's disability and the birth of the deaf child she describes in this essay relevant to her point? Explain. **5.** McElroy's essay can be described as an argument based on deductive reasoning (see pages 26–31). On what fundamental belief or principle does McElroy base her argument? Do you agree with her? Why or why not?

NEGOTIATING DIFFERENCES

The debates surrounding reproductive issues such as prenatal diagnosis, genetic engineering, surrogate parenting, and cloning are so intense in part because they raise questions that challenge some of our most fundamental moral and ethical beliefs. In many instances, these issues give rise to conflicts that seem irreconcilable. Often, the participants in these conflicts seem to occupy positions that offer little room for negotiation or resolution. And although none of the essays in this section overtly reflect such positions, they all address difficult questions that can easily lead to animosity and conflict. The great challenge in addressing such issues is to try to seek some acceptable resolution without conflict. This assignment asks you to take up that challenge.

All the essays in this section address in some way the same basic moral or ethical questions about who has the right to decide what happens to our bodies. Your task is to examine these moral and ethical questions and try to identify the fundamental beliefs or values that come into play in such debates. Write an essay, intended primarily for your classmates, in which you make an argument for an approach to addressing these conflicts about reproductive issues. In other words, your goal is to try to find common ground among the various positions that people take in these debates and to make an argument that might be acceptable, or at least reasonable, to people who hold differing views. Be sure to identify the values or beliefs that you think can be the foundation for accomplishing such a goal.

Keep in mind that it is impossible to resolve these complex issues in a way that would be satisfying to everyone who is concerned about them — especially in a brief essay. But it might be possible to find a way to address these issues that many, if not most, people would find acceptable as a first step. For example, you might argue for a specific first step that would allow interested parties to open up a dialogue about the more difficult issues involved. Such a first step might be a policy to decide when complicated cases (such as the one described in the essay by Wendy McElroy) should be reviewed by a panel of experts or a court. And if you argue effectively, you might be able to persuade even those who hold opposing views that they share values and ideals.

As an alternative, write the same essay described here, but instead of addressing your classmates as your audience, select the readers of a specific publication as your intended audience. You might choose a publication with a very general audience, such as the *New York Times* or *USA Today.* Or you might select a more specialized publication that addresses a more specific audience, such as a magazine devoted to women's issues or a journal with an overt political slant. Or you might decide to write for your local newspaper. Whichever publication you choose, review several issues of it to become familiar with its style and conventions and to get a sense of how it addresses its intended audience.

WHO OWNS

MUSIC?

I n January 2003, in a case known as *Eldred* v. *Ashcroft,* the U.S. Supreme Court upheld a law that extended the term for copyrights for books, movies, music, and other intellectual property for twenty years beyond the fifty years that previous laws already provided for. The case was considered to be one of the most important decisions involving intellectual property in recent decades, and the intense debate surrounding it reflects the importance of copyright law in the United States and the deep concerns many citizens have about it. Those concerns seem especially deep when it comes to copyrights involving music. ■ Although creative works of all kinds are protected under copyright law, music seems to generate particularly intense controversy. Perhaps that's because music is so much a part of the lives of most people; for many people, music is not so much a product as a cultural treasure to which everyone has a right. (See Con-Text on page 255.) It can also be difficult to distinguish among the many different forms of music and the variety of media in which it exists. For example, is a song that is played on the radio subject to the same copyright rules as a song that is played on a CD in a private home? ■ *Eldred* v. *Ashcroft* highlighted the complexity of questions about who owns music and controls its distribution. While representatives of media corporations praised the ruling as an important protection for songwriters and musicians, others complained that the ruling would prevent the public from enjoying the benefits of musical works. Some scholars believe that the framers of the Constitution intended copyright to encourage scientific and creative work and to ensure that such work would eventually benefit the public. But copyright law can also mean profits. It gives songwriters and musicians — and the media companies that produce and distribute their work — the right to earn money from their songs or performances, and it prevents others from profiting unfairly from copyrighted music. And the great popularity of music means that there is a great deal of money at stake. ■ Recent technological developments have added to the difficulty of sorting through these issues. The capabilities of new computer technologies have made it easier than ever for consumers to reproduce and share music. Like millions of other consumers, you might have visited Web sites where you can download, free of charge, copies of your favorite songs that someone else has made available on that site. Such capabilities raise questions about when a copy of a song is being used illegally. Is it a violation of copyright law to download a music file that was copied from a CD that another person legally purchased and then made available on a private Web site? Or is downloading a file the same thing as letting a friend borrow a CD you have purchased so that he or she can record it? The media companies supporting the decision in *Eldred* v. *Ashcroft* believe that they are losing profits whenever someone downloads a song in this way. Others argue that consumers have the right to share music through the Internet. Although the copyright to a song indicates clearly who "owns" that song, it is less clear how far that copyright extends. Must be permission be granted every time that song is played or copied, no matter what the circumstances? Such questions involve legal and economic complexities that will become even more difficult to sort out as new technologies develop. ■ But as the essays in this section indicate, controversies involving the ownership of music are not limited to legal or economic issues. Music can also be considered an expression of cultural identity. But who owns that identity? That question emerged as hip hop and rap music gained popularity in the 1980s and 1990s.

These musical forms "borrowed" from other kinds of music in the form of sampling, a practice whereby an artist incorporates or "quotes" from other songs. Some artists believe that such sampling requires payment, because parts of songs are protected by copyright law. In turn, rap music, which many consider to be a form of Black cultural expression, influenced other musicians, who then "borrowed" from rap — raising questions about whether such borrowing is simply the influence of one form of music on another or constitutes "stealing" an artist's racial or cultural identity. ■ Like certain written works, music has also been subject to censorship in the United States and elsewhere in the world. Sometimes such censorship is based on concerns about morality; sometimes it is driven by political beliefs. Whatever the case, censoring music raises questions not only about free speech but also about who has the right to control artistic expression. ■ Obviously, as such an important and widespread part of culture, music is much more than entertainment. Thus, the questions about the ownership of music raised by the essays in this section reflect important social, legal, economic, and even moral concerns that affect all of us, regardless of our musical tastes. These essays might not provide answers to the kinds of difficult questions regarding intellectual property and music that we have discussed here. But they can help us to understand the issues so that we can seek our own answers in a more informed manner.

CON-TEXT: The Importance of Music

1 Music is a basic function of human existence, arising from the physiological, psychological, and sociological needs of human kind. As such, the value of musical pursuit derives not only from the endeavor to achieve the highest forms of the musical art according to socially accepted norms, but also from the everyday musical encounters of every person. To this end, music is a necessary, life-enhancing experience which should be nurtured in all individuals, not only in those gifted with musical aptitude.

Music is an invariant. It has been present in all cultures, at all times, and throughout the known historical development of the human species, facilitating emotional, physical, and social expression. Music satisfies the human need for aesthetic enjoyment, provides for communication of cultural ideals, integrates, and enculturates.

SOURCE: Kenneth Liske, "Philosophy of Music Education."

① JANIS IAN, "Free Downloads Play Sweet Music"

In the late 1990s, as digital technologies began to influence the consumer market for music, listeners began to take advantage of the capabilities of the Internet to share music with each other. With powerful new computer technologies, a consumer could purchase a CD by a favorite musician, copy a song from that CD to a computer hard drive, then send that song to a friend — and to many other people as well — through the Internet. Eventually, Web sites were established that became clearinghouses for music, usually as MP3 files, a digital format that is well suited to reproducing sound. The best-known of these Web sites was Napster, which at the height of its popularity was visited by hundreds of thousands of users each day, many of whom would download music files via Napster's peer-to-peer software. But even after a legal suit curtailed much of the file-downloading activity enabled by Napster's software in 2000, consumers have continued to find ways to share music files digitally, raising concerns among some musicians and among media companies about copyright violations and about lost profits. As media companies seek ways to prevent the exchange of music files, advocates of free speech and privacy — including some musicians, like Janis Ian — argue that music should be freely available on the Internet, even if that music is protected by copyright. In the following essay, Ian, herself an accomplished musician and recording artist who has won two Grammy awards, argues that musicians and consumers can all benefit from free music downloads; moreover, she suggests that free downloads are good for the art itself by making music more widely available. Her essay encourages us to consider some of the economic issues involving music downloads. But her argument might also be cause to wonder about who should control the distribution of music, once a song has been protected by copyright. This article appeared on *ZDNet*, an Internet technology network, in 2002. It is a shorter version of the original article, which was published in *Performing Songwriter Magazine* in 2002.

Free Downloads Play Sweet Music
JANIS IAN

1 When researching an article, I normally send e-mails to friends and acquaintances, who answer my request with opinions and anecdotes. But when I said I was planning to argue that free Internet downloads are good for the music industry and its artists, I was swamped.

I received over 300 replies — and every single one from someone legitimately in the music business.

Even more interesting than the

e-mails were the phone calls. I don't know anyone at the National Academy of Recording Arts & Sciences (NARAS, home of the Grammy Awards), and I know Hilary Rosen (head of the Recording Industry Association of America, or RIAA)* only in passing. Yet within 24 hours of sending my original e-mail, I'd received two messages from Rosen and four from NARAS, requesting that I call to "discuss the article."

Huh. Didn't know I was that widely read.

5 Ms. Rosen, to be fair, stressed that she was only interested in presenting RIAA's side of the issue, and was kind enough to send me a fair amount of statistics and documentation, including a number of focus group studies RIAA had run on the matter.

However, the problem with focus groups is the same problem anthropologists have when studying peoples in the field: the moment the anthropologist's presence is known, everything changes. Hundreds of scientific studies have shown that any experimental group *wants to please the examiner.* For focus groups, this is particularly true. Coffee and donuts are the least of the payoffs.

The NARAS people were a bit more pushy. They told me downloads were "destroying sales," "ruining the music industry," and "costing *you* money."

Costing *me* money? I don't pretend to be an expert on intellectual property law, but I do know one thing. If a music industry executive claims I should agree with their agenda because it will make me more money, I put my hand on my wallet . . . and check it after they leave, just to make sure nothing's missing.

Am I suspicious of all this hysteria? You bet. Do I think the issue has been badly handled? Absolutely. Am I concerned about losing friends, opportunities, my 10th Grammy nomination, by

publishing this article? Yeah. I am. But sometimes things are just wrong, and when they're that wrong, they have to be addressed.

10 The premise of all this ballyhoo is that the industry (and its artists) are being harmed by free downloading.

Nonsense.

Let's take it from my personal experience. My site gets an average of 75,000 hits a year. Not bad for someone whose last hit record was in 1975. When Napster was running full-tilt, we received about 100 hits a month from people who'd downloaded Society's Child or At Seventeen for free, then decided they wanted more information. Of those 100 people (and these are only the ones who let us know how they'd found the site), 15 bought CDs.

Not huge sales, right? No record company is interested in 180 extra sales a year. But that translates into $2,700, which is a lot of money in my book. And that doesn't include the people who bought the CDs in stores, or came to my shows.

RIAA, NARAS and most of the entrenched music industry argue that free

*According to its Web site, "The Recording Industry Association of America is the trade group that represents the U.S. recording industry. Its mission is to foster a business and legal climate that supports and promotes our members' creative and financial vitality. Its members are the record companies that comprise the most vibrant national music industry in the world. RIAA© members create, manufacture and/or distribute approximately 90% of all legitimate sound recordings produced and sold in the United States." The RIAA filed the lawsuit against Napster that ended Napster's online music sharing service.

NAPSTER

An Internet service for sharing music files (in MP3 format), Napster was founded in 1999 by a college student named Shawn Fanning, who established a Web site where users could exchange their private music files. Napster quickly became an Internet phenomenon as thousands of users began to use Napster's file-sharing software to share music. As many as 60 million users were visiting the site by early 2001. In 2000, the Recording Industry Association of America (RIAA) filed suit against Napster, alleging copyright infringement, and a drawn-out court battle ensued. A court ruled in favor of the RIAA in 2000 and stopped the free exchange of copyrighted files via Napster's software, but Napster continued to operate in a more limited way until 2002, when additional court rulings finally shut it down. But the issues regarding intellectual property, copyright law, and consumer privacy that the Napster case raised generated intense debate that continued well after Napster ceased its operations.

The music industry had exactly the same response to the advent of reel-to-reel home tape recorders, cassettes, DATs, minidiscs, videos, MTV ("Why buy the record when you can tape it?") and a host of other technological advances designed to make the consumer's life easier and better. I know because I was there.

The only reason they didn't react that way publicly to the advent of CDs was because they believed CDs were uncopyable. I was told this personally by a former head of Sony marketing, when they asked me to license Between the Lines in CD format at a reduced royalty rate. ("Because it's a brand new technology.")

Realistically, why do most people download music? To hear new music, and to find old, out-of-print music — not to avoid paying $5 at the local used CD store, or taping it off the radio, but to hear music they can't find anywhere else. Face it: Most people can't afford to spend $15.99 to experiment. And an awful lot of records are out of print; I have a few myself!

downloads hurt sales. More than hurt — it's destroying the industry.

15 Alas, the music industry needs no outside help to destroy itself. We're doing a very adequate job of that on our own, thank you.

Everyone is forgetting the main way an artist becomes successful — exposure. Without exposure, no one comes to shows, no one buys CDs, no one enables you to earn a living doing what you love. 20 Again, from personal experience: In 37 years as a recording artist, I've created 25-plus albums for major labels, and I've *never* received a royalty statement that didn't show I owed *them* money. Label accounting practices are right up there with Enron. I make the bulk of my living from live touring, doing my own show. Live shows are pushed by my Web site, which is pushed by the live shows, and both are pushed by the availability of my music, for free, online.

Who gets hurt by free downloads? Save a handful of super-successes like Celine Dion, none of us. We only get helped.

Most consumers have no problem paying for entertainment. If the music industry had a shred of sense, they'd have addressed this problem seven years ago, when people like Michael Camp were trying to obtain legitimate licenses for music online. Instead, the industrywide attitude was, "It'll go away." That's the same attitude CBS Records had about rock 'n' roll when Mitch Miller was head of A&R. (And you wondered why they passed on The Beatles and The Rolling Stones.)

NARAS and RIAA are moaning about the little mom-and-pop stores being shoved out of business; no one worked harder to shove them out than our own industry, which greeted every new mega-music store with glee, and offered steep discounts to Target, WalMart, et al, for stocking their CDs. The Internet has zero

> ### CONTEXT
>
> **Born in 1951, singer and songwriter Janis Ian released the first of her seventeen albums in 1967. Her 1975 hit song "At Seventeen" earned her the first of two Grammy Awards. She has recorded music for many movie soundtracks, and she has received acclaim as a jazz musician as well as for her children's music. Despite her own success, she has been an outspoken critic of many of the practices of the music industry.**

to do with store closings and lowered sales.

And for those of us with major label contracts who want some of our music available for free downloading . . . well, the record companies own our masters, our outtakes, even our demos, and they won't allow it. Furthermore, they own our voices for the duration of the contract, so we can't post a live track for downloading even if we want to.

25 If you think about it, the music industry should be rejoicing at this new technological advance. Here's a foolproof way to deliver music to millions who might otherwise never purchase a CD in a store. The cross-marketing opportunities are unbelievable. Costs are minimal, shipping nonexistent — a staggering vehicle for higher earnings and lower costs. Instead, they're running around like chickens with their heads cut off, bleeding on everyone and making no sense.

There is *zero* evidence that material available for free online downloading is financially harming anyone. In fact, most of the hard evidence is to the contrary.

The RIAA is correct in one thing — these are times of great change in our industry. But at a time when there are arguably only four record labels left in America (Sony, AOL Time Warner, Universal, BMG — and where is the

> ### COMPLICATION
>
> "I admit it, I love technology. Technologically speaking, I think MP3s are a great idea. But I hate music piracy.
>
> "I believe that it is wrong to copy an artist's intellectual property (their music) without their permission. I believe the same about all intellectual property, such as computer software. I think that all intellectual property owners have the absolute right to decide how their creations are distributed.
>
> "Because of the nature of intellectual property, stealing some of that property doesn't physically remove anything. So there's obviously nothing wrong with music piracy, right? To the contrary. Because intellectual property is just an idea or a representation of that idea, distribution rights is the only thing an intellectual property owner actually owns. In other words, downloading music when the artist doesn't give permission robs them of the only thing they actually have — the right to decide who gets to hear their music and how much it costs them." Source: Kevin Markham, "MP3s Great Technology, but Use Must Be Ethical." (2000).

RICO act when we need it?), when entire genres are glorifying the gangster mentality and losing their biggest voices to violence, when executives change positions as often as Zsa Zsa Gabor changed clothes, and "A&R" has become a euphemism for "Absent & Redundant," we have other things to worry about.

We'll turn into Microsoft if we're not careful, folks, insisting that any household wanting an extra copy for the car, the kids, or the portable CD player, has to go out and "license" multiple copies.

As artists, we have the ear of the masses. We have the trust of the masses. By speaking out in our concerts and in the press, we can do a great deal to dampen this hysteria, and put the blame for the sad state of our industry right back where it belongs — in the laps of record companies, radio programmers, and our own apparent inability to organize ourselves in order to better our own lives — and those of our fans.

30 If we don't take the reins, no one will.

Questions for Discussion

1. Ian draws heavily on her own experience as a musician and a recording artist to support her position on music downloads. Evaluate her use of personal experience as evidence. How effective do you think it is? Is it adequate for her main argument? Do you think she could have used other kinds of evidence to support her argument? Explain. (In answering these questions, you might wish to review the discussion of appraising evidence on pages 76–82). **2.** Ian begins her essay by telling an anecdote about the number of messages she received from people who learned that she was writing about free music downloads. Why do you think she begins her essay in this way? Do you think this beginning is an effective way for her to introduce her subject? Explain. **3.** Ian writes, "There is *zero* evidence that material available for free online downloading is financially harming anyone. In fact, most of the hard evidence is to the contrary." To what extent do you think Ian provides such "hard evidence" in her essay? Do you think she is persuasive on this point? Why or why not? **4.** How would you describe Ian's writing style in this essay? In what ways do you think her style might make her argument more effective? What sort of persona, or *ethos* (see pages 73–75) does her style establish? How might her background and experience as a recording artist contribute to that persona? **5.** Ian devotes a considerable amount of her essay to discussing the positions of music industry people who oppose free music downloads. Why do you think she does so? Do you think she presents their concerns fairly? Explain. How does she characterize the music industry people who oppose her position? In what ways might her argument be strengthened — or weakened — by the way she characterizes these people and their interests? **6.** This essay was published in *ZDNet,* a network of Internet sites that is, according to its Web site, intended for "IT [information technology] professionals and business influencers" and "provides an invaluable perspective and resources so that users can get the most out of their investments in technology." In what ways do you think Ian addresses this audience? Do you think she does so effectively? Explain.

(2) RICHARD TARUSKIN, "Music Dangers and the Case for Control"

Efforts by governments or institutions (such as religious organizations) to ban certain kinds of music are nothing new. So when the Taliban, the Islamic group that ruled Afghanistan from 1996 to 2002, instituted severe and often brutal restrictions on music, many observers saw the move as just another example of censorship. Western critics condemned the ban as a repressive attempt by the Taliban to impose its religious views on the Afghani people, and they argued that free expression — in this case, in the form of music — is a right that should be guaranteed to all people. But is censoring or restricting music ever justified? Music professor Richard Taruskin thinks so. Although he doesn't condone repressive measures such as the Taliban instituted, Taruskin believes that governments can have a compelling — and justifiable — interest in controlling music to serve the public good. This position might seem dramatically out of step with Western values of free speech. But Taruskin argues that music, like other kinds of art, isn't just a form of artistic expression but a means of conveying ideas or beliefs as well. He contends that governments routinely try to control the distribution of certain ideas — with good reason; therefore, governments have reason to control music. Many Americans will likely disagree with Taruskin. But as you read, consider his view of what music is and why it might justifiably be controlled in the public interest. Richard Taruskin teaches music history at the University of California at Berkeley. This essay appeared in the *New York Times* in December, 2001.

Music Dangers and the Case for Control
RICHARD TARUSKIN

1 And on top of everything else, the Taliban hate music, too. In an interview in October with Nicholas Wroe, a columnist for the British newspaper *The Guardian,* John Baily, an ethnomusicologist on the faculty of Goldsmiths College, London, gave the details. After taking power in 1996, the Islamic fundamentalists who ruled most of Afghanistan undertook search-and-destroy missions in which musical instruments and cassette players were seized and burned in public pyres. Wooden poles were festooned with great ribbons of confiscated audio and video tape as a reminder of the ban, imposed in keeping with a maxim attributed to the prophet Muhammad warning "those who listen to music and songs in this world" that "on the Day of Judgment molten lead will be poured into their ears."

Musicians caught in the act were beaten with their instruments and imprisoned for as many as 40 days. The interdiction on professional music-making closed off yet another avenue to women's participation in public life. The only sounds on the Taliban-dominated radio that Western ears would recognize as musical were those of ritual chanting (something quite distinct from "music," both conceptually and linguistically, in Islamic thought as in many of the world's cultures).

So what else is new? Utopians, puritans and totalitarians have always sought to regulate music, if not forbid it outright. Ayatollah Ruhollah Khomeini, probably the Taliban's immediate model, banned it from Iranian radio and television in 1979, because its effects, he said, were like those of opium, "stupefying persons listening to it and making their brains inactive and frivolous."

But our own "Western" tradition is just as full of suspicion toward music, much of it religious. In the fourth century, St. Augustine confessed that as a result of his sensuous enjoyment of the melodies he heard in church, "I have become a problem unto myself." In the 12th, John of Salisbury complained that the spectacular music sung in the Paris Cathedral of Notre Dame could "more easily occasion titillation between the legs than a sense of devotion in the brain." Protestant reformers in England and Switzerland seized and burned books containing "popish ditties" with Talibanish zeal. Somewhat later, the Orthodox patriarch of Moscow ordered bonfires of musical instruments, thought to be avatars of paganism.

5 Religious distrust of music often arises out of distrust of its conduits, especially when female. St. John Chrysostom, the great Father of the Greek Orthodox Church, complained that when marriages were solemnized, "dancing, and cymbals and flutes, and shameful words and songs from the lips of painted girls" were introduced, and with them "all the Devil's great heap of garbage." Near the beginning of my career as a college music teacher, a young Hasidic man in fringes and gabardines approached me on the first day of class to inform me that he was willing to take my course, but that he would sit near the door, and I was to warn him whenever I would play a record that contained the sound of a woman's voice so that he could slip into the hall and avoid it. (Don't do me any favors, I replied.)

Secular thinkers have been no less leery of music. In a famous passage from Plato's "Republic," Socrates advocates banning most of the musical modes or scales, "because more than anything else rhythm and harmony find their way to the inmost soul and take strongest hold upon it, bringing with them and imparting grace, if one is rightly trained, and otherwise the contrary." If Plato were writing today (or less euphemistically),

AYATOLLAH KHOMEINI AND THE TALIBAN

In 1979, exiled Islamic leader Ayatollah Ruhollah Khomeini returned to Iran after his supporters overthrew the U.S.-backed government of the Shah of Iran. Khomeini imposed a government based on his interpretation of the Koran, the holy book of Islam, and harshly criticized Western culture, especially American culture, as decadent, irreligious, and dangerous. Many scholars believed that his model of an Islamic theocracy was adopted by the Taliban when they took power in Afghanistan in 1996. By then, Khomeini had died, but the government he had established in Iran remained in power and served as an inspiration to Moslems elsewhere who shared his interpretation of the Koran. Although many Western and even some Arab nations condemned the Taliban for what they believed were repressive and brutal controls over the people of Afghanistan, some Moslems looked to the Taliban as another model for establishing an Islamic state. The Taliban were removed from power after the United States and its allies invaded Afghanistan in 2002.

arts into a delivery system for political propaganda. Here is how one of Plato's heirs, Joseph Goebbels, retorted to the conductor Wilhelm Furtwängler's plea for moderation in implementing Nazi arts policies:

"Art, in an absolute sense, as liberal democracy knows it, has no right to exist. Any attempt to further such an art could, in the end, cause a people to lose its inner relationship to art and the artist to isolate himself from the moving forces of his time, shut in the airless chambers of 'art for art's sake.' Art must be good but, beyond that, conscious of its responsibility, competent, close to the people and combative in spirit."

10 The same kind of pronouncements and policy directives emanated from the Soviets, nominally the Nazis' enemies. Awful memories of the 1948 show trials convened by Andrei Zhdanov, Stalin's de facto cultural commissar, at which the leading Soviet composers (among them Prokofiev and Shostakovich) were humiliated for their "formalist" misdeeds, feed the current mania for vindicating the same composers, absurdly, as dissidents. The similarity of Nazi and Soviet views on the arts is only one reason political classifications nowadays tend to group the old far right and far left together, in opposition to the "liberal democracy" that appeared, until Sept. 11, to have beaten all of its opponents into submission.

he might have put body in place of soul. For surely it is the all but irresistible kinesthetic response that music evokes that makes it such a potent influence on behavior, thence on morals and belief.

That is what sets music off from literature and painting, and attracts the special attention of censors despite its relative abstractness, which might seem to exempt it from the need for political policing. Tolstoy compared its effects to those of hypnosis, linking right up with Ayatollah Khomeini's strictures. And it can only be a similar discomfort about music's affinity with our grosser animal nature that led so many musical modernists to put so much squeamish distance between their cerebral art and viscerally engaging popular culture.

In any case, Plato's mingled awe and suspicion of music's uncanny power over our minds and bodies have echoed through the ages wherever governments have tried to harness music to uphold the public order (or at least keep music from disrupting it). They found the greatest resonance in those 20th-century totalitarian states that tried to turn the

That is probably why the Taliban's ban on musical performances, while in no way an unusual historical event (and not even really news), has suddenly drawn so much comment. It symbolizes the survival of impulses we might naïvely have thought discredited for good and all — as dead, in their way, as smallpox, with whose revival we are also unexpectedly threatened in these unsettled times.

Anything that conjures up both Nazis and Soviets, and now the Taliban, can have few friends in contemporary Western society. As Mayor Giuliani found out before he became our hero, hardly anything a politician can do will elicit a more dependable outcry across the political spectrum than a move in the direction of arts censorship, even if it threatens no direct intervention in the affairs of artists but only the withholding of municipal largess from institutions (like the Brooklyn Museum of Art) that support them. There is near unanimity in the West today that when it comes to the arts, laissez-faire (coupled, perhaps illogically, with handouts) is the way to go.

But who takes art more seriously? Those who want it left alone or those who want to regulate it? Moreover, the laissez-faire position entails some serious denials. Some say that art is inherently uplifting (if it is really art). Others say that art is inherently transgressive (if it is really art). The words in parentheses, designed to discourage counterexamples and make refutation impossible, merely empty the statements of real meaning. Does such a defense really show a commitment to the value of

art or merely an unwillingness to think about it?

And what about public opinion, which sometimes demands abstentions from the performance or exhibit of artworks? Is that just another censorship tribunal? **15** The musical test case par excellence has always been the taboo on Wagner performances in Israel. Breaching it makes headlines, as the conductor Daniel Barenboim knows very well. He did it last summer to a great din of public protest and righteous indignation. But those who defended Mr. Barenboim's provocation often failed to distinguish between voluntary abstinence out of consideration for people's feelings and a mandated imposition on people's rights.

It was only a social contract that Mr. Barenboim defied, but he seemed to want credit for defying a ban. His act implied that the feelings of Holocaust survivors had been coddled long enough and that continuing to honor them was both an intolerable infringement on his career and an insult to artistic greatness. To agree with him, one had to stretch the definition of censorship way beyond that associated with Nazis, Soviets and Islamic fundamentalists, into moral terrain usually associated with forbearance or discretion or mutual respect.

Now the issue has been joined again, even more pointedly and painfully, in the aftermath of the Sept. 11 terrorist attacks. Announcing that it preferred "to err on the side of being sensitive," the management of the Boston Symphony Orchestra recently canceled its scheduled performances of choruses from "The Death of Klinghoffer," the notoriously controversial opera — masterminded by the director Peter Sellars, with a libretto by the poet Alice Goodman and a score by John Adams — that re-enacts and comments on the murder of an American Jew by Palestinian terrorists aboard the cruise ship Achille Lauro in the fall of 1985.

For thus showing forbearance and discretion, the Boston Symphony has taken some pies in the face. In an exceptionally vulgar rant that appeared in *The San Francisco Chronicle,* the arts columnist David Wiegand, enraged at what he perceived as a slight to Mr. Adams (a Bay Area luminary), wrote, "There is something deeply wrong when a nation galvanizes its forces, its men and women, its determination and its resolve, to preserve the right of the yahoos at the Boston Symphony Orchestra to decide to spare its listeners something that might challenge them or make them think." What nation had done this? And why shouldn't people be spared reminders of recent personal pain when they attend a concert?

A month earlier, Mark Swed, the chief music critic for *The Los Angeles Times,* had expressed a similar opinion, only slightly more decorously, when he boasted that, "preferring answers and understanding to comfort," he had listened to the Nonesuch recording of "Klinghoffer" the day after the World Trade Center had collapsed. But whence this quaintly macho impulse to despise comfort (women's work?) and even deny it haughtily to sufferers? And whence the idea of seeking answers and understand

ing in an opera peopled by wholly fictional terrorists and semifictionalized victims, rather than in more relevant sources of information?
20 Anthony Tommasini, in the *New York Times,* endorsed Mr. Adams's contention that his opera offers "the sad solace of truth." What truth? "The Death of Klinghoffer" trades in the tritest undergraduate fantasies. If the events of Sept. 11 could not jar some artists and critics out of their habit of romantically idealizing criminals, then nothing will. But isn't it time for artists and critics to grow up with the rest of us, now that the unthinkable has occurred?

THE DEATH OF KLINGHOFFER

In 1985, armed members of the Palestine Liberation Front hijacked a commercial cruise ship called the *Achille Lauro,* which was carrying more than 400 tourists on a Mediterranean Sea cruise. The hijackers demanded that fifty Palestinians imprisoned by Israel be released, and they killed Leon Klinghoffer, a sixty-nine-year-old disabled American passenger, subsequently throwing his body and wheelchair overboard. The opera based on the incident, *The Death of Klinghoffer,* by Alice Goodman with music by John Adams, has been controversial since its premiere in 1991.

Protesting the decision of the Boston Symphony Orchestra to cancel its performance of the opera *The Death of Klinghoffer* in 2001, Anthony Tommasini wrote,

But how patronizing for the orchestra's directors to presume what audiences will or will not find offensive. Of course, art can provide solace and comfort. Yet art can also incense and challenge us, make us squirm, make us think. The Boston Symphony missed an opportunity to present an acutely relevant work. . . .

Some have found "Klinghoffer" too soft on the terrorists, too quick to caricature Jews. What do three white Westerners know about ancient conflicts in the Middle East?

Yet a few days after the [September 11, 2001 terrorist] attacks, Senator John Kerry, Democrat of Massachusetts, while calling for decisive military action, courageously suggested that we Americans have not really tried to understand why so many Muslims hate us. That is exactly what Mr. Adams and his co-creators tried to do in "Klinghoffer." Source: Anthony Tommasini, "John Adams, Banned in Boston" (2001).

If terrorism — specifically, the commission or advocacy of deliberate acts of deadly violence directed randomly at the innocent — is to be defeated, world public opinion has to be turned decisively against it. The only way to do that is to focus resolutely on the acts rather than their claimed (or conjectured) motivations, and to characterize all such acts, whatever their motivation, as crimes. This means no longer romanticizing terrorists as Robin Hoods and no longer idealizing their deeds as rough poetic justice. If we indulge such notions when we happen to agree or sympathize with the aims, then we have forfeited the moral ground from which any such acts can be convincingly condemned.

Does "The Death of Klinghoffer" romanticize the perpetrators of deadly violence toward the innocent? Its creators tacitly acknowledged that it did, when they revised the opera for American consumption after its European premieres in Brussels and Paris. In its original version, the opening "Chorus of Exiled Palestinians" was followed not by a balancing "Chorus of Exiled Jews" but by a scene, now dropped from the score, that showed the Klinghoffers' suburban neighbors gossiping merrily about their impending cruise ("The dollar's up. Good news for the Klinghoffers") to an accompaniment of hackneyed pop-style music.

That contrast set the vastly unequal terms on which the conflict of Palestinians and Jews would be perceived throughout the opera. The portrayal of suffering Palestinians in the musical language of myth and ritual was immediately juxtaposed with a musically trivial portrayal of contented, materialistic American Jews. The paired characterizations could not help linking up with lines sung later by "Rambo," one of the fictional terrorists, who (right before the murder) wrathfully dismisses Leon Klinghoffer's protest at his treatment with the accusation that "wherever poor men are gathered you can find Jews getting fat."

Is it unfair to discuss a version of the opera that has been withdrawn from publication and remains unrecorded? It would have been, except that Mr. Adams, throwing his own pie at the Boston Symphony in an interview published recently on the Andante.com Web site, saw fit to point out that the opera "has never seemed particularly shocking to audiences in Europe." He was playing the shame game, trying to make the Boston cancellation look provincial. But when one takes into account that the version European audiences saw in 1991 catered to so many of their favorite prejudices — anti-American, anti-Semitic, anti-bourgeois — the shame would seem rather to go the other way.

25 Nor have these prejudices been erased from the opera in its revised form. The libretto commits many notorious breaches of evenhandedness, but the greatest one is to be found in Mr. Adams's music. In his interview, the composer repeats the oft drawn comparison between the operatic Leon Klinghoffer and the "sacrificial victim" who is "at the heart of the Bach Passions." But his music, precisely insofar as it relies on Bach's example, undermines the facile analogy.

In the "St. Matthew Passion," Bach accompanies the words of Jesus with an aureole of violins and violas that sets him off as numinous, the way a halo would do in a painting. There is a comparable effect in "Klinghoffer": long, quiet, drawn-out tones in the highest violin register (occasionally spelled by electronic synthesizers or high oboe tones). They recall not only the Bachian aureole but also effects of limitless expanse in time or space, familiar from many Romantic scores. (An example is the beginning of Borodin's "In the Steppes of Central Asia.") These numinous, "timeless" tones accompany virtually all the utterances of the choral Palestinians or the terrorists, beginning with the opening chorus.

They underscore the words spoken by the fictitious terrorist Molqui: "We are not criminals and we are not vandals, but men of ideals." Together with an exotically "Oriental" obbligato bassoon, they accompany the fictitious terrorist Mamoud's endearing reverie about his favorite love songs. They add resonance to the fictitious terrorist Omar's impassioned yearnings for a martyr's afterlife; and they also appear when the ship's captain tries to mediate between the terrorists and the victims.

They do not accompany the victims, except in the allegorical "Aria of the Falling Body," sung by the slain Klinghoffer's remains as they are tossed overboard by the terrorists. Only after death does the familiar American middle-class Jew join the glamorously exotic Palestinians in mythic timelessness. Only as his body falls lifeless is his music exalted to a comparably romanticized spiritual dimension.

Why should we want to hear this music now? Is it an edifying challenge, as Mr. Wiegand and Mr. Tommasini contend? Does it give us answers that we should prefer, with Mr. Swed, to comfort? Or does it express a reprehensible contempt for the real-life victims of its imagined "men of ideals," all too easily transferable to the victims who perished on Sept. 11?

30 In a fine recent essay, the literary critic and queer theorist Jonathan Dollimore writes that "to take art seriously — to recognize its potential — must be to recognize that there might be reasonable grounds for wanting to control it." Where should control come from? Unless we are willing to trust the Taliban, it has to come from within. What is called for is self-control. That is what the Boston Symphony laudably exercised; and I hope that musicians who play to Israeli audiences will resume exercising it. There is no need to shove Wagner in the faces of Holocaust survivors in Israel and no need to torment people stunned by previously unimaginable horrors with offensive "challenges" like "The Death of Klinghoffer."

Censorship is always deplorable, but the exercise of forbearance can be noble. Not to be able to distinguish the noble from the deplorable is morally obtuse. In the wake of Sept. 11, we might want, finally, to get beyond sentimental complacency about art. Art is not blameless. Art can inflict harm. The Taliban know that. It's about time we learned.

CONTEXT

Andante.com describes itself as "a new type of classical music venture. Its aim is to document and preserve the world's recorded classical musical heritage and to become the definitive online resource for information about classical music and opera. . . . The mission of the andante Web site is to provide a single, convenient location for in-depth information, stimulating ideas and opinions, and exclusive performances in the world of classical music."

Questions for Discussion

1. Taruskin asserts that Western culture "is full of suspicion toward music." What kinds of evidence does he offer to support that point? Do you think the nature and amount of his evidence are sufficient for his point? Do you find his evidence convincing? Why or why not? (In answering this question, you might refer to "Appraising Evidence" on pages 76–82.) **2.** What makes music such a potentially powerful influence on behavior and belief, according to Taruskin? Why is this point important to his main argument? Do you agree with him? Explain. **3.** Taruskin discusses an incident in which a conductor, Daniel Barenboim, led a performance of Richard Wagner's music in Israel in 2001, and he uses that incident to distinguish between refraining from doing something out of consideration for others ("a voluntary abstinence") and an outright ban on something. Why is this distinction important for Taruskin? How does it relate to his larger point about the control of art? **4.** How does Taruskin justify his assertion that the opera *The Death of Klinghoffer* romanticizes terrorism? How convincing is his support for this assertion? Other forms of music — especially rap music in recent years — have been criticized for romanticizing violence in this way. Think of some examples of music that might do so. Do these examples strengthen or weaken Taruskin's claims, in your view? Explain.
5. In paragraphs 26 through 28, Taruskin focuses on musical elements of the opera *The Death of Klinghoffer* as well as other operas to show how operas can reflect a particular ideological viewpoint — in this case, he believes, a viewpoint that is sympathetic to the terrorists who killed Mr. Klinghoffer. Evaluate the way Taruskin uses his knowledge of musical techniques to make this point. How effective is his argument in this case? **6.** Using the Toulmin model of argumentation (see pages 31–35), identify Taruskin's main reasons for his claim that music should be controlled. Also, identify his warrant for his claim. Do you think most American readers would accept Taruskin's warrant? Explain. **7.** How would you describe Taruskin's tone in this essay? In what ways do you think his tone might enhance or weaken his main argument about controlling music? Cite specific passages from his essay to support your answer.

③ JEFFREY O.G. OGBAR AND VIJAY PRASHAD, **"Black Is Back"**

Arguments about intellectual property that involve rap or hip hop music usually focus on the practice of sampling, a technique that artists use to incorporate into their own songs segments, or "samples," of songs from other artists. Some critics believe that sampling violates copyright law and therefore amounts to intellectual property theft: A musician "owns" a song he or she recorded, and no one else may use that song, or even a part of it, without permission. But scholars Jeffrey Ogbar and Vijay Prashad have a different concern about the ownership of this music: They worry about who owns — or controls — the *meaning* of rap and hip hop music. If these musical styles are, as Ogbar and Prashad believe, forms of cultural expression that give voice to the concerns of Blacks, especially Black youth, then the commercialization of rap and hip hop and its popularity among mainstream groups amount to the theft of black identity as expressed in that music. If this argument seems far-fetched, consider the fact that some critics have argued that the use of folk tunes by great classical composers such as Mozart was also a kind of stealing that benefited Mozart but not the peasants whose music he used. However you feel about such arguments, Ogbar and Prashad remind us that popular music can be much more than entertainment. As a result, arguments about who controls music and how that music is used are much more than arguments about copyright. Jeffrey Ogbar, a history professor at the University of Connecticut, is also a W.E.B. Du Bois research fellow at Harvard University; Vijay Prashad, who is a professor at Trinity College (Connecticut), is the author of *Karma of Brown Folk* (2000) and *Untouchable Freedom* (2000).

Black Is Back
JEFFREY O.G. OGBAR AND VIJAY PRASHAD

1 From Bogota to Beijing, hip-hop's apostles are spreading "the word," striking chords of rage and rebellion in privileged and poor kids alike, in rich countries and poor. The world, it seems, is in love with black America. But this is a treacherous affair. Back in the homeland, a war is being waged against this very same group. One of the frontlines is the prison-industrial complex — an expanding fortress, with the U.S. rate of incarceration (682 per 100,000) six to ten times higher than that of most industrialised nations. Of the two million prisoners, 49 per cent are black and 17 per cent are Latino even though they respectively represent 13 and 11 per cent of the population. Almost one in three

*Janus, a god from Roman mythology who was identified with doors, gates, and beginnings, is often represented artistically with two opposite faces.

black men between the ages of 20 and 29 are caught in the web of correctional control (incarceration, probation or parole). These men lose their right to vote, lose their place as citizens, both in the eyes of the State and in white society.

Outside of the penitentiaries, unemployment is a prison of its own. At seven per cent, the rate may seem low, but look closer and you find that this does not recognise the "disposable" part-time workers, generally composed of ethnic minorities and women. About eight per cent of African Americans are officially unemployed, but the real bombshell is reserved for black youth: almost 32 per cent cannot find a job.

Hip-hop is the "CNN of Black America", raps Chuck D of Public Enemy. Read this line with a metaphorical eye to catch a crucial but not complete reflec-

tion of the world's Janus-like* attraction to rap's art of rebellion. On the one hand, CNN offers constant news coverage world-wide. In symbolic terms, we find rappers cast as reporters on the frontline, offering live updates through their music of the trials, tribulations and peculiarities of neighbourhoods and cities, from Lagos to Frankfurt. On the other hand, global media networks, like CNN, just scratch the surface and cater to mainstream political "tastes" by offering easily digestible nuggets of infotainment. Illustrating this negative side, we find a few posses of Tokyo rappers and fans, for example, literally burning their skin in tanning salons. This is an extreme example reflecting the international mantra: "Be black for a day, wigger for an afternoon!" [Wigger refers to white people who copy black fashions.]

CONTEXT

This essay was published in 2000 in the UNESCO *Courier*, a publication of the United Nations Educational, Scientific and Cultural Organization (UNESCO). UNESCO, which includes 188 member nations, describes its purpose as "to contribute to peace and security in the world by promoting collaboration among nations through education, science, culture and communication in order to further universal respect for justice, for the rule of law and for the human rights and fundamental freedoms which are affirmed for the peoples of the world, without distinction of race, sex, language or religion, by the Charter of the United Nations." Consider the extent to which this essay by Ogbar and Prashad is consistent with UNESCO's stated mission.

Contradictory impulses

Much like jazz and rock 'n' roll in the past, hip-hop has made working class U.S. youth in general and African Americans in particular a cultural hearth for the international market. Its iconic power takes many forms, depending upon the particular political goals and constraints of its practitioners. For some, hip-hop is used to attack poverty, oppression and government corruption. Other fans and musicians take aim at cultural orthodoxy by glorifying gang violence, hyper-materialism and explicit misogyny. Often these contradictory elements take shape simultaneously.

5 In the heart of advanced industrial countries, hip-hop serves as a liberation anthem for those oppressed by racism and poverty. In the disadvantaged suburbs of Paris, the lilting sounds of Senegalese MC Solaar radiate beside North African-inspired rai rap, while NTM (Nique Ta Mère — "screw your mother") besiege the fascism of Jean-Marie Le Pen's Front National party. Across the Channel, British Asian rappers Fun^Da^Mental enshrine the right to self-defence against racist attacks, while German hip-hoppers incite respect for their Turkish origins.

Yet at the same time, hip-hop is also just one of many commercial products or props used for youth rebellion against the established orders of parents. The music, dress and attitude are used to visibly divide one generation from another. In Thailand, male teens speed through the streets in swanky cars, pumped on the raw energy and anger of U.S. rap without the slightest connection to the underlying politics. In Kathmandu,[†] teens use rap's breakbeats to break with tradition, perhaps temporarily, in forging a "modern" identity.

As U.S. rapper L.L. Cool J rhymed, "there's no category, for this story. It will rock in any territory." Cuba offers an "academic's delight" in contradictions. Since 1996, the government has helped

[†]**Kathmandu is the capital city of Nepal.**

As rap and hip hop have grown in popularity, the significance of these musical forms as a social and political movement has been debated. Critics have long condemned rap and hip hop music on the grounds that it expresses racist and misogynistic views and glorifies violence. But Yvonne Bynoe of Urban Think Tank, Inc. expresses the view of many observers that hip hop music has helped to spawn a broader political movement focused on Black rights and economic advancement; she advocates an even more deliberate political commitment among hip hop artists and fans:

> Serious civic engagement means that strategists from the Hip Hop generation become crucial to shifting the political current paradigm of exclusion and marginalization. Black Arts Movement writer, Larry Neal said, "artist and the political activist are one." The scholar/activist therefore must be embraced by the Hip Hop community in conversations about politics with the same fervor that the rap artist and the activist are.

Russell Simmons, the founder of Def Jam Records and one of hip hop's most influential figures, agrees with the need for broader political activism among hip hop fans but also sees the popularity of hip hop as economic power. In an interview with Africana.com, he said,

> Eighty percent of my records are sold to non-African Americans. It's important that I recognize that there's a big market out here culturally, especially since I'm working in the culture business. We have penetrated the mainstream, and if I'm using a black artist, he's not limited to black people, or black ideas that came from the black community. Black people have a take on America, they were born here.

to sponsor an annual National Hip-Hop Conference showcasing local and international stars, mostly from Latin America. According to the U.S. hip-hop magazine *The Source,* Fidel Castro "sees rap music as the existing revolutionary voice of Cuba's future." Yet hip-hop also challenges the socialist vision when fans at concerts proudly wear images of the U.S. dollar bill on their hats and shirts and scream "it's all about the Benjamins" (referring to the image of Benjamin Franklin printed on $100-bills).

Ironically, as post-Cold War hyper-materialism endangers the destiny of young people everywhere, the contradictory message of hip-hop begins to make sense. A decisive feature of the music/culture's ethic is: to "want mine", meaning a share of society's wealth. This desire operates at both the individualist and collective levels. Do you want "it" (luxury, security, etc.) for yourself, or do you want a fair share for your community or society? The urge is so complex that it's difficult, if not impossible, to find one without the other.

Take the case of South Africa, whose townships only recently produced some of the most disciplined and inspirational fighters for social justice. Now in "mixed-race" areas around Cape Town, gangs take their cue from gangsta rap, calling themselves "the Americans" and "throwing up the W", a hand signal from West Coast gangsta rappers of the U.S. The South African example shows us that hip-hop's art of rebellion does not only lead to antiracist and anti-capitalist rebellion, but it often falls victim to the pitfalls of systemic oppression against which it attempts to rebel.

10 Hip-hop alone cannot rise up to the task of political transformation — this is pop culture, not a manifesto. However, by looking at the particular political situations and aspirations of its musicians, we can trace its rise as an iconic power and its demise when the assimilationist powers of the capitalist economy flatten out the music's richness to render it a message of personal gain.

Questions for Discussion

1. This essay focuses on the popularity and commercialization of rap and hip hop music, but Ogbar and Prashad begin with a discussion of the incarceration and unemployment rates of Blacks in the United States. Why do they begin their essay in this way? How effectively do you think this beginning introduces their argument? **2.** According to Ogbar and Prashad, what social and cultural purposes do rap and hip hop music serve? What similarities do Ogbar and Prashad see in how these musical forms are used in different countries? Why are these similarities important to their main argument? What purpose do they believe rap and hip hop *should* serve? (Cite specific passages from the essay to support your answer.) 3. What is the contradictory message that Ogbar and Prashad see in rap and hip hop music? Why, according to them, should we be concerned about this contradictory message? Do you think they value one side or the other of this contradictory message? Explain. **4.** How would you describe the political views of Ogbar and Prashad on the basis of this essay? In what ways do you see those views influencing their argument about rap and hip hop music? What counterarguments might you offer to their position? **5.** Do you think that the argument Ogbar and Prashad make in this essay is similar in any way to Richard Taruskin's argument in his essay (see page 261)? Explain.

④ **JENNY TOOMEY, "Empire of the Air"**

If you have had the opportunity to travel from one part of the United States to another, you probably noticed that wherever you were, you could usually find a radio station that was similar to your favorite hometown radio station. One reason for the similarities among radio stations across the country is that an increasing number of them are owned by a few large media companies. Jenny Toomey thinks that is cause for concern. She isn't worried so much that radio stations today tend to play similar music by the same artists; rather, she is concerned that such similarity reflects a concentration of control of the radio airwaves in the United States. As she points out in her essay, which appeared in the public affairs magazine *The Nation* in 2003, a majority of radio stations are now owned by a small number of media companies. According to Toomey, such a concentration of many stations in the hands of a few companies gives those companies too much control over what we hear on the radio. She argues that radio is not just a business but also a public asset. Whether or not you share Toomey's concerns, her essay asks you to consider who should have control over what we hear on the radio. A musician and leader of the band Tsunami, Jenny Toomey is the former owner of the Simple Machines record label and the founder and executive director of the Future of Music Coalition, an advocacy group that works on behalf of musicians.

Empire of the Air
JENNY TOOMEY

1 For too long, musicians have had too little voice in the manufacture, distribution and promotion of their music and too little means to extract fair support and compensation for their work. The Future of Music Coalition was formed in June 2000 as a not-for-profit think tank to tackle this problem, advocating new business models, technologies and policies that would advance the cause of both musicians and citizens. Much of the work the FMC has done in the past two years has focused on documenting the structures of imbalance and inequity that impede the development of an American musicians'

middle class, and translating legislative-speak into language that musicians and citizens can understand. Our most challenging work, however, and the project of which we are most proud, is our analysis of the effects of radio deregulation on musicians and citizens since the passage of the 1996 Telecommunications Act* (see page 275).

Radio is a public resource managed on citizens' behalf by the federal government. This was established in 1934 through the passage of the Communications Act, which created a regulatory body, the Federal

Communications Commission, and laid the ground rules for the regulation of radio. The act also determined that the spectrum would be managed according to a "trusteeship" model. Broadcasters received fixed-term, renewable licenses that gave them exclusive use of a slice of the spectrum for free. In exchange, they were required to serve the "public interest, convenience and necessity." Though they laid their trust in the mechanics of the marketplace, legislators did not turn the entire spectrum over to commercial broadcasters. The 1934 act included some key provisions that were designed to foster localism and encourage diversity in programming.

Although changes were made to limits on ownership and FCC regulatory control in years hence, the Communications Act of 1934 remained essentially intact until it was thoroughly overhauled in 1996 with the passage of the Telecommunications Act. But even before President Clinton signed the act into law in February 1996, numerous predictions were made regarding its effect on the radio industry:

§ The number of individual radio-station owners would decrease. Those in the industry with enough capital would begin to snatch up valuable but underperforming stations in many markets — big and small.

5 § Station owners — given the ability to purchase more stations both locally and nationally — would benefit from economies of scale. Radio runs on many fixed costs: Equipment, operations and staffing costs are the same whether broadcasting to one person or 1 million. Owners knew that if they could control more than one station in a local

market, they could consolidate operations and reduce fixed expenses. Lower costs would mean increased profit potential. This would, in turn, make for more financially sound radio stations, which would be able to compete more effectively against new media competitors: cable TV and the Internet.

§ There was a prediction based on a theory posited by a 1950s economist named Peter Steiner that increased ownership consolidation on the local level would lead to a subsequent increase in the number of radio format choices available to the listening public. (Steiner, writing in 1952, was not talking about oligopolistic control of the market by a few firms, as we have in the United States; rather, he was basing his predictions on an analysis of BBC radio, which is a nationally owned radio monopoly, not an oligopoly.) According to Steiner's theory, a single owner with multiple stations in a local market wouldn't want to compete against himself. Instead, he would program each station differently

*In 1996 Congress passed the Telecommunications Act, which was intended to update the original Communications Act of 1934 that established laws regarding broadcasting and communications. One provision of the 1996 act is "to make available, so far as possible, to all the people of the United States without discrimination on the basis of race, color, religion, national origin, or sex a rapid, efficient, nation-wide, and world-wide wire and radio communication service with adequate facilities at reasonable charges." As Jenny Toomey notes in her essay, the effects of this and related provisions of the act are still a matter of much debate.

CLEAR CHANNEL COMMUNICATIONS

Clear Channel Communication is the largest owner of radio stations in the United States, with more than 1,200 stations of its own and 100 shows on its Radio Premier Network, which reaches an additional 6,600 stations. It claims to reach 54 percent of all people between the ages of eighteen and forty-nine in the United States. However, it has been the target of much criticism and several lawsuits as a result of its business practices. According to Eric Boehlert, who wrote a series of reports about the company for *Salon* magazine, "radio has never seen anything quite like Clear Channel, which has swallowed up nearly 1,200 radio stations while putting its unique — and some say nasty — stamp on the business. In a series of recent *Salon* reports, insiders from the radio, record and concert industries have voiced concerns about the juggernaut's unmatched power, and how the company uses it."

to meet the tastes of a variety of listeners.

But what really happened?

Well, one prediction certainly came true: The 1996 act opened the floodgates for ownership consolidation. Ten parent companies now dominate the radio spectrum, radio listenership and radio revenues, controlling two-thirds of both listeners and revenue nationwide. Two parent companies in particular — Clear Channel and Viacom — together control 42 percent of listeners and 45 percent of industry revenues.

Consolidation is particularly extreme in the case of Clear Channel. Since passage of the Telecommunications Act, Clear Channel has grown from forty stations to 1,240 stations — thirty times more than Congressional regulation previously allowed. No potential competitor owns even one-quarter the number of Clear Channel stations. With more than 100 million listeners, Clear Channel reaches more than one-third of the US population.

10 Even more bleak is the picture at the local level, where oligopolies control almost every market. Virtually every local market is dominated by four firms controlling 70 percent of market share or greater. In smaller markets, consolidation is more extreme. The largest four firms in most small markets control 90 percent of market share or more. These companies are sometimes regional or national station groups and not locally owned.

Only the few radio-station owners with enough capital to buy additional stations have benefited from deregulation. Station owners have consolidated their operations on a local level, frequently running a number of stations out of a single building, sharing a single advertising staff, technicians and on-air talent. In some cases, radio-station groups have further reduced costs by eliminating the local component almost entirely. Local deejays and program directors are being replaced by regional directors or even by voice-tracked or syndicated programming, which explains a marked decrease in the number of people employed in the radio industry.

Prior to 1996, radio was among the least concentrated and most economically competitive of the media industries. In 1990 no company owned more than fourteen of the more than 10,000 stations nationwide, with no more than two in a single local market. But we found that local markets have now consolidated to the point that just four major radio groups control about 50 percent of the total listener audience and revenue. Clearly, deregulation has reduced competition within the radio industry.

As a result, listeners are losing. With an emphasis on cost-cutting and an effort to move decision-making out of the hands of local station staff, much of radio has become bland and formulaic. Recall Steiner's hopeful theory that an owner would not want to compete against his own company and would therefore operate stations with different programming. We found evidence to the contrary: Radio companies regularly operate two or more stations with the same format — for example, rock, country, adult contemporary, top 40 — in the same local market. In a recent *New York Times* article, "Fewer Media Owners, More Media Choices," FCC chairman Michael Powell denied this, propping up Steiner's theory by saying things like, "Common ownership can lead to more diversity — what does the owner get for having duplicative products?" But we found 561 instances of format redundancy nationwide — a parent company operating two or more stations in the same market, with the same format — amounting to massive missed opportunities for variety.

Still, from 1996 to 2000, format variety — the average number of formats available in each local market — actually increased in both large and small markets. But format variety is not equivalent to true diversity in programming, since formats with different names have similar playlists. For example, alternative, top 40, rock and hot adult contemporary are all likely to play songs by the band Creed, even though their formats are not the same. In fact, an analysis of data from charts in *Radio and Records* and *Billboard's Airplay Monitor* revealed considerable playlist overlap — as much as 76 percent — between supposedly distinct formats. If the FCC or the National Association of Broadcasters are sincerely trying to measure programming "diversity," doing so on the basis of the number of formats in a given market is a flawed methodology.

15 This final point may be the most critical one as we face an FCC that is poised to deregulate media even further in the next few months. (In September [2002], the commissioners voted unanimously to open review of the FCC's media ownership rules.) It is time to put to bed the commonly held yet fundamentally flawed notion that consolidation promotes diversity — that radio-station owners who own two stations within a marketplace will not be tempted to program both stations with the same songs. There's a clear corporate benefit in "self-competition," and it's time we made regulatory agencies admit that fact.

Even in the beginning, radio was regulated to cultivate a commercial broadcast industry that could grow to serve the greatest number of Americans possible. As the decades have passed, most calls for deregulation have come from incumbent broadcasters interested in lifting local and national ownership caps that protect against the competitive pressures of other media.

While the effects of deregulation have been widely studied and discussed, scrutiny is focused on the profitability of the radio industry. But the effect of increased corporate profitability on citizens is rarely, if ever, discussed. Radical deregulation of the radio industry allowed by the Telecommunications Act of 1996 has not benefited the public. Instead, it has led to less competition, fewer viewpoints and less diversity in programming. Substantial ethnic, regional and economic populations are not provided the services to which they are entitled. The public is not satisfied, and possible economic efficiencies of industry consolidation are not being passed on to the public in the form of improved local service. Deregulation has damaged radio as a public resource.

Musicians are also suffering because of deregulation. Independent artists have found it increasingly difficult to get airplay; in payola-like schemes, the "Big Five" music companies, through third-party promoters, shell out thousands of

---

C O N T E X T

The 1996 Telecommunications Act is one of many efforts by U.S. lawmakers since the early 1980s to reduce federal regulation of the radio industry. In part as a response to the kinds of the concerns about deregulation that Toomey expresses in this essay, a bill titled "The Competition in Radio and Concert Industries Act of 2002" was introduced to the U.S. Senate in July 2002. The American Federation of Television and Radio Artists (AFTRA) endorsed the legislation as a way to curtail the consolidation of the radio industry, which AFTRA argued has hurt both the public and the artists whose music is played on radio stations. Supporters of deregulation maintain that the industry today is vibrant and profitable, with fierce competition for listeners in urban markets that benefits consumers by providing them with many choices addressing their listening interests. In 2003, Congress relaxed regulations on all media companies, making it easier for companies to acquire additional media outlets, including radio stations.

dollars per song to the companies that rule the airwaves. That's part of why the Future of Music Coalition undertook this research. We at the FMC firmly believe that the music industry as it exists today is fundamentally anti-artist. In addition to our radio study, our projects — including a critique of standard major-label contract clauses, a study of musicians and health insurance, and a translation of the complicated Copyright Arbitration Royalty Panel proceedings that determined the webcasting royalty rates —

were conceived as tools for people who are curious about the structures that impede musicians' ability to both live and make a living. Understanding radio deregulation is another tool for criticizing such structures. We have detailed the connections between concentrated media ownership, homogenous radio programming and restricted radio access for musicians. Given that knowledge, we hope artists will join with other activists and work to restore radio as a public resource for all people.

NEGOTIATING DIFFERENCES

In 1999 and 2000, as the controversy over Napster intensified (see the sidebar about Napster on page 257), many universities and colleges began to prevent students on their campuses from using Napster to download music. These universities and colleges were concerned that they, too, could become the focus of lawsuits for copyright infringement if students used the schools' computer systems for downloading copyrighted music. Some critics condemned these actions, arguing that the schools were serving the interests of commercial companies rather than the public. The controversy underscored how complicated intellectual property rights issues can become

when it comes to music and when new technologies emerge for sharing music.

For this assignment, you will try to examine these complexities by looking at how students at your school use music. Your task is to write an essay in which you take and justify a position on the use of music. Your specific focus for this argument is up to you. The essays in this section provide several alternatives for you:

- You can focus on the question of digital copying of music and the downloading of music on the Internet, as Janis Ian does in her essay (page 256).

Questions for Discussion

1. In the first sentence of her essay, Toomey unequivocally states her position regarding who should control music. Evaluate the effectiveness of this approach to introducing her subject. How might Toomey's introduction enhance the effectiveness of her argument? In what ways might it weaken her argument? What other strategies might she have used to introduce her argument? **2.** Why does Toomey believe that "listeners are losing" as a result of the consolidation of the radio industry? Do you agree with her? Why or why not? **3.** According to Toomey, the deregulation of the radio industry as a result of the 1996 Telecommunication Act has not benefited citizens, even though it has resulted in greater profits for companies. On what grounds does she make that claim? How convincing do you think Toomey is on this point? **4.** Toomey structures her essay around several predictions that were made about the impact of the 1996 telecommunications act on the radio industry in the United States. Do you think this approach to structuring her essay makes her argument more persuasive? Explain. **5.** Evaluate Toomey's use of statistical information as evidence for her claims. How appropriate to her argument are the kinds of statistics she cites? How do those statistics affect her argument? **6.** Toomey's essay can be considered an example of an argument based on deductive reasoning. (See pages 26–31 for an explanation of this kind of argument.) What is the basic principle or belief on which Toomey bases her argument? Does she state this principle overtly anywhere in her essay? What syllogism does her argument rest on? (See pages 28–29 for a discussion of the syllogism.)

- You can address the question of whether some kinds of music should be restricted from distribution or even banned, as Richard Taruskin argues in his essay (page 261).
- You might focus on cultural aspects of music, as Ogbar and Prashad do in their essay (page 269), perhaps addressing some of the controversies about hip hop music.
- You might address the issue of ownership of radio stations, as Jenny Toomey does (page 274).

Whichever specific issue you choose to focus on, do some investigation to learn how other students at your university feel about the issue. You can talk informally to students you know, or you can conduct more formal research in the form of interviews or a survey. (See pages 175–177 for a discussion of these techniques for gathering information.) Then use this information, along with any relevant published materials you find (including the essays in this section) to help make your case for your position on this issue. Write your essay with the students at your school in mind as your audience. You might intend your essay as an editorial for your student newspaper, if your school has one.

9

EDUCATION

Cluster 1
WHAT SHOULD BE TAUGHT IN SCHOOLS?

① Richard Just, "Enroll: Why Berkeley Students Should Punish a Teacher by Taking His Class"

② Stanley Kurtz, "Balancing the Academy"

③ bell hooks, "Toward a Radical Feminist Pedagogy"

④ Ronald Takaki, "An Educated and Culturally Literate Person Must Study America's Multicultural Reality"

CON-TEXT
John Dewey on Democracy and Education

Cluster 2
HOW SHOULD WE DETERMINE WHAT OUR CHILDREN LEARN?

① Eleanor Martin. " 'No' Is the Right Answer"

② Patricia Williams, "Tests, Tracking, and Derailment"

③ Gregory Cizek, "Unintended Consequences of High Stakes Testing"

④ Bertell Ollman, "Why So Many Exams? A Marxist Response"

CON-TEXT
The Report of the Committee of Ten, 1892

Cluster 3
HOW SHOULD WE PAY FOR EDUCATION?

① Milton Friedman, "The Market Can Transform Our Schools"

② Thomas Sowell, "Flagging Flagships"

③ Andrew Stark, "Pizza Hut, Domino's, and the Public Schools"

④ John Sheehan, "Why I Said No to Coca-Cola"

CON-TEXT
Horace Mann and Public Education

ATION

WHAT SHOULD BE TAUGHT IN SCHOOLS?

The question of what should be taught in schools is as old as formal education itself. In the United States the emergence of the public school in the 19th century was accompanied by intense debates about the nature and content of the curriculum. Some argued that schools should impart values as well as knowledge; others believed that schools should focus on teaching students the skills needed to be productive workers; still others saw schools as places where immigrants could learn to become Americans. And many believed that public education is central to American democracy; the curriculum, therefore, should foster good citizens. One influential voice who supported this connection between education and democracy was philosopher John Dewey, who argued that the school curriculum should do more than supply students with practical knowledge. For Dewey, schools were places where students learned how to live and work together, where they learned about democracy as a way of life rather than an idea or a set of principles (see Con-Text on page 283). Accordingly, Dewey believed that *how* students are taught is as important as what they are taught. ■ Nearly a century after Dewey formulated his extensive philosophy of education, many Americans share his belief in the connection between education and democracy, even if they do not share his vision for a progressive public school system. It might be that this deeply held belief in education as central to democracy is a reason that education has been such a fierce political battleground in the United States. Conflicts about what students should be taught have been waged in classrooms, town halls, school board meetings, state legislatures, and the U.S. Congress. Sometimes these conflicts focus on a specific idea or theory, such as the longstanding debates about the teaching of evolution as opposed to creationism in science courses. Sometimes, conflicts arise around a particular book that students are asked to read; for example, Mark Twain's *The Adventures of Huckleberry Finn* and *The Diary of Anne Frank* are commonly challenged by groups that believe, for various religious or political reasons, that these books should not be required reading in U.S. schools. The testing of students has also caused conflict among parents, educators, government officials, and scholars. And very often controversy surrounds the funding of education. ■ In one way or another, all of these battles are about the purpose of education. As the authors of the essays in this section suggest, to make an argument about what to teach students is to make a statement about what you believe education is — or should be — for. If Dewey was correct in believing that education is ultimately about democracy, then one question to be answered is "What kind of democracy do we want?" There is rarely unanimous agreement among Americans about how to answer that question. As you read the following essays, think about how you might answer it. These writers make arguments about specific issues or ideas that should be taught in American classrooms, but their arguments all rest on beliefs — implied or explicitly stated — about the kind of society we want our schools to help us build. Their views will help you to appreciate the always political nature of formal education; they might also help you to see common beliefs about education that can become the basis for solutions to these longstanding controversies about what we should teach our children.

CON-TEXT: John Dewey on Democracy and Education

Democratic society is peculiarly dependent for its maintenance upon the use in forming a course of study of criteria which are broadly human. Democracy cannot flourish where the chief influences in selecting subject matter of instruction are utilitarian ends narrowly conceived for the masses, and, for the higher education of the few, the traditions of a specialized cultivated class. The notion that the "essentials" of elementary education are the three R's mechanically treated, is based upon ignorance of the essentials needed for realization of democratic ideals. Unconsciously it assumes that these ideals are unrealizable; it assumes that in the future, as in the past, getting a livelihood, "making a living," must signify for most men and women doing things which are not significant, freely chosen, and ennobling to those who do them; doing things which serve ends unrecognized by those engaged in them, carried on under the direction of others for the sake of pecuniary reward. For preparation of large numbers for a life of this sort, and only for this purpose, are mechanical efficiency in reading, writing, spelling and figuring, together with attainment of a certain amount of muscular dexterity, "essentials." Such conditions also infect the education called liberal, with illiberality. They imply a somewhat parasitic cultivation bought at the expense of not having the enlightenment and discipline which come from concern with the deepest problems of common humanity. A curriculum which acknowledges the social responsibilities of education must present situations where problems are relevant to the problems of living together, and where observation and information are calculated to develop social insight and interest.

SOURCE: Chapter 7 of John Dewey, *Democracy and Education* (1916).

① **RICHARD JUST, "Enroll: Why Berkeley Students Should Punish a Teacher by Taking His Class"**

In May 2002 a graduate student in English at the University of California at Berkeley, one of the most prestigious public universities in the United States, sparked a nationwide controversy when he published a description for an undergraduate course entitled "The Politics and Poetics of Palestinian Resistance." The graduate student, Snehal Shingavi, wrote in his course description that "conservative thinkers are encouraged to seek other sections." After many press reports and columns criticized Shingavi's course, Berkeley chancellor Robert Berdahl announced that the course would be monitored so that qualified students were not kept from enrolling in it. Eventually, Shingavi rewrote his course description, but the controversy continued in the popular press and on the Berkeley campus. As the following essay by columnist Richard Just indicates, the controversy prompted debate about whether or not a college course should be overtly political; it raised questions about the role of politics in teaching and learning in American colleges and universities. This is an old debate, but Richard Just reveals that it is as timely as ever. Drawing on his own college experiences, he asks us to think about what should happen in college courses — and to what end. His essay originally appeared in May 2002 in *The American Prospect Online*.

Enroll: Why Berkeley Students Should Punish a Teacher by Taking His Class

RICHARD JUST

1 During the spring of my senior year in college, I signed up for a class called "Cinema, Politics and Society in the Middle East." The professor was unabashedly pro-Palestinian, and the way she taught the region's history reflected her political bias. As the only defender of Israel in the class, I frequently found myself challenging her assertions and those of my classmates. At the same time, I also found myself exposed to the Arab narrative of modern Middle Eastern history, which was quite different from the one I had previously learned. I emerged from the course as staunchly pro-Israel as I had been before, but better able to articulate my views and to understand, if not necessarily agree with, the other side. Taking the class was among the best academic decisions I made at Princeton.

The recent exploits of Snehal Shingavi — the Berkeley grad student whose course description for "The Politics and Poetics of Palestinian Resistance" included a warning that "conservative thinkers are encouraged to seek other sections" — prompted me to think back to my experience studying the Middle East's politics and cinema in college. In trying to restrict the range of opinion in his classroom, Shingavi not only took a hearty swipe at important principles of unfettered academic debate, he also demonstrated a fundamental misunderstanding of the educational role of universities.

At their best, undergraduates come to class to have their views challenged, debated, and, ultimately, deepened. A course offering like Shingavi's that seeks to limit the range of views among students makes, by its very nature, for a less intellectually worthwhile class. It's not just those pro-Israel students (like me) who would have loved to take a course called "The Politics and Poetics of Palestinian Resistance" who are harmed by Shingavi's shenanigans; such behavior also harms those pro-Palestinian students who would have benefited from the intellectual confrontation that the presence of opposing views in a classroom provokes.

But if Shingavi doesn't get it, then I'm not sure his right-wing critics, so quick to seize on any example of liberal bias in the academy, quite get it either. Writing in *National Review Online*, Roger Kimball quickly disposes of Shingavi's trampling of academic freedom before getting to what he believes is the real problem: that Berkeley was offering a class called "The Politics and Poetics of Palestinian Resistance" — "with a read-

ing list featuring no fewer than three books by the Palestine apologist Edward Said"* — in the first place. For Kimball, this is a clear example of the unfortunate politicization of the academy.

5 Kimball, however, is unwilling to distinguish between indoctrination and provocative education. Apparently, in his view, any presentation of politically charged material by a politically charged professor is, on its face, indoctrination. I submit my own experience studying with a pro-Palestinian professor as evidence that this need not be the case. (Or my experience studying with a conservative economist. Or a radical utilitarian bioethicist.) Had these professors awarded better grades to students who agreed with them or otherwise coerced undergraduates into following their intellectual lead, they would have been crossing the line into indoctrination. But in my college experience that was never the case.

*An internationally known scholar, Edward Said is University Professor at Columbia University. His many books about the Middle East include *Orientalism* (1978), *The Question of Palestine* (1980), and *Covering Islam* (1981). Born in Palestine in 1935 and an outspoken critic of U.S. policies in the Middle East, Said has been an influential literary scholar whose work has focused on interpretations of Arabs and of Islam in literature.

"THE DEATH OF OBJECTIVITY,"
BY ROGER KIMBALL

In May 2002 the *National Review Online* published an essay by Roger Kimball entitled "The Death of Objectivity," in which Kimball harshly criticized Snehal Shingavi and his course "The Politics and Poetics of Palestinian Resistance" at the University of California at Berkeley. Kimball argued that

what the people running Berkeley really ought to be worried about — but what no one there has uttered a word to criticize — is the patent politicization of the curriculum implicit in courses like "The Politics and Poetics of Palestinian Resistance."

In my article for the *Wall Street Journal*, I contrasted such efforts to politicize education with Matthew Arnold's ideal of "disinterestedness" — a habit of inquiry, Arnold said, that refused "to lend itself to any . . . ulterior, political, practical considerations about ideas." Traditionally, some such ideal was at the center of the educational enterprise and the search for truth.

To what extent our colleges and universities can still be said to be engaged in the search for truth is an open question, to say the least. The controversy over "The Politics and Poetics of Palestinian Resistance" provided a vivid illustration of what I mean.

I have to confess to being puzzled by Kimball's allegation that politicized college courses are, in and of themselves, a bad thing. In even my most straightforward social-science classes, it was usually possible to discern where a professor fell on the political spectrum. I personally preferred those courses in which the professor let students know where he stood from the first day of class; those were the classes where I thought the hardest and learned the most. But to expect professors of any temperament to check their politics at the classroom door, as Kimball seems to be suggesting they do, is both impractical and anti-educational.

As for Shingavi, where he crossed the line was not in proposing to use his course as a bully pulpit for his controversial views — provided that those views are indeed founded in serious academic inquiry and scholarship (I will give him the benefit of the doubt). Nor did his transgression lie in designing a reading list or curriculum that would support those views. Rather, it was in his attempt to ensure that no one in his classroom would ever disagree with his opinions that Shingavi's lack of respect for the educational process was revealed.

There is only one correct response now for Berkeley's pro-Israel partisans: They should sign up for Shingavi's class. They should do so both to learn from Shingavi — by having their own views challenged — and to teach him a lesson about the value of vigorous intellectual discourse. They should maintain an open mind in grappling with what he has to say, but they should not be afraid to retort with their own views as well.

If their experience is anything like mine, it will be well worth their time and effort. I once caught my Middle Eastern cinema professor smiling ever so slightly as she finished presenting her interpretation of some historical event and then turned toward me, anticipating that a challenge was already on its way. She knew that I disagreed with her, but she also knew that I was in her classroom because I cared enough to grapple with — and learn from — the opposing side. I suppose Roger Kimball would call her approach "the patent politicization of the curriculum." I would call it education.

Questions for Discussion

1. What is the distinction that Richard Just makes between indoctrination and what he calls "provocative education"? Why is this distinction important, in his view? How does it contribute to his main argument about a college education? **2.** Richard Just refers to his own experiences as evidence to support his argument about the benefits of an overtly politicized college class. Evaluate the effectiveness of this use of personal experience as evidence. How do Just's experiences compare to your own? In what ways might your experiences in college courses influence how you respond to Just's use of his own experience as evidence? (In answering these questions, you might refer to the discussion of personal experience as evidence on pages 78–79.) **3.** Richard Just devotes a significant portion of this essay to responding to the arguments of Roger Kimball, who criticized the overtly pro-Palestinian view of the course taught at the University of California at Berkeley. What does Just accomplish by responding to Kimball's criticisms? How do his comments about Kimball contribute to his main argument? How might these comments strengthen his argument? **4.** This essay is an example of an argument based on deductive reasoning (see pages 26–31). What is the fundamental premise on which the author bases his main argument? Do you think most readers would agree to this premise? Explain. **5.** Do you agree with Richard Just's view of the course taught by Shingavi? Why or why not? What counterarguments might you offer in response to Just's main argument about the political nature of college courses?

② STANLEY KURTZ, "Balancing the Academy"

American higher education has long enjoyed a tradition of the free exchange of ideas. In theory, American colleges and universities are places where scholars explore and debate ideas without economic and political restrictions. In reality, the exchange of ideas is never free of political or economic concerns; moreover, ideas have great power in the sense that they affect how people understand the world around them and influence the decisions people make as they interact with one another. According to Stanley Kurtz, that is why we should pay attention to what scholars at American universities say and write, and he supports the efforts of people who keep watch over the apparent political content of college courses. In the following essay, Kurtz, a research fellow at the Hoover Institution at Stanford University, expresses deep concern about what he believes is an anti-American bias among scholars who study the Middle East, which has long been an arena of intense political and military conflict. For Kurtz arguments about the Middle East among scholars are as important as the ongoing conflicts in that region because scholars have the potential to shape public opinion. As you read Kurtz's argument about the anti-American bias he perceives in American higher education, pay attention to the vision of education that he implicitly presents. How does his vision compare to your own? This essay appeared in the *National Review* in 2002.

Balancing the Academy
STANLEY KURTZ

1 An important new organization that promises to focus public concern on "blame America first" bias in the academy is in danger of being discredited. The Middle East Forum, under the direction of Daniel Pipes, has established a project and website called, "Campus Watch." Campus Watch is designed to monitor Middle East Studies in the United States, analyzing and criticizing errors and biases, and drawing public attention to controversies over funding, academic appointments, etc. Campus Watch maintains that Middle East Studies in the United States is dominated by professors who are actively hostile to America's interests in the world. The organization's purpose is to make this problem known to the American public

Already, however, as reported by *The Chronicle of Higher Education,* the Muslim Public Affairs Council, and a number of professors whose work is listed and criticized on the Campus Watch website, have begun a campaign of attack. Campus Watch, they say, is "a hate website," an inappropriate "blacklist," and a "fear mongering" enterprise that could have a "chilling effect" on campus free speech, especially for faculty without tenure.

For those unfamiliar with the upside-down world of today's academy, these complaints might seem plausible. After all, if some scholars of the Middle East are biased or in error, wouldn't it be better for other scholars to challenge them to reasoned debate within the walls of the academy itself? Why stir up partisan passions on matters best fought out in seminar rooms, scholarly journals, and university press books?

Well, yes. The best way to challenge anti-American bias within the academy would be to do so in scholarly venues. Trouble is, there are virtually no scholars left in the field of Middle East Studies (or anywhere else) to mount such a challenge. For the most part, scholars who actually share the perception of America's vital interests held by the vast majority of the American people have long since been purged from the discipline of Middle East Studies.

5 As for blacklisting* and its chilling effect on speech, Middle East Studies today is a field literally founded upon the principle of the blacklist. Edward Said's "post-colonial theory,"† which provides the intellectual framework for contemporary Middle Eastern Studies, is nothing but the program of a blacklist, disguised as high theory.

Edward Said objected to the view of the Middle East portrayed in the work of such renowned scholars as Bernard Lewis and Ernest Gellner. But instead of presenting a competing portrayal of the Middle East, Said proceeded to attack Lewis, Gellner — and a whole list of other scholars — as anti-Muslim bigots in league with "the Zionist lobby." And Said named names, from Lewis and Gellner to such eminent scholars and

CAMPUS WATCH

According to its Web site, Campus Watch "consists of American academics concerned about US interests and their frequent denigration on campus. . . . Campus Watch will henceforth monitor and gather information on professors who fan the flames of disinformation, incitement and ignorance. Campus Watch will critique these specialists, and make available its findings on the internet and in the media." Established by the Middle East Forum (www.meforum.org), Campus Watch believes that "American scholars of the Middle East, to varying degrees, reject the views of most Americans and the enduring policies of the U.S. government about the Middle East"; its Web site publicizes what it sees as the anti-American bias of scholars in American universities. (See www.campus-watch.org.)

public intellectuals as Elie Kedourie, Walter Laqueur, Connor Cruise O'Brien, Martin Peretz, Norman Podhoretz . . . and of course, Daniel Pipes himself.

What Said saw as shameful and bigoted in the work of these scholars and writers was the way they insisted on connecting Islam with terrorism. (Osama bin Laden is the fellow Said ought to be complaining about on that score.) Having labeled a long series of respected scholars as anti-Muslim bigots for their daring to note connections between some strains of contemporary Islam and terrorism, Said concocted the name "Orientalism" to describe their alleged crime. And Said made it clear that "Orientalism" was indeed an accusation of bigotry — a word meant to denote a form of "scarcely concealed racism."

What bothered Said was that "the Zionist lobby," working in league with these (racist) "Orientalist" scholars, had garnered "a vastly disproportionate strength," given how few Middle Easterners were actually Israelis. How, fumed Said, could important public journals and newspapers make themselves open to such bigoted scholars, "with no counterweight" to oppose them?

*Blacklisting is the practice of censoring or somehow excluding certain persons from an activity because of their views. The term grows out of the idea of a "black list" of the names of people to be censored or excluded. Here, Kurtz suggests that scholars with pro-American views are effectively censored in Middle Eastern Studies.

†Post-colonial theory is a school of thought in the humanities that seeks to examine the art and culture of societies such as India and Algeria that were once colonies of Western European nations. Edward Said has been an influential proponent of post-colonial theory as it applies to the Middle East. For more information about Edward Said, see the margin gloss on page 285.

ORIENTALISM

In *Orientalism* (1987), Edward Said defines Orientalism as

a way of coming to terms with the Orient that is based on the Orient's special place in European Western Experience. . . . Orientalism is a style of thought based upon ontological and epistemological distinction made between "the Orient" and (most of the time) "the Occident" Thus a very large mass of writers, among whom are poets, novelists, philosophers, political theorists, economists, and imperial administrators, have accepted the basic distinction between East and West as the starting point for elaborate accounts concerning the Orient, its people, customs, "mind," destiny, and so on. . . . Orientalism as I study it here deals principally, not with a correspondence between Orientalism and Orient, but with the internal consistency of Orientalism and its ideas about the Orient.

*Ernest Gellner was an influential philosopher and theorist who championed rationalism and the scientific method in scholarly inquiry. Born in 1925, he taught at the London School of Economics and Cambridge University and authored many books on philosophy, anthropology, and political affairs. In the 1990s he clashed with Edward Said over his criticisms of Said's idea of "Orientalism."

Having successfully branded nearly all Middle Eastern scholars who did not fall in with his perspective as scarcely concealed racists in league with the Zionist lobby, Said and his followers went about taking over the discipline of Middle East Studies (and many other precincts of the academy as well).

10 The extent of the blacklisting was truly breathtaking. In South Asian Studies, for example, scholars who had nothing at all to say about politics or foreign policy were branded as bigoted and neo-colonial "Orientalists," simply for studying religious ritual or family psychology. The very practice of scholarship outside of Said's leftist political framework was considered to be a subtle form of imperialism. For example, by writing about Hinduism, or by dissecting the dynamics of Indian family life, scholars were said to be turning Asians into "exotic" foreigners — with the subtle implication that such strange and irrational creatures deserved to be deprived of the right to self-rule.

Perhaps most extraordinary of all, under the dominance of Said's post-colonial theory, the very subject of scholarship was transformed. Although some studies of the Middle East or South Asia continued to be written, much of the work of post-colonialists was taken up with critiques of previous scholarship. Study after study was produced, the subject of which was the "subtle" bigotry of conventional scholarly treatments of non-Western societies.

In effect, the message of Said's followers to other scholars was, if you're not with us, you're against us. Having dismissed conventions of liberal tolerance as window dressing for the oppression of the powerful; having branded nearly all scholarship from other perspectives as a species of bigotry; having condemned those who refused to mouth the new academic catechism as fellow-travelers of the despised Israeli lobby; and having named names and written volumes detailing the supposed ethical and political sins of the most respected scholars in several fields, the post-colonialists succeeded in delegitimizing and purging their opponents, thereby taking over much of the academy.

Nothing Daniel Pipes's Campus Watch has come up with can hold a candle to the hate-filled, fear-mongering, intellectually intimidating technique of blacklisting already invented by Edward Said. And you know what? As deeply as I reject and repudiate the views of Edward Said and his many followers, I do not argue, and have not argued, that the post-colonialists ought to be banned from making their case. Let them name names. Let them attack the Zionist lobby. Let them write volumes that purport to reveal the subtle racism of anyone who dares refuse to follow them.

My only concern is that a substantial number of scholars who take issue with the post-colonialists — scholars who see things more along the lines of Bernard Lewis, Ernest Gellner,* and the rest (yes, and even Dan Pipes!), be allowed back in to the academy. My hope is that someday, the argument with Said's followers that today can play out only on the website of Campus Watch might someday be readmitted to the academy itself.

15 How piddling and pathetic are the few and brief little "dossiers" that Pipes has compiled on the most egregiously biased scholars of Middle Eastern Studies. How these "dossiers" pale by comparison to the battalions of university-press books already launched against Dan Pipes and his colleagues. And how unsurprising that even Pipes's limited efforts to start a real debate should have brought down on him the same old bogus accusations of bigotry by which a generation of less-than-leftist scholars have already been purged from the academy.

Post-colonialists without tenure afraid of a challenge from someone who actually disagrees with their premises? Perish the thought! But where were the reporters when grad students who refused to hold with post-colonial theory were prevented by tenured radicals from ever making it into junior faculty positions to begin with? The most effective way to stifle debate, after all, is to deprive a scholar of the chance of trying for tenure in the first place.

Come to think of it, why aren't our finest colleges and universities wooing scholars like Daniel Pipes and Martin Kramer with offers of fabulous salaries and department chairmanships? Why does this happen only to Cornell West? When Daniel Pipes steps onto a college campus, he's got to be surrounded by body guards and protected from attack — no doubt, attack by the same sort of people who recently prevented former Israeli Prime Minister Benjamin Netanyahu from speaking at Montreal's Concordia University. But maybe — just maybe — if proponents of more than one point of view on matters Middle Eastern were actually allowed to teach on our college campuses, we would see less shouting down of speakers, and more civil debate. That is the state of affairs Campus Watch is trying to bring about.

As for me, I very much hope that college administrators do take Campus Watch seriously when it comes to tenure decisions. If some untenured follower of Edward Said has made statements worthy of criticism, let him be criticized. He is free to answer back. The debate will be healthy (and in today's academy, unfortunately, totally unprecedented). But what administrators really need to attend to is the dearth of scholars on campus with views compatible with mainstream public opinion. There is nothing wrong, and everything right, with Campus Watch's claim that our colleges and universities are failing if they cannot make a place for honest debate between scholars of many shades of opinion — certainly including mainstream opinion.

And more power to Campus Watch for inviting students to alert it to egregious cases of professorial bias. True, such reports must be taken with a grain of salt. Student complaints about professors are often themselves biased and self-interested. In only very rare circumstances should a professor be disciplined for a statement made in class. It is important that Campus Watch exercise caution in vetting students complaints. But it is fair to criticize professors for their substantive views, and fair as well to express concern about professors who do not allow balanced discussion in their classes. Students are often at the mercy of professors for grades and recommendations, and are themselves often under tremendous pressure to toe a professor's political line.

20 No, it is not ideal to have to create an organization like Campus Watch. Far better to have the kind of intellectually diverse faculty that would make honest and substantive intellectual debate possible on campus. Far better to have professors with sufficiently diverse views that students could find and work with like-minded mentors, while also challenging themselves by taking classes with professors with whom they disagree. Far better to have a college or university that functions the way an educational institution was meant to, instead of as a training camp for leftist activists. But that is not the world we live in. And until it is, projects like Campus Watch must be welcomed and nurtured.

Edward Said was concerned about the disproportionate influence of a few million Israelis on American opinion. (Could it have had something to do with Israel being a democracy?) Edward Said was concerned about exposing Americans to divergent perspectives on the Middle East. Edward Said named names. And Edward Said and his followers prepared prosecutorial dossiers at multi-volume length. The problem is that Edward Said got his way — and proceeded to commit every sin he once condemned. Divergent opinions were driven out of the academy, a minority opinion was allowed to silence mainstream American views, and blacklisting was raised to a high art.

Daniel Pipes's attempt to right these wrongs isn't even close to committing the sins of Said. And the very folks now screaming about Pipes are the ones who have prosecuted the most vicious and successful campaign of blacklisting in the history of the American academy. Long live Campus Watch — as long as it takes.

Questions for Discussion

1. Why is Kurtz concerned about criticisms of Campus Watch? What do these criticisms of Campus Watch reveal about the state of U.S. higher education, according to Kurtz? In your view, how effectively does the example of Campus Watch illustrate Kurtz's concerns? **2.** Summarize Kurtz's main argument in this essay. What fundamental beliefs about higher education inform Kurtz's argument? Do you think most Americans share those beliefs? Do you share them? Explain. **3.** Kurtz asserts that anti-American bias in higher education is rarely challenged because "there are virtually no scholars left in the field of Middle East Studies (or anywhere else) to mount such a challenge." Why is this assertion important to his main argument? What evidence does he offer to support this assertion? **4.** How would you characterize Kurtz's tone in this essay? To what extent do you think his tone strengthens or weakens his argument? Cite specific passages from his essay in your answer. **5.** Examine how Kurtz describes Edward Said and Daniel Pipes, the two people who figure most prominently in his argument. How do his descriptions of these men contribute to his main argument? Do you think he could have made his argument effectively without lengthy references to Edward Said and his work? Explain. (In answering these questions, you might wish to refer to the discussion of ethos on pages 73–75.)

③ **BELL HOOKS, "Toward a Radical Feminist Pedagogy"**

In the late 1970s and early 1980s colleges and universities began to establish new programs in Women's Studies. These programs, which grew out of the feminist movement, encouraged students to examine the role of gender and power relations in society and challenged longstanding ideas about teaching and learning in American education. But like the women's movement itself, Women's Studies faced resistance and often struggled to gain acceptance as a legitimate academic discipline. That sense of struggle is a central part of the vision of feminist teaching presented in the following essay by scholar and writer bell hooks. hooks argues for a kind of education that is both collaborative and confrontational, one that intentionally challenges convention. The very title of hooks's essay is provocative, suggesting that the purpose of her approach to education is radical change. Perhaps it is that sense of purpose that continues to invite controversy, for despite the growth of Women's Studies programs in American higher education and despite the acceptance of feminism as a school of thought, both Women's Studies and feminist theory continue to face criticism in and outside educational circles. A distinguished Professor of English at City College of New York, bell hooks has been an insistent voice for a progressive view of education based on feminist theory. Her many books about education and culture focus attention on issues of race, gender, and social class. As you read the following essay, which was published in 1989 in her book *Talking Back*, compare her sense of the purpose of education to your own view.

Toward a Radical Feminist Pedagogy
BELL HOOKS

1 My favorite teacher in high school was Miss Annie Mae Moore, a short, stout black woman. She had taught my mama and her sisters. She could tell story after story about their fast ways, their wildness. She could tell me ways I was like mama, ways I was most truly my own self. She could catch hold of you and turn you around, set you straight (these were the comments folk made about her teaching) — so that we would know what we were facing when we entered her classroom. Passionate in her teaching, confident that her work in life was a pedagogy of liberation (words she would not have used but lived instinctively), one that would address and confront our realities as black children growing up in the segregated South, black children growing up within a white-supremacist culture. Miss Moore knew that if we were to be fully self-realized, then her work, and the work of all our progressive teachers, was not to teach us solely the knowledge in books, but to teach us an oppositional world view — different from that of our exploiters and oppressors, a world view that would enable us to see ourselves not through the lens of racism or racist stereotypes but one that would enable us to focus clearly and succinctly, to look at ourselves, at the world around us, critically — analytically — to see ourselves first and foremost as striving for wholeness, for unity of heart, mind, body and spirit.

It was as a student in segregated black schools called Booker T. Washington and Crispus Attucks that I witnessed the transformative power of teaching, of pedagogy. In particular, those teachers who approached their work as though it was indeed a pedagogy, a science of teaching, requiring diverse strategies, approaches, explorations, experimentation, and risks, demonstrated the value — the political power — of teaching. Their work was truly education for critical consciousness. In these segregated schools, the teachers were almost all black women. Many of them had chosen teaching at a historical moment when they were required by custom to remain single and childless, to have no visible erotic or sexual life. Among them were exceptional teachers who gave to their work a passion, a devotion that made it seem a true calling, a true vocation. They were the teachers who conceptualized oppositional world views, who taught us young black women to exult and glory in the power and beauty of our intellect. They offered to us a legacy of liberatory pedagogy that demanded active resistance and rebellion against sexism and racism. They embodied in their work, in their lives (for none of them appeared as tortured spin-

PAULO FREIRE

One of the most influential educational theorists of the 20th century, Paulo Freire (1921–1997) was a teacher, activist, and writer whose many books and articles outlined a revolutionary theory of education. Born in Brazil, Freire developed his early ideas about "liberatory education" by working with illiterate Brazilian peasants, for which he was jailed and then exiled in 1964. He returned to Brazil in 1979 and later served as minister of education. His best-known book is *Pedagogy of the Oppressed* (1970), in which he describes his theory of education as a means of personal and political transformation. Some scholars consider Freire's ideas to be the basis for feminist education of the kind that bell hooks describes in this essay.

sters estranged and alienated from the world around them) a feminist spirit. They were active participants in black community, shaping our futures, mapping our intellectual terrains, sharing revolutionary fervor and vision. I write these words, this essay to express the honor and respect I have for them because they have been my pedagogical guardians. Their work has had a profound impact on my consciousness, on my development as a teacher.

During years of graduate schools, I waited for that phase of study when we would focus on the meaning and significance of pedagogy, when we would learn about teaching, about how to teach. That moment never arrived. For years I have relied on those earlier models of excellent teaching to guide me. Most specifically, I understood from the teachers in those segregated schools that the work of any teacher committed to the full self-realization of students was necessarily and fundamentally radical, that ideas were not neutral, that to teach in a way that liberates, that expands consciousness, that awakens is to challenge domination at its very core. It is this pedagogy that Paulo Freire calls "education as the practice of freedom." In his introduction to Freire's *Pedagogy of the Oppressed*, Richard Shaull writes:

> Education either functions as an instrument which is used to facilitate the integration of the younger generation into the logic of the present system and bring about conformity to it, or it becomes "the practice of freedom," the means by which men and women deal critically and creatively with reality and discover how to participate in the transformation of their world.

A liberatory feminist movement aims to transform society by eradicating patriarchy, by ending sexism and sexist oppression, by challenging the politics of domination on all fronts. Feminist pedagogy can only be liberatory if it is truly revolutionary because the mechanisms of appropriation within white-supremacist, capitalist patriarchy are able to co-opt with tremendous ease that which merely appears radical or subversive. Within the United States, contemporary feminist movement is sustained in part by the efforts academic women make to constitute the university setting as a central site for the development and dissemination of feminist thought. Women's Studies has been the location of this effort. Given the way universities work to reinforce and perpetuate the status quo, the way knowledge is offered as commodity, Women's Studies can easily become a place where revolutionary feminist thought and feminist activism are submerged or made secondary to the goals of academic careerism. Without diminishing in any way our struggle as academics striving to succeed in institutions, such effort is fully compatible with liberatory feminist struggle only when we consciously, carefully, and strategically link the two. When this connection is made

initially but not sustained, or when it is never evident, Women's Studies becomes either an exotic terrain for those politically chic few seeking affirmation or a small settlement within the larger institutional structure where women (and primarily white women) have a power base, which rather than being oppositional simply mirrors the status quo. When feminist struggle is the central foundation for feminist education, Women's Studies and the feminist classroom (which can exist outside the domain of Women's Studies) can be places where education is the practice of freedom, the place for liberatory pedagogy.

5   At this historical moment, there is a crisis of engagement within universities, for when knowledge becomes commoditized, then much authentic learning ceases. Students who want to learn hunger for a space where they can be challenged intellectually. Students also suffer, as many of us who teach do, from a crisis of meaning, unsure about what has value in life, unsure even about whether it is important to stay alive. They long for a context where their subjective needs can be integrated with study, where the primary focus is a broader spectrum of ideas and modes of inquiry, in short a dialectical context where there is serious and rigorous critical exchange. This is an important and exciting time for feminist pedagogy because in theory and practice our work meets these needs.

Feminist education* — the feminist classroom — is and should be a place where there is a sense of struggle, where there is visible acknowledgement of the union of theory and practice, where we work together as teachers and students to overcome the estrangement and alienation that have become so much the norm in the contemporary university.

Feminist education is a general term referring to an approach to teaching based on feminist theory. Often, programs based on feminist theory are called Women's Studies programs. According to the Center for Women's and Gender Studies at the University of Texas at Austin, there are more than 600 Women's Studies programs in the United States. The Center defines the purposes of Women's and Gender Studies as fostering "multi-disciplinary research and teaching that focuses on women, gender, sexuality, and feminist issues [and supporting] the intersections of the above with age, class, race, ethnicity, and nationality."

Most importantly, feminist pedagogy should engage students in a learning process that makes the world "more rather than less real." In my classrooms, we work to dispel the notion that our experience is not a "real world" experience. This is especially easy since gender is such a pressing issue in contemporary life. Every aspect of popular culture alerts us to the reality that folks are thinking about gender in both reactionary and progressive ways. What is important is that they are thinking critically. And it is this

space that allows for the possibility of feminist intervention, whether it be in our classroom or in the life of students outside the classroom. Lately there has been a truly diverse body of students coming to my classes and other feminist classes at universities all around the United States. Many of us have been wondering "what's going on" or "why are all these men, and white men in the class." This changing student body reflects the concern about gender issues, that it is one of the real important issues in people's private lives that is addressed academically. Freire writes, "Education as the practice of freedom — as opposed to education as the practice of domination — denies that we are abstract, isolated, independent, and unattached to the world; it also denies that the world exists as a reality apart from us."

To make a revolutionary feminist pedagogy, we must relinquish our ties to traditional ways of teaching that reinforce domination. This is very difficult. Women's Studies courses are often viewed as not seriously academic because so much "personal stuff" is discussed. Fear that their courses will be seen as "gut" classes has led many feminist professors to rely more on traditional pedagogical styles. This is unfortunate. Certainly, the radical alternative to the status quo should never have been simply an inversion. That is to say, critical of the absence of any focus on personal experience in traditional classrooms, such focus becomes the central characteristic of the feminist classroom. This model must be viewed critically because a class can still be reinforcing domination, not transforming consciousness about gender, even as the "personal" is the ongoing topic of conversation.

To have a revolutionary feminist pedagogy we must first focus on the teacher-student relationship and the issue of power. How do we as feminist teachers use power in a way that is not coercive, dominating? Many women have had difficulty asserting power in the feminist classroom for fear that to do so would be to exercise domination. Yet we must acknowledge that our role as teacher is a position of power over others. We can use that power in ways that diminish or in ways that enrich and it is this choice that should distinguish feminist pedagogy from ways of teaching that reinforce domination. One simple way to alter the way one's "power" as teacher is experienced in the classroom is to elect not to assume the posture of all-knowing professors. This is also difficult. When we acknowledge that we do not know everything, that we do not have all the answers, we risk students leaving our classrooms and telling others that we are not prepared. It is important to make it clear to students that we are prepared and that the willingness to be open and honest about what we do not know is a gesture of respect for them.

To be oppositional in the feminist classroom one must have a standard of valuation that differs from the norm. Many of us tried new ways of teaching without changing the standards by which we evaluated our work. We often left the classroom feeling uncertain about the learning process or even concerned that we were failing as teachers. Let me share a particular problem I have faced. My classroom style is very confrontational. It is a model of pedagogy that is based on the assumption that many students will take courses from me who are afraid to assert themselves as critical thinkers, who are afraid to speak (especially students from oppressed and exploited groups). The revolutionary hope that I bring to the classroom is that it will become a space where they can come to voice. Unlike the stereotypical feminist model that suggests women best come to voice in an atmosphere of safety (one in which we are all going to be kind and nurturing), I encourage students to work at coming to voice in an atmosphere where they may be afraid or see themselves at risk. The goal is to enable all students, not just an assertive few, to feel empowered in a rigorous, critical discussion. Many students find this pedagogy difficult, frightening, and very demanding. They do not usually come away from my class talking about how much they enjoyed the experience.

10 One aspect of traditional models of teaching that I had not surrendered was that longing for immediate recognition of my value as a teacher, and immediate affirmation. Often I did not feel liked or affirmed and this was difficult for me to accept. I reflected on my student experiences and the reality that I often learned the most in classes that I did not enjoy and complained about, which helped me to work on the traditional assumption that immediate positive feedback is a

signifier of worth. Concurrently, I found that students who often felt that they hated a class with me would return later to say how much they learned, that they understood that it was the different style that made it hard as well as the different demands. I began to see that courses that work to shift paradigms, to change consciousness, cannot necessarily be experienced immediately as fun or positive or safe and this was not a worthwhile criteria to use in an evaluation.

In the feminist classroom, it is important to define a term of engagement, to identify what we mean when we say that a course will be taught from a feminist perspective. Often the initial explanations about pedagogy will have a serious impact on the way students experience a course. It is important to talk about pedagogical strategy. For a time, I assumed that students would just get the hang of it, would see that I was trying to teach in a different way and accept it without explanation. Often, that meant I explained after being criticized. It is important for feminist professors to explain not only what will differ about the classroom experience but to openly acknowledge that students must consider whether they wish to be in such a learning space. On a basic level, students are often turned off by the fact that I take attendance, but because I see the classroom experience as constituting a unique learning experience, to miss class is to really lose a significant aspect of the process. Whether or not a student attends class affects grading and this bothers students who are not accustomed to taking attendance seriously. Another important issue for me has been that each student participate in classroom discussion, that each student have a voice. This is a practice that I think is important not because every student has something valuable to say (this is not al-

ways so), but often students who do have meaningful comments to contribute are silent. In my classes, everyone's voice is heard as students read paragraphs which may explore a particular issue. They do not have the opportunity to refuse to read paragraphs. When I hear their voices, I become more aware of information they may not know that I can provide. Whether a class is large or small, I try to talk with all students individually or in small groups so that I have a sense of their needs. How can we transform consciousness if we do not have some sense of where the students are intellectually, psychically?

Concern with how and what students are learning validates and legitimates a focus, however small, on personal confession in classroom discussions. I encourage students to relate the information they are learning to the personal identities they are working to socially construct, to change, to affirm. If the goal of personal confession is not narcissim, it must take place within a critical framework where it is related to material that is being discussed. When, for example, I am teaching Toni Morrison's novel, *The Bluest Eye,* I may have students write personal paragraphs about the relationship between race and physical beauty, which they read in class. Their paragraphs may reveal pain, woundedness as they explore and express ways they are victimized by racism and sexism, or they may express ideas that are racist and sexist. Yet the paragraphs enable them to approach the text in a new way. They may read the novel differently. They may be able to be more critical and analytical. If this does not happen, then the paragraphs fail as a pedagogical tool. To make feminist classrooms the site of transformative learning experiences, we must constantly try new methods, new approaches.

Finally, we cannot have a revolutionary feminist pedagogy if we do not have revolutionary feminists in the classroom. Women's Studies courses must do more than offer a different teaching style; we must really challenge issues of sexism and sexist oppression both by what we teach and how we teach. This is truly a collective effort. We must learn from one another, sharing ideas and pedagogical strategies. Although I have invited feminist colleagues to come and participate in my classes, they do not. Classroom territoriality is another traditional taboo.

Yet if we are to learn from one another, if we are to develop a concrete strategy for radicalizing our classrooms, we must be more engaged as a group. We must be willing to deconstruct this power dimension, to challenge, change and create new approaches. If we are to move toward a revolutionary feminist pedagogy, we must challenge ourselves and one another to restore to feminist struggle its radical and subversive dimension. We must be willing to restore the spirit of risk — to be fast, wild, to be able to take hold, turn around, transform.

Questions for Discussion

1. What crisis does hooks see in education? How can Women's Studies programs help to address that crisis, in her view? **2.** What does hooks mean when she writes that knowledge has become a commodity? What evidence does she offer to support this assertion? Do you agree with her? Why or why not? **3.** Why does hooks teach in way that is confrontational? What is the goal of such an approach to teaching? hooks states that many students find her approach uncomfortable. Why does it not concern her that some of her students do not enjoy her classes? Should it concern her, in your view? Explain. **4.** hooks argues that personal experience should be the central focus of the kind of feminist classroom she advocates. Evaluate the way in which hooks uses her own experience as a student and a teacher to help her make her argument. How effective is her use of personal experience in this essay? **5.** hooks has been both praised and criticized for her unconventional writing style as a scholar. How would you characterize her style? In what ways might her writing style be considered appropriate for the argument she is making about education in this essay? **6.** How effectively does hooks address possible objections to her view? What questions would you raise about hooks's approach to education? What might your reaction to her essay reveal about your own views regarding the purpose of education?

④ **RONALD TAKAKI, "An Educated and Culturally Literate Person Must Study America's Multicultural Reality"**

To what extent should schools teach Americans about their own diversity? In a sense, the emergence of multicultural education in the United States in the past two decades is an answer to that question. When Ronald Takaki published the following essay in 1989, many American colleges and universities were beginning to require students to take courses in which they learned about other cultures. The purpose of such requirements, as Takaki suggests, was to help students to understand diversity in order to be able to live and work together. More than a decade after Takaki's essay was published, such diversity requirements are common, suggesting that multicultural education has become widely accepted by Americans. Yet these requirements continue to spark controversy. Perhaps that is because they force us to reconsider our beliefs about the purpose of education, or perhaps these requirements do not fit in with what we believe schools should teach. Whatever the case, Takaki's argument about the importance of multicultural education is part of the larger discussion that Americans continue to have about what should be taught in schools. Ronald Takaki is Professor of Ethnic Studies at the University of California at Berkeley and the author of many books about race, ethnicity, and education, including *A Different Mirror: A History of Multicultural America* (1993) and *From Different Shores: Perspectives on Race and Ethnicity in America* (1994). This essay was first published in the *Chronicle of Higher Education*.

An Educated and Culturally Literate Person Must Study America's Multicultural Reality
RONALD TAKAKI

1 In Palolo Valley, Hawaii, where I lived as a child, my neighbors were Japanese, Chinese, Portuguese, Filipino, and Hawaiian. I heard voices with different accents and I heard different languages. I played with children of different colors. Why, I wondered, were families representing such an array of nationalities living together in one little valley? My teachers and textbooks did not explain our diversity.

After graduation from high school, I attended a college on the mainland where students and even professors would ask me how long I had been in America and where I had learned to speak English. "In this country," I would reply. "I was born in America, and my family has been here for three generations."

Today, some twenty years later, Asian and also Afro-Americans, Chicano/Latino, and Native-American students continue to find themselves perceived as strangers on college campuses. Moreover, they are encountering a new campus racism. The

*Influential scholars
Allan Bloom and E. D.
Hirsch achieved na-
tional prominence dur-
ing the 1980s by
arguing that U.S. col-
leges were failing to
produce culturally liter-
ate citizens. Bloom is
best known for *The
Closing of the
American Mind* (1987),
Hirsch for *Cultural
Literacy: What Every
American Needs to
Know* (1987). Both
books continue to be
controversial and
widely read.

targets of ugly racial slurs and violence, they have begun to ask critical questions about why knowledge of their histories and communities is excluded from the curriculum. White students are also realizing the need to understand the cultural diversity of American society.

In response, colleges and universities across the country, from Brown to Berkeley, are currently considering requiring students to take courses designed to help them understand diverse cultures.
5 The debate is taking place within a general context framed by academic pundits like Allan Bloom and E. D. Hirsch.* Both of them are asking: What is an educated, a culturally literate person?

I think Bloom is right when he says: "There are some things one must know about if one is to be educated. . . . The university should try to have a vision of what an educated person is." I also agree with Hirsch when he insists that there is a body of cultural information that "every American needs to know."

But the question is: What should be the content of education and what does cultural literacy mean? The traditional curriculum reflects what Howard Swearer, former president of Brown University, has described as a "certain provincialism," an overly Eurocentric perspective. Concerned about this problem, a Brown University visiting committee recommended that the faculty consider requiring students to take an ethnic-studies course before they graduate. "The contemporary definition of an educated person," the committee said, "must include at least minimal awareness of multicultural reality."

This view now is widely shared. Says Donna Shalala, chancellor of the University of Wisconsin at Madison: "Every student needs to know much more about the origins and history of the particular cultures which, as Americans, we will encounter during our lives."

This need is especially felt in California, where racial minorities will constitute a majority of the population by 2000, and where a faculty committee at the University of California at Berkeley has proposed an "American-cultures requirement" to give students a deeper understanding of our nation's racial and cultural diversity. Faculty opposition is based mainly on a disdain for all requirements on principle, an unwillingness to add another requirement, an insistence on the centrality of Western civilization, and a fear that the history of European immigrant groups would be left out of the proposed course.[†]
10 In fact, however, there are requirements everywhere in the curriculum (for reading and composition, the major, a foreign language, breadth of knowledge, etc.). The American-cultures requirement would not be an additional course, for students would be permitted to use the course to satisfy one of their social-sciences or humanities requirements. Western civilization will continue to dominate the curriculum, and the proposed requirement would place the expe-

riences of racial minorities within the broad context of American society. Faculty support for some kind of mandatory course is considerable, and a vote on the issue is scheduled this spring.

But the question often asked is: What would be the focus and content of such multicultural courses? Actually there is a wide range of possibilities. For many years I have been teaching a course on "Racial Inequality in America: A Comparative Historical Perspective." Who we are in this society and how we are perceived and treated have been conditioned by America's racial and ethnic diversity. My approach is captured in the phrase "from different shores." By "shores," I intend a double meaning. One is the shores that immigrants left to go to America — those in Europe, Africa, Latin America, and Asia. The second is the different and often conflicting shores or perspectives from which scholars have viewed the experiences of racial and ethnic groups.

In my course, students read Thomas Sowell's[‡] *Ethnic America: A History* along with my *Iron Cages: Race and Culture in 19th-Century America*. Readings also include Winthrop Jordan on the colonial origins of racism, John Higham on nativism, Mario Barrera on Chicanos, and William J. Wilson on the black underclass. By critically examining the different "shores," students are able to address complex comparative questions: How have the experiences of racial minorities such as blacks and Asians been similar to, and different from, one another? Is "race" the same as "ethnicity"? How have race relations been shaped by economic developments, as well as by culture? What impact have these forces had on moral values about how people should think and behave, beliefs about human nature and society, and images of the past as well as the future?

Other courses could examine racial diversity in relation to gender, immigration, urbanization, technology, or the labor market. Courses could also study specific topics such as Hollywood's racial images, ethnic music and art, novels by writers of color, the civil rights movement, or the Pacific Rim. Regardless of theme or topic, all of the courses should address the major theoretical issues concerning race and should focus on Afro-Americans, Asians, Chicanos/Latinos, and Native Americans.

Who would teach these courses? Responsibility could be located solely in ethnic-studies programs. But this would reduce them to service-course programs and also render even more remote the possibility of diversifying the traditional curriculum. The sheer logistics of meeting the demand generated by an institution wide requirement would be overwhelming for any single department.

15 Clearly, faculty members in the social sciences and humanities will have to be involved. There also are dangers in this approach, however. The diffusion of ethnic studies throughout the traditional disciplines could undermine the coherence and identity of ethnic studies as a field of teaching and scholarship. It could also lead to area-studies courses on Africa or Asia disguised as ethnic studies, to revised but essentially intact Western-civilization courses with a few "non-Western" readings tacked on, or to amorphous and bland "American studies" courses taught by instructors with little or no training in multicultural studies. Such courses, though well-intentioned, could result in the unwitting perpetuation of certain racial stereotypes and even to the transformation of texts by writers and scholars of color into "mistexts." This would only reproduce multicultural illiteracy.

But broad faculty participation in such a requirement can work if there is a sharply written statement of purpose, as

CONTEXT

According to the U.S. Census Bureau, as of 2000, 49.9 percent of the 33.1 million residents of California were classified as White, 31.6 percent were Latino, 11.4 percent were Asian, 6.7 percent were Black, and fewer than 1 percent were Native American. During the 1990s the Latino population in California grew by 35 percent, and the Asian population grew by 36 percent. These figures mirrored population changes in the United States as a whole: Nationally, the Latino population grew by 38.8 percent during the 1990s, and the Asian population grew by 43 percent; during the same period the White population increased by 7.3 percent.

[†] The proposal for an American-cultures requirement to which Takaki refers in this essay was subsequently passed and adopted by the University of California at Berkeley. Since 1993 all students entering the university have had to satisfy this requirement by taking an approved course focusing on issues of race, culture, and ethnicity in American society.

[‡] See Thomas Sowell's essay about funding higher education on pages 342–345.

well as clear criteria for courses on the racial and cultural diversity of American society. We also need interdisciplinary institutes to offer intellectual settings where faculty members from different fields can collaborate on new courses and where ethnic-studies scholars can share their expertise. More importantly, we need to develop and strengthen ethnic-studies programs and departments as academic foundations for this new multicultural curriculum. Such bases should bring together a critical mass of faculty members committed to, and trained in ethnic studies, and should help to preserve the alternative perspectives provided by this scholarly field.

In addition, research must generate knowledge for the new courses, and new faculty members must be trained for ethnic-studies teaching and

scholarship. Berkeley already has a doctoral program in ethnic studies, but other graduate schools must also help prepare the next generation of faculty members. Universities will experience a tremendous turnover in teachers due to retirements, and this is a particularly urgent time to educate future scholars, especially from minority groups, for a multicultural curriculum.

The need to open the American mind to greater cultural diversity will not go away. We can resist it by ignoring the changing ethnic composition of our student bodies and the larger society, or we can realize how it offers colleges and universities a timely and exciting opportunity to revitalize the social sciences and humanities, giving both a new sense of purpose and a more inclusive definition of knowledge.

If concerted efforts are made, someday students of different racial backgrounds will be able to learn about one another in an informed and systematic way and will not graduate from our institutions of higher learning ignorant about how places like Palolo Valley fit into American society.

NEGOTIATING DIFFERENCES

The writers in this chapter address issues that have sparked intense controversies in American schools. In many instances these controversies have emerged as a result of new course requirements or other changes in the curriculum. For example, in his essay Ronald Takaki refers to a controversial proposal for a required multicultural course in the University of California system. As Takaki suggests, the debates about such a proposal are really about what students should be taught — and about what purposes schools really serve.

Imagine that your college or university has decided to revise its own curriculum. You have been given the opportunity to review the requirements of the current curriculum and to decide whether those requirements are adequate or should be changed in some way. But you have not been asked simply for your own opinion about the kind of curriculum your

Questions for Discussion

1. Takaki opens his essay by drawing on personal experience from twenty years earlier. In what ways is this experience relevant to his main argument? How effective is his use of personal experience in helping him make his argument? **2.** Why does Takaki believe that a required course in American cultures is important? How does he establish the need for such a requirement? **3.** What risks does Takaki see in giving responsibility for such courses to a single department? Why is he concerned about locating such courses within traditional academic disciplines? **4.** Why do you think Takaki chooses Brown and Berkeley as examples of "colleges and universities across the country"? Does his use of these examples strengthen or weaken his argument? Explain. **5.** In his essay, Takaki refers to two scholars — Allan Bloom and E. D. Hirsch — who have criticized multicultural education. Why does he do so? What do you think he accomplishes with these references?

school should have; rather, you have been specifically asked to consider whether the curriculum serves the needs of the students who attend your school.

Your task, then, is to write an essay in which you propose and justify changes to your school's curriculum that would make that curriculum more appropriate and useful for the students at your school at this point in time or an essay in which you argue in favor of keep-ing the curriculum as it currently exists. To make your argument for curriculum changes or for maintaining the current curriculum, you will obviously have to examine the curriculum. You should also consider the kinds of students who attend your school and the reasons they do. And you should think about what purpose your school serves in your community. In your es-say, try to make a case for a curriculum that would best serve these different needs.

HOW SHOULD WE DETERMINE
WHAT OUR CHILDREN LEARN?

During the 1990s many states began implementing new tests that were intended to set higher standards for both students and teachers. Many of these new standardized tests were so-called high-stakes tests — that is, students had to pass these tests to advance to the next grade or to earn a high school diploma. In the past many states allowed students to graduate or advance to the next grade level even if they did not pass the state-mandated exams, but these new high-stakes tests made that impossible in many cases. Proponents of such tests argue that setting high standards benefits students by encouraging schools to prepare all their students for the tests rather than only those students who intend to go to college. Without such tests, proponents say, struggling students or students without plans to attend college are placed in less rigorous programs than their college-bound classmates. The result is tracking: a two-tiered (or three- or four-tiered) system that favors some students and places others at a disadvantage. High-stakes tests can remedy that problem by requiring all students to meet the same high standards. ■ Of course, many critics argue just the opposite. They maintain that high-stakes tests not only harm some students, but also make tracking even more widespread. What happens, they ask, to students who complete the curriculum requirements but do not pass the standardized tests? Should they simply be sent on their way without a diploma after twelve years of schooling? And won't the curriculum itself become overly influenced by those tests so that all students will indirectly be shortchanged by teachers who must "teach to the test"? These critics argue that when high-stakes tests are mandated, the focus in schools shifts to test preparation; as a result, important aspects of student learning are ignored. ■ The increased popularity of high-stakes testing in recent years and the intensity of the debates surrounding them can make these problems seem new. In fact, however, educators, parents, students, and politicians have been wrestling with these questions about standards and assessment for many years. In the late 19th century, for example, a special panel of experts called the Committee of Ten was commissioned to look into what at the time was believed to be a crisis in education marked by low student achievement and low standards. The committee members recommended a common curriculum for all students — which is a recommendation that we continue to hear today. (See Con-Text on page 307.) Although much has changed since the Committee of Ten submitted its report in 1892, there is little question that concerns about what curriculum is best for students and how students should be tested have not disappeared. If anything, they have intensified, perhaps because those concerns relate to the important task of educating the nation's children. ■ The essays in this section address those concerns about curriculum and assessment. The authors of these essays offer their views on testing and tracking more than 100 years after the Committee of Ten's famous report. But in effect these authors are doing the same thing that the Committee of Ten did: trying to come to terms with how best to educate and test students. Ultimately, then, these essays reveal that arguments about testing and tracking are really arguments about what education should be.

CON-TEXT: The Report of the Committee of Ten, 1892

1 On one very important question of general policy which affects profoundly the preparation of all school programmes, the Committee of Ten and all the Conferences are absolutely, unanimous. Among the questions suggested for discussion in each Conference were the following: —

7. Should the subject be treated differently for pupils who are going to college, for those who are going to a scientific school, and for those who, presumably, are going to neither?

8. At what age should this differentiation begin, if any be recommended?

The 7th question is answered unanimously in the negative by the Conferences, and the 8th therefore needs no answer. The Committee of Ten unanimously agree with the Conferences. Ninety-eight teachers, intimately concerned either with the actual work of American secondary schools, or with the results of that work as they appear in students who come to college, unanimously declare that every subject which is taught at all in a secondary school should be taught in the same way and to the same extent to every pupil so long as he pursues it, no matter what the probable destination of the pupil may be, or at what point his education is to cease. Thus, for all pupils who study Latin, or history, or algebra, for example, the allotment of time and the method of instruction in a given school should be the same year by year. Not that all the pupils should pursue every subject for the same number of years; but so long as they do pursue it, they should all be treated alike. It has been a very general custom in American high schools and academies to make up separate courses of study for pupils of supposed different destinations, the proportions of the several studies in the different courses being various. The principle laid down by the Conferences will, if logically carried out, make a great simplification in secondary school programmes. It will lead to each subject's being treated by the school in the same way by the year for all pupils, and this, whether the individual pupil be required to choose between courses which run through several years, or be allowed some choice among subjects year by year.

SOURCE: National Education Association. Available at The Memory Hole, http://www.blancmange.net/tmh/books/commoften/mainrpt.html.

① ELEANOR MARTIN, "No" Is the Right Answer

In the late 1990s Massachusetts became one of many states to implement new standardized exams for its students. Part of a nationwide trend toward higher standards and "accountability," the Massachusetts Comprehensive Assessment System (MCAS) represented a significant change for Massachusetts students because high school students who failed the test could not receive a diploma. This new high-stakes test sparked intense controversy as parents, students, and teachers worried about what would happen to students who could not pass the exam. In 1999, as the new tests were administered, a small but vocal opposition emerged. Many opponents called for students to boycott the tests. Eleanor Martin, a high school sophomore at the time, was one of twelve students at Cambridge Rindge and Latin High School who refused to take the test. In the following essay she explains why, making a case against standardized tests such as the MCAS. Although her essay focuses on the required state tests in Massachusetts, her argument addresses larger questions about standardized testing and student learning — questions that continue to stir up heated debate nationwide as more states follow the lead of Massachusetts and implement their own high-stakes tests. Martin's essay was first published in the *Boston Globe* in 1999.

"No" Is the Right Answer
ELEANOR MARTIN

1 On May 17, a dozen sophomores at Cambridge Rindge and Latin High School decided not to take the state-mandated Massachusetts Comprehensive Assessment Test, better known as the MCAS. I was one of them.

For weeks we had carefully researched the political and moral issues at stake. We were aware that it was going to be difficult to refuse the test. When you are a sophomore in high school, it is not easy to go against the orders of your teachers, your advisors, your school, and your state. We were not certain of the punishment that we would receive. Detention, suspension, expulsion? All had been mentioned as possibilities.

When we announced what we were going to do, we received a lot of opposition. We were told that we were going to bring down the cumulative score of our house and of the entire school. But we believed, and still do, that the reasons for fighting this test are more important than any score.

Beginning with the class of 2003, high school students who fail the MCAS test will not be able to graduate. We be-

THE MASSACHUSETTS COMPREHENSIVE ASSESSMENT SYSTEM (MCAS)

The MCAS was developed in the late 1990s as part of the Massachusetts Education Reform Law of 1993, which mandates that all public school students, including students with disabilities and limited English proficiency, be tested in grades 4, 8, and 10 to determine whether they meet the Massachusetts state education standards. Beginning in 2003, students in grade 10 must pass the MCAS exams in English and mathematics to be eligible for a high school diploma; students will be given several opportunities to pass the exams between grade 10 and the end of their senior year. According to the Massachusetts Department of Education, "Parents may *not* legally refuse their child's participation in MCAS. Massachusetts General Laws chapter 76, Sections 2 and 4, establish penalties for truancy as well as for inducing unlawful absence of a minor from school. In addition, school discipline codes generally define local rules for school attendance and penalties for unauthorized absence from school or from a required part of the school day." The MCAS was first administered in 1998.

lieve that a single test should not determine the success and future of a student. **5** How can four years of learning and growing be assessed by a single standardized test? There are so many things that students learn throughout high school — how to play an instrument, act, draw, paint. They learn photography, how to program a computer, fix a car engine, cook tortellini Alfredo, throw a pot, or design a set for a play. Many students say these are among the most important skills they learn in high school, yet all are skills the MCAS fails to recognize.

The MCAS test is expected to take over 20 hours of class time. No test should take that much time out of learning, especially not one whose supposed rationale is that students are not learning enough in school.

The material on the MCAS is very specific. For students to do well, teachers must redesign their curriculums to teach to the test. Districts and school administrators, eager to show high scores, have pressured teachers to create units based on the material. Because the test is based largely on memorization of facts, teachers will have to teach their students these specific facts instead of teaching for deep comprehension and understanding of the material.

Students who have been in this country for only three years are required to take the test. How can someone who has been speaking English for three years be expected to write essays with correct spelling and grammar, which is a requirement to receive a proficient score? Special needs students are also required to take this test to graduate.

Supposedly, this test will be used to evaluate teachers as well as students. However, a test like this simply measures whether a teacher teaches to the test. **10** If the MCAS test is instituted in Massachusetts, the scores will become a major consideration for parents when they choose a school for their children. Schools will therefore want their scores to be as high as possible. Programs such as Metco,* which integrates inner-city students into suburban schools, may be discouraged since it has been shown that inner-city students do not score as well as suburban students.

We are also concerned about the future of innovative programs, such as the Interactive Math Program, or IMP, which does not follow the traditional progression of algebra, geometry, trigonometry, and calculus, but integrates these throughout all four years. Therefore, a sophomore IMP student will not know the expected geometry curriculum, but will

*The Metropolitan Council for Educational Opportunity (Metco) sponsors special educational programs for at-risk students in Massachusetts.

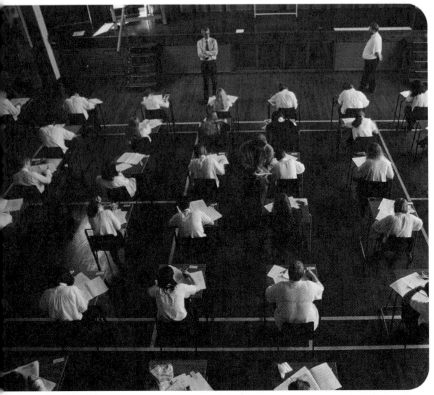

know some trigonometry and calculus that is not included on the MCAS.

Also, certain in-depth courses, such as "Bible as Literature," "The Holocaust," "Reading and Writing on Human Values," Women in Literature," and "African-American Literature" will no doubt be off-limits to freshmen and sophomores because they are not geared to the MCAS.

My humanities teacher in eighth grade used the "Facing History and Ourselves" curriculum, which spends about eight weeks teaching in incredible depth about the Holocaust. We learned about Nazi propaganda and how it compares to propaganda used today. We examined the causes of the Holocaust, confronted the difficult philosophical and moral issues it raises, and focused on what we can do to prevent it from happening again.

This is one of the best educational experiences I have ever had. Because of it, I have a deep and complex understanding of the Holocaust. All the dates and facts that I learned may not stay with me, but I feel certain that my understanding of the event will.

15 We are worried that such innovative and respected curriculums as IMP and "Facing History" will become casualties of the MCAS test mentality.

We are not saying nothing should be done to improve public education in Massachusetts. We are simply saying that taking a paper and pencil test to graduate is not the way to amend education. Massachusetts has already spent $24 million on the MCAS test, and an estimated $14 million more is being spent this year. Roughly that same amount will be spent every year the test is given. We could use that money in better ways — for more staff developers, teacher workshops, improved bilingual education, better school supplies, and better fine arts and technical arts programs.

This is our last chance to raise awareness about getting an education that is not standardized, but meaningful, deep, and personalized. We believe an education like that is worth working for.

Questions for Discussion

1. How does Martin justify her decision to boycott the MCAS? Do you find her justification convincing? Why or why not? **2.** What specific reasons does Martin provide for her opposition to the standardized test in Massachusetts that she refused to take? What do her reasons indicate about her view of what students should learn in school? **3.** What are some of the possible effects of the MCAS that concern Martin? Do you think her concerns are valid? How do they contribute to her main argument against standardized testing? **4.** Evaluate the tone of this essay. To what extent do you think the tone contributes to the essay's main argument? How does it influence your sense of Martin's credibility? **5.** Using the Toulmin model of argumentation (see pages 31–35). What do you think is Martin's central claim in her essay? What is her warrant? Do you think that most readers in Massachusetts would accept her warrant? Explain.

② PATRICIA WILLIAMS, "Tests, Tracking, and Derailment"

If you have gone to school in the United States, chances are that you have encountered some form of tracking: Advanced Placement or honors classes, special education programs for students with special needs, remedial courses for struggling students, enrichment programs for gifted and talented students. Even if you were not tracked into such a program, it is likely that your school's curriculum offered different options for college-bound students and students who did not intend to go to college. The purpose of all these educational tracks is to match the curriculum to students' needs and abilities. But tracking has always been controversial, in part because it is not clear that special programs or tracks serve their intended purposes. Writer Patricia Williams, for example, believes that tracking students — for whatever purpose — ultimately leads to more problems than it solves. In her essay, which was published in *The Nation* in 2002, she traces what she sees as some of those problems and argues that educational resources can be better spent to ensure that all children benefit from schooling. In one sense her essay suggests that debates about how to allocate educational monies inevitably raise larger questions about the goals of schooling. As you read, consider how Williams's sense of the purpose of education informs her argument against educational tracking.

Tests, Tracking, and Derailment
PATRICIA WILLIAMS

1 As state budgets around the country are slashed to accommodate the expense of the war on terror, the pursuit of educational opportunity for all seems ever more elusive. While standardized tests are supposed to be used to diagnose problems and facilitate individual or institutional improvement, too often they have been used to close or penalize precisely the schools that most need help; or, results have been used to track students into separate programs that benefit the few but not the many. The implementation of gifted classes with better student-teacher ratios and more substantial resources often triggers an unhealthy and quite bitter competition for those unnaturally narrowed windows of opportunity. How much better it would be to have more public debate about why the pickings are so slim to begin with. In any event, it is no wonder there is such intense national anxiety just now, a fantastical hunger for children who speak in complete sentences by the age of six months.

A friend compares the tracking of students to the separation of altos from sopranos in a choir. But academic ability and/or intelligence is both spikier and more malleably constructed than such an analogy allows. Tracking students by separating the high notes from the low only works if the endgame is to teach all children the "Hallelujah Chorus." A system that teaches only the sopranos because no parent wants their child to be less than a diva is a system driven by the shortsightedness of narcissism. I think we make a well-rounded society the same way we make the best music: through the harmonic combination of differently pitched, but uniformly well-trained voices.

A parsimony of spirit haunts education policy, exacerbated by fear of the extremes. Under the stress of threatened budget cuts, people worry much more about providing lifeboats for the very top and containment for the "ineducable" rock bottom than they do about properly training the great masses of children, the vibrant, perfectly able middle who are capable of much more than most school systems offer. In addition, discussions of educational equality are skewed by conflation of behavioral problems with IQ,* and learning disabilities with retardation. Repeatedly one hears complaints that you can't put a gifted child in a class full of unruly, noisy misfits and expect anyone to benefit. Most often it's a plea from a parent who desperately wants his or her child re-

moved from a large oversubscribed classroom with a single, stressed teacher in an underfunded district and sent to the sanctuary of a nurturing bubble where peace reigns because there are twelve kids in a class with two specialists and everyone's riding the high of great expectations. But all children respond better in ordered, supportive environments; and all other investments being equal, gifted children are just as prone to behavior problems — and to learning disabilities — as any other part of the population. Nor should we confuse exceptional circumstances with behavior problems. The difficulty of engaging a child who's just spent the night in a homeless shelter, for example, is not productively treated as chiefly an issue of IQ.

The narrowing of access has often resulted in peculiar kinds of hairsplitting. When I was growing up, for example, Boston's Latin School was divided into two separate schools: one for boys and one for girls. Although the curriculum was identical and the admissions exam

*IQ, or intelligence quotient, is a measure of intelligence based partly on the ideas of 19th century French psychologist Alfred Binet. Drawing on his observations of children with and without various disabilities, Binet developed a test to measure a child's "mental age." His test was adapted by several American psychologists and used by the U.S. Army to measure the intelligence levels of its recruits during World War I. IQ tests have long been criticized as inaccurate and unfair, and criticisms of the tests as racially biased intensified in the 1960s and 1970s.

the same, there were some disparities: The girls' school was smaller and so could admit fewer students; and the science and sports facilities were inferior to those of the boys.

5 There was a successful lawsuit to integrate the two schools about twenty years ago, but then an odd thing happened. Instead of using the old girls' school for the middle school and the larger boys' school for the new upper school, as was originally suggested, the city decided to sever the two. The old boys' school retained the name Boston Latin, and the old girls' school — smaller, less-equipped — was reborn as Boston Latin Academy. The entrance exam is now administered so that those who score highest go to Boston Latin; the next cut down go to what is now, unnecessarily, known as the "less elite" Latin Academy.

One of the more direct consequences of this is that the new Boston Latin inherited an alumni endowment of $15 million dollars, much of it used to provide college scholarships. Latin Academy, on the other hand, inherited the revenue of the old Girls' Latin alumni association — something under $200,000. It seems odd: Students at both schools are tremendously talented, the cutoff between them based on fairly insignificant scoring differences. But rather than pool the resources of the combined facilities — thus maximizing educational opportunity, in particular funding for college — the resolution of the pre-existing gender inequality almost purposefully reinscribed that inequality as one driven by wealth and class.

There are good models of what is possible. The International Baccalaureate curriculum, which is considered "advanced" by most American standards, is administered to a far wider range of students in Europe than here, with the result that their norm is considerably higher than ours in a number of areas. The University of Chicago's School Mathematics Project, originally developed for gifted students at the Chicago Lab School, is now recommended for all children — all children, as the foreword to its textbooks says, can "learn more and do more than was thought to be possible ten or twenty years ago." And educator Marva Collins's widely praised curriculum for inner-city elementary schools includes reading Shakespeare.

Imparting higher levels of content requires nothing exceptional but rather normal, more-or-less stable children, taught in small classes by well-trained, well-mentored teachers who have a sophisticated grasp of mathematics and literature themselves. It will pay us, I think, to stop configuring education as a battle of the geniuses against the uncivilized. We are a wealthy nation chock-full of those normal, more-or-less stable children. The military should not be the only institution that teaches them to be all that they can be.

CONTEXT

According to its Web site, "The Nation will not be the organ of any party, sect, or body. It will, on the contrary, make an earnest effort to bring to the discussion of political and social questions a really critical spirit, and to wage war upon the vices of violence, exaggeration, and misrepresentation by which so much of the political writing of the day is marred." Founded in 1865, The Nation is a respected magazine of political affairs that is generally considered to espouse a liberal viewpoint. In what ways does Patricia Williams's argument against tracking reflect the editorial slant of this magazine and its expressed purpose?

Questions for Discussion

1. Williams compares tracking to separating the singers in a choir. How effectively do you think this comparison helps Williams to make her point about the disadvantages of tracking? What does this comparison reveal about her beliefs about the purposes of schooling? 2. Williams refers to "the great masses of children, the vibrant, perfectly able middle who are capable of much more than most school systems offer." What evidence does she offer to support this assertion? Do you think she is right? Why or why not? 3. What point does Williams use the example of the Boston Latin School to illustrate? How effectively does this example help her to make her point? How does it contribute to her main argument about tracking? 4. In her final paragraph Williams argues that we should not think of education "as a battle of the geniuses against the uncivilized." To what extent do you think Bertell Ollman and Gregory Cizek, whose essays appear later in this chapter, would agree with Williams? Cite specific passages from their essays to support your answer.

5. Williams's essay might be considered an essay based on inductive reasoning (see pages 25–26). How effective do you think her essay is as such an argument? How persuasively does she compile evidence to reach her conclusion?

③ GREGORY CIZEK, "Unintended Consequences of High Stakes Testing"

As author Gregory Cizek himself notes, the title of the following essay is misleading. We tend to think of "unintended consequences" as negative. But Cizek makes a vigorous case in favor of standardized testing, arguing that high-stakes tests lead to a number of important and beneficial consequences for students, schools, and teachers alike. Like many proponents of such tests, Cizek believes that carefully constructed standardized tests are a crucial element in efforts to improve public education. As you read through his discussion of the benefits of testing, consider what his list of these benefits reveals about his view of the purpose of formal education. Consider, too, the extent to which his fundamental beliefs about education match — or diverge from — the views of the other writers in this section. Gregory Cizek is an associate professor of education at the University of North Carolina and the author of *Detecting and Preventing Classroom Cheating* (1999). This essay originally appeared in 2002 at EducationNews.org, an online news service devoted to educational issues.

Unintended Consequences of High Stakes Testing
GREGORY CIZEK

*Eschatology is a branch of theology concerned with the end of the world or of humankind.

1   It's eschatological.* In one tract after another, the zealous proclaim that there is a dire threat posed by the anti-Christ of postmodern education: testing. To be more precise, the Great Satan does not comprise *all* testing, only testing *with consequences* — consequences such as grade retention for students, salaries for educators, or the futures of (in particular) low-performing schools. In this fevered and frenzied battle, what is clear is that any sort of high-stakes test is the beast. On the side of the angels are those who take the path of beast-resistance.

As I reflect on my own writing here, I wondered if I would need to make a confession for the sin of hyperbole. Then I re-read some of the sacred texts.

According to Alfie Kohn in a recent issue of the *Kappan,* we must "make the fight against standardized tests our top priority . . . until we have chased this monster from our schools."[1] A companion article in the same issue discussed high-stakes testing in an article titled "the authentic standards movement and its evil twin."[2] Still another canonized a list of 22 martyrs and described their sacrifices of resistance to testing.[3] I concluded that there was no need for me to repent.

In addition to the zealotry, there is also heresy. This article is one example. Testifying to the truth of that label, I confess that the very title of this article is somewhat deceptive. Perhaps many readers will, like me, recall having reviewed several articles with titles like the one used here. In those epistles the faithful are regaled with the travails of students who were denied a diploma as a result of a high-stakes test. They illustrate how testing narrows the curriculum, frustrates our best teachers, produces gripping anxiety in our brightest students, and makes young children vomit or cry, or both. This article will not repeat any of those parables, either in substance or perspective. We now turn to the apocrypha.

Reports from the Battlefield

If nothing else, published commentary concerning high-stakes testing has been remarkable for its uniformity. The conclusion: high-stakes tests are uniformly bad. A recent literature search to locate information about the effects of high-stakes tests turned up 59 entries over the last 10 years. A review of the results revealed that only 2 of the 59 could even remotely be categorized as favorably inclined toward testing. The two entries included a two-page, 1996 publication in a minor source, which bore the straightforward title, "The Case for National Standards and Assessments."[4] The other nominally favorable article simply reviewed surveys of public opinion about high-stakes tests and concluded that broad support for such tests persists.[5] The other 57 entries reflected the accepted articles of faith concerning high-stakes tests. Examples of the titles of these articles include:

"Excellence in Education versus High-stakes Testing"[6] (which carries the obvious implication that testing is antithetical to high-quality education);

"The Distortion of Teaching and Testing: High-stakes Testing and Instruction"[7] (ditto);

"Burnt at the High-Stakes"[8] (no explanation required);

"Judges Ruling Effectively Acquits High-stakes Test: To the Disadvantage of Poor and Minority Students in Texas"[9] (personally, I thought that the less equivocal title, "Analysis Reveals High-quality Test: Everyone Gets the Shaft" could have been used); and

"I Don't Give a Hoot If Somebody is Going to Pay Me $3600: Local School District Reactions to Kentucky's High-stakes Accountability Program."[10]

The Roots of All Evil

5   There have always been high-stakes tests. Testing history buffs have traced high-stakes testing to civil service examinations of 200 B.C., military selection dating to 2000 B.C., and Biblical accounts of the Gilead guards. Mehrens and Cizek relate the story of the minimum competency exam that took place when the Gilead Guards challenged the fugitives from the tribe of Ephraim who tried to cross the Jordan river.

COMPLICATION

Alfie Kohn, to whom Cizek refers several times in this essay, is one of the most visible and respected (or vilified) critics of high-stakes tests in the United States. He has argued against such tests on the grounds that their popularity is driven by profits for testing companies and by the desire for votes among political officials who publicly call for "accountability" in education. In one article (which Cizek cites in his essay), Kohn argues that in addition to several other flaws, standardized tests do not accurately measure student achievement:

The central problem with most standardized tests, however, is simply that they fail to assess the skills and dispositions that matter most. Such tests are generally contrived exercises that measure how much students have managed to cram into short-term memory. Reading comprehension exams usually consist of a concatenation of separate questions about short passages on unrelated topics that call on students to ferret out right answers rather than to engage in thoughtful interpretation. In mathematics, the point is to ascertain that students have memorized a series of procedures, not that they understand what they are doing. Science tests often focus on recall of vocabulary, stressing "excruciatingly boring material," failing to judge the capacity of students to think, and ultimately discouraging many of them from choosing a career in the field, according to Bruce Alberts, president of the National Academy of Science.

In light of all this, it should not be surprising — but it is seldom realized — that the students who perform well on tests are often those who are least interested in learning and least likely to learn deeply. Studies of elementary, middle school, and high school students have found a statistical association between high scores on standardized tests and relatively superficial thinking. (From Alfie Kohn, "Burnt at the High Stakes.")

"Are you a member of the tribe of Ephraim?" they asked. If the man replied that he was not, then they demanded, "Say Shibboleth." But if he couldn't pronounce the H and said Sibboleth instead of Shibboleth he was dragged away and killed. So forty-two thousand people of Ephraim died there."[11]

In the scriptural account of this assessment, nothing is reported concerning the professional and public debates that may have occurred regarding: what competencies should have been tested; how to measure them; how minimally-proficient performance should be defined; whether paper/pencil testing might have been cheaper and more reliable than performance assessment; whether there was any adverse impact against the people of Ephraim; or what remediation should be provided for those judged to be below the standard. Maybe the Gilead Guards should have abandoned their test altogether because it was unclear whether Ephraimites really had the opportunity to learn to pronounce "shibboleth" cor-

rectly, because the burden of so many oral examinations was a top-down mandate, or because listening to all those Ephraimites try to say "shibboleth" reduced the valuable instructional time available for teaching young members of the tribe of Gilead the real-life skills of sword fighting and tent making.[12]

While it is certain that high-stakes testing as been around for some time, it is curious that current high-stakes tests in American education face such an inquisition from, primarily, educators. Ironically, for this, too, we should blame those in the field of testing. Those who know and make high-stakes tests have done the least to make known the purposes and benefits of testing. The laws of physics apply: for every action in opposition to tests, there has been and equal and opposite silence.

A Revelation

One assumption underlying high-stakes testing has received particularly scant attention: the need to make decisions. There is simply no way to escape making decisions about students. These decisions, by definition, create categories. If, for example, some students graduate from high school and others do not, a categorical decision has been made, even if a graduation test was not used. (The decisions were, presumably, made on *some* basis.) High school music teachers make decisions such as who should be first chair for the clarinets. College faculties make decisions to tenure (or not) their colleagues. We embrace decision making regarding who should be licensed to practice medicine. All of these kinds of decisions are unavoidable; each should be based on sound information; and the information should be combined in some deliberate, considered fashion.

10 It is currently fashionable to talk as if high-stakes tests are the *single* bit of in-

formation used to make categorical decisions that wreak hellacious results on both people and educational systems. But simple-minded slogans like "high stakes are for tomatoes" are, well, simple-minded. One need only examine the context in which high-stakes tests are given to see that they are almost never the single bit of information used to make decisions. In the diploma example, multiple sources of information are used to make decisions, and success on each of them is necessary. For instance: So many days of attendance are required. Just one too few days?: No diploma. 2) There are course requirements. Didn't take American Government?: No diploma. 3) There are credit hour requirements. Missing one credit?: No diploma. 4) And, increasingly, there are high-stakes tests. Miss one too many questions on a test?: No diploma. Categorical decisions are made on each of these four criteria. It makes as much sense to single out a single test as the sole barrier as it does to single out a student's American Government examination as "the single test used to make the graduation decision."

We could, of course, not make success on each of the elements essential. One could get a diploma by making success on, say, three out of the four. But which three? Why three? Why not two? The same two for everyone? That seems unfair, given that some people would be denied a diploma simply on the basis of the arbitrary two that were identified. Even if all other criteria were eliminated, and all that remained was a requirement that students must attend at least 150 out of 180 days in their senior year to get a diploma, then what about the student who attends 149 and is a genius? In the end, as long as any categorical decisions must be made, there is going to be subjectivity involved. If there is going to

be subjectivity, most testing specialists — and most of the public — simply favor coming clean about the source and magnitude of the subjectivity, and trying to minimize it.

In the end, it cannot be that high-stakes tests themselves are the cause of all the consternation. It is evident that categorical decisions will be made with or without tests. The real reasons are two-fold. One reason covers resistance to high-stakes testing within the education profession; the second explains why otherwise well-informed people would so easily succumb to simplistic rhetoric centering on testing. On the first count, the fact that high-stakes tests are increasingly used as part of accountability systems provides a sufficient rationale for resistance. Education is one of the few (only?) professions for which advancement, status, compensation, longevity, and so on are not related to personal performance. The entire accountability movement — of which testing has been the major element — has been vigorously resisted by many in the profession. The rationale is rational when there is a choice between being accountable for performance or maintaining a status quo without accountability.

Two Tables of Stone

There is much to be debated about professionalization of teaching and its relationship to accountability. My primary focus here, however, is on the second count — the debate about testing. As mentioned previously, those who know the most about testing have been virtually absent from the public square when any criticism surfaces. In response to 57 bold articles nailed to the cathedral door, 2 limp slips of paper are slid under it. The benefits of high-stakes tests have been assumed, unrecognized, or unarticulated. The following paragraphs present

10 unanticipated consequences of high-stakes testing — consequences that are actually *good* things that have grown out of the increasing reliance on test data concerning student performance.[13]

I. Professional Development   I suspect that most educators painfully recall what passed as professional development in the not-too-distant past. Presentations with titles like the following were all-too-common:

- Vitamins and Vocabulary: Just Coincidence that Both Begin with "V"?
- Cosmetology across the Curriculum
- Horoscopes in the Homeroom
- The Geometry of Rap: 16 Musical Tips for Pushing Pythagoras
- Multiple Intelligences in the Cafeteria

In a word, much professional development was spotty, hit-or-miss, of questionable research base, of dubious

effectiveness, and thoroughly avoidable.

15 But professional development is increasingly taking a new face. Much of it is considerably more focussed on what works, curriculum-relevant, and results-oriented. Driven by the demands of high-stakes tests, the press toward professional development that helps educators hone their teaching skills and content area expertise is clear.

II. Accommodation   Recent federal legislation enacted to guide the implementation of high-stakes testing has been a catalyst for increased attention to students with special needs. Describing the impact of that legislation, researchers Martha Thurlow and James Ysseldyke observe that, "Both Goals 2000* and the more forceful IASA indicated that high standards were to apply to *all* students. In very clear language, these laws defined "all students" as including students with disabilities and students with limited English proficiency."[14]

Because of these regulations applied to high-stakes tests, states across the US are scurrying to adapt those tests for all students, report disaggregated results for subgroups, and implement accommodations so that tests more accurately reflect the learning of all students. The result has been a very positive diffusion of awareness. Increasingly, at the classroom level, educators are becoming more sensitive to the needs and barriers faced by special needs students when they take tests — even the ordinary assessments they face in the classroom. If not forced by the context of once-per-year, high-stakes tests, it is doubtful that such progress would have been witnessed in the daily experiences of many special needs learners.

III. Knowledge about Testing For years, testing specialists have documented a lack of knowledge about assessment on the part of many educators. The title of a 1991 *Kappan* article bluntly asserted educators' "Apathy toward Testing and Grading."[15] Other research has chronicled the chronic lack of training in assessment for teachers and principals and has offered plans for remediation.[16] Unfortunately, for the most part, it has been difficult to require assessment training for pre-service teachers or administrators, and even more difficult to wedge such training into graduate programs in education.

Then along came high-stakes tests. What faculty committees could not enact has been accomplished circuitously. Granted, misperceptions about tests persist (for example, in my state there is a lingering myth that "the green test form" is harder than "the red one"), but I am discovering that more educators know more about testing than ever before. Because many tests now have stakes associated with them, it has become *de rigeur* for educators to inform themselves about their content, construction, and consequences. Increasingly, teachers can tell you the difference between a norm-referenced and a criterion-reference tests; they can recognize, use, or develop a high-quality rubric; they can tell you how their state's writing test is scored, and so on. In this case, necessity has been the mother of intervention.

20 *IV and V. Collection and Use of Information* Because pupil performance on high-stakes tests has become of such prominent and public interest, there has been an intensity of effort directed toward data collection and quality control that is unparalleled. As many states mandate the collection and reporting of this information (and more), unparalleled access has also resulted. Obtaining information about test performance, graduation rates, per-pupil spending, staffing, finance, and facilities is, in most states, now just a mouse-click away. How would you like your data for secondary analysis: Aggregated or disaggregated? Single year or longitudinal? PDF or Excel? Paper or plastic? Consequently, those who must respond to state mandates for data collection (i.e., school districts) have become increasingly conscientious about providing the most accurate information possible — sometimes at risk of penalties for inaccuracy or incompleteness.

This is an unqualified boon. Not only is more information about student performance available, but it is increasingly used as part of decision making. At a recent teacher recruiting event, I heard a recruiter question a teacher about how she would be able to tell that her students were learning. "I can just see it in their eyes," was the reply. Sorry, you're off the island. Increasingly, from the classroom to the school board room, educators are making use of student performance data to help them refine programs, channel funding, and identify roots of success. If the data weren't so important, it is unlikely that this would be the case.

VI. Educational Options Related to the increase in publicly-available information about student performance and school characteristics is the spawning of greater options for parents and students. Complementing a hunger for information, the public's appetite for alternatives has been whetted. In many cases, schools have responded. Charter schools, magnet schools, home schools, and increased offerings of honors, IB and AP courses,[†] have broadened the choices available to parents. And, research is slowly accumulating which suggests that the presence of choices has not spelled doom for traditional options, but has largely raised all boats.[17] It is almost surely the case

***Goals 2000 and IASA.** Goals 2000 refers to the Educate America Act, passed by the U.S. Congress in 1994 and intended to promote coherent educational standards for K–12 schools by supporting efforts in individual states to set standards for student learning. IASA, or the Improving America's Schools Act, which was also passed in 1994, is broad legislation that provided funding and other kinds of support for various initiatives, including improving services for students with disabilities, enhancing basic educational programs, upgrading technology, and strengthening substance abuse prevention efforts.

†IB refers to International Baccalaureate programs, which are described in the margin gloss on page 314. AP refers to Advanced Placement programs, which are rigorous high school courses that can lead to college credit. Founded in 1955, the AP program standards are set by the College Board, which also administers the AP exams that students who complete AP courses must usually take to earn college credit.

that legislators' votes and parents' feet would not be moving in the direction of expanding alternatives if not for the information provided by high-stakes tests — the same tests are being used to gauge the success or failure of these emerging alternatives.

VII. Accountability Systems   No one would argue that current accountability systems have reached a mature state of development. On the contrary, nascent systems are for the most part crude, cumbersome, embryonic endeavors. Equally certain, though, is that even rudimentary accountability systems would not likely be around if it weren't for high-stakes tests. For better or worse, high-stakes tests are often the foundation upon which accountability systems have been built. This is not to say that this relationship between high-stakes tests and accountability is right, noble, or appropriate. It simply recognizes the reality that current accountability systems were enabled by an antecedent: mandated, high-stakes tests.

To many policy makers, professionals, and the public, however, the notion of introducing accountability — even just acknowledging that accountability is a *good* innovation — is an important first step. That the camel's nose took the form of high-stakes tests was (perhaps) not recognized or (almost certainly) viewed as acceptable. Debates continue about the role of tests and the form of accountability.

25 A memory that has helped me to understand both sides of accountability debates involves high school sports physicals. I have vivid memories evoked to this day whenever I drive by a marquee outside a high school on which the notice appears: Boys' Sports Physicals Next Tuesday. As an adolescent male trying out for a high-school baseball team, I recall that event as one at which

dozens of similarly situated guys would line up mostly naked and be checked over by a hometown physician, who volunteered his time to poke, prod, and probe each potential player. The characteristics of the event included that it was: a) somewhat embarrassing; b) performed by an external person; c) somewhat invasive; d) and had the possibility of denying individuals access to an opportunity. I think that these same four characteristics help explain the reaction of many educators to high-stakes tests.

But the analogy can be extended. At the time — and still — I can see that the physicals were necessary to identify small problems, and to prevent potentially bigger problems. But here's the big difference with high-stakes tests: if one of the players was found to have a heart murmur, it was acknowledged that he had a problem and something was done about it. In education, if a student fails a high-stakes test, we assail the test. Now, we all know that achievement tests aren't perfect, but neither are medical tests. Pregnancy tests are often wrong; blood pressure readings are subjective and variable within an individual; even with DNA tests, experts can only say things like "there is 99.93% chance that the DNA is a match." Yet nobody reports their blood pressure as 120/80 with an associated standard error. Maybe I don't really have high blood pressure. Maybe my pressure is 120/80 plus or minus 17.

People seem inclined to accept medical measurements as virtually error-free because there's no finger pointing, only therapy. Maybe his blood pressure is high because he failed to heed the physician's orders to lay off the salt and lose some weight. Maybe her pregnancy test was positive because she was sexually active. Who should be held accountable for the results of the pregnancy test or blood pressure but the person? We seem re-signed to accountability in this context.

Don't get me wrong. When a defective medical measuring device is identified, it gets pulled by the FDA. If there were in-tolerable error rates in home pregnancy test kits, it would create a stir, and the product would be improved, or fall out of use. In education, however, if a pupil doesn't pass a high-stakes test, there are a lot of possible (and confounded) expla-nations: lack of persistence, poor teach-ing, distracting learning environment, inadequate resources, lack of prerequisite skills, poorly-constructed test, dysfunc-tional home situation, and so on. We know that all of these (and more) exist to greater or lesser extents in the mix. Who should be accountable? The teacher for the quality of instruction? I think so. The student for effort and persistence? Yes, again. Administrators for providing safe learning environment? Yep. Assessment specialists for developing sound tests? Bingo. Communities for pro-viding adequate resources? Sure. Parents for establishing a supportive home envi-ronment? Yessirree. The key limitation is that, we can only make policies and products to address those factors that are legitimately under governmental control. And, in education, we understand that intervention may or may not prove effective.

Thus, although high-stakes tests have made a path in the wilderness, the con-troversy clearly hinges on accountability itself. The difficult fits and starts of de-veloping sound accountability systems may actually cause some hearts to mur-mur. Understanding the importance, com-plexity, and difficulties as the accountability infant matures will be surely be trying. How — or if — high-stakes tests will fit into the mature ver-sion is hard to tell, and the devil will be in the details. But it is evident that the presence of high-stakes tests have at least served as a conversation-starter for a policy dialogue that may not have taken place in their absence.

30 *VIII. Educators' Intimacy with Their Disciplines* Once a test has been man-dated in, say, language arts, the first step in any high-stakes testing program is to circumscribe the boundaries of what will be tested. The almost universal strat-egy for accomplishing this is to empanel groups of (primarily) educators who are familiar with the ages, grades, and con-tent to be tested. These groups are usu-ally large, selected to be representative, and expert in the subject area. The groups first study relevant documentation (e.g. the authorizing legislation, state curriculum guides, content standards). They then begin the arduous, time-consuming task of discussing among themselves the nature of the content area, the sequence and content of typical instruction, learner characteristics and developmental issues, cross-disciplinary relationships, and relevant assessment techniques.

These extended conversations help shape the resulting high-stakes tests, to be sure. However, they also affect the discussants, and those with whom they interact when they return to their dis-tricts, buildings, and classrooms. As per-sons with special knowledge of the particular high-stakes testing program, the participants are sometimes asked to replicate those disciplinary and logistic discussions locally. The impact of this trickling-down is just beginning to be noticed by researchers — and the effects are beneficial. For example, at one ses-sion of the 2000 American Educational Research Association conference, scholars reported on the positive effects of a state testing program in Maine on class-room assessment practices[18] and on how educators in Florida were assimilating their involvement in large-scale testing activities at the local level.[19]

These local discussions mirror the large scale counterparts in that they provide educators with an opportunity to become more intimate with the nature and structure of their own disciplines, and to contemplate interdisciplinary relationships. As Martha Stewart would say: it's a good thing. And the impulse for this good thing is clearly the presence of a high-stakes test.

IX. Equity   There is a flip-side to the common concern that high-stakes tests result in the homogenizing of education. The flip-side is that high-stakes tests promote greater homogeneity of education. Naturally, we should be vigilant about the threat posed by common *low* standards that could be engendered, and it is right to worry about gravitating to the lowest common denominator.[20] On the other hand, there is something to be said for increased equity in expectations and experiences for all students. As a result of schools' aligning their curricula and instructional focus more closely to outcomes embodied in high-stakes tests, the experiences of and aspirations for children in urban, suburban, and rural districts within a state are more comparable than they have been in the recent past.

Surely, inequalities — even savage ones — persist. However, some movement toward greater consistency is perceptible. And, the press toward more uniformity of expectation and experience may be particularly beneficial in an increasingly mobile society. The seamlessness with which a student can move from one district to another — even one school to another within a district — may well translate into incremental gains in achievement sufficient enough to spell the difference between promotion and graduation, or retention and dropping out.

35 *X. Quality of Tests*   The final benevolent consequence is the profoundly positive effect that the introduction of high-stakes consequences has had on the tests themselves. Along with more serious consequences has come heightened scrutiny. The high-stakes tests of today are surely the most meticulously developed, carefully constructed, and rigorously reported. Many criticisms of tests are valid, but a complainant who suggests that today's high-stakes tests are "lower-order" or "biased" or "not relevant" are most likely unfamiliar with that which they purport to critique.

If only for its long history and ever-present watch-dogging, high-stakes tests have evolved to a state of being: highly reliable; free from bias; relevant and age appropriate; higher order; tightly related to important, public goals; time and cost efficient; and yielding remarkably consistent decisions. It is fair to say that one strains the gnat in objecting to the characteristics of high-stakes tests, when the characteristics of those tests is compared to what a child will likely experience in his or her classroom the other 176 days of the school year. It is not an overstatement to say that, at least on the grounds just articulated, the high-stakes, state test that a student takes will, by far, be the best assessment that student will see all year.

A secondary benefit of the quality of typical high-stakes tests is that, because of their perceived importance, they become mimicked at lower levels. It is appropriate to abhor teaching to the test. However, it is also important to recognize the beneficial effects of exposing educators to high-quality writing prompts, document-based questions, constructed-response formats, and even challenging multiple-choice items. It is not cheating, but the highest form of praise when educators then rely on these exemplars to enhance their own assessment practices.

Keepin' It Real

It would be foolish to ignore the short-comings and undesirable consequences of high-stakes tests. Current discussions and inquiries are essential, productive, and encouraging. However, amidst the consternation about high-stakes tests, it is equally inappropriate to fail to consider the unanticipated positive consequences, or to fail to incorporate these into any cost-benefit calculus that should characterize sound policy decisions.

Vigorous debates about the nature and role of high-stakes tests and accountability systems are healthy and needed. To these frays, the protestants may bring differing doctrinal starting points and differing conceptions of the source of salvation. It is an exhilarating time of profound questioning. High-stakes tests: we don't know how to live with them; we can't seem to live without them. The oft-quoted first sentence of Charles Dickens' *A Tale of Two Cities* ("It was the best of times, it was the worst of times") seems especially relevant to the juncture at which we find ourselves. The remainder of Dickens' opening paragraph merely extends the piquant metaphor:

> **40** It was the age of wisdom, it was the age of foolishness, it was the epoch of belief, it was the epoch of incredulity, it was the season of Light, it was the season of Darkness, it was the spring of hope, it was the winter of despair, we had everything before us, we had nothing before us, we were all going direct to Heaven, we were all going direct the other way.[21]

Notes

1. Alfie Kohn, "Fighting the Tests: A Practical Guide to Rescuing Our Schools," *Phi Delta Kappan*, vol. 82, 2001, p. 349.
2. Scott Thompson, "The Authentic Testing Movement and Its Evil Twin," *Phi Delta Kappan*, vol. 82, 2001, pp. 358–362.
3. Susan Ohanian, "News from the Test Resistance Trail," *Phi Delta Kappan*, vol. 82, 2001, p. 365.
4. Diane Ravitch, "The Case for National Standards and Assessments," *The Clearing House*, vol. 69, 1996, pp. 134–135.
5. Richard Phelps, "The demand for standardized student testing," *Educational Measurement: Issues and Practice*, vol. 17, no. 3, 1998, pp. 5–23.
6. Asa Hilliard, "Excellence in Education versus High-Stakes Testing," *Journal of Teacher Education*, vol. 51, 2000, pp. 293–304.
7. George Madaus, "The Distortion of Teaching and Testing: High-stakes Testing and Instruction," *Peabody Journal of Education*, vol. 65, 1998, pp. 29–46.
8. Alfie Kohn, "Burnt at the High Stakes," *Journal of Teacher Education*, vol. 51, 2000, pp. 315–327.
9. Karin Chenoweth, "Judge's Ruling Effectively Acquits High-stakes Test: To the Disadvantage of Poor and Minority Students," *Black Issues in Higher Education*, vol. 51, 2000, p. 12.
10. Patricia Kannapel and others, "I Don't Give a Hoot If Somebody Is Going to Pay Me $3600: Local School District Reaction to Kentucky's High-stakes Accountability System." Paper presented at the Annual Meeting of the American Educational Research Association, New York, April 1996 (ERIC Document No. 397 135).
11. Judges 12:5–6, *The Living Bible;* cited in William Mehrens and

CONTEXT

A web portal devoted to education news, EducationNews.org describes itself as "the Internet's leading source of education news." It claims to provide more balanced coverage of education issues than more traditional media, and it seeks to use Internet technologies "to increase interest and subsequent involvement in education reform."

Gregory Cizek, "Standard Setting and the Public Good: Benefits Accrued and Anticipated," in G. J. Cizek (Ed.), *Setting Performance Standards: Concepts, Methods, and Perspectives,* (Mahwah, NJ: Lawrence Erlbaum, 2001).

12. Mehrens and Cizek, pp. 477–478.

13. Ordinarily, the 10 items should probably be presented with appropriate recognition of their downsides, disadvantages, etc. However, for the sake of clarity, brevity, and because most readers are probably already all too aware of the counter arguments, I have chosen to avoid any facade of balanced treatment.

14. Martha Thurlow and James Ysseldyke, "Standard Setting Challenges for Special Populations," in G. J. Cizek (Ed.), *Setting Performance Standards: Concepts, Methods, and Perspectives,* (Mahwah, NJ: Lawrence Erlbaum, 2001), p. 389.

15. John Hills, "Apathy toward Testing and Grading," *Phi Delta Kappan,* vol. 72, 1991, pp. 540-545.

16. See, for example, Rita O' Sullivan and Marla Chalnick, "Measurement-related Course Requirements for Teacher Certification and Recertification," *Educational Measurement: Issues and Practice,* vol. 10, 1991, pp. 17-19, 23; Richard Stiggins, "Assessment Literacy," *Phi Delta Kappan,* vol. 72, 1991, pp. 534-539; James Impara and Barbara Plake, "Professional Development in Student Assessment for Educational Administrators,"

Educational Measurement: Issues and Practice," vol. 15, 1996, pp. 14-20.

17. Chester Finn, Jr., Bruno V. Manno, and Gregg Vanourek, *Charter Schools in Action: Renewing Public Education* (Princeton, N.J.: Princeton University Press, 2000).

18. Jeff Beaudry, "The Positive Effects of Administrators and Teachers on Classroom Assessment Practices and Student Achievement." Paper presented at the annual meeting of the American Educational Research Association, April 2000, New Orleans, LA.

19. Madhabi Banerji, "Designing District-level Classroom Assessment Systems." Paper presented at the annual meeting of the American Educational Research Association, April 2000, New Orleans, LA.

20. Actually, the concern about low expectations may have passed and, if the experiences of states like Washington, Arizona, and Massachusetts are prescient, the concern may be being replaced by a concern that content or performance expectations (or both) are too high and coming too fast. See http://seattletimes. nwsource.com/news/ local/html98/test_19991010.html ; http://www.edweek.org/ew/ ewstory.cfm?slug=13ariz.h20; and Donald C. Orlich, "Education Reform and Limits to Student Achievement," *Phi Delta Kappan,* vol. 81, 2000 pp. 468–472.

21. Charles Dickens, *A Tale of Two Cities* (New York: Dodd, Mead, and Company, 1925), p. 3.

Questions for Discussion

1. Examine the way in which Cizek opens this essay, noting especially his use of religious metaphors. How, specifically, does he introduce his subject and establish his own stance toward it? How does he set the tone for his argument? How effective do you think his introduction is in setting up his argument? In your answer, cite specific words and phrases from his introductory paragraphs. **2.** Cizek devotes much of his essay to summarizing and responding to the arguments of those who are opposed to testing. Evaluate his use of his references to his opponents. How effective are these references in helping him to make his own argument in favor of standardized testing? Do you think he represents his opponents fairly? Explain. **3.** In paragraph 25, Cizek recalls his own experience as a student to introduce an analogy in which he compares high school physical exams to standardized testing. What point does Cizek use this analogy to make? How effectively do you think this analogy helps Cizek to make his point? Would the analogy have been less effective if Cizek had not referred to his own experience as a student? Explain. **4.** In many ways, Cizek's writing style is unusual for a scholarly essay, especially his use of figurative language. How would you describe Cizek's writing style? In what ways do you think it strengthens or weakens his argument? Cite specific passages from his essay in your answer. **5.** Cizek describes the way in which curriculum standards are typically set by panels of experts who determine the appropriate content for specific grade levels in specific subjects. He declares this to be a "good thing." What are some pros and cons that you see in this approach to developing curriculum? Do you think Cizek's discussion of this process enhances his argument? Explain. **6.** Near the end of his essay, Cizek states that vigorous debates about testing "are healthy and needed" and that it is an "exhilarating time of profound questioning" about testing. Do you agree? Why or why not? To what extent do you think Cizek's essay contributes positively to this ongoing debate?

④ **BERTELL OLLMAN, "Why So Many Exams? A Marxist Response"**

Complaints about public education in the United States are so common that the view that schools are in crisis seems to be almost universal. Rarely does anyone describe the schools as working. Critic Bertell Ollman is someone who does. But he doesn't think that's a good thing. Ollman believes that despite constant criticism of schools and calls for reform, public education in the United States effectively serves the basic economic system on which American society is based: capitalism. In his view, the many problems that are typically associated with schools actually reflect of the needs of capitalism rather than the needs of individual students. More specifically, standardized testing is necessary to prepare students for their roles in a capitalist system, and as long as that system remains in place, neither standardized tests nor the problems associated with schooling will go away. Whether or not you agree with Ollman's view of capitalism or his position on testing, his essay is a good example of an argument that reflects a specific theory or political ideology (in this case, Marxism). It suggests as well that educational issues such as testing are related in complex ways to our political and economic lives. Bertell Ollman is a professor of political science at New York University. A well-known Marxist scholar, he has written many books and essays about political and social issues, including *Dialectical Investigations* (1993) and *How to Take an Exam . . . and Remake the World* (2001). The following essay was published in 2002 in *Z Magazine.*

Why So Many Exams? A Marxist Response
BERTELL OLLMAN

1 Psychologist Bill Livant, has remarked, "When a liberal sees a beggar, he [sic] says the system isn't working. When a Marxist does, he [sic] says it is." The same insight could be applied today to the entire area of education. The learned journals, as well as the popular media, are full of studies documenting how little most students know and how fragile are their basic skills. The cry heard almost everywhere is "The system isn't working."

Responding to this common complaint, conservatives — starting (but not ending) with the Bush administration — have offered a package of reforms in which increased testing occupies the central place. The typical liberal and even radical response to this has been to demonstrate that such measures are not likely to have the "desired" effect. The assumption, of course, is that we all want more or less the same thing from a system of education and that conservatives have made an error in the means they have chosen to attain our common end. But what if students are already receiving — more or less — the kind of education that conservatives favor? This would cast their proposals for "reform" in another light. What if, as Livant points out in the case of beggars, the system is working?

Before detailing what young people learn from their forced participation in this educational ritual, it may be useful to dispose of a number of myths that surround exams and exam taking in our society.

(1) *Exams are a necessary part of education.* Education, of one kind or another has existed in all human societies, but exams have not; and the practice of requiring frequent exams is a very recent innovation and still relatively rare in the world.

5 (2) *Exams are unbiased.* In 1912, Henry Goddard, a distinguished psychologist, administered what he claimed were "culture free" IQ* tests to new immigrants on Ellis Island and found that 83 percent of Jews, 80 percent of Hungarians, 79 percent of Italians, and 87 percent of Russians were "feebleminded," adding that "all feebleminded are at least potential criminals." IQ* tests have gotten better since then, but given the character of the testing process, the attitudes of those who make up any test, and the variety of people — coming from so many different backgrounds — who take it, it is impossible to produce a test that does not have serious biases

(3) *Exams are objectively graded.* Daniel Stark and Edward Elliot sent two English essays to 200 high school teachers for grading. They got back 142 grades. For one paper, the grades ranged from 50 to 99; for the other, the grades went from 64 to 99. But English is not an "objective" subject, you say. Well, they did the same thing for an essay answer in mathematics and got back grades ranging from 28 to 95. Though most of the grades they received in both cases fell in the middle ground, it was evident that a good part of any grade was the result of who marked the exam and not of who took it.

(4) *Exams are an accurate indication of what students know and of intelligence in general.* But all sorts of things, including luck in getting (or not getting) the questions you hoped for and one's state of mind and emotions the day of the exam, can have an important effect on the result.

(5) *All students have an equal chance to do well on exams,* that even major differences in their conditions of life have a negligible impact on their performance. There is such a strong correlation between students' family income and their test scores, however, that the radical educational theorist, Ira Shor, has suggested (tongue-in-cheek) that college applications should ignore test scores altogether and just ask students to enter their family income. The results would be the same — with relatively few exceptions, the same people would get admitted into college, but then, of course, the belief that there is equality of opportunity in the classroom would stand forth as the myth that it is.

(6) *Exams are the fairest way to distribute society's scarce resources* to the young, hence the association of exams with the ideas of meritocracy and equality of opportunity. But if some students consistently do better on exams because of the advantages they possess and other students do not outside of school, then directing society's main benefits to these same people compounds the initial inequality.

10 (7) *Exams, and particularly the fear of them, are necessary in order to motivate students to do their assignments.* Who can

*See the margin gloss on IQ tests on page 313.

ams work. They know, for example, that exams don't only involve reading questions and writing answers. They also involve forced isolation from other students, prohibition on talking and walking around and going to the bathroom, writing a lot faster than usual, physical discomfort, worry, fear, anxiety, and often guilt.

They are also aware that exams do a poor job of testing what students actually know. But it is here that most of their criticisms run into a brick wall, because most students don't know enough about society to understand the role that exams — especially taking so many exams — play in preparing them to take their place in it.

But if exams are not what most people think they are, then what are they? The short answer is that exams have less to do with testing us for what we are supposed to know than teaching us what the other aspects of instruction cannot get at (or get at as well). To understand what that is we must examine what the capitalist class require from a system of education.* Here, it is clear that capitalists need a system of education that provides young people with the knowledge and skills necessary for their businesses to function and prosper. But they also want schools to give youth the beliefs, attitudes, emotions, and associated habits of behavior that make it easy for capitalists to tap into this store of knowledge and skills. They need all this not only to maximize their profits, but to help reproduce the social, economic, and even political con-

doubt that years of reacting to such threats have produced in many students a reflex of the kind depicted here? The sad fact is that the natural curiosity of young people and their desire to learn, develop, advance, master, and the pleasure that comes from succeeding — which could and should motivate all studying — has been progressively replaced in their psyches by a pervasive fear of failing. This needn't be. For the rest, if the only reason a student does the assignments is that he/she is worried about the exam, he/she should not be taking that course in the first place.

(8) *Exams are not injurious, socially, intellectually, and psychologically.* Complaining about exams may be most students' first truly informed criticism about society because they are its victims and know from experience how ex-

*The term *capitalism* can be used to refer to an economic system based on a free market in which supply and demand dictate the movement of goods and services. The term can be used more broadly to refer to a social system based on the ideas of individual rights and free choice.

ditions and accompanying processes that allow them to extract profits. Without workers, consumers and citizens who are well versed in and accepting of their roles in these processes, the entire capitalist system would grind to a halt. It is here — particularly as regards the behavioral and attitudinal prerequisites of capitalist rule — that the culture of exams has become indispensable. So what do exams "teach" students?

(1) The crush of tests gets students to believe that one gets what one works for, that the standards by which this is decided are objective and fair, and therefore that those who do better deserve what they get; and that the same holds for those who do badly. After a while, this attitude is carried over to what students find in the rest of society, including their own failures later in life, where it encourages them to "blame the victim" (themselves or others) and feel guilty for what is not their fault.

15 (2) By fixing a time and a form in which they have to deliver or else, exams prepare students for the more rigorous discipline of the work situation that lies ahead.

(3) In forcing students to think and write faster than they ordinarily do, exams get them ready mentally, emotionally, and also morally for the speed-ups they will face on the job.

(4) The self-discipline students acquire in preparing for exams also helps them put up with the disrespect, personal abuse, and boredom that awaits them on the job.

(5) Exams are orders that are not open to question — "discuss this," "outline that," etc. — and taking so many exams conditions students to accept unthinkingly the orders that will come from their future employers.

(6) By fitting the infinite variety of answers given on exams into the strait-jacket of A, B, C, D, and F, students get accustomed to the standardization of people as well as of things and the impersonal job categories that will constitute such an important part of their identity later on.

20 (7) Because passing an exam is mainly good for enabling students to move up a grade so they can take a slightly harder exam, which — if they pass — enables them to repeat the exercise *ad infinitum,* they begin to see life as an endless series of ever more complicated exams, where one never finishes being judged and the need for being prepared and respectful of the judging authorities only grows.

(8) Because their teachers know all the right answers to the exams, students tend to assume that those who are above them in other hierarchies also know much more than they do.

(9) Because their teachers genuinely want them to do well on exams, students also mistakenly assume that those in relation of authority over them in other hierarchies are also rooting for them to succeed, that is, have their best interests at heart.

(10) Because most tests are taken individually, striving to do well on a test is treated as something that concerns students only as individuals. Cooperative solutions are equated with cheating, if considered at all.

(11) Because one is never quite ready for an exam, there is always something more to do, students often feel guilty for reading materials or engaging in activities unrelated to the exam. The whole of life, it would appear, is but preparation for exams or doing what is required in order to succeed (as those in charge define "success").

25 (12) With the Damocles[†] sword of a failing (or for some a mediocre) grade hanging over their heads throughout

[†]According to Roman myth, Damocles was a courtier in Syracuse, Greece, in the 4th century B.C.E. who envied the life of his ruler Dionysius. Given the chance to experience that life, Damocles agreed until he realized that, once seated in the ruler's throne, a large sword was suspended over his head by a single horse hair. The experience prompted him to reevaluate his beliefs about what constitutes a good life.

their years in school (including university), the inhibiting fear of swift and dire punishment never leaves students, no matter their later situation.

(13) Coupled with the above, because there is always so much to be known, exams — especially so many of them — tend to undermine students' self-confidence and to raise their levels of anxiety, with the result that most young people remain unsure that they will ever know enough to criticize existing institutions and become even physically uncomfortable at the thought of trying to put something better in their place.

(14) Exams also play a key role in determining course content, leaving little time for material that is not on the exam. Among the first things to be omitted in this "tightening" of the curriculum are students' own reactions to the topics that come up, collective reflection on the main problems of the day, alternative points of view and other possibilities generally, the larger picture (where everything fits), explorations of topics triggered by individual curiosity, and anything else that is likely to promote creative, cooperative, or critical thinking.

(15) Exams also determine the form in which most teaching goes on, since for any given exam there is generally a best way to prepare for it. Repetition and forced memorization, even learning by rote, and frequent quizzes (more exams) leave little time for other more imaginative approaches to conveying, exchanging and questioning facts and ideas.

(16) Multiple exams become one of the main factors determining the character of the relation between students (with students viewing each other as competitors for the best grades), the relation between students and teachers (with most students viewing their teachers as examiners and graders first, and most teachers viewing their students largely in terms of how well they have done on exams), also the relation between teachers and school administrators (since principals and deans now have an "objective" standard by which to measure teacher performance), and even the relation between school administrations and various state bodies (since the same standard is used by the state to judge the work of schools and school systems). Exams mediate all social relations in the educational system in a manner similar to the way money mediates relations between people in the larger society with the same dehumanizing results.

30 While exams have been with us for a long time, socializing students in all the ways that I have outlined above, it is only recently that the mania for exams has begun to affect government policies. Why now? Globalization, or whatever it is one chooses to call this new stage, has arrived. But to which of its aspects is the current drive for more exams a carefully fashioned response? The proponents of such educational "reform" point to the intensified competition between industries and workers worldwide and the in-

GLOBALIZATION

The term *globalization* has been used to refer to a complex set of political, social, and economic developments in the last decade or so that have made nations, societies, and regions of the world more interdependent. Commerce, communication, and travel between various regions of the world have increased, and international trade agreements have facilitated economic and social contacts across national borders. According to journalist Thomas Friedman, whose 1999 book *The Lexus and the Olive Tree* examines the effects of globalization, "Globalization is not a phenomenon. It is not just some passing trend. Today it is an overarching international system shaping the domestic politics and foreign relations of virtually every country, and we need to understand it as such." Whether or not globalization is a good thing is intensely debated. You can find a sampling of the debate at http://globalization.about.com/library/weekly/aa080701a.htm. (Also see Chapter 13 for essays on various issues associated with globalization.)

creasingly rapid pace at which economic changes of all kinds are occurring. To survive in this new order requires people, they say, who are not only efficient, but also have a variety of skills (or can quickly acquire them) and the flexibility to change tasks whenever called upon to do so. Thus, the only way to prepare our youth for the new economic life that awaits them is to raise standards of education, and that entails, among other things, more exams.

A more critical approach to globalization begins by emphasizing that the intensification of economic competition worldwide is driven by capitalists' efforts to maximize their profits. It is this that puts all the other developments associated with globalization into motion. It is well known that, all things being equal, the less capitalists pay their workers and the less money they spend on improving work conditions and reducing pollution, the more profit they make. Recent technological progress in transportation and communication, together with free trade and the abolition of laws restricting the movement of capital, allow capitalists to consider workers all over the world in making their calculations. While the full impact of these developments is yet to be felt, we can already see two of its most important effects in the movement of more and more companies (and parts of companies) out of the U.S. and a rollback of modest gains in wages, benefits, and work conditions that American workers have won over the last 50 years.

The current rage for more exams needs to be viewed as part of a larger strategy that includes stoking patriotic fires and chipping away at traditional civil liberties (both rationalized by the so-called war on terrorism), the promotion of "family values," restrictions on sexual freedom (but not, as we see, on sexual hypocrisy), and the push for more prisons and longer prison sentences for a whole range of minor crimes.

Is there a connection between exams and the privatization of public education? They appear to be separate, but look again. With new investment opportunities failing to keep up with the rapidly escalating surpluses in search of them (a periodic problem for a system that never pays its workers enough to consume all the wealth they produce), the public sector has become the latest "last" frontier for capitalist expansion. Given its size and potential for profit, what are state prisons or utilities or transport or communication systems or

C O N T E X T

Founded in 1987, *Z Magazine* describes its mission as follows: "Z is an independent monthly magazine dedicated to resisting injustice, defending against repression, and creating liberty. It sees the racial, gender, class, and political dimensions of personal life as fundamental to understanding and improving contemporary circumstances; and it aims to assist activist efforts for a better future." To what extent does Ollman's essay fit this mission? In what ways do you think Ollman's argument might be effective for a wider audience than the readers of *Z Magazine*?

other social services next to public education? But how to convince the citizenry that companies whose only concern is with the bottom line can do a better job educating our young than public servants dedicated to the task? What seems impossible could be done if somehow education were redefined to emphasize the qualities associated with business and its achievements. Then — by definition — business could do the "job" better than any public agency.

Enter exams. Standardization, easily quantifiable results, and the willingness to reshape all intervening processes to obtain them characterize the path to success in both exams and business. When that happens (and to the extent it has already happened), putting education in the hands of businesspeople who know best how to dispense with "inessentials" becomes a perfectly rational thing to do.

35 What should students do about all this? Well, they shouldn't refuse to take exams (unless the whole class gets involved) and they shouldn't drop out of school. Given the relations of power inside education and throughout the rest of society, that would be suicidal and suicide is never good politics. Rather, they should become better students by learning more about the role of education, and exams in particular, in capitalism. Nowhere does the contradiction between the selfish and manipulative interests of our ruling class and the educational and developmental interests of students stand out in such sharp relief as in the current debate over exams. Students of all ages need to get involved in this debate in order to raise the consciousness of young people regarding the source of their special oppression and the possibility of uniting with other oppressed groups to create a truly human society. Everything depends on the youth of today doing better on this crucial test than my generation did, because the price for failure has never been so high. Will they succeed? Can they afford to fail?

NEGOTIATING DIFFERENCES

As a student, you have undoubtedly had direct experiences with standardized tests as well as the many other kinds of tests given in schools. Like every student, you know from those experiences how great the impact of testing can be.

But testing affects others as well: teachers, parents, school administrators, and politicians, to name a few. In many states, if students perform poorly on standardized tests, school funding can be affected, and teachers' and administrators' jobs can be at stake. The consequences of testing are great indeed. And given the trend in the United States toward more rather than fewer high-stakes tests, the debates about testing and its consequences are likely to intensify in the coming years.

With that in mind, and drawing on your own experiences, write an essay in which you state your own position about the need for and use of standardized tests. Imagine that your audience is a general audience of students, educators, and parents who have some direct interest in testing and in education generally.

1. Ollman discusses eight "myths" that he believes surround testing in the United States. Evaluate his discussion of these "myths." How widespread do you think the eight beliefs he calls "myths" really are? How effectively does he dispel each of these beliefs? To what extent does his discussion of these beliefs — and his description of them as "myths" — enhance or weaken his argument? How does his discussion of these "myths" compare to Gregory Cizek's discussion of the ten benefits of standardized testing (see pages 316–327)?

2. Ollman asserts that "most students don't know enough about society to understand the role that exams . . . play in preparing them to take their place in it." How does this point contribute to his main argument about testing? How might it reflect his Marxist perspective? Do you agree with him? **3.** Ollman claims that a capitalist system requires citizens with certain beliefs, attitudes, and skills who also accept specified roles in American society. He then offers a list of sixteen ways in which testing teaches students what they need to know to serve the capitalist system. How persuasive do you find this list? What responses might you offer to Ollman's lessons? Do you think Ollman expects most Americans to reject his list? **4.** Why does Ollman believe that globalization is an important factor influencing standardized testing? What evidence does he offer in support of this position? Evaluate the effectiveness of that evidence. Do you agree with Ollman about the connection between globalization and testing? Why or why not? **5.** Ollman offers advice to students about what they should do about standardized tests. In what ways do you think this advice might enhance the effectiveness of his argument? How realistic do you think his advice is? **6.** Ollman's essay can be described as an argument based on deductive reasoning (see pages 26–31). What is the basic premise of his argument? Do you think most Americans would agree with him? Explain. **7.** Using the Toulmin Model of argumentation (see pages 31–35), identify Ollman's central claim and the warrant (or warrants) on which that claim is based. Do you think most Americans would accept his warrant(s)? Explain.

If you live in a state where standardized tests are mandated, such as New York or California, consider using your experiences with your state tests to help make your argument. You can also draw on the essays in this section to support your position. As you formulate your argument, keep in mind the different reasons for — or against — the use of testing, such as Eleanor Martin, Patricia Williams, Gregory Cizek, and Bertell Ollman have discussed in their arguments in this section. In stating and justifying your own position on testing, try to address the concerns of others who have a legitimate interest in the kinds of standardized tests that you have had to take as a student — for example, the administrators and teachers at your school or members of the community where you live.

Alternatively, construct a Web site intended to present your position on testing. Be sure to design your Web site in a way that will present your position effectively to a specific audience that you wish to address.

HOW SHOULD WE PAY FOR EDUCATION?

Horace Mann is often referred to as the father of American public education. A well-known political figure in Massachusetts in the early 19th century, Mann became the first Secretary of the State Board of Education in 1837. In his twelve years in this position, Mann worked ceaselessly to improve public education in Massachusetts. He helped to establish the first "normal schools" to train teachers, was instrumental in founding school district libraries, and won increased state funding for improved textbooks, facilities, and teachers' wages. But it was Mann's ideas about the importance of public education that constituted his most lasting influence. He helped to establish the idea that education was the natural right of all children and that well-educated children led to a wealthier society. (See Con-Text on page 337.) In 1948 he proposed that public education be funded through taxation — a radical idea at the time that would eventually become widely accepted in the United States. Today, taxes of various kinds, but especially taxes on property, are the primary means by which public schools are funded in the United States. ■ The fact that taxes pay for just about all American schools should not be taken as a sign that Americans agree on education funding. As the essays in this section make clear, education funding remains a hotly contested issue in the United States. In the past two decades, taxpayer anger about rising school taxes in several states has led to referendums and legal challenges that have resulted in changes in the way schools are funded in those states. Meanwhile, in the late 1990s a few cities, including Baltimore and Philadelphia, hired for-profit companies to run some of their schools. During the same time some school districts struck deals with soft drink companies and other businesses as a way to supplement funding sources to pay for computers, books, extracurricular activities, and other school needs. (The essays by Andrew Stark and John Sheehan present arguments about whether to allow companies to help fund schools in this way.) And despite Horace Mann's warning more than 150 years ago that taxpayers should not fund religious schools, proposals for school vouchers, which would use tax dollars to help pay tuition at private and religious schools, have again become common, as Milton Friedman's essay indicates. And as Thomas Sowell suggests in his essay, debates about education funding are not limited to elementary and secondary schools; universities and colleges wrestle with the same questions. ■ As schools struggle to pay for the education they provide, these debates are likely to intensify, and perhaps new ideas for funding education will emerge. Ultimately, these debates remain intense not only because the economics of schooling are often complicated and difficult, but also because Americans continue to believe, as Horace Mann did, that education is a public obligation.

CON-TEXT: Horace Mann and Public Education

1 Now surely nothing but universal education can counterwork this tendency to the domination of capital and the servility of labor. If one class possesses all the wealth and the education, while the residue of society is ignorant and poor, it matters not by what name the relation between them may be called: the latter, in fact and in truth, will be the servile dependents and subjects of the former. But, if education be equally diffused, it will draw property after it by the strongest of all attractions; for such a thing never did happen, and never can happen, as that an intelligent and practical body of men should be permanently poor. Property and labor in different classes are essentially antagonistic; but property and labor in the same class are essentially fraternal. . . . Education then, beyond all other devices of human origin, is a great equalizer of the conditions of men, — the balance wheel of the social machinery.

SOURCE: Horace Mann, *Education and National Welfare*, 1848.

① MILTON FRIEDMAN, "The Market Can Transform Our Schools"

Arguments about school funding are often connected to arguments about school reform. The idea of school vouchers, which refers to using public funding to help some students pay tuition at private schools, gained force in the 1990s as Americans debated ways to improve struggling public schools, especially those in urban areas. Vouchers, proponents argued, will force poor public schools to improve because students will use vouchers to go to private schools if their public schools are inadequate. In this way, vouchers encourage school reform even as they help individual students to attend private schools. Some cities, notably Milwaukee and Cleveland, implemented vouchers in efforts to rescue failing schools. But these voucher programs were controversial, in part because students could use vouchers to pay tuition at religious schools. The Cleveland program was challenged in court on the grounds that it violated the Constitutional separation of church and state.

Milton Friedman, the 1976 recipient of the Nobel Prize for Economics, has become one of the most prominent proponents of vouchers. He wrote the following essay in 2002 after the U.S. Supreme Court upheld the Cleveland voucher program. As he explains in his essay, which was first published in the *New York Times*, Friedman believes that the principles of the free market will ultimately lead to better schools. In a sense Friedman shares Horace Mann's belief in a child's right to education (see Con-Text on page 337). But he believes that it is the free market that will ensure that right to education. Friedman has been a research associate at the Hoover Institution at Stanford University since 1977 and is also Distinguished Professor Emeritus of Economics at the University of Chicago. With his wife Rose Friedman he established the Milton & Rose D. Friedman Foundation, which supports vouchers and related public initiatives to fund private education.

The Market Can Transform Our Schools
MILTON FRIEDMAN

1 The Supreme Court's voucher decision clears the way for a major expansion of parental school choice. Opponents of choice can no longer use the First Amendment's religious Establishment Clause to attack voucher programs, now that the Supreme Court has declared the Cleveland program constitutionally acceptable even though most voucher recipients went to parochial schools.

The state of Ohio provided vouchers worth up to $2,250 to low-income parents in Cleveland who chose to send their children to private schools that charge them tuition of no more than $2,500 per child. The voucher was offered as an alternative to government schooling costing nearly three times as much per student. Yet some 4,000 low-income parents still found the private alternative preferable — enough so to pay 10 percent of private school tuition out of their own pockets. What an indictment of government schools.

Most schools that accept vouchers are religious for a simple reason, and one that is easily corrected. That reason is the low value of the voucher. It is not easy, perhaps not possible, to provide a satisfactory education for $2,500 per student. Most private schools spend more than that. But parochial schools are able to accept that low voucher amount because they are subsidized by their churches.

Raise the voucher amount to $7,000 — the sum that Ohio state and local governments now spend per child in government schools — and make it available to all students, not simply to students from low-income families, and most private schools accepting vouchers would no longer be religious. A host of new nonprofit and for-profit schools would emerge. Voucher-bearing students would then be less dependent on low-tuition parochial schools.

CONTEXT

In 1996 the Cleveland public school system launched a program that provided state funds to pay private school tuition for students who met certain income requirements. Proponents described the program as a way for poor students to choose alternatives to their unsuccessful public schools. The following year, the program was ruled unconstitutional by an Ohio state appeals court. The case eventually made its way to the U.S. Supreme Court, which reversed the lower court decision in June 2002 and upheld the Cleveland voucher program as constitutional. The Supreme Court's ruling, which was criticized by opponents of voucher programs who were concerned about the public funding of religious schools, was widely considered to be a landmark decision that paved the way for other voucher programs.

5 Parents would then truly have a choice, and the quality of schooling — in both public and private schools — would soar as competition worked its magic. This has happened in Milwaukee, where the voucher program has evolved over the past 10 years. Since that program's creation, 37 new schools have opened, nearly two-thirds of them nonreligious.

Assumption of responsibility by government for educating all children does not require that schooling be delivered in government-run institutions — just as government food stamps need not be spent in government grocery stores.

Besides, an emphasis on school choice is not new, even in public programs. The G.I. Bill enacted at the end of World War II demonstrates how well choice can work. That program provided vouchers for higher education — for use in religious and nonreligious institutions — to millions of veterans; it transformed higher education and provided the educational leadership that has played a major role in political and economic change in the postwar period.

When the G.I. Bill* was enacted, doubts were expressed that the colleges could expand rapidly enough to handle the flood of new students. Yet the number of students enrolled in colleges nearly doubled in the two years after the end of the war. The supply expanded to meet the surge in demand.

*The Servicemen's Readjustment Act of 1944, also called the GI Bill of Rights, provided money for tuition and other educational expenses to veterans who served with the U.S. armed forces in World War II. The effect of the bill on higher education was enormous. Millions of U.S. veterans took advantage of the bill to attend colleges and universities, whose enrollments increased dramatically in the late 1940s and 1950s. Some scholars credit the G.I. Bill with helping improve the socioeconomic status of the U.S. working class.

10 School vouchers can push elementary and secondary education out of the 19th century and into the 21st by introducing market competition on a broad scale, just as competition has made progress possible in every other area of economic and civic life.

The biggest winner from such an educational revolution would be American society as a whole. A better schooled work force promises higher productivity and more rapid economic growth. Even more important, improved education could help narrow the income gap between the less skilled and more skilled workers and would fend off the prospect of a society divided between the haves and have-nots, of a society in which an educated elite provides for a permanent class of unemployables.

The market will respond as fully and rapidly to the increased demand for private schools generated by the expansion of vouchers for elementary and secondary education. Private voucher programs, financed by foundations and individuals, plus the limited government programs so far enacted have already brought forth a market response.

COMPLICATION

"There has been a breakdown in the accord that guided a good deal of educational policy since World War II. Powerful groups within government and the economy and within authoritarian populist social movements have been able to redefine — often in very retrogressive ways — the terms of debate in education, social welfare, and other areas of the common good. What education is *for* is being transformed. No longer is education seen as part of a social alliance in which many minority groups, women, teachers, community activists, progressive legislators and government officials, and others joined together to propose (limited) social democratic policies for schools: expanding educational opportunities, attempts at equalizing outcomes, developing special programs in bilingual and multicultural education, and so on. . . . An alliance has been formed, one that has increasing power in educational and social policy. This power bloc combines business with the New Right and with neoconservative intellectuals. Its interests are not in increasing the life chances of women, people of color, or labor. Rather it aims at providing the educations conditions believed necessary both for increasing international competitiveness, profit, and discipline and for returning us to a romanticized past of the ideal home, family, and school." Source: Michael Apple, *Cultural Politics and Education* (1996).

Questions for Discussion

1. In paragraph #2, Friedman refers to public education as "government schooling." What do you think that term suggests about Friedman's political views? Given that this essay first appeared in the *New York Times*, a newspaper that is distributed nationally but sometimes considered to support a liberal political viewpoint, do you think Friedman intended this term to be provocative? How did you react to the term? What might your reaction suggest about your own political viewpoint? **2.** Friedman is an internationally renowned economist, and he rests his argument in large part on free market principles. What effect do you think Freidman's reputation as an economist might have on readers? What effect does it have on you? Do his accomplishments as an economist give him more or less credibility on the issue of education funding, in your view? Explain. **3.** What does Friedman see as the benefits of vouchers? What evidence does he supply to support his assertions about those benefits? How effective do you think his evidence is? To what extent might your answer to that question depend on whether you agree with his views about free markets? **4.** Friedman cites various figures in making his argument about vouchers. Evaluate the effectiveness of these figures as evidence to support his argument. How convincing do you find these figures? To what extent do you think these figures strengthen or weaken his argument?

② T H O M A S   S O W E L L , "Flagging Flagships"

The ongoing debates about funding public schools focus on K–12 education. But colleges and universities increasingly face their own fiscal challenges, and some measures that they have taken in recent years to meet their rising costs have sparked controversies to match the fights over school vouchers and taxes. More and more colleges and universities now turn to private sources, including businesses and corporations, to fund their programs. And as Thomas Sowell points out in the following essay, even state universities, which have traditionally been funded with public money, pay less and less of their costs with tax dollars. These developments might seem inevitable in an age of privatization and globalization. But many critics worry that higher education, long considered an arena for free and open inquiry, is becoming beholden to the private interests whose money colleges and universities take. Sowell is concerned that as universities stray from their traditional mission, the taxpayer is increasingly being asked to fund activities, such as research, that are not central to the educational mission of state universities. His essay implicitly raises questions about what the mission of public higher education really is and who should pay for it. A well-known conservative scholar, Thomas Sowell is a senior fellow at the Hoover Institution at Stanford University and the author of many books and essays on public policy issues. This essay first appeared as a syndicated column in 2002.

Flagging Flagships
THOMAS SOWELL

1 Some state universities are having smaller and smaller proportions of their costs paid for by the states, and some people are talking about the possibility of their ceasing to be state universities at all.

The University of Texas at Austin, for example, gets more money from student tuition than it gets from the state government. That's not counting how much money it gets from the federal government, from foundations, from alumni do-nations, from the earnings of its own endowment, and from other sources.

More than one-fourth of the students on this flagship campus of the University of Texas system have parents who make $100,000 a year and up. It is not immediately obvious why the average taxpayer should be subsidizing the education of these students, much less the research of their professors.

The image of a state university, as a place where those unable to afford a pricey private college can nevertheless get a good education, applies less and less to flagship universities like the University of Texas at Austin, the University of California at Berkeley, or the University of Michigan at Ann Arbor. These are places whose main output is research, not undergraduate education.

5 During my years as a tenured faculty member at UCLA, I never saw a junior faculty member whose contract was not renewed because he was not a good teacher. But I saw many who were terminated because their research was not of the quantity or quality that was expected — regardless of how good they were at teaching. It was strictly publish or perish.

UCLA was not at all unique in this. It is common at both state and private universities for the "teacher of the year" award to be regarded by some as the kiss of death. That is because so many people who have received this award have also been terminated.

Good teaching takes up time — in preparation for class and in student conferences — which reduces the time available for research. A professor at the University of Michigan put it bluntly: "Every minute I spend in an

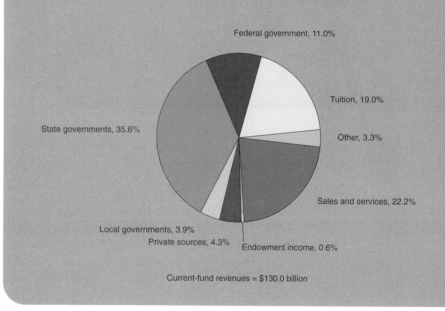

UNIVERSITY FUNDING

The accompanying chart shows percentages of funding sources for public colleges and universities as of 1997. According to a survey conducted by the National Center for Education Statistics in 2001, full-time faculty at research universities, such as the "flagship" state universities Thomas Sowell refers to, devoted 45 percent of their time to teaching and 27 percent to research; full-time faculty at private liberal arts colleges spent 66 percent of their time on teaching and 8 percent on research.

Sources of current-fund revenue for public degree-granting institutions: 1996–97

Federal government, 11.0%
Tuition, 19.0%
Other, 3.3%
Sales and services, 22.2%
Endowment income, 0.6%
Private sources, 4.3%
Local governments, 3.9%
State governments, 35.6%

Current-fund revenues = $130.0 billion

A strong case can be made for research institutions such as Brookings or RAND, and a case can be made for having some of them located on a university campus. The Hoover Institution, ranked number one in the world by *The Economist* magazine, is located on the campus of Stanford University.

10 It is a lot harder to make a case for having research institutions supported by taxpayers under the false pretense that their main job is teaching students — as happens with flagship state universities. When students and their parents are choosing a college, they need to understand that these students are less likely to be taught by the famous professors at famous state universities than they are to be taught by graduate students who are there primarily to study under those professors.

Research universities could be allowed to privatize and sell off some of their operations, such as teaching. Responsibility for teaching undergraduates could thus be taken out of the hands of graduate students and junior faculty, and transferred to teaching institutions, including on-line institutions like the University of Phoenix.

On-line teaching may never be as good as direct contact with a professor dedicated to teaching. But it may still be

undergraduate classroom is costing me money and prestige."

Parents and taxpayers may not understand what their state universities are doing, but those inside these institutions know all too well what pays off and what doesn't. Nor is there anything wrong with research in general, though much academic research is dubious. The real question is: What kinds of activities should take place in what kinds of institutions — and at whose expense?

BROOKINGS AND RAND

The Brookings Institution and the RAND Corporation are two of the most prestigious "think tanks" on public policy in the United States. The Brookings Institution, founded in 1916 and known for its liberal viewpoint, describes itself as "an independent, nonpartisan organization devoted to research, analysis, education, and publication focused on public policy issues in the areas of economics, foreign policy, and governance. The goal of Brookings activities is to improve the performance of American institutions and the quality of public policy by using social science to analyze emerging issues and to offer practical approaches to those issues in language aimed at the general public." The RAND Corporation, which describes itself as "a nonprofit institution that helps improve policy and decision-making through analysis and research," was created in 1946 by the U.S. Air Force and has worked closely with the U.S. military since then.

C O N T E X T

Located at Stanford University, the Hoover Institution is a think tank devoted to research and analysis on U.S. public policy and international affairs. Founded in 1959, it is well known for the work of its prestigious scholars and for its conservative viewpoint. It espouses "the principles of individual, economic, and political freedom; private enterprise; and representative government." Thomas Sowell has been a research fellow at the Hoover Institution since 1980.

an improvement over being taught by a graduate student who gives top priority to completing his own education and beginning a career. A research institution does not need a costly football stadium or student dormitories or a swimming pool.

What stands in the way of such rational reorganizations are inertia, false impressions, traditions and politics. As the president of Texas A & M University said of the state legislature: "They pay 20 percent and control 100 percent. Why would they give that up?"

C O N T E X T

Founded in 1976, the University of Phoenix claims to be the largest private university in the United States, with 125,000 students on 117 campuses. It generated controversy in the 1990s by offering degree programs exclusively online; critics questioned the University of Phoenix's use of a large percentage of part-time faculty to deliver its programs.

Questions for Discussion

1. What is Sowell's primary concern about the use of tax dollars to support large state universities? What does this concern suggest about Sowell's view of the purpose of higher education in general? **2.** Evaluate the evidence Sowell presents in this essay to support his claims about the focus on research at "flagship" state universities. What kind of evidence does he present? How effective is this evidence in helping him make his main argument about large state universities? **3.** In paragraph 9, Sowell refers to the Hoover Institution as an example of a research institution located on a university campus. What point does Sowell use this example to make? Is this example an appropriate and convincing one for him to use in this case? Explain. Is your answer to that question influenced by the knowledge that Sowell himself works at the Hoover Institution? **4.** Sowell asserts that teaching is not the main job of the faculty at flagship state universities. What support does he offer for this assertion? Do you think he is right? Why or why not? How might your own experience influence your answer to that question? **5.** What alternatives does Sowell propose for funding flagship state universities? Do you think these alternatives would solve the problems that Sowell describes in this essay? Explain. What counterarguments can you offer to Sowell's proposals for alternative funding?

③ ANDREW STARK, "Pizza Hut, Domino's, and the Public Schools"

Controversies about school funding are as old as public education itself in American society, but in the 1990s a new twist developed. As school districts struggled to find ways to pay the rising costs of instruction, teachers' salaries, facilities, and extracurricular activities, some schools turned to the private sector for new sources of revenue. Many businesses, such as IBM and Apple Computers, have had a presence in schools for many years, often providing technology for students in return for little more than good public relations. But in the 1990s some businesses began to establish much more intimate relationships with schools. For example, soft drink companies such as Coca Cola have purchased exclusive rights to sell their products to students in some school districts. And some companies sell educational services directly to schools. The most famous (or notorious — depending on your viewpoint) of these companies is Channel One, which provides educational television and related technology to schools in return for the right to sell advertising to companies that wish to market their products to students. Such arrangements have sparked intense controversy. Although schools reap financial benefits and perhaps educational advantages from arrangements with companies such as Channel One, critics charge that such arrangements amount to the commercialization of schools, which in effect provide companies with a captive audience of budding consumers. In the following essay writer Andrew Stark carefully reviews the controversy and acknowledges some of the potential problems associated with these commercial arrangements. But he sees advantages for schools as well. As you read his essay, consider the vision of schools that Stark seems to have. Consider, too, the extent to which his argument matches your own perspective about what should — and shouldn't — happen in schools. His essay, which was first published in *Public Policy Online* in 2001, provides a compelling reminder that debates about school funding always run deeper than questions of finance. Stark teaches in the Division of Management at the University of Toronto at Scarborough and is the author of *Conflict of Interest in American Public Life* (2000).

Pizza Hut, Domino's, and the Public Schools
ANDREW STARK

1 Los Angeles-based Tooned-In Menu Team, Inc., prints 4 million menus each month for school cafeterias around the country, each one laden with ads for products such as Pillsbury cookies or Pokemon. The deal is this: In exchange for getting their menus done up for free, participating schools provide Tooned-In with a ready market for its advertisers. It's just one of a proliferating number of arrangements forged each year between schools (or school boards) and companies. Consider McDonald's All-American Reading Challenge, in which McDonald's gives hamburger coupons to elementary-school students in exchange for their reading a certain number of books. Or Piggly Wiggly's offer to donate money to a school in return for sales receipts — indicating proof of purchase at the store — from the school community. Or the American Egg Board's "Incredible Journey from Hen to Home" curricular material, which is provided to schools for free while also promoting egg consumption. Or ZapMe!, which furnishes schools with free computer labs in return for the opportunity to run kid-oriented banner ads on the installed browsers and collect aggregate demographic information on students' web-surfing habits.

In each case, the school gets something — money, equipment, incentives for kids to learn, curricular material — at a time of shrinking public-education budgets. And the companies also get something: access to a lucrative market. American teenagers spend $57 billion of their own money annually while influencing family expenditures of $200 billion more. As important, these commercial deals enable companies to build brand loyalty in a new generation of consumers. That is why the term "commercialism in the schools," with its controversial connotations, never gets applied to the sorts of universally praised deals — such as company-sponsored scholarship, internship, or training programs — in which companies treat students not as future consumers but as future employees.

And indeed commercialism in the schools is controversial; it attracts fierce

THE TOONED-IN MENU

Image from a school lunch menu provided by Tooned-In, Inc.

criticism. National organizations such as the Yonkers-based Consumers Union* or Oakland's Center for Commercial-Free Public Education — as well as numerous ad hoc parental movements at the local level — have taken up arms against commercial deals, battling companies in school board hearings and courtrooms. Their concerns: that commercial deals cede control of the education agenda to nonteachers, that they prey upon a captive audience, that they distort kids' and families' consumer choices, that they foster materialistic values, and that kids should not be bombarded by biased, commercially motivated messages in a place where they expect the information disseminated to be objective and confined to pedagogical purposes. The debate has become shrill and polarized. "I was speaking to one of my critics not long ago," says Tooned-In's director of school relations, Frank Kohler. "She doesn't own a car because she's opposed to the use of fossil fuels. She doesn't go to the movies because she resents the commercials. I said to her, 'Lady, you don't represent America!'"

*Founded in 1936, Consumers Union is an independent, nonprofit organization devoted to consumer issues. It defines its mission as testing products, informing the public about products and about policy issues of concern to consumers, and protecting consumers: "We are a comprehensive source for unbiased advice about products and services, personal finance, health and nutrition, and other consumer concerns."

Yet there is a big problem with both commercialism's critics and its defenders. Neither side adequately distinguishes — among the many kinds of deals out there — between those that are genuinely troubling and those that are not; both paint with a broad brush. In the eyes of Ernest Fleishman, senior vice president for education at Scholastic, Inc., a New York-based company that sells books and posters through the schools, many of his antagonists "tend to use shotguns" in their attacks. "They draw no distinctions," Fleishman complains, between the "very, very different kinds of deals schools strike with companies." But what kind of discriminations should commercialism's critics be making? As Fleishman himself notes, "very few school districts have guidelines covering these matters." And certainly, defenders of commercialism in the public schools are themselves not always prone to drawing boundaries and ceding some ground to the opposition. Paul Folkemer, spokesman for the controversial "Channel One" — which beams a 12-minute newscast including two minutes of paid advertising into 12,000 schools daily — justifies his company's business this way: "Commercialism has always existed in the schools; think of the local drugstore that used to advertise in the high school yearbook." But is there no pertinent way of distinguishing Channel One from the high school yearbook?

5 If we were going to draw lines between the various kinds of commercialism so understood, the best way to begin would be to distinguish two basic types of commercial deal, types well exemplified by the contrary arrangements Pizza Hut and Domino's have struck with American schools. On the one hand, Pizza Hut will reward children who read a certain number of books in a particular pe-

riod of time with free pizza. On the other, Domino's will reward kids who buy pizza — or more exactly their school, which sends the receipts in to the local franchise — with free books. The dynamics of these two programs precisely reverse one another. In the Pizza Hut deal, students perform an act that is supposedly part of their role in the public schools: They read. In return, what the company offers is a private-market commodity: pizza. With the Domino's arrangement, kids slip outside of their public-school roles and perform a private-market act by buying pizza. In return, the company furnishes schools with the wherewithal to buy public goods — goods which are of value to the teaching role of the public schools, such as books.

As it turns out, the Pizza Hut and Domino's programs aptly symbolize the two basic kinds of arrangements companies invariably make with schools; almost every instance of commercialism falls into one or the other category. Either, as in the Pizza Hut deal, the school offers a public good — students' reading time, or classroom space, or curricular access — and the company reciprocates with whatever private-market commodity it happens to sell, whether pizza, coupons for orange juice, or samples of spaghetti sauce, sometimes dressed up as curricular material. Or, as with the Domino's deal, the school offers the company something of private-market value — namely, its own students as consumers — and what the company offers the school is materiel or monies of public value: books, equipment, computers, or outright cash gifts that have no connection with whatever it is the company sells. The first kind of deal can be troubling, but not for the reason most critics believe. The second, however, is simply far less disturbing than critics allow.

From Public Good to Private Benefit

Begin by considering a few examples of the first kind of deal, the Pizza Hut-type. Minute Maid, for instance, has staged its own version of the Pizza Hut arrangement: Students would read — that is, they would do something that is part of their role in the public schools — and what they would get in return were book covers advertising Minute Maid's private-market commodity, orange juice, or rebates on purchases. A few years ago, in a similar vein, schools across the country struck an agreement with General Mills, according to which they would devote classroom time — a public good — to a science experiment in which students would pop free samples of Fruit Gushers (the company's new private-market commodity) into their mouths, making comparisons between the resulting sensation and the dynamics of volcanic eruptions. A prominent Campbell's Soup deal — which offered schools a science experiment purporting to show that its Prego spaghetti sauce is thicker than Unilever's Ragu — fell into the same category. As did a sixth-grade math textbook, published by McGraw Hill and introduced into public curricula around the country, which featured a passel of references to brand-name private-market commodities such as Nike and Gatorade.

In all of these cases, the school offered something in its public capacity — its own classroom time and space — and the company reciprocated with whatever it happened to sell on the private market — orange juice, spaghetti sauce — wrapped in some form of curricular material. The typical deal struck by Channel One, the 800-pound bête noire of commercialism critics, falls into the same category. What the school turns over to Channel One is the public good of

CHANNEL ONE

Owned by Primedia, Inc., Channel One is broadcast to more than eight million students in 12,000 middle, junior, and high schools in the United States. First broadcast in 1990, Channel One features twelve-minute shows on contemporary news stories; it also runs two minutes of advertisements from various companies, such as Nike and Reebok. According to its Web site, Channel One has won more than 150 awards for its programming since 1990.

classroom time: The typical Channel One deal calls for 90 percent of a school's students to watch the show, beamed daily by satellite, on 90 percent of schooldays. In return, what Channel One furnishes is its own private-market commodity — namely, two minutes daily of advertising for other private commodities such as Reebok or Nintendo — wrapped in current-events curricular material, the ten minutes daily of news coverage its programs provide.

It's true that Channel One also gives each subscribing school approximately $17,000 worth of wholly *public* goods, in the form of free TV and satellite dish equipment. Yet both Channel One and its critics deny that these public goods are of much value to schools. Noting that "a couple of hundred schools haven't even asked for [the equipment]," Channel One's Folkemer says that "if the deal was just to get the equipment, schools wouldn't continue it. Equipment is not that significant." Channel One's opponents, such as Alex Molnar of the University of Wisconsin at Milwaukee, agree, denying that the equipment Channel One offers is "valuable to the school[s even] in the most crass commercial terms." Of course, the two sides have different motives for dismissing the utility of Channel One's gifts of videos and satellite equipment. Channel One does so

to allay any charge that schools are taking its programs because of the free equipment rather than the educational merits of the programming; critics, for their part, want to argue that Channel One is exploiting schools, getting valuable advertising access to children's minds in exchange for virtually nothing. But the bottom line is this: If indeed the public good of free equipment means so little, as both Channel One and its critics seem to agree, then the Channel One deal remains essentially identical to the Pizza Hut, Minute Maid, and Fruit Gusher arrangements. What the school turns over is public curricular space and classroom time, and what the company provides in return is essentially a private-market commodity — in this case, advertising — fashioned in a curricular package that inserts itself into the public time and space made available.

10 What's so wrong with these kinds of deals? Critics have a full quiver, but the most prominent salvo misses. On it, the problem with Channel One — or Minute Maid's book covers or Campbell's curricular material — is that, installed as they are inside the classroom, their promotional efforts prey upon a captive audience. If the company's pitch were removed even to the cafeteria, as with Kohler's menus, that would be a different story: Students don't have to eat lunch there. Better still that the ads should move onto the school roof: There is little to say against the two suburban Dallas school rooftops that feature Dr. Pepper ads for overflying planes. But as the public space which the school makes available to a private commodity's promotional material moves from the outer perimeters of the building to the inner sanctum of the classroom, the audience grows more captive; the private-market advertisements, consequently, more allegedly harmful. In a 1995 memo concerning Channel One, the New York State Department of Education put it this way: "It's [sic] mission is to . . . deliver up a large, captive . . . audience to advertisers." And this, presumably, is a bad thing.

But is it? Captivity is double-edged. If a captive audience means that Channel One's ads might carry more suasive clout than otherwise — because students can't avoid them — it also means that the content of the surrounding news material might be of greater quality than otherwise. It is harder to accuse Channel One, as some accuse PBS, of feeling under pressure to water down the quality of its programming to attract the audiences that corporate sponsors desire, precisely because Channel One's viewers can't go anywhere.

Accordingly, some critics of Channel One backpedal. Far from berating Channel One for exploiting a captive audience, they instead adopt an assault based on *denying* that its audience is all that captive. Students, they say, actually have a tendency to mentally wander, do homework, gossip, or simply space out during the Channel One broadcast; and this, they worry, means that Channel One faces an enormous incentive to dilute its news content, rendering it ever more glitzy and gimmicky, in order to attract student attention. Channel One's news broadcasts, the media critic Mark Crispin Miller has written, rely on "brilliant, zippy graphics," a "young and pretty . . . team of anchors," and content that is "compressed and superficial" in order to compel the attention of students — precisely because they tend to "zone out," as Miller puts it, during broadcasts. "The content of Channel One News," says William Hoynes, a Vassar sociologist who has studied the company's programming, "suggests the difficulties of holding the attention of even captive audiences"; it's clear, Hoynes writes, "that Channel One has consequently tailored a [news] product that is, first and foremost, about inducing students to pay attention, with a relentlessly hip style and . . . gimmicks."

If, however, students' attention can and does wander, is it not misconceived to describe them as constituting a "captive" audience? Either the audience is captive, in which case the ads are potent but the news programming encounters less of a need to be diluted — or else students' minds are free to roam, in which case programmers might be tempted to water down the news content but the ads likely have less impact. It's true that one study has shown that students tend to remember more about Channel One's ads than about the news content; but since they are equally captive (or noncaptive) in either case, captivity per se — notwithstanding its mantra-like appearance in criticisms of

Channel One — isn't the issue. The captivity critique is not quite ready for prime time.

There is, however, a qualified critique of the Channel One deal — and, by extension, the McGraw Hill or Minute Maid arrangements — that has some merit. In a much cited 1993 study, Michael Morgan, a professor of communications at the University of Massachusetts at Amherst, reported that "Channel One is most often found in schools . . . that have the least amount of money to spend on conventional educational resources." Among poorer schools — where total spending per student is $2,599 per year or less — about six in 10 take Channel One. But among wealthier schools — those that spend at least $6,000 — only about one in 10 subscribe. Morgan's conclusion: For those schools that cannot even afford books and maps, the free 10 minutes of news content itself — forget the TV sets and the satellite dishes — may, by filling a curricular void, prove sufficient to overcome any reservations teachers harbor about Channel One's content. As the Center for Commercial-Free Public Education puts it, in "schools where text books are old or there is no money for supplemental materials," Channel One — or Campbell's Soup or General Mills curricular material — "can be a popular way for teachers to brighten a subject up." David Shenk, a fellow at the Freedom Forum Media Studies Center, agrees: "Poorly funded school districts are the most likely [to take Channel One or Campbell's or Minute Maid curricular products] because prefabricated lesson plans save preparation time and provide relief for overburdened teachers." A *Wall Street Journal* article a few years back reported on the case of Laurie Bjoriykke, a third grade teacher in Gaithersburg, Md., who "says she has no textbooks for her history and science classes" and so "shows two corporate tapes a month to supplement her resources."

15 What all of this means, says the Consumers Union's Charlotte Baecher, is that schools taking Channel One have put themselves into a kind of "conflict of interest." As with all public officials, teachers should make their official decisions — including their decisions about how to allocate curricular time and classroom space — on the merits, according to the public interest, and not on the basis of their need for private support. Of course, the kind of deal represented by Channel One is not the most serious kind of conflict of interest imaginable: That's the kind where an official has the capacity to use her public role to benefit a private company in return for a personal payment. Instead, the Channel One arrangement resembles the milder form of conflict (but one still statutorily regulated at the federal level) in which officials take something of value from a private company not for themselves personally, but to help serve the purposes of their cash-strapped public agency. The rule is that the public agenda should never be skewed by an agency's need for private assistance, let alone the official's personal desire for private gain. As Sen. Richard Shelby, Republican of Alabama, recently put it, "I want [school] decision makers to be able to

decide for themselves rather than have to settle for a 'deal.'"

The fact that Channel One makes its way preponderantly into poorer schools, however, confronts not only those schools but the company itself with a problem. Jim Metrock, a former steel industry executive who now heads an Alabama-based anti-Channel One organization called Obligation, notes that because Channel One "is going into school systems where kids may not be able to pay for the product, Channel One's advertisers" might not be "getting the audience they paid for . . . probably the demographics are different." Kevin Gordon of the California School Boards Association agrees: "Their hope was that they'd be in all sorts of markets," Gordon says, "but that hasn't happened." William Hoynes adds that Channel One wanted to "be seen to reach the youth market, not the *poor* youth market."

Ironically, then, while the Channel One-type deal might skew the curricular path taken by poorer schools, it also, in a way, threatens to skew the marketing path taken by the company. Just as schools risk making public decisions based not on the public-interest merits but on extraneous private inducements, companies like Channel One risk making their private-market decisions — their decisions as to where to prospect for consumers — based not on which schools

COMPLICATION

"Corporate-sponsored teaching materials are reaching more than 20 million students in elementary and high schools every year. Product samples and coupons are distributed to more than two million students. TV commercials and magazine ads in the classroom reach countless millions more. . . . On a larger scale, schools are bartering students' ability to make rational marketplace choices in exchange for equipment they couldn't otherwise afford. The result: Schools are becoming heavily sponsored by corporations marketing products. They're selling the kids entrusted to them to any bidder. Sponsored materials' advertising is disguised as educational materials, which kids are less likely to question." Source: "Selling America's Kids: Commercial Pressures on Kids of the 90's," *Consumer Reports.*

are the most privately lucrative, but on the extraneous consideration as to which are most publicly needy. Channel One's former president for programming, Andy Hill, acknowledges that if the company "went to advertisers and said 'poorer kids watch our programs,' that would be insane." Yet he maintains that he "hasn't seen a demographic breakdown" of Channel One's audience and concedes that "all other things being equal, a wealthier school is less likely to be enticed" by the curricular material Channel One offers. Indeed, Hill says, if the "far left-wing Democrats who oppose Channel One instead devoted their energy to electing politicians who would raise funding for public schools, Channel One would be gone quickly."

The typical Channel One deal, then, embarks the company on a mild perversion of its purposes, leading it to prospect for markets not where the private capacity to pay for the products it advertises is highest, but where the public needs for its curricular material are greatest. In the same way, it is likely that Channel One embarks some schools on a mild perversion of their purposes, causing them to make decisions on how to allocate public space and time not on the basis of the public interest — the pedagogical merits — but according to the blandishments offered by a private enterprise. In this sense, this first type of "commercialism" arrangement — where what the school offers is its own public space and time, and what the company supplies is its own private-market commodity or advertising for it — can rankle on both sides.

From Private Market to Public Benefit

In the second form of school commercialism, however, the school does not offer the company its students in their public

role as students — or public curricular time or public classroom space — but rather centers exclusively on students and parents in their private-market role, as active purchasers of commodities. And what the company offers the school is a public good, pure and simple — such as equipment, computers, or a cash bequest — purged of any association with the company's own private-market commodity. In the Domino's example, students buy pizza, the school gets books. Or take another example: Parents in many states purchase products from their local Wal-Mart and return the receipts to the neighborhood school, which then sends the receipts back to Wal-Mart, which in turn rewards the school with free computer lessons for its students. Apple's "Apples for Students Program" does much the same with Apple computers: Students and their families purchase produce from a local grocery store which then, in a deal with Apple, provides the school with free or reduced-price computers once a certain threshold of purchases has been reached. Hershey or Orville Redenbacher, likewise, will give a school cash for every candy wrapper or popcorn label its parents and children send in.

20 Brita Butler-Wall, who led an ultimately unsuccessful fight to keep advertising out of Seattle's schools, calls such arrangements "travesties." She and other critics indict them both because of what they mean for the students and because of what they imply about the companies. As far as the students are concerned, Consumers Union complains, deals such as Apple's or Wal-Mart's teach them "to choose products or stores for all the wrong reasons" — not on the basis of the private-market criteria of price and quality, which is what they should be learning to use, but rather skewed by the hope of gaining some form of public benefit for the school. As for the companies providing cash or equipment to schools in exchange, Consumers Union argues, they are not doing so for purely altruistic reasons but rather are engaging in "self-serving philanthropy," giving because they expect to reap a return in goodwill. Companies' gifts of public goods such as books, equipment, or the cash to buy them — which should be made purely on the public-spirited criteria of generosity and benevolence — are instead being skewed by the hope of gaining some private benefit.

But the critics say too much. In such arrangements, both the school and the company are no longer compromising their principal roles, having stepped outside of them. The school is no longer a public forum but a private market; the company no longer a private enterprise

but a public philanthropist. As far as the school is concerned, there is thus no turning over of any kind of public space — let alone the sanctum of the classroom — to the service of private ends. Rather, the school community's private-market decisions are being diverted to serve public ends. And this is no more troubling than, say, someone's holding in his wallet a Sierra Club or Multiple Sclerosis Society affinity credit card, where his determination as to whether to buy a particular private-market commodity can get colored, at the margins, by his knowledge that in paying for it he'll benefit a favored public cause.

As for the company — say Wal-Mart or Apple — it does not (as does Channel One) find itself directing a promotional campaign to markets where the public needs for curricular filler may be large but the private capacity to buy its products meager. Instead, in these arrangements, the company steps entirely outside of its profit-making role and enters a philanthropic one. And in distributing its public largesse, it simply does what many a company does, namely, allow itself to be guided by the need to cultivate a private market. This is no more troubling than what happens when a mogul builds a hospital wing named after his company.

But there is a further wrinkle here. Even with deals of this relatively benign sort — in which the school offers a private market and the company a public good — there lurks, critics say, an insidious danger. There is a tendency, they argue, for the private market in question to move from outside the school to inside. During the 1997–98 school year, South Fork High School in Florida's Marlin County executed a deal with Pepsi in which — instead of students buying Pepsi at local stores in return for a corporate gift to the school — Pepsi got the exclusive right to sell drinks to students *within* the school itself, in return for which the school got $155,000 cash. A year later, the Colorado Springs school district awarded Coke a similar privilege in return for $8 million over 10 years.

More and more such arrangements are cropping up. And here, critics say, an added problem emerges. Unlike the Wal-Mart and Apple deals, where students and parents buy products outside of the school — and where they retain the option of shopping at Sears or buying from IBM should they prefer — when the market moves inside the school, such choices often evaporate. When Coke won its contract with Colorado Springs, 53 schools had to jettison their Pepsi machines as part of the arrangement. "Exclusivity," says Brita Butler-Wall, "is against free enterprise; it means a lack of consumer choice." The Consumers Union's Charlotte Baecher agrees. "Look at the great diversity of beverages you and I had when we were kids after a school football game," Baecher says; "today, with exclusive pouring arrangements, kids don't have the same broad range of choice." Echoing this concern, the Berkeley school board recently tried to make an in-school marketing deal with Pepsi more palatable by requiring the company to offer a variety of drink alternatives in its school vending machines.

25 It is, though, a little hard to take this "exclusivity" complaint seriously. Critics of commercialism in the schools are (or at least should be) coming from a perspective on which there's too much consumerism — too *much* commodity choice — in the schools, not too little. A critic of commercialism in the schools who complains that a particular deal is "against free enterprise," or that it fails to offer students a range of soft-drink alternatives, needs to do a little more work on her argument. It was, after all, the

city of Berkeley that 30 years ago gave prominence to the Marxist philosopher Herbert Marcuse.* Choices such as the one between Coke and Pepsi, Marcuse famously declared, are a form of "repressive tolerance," a false dichotomy staged by capitalists to distract people from the real, more fundamental choice between "wage slavery" and socialism. Odd that Berkeley should now be passing laws designed to preserve such small-beer choices in the school, as if the presence of Coke but not Pepsi were some form of deprivation. "Anticommercialism" is the last movement that should be taking such a position.

It's true that some critics zero in on Coke or Pepsi deals because the drinks are so lacking in nutritional value. "Calcium intake among active girls who have switched from milk to soft drinks," declares Maryland anti-commercialism activist Michael Tabor, "has decreased bone density." This attack, however, would have more credibility if the Consumers Union publication *Captive Kids* hadn't also scrutinized the Dairy Council of Wisconsin's "Delicious Decisions" curricular material for signs of "bias toward milk products."

What concerns over captivity are to the first kind of deal — where what the school offers is its public space — concerns about exclusivity are to the second kind of deal, where what the school offers is a private market. Both worries are red herrings. In witness whereof, it's worth noting that corporate practitioners of the first kind of deal — such as Channel One vice president Jeff Ballabon — defend themselves in a backhanded way by assailing the second kind of deal, the Coke or Pepsi arrangements, precisely for their exclusivity. "The deals schools make with vendors to feature only their products in the schools," Ballabon says: "*that* smacks to me of commercialism."

CONTEXT

See John Sheehan's essay on page 358 in this section for a discussion of the Colorado school districts' decision about selling Coke in their schools.

*A philosopher and scholar, Herbert Marcuse (1898–1979) became well known in the 1960s for his leftist critiques of American capitalism. His best-known book is *One-Dimensional Man* (1964).

Returning the compliment, practitioners of the second kind of deal — such as Dan DeRose, whose dd Marketing helps forge Coke and Pepsi arrangements — take aim at the first kind of deal, the Channel One arrangement, for preying on a captive audience. "Personally," DeRose told a 1998 symposium, "we feel that [commercialism] should stay out of the classroom."

Frank Kohler's fretfulness notwithstanding, when it comes to commercialism in the schools, it is possible to draw lines. When a school gives over classroom space to a company like Minute Maid — in return for book covers advertising Minute Maid's orange juice products — each party hazards the perversion of its principal role: its role as a public entity in the case of the school; its role as a private profit-making entity in the case of the company. The school risks suborning public space to private purposes, not public criteria. And the company risks aiming its promotions at student bodies which are the most publicly needy, not necessarily the most privately lucrative.

On the other hand, when a school steps out of its public role to create a private market for a grocery store's products — and when in turn the store steps out of its private profit-making role and contributes something of public value, such as Apple computers, to the school — what happens is relatively benign. It should be difficult to find fault with students whose private market purchases are guided by their hope of winning some public goods for their school. Likewise with businesses whose public philanthropy is affected by their desire for private gain.

30 Of course, just because it is possible to draw lines between the two types of deal doesn't mean they never get blurred. General Mills once had an arrangement whereby children would collect box tops from its cereal products — acting in their private-market roles as consumers, not their public roles as students — yet what they got in return were not public goods such as books, equipment or cash, but school visits from the Trix Bunny, who would urge them to consume more of the company's private-market commodities.

It is hard not to raise one's eyebrows at such a deal. But beyond this rare line-blurring instance, most commercialism arrangements fall into either one class or the other, resembling either the Minute Maid or the Apple deal. The problem with commercialism's critics is that they tend to place the two on a par — finding fault equally with the Minute Maid orange juice and the Apple Computer arrangements. In so doing, they paint with too broad a brush. When it comes to commercialism in the schools, as in so many other areas of life, it's important not to mix apples with oranges.

Questions for Discussion

1. In his essay Stark distinguishes between two basic types of commercial deals between public schools and private companies. Why is this distinction important, in Stark's view? What support does Stark provide that "almost every instance of commercialism falls into one or the other category"? Summarize Stark's view of the main advantages or disadvantages of each type of commercial deal. What does his discussion of these deals indicate about his view of the purpose of public education? **2.** Stark organizes his entire essay around the distinction between two different kinds of deals between public schools and private companies. How effective is this strategy in helping him to make his main argument about commercialism in schools? **3.** Stark uses many examples to illustrate the two different types of arrangements between schools and private companies. Evaluate Stark's use of these examples. How effective are they in illustrating his points? How well do they contribute to his main argument? Where appropriate, draw on your own experiences with the products or companies Stark mentions to answer these questions. **4.** How does Stark respond to the criticism that students are a captive audience for Channel One's broadcasts? Why is Stark not worried about the fact that deals between public schools and private companies in effect provide a captive audience of students for the companies' products or advertising? Do you agree? Why or why not? **5.** Stark claims that exclusivity is a primary concern of critics of the second kind of deal between schools and companies that he describes in this essay. What does he mean by *exclusivity* here? How does he answer the concerns of critics on this issue? How persuasive are Stark's responses to those critics, in your view? **6.** Stark asserts that when commercial deals are made between public schools and private companies, both schools and companies risk a perversion of their principle roles. What does he mean by "*perversion*" in this context? Why is this point important to his main argument? Do you think he is right? Explain. **7.** Stark devotes much of his essay to summarizing and responding to some of the critics of deals between public schools and private companies. How fairly do you think Stark presents the views of these critics? How persuasive are Stark's responses to these critics, in your view? To what extent do you think Stark strengthens or weakens his main argument with his discussions of these critics? Cite specific passages from Stark's essay in your answer.
8. On several points related to the question of deals between private companies and public schools, Stark either finds agreement between supporters and opponents of such deals or identifies concerns about such deals that both sides have. With that in mind, evaluate the effectiveness of Stark's essay as an example of a Rogerian argument. Do you think Stark's essay points to a resolution of this controversy that can satisfy all sides of the issue? Explain, citing specific passages in the essay to support your answer. (You might wish to refer to the discussion of Rogerian argument on pages 127–132.)

358 CHAPTER 9 EDUCATION

④ **JOHN SHEEHAN, "Why I Said No to Coca-Cola"**

In early 1999 three public school districts in Colorado signed a contract with Coca-Cola that gave the soft drink company exclusive rights to sell its products in the schools in those districts. In return, the districts were to receive more than $27 million dollars. It was a dramatic example of a recent trend in the funding of education: commercial deals between public schools and private companies. The great financial pressures on schools can make such deals very difficult for schools to turn down. But these deals have many critics, including John Sheehan. Sheehan, a school board vice president in one of the three Colorado districts that signed the deal with Coca-Cola, voted against the contract. He explains why in the following essay, which was originally published in the *American School Board Journal* in 1999. As Sheehan's essay makes clear, commercial deals between schools and companies raise a number of complicated and difficult questions. His concerns about such deals grow out of his beliefs about the purposes of public education and how those beliefs should ultimately drive decisions about school funding.

Why I Said No to Coca-Cola
JOHN SHEEHAN

1 Last February, a consortium of three Colorado school districts approved one of the most lucrative beverage contracts in the nation. The vote on the 10-year, $27.7 million pact with Coca-Cola was unanimous — almost. I was the only one of the consortium's 17 board members to vote against it.

Why was I opposed? The reasons are not simple, and indeed, the issue is not a simple one. I started out relatively supportive of the use of advertising in schools, as long as it was done "judiciously." But gradually, I changed my opinion. Now I can no longer accept the notion of our schools becoming brokers for advertising space or, worse yet, middlemen in the merchandising of products

directly to our students. It is better, in my opinion, to walk away from the short-term opportunity for money than to open our schools to the long-term consequences that come with the dollars. Here are my concerns:

■ **Education and marketing are like oil and water.**
Public education has an agenda that is already crowded enough. When we become marketers and distributors, we confuse our mission. I worry about a time when our educational goals might be influenced or even set by private companies targeting our students with their own narrow messages. And before you think I

am simply being paranoid, consider some of the advertisements from companies that already specialize in marketing to students in schools.

"School is . . . the ideal time to influence attitudes, build long-term loyalties, introduce new products, test-market, promote sampling and trial usage, and — above all — to generate immediate sales," says an ad to clients of Lifetime Learning Systems.* "Reach him in the office," an ad for Modern Talking Picture Service, Inc., says above a photo of a five-year-old Asian-American boy dressed in a three-piece suit and armed with a briefcase. "His first day job is kindergarten. . . . If he's in your target market, call us. . . ." 5 How long will it be before these messages become our message?

■ **We are opening the floodgates of consumerism.**
We have all become inured to the constant barrage of advertising, but for me, consumerism is a real problem. The pressure to buy and measure our success in life through the things we acquire is overwhelming. Education should offer a way for students to seek a good life that means more than just wealth. It saddens me to see our schools become part of this marketing machinery. Public schools should be a respite from the constant onslaught of advertisers.

And there is no such thing as opening the floodgates just a little bit. The driving force behind the marketing machine is immense. Once in the door, businesses will be ceaseless in their efforts to gain more ground. In our high schools, Coca-Cola has already won the opportunity to put 20 Coke machines in each building. Our contract with the company alludes to the idea that Coke sales in the lunchroom could become a reality if the U.S. Department of Agriculture were to sanction Coke products within the federal lunch program.

■ **Businesses are targeting a captive audience.**
There is something unethical, in my opinion, about viewing our captive audience of students as targets for current and future marketing efforts. These students are captive only because our schools have been entrusted with the responsibility of educating them. Taking financial advantage of this unique situation is a breach of that trust.

■ **We are letting our legislators and the public off the hook.**
Yes, schools need money, but turning to commercial sales for

*See the Complication on page 352.

COMPLICATION

In 1998 Steve Morrison, a Colorado school administrator whose district also signed a contract with Coca-Cola, wrote an essay in which he examined the benefits of such commercial deals:

In the 12 months that it took to develop the sponsorship proposal, negotiate the contract and sign the deal, we learned a lot. The major lesson was to shift from thinking like educators to thinking more like businesses. . . .

Visitors to school districts that claim to have no commercialism in their buildings will spot any number of corporate logos on student clothing, corporate emblems on almost every piece of equipment in the school (have you ever seen a computer without a brand name plainly visible?) or book covers that extol the virtues of careers in the armed forces. One would be hard pressed to find a school that truly has no commercial links. If commercialism already exists in education, then the real decision may be how to monitor and control the level of commercialism that students are exposed to so that the primary educational mission is not compromised and new sources of funding can be developed to support student programs. Source: "A Corporate Pitch for Athletics" by Steve Morrison.

income is a cop-out. It sends the message to our voters and legislators that we can let them off the hook — that advertising and sales of consumer products can fill the gap when it comes to supporting education. My state ranks pitifully low in funding for public schools, but when we sign up with corporate giants like Coke, we are sending the message that a multimillion-dollar market is ours for the taking. What incentive is there for our legislators to rethink their priorities?

10 Most of the decisions school boards make are not grand decisions that have a huge and immediate impact; they are in-cremental. The decision to sign a contract with Coca-Cola is also incremental. Today, we feel reasonably safeguarded from abuses in advertising and sales. But let's put things in context. I have already heard from our administration that this decision is no big deal because schools already sell soda. Some 20 years ago or so, an administrator decided to put a vending machine in the building to raise a little loose change. Do you suppose anyone saw that decision as the harbinger of a multimillion-dollar marketing arrangement among three major Colorado school districts and Coca-Cola?

I doubt it. And I can't imagine what things might look like 20 years from now.

NEGOTIATING DIFFERENCES

The essays in this section address three controversies related to the funding of public education: the use of public money to fund private schools, the use of tax dollars to support research-oriented state universities, and commercial deals between public schools and private companies to help pay the costs of public education. These controversies grow out of larger questions about the purpose of public schooling and whose responsibility it is to fund and manage schools. For some, public schools must remain public and should have no connection to private or sectarian interests. For others, private interests are at the core of American society and offer a viable alternative to govern-ment control of schools. Still others believe that local districts should make their own decisions about these matters. Yet very few suggest that the government should get out of education altogether or that public education should be abolished in favor of an exclusively private system. For most people who are concerned about these issues, then, the basic problem remains more or less the same: How can we pay for education in a way that enables us to accomplish the goals of public education?

Drawing on the essays in this section and on any other appropriate resources, write an essay in which you answer that question. In your essay, focus on public education in gen-

Questions for Discussion

1. Sheehan states that "education should offer a way for students to seek a good life that means more than just wealth." Why is this statement important to Sheehan's main argument against commercial deals between schools and private companies? Do you agree with him? Why or why not? **2.** Sheehan claims that marketing products in schools is a breach of trust. What exactly does he mean by that statement? What does that statement reveal about Sheehan's views about public education? **3.** Sheehan asserts that schools "confuse" their mission when they make deals with private companies. In some ways, Sheehan's assertion is similar to the point Andrew Stark makes about schools "perverting" their purpose (see page 353). However, these two authors reach different conclusions about commercial deals. Why? What differences do you see in the fundamental beliefs each author has about education and school funding? Which author do you find more convincing? Why? **4.** Sheehan ends his essay by looking toward the future, expressing the concern that the deal with Coca-Cola will lead to more and more such deals. How effectively do you think this ending supports Sheehan's main argument? **5.** Sheehan's essay can be considered an argument based on inductive reasoning. Explain how Sheehan arrives at his conclusion. What evidence does he cite that eventually leads him to conclude that commercial deals with private companies are a bad idea for public schools?

eral or on a specific level of education, such as elementary, secondary, or higher education. Make an argument about how you believe schools should be funded: whose responsibility paying for public education is, where funds should come from, how they should be allocated, and — most important — why. In making your argument, try to articulate your fundamental beliefs about education and its role in American culture.

In completing this assignment, you might wish to speak to school administrators, school board members, education professors, or others who might have experience with or knowledge about education funding. You might also draw on your own experiences to help support your argument. For example, you may have attended a public school that eliminated a sports team or arts program because of a lack of funding. Or perhaps you live in a town where high property taxes created a public controversy. Such experiences can help make your argument more concrete and provide evidence for your position. Above all, keep in mind that your argument should ideally try to find what you consider to be a resolution to this issue that might be acceptable to others who are concerned about education funding.

10

ENVIRONMENTS

ENVIRO

NMENTS

WHAT IS

COMMON GROUND?

I n his famous 1968 essay "The Tragedy of the Commons" (see Con-Text on page 365), biologist Garrett Hardin laid out the central dilemma caused by a growing human population: **"We want the maximum good per person; but what is good? To one person it is wilderness, to another it is ski lodges for thousands. To one it is estuaries to nourish ducks for hunters to shoot; to another it is factory land. Comparing one good with another is, we usually say, impossible because goods are incommensurable. Incommensurables cannot be compared."** But Hardin goes on to say that in reality we *must* find some way to compare the incommensurables. We have no choice, because our earth is a finite resource. And that's the challenge: How do we compare incommensurables? How do we decide what's best for *all* of us, even if it means that our decisions will not be good for *some* of us? What is the common good? And how should we use our common ground? ■ The essays in this section address these questions. They challenge us to reexamine what we mean when we speak of the "common good," and they remind us that what we consider to be good for all might only reflect our own cultural perspectives. These essays also reveal that the idea of the commons can include a specific plot of land with historical and cultural significance as well as a technological space such as the Internet that seems to occupy no physical place. Together, these essays underscore the complexity of "the commons," which is an idea as old as human society itself. They also help us see why arguments about the common good and common ground are often so difficult — and so important.

CON-TEXT: The Tragedy of the Commons

1 The tragedy of the commons develops in this way. Picture a pasture open to all. It is to be expected that each herdsman will try to keep as many cattle as possible on the commons. Such an arrangement may work reasonably satisfactorily for centuries because tribal wars, poaching, and disease keep the numbers of both man and beast well below the carrying capacity of the land. Finally, however, comes the day of reckoning, that is, the day when the long-desired goal of social stability becomes a reality. At this point, the inherent logic of the commons remorselessly generates tragedy.

As a rational being, each herdsman seeks to maximize his gain. Explicitly or implicitly, more or less consciously, he asks, "What is the utility to *me* of adding one more animal to my herd?" . . .

The rational herdsman concludes that the only sensible course for him to pursue is to add another animal to his herd. And another; and another. . . . But this is the conclusion reached by each and every rational herdsman sharing a commons. Therein is the tragedy. Each man is locked into a system that compels him to increase his herd without limit — in a world that is limited.

Ruin is the destination toward which all men rush, each pursuing his own best interest in a society that believes in the freedom of the commons. Freedom in a commons brings ruin to all. . . .

Education can counteract the natural tendency to do the wrong thing, but the inexorable succession of generations requires that the basis for this knowledge be constantly refreshed. . . .

SOURCE: Garrett Hardin, "The Tragedy of the Commons" (1968).

① GEORGE WILL, "In Defense of Hallowed Ground"

When we preserve the ground on which a great battle is fought, such as at Gettysburg in Pennsylvania or Saratoga in New York, we memorialize the important events that took place there and honor those who lost their lives. Well-known columnist and political commentator George Will believes that we do something more when we preserve those battlefields: We preserve our nation's collective memory. For Will the hallowed ground of such battlefields is an important part of our identity as Americans, and that belief provides a twist to the typical arguments about whether to preserve special places like battlefields or to develop them for our economic benefit. In the following essay, which appeared as a syndicated column in 2002, Will makes a case against building residential housing and corporate offices on the site of one of the great Civil War battles at Chancellorsville, Virginia. At the time Will wrote his essay, residents of the area were debating proposals for development of that land, and many opponents argued against those proposals on the grounds that new development would destroy the rural character of that region. Will complicates the debate by reminding us that some common ground is special to us for reasons that have nothing to do with lifestyle, economic growth, or environmental preservation. They matter to us for less tangible reasons. In making his argument, he invites us to consider what we value most when we decide how to use land and resources that belong to all of us. Will is a well-known political commentator whose syndicated columns appear in hundreds of newspapers each week.

In Defense of Hallowed Ground
GEORGE WILL

"Why did we run? Well, those who didn't run are there yet."
— AN OHIO SOLDIER

1 The 12-mile march on May 2, 1863, took Stonewall Jackson from the clearing in the woods where he conferred for the last time with Robert E. Lee, to a spot from which Jackson and 30,000 troops surveyed the rear of the Union forces. Those forces, commanded by a blowhard, Joe Hooker* ("May God have mercy on General Lee, for I shall have none"), were about to experience one of the nastiest shocks of the Civil War.

Two hours before dusk, Federal soldiers were elated when deer, turkeys and rabbits came pelting out of the woods into their lines. It was not dinner but death approaching. By nightfall Federal forces were scattered. When the fighting subsided four days later, Lee was emboldened to try to win the war with an invasion of Pennsylvania. The invasion's high-water mark came at the crossroads town of Gettysburg.

One hundred and thirty-nine years after the battle here, a more protracted struggle is under way. In 1863 the nation's survival was at stake. Today, only the nation's memory is at stake.

"Only?" Without memory, the reservoir of reverence, what of the nation survives?

5   Hence the urgency of the people opposing a proposal to build, on acreage over which the struggle surged, 2,350 houses and 2.4 million square feet of commercial and office space. All this would bring a huge increase in traffic, wider highways and the further submergence of irrecoverable history into a perpetually churned present.

Northern Virginia, beginning about halfway between Richmond and Washington, is a humming marvel of energy and entrepreneurship, an urbanizing swirl of commerce and technology utterly unlike the static rural society favored by Virginia's favorite social philosopher, Thomas Jefferson. Chancellorsville is in an east-west rectangle of terrain about 15 miles long and 10 miles wide, now divided by Interstate 95, that saw four great battles — Fredericksburg, Chancellorsville, Spotsylvania, the Wilderness — involving 100,000 killed, wounded or missing.

Where a slavocracy once existed, Northern dynamism now prevails. But Northern Virginia has ample acreage for development, without erasing the landscapes where the Army of Northern Virginia spent its valor. As for the Federals' side, it is a scandal that the federal government's cheese-paring parsimony has prevented the purchase of his-

torically significant land — 20,000 acres, maximum — at Civil War battlefields from Maryland to Mississippi.

Just $10 million annually for a decade — a rounding error for many Washington bureaucracies — would preserve much important battlefield land still outside National Park Service boundaries. The government's neglect can be only partially rectified by the private work of the Civil War Preservation Trust, just 3 years old. (You can enlist at http://www. civilwar.org. Also check http://www. chancellorsville.org.)

CWPT's President James Lighthizer, a temperate, grown-up realist, stresses that

*Union General Joseph Hooker (1814–1879) was known both for looking after the men he commanded and for quarreling with the superiors to whom he reported. He was also associated with heavy drinking and sexual misconduct. Although military historians credit him with some successes, he is widely believed to have lost his nerve at Chancellorsville.

*In addition to serving as the third President of the United States, Thomas Jefferson (1743–1826) was governor of Virginia and founder of the University of Virginia. "Jeffersonian" means characteristic of his political attitudes, which included a belief in democracy and faith in our country's future.

CWPT's members are "not whacked-out tree-huggers" who hate development and want to preserve "every piece of ground where Lee's horse pooped." But regarding commemorations, Americans today seem inclined to build where they ought not, and to not build where they should, as at the site of the World Trade Center.

10 In New York City, many people who are anti-growth commerce-despisers want to exploit ground zero for grinding their old ideological axes. They favor making all or most of the 16-acre parcel a cemetery without remains, a place of perpetual mourning — what Richard Brookhiser disapprovingly calls a "deathopolis" in the midst of urban striving.

But most who died at ground zero were going about their private pursuits of happiness, murdered by people who detest that American striving. The murderers crashed planes into the twin towers, Brookhiser says, "in the same spirit in which a brat kicks a beehive. They will be stung, and the bees will repair the hive." Let the site have new towers, teeming with renewed striving.

But a battlefield is different. A battlefield is hallowed ground. Those who were there gave the last full measure of devotion and went there because they were devoted unto death to certain things.

Those who clashed at Chancellorsville did so in a war that arose from a clash of large ideas. Some ideas were noble, some were not. But there is ample and stirring evidence that many of the young men caught in the war's whirlwind could articulate what the fight was about, on both sides. . . .

Local government here can stop misplaced development from trampling out the contours of the Confederacy's greatest victory. A Jeffersonian* solution.

WORLD TRADE CENTER

As the ruins of the World Trade Center were cleared away in 2002, the Port Authority of New York and New Jersey, which owned the site, sponsored an international design competition to find a plan for the multipurpose use of the land in question. Some of the early plans offended Americans who had lost family members when the towers were suddenly destroyed; they felt that commercial use of the site failed to show respect for the dead. Others complained that early plans were ugly and that an opportunity for bringing more beauty to New York was being thrown away. And many residents argued that the site should become a multiuse neighborhood, with apartments and businesses as well as a memorial to the victims. In February 2003 a design by architect Daniel Libeskind featuring a 1776-foot tower was selected for the site.

Questions for Discussion

1. How does Will provide support for his claim that Joe Hooker was a "blowhard"? How does this kind of language affect Will's credibility as an author? **2.** Will describes memory as "the reservoir of reverence." If memory does indicate what we value, what conclusions can you make about the American public? What kinds of things do we tend to remember, and what are we likely to forget? **3.** Consider how Will uses numbers in paragraphs 5–7. What role do these numbers play in his argument? Do you think Will uses these numbers effectively in supporting his point? Explain. **4.** How does Will establish that his interest in preserving Chancellorsville is not based on which side won that battle? **5.** Why does Will compare the controversy over the fate of Chancellorsville battlefield with the controversy over how the site of the World Trade Center should be treated? How effective do you think this comparison is in helping to make Will's main argument?

② RADHA D'SOUZA, "Global Commons: But Where Is the Community?"

By the start of the 21st century the idea of a "global commons" had become almost cliché. The rapid growth of international trade, spurred on by agreements such as the North American Free Trade Agreement (NAFTA) and the General Agreement of Trade and Tariffs (GATT), and the emergence of communications media such as the Internet seemed to break down national borders and challenge traditional ideas about community and citizenship. For many people the idea of the commons no longer seemed connected exclusively to local places or cultures; instead, the earth itself seemed to have become our commons. Radha D'Souza, a writer and activist who lectures in law at Waikato University in New Zealand, expresses deep reservations about the development of this idea of a global commons. In the following essay, which appeared in 2002 on NoLogo.org, a Web site devoted to human rights activism, D'Souza traces the idea of the commons in her native India and reveals that different cultures have different ways of understanding what constitutes common ground. In examining this idea, D'Souza challenges us to think carefully about what we really mean by "the common good" in a changing and diverse world. As you read D'Souza's essay, consider how her experience as someone who grew up in a nation that was once a colony of Great Britain shapes her views about developments such as the growth of international trade. Consider, too, how your own cultural background might influence your views about the common good.

Global Commons: But Where Is the Community?
RADHA D'SOUZA

*Non-government organizations (NGOs) are advocacy groups, usually nonprofit, that address social, political, economic, cultural, and environmental issues. These groups are not affiliated with any national governments.

1 It is everywhere these days, this idea of a global commons. It started with the environment, now it has spread to all sorts of other issues. It is an idyllic idea too — one humanity, one world, one nature. It erases troublesome differences and intractable histories, just like heaven. Like heaven, it is not a new idea. It has been around for a long, long time, as long as the East India Company, the New Zealand Company and others;

yet it continues to resurface with a spanking new look whenever there is turbulence in the world.

Historically, the idea of "commons" is closely bound together with the idea of a "community": people bound together by time and place, a common history and geography. Capitalism destroyed communities bound to time and place, tied to history and geography. Instead it created communities that were based on "interests" located within wider market transactions. Trade Unions, for example, are "communities" of workers, whose interest is in the labour markets, consumer organisations are communities founded on people with interest in the products they consume, industry organisations are communities with a common interest in maintaining conditions for industries and so on. For communities formed on the basis of market interests their primary allegiance is to the "interest" that constitutes them into a "community" and not to place or their histories. Their histories deal with economics and politics not ancestors, place and genealogies. The idea of "commons" as it is used in the NGO* parlance does not examine the "community" that seeks "commons."

In pre-colonial India, the village was the basic social unit that formed the building block of society. The village was the unit of taxation, the unit where resource allocation including land, labour and water took place besides social codes of conduct. The British saw it differently. In their view the village was the "owner" of land and therefore land was communally owned in India. Through the Ryotwari Acts,[†] the colonial government substituted itself for the "community" and all land, forests and water became "commons" that the state could regulate in the interest of the community. And, of course since the British had come to India to stay they were now part of the community — presto!

Historically, de-linking the idea of commons from a critical understanding of communities underpins colonisation. Since the advent of colonisation, the ideological rationale has always been in a universalistic language. Such a language avoids dealing with the causes of the problem, whether it be natural resources or the human conditions. It holds out the false hope that those causes can be swept under the carpet, and the problems

THE EAST INDIA COMPANY

Created in 1600, the British-run East India Company acquired numerous trading privileges in India and eventually came to rule the entire country. The power of this private company reached its height between 1757 and 1857, but it was dissolved after a rebellion by the peoples of India. From 1858 to 1947 India was ruled by the British government. Many scholars believe that the East India Company exploited India and that colonial exploitation continued after India was absorbed into the British Empire. Like India, New Zealand was once governed by the British.

can be dealt with without reference to where they come from and whence they come from. The politics of commons therefore denies self-determination of oppressed people because it assumes that the oppressors and the oppressed form a "community" that can live together without dealing with their histories or geographies.

5 For "Northern" NGOs, the idea of commons is appealing because it avoids self-critical reflection on how they are better off than the rest of the world. Worse still, it avoids the even more difficult spectre of having to confront the reality that they will continue to do better than the others as a result of the "commons." Above all the idea of a global "commons" does not call upon the "civil society" of the "North" to renounce or give up any-

[†]Implemented by the British rulers of India in the late 18th century, the Ryotwari Acts established a system for tax collection in which local Indian peasants, or *ryots*, were required to contribute a share of their produce to a village leader, who would then turn the revenues over to the state.

DEFINING NATIONAL BORDERS

After World War I the countries that emerged as victors redrew national boundaries in the defeated German, Austro-Hungarian, and the Ottoman empires. Many historians believe that the diplomats who created new nations at that time failed to consider religious and ethnic differences within the states they were mapping out. These new nations included Yugoslavia, Czechoslovakia, Turkey, Syria, and Iraq. After World War II, states such as India, Pakistan, and Israel were created. In some of these cases religious or ethnic differences have caused nations to split apart; in others ongoing violence has deepened differences between diverse groups living within a single state.

*The husk or shell of something is traditionally considered worthless, so in this proverb one of the people in question has brought nothing useful to the shared meal. The Tamil are an ethnic group who live on the Indian subcontinent.

thing, least of all power. Tigers and sheep graze in the commons, but they do so only in God's wonderland.

There is a Tamil proverb* that captures the idea of partnership in the following way: you contribute the flattened rice, and I will contribute the husk, and the two of us can sit by the riverside, watch the sunset, blow the husk from the rice and eat it together. To those of us who are products of colonisation, that is just what the idea of "commons" sounds like.

CONTEXT

This essay appeared on NoLogo.org, a Web site that was launched by Naomi Klein, the author of *No Logo: Taking Aim at the Brand Bullies* (1999). NoLogo.org describes itself as a "portal to various segments of the global justice movement. It was intended as a forum for readers of *No Logo* who wanted to read further or get involved in the global movement against corporate exploitation and neoliberal globalization documented in the book." To what extent does D'Souza's essay reflect the viewpoint of this Web site?

Questions for Discussion

1. How many claims does D'Souza make in this argument? What support does she offer for these claims?

2. D'Souza makes a spiritual reference in paragraph 1. What does it imply about the relationship between spirituality and politics? In what sense is this relationship important to D'Souza's main argument? 3. How would you describe the tone of this argument? Is it effective? Cite specific passages from the text to support your answer. 4. To what extent do you think D'Souza's argument reflects her own background as an Indian woman? How effectively do you think she addresses readers who are from Western or "Northern" nations? 5. D'Souza's essay was published on NoLogo.org, a Web site that supports activism against multinational corporations. (see Context on page 371.) In what sense is D'Souza's argument appropriate for readers who are likely to visit NoLogo.org? In what ways is her argument consistent with the stated mission of that Web site? Do you think her essay would be equally effective for a more general audience? Explain.

③ DAVID BOLLIER, "Rediscovery of the Commons: Managing for the Common Good, Not Just for the Corporate Good"

Discussions about the common interest, whether they take the form of debates about preserving natural areas or protecting the airwaves for public use, often refer to private property, government regulation, and free markets. In fact, *the market*, a term referring generally to economic activity, can be thought of as a commons, in the same way we might think of a national park as a commons. But journalist David Bollier argues that there are some things — property, resources, even ideas — to which neither governments nor businesses have an exclusive right; there are some things that belong to everyone. The difficult question is "What are those things?" In the following essay Bollier offers his answer to that question. He argues against a market-driven view of the commons, which he contends has become the dominant way of thinking about the common interest. In place of that view he proposes a more sweeping vision of a commons in which "ecological stability, social values, aesthetic concerns and democratic traditions should carry as much weight around the policymaking table as economic analysis." Whether you find that argument persuasive might depend more on your own vision of what U.S. society should aspire to than on the evidence that Bollier offers to support his claim. Bollier is a journalist and public policy activist who serves as a senior fellow at the Norman Lear Center of the Annenberg School for Communications at the University of Southern California. He is the author of a number of books, including *Silent Theft: The Private Plunder of Our Common Wealth* (2002), from which the following essay is adapted. This essay was published in 2002 at TomPaine.com.

Rediscovery of the Commons: Managing for the Common Good, Not Just for the Corporate Good
DAVID BOLLIER

1 For at least the past 20 years, it has been a mantra in our national political life that the so-called free market is our best hope for a brighter, more beautiful tomorrow. From Ronald Reagan's sermons on the "magic of the marketplace" to the giddy euphoria of the Internet revolution, politicians and business leaders have locked arms in praise of strong property rights, deregulation, globalization and the marketization of everything.

But even before the dot-com bust and the astonishing financial and ethical meltdown of some leading American corporations, there has been a growing counter-movement afoot. This insurgency not only insists that markets have distinct limits, but that there are serious alternative ways of creating and managing wealth in socially benign ways. Call it a rediscovery of the commons.

It is a quiet trend with diverse manifestations. But at heart its goal is to prevent the private plunder of resources that belong to everyone and to erect new mechanisms for assuring their popular control.

The issues that surround the commons "are very likely going to drive the next big turn of the political wheel," predicts Jonathan Rowe, a former top Senate staffer and now director of the Tomales Bay Institute. "In recent decades, the market has been penetrating into realms previously thought off-limits. It is claiming every last inch of physical and psychological space, from the outer reaches of the solar system to the most intimate interiors of daily experience."

5 Broadly speaking, the commons identifies a set of interests that are distinct from the state and the market. A good shorthand might be "we the people." The state may intervene as a trustee on behalf of the commons — to protect widely shared interests or resources — and "market populists" may like to claim that markets are more democratically empowering than democracy itself. To whatever extent these claims may or may not be true, the point is that the people have sovereign interests that are separate from those of government and markets. "The commons" offers a conceptual framework for expressing these interests.

Unlike the market, which is dedicated to private economic gain, the commons is about communities managing their shared property for the benefit of all, as a civic entitlement. It's about managing for the common good, not just for the corporate good. It's about assuring popular enfranchisement, not granting privileges according to one's ability to pay or invest.

CORPORATE MELTDOWNS

After reaching record highs in the late 1990s, U.S. stock markets went into a serious decline that was triggered by various causes, including artificially high prices and troubling world events. But many analysts agree that corporate scandals played a significant role in the loss of investor confidence at that time. Executives at major corporations such as Enron and WorldCom were proven to have used dishonest accounting methods. Other kinds of corporate dishonesty subsequently emerged. Billions of dollars disappeared from the U.S. economy — and from the retirement plans of many Americans.

Just as "the market" can refer to anything from stock markets and furniture retailing to lemonade stands, so "the commons" has many tiers of meaning. Three of the more important types of common assets include:

Public Assets

These are resources that the people own and that government manages as a trustee and steward.* For example, Americans collectively own the electromagnetic spectrum used by broadcasters. (See "Complication" on page 376.) Even though it is worth tens of billions of dollars, Congress has essentially surrendered huge swaths of the spectrum to broadcasters for free. The inequity is immediately obvious because wireless companies, in sharp contrast, pay huge sums of money for use of the spectrum.

*A trustee has legal power to administer property for an individual beneficiary (such as a minor) or to supervise the administration of an institution (such as a college). A steward is also charged with the management of property but usually with less power than a trustee. For example, a trustee could decide to sell a piece of property, but a steward is more likely to manage it.

"WE THE PEOPLE"

The U.S. Constitution begins, "We the people of the United States, in order to form a more perfect union, establish justice, insure domestic tranquility, provide for the common defense, promote the general welfare, and secure the blessings of liberty to ourselves and our posterity, do ordain and establish this Constitution for the United States of America." Seven sections, or "articles" then follow. Additional sections have been added by amendment.

COMPLICATION

For an argument that addresses the question of ownership of the radio airwaves, see Jenny Toomey's "Empire of the Air" on page 274.

Millions of acres of public lands containing minerals, timber, oil and grazing areas also belong to the public. But like the airwaves, government allows major corporations to use and abuse these resources for far less than their market value. It has also allowed public lands to be used even though ecological harm is likely to result.

10 The federal government is also the sponsor and steward of enormous stores of federally sponsored research, reports and databases. Taxpayers have paid hundreds of millions of dollars for risky basic research for new medications, often resulting in major breakthroughs. Yet the profits — and they are hefty — typically accrue to the drug companies alone. "Such a deal!," exclaims James Love, director of the Consumer Project on Technology. "The taxpayers pay to invent a promising drug, then give a monopoly to one company. And the company's role? To agree to sell it back to us." Love has extensively documented how exclusive licensing deals for federally developed drugs force taxpayers to pay higher prices for AZT and ddI (HIV and AIDS-related drugs), Prozac (depression), Capoten (hypertension), Taxol (cancer) and many other medications.

Common Assets

These are "unowned" resources — the atmosphere, life forms, genes — that have not been formally brought under the control of either markets or government. They are resources that all humans own as a moral right, but which have no formal recognition in law and no historic role as a market commodity. The human genome and the genetic structures that make up agricultural crops, for example, are common assets that are now being converted into private property.

As Maude Barlow and Tony Clarke revealed in their remarkable report, *Blue Gold*, some companies are trying to lock up vast quantities of water in Canada and Scotland in order to transport and sell it to "thirsty" regions of the world. Once "marketized" as a global commodity, water — a basic necessity of life — may become too expensive for local communi-

ties to afford, especially when an affluent region halfway around the globe is willing to buy it. The disruptive effects on regional ecosystems are given little consideration. This is a classic model of how an aspect of nature that once belonged to everyone is being converted into private property.

Social Commons

Many commons have less to do with managing a physical resource than with communities of people pursuing a shared mission. Examples include scientific disciplines, Internet affinity groups and local communities. Through the exchange of gifts — time, energy, resources — members of social commons create special interpersonal bonds among each other, which over time are the basis for creating value in highly efficient, socially satisfying ways. Online genealogical Web sites and blood donation systems, for instance, are based on people freely "giving" to the commons — and eventually reaping benefits later. Not all forms of "self-interest" resemble the selfish, acquisitive behavior of the market.

Why a Commons Movement Now?

Why is the fledgling commons movement arising now? Much has to do with the palpable excesses of our market culture. Not only has American material output reached new pinnacles, as represented by SUVs and McMansion homes, American obsessions with private property are reaching some absurd new levels.
15 A family with a rare genetically transmitted disease has actually patented the disease gene so that patent-hungry university researchers couldn't do so. A German publisher of a magazine called "O" has gone after Oprah for control of the letter "O" as a magazine title. The World Wildlife Federation challenged the World Wrestling Federation over control of the letters "WWF."

Many proponents of the commons are revolted by the new frontiers of property-grubbing. It's unseemly and a denial of some of our most appealing public-spirited American traditions. That's one reason why the American Library Association recently started an Information Commons Project. The ALA's immediate past president Nancy Kranich points out that "libraries provide the real and virtual spaces in communities for free and open exchange of ideas fundamental to democratic participation and civil society" — a function that expansions in copyright law now threaten.

Others are animated by the ripoff and abuse of public resources — airwaves, public lands, the Internet, public spaces, schools and libraries, and more. That's why policy entrepreneur Peter Barnes proposed the idea of a congressionally chartered "Sky Trust" that would help the public assert ownership over the atmosphere and collect fees from companies that pollute our shared atmosphere.

Champions of the commons want to regain public control over public resources and preserve them for public benefit. Marketeers tend to want to

For other arguments that address copyright law, see pages 212–231.

monetize these resources for private gain.

The new conversation about the commons is burgeoning for cultural reasons as well. Now that communism is dead, it has become more permissible to talk in respectable company about cooperation and collaboration. To be sure, Microsoft still Red-baits Linux users as un-American, and representatives of the film and recording industries cry "piracy" when people share digital information, even when that sharing is entirely legal. **20** Paradoxically, much of the economic growth of the 1990s stemmed from the Internet, the biggest and most robust commons in history. The idea that a commons can be a valuable resource for wealth-creation in the market calls into question some core assumptions of economic theory.

Economists, for example, routinely claim that people will have no incentives to create valuable information or creative works unless they have strict copyright protection and the ability to participate in markets. But this simply is not true on the Internet. The biggest effusion of creativity and knowledge in history has occurred precisely because there were weak copyright protections and a general absence of markets. Yes, e-commerce has flourished in some sectors and many kinds of information will not be created without copyright protection. But the Internet has demonstrated that a commons of digital content and infrastructure is critical to competitive, well-functioning markets, not to mention a healthy democracy.

It should be remembered that the Internet was not the brainchild of Larry Ellison or Bill Gates,* but of public servants and academics operating in an environment far removed from the market. As a result, the open, end-to-end architecture of the Internet has facilitated the free and easy sharing of information. It has unleashed a creative explosion of Web sites, listservs, open source software development, peer-to-peer file sharing communities — a robust ecosystem of innovation that no market could or did create on its own. (Thought experiment: Compare diversity of expression on television or radio with that of the Internet.)

The commons movement is about reconceptualizing what should be public and shared and what limits should constrain the expansion of markets. Contrary to the Milton Friedman† acolytes, not all aspects of life should be controlled by markets. That's why the commons movement insists upon pioneering new models of community control of resources. It also challenges the presumption that virtually everything should be for sale in the market.

Naturally, the strategies and styles of this eclectic movement vary. Yet the groups that are most active — environmentalists, biotech activists, anti-

*Larry Ellison founded Oracle, which became one of the world's leading suppliers of software. Ellison and Bill Gates, the founder of Microsoft, are among the richest men in the world.

COMMUNISM

As an economic theory, Communism called for public ownership of natural resources and the means of production. In practice, it became associated with totalitarianism and favoritism of government insiders. Communism drew international attention after Bolsheviks seized power in Russia in 1918 and subsequently formed both the Union of Soviet Socialist Republics (U.S.S.R.) and the Comintern, an agency dedicated to spreading Communism to other countries. Although Communism attracted many followers as late as the 1940s, it began losing appeal after the death of Soviet dictator Joseph Stalin in 1953. Nevertheless, resistance movements seeking to establish communist governments sprang up in countries around the world through the 1980s. The U.S.S.R. remained one of the world's superpowers until the late 1980s when Eastern European countries broke free of Soviet control, and the Soviet Union broke apart, revealing internal weakness caused by bad economic planning. Political parties calling themselves "Communist" remained in place elsewhere — in China, for example, and Cuba — but their economic polices became more sympathetic to private enterprise. When Bollier writes, "communism is dead," he means that it is no longer taken seriously by economists or government planners, including those who still call themselves "Communist."

commercialization advocates, media reform advocates, open source programmers, defenders of the public domain in copyright law — share a commitment to fighting pernicious market excesses. It's gotten so bad that the only viable protest option, writes *Baffler* editor Thomas Frank, is to "commodify our dissent" — the title of a book of essays critiquing the "gilded age" of the 1990s. 25 But "the commons" is not just a reactive critique of the market. It is also about advancing a new and positive vision. The idea is to instigate a broader vector of conversation than the sterile, misleading debate about free markets ("good") versus regulation ("bad"). The concept of "the commons" insists that ecological stability, social values, aesthetic concerns and democratic traditions should carry as much weight around the policymaking table as economic analysis. At this early stage, it is unclear how the commons movement will evolve and perhaps consolidate. But one thing is clear: the scope and ferocity of market activity is rapidly expanding into every nook and cranny of nature and culture. As market imperialism intensifies and transforms nature, communities and culture in new ways, the commons is likely to become a more frequently invoked organizing principle for resisting — and for imagining better, more humane alternatives.

†The winner of the 1976 Nobel Prize for Economics and a prolific writer who taught for many years at the University of Chicago, Milton Friedman (b. 1912) has argued on behalf of free enterprise and monetary policies that are likely to favor economic growth without causing inflation. (You can read an essay by Friedman on pages 338–341.)

Questions for Discussion

1. How would you summarize Bollier's main argument? On what fundamental beliefs about how a society should work does Bollier base his argument? **2.** What kind of audience do you think is most likely to object to Bollier's argument? Does he do anything to reassure such an audience? **3.** Bollier argues that we need "to erect new mechanisms" for assuring democratic control over commonly held resources. What kind of mechanisms do you think are likely to gain political support today? How realistic do you find Bollier's proposals for such new mechanisms? **4.** In paragraph 4, Bollier quotes a source claiming that the debate over common ground is "likely going to drive the next big turn of the political wheel." After these words were published, the United States was attacked by terrorists, and public attention turned to domestic security and foreign affairs. Do these events make Bollier seem less credible today? To what extent does his argument depend on a historical context in which Americans enjoyed economic and military security? **5.** In paragraph 10, Bollier refers to the high cost of prescription drugs in the United States. Drug manufacturers traditionally argue that these prices support research and development, but Bollier claims that part of this research is funded by taxpayers. Do you think the federal government should support drug research? Do you think it should regulate drug pricing? Why or why not? **6.** Of the various kinds of commons that Bollier discusses, which ones concern you the most? What might your response to this question indicate about your own political views? **7.** In paragraph 25, Bollier claims, "The concept of 'the commons' insists that ecological stability, social values, aesthetic concerns and democratic traditions should carry as much weight around the policymaking table as economic analysis." On what grounds does Bollier make this claim? Do you agree with him? Why or why not?

④ CASS SUNSTEIN, "The Daily We: Is the Internet Really a Blessing for Democracy?"

Democracy is based on the idea that citizens have the right to decide what is in the public interest. Yet studies regularly show that only about half of all eligible Americans vote in national elections and even fewer in local elections. You might put it this way: Citizens have the power to determine what is in their interests as a society, but few exercise that power. Why? One answer might be that we currently do not have a genuine public forum in which we can debate the issues that affect our common interests. That answer might seem surprising in an age characterized by new forms of technology and media that seem to keep us informed and connected "24-7." But Cass Sunstein suggests that despite the power of new media — specifically, the Internet — to inform and connect, we lack a true public sphere in which, as he writes, "a wide range of speakers have access to a diverse public." The Internet has the potential to be part of that public sphere, a commons for ideas, but according to Sunstein, for most Americans it has become a means for accessing only the information that interests them. As a result, it is not a forum for confronting the diversity of views on which a healthy democracy depends. Sunstein's well-documented argument rests on a particular vision of what a democracy should be. As you read, ask yourself whether you share his vision. Ask yourself, too, what role media like the Internet should play in a democracy. Sunstein is the Karl N. Llewellyn Distinguished Service Professor of Jurisprudence, Law School and Department of Political Science, University of Chicago. He has written widely on civil rights, technology, and social justice. The following essay is a slightly shortened version of an article that appeared in the *Boston Review* in 2001.

The Daily We: Is the Internet Really a Blessing for Democracy?
CASS SUNSTEIN

1 Is the Internet a wonderful development for democracy? In many ways it certainly is. As a result of the Internet, people can learn far more than they could before, and they can learn it much faster. If you are interested in issues that bear on public policy — environmental quality, wages over time, motor vehicle safety — you can find what you need to know in a matter of seconds. If you are suspicious of the mass media, and want to discuss issues with like-minded people, you can do that, transcending the limitations of geography in ways that could barely be imagined even a decade ago. And if you want to get information to a wide range of people, you can do that via email and websites; this is another sense in which the Internet is a great boon for democracy.

But in the midst of the celebration, I want to raise a note of caution. I do so by emphasizing one of the most striking powers provided by emerging technologies: the growing power of consumers to "filter" what they see. As a result of the Internet and other technological developments, many people are increasingly engaged in a process of "personalization" that limits their exposure to topics and points of view of their own choosing. They filter in, and they also filter out, with unprecedented powers of precision. Consider just a few examples:

1. Broadcast.com has "compiled hundreds of thousands of programs so you can find the one that suits your fancy. . . . For example, if you want to see all the latest fashions from France 24 hours of the day you can get them. If you're from Baltimore living in Dallas and you want to listen to WBAL, your hometown station, you can hear it."

2. Sonicnet.com allows you to create your own musical universe, consisting of what it calls "Me Music." Me Music is "A place where you can listen to the music you love on the radio station YOU create. . . . A place where you can watch videos of your favorite artists and new artists."

3. Zatso.net allows users to produce "a personal newscast." Its intention is to create a place "where you decide what's news." Your task is to tell "what TV news stories you're interested in," and Zatso.net

turns that information into a specifically designed newscast. From the main "This is the News I Want" menu, you can choose stories with particular words and phrases, or you can select topics, such as sports, weather, crime, health, government/politics, and much more.

4. Info Xtra offers "news and entertainment that's important to you," and it allows you to find this "without hunting through newspapers, radio and websites." Personalized news, local weather, and "even your daily horoscope or winning lottery number" will be delivered to you once you specify what you want and when you want it.

5. TiVo, a television recording system, is designed, in the words of its website, to give "you the ultimate control over your TV viewing." It does this by putting "you at the center of your own TV network, so you'll always have access to whatever you want, whenever you want." TiVo "will automatically find and digitally record your favorite programs every time they air" and will help you create "your personal TV line-up." It will also learn your tastes, so that it can "suggest other shows that you may want to record and watch based on your preferences."

6. Intertainer, Inc. provides "home entertainment services on demand," including television, music, movies, and shopping. Intertainer is intended for people who want "total control" and "personalized experiences." It is "a new way to get whatever movies, music, and television you want anytime you want on your PC or TV."

7. George Bell, the chief executive officer of the search engine Excite, exclaims, "We are looking for ways to be able to lift chunks of content off other areas of our service and paste them onto your personal page so you can constantly refresh and update that 'newspaper of me.' About 43 percent of our entire user data base has personalized their experience on Excite."

Of course, these developments make life much more convenient and in some ways much better: we all seek to reduce our exposure to uninvited noise. But from the standpoint of democracy, filtering is a mixed blessing. An understanding of the mix will permit us to obtain a better sense of what makes for a well-functioning system of free expression. In a heterogeneous society, such a system requires something other than free, or publicly unrestricted, individual choices. On the contrary, it imposes two distinctive requirements. First, people should be exposed to materials that they would not have chosen in advance. *Unanticipated encounters,* involving topics and points of view that people have not sought out and perhaps find irritating, are central to democracy and even to freedom itself. Second, many or most citizens should have a range of *common experiences*. Without shared experiences, a heterogeneous society will have a more difficult time addressing social problems and understanding one another.

Individual Design
Consider a thought experiment — an apparently utopian dream, that of complete individuation, in which consumers can entirely personalize (or "customize") their communications universe.

5 Imagine, that is, a system of communications in which each person has unlimited power of individual design. If some people want to watch news all the time, they would be entirely free to do exactly that. If they dislike news, and want to watch football in the morning and situation comedies at night, that would be fine too. If people care only about America, and want to avoid international issues entirely, that would be very simple; so too if they care only about New York or Chicago or California. If people want to restrict themselves to certain points of view, by limiting themselves to conservatives, moderates, liberals, vegetarians, or Nazis, that would be entirely feasible with a simple point-and-click. If people want to isolate themselves, and speak only with like-minded others, that is feasible too.

At least as a matter of technological feasibility, our communications market is moving rapidly toward this apparently utopian picture. A number of newspapers' websites allow readers to create filtered versions, containing exactly what they want, and no more. If you are interested in getting help with the design of an entirely individual paper, you can consult a number of sites, including Individual.com and Crayon.net. To be sure, the Internet greatly increases people's ability to expand their horizons, as millions of people are now doing; but many people are using it to produce narrowness, not breadth. Thus MIT professor Nicholas Negroponte refers to the emergence of the "Daily Me" — a communications package that is personally designed, with components fully chosen in advance.

Of course, this is not entirely different from what has come before. People who read newspapers do not read the same newspaper; some people do not read any newspaper at all. People make choices among magazines based on their tastes and their points of view. But in the emerging situation, there is a difference of degree if not of kind. What *is* different is a dramatic increase in individual control over content, and a corresponding decrease in the power of general interest intermediaries, including newspapers, magazines, and broadcasters. For all their problems, and their unmistakable limitations and biases, these intermediaries have performed some important democratic functions.

People who rely on such intermediaries have a range of chance encounters, involving shared experience with diverse others and exposure to material that they did not specifically choose. You might, for example, read the city newspaper and in the process come across a range of stories that you would not have selected if you had the power to control what you see. Your eyes may come across a story about Germany, or crime in Los Angeles, or innovative business practices in Tokyo, and you may read those stories although you would hardly have placed them in your "Daily Me." You might watch a particular television channel — perhaps you prefer Channel 4 — and when your favorite program ends, you might see the beginning of another show, one that you would not have chosen in advance. Reading *Time* magazine, you might come across a discussion of endangered species in Madagascar, and this discussion might interest you, even affect your behavior, although you would not have sought it out in the first instance. A system in which you lack control over the particular content that you see has a great deal in common with a public street, where you might encounter not only friends, but a heterogeneous

variety of people engaged in a wide array of activities (including, perhaps, political protests and begging).

In fact, a risk with a system of perfect individual control is that it can reduce the importance of the "public sphere" and of common spaces in general. One of the important features of such spaces is that they tend to ensure that people will encounter materials on important issues, whether or not they have specifically chosen the encounter. When people see materials that they have not chosen, their interests and their views might change as a result. At the very least, they will know a bit more about what their fellow citizens are thinking. As it happens, this point is closely connected with an important, and somewhat exotic, constitutional principle.

Public (and Private) Forums

10 In the popular understanding, the free speech principle forbids government from "censoring" speech of which it disapproves. In the standard cases, the government attempts to impose penalties, whether civil or criminal, on political dissent, and on speech that it considers dangerous, libelous, or sexually explicit. The question is whether the government has a legitimate and sufficiently weighty basis for restricting the speech that it seeks to control.

But a central part of free speech law, with large implications for thinking about the Internet, takes a quite different form. The Supreme Court has also held that streets and parks must be kept open to the public for expressive activity.[1] Governments are obliged to allow speech to occur freely on public streets and in public parks — even if many citizens would prefer to have peace and quiet, and even if it seems irritating to come across protesters and dissidents whom

CONTEXT

The First Amendment to the U.S. Constitution reads, "Congress shall make no law respecting an establishment of religion, or prohibit the free exercise thereof; or abridging the freedom of speech, or of the press; or of the right of the people peacefully to assemble, and to petition the government for a redress of grievances."

one would like to avoid. To be sure, the government is allowed to impose restrictions on the "time, place, and manner" of speech in public places. No one has a right to use fireworks and loudspeakers on the public streets at midnight. But time, place, and manner restrictions must be both reasonable and limited, and government is essentially obliged to allow speakers, whatever their views, to use public property to convey messages of their choosing.

The public forum doctrine serves three important functions.[2] First, it ensures that speakers can have access to a wide array of people. If you want to claim that taxes are too high, or that police brutality against African Americans is common, you can press this argument on many people who might otherwise fail to hear the message. Those who use the streets and parks are likely to learn something about your argument; they might also learn the nature and intensity of views held by one of their fellow citizens. Perhaps their views will be changed; perhaps they will become curious, enough to investigate the question on their own.

Second, the public forum doctrine allows speakers not only to have general access to heterogeneous people, but also to specific people, and specific institutions, with whom they have a complaint. Suppose, for example, that you believe that the state legislature has behaved irresponsibly with respect to crime or health care for children. The public forum ensures that you can make your views heard by legislators simply by protesting in front of the state legislature building.

Third, the public forum doctrine increases the likelihood that people generally will be exposed to a wide variety of people and views. When you go to work, or visit a park, it is possible that you will have a range of unexpected encounters, however fleeting or seemingly inconsequential. You cannot easily wall yourself off from contentions or conditions that you would not have sought out in advance, or that you would have chosen to avoid if you could. Here, too, the public forum doctrine tends to ensure a range of experiences that are widely shared — streets and parks are public property — and also a set of exposures to diverse circumstances. In a pluralistic democracy, an important shared experience is in fact the very experience of society's diversity. These exposures help promote understanding and perhaps, in that sense, freedom. And all of these points are closely connected to democratic ideals.

15 Of course, there is a limit to how much can be done on streets and in parks. Even in the largest cities, streets and parks are insistently *local*. But many of the social functions of streets and parks as public forums are performed by other institutions, too. In fact, society's general interest intermediaries — newspapers, magazines, television broadcasters — can be understood as public forums of an especially important sort, perhaps above all because they expose people to new, unanticipated topics and points of view.

When you read a city newspaper or a national magazine, your eyes will come across a number of articles that you might not have selected in advance, and if you are like most people, you will read some of those articles. Perhaps you did not know that you might have an interest in minimum wage legislation, or Somalia, or the latest developments in the Middle East. But a story might catch your attention. And what is true for topics of interest is also true for points of view. You might think that you have nothing to learn from someone whose view you abhor; but once you come across the editorial pages, you might read what they have to say, and you might benefit from the experience. Perhaps you will be persuaded on one point or another. At the same time, the front-page headline or the cover story in *Newsweek* is likely to have a high degree of salience for a wide range of people.

Television broadcasters have similar functions. Most important in this regard is what has become an institution: the evening news. If you tune into the evening news, you will learn about a number of topics that you would not have chosen in advance. Because of their speech and immediacy, television broadcasts perform these public forum-type functions more than general interest intermediaries in the print media. The "lead story" on the networks is likely to have a great deal of public salience; it helps to define central issues and creates a kind of shared focus of attention for millions of people. And what happens after the lead story — dealing with a menu of topics both domestically and internationally — creates something like a speakers' corner beyond anything imagined in Hyde Park. As a result, people's interest is sometimes piqued, and they might well become curious and follow up, perhaps changing their perspective in the process.

None of these claims depends on a judgment that general interest intermediaries are unbiased, or always do an excellent job, or deserve a monopoly over the world of communications. The Internet is a boon partly because it breaks that monopoly. So too for the proliferation of television and radio shows, and even channels, that have some specialized identity. (Consider the rise of Fox News, which appeals to a more conservative audience.) All that I am claiming is that general interest intermediaries expose people to a wide range of topics and

views and at the same time provide shared experiences for a heterogeneous public. Indeed, intermediaries of this sort have large advantages over streets and parks precisely because they tend to be national, even international. Typically they expose people to questions and problems in other areas, even other countries.

Specialization and Fragmentation

In a system with public forums and general interest intermediaries, people will frequently come across materials that they would not have chosen in advance — and in a diverse society, this provides something like a common framework for social experience. A fragmented communications market will change things significantly.

20 Consider some simple facts. If you take the ten most highly rated television programs for whites, and then take the ten most highly rated programs for African Americans, you will find little overlap between them. Indeed, more than half of the ten most highly rated programs for African Americans rank among the ten *least* popular programs for whites. With respect to race, similar divisions can be found on the Internet. Not surprisingly, many people tend to choose like-minded sites and like-minded discussion groups. Many of those with committed views on a topic — gun control, abortion, affirmative action — speak mostly with each other. It is exceedingly rare for a site with an identifiable point of view to provide links to sites with opposing views; but it is very common for such a site to provide links to like-minded sites.

With a dramatic increase in options, and a greater power to customize, comes an increase in the range of actual choices. Those choices are likely, in many cases, to mean that people will try to find material that makes them feel comfortable, or that is created by and for people like themselves. This is what the Daily Me is all about. Of course, many people seek out new topics and ideas. And to the extent that people do, the increase in options is hardly bad on balance; it will, among other things, increase variety, the aggregate amount of information, and the entertainment value of actual choices. But there are serious risks as well. If diverse groups are seeing and hearing different points of view, or focusing on different topics, mutual understanding might be difficult, and it might be hard for people to solve problems that society faces together. If millions of people are mostly listening to Rush Limbaugh* and others are listening

to Fox News, problems will arise if millions of other people are mostly or only listening to people and stations with an altogether different point of view.

We can sharpen our understanding of this problem if we attend to the phenomenon of *group polarization*. The idea is that after deliberating with one another, people are likely to move toward a more extreme point in the direction to which they were previously inclined, as indicated by the median of their predeliberation judgments. With respect to the Internet, the implication is that groups of people, especially if they are like-minded, will end up thinking the same thing that they thought before — but in more extreme form.

Consider some examples of this basic phenomenon, which has been found in over a dozen nations.[3] (a) After discussion, citizens of France become more critical of the United States and its intentions with respect to economic aid. (b) After discussion, whites predisposed to show racial prejudice offer more negative responses to questions about whether white racism is responsible for conditions faced by African Americans in American cities. (c) After discussion, whites predisposed not to show racial prejudice offer more positive responses to the same question. (d) A group of moderately profeminist women will become more strongly profeminist after discussion. It follows that, for example, after discussion with one another, those inclined to think that President Clinton was a crook will be quite convinced of this point; that those inclined to favor more aggressive affirmative action programs will become more extreme on the issue if they talk among one another; that those who believe that tax rates are too high will, after talking together, come to think that large, immediate

*Rush Limbaugh (b. 1951) broadcasts conservative political commentary on over 600 radio stations and though a daily updated web site.

tax reductions are an extremely good idea.

The phenomenon of group polarization has conspicuous importance to the current communications market, where groups with distinctive identities increasingly engage in within-group discussion. If the public is balkanized,[†] and if different groups design their own preferred communications packages, the consequence will be further balkanization, as group members move one another toward more extreme points in line with their initial tendencies. At the same time, different deliberating groups, each consisting of like-minded people, will be driven increasingly far apart, simply because most of their discussions are with one another. . . .

25 Group polarization is a human regularity, but social context can decrease, increase, or even eliminate it. For present purposes, the most important point is that group polarization will significantly increase if people think of themselves, antecedently or otherwise, as part of a group having a shared identity and a degree of solidarity. If, for example, a group of people in an Internet discussion group think of themselves as opponents of high taxes, or advocates of animal rights, their discussions are likely to move toward extreme positions. As this happens to many different groups, polarization is both more likely and more extreme. Hence significant movements should be expected for those who listen to a radio show known to be conservative, or a television program dedicated to traditional religious values or to exposing white racism.

This should not be surprising. If ordinary findings of group polarization are a product of limited argument pools and social influences, it stands to reason that when group members think of one an-

other as similar along a salient dimension, or if some external factor (politics, geography, race, sex) unites them, group polarization will be heightened.

Group polarization is occurring every day on the Internet. Indeed, it is clear that the Internet is serving, for many, as a breeding ground for extremism, precisely because like-minded people are deliberating with one another, without hearing contrary views. Hate groups are the most obvious example. Consider one extremist group, the so-called Unorganized Militia, the armed wing of the Patriot movement, "which believes that the federal government is becoming increasingly dictatorial with its regulatory power over taxes, guns and land use." A crucial factor behind the growth of the Unorganized Militia "has been the use of computer networks," allowing members "to make contact quickly and easily with like-minded individuals to trade information, discuss current conspiracy theories, and organize events."[4] The Unorganized Militia has a large number of websites, and those sites frequently offer links to related sites. It is clear that websites are being used to recruit new members and to allow like-minded people to speak with one another and to reinforce or strengthen existing

[†]*Balkanization* **is a term that is used to describe small-scale independence movements that divide countries into several nations. A clear example is Yugoslavia, located in the Balkans, which broke into the conflict-ridden states of Bosnia, Kosovo, Serbia, and Montenegro.**

MILITIA GROUPS

Officials estimate that there are more than 400 militia groups active in the United States. Some are open, with their own Web sites; others are underground. Most are dedicated to the defense of individual liberty from what they perceive as the threat of an oppressive federal government. Some militia groups have been associated with terrorist attacks within the United States. Militia members, many of whom are on the extreme right, tend to see themselves as patriots. The FBI sees them as a threat to national security.

convictions. It is also clear that the Internet is playing a crucial role in permitting people who would otherwise feel isolated and move on to something else to band together and spread rumors, many of them paranoid and hateful. . . .

Of course we cannot say, from the mere fact of polarization, that there has been a movement in the *wrong* direction. Perhaps the more extreme tendency is better; indeed, group polarization is likely to have fueled many movements of great value, including the movement for civil rights, the antislavery movement, the movement for sex equality. All of these movements were extreme in their time, and within-group discussion bred greater extremism; but extremism need not be a word of opprobrium. If greater communications choices produce greater extremism, society may, in many cases, be better off as a result.

But when group discussion tends to lead people to more strongly held versions of the same view with which they began, and if social influences and limited argument pools are responsible, there is legitimate reason for concern. Consider discussions among hate groups on the Internet and elsewhere. If the underlying views are unreasonable, it makes sense to fear that these discussions may fuel increasing hatred and a socially corrosive form of extremism. This does not mean that the discussions can or should be regulated. But it does raise questions about the idea that "more speech" is necessarily an adequate remedy — especially if people are increasingly able to wall themselves off from competing views.

30 The basic issue here is whether something like a "public sphere," with a wide range of voices, might not have significant advantages over a system in which isolated consumer choices produce a highly fragmented speech market. The most reasonable conclusion is that it is extremely important to ensure that people are exposed to views other than those with which they currently agree, that doing so protects against the harmful effects of group polarization on individual thinking and on social cohesion. This does not mean that the government should jail or fine people who refuse to listen to others. Nor is what I have said inconsistent with approval of deliberating "enclaves," on the Internet or elsewhere, designed to ensure that positions that would otherwise be silenced or squelched have a chance to develop. Readers will be able to think of their own preferred illustrations. Consider, perhaps, the views of people with disabilities. The great benefit of such enclaves is that positions may emerge that otherwise would not and that deserve to play a large role in the heterogeneous public. Properly understood, the case of "enclaves," or more simply discussion groups of like-minded people, is that they will improve social deliberation, democratic and otherwise. For these improvements to occur, members must not insulate themselves from competing positions, or at least any such attempts at insulation must not be a prolonged affair.

Consider in this light the ideal of "consumer sovereignty," which underlies much of contemporary enthusiasm for the Internet. Consumer sovereignty means that people can choose to purchase, or to obtain, whatever they want. For many purposes this is a worthy ideal. But the adverse effects of group polarization show that, with respect to communications, consumer sovereignty is likely to produce serious problems for individuals and society at large — and these problems will occur by a kind of iron logic of social interactions. . . .

I hope that I have shown enough to demonstrate that for citizens of a hetero-

SUNSTEIN 389

THE DAILY WE: IS THE INTERNET REALLY A BLESSING FOR DEMOCRACY?

geneous democracy, a fragmented communications market creates considerable dangers. There are dangers for each of us as individuals; constant exposure to one set of views is likely to lead to errors and confusions, or to unthinking conformity (emphasized by John Stuart Mill). And to the extent that the process makes people less able to work cooperatively on shared problems, by turning collections of people into non-communicating confessional groups, there are dangers for society as a whole.

Common Experiences

In a heterogeneous society, it is extremely important for diverse people to have a set of common experiences.[5] Many of our practices reflect a judgment to this effect. National holidays, for example, help constitute a nation, by encouraging citizens to think, all at once, about events of shared importance. And they do much more than this. They enable people, in all their diversity, to have certain memories and attitudes in common. At least this is true in nations where national holidays have a vivid and concrete meaning. In the United States, many national holidays have become mere days-off-from-work, and the precipitating occasion — President's Day, Memorial Day, Labor Day — has come to be nearly invisible. This is a serious loss. With the possible exception of the Fourth of July, Martin Luther King Day is probably the closest thing to a genuinely substantive national holiday, largely because that celebration involves something that can be treated as concrete and meaningful — in other words, it is *about* something.

Communications and the media are, of course, exceptionally important here. Sometimes millions of people follow the presidential election, or the Super Bowl, or the coronation of a new monarch;

many of them do so because of the simultaneous actions of others. The point very much bears on the historic role of both public forums and general interest intermediaries. Public parks are places where diverse people can congregate and see one another. General interest intermediaries, if they are operating properly, give a simultaneous sense of problems and tasks.

35 Why are these shared experiences so desirable? There are three principal reasons:

1. Simple enjoyment is probably the least of it, but it is far from irrelevant. People like many experiences more simply because they are being shared. Consider a popular movie, the Super Bowl, or a presidential debate. For many of us, these are goods that are worth less, and possibly worthless, if many others are not enjoying or purchasing them too. Hence a presidential debate may be worthy of individual attention, for many people, simply because so many other people consider it worthy of individual attention.

2. Sometimes shared experiences ease social interactions, permitting people to speak with one another, and to congregate around a common issue, task, or concern, whether or not they have much in common with one another. In this sense they provide a form of social glue. They help make it possible for diverse people to believe that they live in the same culture. Indeed they help constitute that shared culture, simply by creating common memories and experiences, and a sense of common tasks.

3. A fortunate consequence of shared experiences — many of them

produced by the media — is that people who would otherwise see one another as unfamiliar can come to regard one another as fellow citizens, with shared hopes, goals, and concerns. This is a subjective good for those directly involved. But it can be objectively good as well, especially if it leads to cooperative projects of various kinds. When people learn about a disaster faced by fellow citizens, for example, they may respond with financial and other help. The point applies internationally as well as domestically; massive relief efforts are often made possible by virtue of the fact that millions of people learn, all at once, about the relevant need.

How does this bear on the Internet? An increasingly fragmented communications universe will reduce the level of shared experiences having salience to a diverse group of Americans. This is a simple matter of numbers. When there were three television networks, much of what appeared would have the quality of a genuinely common experience. The lead story on the evening news, for example, would provide a common reference point for many millions of people. To the extent that choices proliferate, it is inevitable that diverse individuals, and diverse groups, will have fewer shared experiences and fewer common reference points. It is possible, for example, that some events that are highly salient to some people will barely register on others' viewscreens. And it is possible that some views and perspectives that seem obvious for many people will, for others, seem barely intelligible.

This is hardly a suggestion that everyone should be required to watch the

same thing. A degree of plurality, with respect to both topics and points of view, is highly desirable. Moreover, talk about "requirements" misses the point. My only claim is that a common set of frameworks and experiences is valuable for a heterogeneous society, and that a system with limitless options, making for diverse choices, could compromise the underlying values.

Changing Filters

My goal here has been to understand what makes for a well-functioning system of free expression, and to show how consumer sovereignty, in a world of limitless options, could undermine that system. The point is that a well-functioning system includes a kind of public sphere, one that fosters common experiences, in which people hear messages that challenge their prior convictions, and in which citizens can present their views to a broad audience. I do not intend to offer a comprehensive set of policy reforms or any kind of blueprint for the future. In fact, this may be one domain in which a problem exists for which there is no useful cure: the genie might simply be out of the bottle. But it will be useful to offer a few ideas, if only by way of introduction to questions that are likely to engage public attention in coming years.

In thinking about reforms, it is important to have a sense of the problems we aim to address, and some possible ways of addressing them. If the discussion thus far is correct, there are three fundamental concerns from the democratic point of view. These include:

(a) the need to promote exposure to materials, topics, and positions that people would not have chosen in advance, or at least enough exposure to produce a degree of understanding and curiosity;

(b) the value of a range of common experiences;

(c) the need for exposure to substantive questions of policy and principle, combined with a range of positions on such questions.

Of course it would be ideal if citizens were demanding, and private information providers were creating, a range of initiatives designed to alleviate the underlying concerns. Perhaps they will; there is some evidence to this effect. New technology can expose people to diverse points of view and creates opportunities for shared experiences. People may, through private choices, take advantage of these possibilities. But, to the extent that they fail to do so, it is worthwhile to consider private and public initiatives designed to pick up the slack.

40 Drawing on recent developments in regulation generally, we can see the potential appeal of five simple alternatives. Of course, different proposals would work better for some communications outlets than others. I will speak here of both private and public responses, but the former should be favored: they are less intrusive, and in general they are likely to be more effective as well.

Disclosure: Producers of communications might disclose important information on their own, about the extent to which they are promoting democratic goals. To the extent that they do not, they might be subject to disclosure requirements (though not to regulation). In the environmental area, this strategy has produced excellent results. The mere fact that polluters have been asked to disclose toxic releases has produced voluntary, low-cost reductions. Apparently fearful of public opprobrium, companies have been spurred to reduce toxic emis-

sions on their own. The same strategy has been used in the context of both movies and television, with ratings systems designed partly to increase parental control over what children see. On the Internet, many sites disclose that their site is inappropriate for children. . . .

Self-Regulation: Producers of communications might engage in *voluntary self-regulation.* Some of the difficulties in the current speech market stem from relentless competition for viewers and listeners, competition that leads to a situation that many broadcast journalists abhor about their profession, and from which society does not benefit. The competition might be reduced via a "code" of appropriate conduct, agreed upon by various companies, and encouraged but not imposed by government. In fact, the National Association of Broadcasters maintained such a code for several decades, and there is growing interest in voluntary self-regulation for both television and the Internet. The case for this approach is that it avoids government regulation while at the same time reducing some of the harmful effects of market pressures. Any such code could, for example, call for an opportunity for opposing views to speak, or for avoiding unnecessary sensationalism, or for offering arguments rather than quick soundbites whenever feasible. On television, as distinct from the Internet, the idea seems quite feasible. But perhaps Internet sites could also enter into informal, voluntary arrangements, agreeing to create links, an idea to which I will shortly turn.

Subsidy: The government might *subsidize speech,* as, for example, through publicly subsidized programming or publicly subsidized websites. This is, of course, the idea that motivates the Public Broadcasting System. But it is reasonable to ask whether the PBS model is not outmoded. Other approaches, similarly designed to promote educational, cultural, and democratic goals, might well be ventured. Perhaps government could subsidize a "Public.net" designed to promote debate on public issues among diverse citizens — and to create a right of access to speakers of various sorts.[6]

Links: Websites might use links and hyperlinks to ensure that viewers learn about sites containing opposing views. A liberal magazine's website might, for example, provide a link to a conservative magazine's website, and the conservative magazine might do the same. The idea would be to decrease the likelihood that people will simply hear echoes of their own voices. Of course many people would not click on the icons of sites whose views seem objectionable; but some people would, and in that sense the system would not operate so differently from general interest intermediaries and public forums. Here, too, the ideal situation would be voluntary action. But if this proves impossible, it is worth considering both subsidies and regulatory alternatives.

45 *Public Sidewalk:* If the problem consists in the failure to attend to public issues, the most popular websites in any given period might offer links and hyperlinks, designed to ensure more exposure to substantive questions. Under such a system, viewers of especially popular sites would see an icon for sites that deal with substantive issues in a serious way. It is well established that whenever there is a link to a particular webpage from a major site, such as MSNBC, the traffic is huge. Nothing here imposes any requirements on viewers. People would not be required to click on links and hyperlinks. But it is reasonable to expect that many viewers would do so, if only to satisfy their curiosity. The result would be to create a kind of Internet "sidewalk" that promotes some of the purposes of the public forum doctrine. Ideally, those who create websites might move in this direction on their own. To those who believe that this step would do no good, it is worth recalling that advertisers are willing to spend a great deal of money to obtain brief access to people's eyeballs. This strategy might be used to create something like a public sphere as well.

These are brief thoughts on some complex subjects. My goal has not been to evaluate any proposal in detail, but to give a flavor of some possibilities for those concerned to promote democratic goals in a dramatically changed media environment.[7] The basic question is whether it might be possible to create spaces that have some of the functions of public forums and general interest intermediaries in the age of the Internet. It seems clear that government's power to regulate effectively is diminished as the number of options expands. I am not sure that any response would be worthwhile, all things considered. But I am sure that if new technologies diminish the number of common spaces, and re-

duce, for many, the number of unanticipated, unchosen exposures, something
important will have been lost. The most
important point is to have a sense of
what a well-functioning democratic order
requires.

Beyond Anticensorship
My principal claim here has been that a
well-functioning democracy depends on
far more than restraints on official censorship of controversial ideas and opinions. It also depends on some kind of
public sphere, in which a wide range of
speakers have access to a diverse public
— and also to particular institutions, and
practices, against which they seek to
launch objections.

Emerging technologies, including the
Internet, are hardly an enemy here. They
hold out far more promise than risk, especially because they allow people to
widen their horizons. But to the extent
that they weaken the power of general interest intermediaries and increase people's ability to wall themselves off from
topics and opinions that they would prefer to avoid, they create serious dangers.
And if we believe that a system of free
expression calls for unrestricted choices
by individual consumers, we will not even
understand the dangers as such. Whether
such dangers will materialize will ultimately depend on the aspirations, for
freedom and democracy alike, by whose
light we evaluate our practices. What I

have sought to establish here is that in a
free republic, citizens aspire to a system
that provides a wide range of experiences
— with people, topics, and ideas — that
would not have been selected in advance.

1. *Hague v. CIO,* 307 US 496 (1939).
2. I draw here on the excellent treat-
   ment in Noah D. Zatz, "Sidewalks
   in Cyberspace: Making Space for
   Public Forums in the Electronic
   Environment," *Harvard Journal of
   Law and Technology* 12 (1998):
   149.
3. For a general discussion, see Cass
   R. Sunstein, "Deliberative Trouble?
   Why Groups Go To Extremes," *Yale
   Law Journal* (2000).
4. See Matthew Zook, "The
   Unorganized Militia Network:
   Conspiracies, Computers, and
   Community," *Berkeley Planning
   Journal* 11 (1996), available at
   http://socrates.berkeley.edu/zook/
   pubs/Militia_paper.html.
5. I draw here on Cass R. Sunstein
   and Edna Ullmann-Margalit,
   "Solidarity Goods," *Journal of
   Political Philosophy* (forthcoming in
   2001).
6. See Andrew Shapiro, *The Control
   Revolution* (New York: Basic Books,
   1999).
7. See Sunstein, *Republic.com,* for
   more detail.

Questions for Discussion

1. Early in his essay, Sunstein raises a warning about what he calls the "personalization" of the Internet. What does he mean by that term? Why is that idea of personalizing the Internet important to his main argument? Is his concern valid, in your view? Why or why not? To what extent do you think you "personalize" the Internet? **2.** Notice that Sunstein opens his essay with a summary of the benefits of the Internet. How does this opening contribute to his main argument? What advantages and disadvantages do you see to this approach to opening his essay? **3.** In paragraphs 24–29, Sunstein discussed the dangers of "group polarization." What does Sunstein mean by this term? In what ways is it important to his main argument? Have you experienced a situation in which group discussion led to reinforcement — or change — of a belief you already had? How might that experience influence your reaction to Sunstein's argument? **4.** Sunstein offers five possible solutions to the problems he sees with current trends in media. How effective do you think these measures would be in addressing Sunstein's concerns? What does he achieve by presenting these measures as possibilities rather than certainties? **5.** Although Sunstein describes this argument as "brief

NEGOTIATING DIFFERENCES

The writers in this cluster have shown that the term *common ground* can be defined in different ways. An open piece of land can provide common ground, as in a park. (In fact, one of the oldest parks in the United States is an urban park called Boston Common, which was once a true common — a public area where residents of 17th century Boston could graze their livestock.) But as David Bollier shows, common ground can also include public resources such as airwaves, minerals, and water. And Cass Sunstein demonstrates that the Internet provides a kind of virtual common ground.

Keeping in mind that complexity of the idea of "common ground," imagine that administrators at your college or university have decided that your school needs a new gymnasium. They believe that the lack of good athletic facilities is a big reason why many prospective students choose to attend other schools. However, your school has little room to expand. For a variety of reasons, it would be prohibitively expensive for the school simply to buy adjacent land for a new gym.

Accordingly, the administration is considering two possibilities: Demolish the old gym (or

thoughts on some complex subjects," it nevertheless runs for many pages. Why is this argument so long? What strategies does Sunstein use to help readers make their way through it? Do you find those strategies effective? Explain. **6.** At the end of his argument, Sunstein writes, "My principal claim here has been that a well-functioning democracy depends on far more than restraints on official censorship of controversial ideas and opinions. It also depends on some kind of public sphere, in which a wide range of speakers have access to a diverse public — and also to particular institutions, and practices, against which they seek to launch objectives." To what extent does the argument as a whole depend on readers accepting this principle as a premise? **7.** Sunstein's essay might be described as an argument based on inductive reasoning. (See pages 25–26 for a discussion of arguments based on inductive reasoning.) How effective do you think his essay is as such an argument? Does he offer sufficient evidence to lead us to his conclusions about the Internet as a public sphere in a democracy? Explain, citing specific passages from his essay in your answer.

another old building on campus) and build a medium-sized gym on its site, or build a large, state-of-the art gym on the remaining open space on campus, a common ground where students like to read and relax in fair weather. Obviously, either option would generate protests.

Wishing to resolve this situation in a way that best addresses the interests of your campus community, the administration has solicited opinions from students and others on campus. You have decided to submit a proposal for what you believe should be done in this situation. In your proposal, make a case for your point of view about which option would be best for the school. Be sure to address the issue of what you see as the value of common space on campus (if any), drawing on the essays in this section to help support your argument.

Alternatively, if your campus has had a similar situation, you may choose to write an essay addressing that specific situation rather than the hypothetical situation we have described here.

HOW DO WE

DESIGN COMMUNITIES?

Visitors to Washington, D.C., sometimes complain about how difficult it can be to drive in that city. The streets seem to be laid out in a confusing pattern, with several main thoroughfares cutting across otherwise parallel streets at odd angles. It might surprise those visitors to learn that Washington, D.C. was originally designed from scratch by French architect Pierre L'Enfant, who was commissioned by President Washington in 1791. If you look at a street map of the city, you can make out the main features of that original design. For instance, those angled thoroughfares radiate from the central location of the Capitol Building; the famous Mall in front of the Capitol reflects L'Enfant's vision for a wide, central avenue. L'Enfant's original design was changed in several ways even as the city was being built, and in the years since it was constructed, the city, like many American cities, has grown dramatically. The confusing street patterns partially reflect the lack of planning and regulation as the city has grown; other oddities have occurred as builders and city leaders have tried to accommodate to the original design. For example, some buildings, such as the FBI Building and the East Building of the National Gallery of Art, are not square or rectangular but have unusual angles (such as a trapezoid) to fit into the odd-shaped city blocks created by those radiating thoroughfares. If you live in a city or town that has experienced recent growth, you might have seen the same phenomenon. ■ The growth of cities and towns tends to be seen as a good thing. But as the example of Washington, D.C., indicates, growth can create problems too. As cities and towns expand, new residents and businesses require more services, which lead to even more growth. There is an increasing need for more energy and more space. Not surprisingly, such growth often occurs at the edges of cities, where farmland and rural communities once existed. Despite the economic benefits, residents sometimes resist growth because it inevitably changes the quality of life in their communities. Famous architect Frank Lloyd Wright, whose building designs reflected his belief that our structures should be part of the natural environment where they are located, once scolded the people of Miami about the unnatural way in which their city developed (see *Con-Text* on page 397). Wright's argument was really a call to create livable communities that foster a certain kind of quality of life. But "quality of life" might not be the same for all people, and that is where conflicts can arise. Ultimately, growth raises questions about the kinds of communities we want. And how do we determine what kinds of communities we should have? ■ In a sense, all the essays in this section address that question. Ostensibly, these essays are about the problems associated with the growth of our communities. A few of the writers discuss "sprawl," which is the rapid and seemingly unchecked growth of cities and towns into surrounding rural areas. Others describe the "smart growth" movement that emerged in the 1990s, partly as a reaction to sprawl. In making their arguments, these writers offer their respective visions for the kinds of communities we should have. Their essays remind us that when we argue about practical problems such as sprawl, we are really addressing deeper — and often more difficult — questions about how we should live together.

CON-TEXT: "A Beautiful Place Made Ugly"

1 We were coming in on the plane looking over this great, marvelous and very beautiful plateau and what do we see? Little tiny subdivisions of squares, little pigeonholes, little lots, everything divided up into little lots, little boxes on little lots, little tacky things.

And you come downtown and what's happening? Plenty of skyscrapers. You call them hotels. You can't tell whether they're hotels or office buildings or something in a cemetery. They have no feelings, no richness, no sense of this region.

And that, I think is happening to the country. It's not alone your misfortune. . . .

You want to live in a way becoming to human beings with your spirit and a devotion to the beautiful, don't you? Well, why don't you? Why would you accept this sort of thing? Why would you let them put it over on you? You say because of economic reasons.

Well, if that's what this country talks about as the highest standard of living in the world, then I think it isn't at all the highest,

it's only biggest — and quite ignorant.

Nature must be ashamed of these hotels that you're building down here. Nature must be ashamed of the way this place has been laid out and patterned after a checkerboard and parceled out in little parcels where you stand on each other's toes, face the sidewalk, your elbows in the next neighbor's ribs. . . .

SOURCE: Frank Lloyd Wright, public address, Miami, Florida (1955).

① **DAVID PLOTZ, "A Suburb Grown Up and All Paved Over"**

The tension between individual rights and the interests of the state is an old one in American society. And it often emerges in the form of controversies about the rights of property owners to determine how to use their land. In the following essay, journalist Dave Plotz describes one such controversy: a law prohibiting homeowners in Fairfax County, Virginia, one of the wealthiest counties in the country, from paving their yards. At first glance, the purpose of the law, reasonably enough, seems to be to protect property values and preserve the character of a community. But Plotz argues that much more is involved. He traces the origins of the law to concerns about growth, development, and especially immigration — longstanding issues that have often caused conflict among Americans. In his essay, which was published in the *New York Times* in 2002, Plotz raises questions about the social effects of economic development. He also prompts us to consider what kinds of communities we wish to have. Plotz is the Washington bureau chief of Slate.com, an online public affairs magazine.

A Suburb Grown Up and All Paved Over
DAVID PLOTZ

1 The first commandment of the suburbs used to be Not in My Back Yard. Apparently now it is Not in Your Front Yard — at least here in Fairfax County, Va., just over the Potomac from Washington.

Earlier this month the county council passed a law forbidding homeowners from paving over their front yards to create extra parking spaces. This legislation is directed not at the mansion-owners of Reston, who have ample room for their fleets of Beemers, but at the immigrants sardined into houses in the county's less tony neighborhoods, like Groveton. There has apparently been a rash of yard-paving: the owners of these houses have asphalted the lawn so they have a place to put the three, four or six cars that their sisters and husbands and cousins need to get to work.

Fairfax isn't the only jurisdiction that is fighting yard-paving; Boston and San Francisco are, too. But there is something absurd in the idea of Fairfax trying to limit car ownership. Like most suburbs, Fairfax County owes not just its existence but its prosperity to the automobile. Its major landmarks are intersections (Bailey's Crossroads, Tysons Corner, Seven Corners and so on). And there's something equally silly in the notion that stopping pave-overs somehow preserves Fairfax's natural beauty — as if any remained. One councilwoman said she supported the bill because pave-overs had "nibbled away" at Fairfax's green space.

Nibbled is right: When you add up the malls and highways and condos and office parks and malls and malls, what's left is enough greenery for a side salad. Every neighborhood in Fairfax is named after the nature that was destroyed to build it: Rose Hill, Blueberry Farm, Sycamore Lakes — every place but Money's Corner.

5 The paving regulation stems partly, of course, from the usual paranoia about property values. Grass sells better than asphalt. But the regulation may succeed only in moving cars from the front lawn to the front curb. As soon as the pave-over law passed, at least one resident griped that it would encourage people to park on the street. No doubt the council will be weighing street parking bans next.

The true cause of the pave-over law, however, is not parking. It's Fairfax's midlife crisis. Fairfax County, which strutted and preened through the 1990's, is having some bad years. America Online, which was born and raised here, married Time Warner and moved its headquarters to New York City. Michael Saylor, Fairfax County's very own Internet billionaire, has become a pariah, his crippled company, Microstrategy, a symbol of all that was wrong with the tech bubble. The richest county in America according to the 1990 census, Fairfax discovered a few weeks ago that it has now dropped to No. 2.

Yet the roots of the crisis here go even deeper. Since the 1970's, Fairfax

has morphed from a bucolic exurb into its own metropolis, a hotbed of industry and commerce. The typical lazy comforts of the distant suburb have vanished; the

U.S. POVERTY RATE

The U.S. Bureau of Labor Statistics determines the U.S. poverty rate, or the percentage of poor people in the United States, by calculating the number of households below the poverty line. That line varies according to the number of people in a household. In 2002 a family of four fell below the poverty line if its total income was less than $18,104. A single person was considered poor if he or she earned less than $9,044 a year. In 2001 only 4.6 percent of the residents met these criteria in Fairfax County, Virginia; by contrast, the U.S. national poverty rate in 2001 was 11.7 percent.

COMPLICATION

Gerald Gordon, president of the Fairfax County Economic Development Authority, responded to Plotz's essay by pointing out that 11,500 jobs were created in Fairfax County in 2001. He also noted that "the county has more than 30,000 acres of dedicated parkland, including a national wildlife refuge established to protect bald eagles and one of the largest urban marshes on the east coast." (See an excerpt from his letter in Chapter 2, page 24.)

danger and disorder of the city always seem to be encroaching. The county's population will top a million any day now — nearly twice that of Washington itself.

Growth is not new to the county, but immigrants are. The number of immigrants in Fairfax jumped 86 percent in the 90's, to nearly a quarter of the population. (Essentially all the population growth came from immigrants and their children.) A third of county residents now speak a language other than English at home, more than twice the national average.

Fairfax is the very model of the benefits of immigration. Southeast Asians, Indians, Arabs, Pakistanis, West Africans, East Africans and Latin Americans have all settled here in huge numbers, but the county remains wonderfully mixed up. It lacks ethnic enclaves. Immigration has accomplished the impossible in Fairfax: it has made the county interesting, with the area's best and oddest ethnic restaurants and stores.

10 Fairfax's high-tech industry has relied heavily on highly educated foreign workers. At the same time, though without the same eagerness, Fairfax has accepted tens of thousands of low-skill immigrants. They are the backbone of the county's service sector. Working-class immigrants move to Fairfax because that is where the jobs are. They pack houses because rents and home prices are so high they can't afford to live in less cramped conditions. They buy cars because that's the only way they can get to the jobs that everyone wants them to do. And so they pave driveways.

Poverty rates have climbed with the arrival of these immigrants, and middle-class neighbors feel squeezed. The pave-over bill is only the most recent manifestation of their worry. Last year a state senator from Fairfax introduced a bill to the Virginia Legislature that would forbid Virginians from sleeping in living rooms, dining rooms, kitchens and closets. The measure was withdrawn immediately after loud complaints from civil libertarians and immigrant groups.

Fairfax is growing up faster than its residents can adjust. Like many sprawled suburbs, it has consumed its youthful vim and isn't quite sure what to do now. In the space of a generation, Fairfax lost its rural character and its middle-class white identity. In exchange it has won jobs, businesses and bustling, hustling immigrants.

The pave-over battle is a small rearguard action to preserve some vision of a Fairfax past, and in a way it's oddly encouraging. It signals the success of the American melting pot: Fairfax County has undergone great change, causing enormous upheaval, and all anyone can find to fight about is parking.

Questions for Discussion

1. To what extent is social class relevant to the conflicts that Plotz describes in Fairfax County, Virginia? In your experience, does social class determine what people expect from government regulations about housing and zoning? Should government set different standards for different neighborhoods based on the value of property? **2.** On what grounds does Plotz criticize the Fairfax County law that prevents homeowners from paving their lawns? Do you think most people would agree with him? Do you? Why or why not? **3.** Plotz writes that Fairfax Country "lacks ethnic enclaves" and that races within the county are "wonderfully mixed up." What do these statements reveal about his values? Do you think residents of Fairfax County are likely to agree that the lack of ethnic enclaves is a benefit? Explain. **4.** How would you describe the tone of Plotz's essay? In what ways do you think his tone affects his main argument? Given his broad audience (this essay was published in the *New York Times,* a widely circulated newspaper), do you think his tone is appropriate. Explain, citing specific words and phrases from his essay in your answer. **5.** Is Fairfax County a special case? Or is rapid growth causing conflicts in a county in your own state? What do your answers to these questions indicate about the validity of Plotz's argument? What indication can you find in the essay that Plotz sees Fairfax County as one example of a larger problem?

② VIRGINIA POSTREL, "Misplacing the Blame for Our Troubles on 'Flat, Not Tall' Spaces"

In 1999 Vice President Al Gore announced a federal "smart growth" initiative. It was intended to help cities and towns combat the effects of unchecked development and to manage their growth to create more livable communities. Gore's smart growth initiative reflected a belief in the possibility of sustaining economic growth while maintaining healthy communities and protecting the environment. Writer Virginia Postrel calls this possibility a myth. Contemporary life, she suggests in the following essay, requires tradeoffs; our lifestyle choices will have both positive and negative consequences, she says. Postrel is making what seems to be a common-sensical argument, one that might match your own experience. But Postrel's argument addresses a much larger matter: What kinds of communities do we really wish to live in? Proponents of smart growth, she suggests, embrace a vision of community that differs from the lifestyle that many suburbanites consciously seek. She suggests that "smart-growthers" wish to impose their vision on others. Although Postrel's starting point for her argument is a 1999 speech by former Vice President Al Gore, a champion of smart growth, the issues that she addresses remain timely and intensely debated today. In late 2002, for example, the New Jersey state legislature was debating a proposed law that would severely restrict suburban sprawl by implementing measures that are based on the idea of smart growth. Whether or not you agree with such measures — or with Postrel — might depend upon your own vision of the ideal community. Postrel is the author of *The Future and Its Enemies* (Free Press, 1998) and a columnist whose essays about business and culture have appeared in the *New York Times, Forbes,* and *D Magazine.* This essay was published in the *Los Angeles Times* in 1999.

Misplacing the Blame for Our Troubles on 'Flat, Not Tall' Spaces
VIRGINIA POSTREL

1 If Al Gore denounced soccer moms, told us everything was better in the good old days and demanded that we let his friends redesign our lives to fit their morality, you might think he'd gone over to the religious right. You'd be wrong, however.

Welcome to the war on sprawl, otherwise known as the suburbs.

Gore describes the problem this way: "Acre upon acre of asphalt have transformed what were once mountain clearings and congenial villages into little more than massive parking lots. The ill-thought-out sprawl hastily developed around our nation's cities has turned what used to be friendly, easy suburbs into lonely cul-de-sacs, so distant from the city center that if a family wants to buy an affordable house they have to drive so far that a parent gets home too late to read a bedtime story."

This tale raises many questions: How did those houses in "easy suburbs" catapult themselves to become "lonely cul-de-sacs" reachable only by hours on the road? Why did that transformation make housing more expensive? How early do those kids go to bed?

5 Gore is clearer on one thing. The problem is that "we've built flat, not tall," putting houses and offices on inexpensive outlying land instead of packing them tighter and tighter in crowded, expensive cities. "Flat, not tall" is the definition of "sprawl." The anti-sprawl critique is that houses with yards and businesses with ample parking are ruining the country.

If you listen only to Gore's speeches, you'd think that the anti-sprawl crusade is about magically making all the nasty trade-offs in life go away. Abandon "ill-planned and ill-coordinated development," and houses will be cheap everywhere. No one will ever sit in traffic. We will all enjoy "livability."

It's a myth, of course. But attacking "sprawl" is a way of blaming an impersonal force for the trade-offs individuals have made in their lives, notably the decisions to work long hours and buy elbow room. The anti-sprawl campaign simultaneously indulges baby boomers' guilt and excuses their life choices, treating them as victims rather than actors. It tells voters that they're bad parents who are destroying the Earth, but then says that it's not their fault.

Harried commuters just want fewer traffic jams. But anti-sprawl technocrats

have something more grandiose in mind. They want everyone to live the way I do: in an urban townhouse off a busy street, with no yard but plenty of shops and restaurants within walking distance. Their "smart growth" planning means confining family life to crowded cities so that the countryside can be left open for wildlife, recreation and a few farmers. They crave "density," which they believe is more efficient and more interesting.

Thus a study highlighted on the Sierra Club's Web site celebrates multi-unit housing: "Sharing walls shares and saves heat. . . . The

CONTEXT

According to the U.S. Census Bureau, as of 2000 the average population density in the United States was about eighty persons per square mile, and the average housing density was about thirty-three units per square mile. The metropolitan area with the highest housing density was Passaic, New Jersey, at 5154 units per square mile; San Francisco, which Postrell mentions, had a housing density of 701 units per square mile. Among the lowest housing densities were Flagstaff, Arizona (2.5 units per square mile), and Casper, Wyoming (5.6 units per square mile).

single-family houses consume four times as much land for streets and roads and 10 times as much for the houses themselves. The single-family houses use nearly six times as much metal and concrete, the mining of which threatens many of our natural areas."

10 The ideal is San Francisco's densities of 50 to 100 units per acre. Crowding is good. Density means more traffic — more cars in a smaller space, plus no new road construction. Given enough pain, anti-sprawlers hope to get people out of their cars. They favor inflexible rail systems and other mass transit. "As traffic congestion builds, alternative travel modes will become more attractive" is how Minnesota's Twin Cities Metropolitan Council justified a decision not to build any more roads for the next 20 years.

"Smart-growthers" have no sympathy for suburban family life, which they find wasteful and sterile. And they have no patience for the way contemporary cities have evolved to spread out jobs and houses, to build "flat not tall" in response to the desire for privacy and personal space. They disapprove not merely of the congestion generated when people flock to a new area, but of the reduction in congestion in the city created at the same time.

The anti-sprawl campaign seeks to impose a static, uniform future through nostalgic appeals to an idealized past. It does indeed have much in common with the least tolerant elements of the religious right. It is just less honest.

Questions for Discussion

1. Postrel first published this argument in 1999, when Al Gore was Vice President of the United States and campaigning for the Democratic nomination for the presidency. How would that context explain why she chose to tie her defense of "sprawl" to a critique of Gore? How do you think that writing decision affects her argument today? **2.** Postrel writes, "Harried commuters just want fewer traffic jams." What evidence does Postrel offer for this statement? Do you think she needs to support this statement in any way? Explain. What purpose do you think this statement serves in Postrel's main argument? **3.** What is the purpose of paragraph 9? How does citing the Sierra Club help Postrel's case? What does it suggest to you about Postrel's values? How did you respond to this paragraph? What might your response to it reveal about your own values? **4.** Postrel suggests that the Twin Cities Metropolitan Council's decision not to build new roads for the next twenty years reflects the inflexibility of smart-growth proponents when it comes to problems such as traffic congestion. You can read an introduction to the study commissioned by the Council at www.me3.org/sprawl/bckgrnd.pdf. Review that introduction and assess how Postrel represents the position of the council. Is her representation fair? Explain, citing passages from the study in your answer. **5.** The opening and concluding paragraphs of this argument link opponents of urban sprawl to the religious right. What do you think Postrel means by "the religious right?" What could it have in common with opponents of urban sprawl? In what ways might Postrel's strategy of linking "smart-growthers" and the religious right strengthen or weaken her argument?

③ DONELLA MEADOWS, "So What Can We Do —
Really Do — About Sprawl?"

Debates about sprawl — a term that refers to the spread of housing developments, strip malls, and office buildings into rural areas — often focus on concerns about quality of life and environmental damage. But Donella Meadows demonstrates that sprawl is also a public policy issue. She is clearly an opponent of unchecked development, but she refuses simply to criticize developers. "We can't blame those who make the money," she writes. "They're playing the game according to the rules." For Meadows combating sprawl means understanding — and changing — those rules, which include tax laws and zoning ordinances. Meadows refuses to reduce the problem of sprawl to a pro-versus-con debate. All of us, she suggests, benefit from municipal services and economic development, no matter how fervently we might support environmental protection. So we cannot simply say that we are for or against development. Her argument encourages us to think about protecting the environment and enhancing our quality of life in terms of such mundane (and perhaps dull) matters as taxes and zoning. In doing so, we might also think about our own responsibilities — as consumers and as citizens of a town or city — for the problems caused by sprawl. In this sense her essay is an effort to address a complex problem by understanding it rather than by opposing those who might disagree with her. Donella Meadows, who died in 2001, was the director of the Sustainability Institute and an adjunct professor of environmental studies at Dartmouth College. Author or co-author of nine books, including the best-selling *Limits to Growth* (1972), she was an internationally known voice for an environmentally conscious lifestyle. This essay appeared in her weekly "Global Citizen" column in 1999.

So What Can We Do — Really Do — About Sprawl
DONELLA MEADOWS

1 In my mind St. Louis is the poster city for sprawl (see photo on page 407). It has a glittering, high-rise center where fashionable people work, shop and party. Surrounding the center are blocks and blocks of empty lots, abandoned buildings, dying stores, a sad wasteland through which the fashionable people speed on wide highways to the suburbs. In the suburbs the subdivisions and shopping centers expand rapidly outward onto the world's best farmland.

When I imagine the opposite of sprawl, I think of Oslo, Norway (see photo on page 408). Oslo rises halfway up the hills at the end of a fjord and then abruptly stops. What stops it is a huge public park, in which no private entity is allowed to build anything. The park is full of trails, lakes, playgrounds, picnic tables, and scattered huts where you can stop for a hot drink in winter or cold drink in summer. Tram lines radiate from the city to the park edges, so you can ride to the end of a line, ski or hike in a loop to the end of another line and ride home.

That is a no-nonsense urban growth boundary. It forces development inward. There are no derelict blocks in Oslo. Space no longer useful for one purpose is snapped up for another. Urban renewal goes on constantly everywhere. There are few cars, because there's hardly any place to park and anyway most streets in the shopping district are pedestrian zones. Trams are cheap and frequent and go everywhere. The city is quiet, clean, friendly, attractive and economically thriving.

How could we make our cities more like Oslo and less like land-gulping, energy-intensive, half-empty St. Louis? There is a long list of things we could do. Eben Fodor, in his new book "Better Not Bigger" (the most useful piece of writing on sprawl control I've seen) organizes them under two categories: taking the foot off the accelerator and applying the brake.

5 The accelerator part comes from widespread public subsidies to sprawl. Fodor lists ten of them, which include:

- Free or subsidized roads, sewer systems, water systems, schools, etc. (Instead charge development impact fees high enough to be sure the taxes of present residents don't

go up to provide public services for new residents.)
- Tax breaks, grants, free consulting services, and other handouts to attract new businesses. (There's al-

BETTER NOT BIGGER

"Our cities and towns keep growing and growing. 'To what end?' you might ask. Are big cities so much better than small cities that we should strive to convert every small city into a bigger one? It seems clear from looking at many of the world's largest cities that we have little reason to envy them. Maybe there is some ideal size where all the best qualities of a community come together to reach an optimal state of urban harmony? If there is such a size, would we know when we've reached it? Would we be less able to stop growing once we were there? The reality is that we just grow and grow, regardless of our community's size or whether further growth is good or bad for us. Endless growth is the only plan on the table." Source: Eben Fodor, *Better Not Bigger* (1999).

most never a good reason for the public to subsidize a private business, especially not in a way that allows it to undercut existing businesses.)

■ Waiving environmental or land-use regulations. (Make the standards strong enough to protect everyone's air, water, views and safety and enforce those standards firmly and evenly.)

■ Federally funded road projects. (The Feds pay the money, but the community puts up with the sprawl. And where do you think the Feds get the money?)

Urban growth accelerators make current residents pay (in higher taxes, lower services, more noise and pollution and traffic jams) for new development. There is no legal or moral reason why they should do that. Easing up on the accelerator should at least guarantee that growth pays its own way.

Applying the brake means setting absolute limits. There are some illegal reasons for wanting to do this: to protect special privilege, to keep out particular kinds of persons; to take private property for public purpose without fair compensation. There are also legal reasons: to protect watersheds or aquifers or farmland or open space, to force growth into places where public services can be efficiently delivered, to slow growth to a rate at which the community can absorb it, to stop growth before land, water, or other resources fail.

Fodor tells the stories of several communities that have limited their growth and lists many techniques they have used to do so. They include:

■ Growth boundaries and green belts like the one around Oslo.
■ Agricultural zoning. Given the world food situation, not another square inch of prime soil should be built upon anywhere.
■ Infrastructure spending restrictions. Why should a Wal-Mart that sucks in traffic force the public to widen the road? Let Wal-Mart do it, or let the narrow road limit the traffic.
■ Downzoning. Usually met with screams of protest from people whose land values are reduced, though we never hear objections when upzoning increases land values.
■ Comprehensive public review of all aspects of a new development, such as required by Vermont's Act 250.
■ Public purchase of development rights.
■ Growth moratoria, growth rate limits, or absolute caps on municipal size, set by real resource limitations.

Boulder, Colorado, may be the American town that has most applied growth controls, prompted by a sober look at the "build-out" implications of the city's zoning plan. Boulder voters approved a local sales tax used to acquire greenways around the city. A building height limitation protects mountain views. Building permits are limited in number, many can be used only in the city center, and 75 percent of new housing permits must be allocated to affordable housing. Commercial and industrial land was downzoned with the realization that if jobs grow faster than housing, commuters from other towns will overload roads and parking facilities.

10 All that and more is possible in any city. But controlling growth means more than fiddling at the margins, "accommodating" growth, "managing" growth. It means questioning myths about growth, realizing that growth can bring more costs than benefits. That kind of growth makes us poorer, not richer. It shouldn't be celebrated or welcomed or subsidized or managed or accommodated; it should be stopped.

We have planning boards. We have zoning regulations. We have urban growth boundaries and "smart growth" and sprawl conferences. And we still have sprawl. Between 1970 and 1990 the population of Chicago grew by four percent; its developed land area grew by 46 percent. Over the same period Los Angeles swelled 45 percent in population, 300 percent in settled area.

Sprawl costs us more than lost farmland and daily commutes through landscapes of stunning ugliness. It costs us dollars, bucks straight out of our pockets, in the form of higher local taxes. That's because our pattern of municipal growth, especially land-intensive city-edge growth, consistently costs more in public services than it pays in taxes.

In his new book "Better Not Bigger," Eben Fodor cites study after study showing how growth raises taxes. In Loudon County, Virginia, each new house on a quarter-acre lot adds $705 per year to a town budget (in increased garbage collection, road maintenance, etc. minus increased property tax). On a five-acre lot

a new house costs the community $2232 per year. In Redmond, Washington, single-family houses pay 21 percent of property tax but account for 29 percent of the city budget. A study in California's Central Valley calculated that more compact development could save municipalities 500,000 acres of farmland and $1.2 billion in taxes.

There are dozens of these studies. They all come to the same conclusion. New subdivisions reach into the pockets of established residents to finance additional schools and services. Commercial and industrial developments sometimes pay more in taxes than they demand in services, but the traffic and pollution they generate reduces nearby property value. New employees don't want to live near the plant or strip, so they build houses and raise taxes in the NEXT town. Large, well-organized companies such as sports teams and Wal-Mart, push city governments to widen roads, provide free water or sewage lines, offer property tax breaks, even build the stadium.

15 Given all the evidence to the contrary, it's amazing how many of us still believe the myth that growth reduces taxes. But then, every myth springs from a seed of truth. Municipal growth does benefit some people. Real estate agents get sales, construction companies get jobs, banks get more depositors and borrowers, newspapers get higher circulations, stores get more business (though they also get more and tougher competition). Landowners who sell to developers can make big money; developers can make even bigger money.

COMPLICATION

Boulder, Colorado, is sometimes listed among America's most desirable cities, but it has also developed a reputation for being an expensive place to live. A 1998 study of the cost of living in Colorado found that Boulder County had an above-average cost-of-living index, which measures the cost of household expenditures for various common items. It ranked seventeenth among Colorado's fifty-six counties in overall cost-of-living. However, housing costs in Boulder County did not have as large an influence on cost of living as the sixteen counties with higher cost-of-living indexes.

PYRAMID SCHEMES

A pyramid scheme is a fraudulent way of making money through which someone creates the illusion of a profitable business by attracting new investment through false claims. Any "profits" are the result of new investment, not because the company is succeeding in producing or selling anything. New investment eventually dries up, and the pyramid collapses. To use a simple analogy, you might use a chain letter to convince five people to give you $1.00 each, promising that they will each receive $5.00 back once they recruit five more investors at a $1.00 apiece as the chain letter continues. Sooner or later, people stop writing back. For more information, visit http://skepdic.com/pyramid.html.

Those folks are every town's growth promoters. Eben Fodor calls them the "urban growth machine" and cites an example of how the machine is fueled. Imagine a proposed development that will cost a community $1,000,000 and bring in $500,000 in benefits. The $500,000 goes to ten people, $50,000 apiece. The $1,000,000 is charged to 100,000 people as a $10 tax increase. Who is going to focus full attention on this project, be at all the hearings, bring in lawyers, chat up city officials? Who is going to believe sincerely and claim loudly that growth is a good thing?

Fodor quotes Oregon environmentalist Andy Kerr, who calls urban growth, "a pyramid scheme in which a relatively few make a killing, some others make a living, but most [of us] pay for it." As long as there is a killing to be made, no tepid "smart-growth" measures are going to stop sprawl. We will go on having strips and malls and cookie-cutter subdivisions and traffic jams and rising taxes as long as someone makes money from them.

We can't blame those who make the money. They're playing the game according to the rules, which are set mainly by the market, which rewards whomever is clever enough to put any cost of doing business onto someone else. They get the store profits, we build the roads. They hire the workers (paying as little as they can get away with, because the market requires them to cut costs), we sit in traffic jams and breathe the exhaust. They get jobs building the subdivision, we lose open lands, clean water, and wildlife. Then we subsidize them with our taxes. That, the tax subsidy, is not the market, it's local politics. Collectively we set out pots of subsidized honey at which they dip. We can't expect them not to dip; we can only expect them to howl if the subsidy is taken away.

The "we-they" language in the previous paragraph isn't quite right. They may profit more than we do, but we flock to the stores with the low prices. We buy dream homes in the ever-expanding suburbs. We use the services of the growth machine. (With some equally amateur friends I'm trying to create a 22-unit eco-development, and I'm learning to appreciate the skills needed and the risks borne by developers.) We want our local builders and banks and stores and newspapers to thrive.

20 So what can we do about this spreading mess, which handsomely rewards a few, which turns our surroundings into blight, which most of us hate but in which most of us are complicit — and which we subsidize with our tax dollars?

Concrete answers to that question take a long chapter in Fodor's book and will take another column here. The general answer is clear. Don't believe the myth that all growth is good. Ask hard questions. Who will benefit from the next development scheme and who will pay? Are there better options, including undeveloped, protected land? How much growth can our roads, our land, our waters and air, our neighborhoods, schools and community support? Since we can't grow forever, where should we stop?

Questions for Discussion

1. In her opening paragraphs, Meadows contrasts St. Louis and Oslo. How effective is this contrast? To what extent does her argument as a whole depend on comparison or contrast? **2.** Meadows devotes much of her space to summarizing the work of Eben Fodor. Evaluate her use of Fodor's ideas. Does she tell you enough about his work that you can understand the principles he advocates? Does Meadows inspire sufficient confidence as a writer for you to believe that her summary of Fodor is accurate? In what ways do you think her argument about sprawl is strengthened or weakened by her use of Fodor's ideas? **3.** Drawing on Eben Fodor's work, Meadows uses the metaphors of growth accelerators and brakes to explain her concerns about sprawl. How effectively does this strategy enable her to review her concerns? Do you think the metaphors of accelerators and brakes are appropriate in this case? Explain. **4.** Meadows asserts that there is "no legal or moral reason" why current residents of an area should be compelled to pay for new development of that area. What does this assertion reveal about Meadows's fundamental beliefs and assumptions about communities and development? Do you agree with her? Why or why not? **5.** Meadows cites various statistics related to development and growth, and she cites several studies as well. How persuasive is her use of such evidence to support her claims? **6.** According to Meadows, who is responsible for urban sprawl? Do you agree? Why or why not? **7.** Meadows ends her argument with a series of questions. How effectively do you think her questions conclude her argument? In what sense might they be appropriate, given her main argument about sprawl? **8.** Meadows asserts that the problem of sprawl is not really a "we-they" problem. In other words, it is not possible to reduce the issue to two sides: one in favor and one against. She encourages us to consider how everyone involved has some responsibility for the problem. In this regard, her argument might be considered a Rogerian argument. Drawing on the explanation of Rogerian argument on pages 19–21, evaluate Meadows's essay as a Rogerian argument. Do you think it can justifiably be described as a Rogerian argument? Explain. How effective do you think it is as such an argument?

④ **R O B E R T   W I L S O N ,** "Enough Snickering. Suburbia Is More Complicated and Varied Than We Think"

When people debate about sprawl, they usually talk about suburbs, since the growth that creates sprawl tends to occur there. But just what do we mean by the term *suburb*? Robert Wilson seeks to answer that question. He argues that we need to understand suburbs in part because they reflect our values and our visions for the lives we wish to have. In the following essay, Wilson explores not only what suburbs are, but also what they mean to our sense of ourselves as Americans. He reveals that although he is not a big fan of the way suburbs have evolved since the early 20th century, he also sees suburbs as an important part of American culture. Furthermore, he points out, many people love them. Notice that Wilson approaches his subject from the perspective of a journalist and citizen who is deeply interested in preserving American culture. At the time this essay was published in the *Architectural Record* in 2000, he was the editor of *Preservation,* the magazine of the National Trust for Historical Preservation, which is devoted to preserving historically and culturally significant buildings and places.

Enough Snickering. Suburbia Is More Complicated and Varied Than We Think

R O B E R T   W I L S O N

*Award-winning novelist John Updike is especially known for a series of novels focused on a character named Harry "Rabbit" Angstrom, who responds with mixed results to the opportunities and challenges of suburban, middle-class life.

1 As the editor of *Preservation* magazine, a publication that sees itself as being about place, I've realized recently that we have been overlooking a pretty significant subject: suburbia, the place where half of Americans live. We have run stories about sprawl and the New Urbanism and made the usual condescending references to cookie-cutter houses and placeless places. But we have failed to look at the suburbs with the same curiosity and courtesy that we've shown to Dubrovnik, say, or Sioux Falls or Paducah. "Why is that?" I now wonder. Snobbery is part of the answer. Nothing can be less hip than suburbia. At a time when our cities are showing new signs of life and our open space is still being chewed up at an exponential rate, whose imagination is going to catch fire over the problems of the suburbs? Part of the answer is also linguistic. The s-word itself has become so ubiquitous and so baggage-laden that it barely means anything anymore. There is a paradox lurking here. The word suburbia has been used to describe the increasingly varied places where more and more of us live — gritty inner suburbs that share many of the problems of their urban neighbors, immigrant neighborhoods at every economic level, and new greenfield developments sporting one McMansion bigger than the next. Yet our definition of the word remains fixed in a former time, decades ago, when women worked at home and men commuted to work. The biggest problem with suburbia is that we are all so certain that we know what it means. We watched *Father Knows Best* and read our Updike,* and even a recent film like the Oscar-laden *American Beauty* confirms what we think we know: suburbia is a dull, sterile, unhappy place.

A Persistent Bias

As this suggests, the problem is also cultural. For the most part, American culture and opinion are still created, even in the Internet age, in cities at either edge of the continent. City dwellers, whether native born or the still more unforgiving recent converts, think of the suburbs as a mediocre place for mediocre people, a place where they will never venture or from which they have happily escaped. Even those who work in cities and live in suburbs (many of which now offer more urban amenities than nine-to-five cities) share this antisuburban frame of mind. If intellectuals do deign to look at the suburbs — whether cleverly in a film like *American Beauty* or clumsily, as in another recent film, the ugly paranoid fantasy *Arlington Road* — they assume that so much banality must be hiding something deeply evil.

Beyond the Movies

I'm really not here to defend suburbia, only to suggest that it is a more complicated, more various, and more quickly evolving place than we think. Two writers

> **CONTEXT**
>
> Many critics saw the Academy Award–winning film *American Beauty*, released in 1999, as a comment on life in white suburbia. In contrast to the seemingly healthy and happy suburban families portrayed in television shows such as *Father Knows Best* or *Ozzie and Harriet*, the family in *American Beauty* displays dysfunction and deep dissatisfaction with their apparently normal lives.

I admire, Witold Rybczynski and Joel Garreau, have helped me reach this state of cautious curiosity. The former, in his recent biography of Frederick Law Olmsted[†] and elsewhere, has reminded me that the suburb was a noble idea that was often, in the first decades of its existence, nobly executed. Many of these places, such as Chevy Chase near Washington, D.C., continue to function admirably well. Garreau's insight is that Venice didn't become Venice the instant it was built, but developed over a period of centuries. If we remember that the suburbs, especially the postwar suburbs over which we do most of our hand-wringing, are still relatively new places, the question becomes not "Why are they so bad?" but, "What is the next step to making them better?"

Who's to Blame?

As a journalist, I am naturally filled with righteous indignation about the subject. My instincts are first to find someone to blame and second to flatter myself that I know the solution. So, here goes: One reason that the suburbs are not better is that the best minds in architecture abandoned them. Once, not just Olmsted but Frank Lloyd Wright, Le Corbusier, Clarence Stein,[‡] and others considered, in an urgent and serious way, the questions of where and how people might live if they didn't live in cities or on farms. Am I wrong in believing that between the Garden City movement of the 1910s and 1920s and the New Towns of the 1960s there was a wasteland of ideas beyond the city limits — just as the suburbs

[†]**Frederick Law Olmsted (1822–1903)** is widely considered one of our country's most important landscape architects. With his partner Calvert Vaux, he created the winning design for the creation of Central Park in New York City. He also designed the grounds for the U.S. Capitol, among many other projects of na-

[‡]**Frank Lloyd Wright (1869–1959), Le Corbusier (1887–1967), and Clarence Stein (1882–1975)** were influential architects in the early twentieth century. Stein, in particular, is associated with the Garden City Movement, which sought to create beautifully landscaped communities within easy access of major cities.

Andres Duany, Elizabeth Plater-Zyberk, and Jeff Speck frankly admit and defend their suburban focus. Whether they helped create the slow-growth, sustainable-growth, antisprawl movements that have captured the imagination of so many voters in recent elections at all levels of government, or whether they merely capitalized on these movements, their book seems timely. In a recent front-page article, the *New York Times* reported that academics have suddenly taken an urgent interest in suburbia. Other major newspapers across the country have latched on to the subject, perhaps as an outgrowth of the widening interest in sprawl.

began to lay waste to vast portions of the American landscape? And that there was precious little between the New Towns and the New Urbanists? Isn't this why the design and execution of suburbs have been so disappointing, because the field was abandoned to the merely avaricious? For anyone who is irritated by how much attention the New Urbanists get, here is the simple answer to their popularity with the media: However retrograde their ideas, however short their accomplishments to date might fall, at least they have an idea and at least they have acted upon it.

5 The New Urbanists spent a certain amount of time reacting to Vincent Scully's suggestion that they should really be thought of as the New Suburbanists, but in their new book, *Suburban Nation: The Rise of Sprawl and the Decline of the American Dream,*

Recent stories in *Preservation,* beginning with a cover story on the new suburban immigrants, have not thrilled hardcore preservationists, for whom suburbia has always been a particular bete noire. For me, this resistance is only a speed bump on the road to the movement's democratization.

Do I foresee the wholesale preservation of postwar suburbs? Probably not. Rapid evolution would be far more desirable. Still, alarms were sounded recently in Houston, where a whole neighborhood of brick ranch houses was under siege. The truth is that most people love their suburban homes and neighborhoods and will fight to save them. And if preservationists have learned anything in the last century or so, it is that the notion of what is worth preserving changes. Just recall how Victorian buildings were despised as recently as a few decades ago.

Perhaps the split-level will be the retro rage in 2050.

Design Creeps in

As money and newly sophisticated consumers pour into the suburbs, good design and architecture are beginning to follow. In my neck of suburbia, northern Virginia, where even a determined electorate has had trouble slowing sprawl, there are nonetheless hopeful signs that good ideas are arriving — from town-center schemes for shopping and living to interesting and appealing buildings for churches, college campuses, and office complexes.

Most welcome of all, perhaps, is the improved architecture for public buildings, including schools, which were the most bereft places we allowed to be built in the bad old days just ending. May all of you who read these words enthusiastically enter the fray, enriching yourselves even as you enrich a vast part of our landscape that urgently needs you.

NEW TOWNS AND THE NEW URBANISTS

The New Towns movement in regional planning gained popularity in the United States in the 1920s. It focused on carefully designed and largely residential communities that were located away from urban centers. These New Towns, also called "Garden Cities," sometimes developed into large suburban areas. The New Urbanism, which emerged in the 1990s, is a reaction to the New Town idea of community planning. As an alternative to sprawl, New Urbanism emphasizes the integration of housing, workplaces, businesses, and recreation into small neighborhoods that are connected by public transportation. According to Ute Angleki Lehrer, a professor of urban and regional planning at the State University of New York at Buffalo, "By establishing specific rules for land use and building design, the architects of New Urbanism believe that they can create diversity and density in neighborhoods of both new suburban development and revitalization projects in existing urban areas."

Questions for Discussion

1. Wilson opens his argument by establishing that he is editor or *Preservation* magazine. To what extent does this information make him a credible source? When considering his argument as a whole, how would you evaluate his credibility? **2.** On what grounds might preservationists try to protect suburban neighborhoods that some critics find ugly? Do you think Wilson does justice to a more positive view of suburban communities? Explain. **3.** Wilson suggests in this essay that suburbs can be better. What exactly does he mean? What does his position reveal about his own beliefs regarding the ideal community? Do you agree with him? Why or why not? **4.** Notice the many references Wilson makes in his essay to films, literature, historical developments, and social movements. What do these references suggest about the audience Wilson is addressing in this essay? Does that audience include you? Explain. **5.** Wilson's essay raises questions about how we think about the communities we live in. How does his argument affect the way you think communities should be designed? Do you think he wishes to challenge conventional views about community design? Explain, citing specific passages from his essay to support your answer.

NEGOTIATING DIFFERENCES

Several of the authors included in this section express concern about the effects of sprawl on open space such as farmland. But urban sprawl can also damage inner cities as people move to distant suburbs and eventually also work and shop many miles from the city center. Moreover, sprawl can also affect older suburbs located at the inner ring around a city. According to one expert, "These are the patterns that many cities in the Rust Belt are carving out — entire rings spreading outward relentlessly, or pie-shaped pieces doing the same. Left behind are devastated neighborhoods in formerly industrial cities. So natural landscapes aren't the only victims of the public policies and private preferences that have suburbanized America. They've also taken a toll on aging built landscapes and the people remaining in them" (Deron Lovass, "Shrinking Cities, Growing Populations").

So sprawl can affect most Americans: city dwellers, suburbanites, and anyone living in a rural area within commuting distance of a metropolitan region.

Imagine now that you are at a public meeting at which a developer is seeking permission to build new housing on 500 acres of farmland an hour's drive from the center of the largest city in your state. This meeting has attracted environmentalists who are concerned about the consequences of development, commuters who are worried that highways are already overcrowded, and residents from the city and older suburbs who believe that continued growth will damage the areas in which they live. Other voices are also heard at this meeting, however. Several people speak about an urgent need for safe, affordable housing, and others insist that additional development is essential for the economic well-being of the metropolitan area as a whole. Finally, someone else points out that new developments do not have to be ugly. On the contrary, they can be well designed and built in an environmentally responsible way.

With this scenario in mind, write an essay in which you advocate a specific plan for the land in question. In your essay, discuss what you see as the primary goals for the community that will be built — and for the use of such land in general. Also try to account for the various perspectives of people who are concerned about how that land will be used. Taking these matters into account, make an argument for what you believe should be done with the land. Ideally, your argument will address the various concerns expressed at the meeting, even if all parties involved would not agree with your proposal.

Alternatively, focus your essay on an actual controversy involving sprawl or development in the area where you live. Follow the same guidelines described in the previous paragraph, but focus on the specific situation in your area.

WHAT IS OUR

RELATIONSHIP TO NATURE?

I n his famous essay, "Walking" (see *Con-Text* on page 419), 19th century American writer Henry David Thoreau announces, "Life consists with wildness. The most alive is the wildest. Not yet subdued to man, its presence refreshes him." Perhaps this idea that we require "the wild" to be truly alive helped to make Thoreau a favorite writer of the environmental movement that emerged in the United States in the 1960s and 1970s. And perhaps it accounts for his high standing among environmentalists even today. Certainly, many people who support wilderness preservation and who venture into wilderness areas find solace and revitalization there. They argue that wilderness helps us to understand who we are. ■ But in "Walking," Thoreau argues that wilderness doesn't help us to understand who we are; for Thoreau wilderness *is* who we are. Indeed, Thoreau criticized the cultivation of farmland and the construction of cities and towns not because they destroyed wilderness areas, but because they destroyed human life as he believed it should be lived: "Hope and the future for me are not in lawns and cultivated fields," he wrote, "not in cities and towns, but in the impervious and quaking swamps." This is a vision not so much of wilderness but of human life. For Thoreau the two — wilderness and humans — are not distinct but the same. ■ The essays in this section explore this connection between humans and the wilderness. In one way or another these writers take up the challenge of defining our relationship to wilderness. It seems to be an especially important challenge at the beginning of the 21st century, since wilderness areas around the world are under great pressure from development and population growth, and many are disappearing altogether. The loss of such areas raises questions about their value to us. Is their value only a function of the economic benefit they might produce — such as the lumber from the trees that are removed from a wilderness area when it is developed? Or does the value of wilderness lie in something more than profit, as Thoreau believed? For some writers the answers to those questions require us to reexamine the very idea of wilderness. And some writers even suggest that the desire to preserve wilderness is really a reflection of Western cultural values — values that might be at odds with the values of people from other cultures. ■ As a group, then, these essays underscore the need to think carefully about our relationship to wilderness as we address the difficult question of what to do about disappearing wilderness areas.

CON-TEXT: Thoreau's Wildness

1 Life consists with Wildness. The most alive is the wildest. Not yet subdued to man, its presence refreshes him. One who pressed forward incessantly and never rested from his labors, who grew fast and made infinite demands on life, would always find himself in a new country or wilderness, and surrounded by the raw material of life. He would be climbing over the prostrate stems of primitive forest trees.

Hope and the future for me are not in lawns and cultivated fields, not in towns and cities, but in the impervious and quaking swamps. . . .

In short, all good things are wild and free. There is something in a strain of music, whether produced by an instrument or by the human voice — take the sound of a bugle in a summer night, for instance — which by its wildness, to speak without satire, reminds me of the cries emit-

ted by wild beasts in their native forests. It is so much of their wildness as I can understand. Give me for my friends and neighbors wild men, not tame ones. The wildness of the savage is but a faint symbol of the awful ferity with which good men and lovers meet.

source: Henry David Thoreau, *Walking*, 1862.

① RACHEL CARSON, "The Obligation to Endure"

If the environmental movement in the latter part of the 20th century can be traced to any single work, it is probably *Silent Spring* (1962), Rachel Carson's widely read analysis of how pesticides and other chemicals were polluting the earth and endangering both wildlife and human life. An aquatic biologist with the U.S. Bureau of Fisheries, Carson (1907–1966) became the editor-in-chief of the publications of the U.S. Fish and Wildlife Service. The values that Carson espouses regarding the natural world — values that deeply influenced a generation of environmental advocates — emerge subtly but powerfully in her discussion of the physical and biological effects of chemicals in the environment. She writes as a scientist, but as you read, consider whether science is the primary perspective from which she examines the problem of pesticides. More important, perhaps, is what Carson conveys about our relationship with the earth. The fact that our relationship with the earth remains a complex and often troubled one might account for the enduring popularity of Carson's book in the more than forty years since its publication. "The Obligation to Endure" is the second chapter of *Silent Spring*.

The Obligation to Endure
RACHEL CARSON

1 The history of life on earth has been a history of interaction between living things and their surroundings. To a large extent, the physical form and the habits of the earth's vegetation and its animal life have been molded by the environment. Considering the whole span of earthly time, the opposite effect, in which life actually modifies its surroundings, has been relatively slight. Only within the moment of time represented by the present century has one species — man — acquired significant power to alter the nature of his world.

During the past quarter century this power has not only increased to one of disturbing magnitude but it has changed in character. The most alarming of all man's assaults upon the environment is the contamination of air, earth, rivers, and sea with dangerous and even lethal materials. This pollution is for the most part irrecoverable; the chain of evil it initiates not only in the world that must support life but in living tissues is for the most part irreversible. In this now universal contamination of the environment, chemicals are the sinister and little-recognized partners of radiation in changing the very nature of the world — the very nature of its life. Strontium 90, released through nuclear explosions into the air, comes to earth in rain or drifts down as fallout, lodges in soil, enters into the grass or corn or wheat grown there, and in time takes up its abode in the bones of a human being, there to remain until his death. Similarly, chemicals sprayed on croplands or forests or gardens lie long in soil, entering into living organisms, passing from one to another in a chain of poisoning and death. Or they pass mysteriously by underground streams until they emerge and, through the alchemy of air and sunlight, combine into new forms that kill vegetation, sicken cattle, and work unknown harm on those who drink from once pure wells. As Albert Schweitzer has said, "Man can hardly even recognize the devils of his own creation."

It took hundreds of millions of years to produce the life that now inhabits the earth — eons of time in which that developing and evolving and diversifying life reached a state of adjustment and balance with its surroundings. The environment, rigorously shaping and directing the life it supported, contained elements that were hostile as well as supporting. Certain rocks gave out dangerous radiation; even within the light of the sun, from which all life draws its energy, there were shortwave radiations with power to injure. Given time — time not in years but in millennia — life adjusts, and a balance has been reached. For time is the essential ingredient; but in the modern world there is no time.

The rapidity of change and the speed with which new situations are created follow the impetuous and heedless pace of man rather than the deliberate pace of nature. Radiation is no longer merely the background radiation of rocks, the bombardment of cosmic rays, the ultraviolet of the sun that have existed before there was any life on earth; radiation is now the unnatural creation of man's tampering with the atom. The chemicals to which life is asked to make its adjust-

NUCLEAR TESTING

More than 2,000 nuclear tests have been conducted since 1945, and over 700 of them were conducted in the earth's atmosphere or under its oceans. When Carson wrote her argument in 1962, above-ground nuclear testing was routine. Since 1980 most nations have agreed to avoid above-ground nuclear testing, but tests are still conducted underground, under the ocean, and in space. In 1996 Greenpeace estimated that the tests that had been conducted by then had left 3,830 kilograms of plutonium in the ground and 4,200 kilograms of plutonium in the air.

ment are no longer merely the calcium and silica and copper and all the rest of the minerals washed out of the rocks and carried in rivers to the sea; they are the synthetic creations of man's inventive mind, brewed in his laboratories, and having no counterparts in nature.

5 To adjust to these chemicals would require time on the scale that is nature's; it would require not merely the years of a man's life but the life of generations. And even this, were it by some miracle possible, would be futile, for the new chemicals come from our laboratories in an endless stream; almost five hundred annually find their way into actual use in the United States alone. The figure is staggering and its implications are not easily grasped — 500 new chemicals to which the bodies of men and animals are required somehow to adapt each year, chemicals totally outside the limits of biologic experience.

Among them are many that are used in man's war against nature. Since the mid-1940s over 200 basic chemicals have been created for use in killing insects, weeds, rodents, and other organisms described in the modern vernacular as "pests"; and they are sold under several thousand different brand names.

These sprays, dusts, and aerosols are now applied almost universally to farms, gardens, forests, and homes — nonselec-

*See the Complication
on page 428.

war is never won, and all life is caught in its violent crossfire.

Along with the possibility of the extinction of mankind by nuclear war, the central problem of our age has therefore become the contamination of man's total environment with such substances of incredible potential for harm — substances that accumulate in the tissues of plants and animals and even penetrate the germ cells to shatter or alter the very material of heredity upon which the shape of the future depends.

Some would-be architects of our future look toward a time when it will be possible to alter the human germ plasm by design. But we may easily be doing so now by inadvertence, for many chemicals, like radiation, bring about gene mutations. It is ironic to think that man might determine his own future by something so seemingly trivial as the choice of an insect spray.

tive chemicals that have the power to kill every insect, the "good" and the "bad," to still the song of birds and the leaping of fish in the streams, to coat the leaves with a deadly film, and to linger on in soil — all this though the intended target may be only a few weeds or insects. Can anyone believe it is possible to lay down such a barrage of poisons on the surface of the earth without making it unfit for all life? They should not be called "insecticides," but "biocides."

The whole process of spraying seems caught up in an endless spiral. Since DDT* was released for civilian use, a process of escalation has been going on in which ever more toxic materials must be found. This has happened because insects, in a triumphant vindication of Darwin's principle of the survival of the fittest, have evolved super races immune to the particular insecticide used, hence a deadlier one has always to be developed — and then a deadlier one than that. It has happened also because, for reasons to be described later, destructive insects often undergo a "flareback," or resurgence, after spraying, in numbers greater than before. Thus the chemical

10 All this has been risked — for what? Future historians may well be amazed by our distorted sense of proportion. How could intelligent beings seek to control a few unwanted species by a method that contaminated the entire environment and brought the threat of disease and death even to their own kind? Yet this is precisely what we have done. We have done it, moreover, for reasons that collapse the moment we examine them. We are told that the enormous and expanding use of pesticides is necessary to maintain farm production. Yet is our real problem not one of *overproduction?* Our farms, despite measures to remove acreages from production and to pay farmers *not* to produce, have yielded such a staggering excess of crops that the American taxpayer in 1962 is paying out more than one billion dollars a year as the total carrying cost of the surplus-food storage program. And is the situation helped when one branch of the Agriculture Department

tries to reduce production while another states, as it did in 1958, "It is believed generally that reduction of crop acreages under provisions of the Soil Bank will stimulate interest in use of chemicals to obtain maximum production on the land retained in crops."

All this is not to say there is no insect problem and no need of control. I am saying, rather, that control must be geared to realities, not to mythical situations, and that the methods employed must be such that they do not destroy us along with the insects.

The problem whose attempted solution has brought such a train of disaster in its wake is an accompaniment of our modern way of life. Long before the age of man, insects inhabited the earth — a group of extraordinarily varied and adaptable beings. Over the course of time since man's advent, a small percentage of the more than half a million species of insects have come into conflict with human welfare in two principal ways: as competitors for the food supply and as carriers of human disease.

Disease-carrying insects become important where human beings are crowded together, especially under conditions where sanitation is poor, as in time of natural disaster or war or in situations of extreme poverty and deprivation. Then control of some sort becomes necessary. It is a sobering fact, however, as we shall presently see, that the method of massive chemical control has had only limited success, and also threatens to worsen the very conditions it is intended to curb.

Under primitive agricultural conditions the farmer had few insect problems. These arose with the intensification of agriculture — the devotion of immense acreages to a single crop. Such a system set the stage for explosive increases in specific insect populations. Single-crop farming does not take advantage of the principles by which nature works; it is agriculture as an engineer might conceive it to be. Nature has introduced great variety into the landscape, but man has displayed a passion for simplifying it. Thus he undoes the built-in checks and balances by which nature holds the species within bounds. One important natural check is a limit on the amount of suitable habitat for each species. Obviously then, an insect that lives on wheat can build up its population to much higher levels on a farm devoted to wheat than on one in which wheat is intermingled with other crops to which the insect is not adapted.

15 The same thing happens in other situations. A generation or more ago, the towns of large areas of the United States lined their streets with the noble elm tree. Now the beauty they hopefully created is threatened with complete destruction as disease sweeps through the elms, carried by a beetle that would have only limited chance to build up large populations and to spread from tree to tree if the elms were only occasional trees in a richly diversified planting.

CONTEXT

The Agricultural Act of 1956, usually called the Soil Bank Act, provided federal funds to farmers to keep certain lands out of agricultural production, sometimes as a way to control the prices of some agricultural products. The act was repealed in 1965, three years after Rachel Carson's *Silent Spring* was published. But the policy of using federal funds to keep agricultural lands out of production continued under subsequent legislation.

INSECTS AND AGRICULTURE

U.S. agricultural production more than doubled between the late 1940s and the 1980s, in part because of the increased use of pesticides to control insects that damaged some agricultural products and lowered agricultural yields. However, concerns about the health risks associated with pesticides grew in the years after *Silent Spring* was published. In addition, some insects have demonstrated resistance to pesticides. And despite increased use of pesticides, some studies show a slight rise in crop losses due to insects among major crops (such as corn) over the past century; these studies show such crop losses between 10 percent and 15 percent, with some estimates as high as 37 percent. These developments, along with the growing influence of the environmental movement in the 1970s and 1980s, have prompted some farmers to consider alternatives to conventional farming methods that rely on pesticides to control insects. "Organic" or "natural" farming uses a variety of methods to control insects, including crop rotation and biological controls (e.g., introducing one kind of insect to control other insects that damage crops). Proponents of such methods argue that crop yields are not reduced when pesticide use is decreased or discontinued, and some studies actually show increased crop yields as a result of organic farming methods.

Another factor in the modern insect problem is one that must be viewed against a background of geologic and human history: the spreading of thousands of different kinds of organisms from their native homes to invade new territories. This worldwide migration has been studied and graphically described by the British ecologist Charles Elton in his recent book *The Ecology of Invasions*. During the Cretaceous Period, some hundred million years ago, flooding seas cut many land bridges between continents and living things found themselves confined in what Elton calls "colossal separate nature reserves." There, isolated from others of their kind, they developed many new species. When some of the land masses were joined again, about 15 million years ago, these species began to move out into new territories — a movement that is not only still in progress but is now receiving considerable assistance from man.

The importation of plants is the primary agent in the modern spread of species, for animals have almost invariably gone along with the plants, quarantine being a comparatively recent and not completely effective innovation (See "Context" on page 426.) The United States Office of Plant Introduction alone has introduced almost 200,000 species and varieties of plants from all over the world. Nearly half of the 180 or so major insect enemies of plants in the United States are accidental imports from abroad, and most of them have come as hitchhikers on plants.

In new territory, out of reach of the restraining hand of the natural enemies that kept down its numbers in its native land, an invading plant or animal is able to become enormously abundant. Thus it is no accident that our most troublesome insects are introduced species.

These invasions, both the naturally occurring and those dependent on human assistance, are likely to continue indefinitely. Quarantine and massive chemical campaigns are only extremely expensive ways of buying time. We are faced, according to Dr. Elton, "with a life-and-death need not just to find new technological means of suppressing this plant or that animal"; instead we need the basic knowledge of animal populations and their relations to their surroundings that will "promote an even balance and damp down the explosive power of outbreaks and new invasions." **20** Much of the necessary knowledge is now available but we do not use it. We train ecologists in our universities and even employ them in our governmental agencies but we seldom take their advice. We allow the chemical death rain to fall as though there were no alternative, whereas in fact there are many, and our ingenuity could soon discover many more if given opportunity.

Have we fallen into a mesmerized state that makes us accept as inevitable that which is inferior or detrimental, as though having lost the will or the vision to demand that which is good? Such thinking, in the words of the ecologist Paul Shepard, "idealizes life with only its head out of water, inches above the limits of toleration of the corruption of its own environment. . . . Why should we tolerate a diet of weak poisons, a home in insipid surroundings, a circle of acquaintances who are not quite our enemies, the noise of motors with just enough relief to prevent insanity? Who would want to live in a world which is just not quite fatal?" Yet such a world is pressed upon us. The crusade to create a chemically sterile, insect-free world seems to have engendered a fanatic zeal on the part of many specialists and most of the so-called control agencies. On every hand there is evidence that those engaged in spraying operations exercise a ruthless power. "The regulatory entomologists . . . function as prosecutor, judge and jury, tax assessor and collector and sheriff to enforce their own orders," said Connecticut entomologist Neely Turner. The most flagrant abuses go unchecked in both state and federal agencies.

It is not my contention that chemical insecticides must never be used. I do contend that we have put poisonous and biologically potent chemicals indiscriminately into the hands of persons largely or wholly ignorant of their potentials for harm. We have subjected enormous numbers of people to contact with these poisons, without their consent and often without their knowledge. If the Bill of Rights contains no guarantee that a citizen shall be secure against lethal poisons distributed either by private individuals or by public officials, it is surely only because our forefathers, despite their con-

siderable wisdom and foresight, could conceive of no such problem.

I contend, furthermore, that we have allowed these chemicals to be used with little or no advance investigation of their effect on soil, water, wildlife, and man himself. Future generations are unlikely to condone our lack of prudent concern for the integrity of the natural world that supports all life.

There is still very limited awareness of the nature of the threat. This is an era of specialists, each of whom sees his own problem and is unaware of or intolerant of the larger frame into which it fits. It is also an era dominated by industry, in which the right to make a dollar at whatever cost is seldom challenged. When the public protests, confronted with some obvious evidence of damaging results of pesticide applications, it is fed little tranquilizing pills of half truth. We urgently need an end to these false assurances, to the sugar coating of unpalatable facts. It is the public that is being asked to assume the risks that the insect controllers calculate. The public must decide whether it wishes to continue on the present road, and it can do so only when in full possession of the facts. In the words of Jean Rostand, "The obligation to endure gives us the right to know."

Questions for Discussion

1. What kinds of evidence does Carson present to support her claim that our environment is at risk? How persuasive do you find her evidence? **2.** Carson asks, "How could human beings seek to control a few unwanted species by a method that contaminated the entire environment and brought the threat of disease and death even to their own kind?" How would you answer her? **3.** Ronald Bailey, whose essay appears on page 427, asserts that the effectiveness of Carson's book was due largely to her language rather than to the strength of her evidence. Evaluate Carson's writing style and tone in this essay. How effective do you find them? In what ways do you think they contribute to her argument? Do you think Bailey is right? **4.** On the basis of the essay, what fundamental values do you think Carson holds about human beings and their relationship to the environment? Do you think most Americans share these values today? Explain. **5.** As the sidebar on page 424 indicates, crop losses due to insect damage can be significant for farmers, and many agricultural experts believe that the appropriate use of pesticides remains the best way to control insects. In what ways does Carson address this concern in her essay? **6.** *Silent Spring* was published in 1962. What elements of Carson's argument do you think are still relevant? Do you think that any of the concerns raised by Carson have been resolved? Explain.

② RONALD BAILEY, "Silent Spring at 40"

Rachel Carson's best-selling and widely influential book *Silent Spring* (see pages 420–426) is usually thought of as a scientific work — a careful analysis of the effects of pesticides. In the following essay, Ronald Bailey suggests that it is something else. Its influence, he argues, lies in its persuasiveness as an argument more than in the quality of its scientific analysis. In fact, Bailey argues that Carson played fast and loose with scientific facts in making her argument against pesticide use, and he offers a detailed and extensive examination of those facts in an effort to call Carson's argument into question. In doing so, Bailey reminds us that any text can be understood as an argument and that even science relies on argument and rhetoric. Whether or not you agree with Bailey's critique of Carson, the real value of his essay might be in the way it reveals the rhetorical and argumentative character of scientific texts. He helps us see, too, that this is as it should be, because issues such as pesticide use are not just scientific issues but social and political issues that can directly affect our lives. Argument, in other words, is one of the means by which we try to address these issues together. Ronald Bailey is the science correspondent for *Reason* magazine, in which the following essay appeared in 2002; he is also the editor of *Earth Report 2000: Revisiting the True State of the Planet.*

Silent Spring at 40
RONALD BAILEY

1 The modern environmentalist movement was launched at the beginning of June 1962, when excerpts from what would become Rachel Carson's anti-chemical landmark *Silent Spring* were published in *The New Yorker*. "Without this book, the environmental movement might have been long delayed or never have developed at all," declared then-Vice President Albert Gore in his introduction to the 1994 edition. The foreword to the 25th anniversary edition accurately declared, "It led to environmental legislation at every level of government."

In 1999 *Time* named Carson one of the "100 People of the Century." Seven years earlier, a panel of distinguished Americans had selected *Silent Spring* as the most influential book of the previous 50 years. When I went in search of a copy recently, several bookstore owners told me they didn't have any in stock because local high schools still assign the book and students had cleaned them out.

Carson worked for years at the U.S. Fish and Wildlife Service, eventually becoming the chief editor of that agency's publications. Carson achieved financial independence in the 1950s with the publication of her popular celebrations of marine ecosystems, *The Sea Around Us* and *The Edge of the Sea*. Rereading *Silent Spring* reminds one that the book's effectiveness was due mainly to Carson's

From a public health statement by the Agency for Toxic Substances and Disease Registry (1989):

Short-term exposure to high doses of DDT affects primarily the nervous system. People who either voluntarily or accidentally swallowed very high amounts of DDT experienced excitability, tremors, and seizures. These effects on the nervous system appeared to be reversible once exposure stopped. Some people who came in contact with DDT complained of rashes or irritation of the eyes, nose, and throat. People exposed for a long-term at low doses, such as people who made DDT, had some changes in the levels of liver enzymes, but there was no indication that DDT caused irreversible harmful (noncancer) effects. Tests in laboratory animals confirm the effect of DDT on the nervous system. However, tests in animals suggest that exposure to DDT may have a harmful effect on reproduction, and long-term exposure may affect the liver. Studies in animals have shown that oral exposure to DDT can result in an increased occurrence of liver tumors. In the five studies of DDT-exposed workers, results did not indicate increases in the number of deaths or cancers. However, these studies had limitations so that possible increases in cancer may not have been detected. Because DDT caused cancer in laboratory animals, it is assumed that DDT could have this effect in humans.

passionate, poetic language describing the alleged horrors that modern synthetic chemicals visit upon defenseless nature and hapless humanity. Carson was moved to write *Silent Spring* by her increasing concern about the effects of pesticides on wildlife. Her chief villain was the pesticide DDT.

The 1950s saw the advent of an array of synthetic pesticides that were hailed as modern miracles in the war against pests and weeds. First and foremost of these chemicals was DDT. DDT's insecticidal properties were discovered in the late 1930s by Paul Muller, a chemist at the Swiss chemical firm J.R. Geigy. The American military started testing it in 1942, and soon the insecticide was being sprayed in war zones to protect American troops against insect-borne diseases such as typhus and malaria. In 1943 DDT famously stopped a typhus epidemic in Naples in its tracks shortly after the Allies invaded. DDT was hailed as the "wonder insecticide of World War II."

5 As soon as the war ended, American consumers and farmers quickly adopted the wonder insecticide, replacing the old-fashioned arsenic-based pesticides, which were truly nasty. Testing by the U.S. Public Health Service and the Food and Drug Administration's Division of Pharmacology found no serious human toxicity problems with DDT. Muller, DDT's inventor, was awarded the Nobel Prize in 1948.

DDT was soon widely deployed by public health officials, who banished malaria from the southern United States with its help. The World Health Organization credits DDT with saving 50 million to 100 million lives by preventing malaria. In 1943 Venezuela had 8,171,115 cases of malaria; by 1958, after the use of DDT, the number was down to 800. India, which had over 10 million cases of malaria in 1935, had 285,962 in 1969. In Italy the number of malaria cases dropped from 411,602 in 1945 to only 37 in 1968.

The tone of a *Scientific American* article by Francis Joseph Weiss celebrating the advent of "Chemical Agriculture" was typical of much of the reporting in the early 1950s. "In 1820 about 72 per cent of the population worked in agriculture, the proportion in 1950 was only about 15 per cent," reported Weiss. "Chemical agriculture, still in its infancy, should eventually advance our agricultural efficiency at least as much as machines have in the past 150 years." This improvement in agricultural efficiency would happen because "farming is being revolutionized by new fertilizers, insecticides, fungicides, weed killers, leaf removers, soil conditioners, plant hormones, trace minerals, antibiotics and synthetic milk for pigs."

In 1952 insects, weeds, and disease cost farmers $13 billion in crops annually. Since gross annual agricultural output at that time totaled $31 billion, it was estimated that preventing this damage by using pesticides would boost food and fiber production by 42 percent. Agricultural productivity in the United States, spurred by improvements in farming practices and technologies, has continued its exponential increase. As a result, the percentage of Americans living and working on farms has dropped from 15 percent in 1950 to under 1.8 percent today.

But DDT and other pesticides had a dark side. They not only killed the pests at which they were aimed but often killed beneficial organisms as well. Carson, the passionate defender of wildlife, was determined to spotlight these harms. Memorably, she painted a scenario in which birds had all been poisoned by insecticides, resulting in a "silent spring" in which "no birds sing." **10** The scientific controversy over the effects of DDT on wildlife, especially birds, still vexes researchers. In the late 1960s, some researchers concluded that exposure to DDT caused eggshell thinning in some bird species, especially raptors such as eagles and peregrine falcons. Thinner shells meant fewer hatchlings and declining numbers. But researchers also found that other bird species, such as quail, pheasants, and chickens, were unaffected even by large doses DDT.

On June 14, 1972, 30 years ago this week, the EPA banned DDT despite considerable evidence of its safety offered in seven months of agency hearings. After listening to that testimony, the EPA's own administrative law judge declared, "DDT is not a carcinogenic hazard to man . . . DDT is not a mutagenic or teratogenic hazard to man . . . The use of DDT under the regulations involved here [does] not have a deleterious effect on freshwater fish, estuarine organisms, wild birds or other wildlife." Today environmental activists celebrate the EPA's DDT ban as their first great victory.

Carson argued that DDT and other pesticides were not only harming wildlife but killing people too. The 1958 passage by Congress of the Delaney Clause, which forbade the addition of any amount of chemicals suspected of causing cancer to food, likely focused Carson's attention on that disease. (See "Context" on page 430.)

For the previous half-century some researchers had been trying to prove that cancer was caused by chemical contaminants in the environment. Wilhelm Hueper, chief of environmental cancer research at the National Cancer Institute and one of the leading researchers in this area, became a major source for Carson. Hueper was so convinced that trace exposures to synthetic chemicals were a

major cause of cancer in humans that he totally dismissed the notion that smoking cigarettes caused cancer. The assertion that pesticides were dangerous human carcinogens was a stroke of public relations genius. Even people who do not care much about wildlife care a lot about their own health and the health of their children.

In 1955 the American Cancer Society predicted that "cancer will strike one in every four Americans rather than the present estimate of one in five." The ACS attributed the increase to "the growing number of older persons in the population." The ACS did note that the incidence of lung cancer was increasing very rapidly, rising in the previous two decades by more than 200 percent for women and by 600 percent for men. But the ACS also noted that lung cancer "is the only form of cancer which shows so definite a tendency." Seven years later, Rachel Carson would call her chapter on cancer "One in Four."

15 To bolster her case for the dangers of DDT, Carson improperly cited cases of acute exposures to the chemical as proof of its cancer-causing ability. For example, she told the story of a woman who sprayed DDT for spiders in her basement and died a month later of leukemia. In

CONTEXT

Part of the Federal Food, Drug and Cosmetic Act, the Delaney Clause sets a standard of "zero cancer risk" for residues of pesticides in food additives. This standard means, in effect, that any residues of any substance that is considered a carcinogen are prohibited from food products. According to the National Council for Science and the Environment,

Such a risk standard does not allow an assessment of any possible agricultural benefits from the use of pesticides. Several groups, including the pesticide and food industries, want Congress to replace the Delaney Clause with a "negligible risk" standard. The pesticide industry claims that a single "negligible risk" standard would set one risk standard for all foods and would allow newer, safer pesticides to be marketed even with some evidence of carcinogenicity. However, Delaney Clause supporters argue that Delaney reduces risks associated with carcinogenic pesticide chemicals and no carcinogenic substances should be added voluntarily to food; there are enough natural carcinogenic toxins already in the food supply.

another case, a man sprayed his office for cockroaches and a few days later was diagnosed with aplastic anemia. Today cancer specialists would dismiss out of hand the implied claims that these patients' cancers could be traced to such specific pesticide exposures. The plain fact is that DDT has never been shown to be a human carcinogen even after four decades of intense scientific scrutiny.

Carson was also an effective popularizer of the idea that children were especially vulnerable to the carcinogenic effects of synthetic chemicals. "The situation with respect to children is even more deeply disturbing," she wrote. "A quarter century ago, cancer in children was considered a medical rarity. Today, more American school children die of cancer than from any other disease." In support of this claim, Carson reported that "twelve per cent of all deaths in children between the ages of one and fourteen are caused by cancer."

Although it sounds alarming, Carson's statistic is essentially meaningless unless it's given some context, which she failed to supply. It turns out that the percentage of children dying of cancer was rising because other causes of death, such as infectious diseases, were drastically declining.

In fact, cancer rates in children have not increased, as they would have if Carson had been right that children were especially susceptible to the alleged health effects of modern chemicals. Just one rough comparison illustrates this point: In 1938 cancer killed 939 children under 14 years old out of a U.S. population of 130 million. In 1998, according to the National Cancer Institute, about 1,700 children died of cancer, out of a population of more than 280 million. In 1999 the NCI noted that "over the past 20 years, there has been relatively little change in the incidence of children diagnosed with all forms of cancer; from 13

cases per 100,000 children in 1974 to 13.2 per 100,000 children in 1995."

Clearly, if cancer incidence isn't going up, modern chemicals can't be a big factor in cancer. But this simple point is lost on Carson's heirs in the environmental movement, who base their careers on pursuing phantom risks. The truth is that both cancer mortality and incidence rates have been declining for about a decade, mostly because of a decrease in the number of cigarette smokers.

20 The Great Cancer Scare launched by Carson, and perpetuated by her environmentalist disciples ever since, should have been put to rest by a definitive 1996 report from the National Academy of Sciences, Carcinogens and Anticarcinogens in the Human Diet. The NAS concluded that levels of both synthetic and natural carcinogens are "so low that they are unlikely to pose an appreciable cancer risk." Worse yet from the point of view of anti-chemical crusaders, the NAS added that Mother Nature's own chemicals probably cause more cancer than anything mankind has dreamed up: "Natural components of the diet may prove to be of greater concern than synthetic components with respect to cancer risk."

Meanwhile, Carson's disciples have managed to persuade many poor countries to stop using DDT against mosquitoes. The result has been an enormous increase in the number of people dying of malaria each year. Today malaria infects between 300 million and 500 million people annually, killing as many 2.7 million of them. Anti-DDT activists who tried to have the new U.N. treaty on persistent organic pollutants totally ban DDT have stepped back recently from their ideological campaign, conceding that poor countries should be able to use DDT to control malaria-carrying mosquitoes.

So 40 years after the publication of *Silent Spring,* the legacy of Rachel Carson is more troubling than her admirers will acknowledge. The book did point to problems that had not been adequately addressed, such as the effects of DDT on some wildlife. And given the state of the science at the time she wrote, one might even make the case that Carson's concerns about the effects of synthetic chemicals on human health were not completely unwarranted. Along with other researchers, she was simply ignorant of the facts. But after four decades in which tens of billions of dollars have been wasted chasing imaginary risks without measurably improving American health, her intellectual descendants don't have the same excuse.

Questions for Discussion

1. Bailey begins this essay with a description of the impact that *Silent Spring* had — and continues to have — after its publication in 1962. He also discusses the praise Rachel Carson received for that book. Why do you think Bailey begins his essay, which is critical of Carson's *Silent Spring*, in this way? In what ways might this beginning help to set up his main argument? **2.** Bailey claims that the effectiveness of *Silent Spring* "was due mainly to Carson's passionate, poetic language describing the alleged horrors that modern synthetic chemicals visit upon defenseless nature and hapless humanity." What evidence does he provide to support that claim? Why, in Bailey's view, should we be concerned that *Silent Spring* was persuasive largely because of Rachel Carson's "passionate, poetic language"? Evaluate Bailey's own use of language in this essay. To what extent does he employ some of the same argumentative strategies that he claims Carson used in her book? Cite specific passages from his essay to support your answer. **3.** Bailey essentially accuses Rachel Carson either of ignoring important facts about the dangers or safety of DDT or of not telling the whole story. What specific kinds of evidence does he present to support this accusation? (See pages 76–82 for a discussion of kinds of evidence.) How persuasive is this evidence, in your view? Do you think Bailey's argument is influenced by his own views about the environment, as he believes Carson's argument was influenced by her views about the environment? Explain, citing specific passages from the essay to support your answer. **4.** In Bailey's view, what are the consequences of the problems that he describes with Rachel Carson's *Silent Spring*? Why is it important for us to understand these consequences? What should be done about this situation, in his opinion? Do you agree? Why or why not? **5.** Bailey's essay was published in *Reason* magazine, which is considered libertarian in its viewpoint and which advocates liberty and individual choice. To what extent do you think Bailey's essay reflects the perspective of *Reason*? How effective do you think his argument would be for an audience that advocates environmental protection — for example, members of the Sierra Club? Do you think Bailey would be concerned if such readers would dismiss his argument? Explain. **6.** Given the intensity of arguments about environmental issues — and given the potential health and economic consequences of environmental damage — evaluate Bailey's contributions to the ongoing debates about protecting our environment. What value do you think Bailey's essay has in these ongoing debates? To what extent does Bailey's essay help us better address the challenge of finding fair and reasonable ways to protect our environment?

③ **JACK TURNER, "In Wildness Is the Preservation of the World"**

In the following essay from his book *The Abstract Wild* (1996), writer and environmentalist Jack Turner states that "most people no longer have much direct experience of wild nature." As a result, he suggests, neither those who seek to preserve wilderness areas nor those who oppose such preservation really know what they're talking about; they simply do not understand the *wild*. What's more, Turner contends, our wilderness is not wild. Instead, it is packaged and managed in parks and preserves that are more like museums than genuine wild areas. In providing his reasons for his unconventional view, Turner challenges us to rethink not only our relationship to wilderness but also our very understanding of what it means to be human. He advocates a sense of self as intimately part of the wild — in a very physical sense. Only this direct experience of the wild — and this sense of ourselves *as* wild — will lead to the kind of passionate commitment to wilderness that Turner believes is essential for preserving wilderness. Turner's argument might seem extreme at times, and you might wonder about the feasibility of the kind of direct experience of the wild that he advocates. Can everyone really have such experience? Yet as extreme as his views might sometimes seem, Turner reminds us that all arguments about wilderness preservation are in a sense about how we understand ourselves in relation to the natural world. A former philosophy professor, Turner is now a mountain guide and writer whose articles and books focus on environmental issues.

In Wildness Is the Preservation of the World
JACK TURNER

I wish my neighbors were wilder.

— HENRY THOREAU

*Created by President John F. Kennedy in 1962, Point Reyes National Seashore in the middle of California's coast is known for its biological diversity and panoramic views.

1 Hanging from the ceiling of the visitors center at Point Reyes National Seashore* are plaques bearing famous quotations about the value of the natural world. The one from Thoreau, from his essay "Walking," reads: "In Wilderness is the preservation of the World." This, of course, is a mistake. Henry didn't say "wilderness," he said "wildness." But the mistake has become a cliché, suitable for T-shirts and bumper stickers. I think this mistake is like a Freudian slip: it serves a repressive function, the avoidance of conflict, in this case the tension between wilderness as property and wildness as quality. I also think we are all confused

about this tension. William Kittredge has been candid enough to admit that "For decades I misread Thoreau. I assumed he was saying wilderness. . . . Maybe I didn't want Thoreau to have said wildness, I couldn't figure out what he meant."[1] I agree.

I believe that mistaking wilderness for wildness is one cause of our increasing failure to preserve the wild earth and that Kittredge's honesty identifies the key issue: we are confused about what Thoreau meant by wildness, we aren't sure what we mean by wildness, and we aren't clear how or what wildness preserves.

If you study the indexes in the recent scholarly edition of Thoreau's works published by Princeton University Press, you will discover that "wild" and "wilderness" do not often occur. Nor do Thoreau's journal entries during the period he was writing "Walking," roughly the spring of 1851, explain what he might have meant. But after reading Richard C. Trench's *On the Study of Words,* published in 1852, Thoreau made the following important note in his "Fact-Book": *"Wild —* past participle of *to will,* self-willed."[2]

We are also confused about what Thoreau meant by "world." I do not believe he meant merely our planet, even in the fashionable sense of Gaia. Near the end of "Walking" he says, "We have to be told that the Greeks called the World Κόσμος, Beauty, or Order, but we do not see clearly why they did so, and we esteem it at best only a curious philological fact."[3] Our modern word is *cosmos,* and the most recent philological studies suggest the meaning of harmonious order.[4] So in the broadest sense we can say that Thoreau's "In Wildness is the preservation of the World" is about the relation of free, self-willed, and self-determinate "things" with the harmonious order of the cosmos. Thoreau claims that the first

HENRY DAVID THOREAU

Best known for *Walden,* his account of living by himself in a cabin by Walden Pond near his home in Concord, Massachusetts, Henry David Thoreau (1817–1862) is remembered for his love of nature and belief in independence of spirit. An individualist who nevertheless took much interest in the world around him, Thoreau advocated living simply — in harmony with nature and with absolute integrity. Thoreau delivered "Walking" as a lecture late in his life, and it was published only after his death. Today it is regarded as one of the texts that shaped the development of the environmental movement. Part of the essay is included in the *Con-Text* on page 419. You can find the full text of "Walking" online at www.ecotopia.org/ehof/Thoreau/walking.html.

preserves the second. The problem is this: it is not clear to any of us, I think, how the wildest acts of nature — earthquakes, wildfires, the plagues, people being killed and eaten by mountain lions and grizzly bears, our lust, the open sea in storm — preserve a harmonious cosmic order.

5 I know of no author who directly addresses this issue, and a cursory examination of our environmental literature will convince anyone that we are not dealing with a saying that, for most preservationists, describes the heart of our ideology. Indeed, it was not until Gary Snyder published *The Practice of the Wild* that we had a general discussion of what nature, wildness, and wilderness mean and how they are connected. This situation shouldn't surprise us, because most people no longer have much direct experience of wild nature, and few meditate on the cosmos. Since language and communication are social phenomena that presume common, shared experience, it follows that clarity about the issue, perhaps even discourse, is impossible. I would go so far as to say that in many inner cities, here and in the developing world, people no longer have a concept of wild nature based on

*Philosopher Ralph Waldo Emerson (1803–1882) is widely considered one of the most influential figures in the development of American ideas about education and nature. He is closely associated with Thoreau, whom he mentored.

personal experience. Mostly, the wild is something bad reported by television. As a New York wit has it, "Nature is something I pass through between my hotel and my taxi." And, needless to say, a growing world population ignorant of the key concepts of our movement will hinder the cause of preservation and render its goals increasingly unrealistic.

"Walking," and also *Walden* and two other essays — "Resistance to Civil Government" (unfortunately called "Civil Disobedience" most of the time) and "Life without Principle" — express the radical heart of Thoreau's life's work, and since he revised "Walking" just before his death, we may assume it accurately represents his ideas.

The most notable fact about these works is that Thoreau virtually ignores our current concerns with the preservation of habitats and species. He would no doubt include them — he says "all good things are wild and free" — but he writes mainly about human beings, their literature, their myths, their history, their work and leisure, and, of course, their walking. His question, which he got from Emerson,* is about human life: "How

ought I to live?" Thoreau is unique because part of his answer to this old question involves wildness. In "Walking," he says, for instance, "Give me for my friends and neighbors wild men, not tame ones. The wildness of the savage is but a faint symbol of the awful ferity with which good men and lovers meet" (122). And listen to the essay's opening lines: "I wish to speak a word for Nature, for absolute freedom and wildness, as contrasted with a freedom and culture merely civil, — to regard man as an inhabitant, or a part and parcel of Nature, rather than a member of society" (93). Absolute freedom. Absolute wildness. Human beings as inhabitants of that absolute freedom and wildness. This is not the usual environmental rhetoric, and Kittredge is surely correct: most of us simply don't know what Thoreau means.

What is equally confounding is that people who have led a life of intimate contact with wild nature — a buckaroo working the Owyhee country, a halibut fisherman plying the currents of the Gulf of Alaska, an Eskimo whale hunter, a rancher tending a small cow/calf operation, a logger with his chain saw — often oppose preserving wild nature. The friends of preservation, on the other hand, are often city folk who depend on weekends and vacations in designated wilderness areas and national parks for their (necessarily) limited experience of wildness. This difference in degree of experience of wild nature, the dichotomy of friends/enemies of preservation, and the notorious inability of these two groups to communicate also indicate the depth of our muddle about wildness. We don't know what we mean, and those who have the most experience with the wild disagree with what we want to achieve.

We also presume that the experience of wildness and wilderness are related, and this is plausible (though it ignores

elements of our personal lives that also might be thought of as wild: sex, dreams, rage, etc.). However, since wilderness is a place, and wildness a quality, we can always ask, "How wild is our wilderness?" and "How wild is our experience there?" My answer? Not very, particularly in the wilderness most people are familiar with, the areas protected by the Wilderness Act of 1964.[†]

10 There are many reasons for this. Some are widely acknowledged, and I will pass over them briefly, but there is one reason that is not widely accepted, a reason that is offensive to many minds, but one that goes to the heart of Thoreau's opening lines, namely, that human beings no longer accept their status as "part and parcel" of a biological realm that is self-willed, self-determined, self-ordered. Instead we have divided ourselves from that realm and make every attempt to control it for our own interests. Wilderness is one of the few places where we can begin to correct this division; hence, despite the rage for wilderness as a bastion for conserving biodiversity, I am inclined to think its primary importance remains what the founders of the conservation movement thought it was: a basis for an important kind of human experience. Without big, wild wilderness I doubt most of us will ever see ourselves as part and parcel of nature.

Why isn't our wilderness wild, and why is there so little experience of wildness there? Well, first of all, the wilderness that most people visit (with the exception of Alaska and Canada) is too small — in space and time. Like all experience, the experience of the wild can be a taste or a feast, and a feast presumes substance and leisure. Yet about a third of our legislated wilderness units are smaller than 10,000 acres, an area approximately four miles long on each side. An easy stroll. Some wilderness areas,

usually islands, have fewer than 100 acres, and I have been told that Point Reyes now has meaningless "wilderness zones" measuring several hundred yards.

Even our largest wilderness areas are small. Only 4 percent are larger than 500,000 acres, an area 27 miles on a side, and since many follow the ridges of mountain ranges, they are so elongated that a strong hiker can cross one in a single day. True, some are adjacent to other wilderness areas and remote BLM lands and national parks, but compared to the Amazon, Alaska, the Northwest Territories, or the Himalayas, most Wilderness Act wilderness seems very small indeed.

Unfortunately, without sufficient space and time the experience of wildness in the wilderness is diminished or simply doesn't exist. Many people agree with Aldo Leopold that it should take a couple of weeks to pack across a true wilderness, something that probably isn't possible in the lower forty-eight now. The law is simple: The farther you are from a road, and the longer you are out, the wilder your experience. Two weeks is the minimum, a month is better. Until then the mind remains saturated with human concerns and blind to the natural world, the body bound to metronomic time and ignorant of natural biological rhythms. A traveler in small wilderness for a weekend backpack trip remains ignorant of these differences between short and long stays in wilderness, yet a long stay is fundamental to seeing ourselves as part of biological nature, for the order of nature is above all a rhythmic order.

Second, small wilderness units usually lack predators. Sometimes this is simply a function of their small size, but sometimes it's a function of artificial borders created according to economic and political, rather than ecological, criteria. The result is the same: the wilderness is

[†]**The Wilderness Act of 1964 defines *wilderness* as follows: "A wilderness, in contrast with those areas where man and his own works dominate the landscape, is hereby recognized as an area where the earth and its community of life are untrammeled by man, where man himself is a visitor who does not remain."**

CONTEXT

The Bureau of Land Management (BLM) is a U.S. government agency in the Department of the Interior that manages 262 million acres of public land, mostly in western states. The BLM describes its mission in part as sustaining "the health, diversity, and productivity of the public lands for the use and enjoyment of present and future generations." Lands under BLM management are used for a variety of purposes, including grazing livestock, mining, logging, and recreation. The BLM's policies have often been the subject of criticism by environmentalists as well as by proponents of the development of wilderness areas.

tamed. Predators are perhaps our most accessible experience of the wild. To come upon a grizzly track is to experience the wild in a most intimate, carnal way, an experience that is marked by gross alterations in attention, perception, body language, body chemistry, and emotion. Which is to say you feel yourself as part of the biological order known as the food chain, perhaps even as part of a meal.

15 Third, this tameness is exacerbated by our current model for appropriate human use of the wild — the intensive recreation that requires trail systems, bridges, signs for direction and distance, backcountry rangers, and rescue operations that in turn generate activities that further diminish wildness — maps, guide books, guiding services, advertising, photography books, instructional films — all of which diminish the discovery, surprise, the unknown, and the often-dangerous Other — the very qualities that make a place wild. Each of these reductions tames and domesticates the wilderness and diminishes wild experience.

Fourth, intensive recreational use influences public policy, leading those with authority to institute artificial methods of control that benefit recreational use. Animal populations are managed by controlled hunting, wildfires are suppressed, predators

moved, and humans treated in a manner best described by the word "surveillance." The wild becomes a problem to be solved by further human intervention — scientific studies, state and federal laws, judicial decision, political compromise, and administrative and bureaucratic procedures. Once this intervention begins, it never ends; it spirals into further and further human intrusion, rendering wilderness increasingly evaluated, managed, regulated, and controlled. That is, tamed. Nibble by nibble, decision by decision, animal by animal, fire by fire, we have diminished the wildness of our wilderness.

Thus diminished, wilderness becomes a special unit of property treated like a historic relic or ruin — a valuable remnant. It becomes a place of vacations (a word related to "vacant, empty"). Humans become foreigners to the wild, foreigners to an experience that once grounded their most sacred beliefs and values. In short, wilderness as relic leads to tourism, and tourism in the wilderness becomes the primary mode of experiencing a diminished wild.

Wilderness as relic always converts places into commodities, because tourism, in its various manifestations, is a form of commerce. All tourism is to some degree destructive, and wilderness tourism is no exception. Virtually

> ### COMPLICATION
>
> Sometimes called "eco-tourism," wilderness tourism has become a multi-billion-dollar industry in the past few decades. A study by the Council for Environmental Cooperation reported in 2000 that tourism was the largest industry worldwide, and nature travel was the fastest-growing segment of that industry. A separate study estimated that nature travel accounted for $260 billions annually in revenues in the United States. Some proponents of wilderness tourism argue that it can support efforts to preserve the environment. For example, Ralph Keller, of the Eco-tourism Association of Vancouver (Canada), where conflicts have erupted between the eco-tourism business and industries such as logging, argued in 1999 that "wilderness, worldwide, is disappearing at an astonishing rate. Those countries with enough foresight to protect wilderness will have a powerful economic edge in years to come."

everyone (including me) in "the Nature business" feeds (literally) on wilderness as commodity. We are enthralled with our ability to make a living with this exchange, but we tend to ignore the practical consequences for wilderness preservation and for ourselves. Wilderness tourism is not a free lunch. Its worse consequence is that it conceals what should be its primary use: the wild as a project of the self. Compared with residency in a wild biological realm, where the experience of wildness is part of everyday life, wilderness tourism is pathetic. It has had some very bad consequences, and we need to acknowledge them.

Wilderness tourism ignores, perhaps even caricatures, the experience that decisively marked the founders of wilderness preservation: Henry Thoreau, John Muir, Robert Marshall, Aldo Leopold, and Olaus Murie.* The kind of wildness they experienced has become very rare — an endangered experience. As a result, we no longer understand the roots of our own cause. Reading the works of these men and then looking at an issue of, say, *Sierra* can cause severe disorientation. The founders had something we lack, something Thoreau called "Indian Wisdom." For much of their lives these men lived in and studied nature before it became a "wilderness area," and their knowledge came not from visitor centers and guidebooks but from intimate, direct personal experience.

20 Thoreau's knowledge of the lands surrounding Concord was so vast that some of the town's children believed that, like God, Henry had created it all. His knowledge of flora was so precise, a rare fern species not seen for a hundred years was recently rediscovered by examining his notes, and his examination of the succession of forest trees is a seminal essay for modern ecology. Muir spent months alone in the wild Sierra Nevada and made origi-

nal contributions to the study of glaciers. The lives of Marshall, Leopold, and Murie similarly exhibit extensive personal experience and knowledge of wilderness and wildness. To a considerable degree their lives were devotions to wild nature. Without such devotion, I do not believe there would be Thoreau's epiphanies on Katahdin, Muir's mystical identification with trees, or Leopold's thinking like a mountain.

Wilderness tourism is completely different. It is devoted to fun. We hunt for fun, fish for fun, climb for fun, ski for fun, and hike for fun. This is the grim harvest of the "fun hog" philosophy that powered the wilderness-recreation boom for three decades, the philosophy of *Outside* magazine and dozens of its ilk, and there is little evidence that either the spiritual or scientific concerns of the original conservationists — or the scientific concerns of conservation biologists — have trickled down to most wilderness fun hogs.

Given the ignorance and arrogance of most fun hogs, it is understandable that those who stand to lose by increased wilderness designation — farmers, ranchers, loggers, commercial fishermen, American Indians — are often enraged. Instead of a clash of needs, the preservation of the wild appears to be a clash of work versus recreation. Lacking a deeper experience of wildness and access to the lore, myth, metaphor, and ritual necessary to share that experience, there is no communication, no vision, that might shatter the current dead-end of wilderness debate. Both groups exploit the wild, the first by consuming it, the second by converting it into a playpen and then consuming it. Worship of wilderness designation thus becomes idolatry, the confusion of a symbol with its essence. In either case the result is the same: destruction of the wild.

*Sometimes called the father of our national park system, John Muir (1838–1914) is credited with inspiring President Theodore Roosevelt to found Yosemite National Park; Muir was also the founder of the Sierra Club. Robert Marshall (1906–1938) founded the Wilderness Society and fought to preserve wilderness in its natural state. Environmental activist Aldo Leopold (1887–1948) wrote *A Sand County Almanac* (1949), which promoted his idea of a "land ethic" and influenced the environmental movement in the 1960s and 1970s. Olaus Murie (1889–1963) helped establish Jackson Hole National Monument and led the campaign to establish the nine million acre Arctic National Refuge in Alaska.

DEEP ECOLOGY

The deep ecology movement, which grew out of the ideas of Norwegian philosopher Arne Naess, emphasizes a holistic view of the relationship between humans and the environment. Deep ecologists embrace all manner of diversity and advocate a set of values that emphasizes harmony in our relationships to each other and to the natural world, of which we are a part. According to philosophy scholar Alan Drengson, "Supporters of the deep ecology movement platform are committed to recognizing and respecting in word and deed the inherent worth of humans and other beings. This leads to actions that try to minimize our own impacts on ecological communities and other human cultures."

With wilderness tourism we also lose our most effective weapon for preserving what little remains of the natural world: emotional identification. At the bedrock level, what drives both reform environmentalism and deep ecology is a practical problem: how to compel human beings to respect and care for wild nature. The tradition of Thoreau and Muir says that the best way to do this is raw, visceral contact with wild nature. True residency in the wild brings identification and a generalized "not in my back yard," or NIMBY, response that extends sympathy to all the wild world. Without this identification, solutions are abstract and impotent — that is, impractical. But because so many of us are obsessed with fun in the wild, there is a lot of impractical, impotent stuff dominating environmental thought. We have fun and we have philosophy, but we have little serious use of wilderness to study our place in nature, to study, that is, the relation between freedom and the cosmos.

For example, giving trees and animals moral rights analogous to the rights of humans has bogged down in a morass of value theory. The aesthetic campaign to preserve the wild has done as much harm as good, since it suggests (especially in a nation of relativists) that preservation is a matter of taste, a preference no more compelling than the choice between vanilla and chocolate. It leads to tedious arguments that begin with "Who are you to say that we shouldn't have snowmobiles in the Teton wilderness?" on the model of "Who are you to say I shouldn't eat chocolate?" This, in turn, leads inevitably to questions of egalitarianism and elitism, and hence directly into the dismal swamp of politics, which, as Thoreau says in "Walking," is the most alarming of man's affairs. Politicians are invariably people of the *polis* — city slickers, those furthest removed from the natural order. 25 Philosophers have been no more helpful. Deep ecologists are desperately attempting to replace the philosophical foundations of a mechanical model of the world with those of an organic model of the world. Unfortunately, these new foundations are not at all obvious to the other philosophers, not to mention the lay public. The search for foundations — for science, mathematics, logic, or the social sciences — has been the curse of rationalism from Descartes to the present, and the foundations of deep ecology will not exorcise that curse. Many explications of deep ecology rely on some of the most obscure ruminations of Spinoza, Whitehead, and Heidegger. This bodes ill for big wilderness.

All these things are reasonable (sort of), but as Hume saw clearly, reason alone is insufficient to move the will. We should repeat this to ourselves every day like a mantra. Reason has not compelled us to respect and care for wild nature, and we have no basis to believe it will in the future. Philosophical arguments, moralizing, aesthetics, political legislation, and abstract philosophies are notoriously incapable of compelling human behavior. Given the choice, I would side with the fun hogs, who are at least out there connecting with the wild on some level.

Wilderness tourism also results in little art, literature, poetry, myth, or lore for many, if not most, of our wild places. In "Walking," Thoreau described "the West" as "preparing to add its fables to those of the East. The valleys of the Ganges, the Nile, and the Rhine, having yielded their crop, it remains to be seen what the valleys of the Amazon, the Platte, the Orinoco, the St. Lawrence, and the Mississippi will produce" (121). Well, nearly 150 years later, it still remains to be seen. If you ask for the art, literature, lore, myth, and fable of where I live, the headwaters of the Snake River, I would answer that we are working on it, but it might be awhile, because art that takes a place as its subject is created by people who live in and develop a sense of that place. And this takes lots of time. This is true of both wilderness and civilization. Joyce grew up in Dublin, Atget lived in Paris, Muir and Adams lived in Yosemite, Henry Beston lived on Cape Code. Many of our best writers on wilderness — Abbey, Snyder, Peacock — worked as fire lookouts for the U.S. Forest Service. (There is probably a doctoral dissertation here: "The Importance of Fire Lookouts in the Development of Western Nature Literature.") But if access to the wild world is limited to weekend tourism, we have no reason to expect a literature and lore of wild nature.

Yet most of us, when we think about it, realize that after our own direct experience of nature, what has contributed most to our love of wild places, animals, plants — and even, perhaps, to our love of wild nature, our sense of our citizenship — is the art, literature, myth, and lore of nature. For here is the language we so desperately lack, the medium necessary for vision. Mere concepts and abstractions will not do, because love is beyond concepts and abstractions. And yet the problem is one of love. As

Stephen Jay Gould wrote, "We cannot win this battle to save species and environments without forging an emotional bond between ourselves and nature as well — for we will not fight to save what we do not love."[5] The conservation movement has put much thought, time, effort, and money into public policy and science, and far too little into direct personal experience and the arts. There is nothing wrong with public policy and science, but since they will not produce love, they must remain secondary in the cause of preservation.

And finally, wilderness tourism produces no phenology of wild places, the study of periodic phenomena in nature — bird migration, mating of animals, leafing of trees, the effects of climate. This is unfortunate, for phenology, as Paul Shepard has reminded us, is the study of the mature naturalist — the gate

*Phenology is the study of periodic biological phenomena such as the flowering of trees and the migration of birds.

through which nature becomes personal.[6] Leopold published phenological studies of two counties in Wisconsin, and Thoreau dedicated the last years of his life to studying the mysterious comings and goings of the natural world. Phenology* requires a complete immersion in place over time so that the attention, the senses, and the mind can scrutinize and discern widely — the dates of arrivals and departures, the births, the flourishings, the decays, and the deaths of wild things, their successions, synchronicities, dependencies, reciprocities, and cycles — the lived life of the earth. To be absorbed in this life is to merge with larger patterns. Here ecology is not studied, but felt, so that truths become known in the same way a child learns hot from cold — truths that are immune from doubt and argument and, most important, can never be taken away. Here is the common wisdom of indigenous peoples, a wisdom that cannot emerge from tourism in a relic wilderness.

30 We are left with the vital importance of residency in wild nature, and a visceral knowledge of that wildness, as the most practical means of preserving the wild. What we need now is a new tradition of the wild that teaches us how human beings live best by living in and studying the wild without taming it or destroying it. Such a tradition of the wild did exist; it is as old as the Pleistocene. Before Neolithic times, human beings were always living in, traveling through, and using lands we now call wilderness; they knew it intimately, they usually respected it, they often cared for it. It is the tradition of the people that populated all of the wilderness of North America, a tradition that influenced Taoism and Hinduism and informed major Chinese and Japanese poetic traditions. It is the tradition that emerged again with

Emerson and Thoreau. In short, it is a tradition that could again compel respect, care, and love for wild nature in a way that philosophical foundations, aesthetics, moral theory, and public policy cannot. It is a tradition we need to recreate for ourselves, borrowing when necessary from native cultures, but making it new — a wild tradition of our own.

A wild bunch is forming, an eclectic tribe returning to the wild to study, learn, and express. From them will come the lore, myth, literature, art, and ritual we so require. Frank Craighead, John Haines, and Gary Snyder are among the elders of this tribe. There is also Richard Nelson on his island, Doug Peacock with his grizzlies, Terry Tempest Williams and her beloved birds, Hannah Hinchman and her illuminated journals, Gary Nabhan and his seeds, Dolores LaChapelle and her rituals, and many others — all new teachers of the wild. Their mere presence is not sufficient, however. It will not help us if this tradition is created for us, to be read about in yet another book. To create a wilder self, the self must live the life of the wild, mold a particular form of human character, a form of life. Relics will not do, tourism will not do, books will not do.

If we want this wilder self, we must begin, in whatever ways we can imagine, to rejoin the natural world. One way is to consider our bodies as food for others. Out there is the great feeding mass of beings we call the Earth. We incorporate, and are incorporated, in ways not requiring legal papers. We are creator and created, terrorist and hostage, victim and executioner, guest of honor and part of the feast. This system of food, which is hidden from the urban mind, is terrifying in its identity and reciprocity. It is a vision that could inform everything from our private spiritual matters to the gross facts of nourishment and death. It at least partly answers Thoreau's question, "How should I live?" Now we have to figure out how we can achieve it here and now, in this place, in these times.

I am convinced that such a life is still possible. I love my Powerbook, my Goretex gear, and my plastic kayak. But I also make a point to eat fritillaria, morels, berries, fish, and elk. I want to feed directly from my place, to incorporate it. When I die, I wish my friends could present my body as a gift to the flora and fauna of my home, Grand Teton National Park, because I want my world to incorporate me.

On my travels in Tibet I was always delighted by the tradition of sky-burial. The human body is cut up and the bones broken to the marrow and left for animals, mostly birds. Later the bones are pounded and mixed with tsampa — a roasted barley — and again offered to the animals. Finally everything is gone, gone back into the cycle. Recently, when a friend lost her beloved dog, she carried it out to a beautiful view of the mountains, covered it with wild flowers, and left it for the coyotes and ravens and bugs. We should have the courage to do the same for ourselves, to re-enter the great cycle of feeding.

35 The moose incorporates the willow, taking the life of the willow into its own life, making the wildness of the willow reincarnate. I kill the moose, its body feeds the willow and grouse wortleberries where it dies, it feeds my body, and in feeding my body, the willow and the moose feed the one billion bacteria that inhabit three inches of my colon, the one million spirochetes that live in my mouth, and the microscopic brontosaurus-like mites that live by devouring the goo on my eyelashes. This great feeding body is the world. It evolved together, mutually, all interdependent, all interrelating ceaselessly, the dust of old stars hurtling through time, and we are the form it chose to make it conscious of itself.

From this vision of a wild order in complete interdependence comes freedom, a freedom unlike our civil freedoms but, I think, close to what Thoreau imagined. Perhaps it is best expressed by the Taittiriya Upanishad:[7]

O wonderful! O wonderful!
O wonderful!
I am food! I am food! I am food!
I eat food! I eat food! I eat food!
My name never dies, never dies,
never dies!
I was born first in the first of the
worlds,
earlier than the gods, in the belly
of what has no death!
Whoever gives me away has helped
me the most!
I, who am food, eat the eater of
food!
I have overcome this world!

He who knows this shines like
the sun.
Such are the laws of mystery!

1. Kittredge, William. "What Do We Mean?" *Northern Lights* 6 (Fall 1990).

2. See Sherman Paul, *The Shores of America: Thoreau's Inward Exploration* (University of Illinois Press, 1958), 412–17, and Robert D. Richardson, Jr., *Henry Thoreau: A Life of the Mind* (University of California Press, 1986), 224–27.

3. Thoreau, Henry David. "Walking." *The Natural History Essays.* Salt Lake City, UT: Peregrine Smith Books, 1984, Page 130.

4. This is the meaning given by Eric Partridge in *Origins: A Short Etymological Dictionary of Modern*

English (New York: Macmillan, 1958).

5. Gould, Stephen Jay, "Unenchanted Evening." *Natural History* (September 1991): 14.

6. Shepard, Paul: *Nature and Madness,* (San Francisco: Sierra Club Books, 1982), 132.

7. Translated by Lewis Hyde and used as an epigraph for his book *The Gift: Imagination and the Erotic Life of Property* (New York: Random House, 1979).

Questions for Discussion

1. What is the importance of distinguishing *wilderness* from *wildness*, according to Turner? What would you have to do if you wanted to experience both? What does this distinction have to do with current debates about environmental preservation, as Turner sees it? **2.** Turner gives a great deal of emphasis to the ideas of Henry David Thoreau in this essay (see the sidebar on page 433). Evaluate his use of Thoreau's work. What do you think he achieves by establishing that Thoreau's meaning is unclear? How does he use Thoreau's ideas to help make his main argument. What does this emphasis on Thoreau suggest about Turner's sense of audience? **3.** Turner asserts that there are at least four reasons that people have little true experience of the wild. What do these four reasons suggest about Turner's beliefs about wilderness? What do they suggest about Turner's values in general? Do you think Turner is right that people today have very little genuine experience with the wild? Why or why not? **4.** Why does Turner criticize wilderness tourism? How do these criticisms support his main argument? Do you agree with him? What benefits do you see to wilderness tourism that Turner overlooks? **5.** Although he admits to wearing Goretex and having a plastic kayak, Turner is critical of "fun hogs," or people who spoil wilderness by using it as "a playpen." What does this imply about how he would like to see wilderness areas managed? How does his position about "fun hogs" influence your sense of him as a credible author? **6.** Turner asserts that the kind of relationship to the wild that he advocates is still possible today. Do you agree with him? Why or why not? What objections to his position can you offer? To what extent do you think Turner adequately addresses these objections? **7.** Using the Toulmin model of argumentation (see pages 31–35), identify the central claims that Turner makes in this essay. Also identify his main warrants. To what extent do you think most Americans would accept these warrants?

④ VANDANA SHIVA, "Values Beyond Price"

Vandana Shiva is an internationally known activist for women's rights and environmental protection. A physicist by training, she founded the Research Foundation for Science, Ecology, and Technology and its affiliated program, Navdanya, to support biodiversity and to protect indigenous foods and local cultures from the effects of globalization and multinational agribusiness. She has been an insistent voice for Third World interests on environmental issues, arguing that environmental activists impose Western values on their efforts to protect the global environment. As a result, she insists, the needs of local inhabitants in places such as her native India are ignored, often with disastrous results. Shiva challenges those who care about the environment to rethink the relationship between humans, nature, culture, and commerce. When she argues that monetary values are at the root of the ecological crisis, as she does in the following essay, she pushes readers to understand environmental protection as something more than a conflict between economic development and wilderness preservation. For Shiva, arguments about environmental protection cannot be separated from issues of social justice. Her essay, which was published in 1996 in the journal *Our Planet*, will no doubt seem provocative to some Western readers. But it reminds us that when we argue about issues as important as the environment, we always do so from a particular cultural perspective that is informed by certain values and beliefs. Identifying those values and beliefs can be the first step toward resolving difficult questions about protecting the earth.

Values Beyond Price
VANDANA SHIVA

1 In the *Vishnu Purana,* the world is destroyed and recreated by the cosmic being when human values fail to maintain nature and society. (See "*Vishnu Purana*" on page 444.) Vishnu, the Creator, assumes the character of Rudra or Shiva, the destroyer, and descends to reunite all his creatures with himself. He enters into the seven rays of the sun and drinks up all the waters of the Earth, leaving the seas and the springs dry.

The reduction of all value to wealth and the exclusion of compassion and care from human relationships are among the factors that cause this dissolution. As the *Vishnu Purana* puts it: "The minds of men will be wholly occupied in acquiring wealth, and wealth will be spent solely on selfish gratification. Men will fix their desires upon riches, even though dishonestly acquired. No man will part with the smallest fraction of the smallest coin, though entreated by a friend. The people will be almost always in dread of dearth and apprehensive of scarcity."

VISHNU PURANA

Composed in the first or second century, and consisting of approximately 23,000 verses, the *Vishnu Purana* is an important Hindu text describing the creation of the universe, the earth, and all living things. Vishnu, who is both a creator and a destroyer, is foremost among Hindu gods and forms part of a trinity with Shiva and Brahma. Although there are several other Puranas, the *Vishnu Purana* has been called Puranartna, or "gem of Puranas." Like the Bible, the *Vishnu Purana* is studied by both theologians and laypeople who are interested in understanding the nature of the universe and the place of human beings within it.

*The World Bank is an international lending agency backed by the governments of the countries that dominate the world's economy. Among other activities, some of which are controversial, the World Bank helps to finance major construction projects in developing nations.

The links between greed, scarcity and destruction that this story brings out are at the heart of the ecological crisis. The reduction of all value to monetary value is an important aspect of the crisis of scarcity generated by the process of increasing affluence.

It is often said that the roots of environmental destruction lie in treating natural resources as "free" and not giving them "value." Most discussions in the dominant paradigm assume that monetary, commercial or market value is the only way of measuring or valuing the environment. It is falsely assumed that value can be reduced to price.

5 However, the market is not the only source of values, and monetary values are not the only ones. Spiritual values treat certain resources and ecosystems as sacred — there are also such social values as those associated with common property resources. In both cases, resources have no price — but a very high value. In fact, it is precisely because their value is high that these resources are not left to the market but are taken beyond the domain of monetary value so as to protect and conserve them.

The proposal to solve the ecological crisis by giving market values to all resources is like offering the disease as the cure. The reduction of all value to commercial value, and the removal of all spiritual, ecological, cultural and social limits to exploitation — the shift that took place at the time of industrialization — is central to the ecological crisis.

This shift is reflected in the change in the meaning of the term "resource," which originally implied life. Its root is the Latin verb, *surgere,* evoking the image of a spring continually rising from the ground. Like a spring, a "resource" rises again and again, even if it has been repeatedly used and consumed. The word highlighted nature's power of self-regeneration and her prodigious creativity. Moreover, it implied an ancient idea about the relationship between humans and nature — that the Earth bestows gifts on humans who, in turn, are well advised not to suffocate her generosity. In early modern times, "resources" therefore suggested reciprocity along with regeneration.

With the advent of industrialism and colonialism, "natural resources" became the parts of nature required as inputs for industrial production and colonial trade. In 1870 John Yeates in his *Natural History of Commerce* offered the first definition of this new meaning: "In speaking of the natural resources of any country, we refer to the ore in the mine, the stone unquarried (etc.)."

Regeneration Denied

By this view, nature has been stripped of her creative power and turned into a container for raw materials waiting to be transformed into inputs for commodity production. Resources are merely any materials or conditions existing in nature which may have potential for "economic exploitation." Without the capacity of regeneration, the attitude of reciprocity has also lost ground: it is now simply human inventiveness and industry which "impart value to nature." Natural resources must be developed and nature will only find her destiny once capital and technology have been brought in. Nature, whose real nature it is to rise again, was transformed by this originally Western world view into dead and manipulatable matter — its capacity to renew and grow denied.

10 The market economy is only one of the world's economies — in addition, there is nature's economy of life-support processes and people's economy in which our sustenance is provided and our needs are met. Nature's economy is the most basic, both in that it is the base of the people's and market economies, and because it has the highest priority to, and claim on, natural resources. However, development and economic growth treat the market economy as the primary one, and either neglect the others or treat them as marginal and secondary.

Capital accumulation does lead to financial growth, but it erodes the natural resource base of all three economies. The result is a high level of ecological instability. The anarchy of growth and the ideology of development based on it are the prime reasons underlying the ecological crises and destruction of natural resources. In order to resolve ecological conflicts and regenerate nature, these economies must be given their due place in the stable foundation of a healthy nature.

Commodification of resources must be replaced by the recovery of commons. This involves the recovery of the domains of nature's economy and the sustenance economy, which, in turn, involves the recovery of the value of nature in its spiritual, ecological and social dimensions.

The dominant model of environmental economics promoted by the World Bank* and major economic powers attempts further to reduce nature's economy and the sustenance economy to the market economy. Preoccupation with "getting the prices right" can lead to a blindness to the fact that the market usually gets the values of justice and sustainability wrong.

The marketization of common resources is based on myths. The first is the equivalence of "value" and "price." Resources — such as sacred forests and rivers — often have very high value while having no price. The second is that

common property resources tend to degrade.[†] Privatization is frequently prescribed for solving "problems" caused by overusing resources under open access and common property. But it is based on the tradeability of private property, while commons are based on the inalienability of shared rights derived from use. The assumption that alienability is more conducive to conservation is derived from the false association of price with value.

15 It has been argued that landowners have little incentive to invest in long-term measures such as soil conservation if they do not have the right to sell or transfer their land, and thus cannot realize the value of any improvements. This is patently false, since the best examples of soil conservation — such as in the hill-terraces of the Himalaya — have been realized for precisely the opposite reasons. Communities who are not threatened by alienation of resources and their benefits have the long-term possibility and interest to conserve them.

Aggravation of Poverty

The dominant paradigm of environmental economics fails to internalize the costs of resource degradation socially and ecologically. Social internalization would imply that those responsible for environmental degradation should bear the costs of it.

Turning commons into commodities is a necessary part of environmental economics in the market paradigm. But it does not stop environmental degradation because

[†]For perspectives on the idea of the "commons," see pages 365–395.

COMPLICATION

According to a 2002 study for the National Bureau of Economic Research, the proportion of the world's population living on less than one dollar per day has dropped from 20 percent to 5 percent in the past twenty-five years, when adjusted for inflation. The report acknowledged that in some countries these trends did not hold, but the global trend seemed clear. In 2001 the Cato Institute, a free market think tank, summed up several studies to report that "in the past 10 years, the percentage of poor people in the developing world fell from 29 to 24 percent."

the economically powerful do not mind paying a higher price for a resource. Other people bear the costs both of the scarcity of a declining resource, to which the rich can continue to have access, and of related scarcities and pollution caused by overexploitation. These ecological costs are not considered in the reductionist model of market internalization.

A genuine internalization would have to include values beyond those of the market, values that put limits on overexploitation. Given the vast gulf between the rich and poor, market prices, no matter how high they rise, will not introduce limits to exploitation. They will therefore not restrict resource exploitation within ecological limits, but will instead allow resource degradation to continue while aggravating poverty and injustice. (See "Complication" on page 445.)

Economic growth takes place through the overexploitation of natural resources, creating a scarcity of them in both nature's economy and the survival economy. Nature shrinks as capital. The growth of

the market cannot solve the very crisis it creates. Furthermore, while natural resources can be converted into cash, cash cannot be converted into nature's ecological processes. Those who offer market solutions to the ecological crisis limit themselves to the market, and look for substitutes to the commercial function of natural resources as commodities and raw material. However, in nature's economy, the currency is not money, it is life.

20 This neglect of the role of natural resources in ecological processes and in people's sustenance economy — and the diversion and destruction of these resources for commodity production and capital accumulation — are the main reasons for both the ecological crisis and the crisis of survival in the developing world. The solution seems to lie in giving local communities control over local resources so that they have the right and responsibility to rebuild nature's economy and, through it, their sustenance. Only this will ensure greater distributive justice, participation and sustainability.

NEGOTIATING DIFFERENCES

As the essays in this section indicate, environmental concerns have not disappeared since Rachel Carson's *Silent Spring* was published in 1962; rather, they have in many ways intensified, despite our increasing awareness of some of the risks that Carson highlighted in her famous book. One of the challenges we now face is how to set environmental priorities and then use them to identify specific actions that can be undertaken to benefit the environment. Part of that challenge is deciding where to place responsibility for some of the environmental problems we face.

For example, whose responsibility is the increased air pollution and greater use of oil that result from the popularity of SUVs? The drivers who purchase such vehicles? The companies that manufacture and sell them? The U.S. government, whose policies allow SUVs to avoid the stricter emissions controls placed on cars? In her essay on page 443, Vandana Shiva argues that "those responsible for environmental degradation should bear the costs for it." But how should we determine that responsibility when so many different people seem to have a hand in that environmental degradation?

Questions for Discussion

1. Shiva opens her argument by drawing on an ancient Hindu text. What effect do you think Shiva achieves by beginning her essay in this way? What do you think this beginning suggests about her sense of her audience? How do you think Western readers might react to this introduction? **2.** Shiva offers a brief history of the idea of "natural resources." What do you think she accomplishes with this history? How might it contribute to her main argument? **3.** What does Shiva mean by the "commodification of resources"? How does this idea fit into her main argument? What does this idea suggest about her own values? **4.** Shiva argues that proposals for treating natural resources as commodities with market value are based on two myths. What are these two myths? Do you think Shiva is justified in calling these ideas or viewpoints "myths"? Why or why not? What might your answer to these questions indicate about your own values and cultural background? **5.** What does Shiva mean by "market internalization"? Why is this idea important to her main argument about market-driven solutions to ecological problems? **6.** What vision for society do you think drives Shiva's argument? To what extent do you think Western readers would share her vision? Cite specific passages from her essay to support your answer; consider especially her second-to-last paragraph.

With these points in mind, identify an environmental problem in your geographic region (or identify a national environmental issue that affects your region), and try to determine who is responsible for this problem. Using whatever sources seem appropriate, try to learn about the problem to identify the factors that seem to have helped create it. Look also for potential solutions to it. Then write an essay to a local audience (e.g., the readers of your local newspaper or residents of an area affected by the problem) in which you argue for what you think is the most feasible solution to the problem. For example, if you were to write your essay about the problem of SUVs that we mentioned in the previous paragraph, you would want to learn about the environmental damage SUVs might cause as well as related problems. And you would want to learn about the extent of those problems in your region. Whatever your topic, try to write an argument that would persuade environmentalists and others affected by the problem that your approach would be a reasonable one.

11

AMERICAN NATIONAL IDENTITY

AMERICAN NAT

Cluster 1
WHO GETS TO BE AN AMERICAN?

(1) Celia C. Perez-Zeeb, "By the Time I Get to Cucaracha"

(2) Peter Brimelow, "A Nation of Immigrants"

(3) Jacob G. Hornberger, "Keep the Borders Open"

(4) Steven Camarota, "Too Many: Looking Today's Immigration in the Face"

CON-TEXT
The New Colossus

Cluster 2
WHAT DOES IT MEAN TO BE A GOOD AMERICAN CITIZEN?

(1) John Balzar. "Needed: informed Voters"

(2) Russ Baker, "Want to Be a Patriot? Do Your Job"

(3) Wilfred M. McClay, "America: Idea or Nation?"

(4) Michael Kazin, "A Patriotic Left"

CON-TEXT
John F. Kennedy's Inaugural Address, 1961

Cluster 3
WHAT KIND OF POWER SHOULD WE GIVE OUR GOVERNMENT?

(1) Martin Luther King, Jr., "Letter from a Birmingham Jail"

(2) Michael Kelly, "Liberties Are a Real Casualty of War"

(3) Heather Green, "Databases and Security vs. Privacy"

(4) Alan M. Dershowitz, "Why Fear National ID Cards?"

CON-TEXT
The Declaration of Independence

ONAL IDENTITY

WHO·GETS·TO·BE

AN AMERICAN?

According to the U.S. Census Bureau, more than 13 million legal and illegal immigrants entered the United States between 1990 and 2000. The Center for Labor Market Studies at Northeastern University determined that immigrants accounted for 50 percent of the 16 million new workers who entered the work force during the 1990s. Those numbers indicate the significant impact that immigrants can have on the U.S. economy. In fact, Andrew Sum, the director of the Center for Labor Market Studies, speaking in 2002 about his center's study of immigrant labor, declared that "the American economy absolutely needs immigrants." ■ Not everyone would agree. The impact of immigrants on U.S. society has long worried many Americans. As Peter Brimelow, whose essay appears on pages 457–462, points out, Americans seem fond of declaring that "we are a nation of immigrants." Indeed, the famous poem inscribed on the Statue of Liberty seems to say unequivocally that America will accept all those who seek a better life here (see *Con-Text* on page 451). Nevertheless, concerns about the effects of immigration on U.S. economic and cultural life have always fueled debates about the extent to which the United States should open its borders to immigrants. Although the patterns of immigration might change from one era to another, the issues surrounding immigration do not. In the late 19th and early 20th centuries, when millions of people came to the United States from eastern European and Mediterranean countries, most of them hoping to escape poverty or political conflict, many Americans saw these new arrivals as a threat to economic stability and even to the values that had shaped the U.S. legal and political systems. As you read through the essays in this section, you will encounter some of those same concerns, expressed more than a century later, at a time when increasing numbers of immigrants are arriving from South America and Asia. ■ But arguments about immigration are not just about policy matters or economic worries. They reflect deeper and more complicated concerns about American identity: What exactly does it mean to be an American? Who decides? And *how* should we decide who will become an American? The authors of the essays in this section address these questions, sometimes focusing on policy and sometimes on ethnicity, race, gender, or national origin. These authors represent a range of views on immigration, but perhaps more important is the fact that their essays reveal how complex the questions about immigration and American national identity can be. In a sense, these authors all seek the same thing: immigration policies that contribute to a society that is consistent with American ideals. The real challenge, though, might be reaching agreement on those ideals. As you read these essays, consider the extent to which these authors help us meet that challenge.

CON-TEXT: "The New Colossus"

This is the famous poem that appears on the pedestal of the Statue of Liberty in New York Harbor:

The New Colossus

by Emma Lazarus

Not like the brazen giant of Greek fame, With conquering
limbs astride from land to land;

Here at our sea-washed, sunset gates shall stand
A mighty woman with a torch, whose flame
Is the imprisoned lightning, and her name
Mother of Exiles. From her beacon-hand
Glows world-wide welcome; her mild eyes command
The air-bridged harbor that twin cities frame.

"Keep ancient lands, your storied pomp!" cries she
With silent lips.

"Give me your tired, your poor,
Your huddled masses yearning to breathe free,
The wretched refuse of your teeming shore.

Send these, the homeless, tempest-tost to me,
I lift my lamp beside the golden door!"

① **CELIA C. PEREZ-ZEEB, "By the Time I Get to Cucaracha"**

Current debates about immigration often focus on the problem of illegal immigrants entering the United States from Mexico and other Central and South American countries. Critics of U.S. immigration policy sometimes charge that the high numbers of illegal immigrants from these countries place a burden on schools and other social services that are paid for by U.S. taxpayers; they also contend that because these immigrants are willing work for low wages, they weaken the job market for legal citizens. These concerns tend to cast the debates about immigration in economic terms. Writer Celia C. Perez-Zeeb, however, believes that concerns about immigration might have more to do with race and gender than with jobs and taxes. In the following essay she focuses attention on the laws governing marriages between immigrants and American citizens, and she points out how those complicated laws can place women at a disadvantage. She also examines the role that ethnic stereotypes about Hispanic people play in public debates about immigration. Although she focuses her argument on how Hispanic people are portrayed in these debates and in the popular media, you might consider whether her argument would apply to other ethnic groups who are associated with immigration. This essay appeared in *Bad Subjects* in 2002.

By the Time I Get to Cucaracha
CELIA C. PEREZ-ZEEB

1 I was watching NBC's *Will and Grace.* It's a show about a woman, Grace, who leaves her fiancé at the chapel on their wedding day and runs off to live with her gay best friend, Will. In this particular episode Karen, Grace's extremely obnoxious socialite assistant, was upset because her housekeeper, Rosario, was going to be deported. In order to keep her in the country they hatched up the old green card* scam, and picked Will's gay friend, Jack, to be the groom. In one scene Karen and Rosario, who have one of those wacky love-hate relationships,

*"Green cards" grant noncitizens the right to live permanently in the United States. (See www.ftc.gov/bcp/conline/pubs/alerts/lottery.htm.)

are arguing and Karen says to Rosario, "If it wasn't for this you'd be flying back to Cucaracha on Air Guacamole with live chickens running up and down the aisle!"

I almost fell off the bed. I could not believe my ears.

The people involved in the creation of the show probably justify such blatantly unfunny and racist remarks by making the Karen character super-annoying, self-absorbed and materialistic, thus excusing her ignorance. Maybe they feel they have a little bit of leeway since they have (gasp!) gay characters in the show, and so, of course, they cannot possibly be racist or discriminatory. But, frankly, I think it's messed up that the maid "just happens" to be Latina because, hey, guess what, Latinas are capable of being more than some yuppie's housekeeper! And that said, we should be grateful to all the women, Latina or otherwise, who earn or have earned a living as house-keepers. My mom was a housekeeper when she first came to this country.

Most of the mainstream media seem to believe it's okay to portray Latinos like dirtballs. Not to mention the fact that Latino characters are usually depicted as being in this country illegally. There are plenty of people out there who already view Latinos as hailing from "Cucaracha" without having their beliefs reinforced by the almighty television. If you think we Latinos have made amazing progress and have many Latino actors on television and in movies that aren't portrayed nega-tively, how about watching the ALMA awards? It pains me to see the as-sociation grasping at straws to have a category in which there are more than two actors and to see how, in most cases, the nominees for awards are supporting actors. Characters not unlike Rosario.

5 But, when I see shows like *Will and Grace,* I wonder where the outrage is? Maybe the right people weren't watching that particular episode and so there was no uproar about it (unlike the whole Taco Bell Chihuahua controversy), but I think there's also something to be said about the fact that people tend to forget that groups other than African-Americans are discriminated against in this country and are often portrayed as racist stereo-types by the media. If the maid had been African-American and "Karen" had made a similarly insulting comment, all hell probably would have broken loose. However, NBC wouldn't have had the balls to even allow such a comment

AMERICAN LATINO MEDIA ARTS (ALMA) AWARDS

The ALMA Awards were created in 1995 as part of an effort among advo-cacy groups to promote fair, accurate, and balanced portrayals of Latinos in television, film, and music. Born as a direct response to negative stereotyp-ing of Latinos in entertainment, these awards honor Latino performers for their outstanding artistic achievement and for enhancing the image of Latinos. The name ALMA, which is Spanish for "spirit" or "soul," is intended to represent the determined spirit of the Latino people as well as the scope of the awards program. (See www.almaawards.com/index.cfm.)

against a black character to air, because it is widely acknowledged that this coun-try has treated black people terribly. And, perhaps more importantly, there are a lot of black activists and groups who would protest. Whatever the reason, it defi-nitely seems to be more acceptable to make fun of certain groups than others.

What's more, pulling this tired and de-ceptive green card story line is ignorant and misleading. They assume (a) that it's easy to become a legal immigrant in such

THE TACO BELL CHIHUAHUA CONTROVERSY

In 1998 the fast-food company Taco Bell ran a series of advertisements fea-turing a talking chihuahua that spoke with a pronounced Spanish accent. Despite the ad campaign's apparent commercial success, many people con-demned the ads as insulting to Latino people. One critic of the ads was Gabriel Cazares the mayor of Clearwater, Florida, who was also a former president of the Tampa, Florida, chapter of the League for United Latin American Citizens. Cazares told an interviewer,

I think it was an unfortunate commercial. I think that the use of a dog to depict Mexicans was very demeaning. If Taco Bell wanted to depict someone that would reflect Mexican culture we have many live, two-legged artists, singers, dancers, musicians — some great people in America that could have been selected to give a testimonial for Taco Bell (and) say, 'Yo quiero un taco.' And that wouldn't have been offensive.

a manner and (b) that illegal immigrants are gaining residency left and right by marrying for green cards. I think it's fucked up that NBC can get away with letting something so insulting and demeaning to Latinos air, but, frankly, I'm not surprised. I'd seen that story line way too many times already in now-defunct shows like *Jesse* and *Beverly Hills 90210*. It's always portrayed as quick, easy, funny, and oh so romantic. Oh look at this wonderful American marrying this poor wetback just so she can stay in the country. How sweet. Yeah, well it isn't.

The rules governing the attainment of residency by non-citizens married to US citizens are not necessarily clear and not necessarily easy to follow. According to US law, marriages between a citizen and non-citizen must be entered into in "good faith." Then, just before a couple's two year anniversary, they must undergo an interview with an immigration officer,

who attempts to make sure their union isn't a sham. The "investigation" includes weird, personal questions like: what side of the bed does your mate sleeps on? Or, what kind of underwear do they wear? During this two-year period the marriage cannot be annulled or terminated unless the spouse dies. And no, permanent resident status isn't automatically granted after two years. A petition has to be entered in order to terminate immigrant status. If it isn't filed then the person can be sent back to their country of origin, unless there's a really good reason for not having filed the petition.

An article in the *Yale Journal of Law and Feminism,* "The Gender Dimensions of U.S. Immigration Policy," argues that female immigrants tend to be at a disadvantage because their entrance into the country often depends more on family ties than other more "legitimate" reasons for entry. For example, employment-based immigration is dominated by men because it tends to favor people who already have advanced degrees in their field, are wealthy, or have much sought after scientific or technological skills. The number of "unskilled" workers who are allowed to enter the country has been lowered; therefore, immigrant women, who tend to come to work as housekeepers or child care providers, have a more difficult time having a "legitimate" reason to enter the United States.

Don't get me wrong, though! The United States does love its immigrants. Of course, on the condition that they can do something for the economy. They don't want to hear about your poverty and persecution, but if you have money or special skills, well, that's a different story. Immigrants are allowed to enter the country legally if they make an outrageous monetary donation. Supermodels are also given special visas as entertainers and as possessors of specialized skills (being skinny and being able to pout on cue, I guess).

10 In 1986 the Immigration Marriage Fraud amendment* was passed by Congress. This is the amendment that made the two-year minimum marriage period mandatory before a person could be considered for permanent resident status. The *Yale Law* article argues that this piece of legislation gives the spouse who is a citizen, most often the male, excessive power over the immigrant spouse because, believe it or not, after the two-year period is over, if the citizen spouse chooses not to sign the petition for resident status then the immigrant spouse and children, if there are any, can be removed from the United States. So for at least two years an immigrant woman can be at the mercy of whatever her spouse wishes.

You get a whole other story from the senators who spoke at the July 26, 1985 session of Congress for the Subcommittee on Immigration and Refugee Policy. According to Senator Alan K. Simpson (chairman of the subcommittee), "United States citizens legitimately petition for 'mail order brides' advertised in the backs of magazines and tabloids sold at the checkout lines of supermarkets. The alien admitted as a fiancé will go through the appearance of wanting to marry and build a future life until after the actual wedding ceremony. The alien then promptly abandons his or her spouse." Now, come on. It's okay for these men to order brides through the mail, but god forbid someone try to marry in order to stay in this country and hope for a better life? Does the idea of ORDERING a bride not seem even slightly disturbing to Senator Simpson?

Throughout his speech Alan Simpson made it seem like those who marry immigrants do so either because they "feel

sorry" for them or because they are being coerced to do so. The "alien" (what's up with that label?) is portrayed as the scheming good-for-nothing, while the United States citizen is just a poor little lamb who is being manipulated. Simpson states that, "Because the alien and the arranger are well aware of the risks and penalties of disclosure . . . , they feel no compunction in intimidating their United States citizen or resident alien spouses or fiancés." Simpson referred to immigrants who sought marriage for residency as "smooth-talking alien(s)" who made it a practice to convince the citizen that they were going into the marriage out of love and then once they obtained their resident status, they dumped the spouse.

It took Simpson awhile, but he eventually got his main concern off his chest when he argued that most of the illegal immigrants attempting to gain residency through marriage were doing so because they could not obtain residency otherwise. The reasons for their inability to obtain visas, according to Simpson, was because "most aliens" have broken the law in some manner — through illegal entry, or due to the fact that they are terrorists, criminals, narcotics users/dealers, or prostitutes. Note the words "MOST ALIENS."

In the early '80s, before the 1986 amendment was passed, the INS estimated that nearly 30% of the cases in which an immigrant had gained resident status through marriage were involved in "suspect marital relationships." When this estimate was revised, the figure was much closer to 8%.

15 Television and movies portray things as if there really are hundreds of thousands of immigrants in the United States getting hitched left and right in order to stay in the country, which is not true. The media makes it seem like a piece of cake to just up and marry and

*Passed by Congress in 1986, the Immigration Marriage Fraud Amendment was intended to deter illegal immigration that occurred through fraudulent marriages between American citizens and immigrants seeking legal status in the United States. The act requires that the U.S. citizen must have met his or her foreign spouse within two years of the marriage, except under certain special circumstances.

CONTEXT

This essay appeared in 2002 in *Bad Subjects: Political Education for Everyday Life*, a journal published by a nonprofit organization that describes itself as "a collective that . . . seeks to revitalize progressive politics in retreat." According to its Web site, *Bad Subjects* believes that "too many people on the left have taken their convictions for granted. So we challenge progressive dogma by encouraging readers to think about the political dimension to all aspects of everyday life. We also seek to broaden the audience for leftist and progressive writing, through a commitment to accessibility and contemporary relevance" (see http://eserver.org/bs/faq/). In what ways do you think this essay addresses the political viewpoints of people who are likely to read this journal?

all of a sudden you're an American, which is also not true. Even sadder is that the media completely trivializes the reasons why people come to this country, or why some women might be so desperate not to return to their countries that they would be willing to marry someone they don't know and potentially endure abuse.

The media rarely, if ever, mentions that many of the Central and South American countries these people are fleeing have been historically terrorized by U.S. supported regimes. The media never bothers to mention that the United States quite often turns a blind eye to the terrorism, the disappearances, the tortures, the rapes, and other abuses being suffered by people who come to this country. Apparently, immigrants are most useful to the U.S. when they are performing backbreaking labor or being the brunt of jokes.

Questions for Discussion

1. What is Perez-Zeeb's main point is this essay? Where in the essay does she state that point most directly? **2.** Using specific examples of Perez-Zeeb's language to support your answer, describe the tone of this essay. Do you think the tone is appropriate to Perez-Zeeb's argument? Explain. **3.** Perez-Zeeb objects to the humor involving Latinos on U.S. television shows, and she specifically criticizes an episode of the television show *Will and Grace* in which a marriage is arranged between two characters, one who is a Latina immigrant and one who is an American citizen. What problem involving immigrants does Perez-Zeeb use this episode to introduce? Do you think her criticism of this television show is an effective strategy, given her main argument? Why or why not? **4.** Perez-Zeeb refers several times to an article from the *Yale Journal of Law and Feminism*. What do you think she accomplishes by making these references? How might these references enhance (or weaken) her argument? **5.** Does the fact that Perez-Zeeb is herself Latina have any effect on her argument? Explain.

② PETER BRIMELOW, "A Nation of Immigrants"

Born and educated in Great Britain, Peter Brimelow now lives and works in the United States. A senior editor of *Forbes* magazine, he is the author of *Alien Nation: Common Sense About America's Immigration Disaster* (1995), *The Patriot Game: Canada and the Canadian Question Revisited* (1987), and *The Wall Street Gurus: How You Can Profit from Investment Newsletters* (1986), among other books. "A Nation of Immigrants" is an editor's title for the following short excerpt from a long, controversial article on immigration that Brimelow published in 1992 in *National Review,* a monthly magazine that reflects politically conservative opinions. Although Brimelow addresses the political debate about immigration policy that was occurring in the early 1990s, his argument really goes beyond policy issues to the complicated question of what constitutes a nation. Does it have to do with ethnic or racial identity? Or is it a matter of political borders and geographic location? Such questions, Brimelow suggests, must be answered if there is to be any acceptable resolution to the continuing conflicts regarding immigration policy in the United States.

A Nation of Immigrants
PETER BRIMELOW

1 Everyone has seen a speeded-up film of the cloudscape. What appears to the naked eye to be a panorama of almost immobile grandeur writhes into wild life. Vast patterns of soaring, swooping movement are suddenly discernible. Great towering cumulo-nimbus formations boil up out of nowhere, dominating the sky in a way that would be terrifying if it were not, in real life, so gradual that we are barely aware that anything is going on.

This is a perfect metaphor for the development of the American nation. America, of course, is exceptional. What is exceptional about it, however, is not the way in which it was created, but the speed.

"We are a nation of immigrants." No discussion of U.S. immigration policy gets far without someone making this helpful remark. As an immigrant myself, I always pause respectfully. You never know. Maybe this is what they're taught to chant in schools nowadays, a sort of multicultural Pledge of Allegiance.

But it secretly amuses me. Do they really think other nations sprouted up out of the ground? ("Autochthonous" is the classical Greek word.) The truth is that *all* nations are nations of immigrants. But the process is usually so slow and historic that people overlook it. They mistake for mountains what are merely clouds.

5 This is obvious in the case of the British Isles, from which the largest single proportion of Americans are still derived. You can see it in the place-names.

Within a few miles of my parents' home in the north of England, the names are Roman (Chester, derived from the Latin for camp), Saxon (anything ending in -ton, town, like Oxton), Viking (-by, farm, like Irby), and Norman French (Delamere). At times, these successive waves of peoples were clearly living cheek by jowl. Thus among these place-names is Wallesey, Anglo-Saxon for "Island of the Welsh" — Welsh being derived from the word used by low-German speakers for foreigners wherever they met them, from Wallonia to Wallachia. This corner of the English coast continued as home to some of the pre-Roman Celtic stock, not all of whom were driven west into Wales proper as was once supposed.

The English language that America speaks today (or at least spoke until the post-1965 fashion for bilingual education) reflects the fact that the peoples of Britain merged, eventually; their separate contributions can still be traced in it. Every nation in Europe went through the same process. Even the famously homogeneous Japanese show the signs of ethnically distinct waves of prehistoric immigration.

But merging takes time. After the Norman Conquest in 1066, it was nearly three hundred years before the invaders were assimilated to the point where court proceedings in London were again heard in English. And it was nearly nine centuries before there was any further large-scale immigration into the British Isles — the Caribbean and Asian influx after World War II. Except in America. Here the process of merging has been uniquely rapid. Thus about 7 million Germans have immigrated to the U.S. since the beginning of the nineteenth century. Their influence has been profound — to my British eye it accounts for the odd American habit of getting up in the morning and starting work. About 50 million Americans told the 1980 Census that they were wholly or partly of German descent. But only 1.6 million spoke German in their homes.

So all nations are made up of immigrants. But what is a nation — the end product of all this merging? This brings us into a territory where words are weapons, exactly as George Orwell pointed out years ago. "Nation" — as suggested by its Latin root *nascere,* to be born — intrinsically implies a link by blood. A nation is an extended family. The merging process through which all nations pass is not merely cultural, but to a considerable extent biological, through intermarriage.

Liberal commentators, for various reasons, find this deeply distressing. They regularly denounce appeals to common ethnicity as "nativism" or "tribalism." Ironically, when I studied African history in college, my politically correct tutor deprecated any reference to "tribes." These small, primitive, and incoherent groupings should, he said, be dignified as "nations." Which suggests a useful definition: tribalism/nativism is nationalism of which liberals disapprove.

10 American political debate on this point is hampered by a peculiar difficulty. American editors are convinced that the term "state" will confuse readers unless reserved exclusively for the component parts of the United States — New York, California, etc. So when talking about sovereign political structures, where the British would use "state," the Germans "*Staat,*" and the French "*l'état,*" journalists here are compelled to use the word "nation." Thus in the late 1980s it was common to see references to "the nation of Yugoslavia," when Yugoslavia's problem was precisely that it was not a nation at all, but a state that contained several different small but fierce nations — Croats, Serbs, etc. (In my constructive

way, I've been trying to introduce, as an alternative to "state," the word "polity" — defined by Webster as "a politically organized unit." But it's quite hopeless. Editors always confuse it with "policy.")

This definitional difficulty explains one of the regular entertainments of U.S. politics: uproar because someone has unguardedly described America as a "Christian nation." Of course, in the sense that the vast majority of Americans are Christians, this is nothing less than the plain truth. It is not in the least incompatible with a secular *state* (polity).

But the difficulty over the N-word has a more serious consequence: it means that American commentators are losing sight of the concept of the "nation-state" — a sovereign structure that is the political expression of a specific ethno-cultural group. Yet the nation-state was one of the crucial inventions of the modern age. Mass literacy, education, and mobility put a premium on the unifying effect of cultural and ethnic homogeneity. None of the great pre-modern multinational empires have survived. (The Brussels bureaucracy* may be trying to create another, but it has a long way to go.)

This is why Ben Wattenberg is able to get away with talking about a "Universal Nation." On its face, this is a contradiction in terms. It's possible, as Wattenberg variously implies, that he means the diverse immigrant groups will eventually intermarry, producing what he calls, quoting the English poet John Masefield a "wondrous race." Or that they will at least be assimilated by American culture, which, while globally dominant, is hardly "universal." But meanwhile there are hard questions. What language is this "universal nation" going to speak? How is it going to avoid ethnic strife? dual loyalties? collapsing like the Tower of Babel? Wattenberg is not asked to reconcile these questions, although he is

not unaware of them, because in American political discourse the ideal of an American nation-state is in eclipse.

Ironically, the same weaknesses were apparent in the rather similar concept of "cultural pluralism" invented by Horace M. Kallen at the height of the last great immigration debate, before the Quota Acts of the 1920s.† Kallen, like many of today's pro-immigration enthusiasts, reacted unconditionally against the cause for "Americanization" that the 1880-to-1920 immigrant wave provoked. He argued that any unitary American nationality had already been dissipated by immigration (sound familiar?). Instead, he said the U.S. had become merely a political state (polity) containing a number of different nationalities. **15** Kallen left the practical implications of this vision "woefully undeveloped" (in the words of the *Harvard Encyclopedia of American Ethnic Groups*). It eventually evolved into a vague approval of tolerance, which was basically how Americans had always treated immigrant groups anyway — an extension, not coincidentally, of how the English built the British nation.

But in one respect, Kallenism is very much alive: he argued that authentic Americanism was what he called "the American Idea." This amounted to an almost religious idealization of "democracy," which again was left undeveloped but which appeared to have as much to do with non-discrimination and equal protection under the law as with elections. Today, a messianic concern for global "democracy" is being suggested to conservatives as an appropriate objective for U.S. foreign policy.

And Kallenism underlies the second helpful remark that someone always makes in any discussion of U.S. immigration policy: "*America isn't a nation like the other nations — it's an idea.*"

*The "Brussels bureaucracy" to which Brimelow refers in this paragraph is the European Community (now called the European Union), which has its administrative offices in the city of Brussels, Belgium.

†The Immigration Quota Acts of 1921 and 1924 established the first limits to the number of legal immigrants who were allowed to enter the United States each year. These laws tended to place greater restrictions on immigration from southern and eastern European countries and fewer restrictions on Nordic and Anglo-Saxon nations.

*Fought in 1415, the Battle of Agincourt was one of the key battles in what has come to be known as the Hundred Years War between France and England. King Henry V of England led an invading army into France over a land dispute and defeated an apparently stronger French force near a fortified town named Agincourt. His exploits were immortalized in Shakespeare's *Henry V*.

Once more, this American exceptionalism is really more a matter of degree than of kind. Many other nations have some sort of ideational reinforcement. Quite often it is religious, such as Poland's Roman Catholicism; sometimes cultural, such as France's ineffable Frenchness. And occasionally it is political. Thus — again not coincidentally — the English used to talk about what might be described as the "English Idea": English liberties, their rights as Englishmen, and so on. Americans used to know immediately what this meant. As Jesse Chickering wrote in 1848 of his diverse fellow-Americans: "English laws and institutions, adapted to the circumstances of the country, have been adopted here. . . . The tendency of things is to mold the whole into one people, whose leading characteristics are English, formed on American soil."

What is unusual in the present debate, however, is that Americans are now being urged to abandon the bonds of a common ethnicity and instead to trust entirely to ideology to hold together their state (polity). This is an extraordinary experiment, like suddenly replacing all the blood in a patient's body. History suggests little reason to suppose it will succeed. Christendom and Islam have long ago been sundered by national quarrels. More recently, the much-touted "Soviet Man," the creation of much tougher ideologists using much rougher methods than anything yet seen in the U.S., has turned out to be a Russian, Ukrainian, or Kazakh after all.

20 Which is why Shakespeare has King Henry V say, before the battle of Agincourt,* not "we defenders of international law and the dynastic principle as it applies to my right to inherit the throne of France," but

We few, we happy few, we band of brothers.

However, although intellectuals may have decided that America is not a nation but an idea, the news has not reached the American people — especially that significant minority who sternly tell the Census Bureau their ethnicity is "American." (They seem mostly to be of British origin, many generations back.) And it would have been considered absurd throughout most of American history.

John Jay in *The Federalist Papers* wrote that Americans were "one united people, a people descended from the same ancestors, speaking the same language, professing the same religion, attached to the same principles of government, very similar in their manners and customs." Some hundred years later, Theodore Roosevelt in his *Winning of the West* traced the "perfectly continuous history" of the Anglo-Saxons from King Alfred to George Washington. He presented the settling of the lands beyond the Alleghenies as "the crowning and greatest achievement" of "the spread of the Englishspeaking peoples," which —

though personally a liberal on racial matters — he saw in explicit terms: "it is of incalculable importance that America, Australia, and Siberia should pass out of the hands of their red, black, and yellow aboriginal owners, and become the heritage of the dominant world races."

Roosevelt himself was an example of ethnicities merging to produce this new nation. He thanked God — he teased his friend Rudyard Kipling — that there was "not a drop of British blood" in him. But that did not stop him from identifying with Anglo-Saxons or from becoming a passionate advocate of an assimilationist Americanism, which crossed ethnic lines and was ultimately to cross racial lines.

And it is important to note that, at the height of the last great immigration wave, Kallen and his allies totally failed to persuade Americans that they were no longer a nation. Quite the contrary: once convinced that their nationhood was threatened by continued massive immigration, Americans changed the public policies that made it possible.

ASSIMILATION

Often, debates about immigration policy in the U.S. focus on the issue of *assimilation*, which refers to the process by which immigrants become American by adopting the values, traditions, ideals, and even the language of the United States. Sometimes, the metaphor of the "melting pot" is used to describe this process: People of many different backgrounds and identities are mixed together to form a single American nation. When Brimelow describes Theodore Roosevelt as an "advocate of an assimilationist Americanism," he is also referring to a belief in the importance of assimilation in maintaining American identity. When he states in paragraph 11 that "the vast majority of Americans are Christians," he is partly defining that American identity. When he refers in paragraph 19 to "a common ethnicity," he is referring to the same "Anglo-Saxons" that he tells us Roosevelt aligned himself with — an ethnic group that, for Brimelow, constitutes the American identity. However, in the last few decades, many Americans, especially those from minority groups, have questioned this idea of one nation in which one's ethnic, racial, and religious identities become subsumed by his or her identity as an "American." Instead, arguing that diversity rather than assimilation is what makes America unique and strong, these critics have proposed the metaphor of a mosaic, in which each person retains his or her racial or ethnic identity while becoming a piece of the larger American cultural "mosaic."

While the national origins quotas were being legislated, President Calvin Coolidge put it unflinchingly: "America must be kept American."

Everyone knew what he meant.

Questions for Discussion

1. In his essay, Brimelow describes words as weapons. What does he mean? In what way is his concern about language — and about the definitions of specific terms — central to his argument? **2.** Brimelow distinguishes between *nation* and *state*. Why does he believe that the distinction is important? How does he use that distinction in building his argument? **3.** According to Brimelow, how has the debate over immigration changed? Why is he concerned about this change? Do you think his concern is justified? Why or why not? **4.** In paragraphs 21 and 22, Brimelow appeals to American figures of historical importance, such as John Jay and Theodore Roosevelt. Has he strengthened his case by making these references? Explain. In what ways might he have left himself open to counterargument on this point? **5.** Brimelow asserts that Americans do not agree with the statement that America is an idea, not a nation. Why is this point important to Brimelow? Do you think he is right? Why or why not? **6.** Brimelow concludes by stating that "everyone" knew what it meant to be American back in the 1920s. What is Brimelow implying here? How effective is that statement as a conclusion to his argument? **7.** Does the fact that Brimelow was born in England influence the way you read his argument? Does it give him more or less credibility, in your view? Explain.

③ JACOB G. HORNBERGER, "Keep the Borders Open"

Arguments about immigration in the United States often focus on concerns about jobs and money. Many Americans worry that immigrants will take jobs away from them; some fear that immigrants will strain city and state budgets for education and unemployment benefits, resulting in higher taxes. These are valid and serious concerns, and Jacob G. Hornberger acknowledges them in the following essay. But unlike many critics of U.S. immigration policy, Hornberger is concerned about a more basic issue: individual freedom. He makes his argument in favor of an open immigration policy from his perspective as a libertarian (see the sidebar on page 464). Hornberger is founder of the Future of Freedom Foundation, an organization that advocates in favor of libertarian positions on issues such as immigration. As you read his essay, pay attention to the way he builds his argument on his fundamental libertarian views about individual citizens and the role of the state. Consider how those views might make his argument more or less effective among readers who have allegiances to other political perspectives.

Keep the Borders Open
JACOB G. HORNBERGER

1 In times of crisis, it is sometimes wise and constructive for people to return to first principles and to reexamine and reflect on where we started as a nation, the road we've traveled, where we are today, and the direction in which we're headed. Such a reevaluation can help determine whether a nation has deviated from its original principles and, if so, whether a restoration of those principles would be in order.

It is impossible to overstate the unusual nature of American society from the time of its founding to the early part of the 20th century. Imagine: no Social Security, Medicare, Medicaid, income taxation, welfare, systems of public (i.e., government) schooling, occupational li-

censure, standing armies, foreign aid, foreign interventions, or foreign wars. Perhaps most unusual of all, there were virtually no federal controls on immigration into the United States.

With the tragic and costly exception of slavery, the bedrock principle underlying American society was that people should be free to live their lives any way they chose, as long as their conduct was peaceful. (See "Libertarianism" on page 464.) That is what it once meant to be free. That is what it once meant to be an American. That was the freedom that our ancestors celebrated each Fourth of July.

Let's examine the issue of immigration because it provides a good model for comparing the vision of freedom of our

LIBERTARIANISM

Hornberger's statement that "the bedrock principle underlying American society was that people should be free to live their lives any way they chose, as long as their conduct was peaceful" reflects his Libertarian beliefs. According to its Web site, the Libertarian Party "is committed to America's heritage of freedom: individual liberty and personal responsibility; a free-market economy of abundance and prosperity; a foreign policy of non-intervention, peace, and free trade" (see www.lp.org). In short, libertarians believe in maximizing individual freedom and minimizing the power of the state. This political philosophy has a long history in American society. Although the Libertarian Party itself does not have sufficient membership to challenge the Democrats and Republicans in national elections, it plays an important political role in some states, and many Americans share its views on issues such as immigration and foreign policy.

*In 1939 the S.S. *St. Louis* sailed for Cuba from Germany carrying 900 Jewish passengers who were fleeing Nazi persecution and who hoped eventually to enter the United States. The passengers were refused entry into Cuba, and after several weeks the ship was forced to return to Germany. The incident came to be known as the "voyage of the damned."

ancestors with that which guides the American people today.

5   In economic terms, the concept of freedom to which our Founders subscribed entailed the right to sustain one's life through labor by pursuing any occupation or business without government permission or interference, by freely entering into mutually beneficial exchanges with others anywhere in the world, accumulating unlimited amounts of wealth arising from those endeavors, and freely deciding the disposition of that wealth.

The moral question is: Why shouldn't a person be free to cross a border in search of work to sustain his life, to open a business, to tour, or simply because he wants to? Or to put it another way, under what moral authority does any government interfere with the exercise of these rights?

Most Americans like the concept of open borders within the United States, but what distinguished our ancestors is that they believed that the principles of freedom were applicable not just domestically but universally. That implied open borders not only for people traveling in-

side the United States but also for people traveling or moving to the United States.

One important result of this highly unusual philosophy of freedom was that throughout the 19th century, people all over the world, especially those who were suffering political tyranny or economic privation, always knew that there was a place they could go if they could succeed in escaping their circumstances.

The American abandonment of open immigration in the 20th century has had negative consequences, both morally and economically. Let's consider some examples.

10 Prior to and during World War II, U.S. government officials intentionally used immigration controls to prevent German Jews from escaping the horrors of Nazi Germany by coming to America. Many of us are familiar with the infamous "voyage of the damned,"* where U.S. officials refused to permit a German ship to land at Miami Harbor because it carried Jewish refugees. But how many people know that U.S. officials used immigration controls to keep German Jews and Eastern European Jews from coming to the United States even after the existence of the concentration camps became well known?

Indeed, how many Americans know about the one million anti-communist Russians whom U.S. and British officials forcibly repatriated to the Soviet Union at the end of World War II, knowing that death or the gulag awaited them?

Ancient history, you say? Well, consider one of the most morally reprehensible policies in the history of our nation: the forcible repatriation of Cuban refugees into communist tyranny, a practice that has been going on for many years and that continues to this day.

Let me restate this for emphasis: Under the pretext of enforcing immigration laws, our government — the U.S. government — the same government that sent tens of thousands of American GIs to their deaths in foreign wars supposedly to resist communism, is now forcibly returning people into communism.

We have seen the establishment of Border Patrol passport checkpoints on highways and airports inside the United States (north of the border), which inevitably discriminate against people on the basis of skin color. We have seen the criminalization of such things as transporting, housing, and hiring undocumented workers, followed by arbitrary detentions on highways as well as raids on American farms and restaurants. 15 We have seen the construction of a fortified wall in California. This wall, built soon after the fall of the ugliest wall in history, has resulted in the deaths of immigrants entering the country on the harsh Arizona desert. Would Washington, Jefferson, or Madison have constructed such a wall?

We have come a long way from the vision of freedom set forth by our Founding Fathers.

Let's consider some of the common objections to open immigration:

1. *Open immigration will pollute America's culture.* Oh? Which culture is that? Boston? New York? Savannah? New Orleans? Denver? Los Angeles? I grew up on the Mexican border (on the Texas side). My culture was eating enchiladas and tacos, listening to both Mexican and American music, and speaking Tex-Mex (a combination of English and Spanish). If you're talking about the danger that my culture might get polluted, that danger comes from the north, not from the south. America's culture

has always been one of liberty — one in which people are free to pursue any culture they want.

2. *Immigrants will take jobs away from Americans.* Immigrants displace workers in certain sectors

U.S. IMMIGRATION POLICY ON CUBA

According to the Close Up Foundation, a nonpartisan citizen education organization,

The island nation of Cuba, located just ninety miles off the coast of Florida, is home to 11 million people and has one of the few remaining communist regimes in the world. Cuba's leader, Fidel Castro, came to power in 1959 and immediately instituted a communist program of sweeping economic and social changes. Castro allied his government with the Soviet Union and seized and nationalized billions of dollars of American property. U.S. relations with Cuba have been strained ever since. A trade embargo against Cuba that was imposed in 1960 is still in place today. . . . All aspects of U.S. policy with Cuba, such as the current trade embargo, immigration practices, and most recently the possibility of a free exchange by members of the media, provoke heated debates across the United States. . . . Some believe that the country's current policy toward Cuba is outdated in its Cold War approach and needs to be reconstructed. However, many still consider Fidel Castro a threat in the hemisphere and a menace to his own people and favor tightening the screws on his regime even more.

Part of the new border fence in California. (Photo by Nic Paget-Clarke. Available at www.inmotionmagazine.com/border.html and www.inmotionmagazine.com/border4.html).

but the displaced workers benefit through the acquisition of higher-paying jobs in other sectors that expand because of the influx of immigrants. It is not a coincidence that historically people's standard of living has soared when borders have been open. Keep in mind also that traditionally immigrants are among the hardest-working and most energetic people in a society, which brings a positive vitality and energy to it.

3. *Immigrants will go on welfare.* Well maybe we ought to reexamine whether it was a good idea to abandon the principles of our ancestors in that respect as well. What would be wrong with abolishing welfare for everyone, including Americans, along with the enormous taxation required to fund it? But if Americans are in fact hopelessly addicted to the government

dole, there is absolutely no reason that the same has to happen to immigrants. Therefore, the answer to the welfare issue is not to control immigration but rather to deny immigrants the right to go on the government dole. In such a case, however, wouldn't it be fair to exempt them from the taxes used to fund the U.S. welfare state?

4. *Immigrants will bring in drugs.* Lots of people bring in drugs, including Americans returning from overseas trips. Not even the harshest police state would ever alter that fact. More important, why not legalize drugs and make the state leave drug users alone? Is there any better example of an immoral, failed, and destructive government program than the war on drugs? Why should one government intervention, especially an immoral, failed one, be used to justify another?

5. *There will be too many people*. Oh? Who decides the ideal number? A government board of central planners, just like in China? Wouldn't reliance on the free market to make such a determination be more consistent with our founding principles? Immigrants go where the opportunities abound and they avoid areas where they don't, just as Americans do.

6. *Open immigration will permit terrorists to enter our country*. The only permanent solution to terrorism against the United States, in both the short term and long term, is to abandon the U.S. government's interventionist foreign policy, which is the breeding ground for terrorism against our country. No immigration controls in the world, not even a rebuilt Berlin Wall around the United States, will succeed in preventing the entry of people who are bound and determined to kill Americans.

More than 200 years ago, ordinary people brought into existence the most unusual society in the history of man. It was a society based on the fundamental moral principle that people everywhere are endowed with certain inherent rights that no government can legitimately take away.

Somewhere along the way, Americans abandoned that concept of freedom, especially in their attachment to such programs and policies as Social Security, Medicare, Medicaid, income taxation, economic regulation, public (i.e., government) schooling, the war on drugs, the war on poverty, the war on wealth, immigration controls, foreign aid, foreign intervention, and foreign wars — none of which our founders had dreamed of. 20 The current crisis provides us with an opportunity to reexamine our founding principles, why succeeding generations of Americans abandoned them, the consequences of that abandonment, and whether it would be wise to restore the moral and philosophical principles of freedom of our Founders. A good place to start such a reexamination would be immigration.

Questions for Discussion

1. On what fundamental principle does Hornberger rest his main argument about immigration? Do you share his belief in this principle? Do you think most Americans do? **2.** What main reasons does Hornberger cite in support of his position on immigration? Identify the kinds of evidence he provides (see "Appraising Evidence" on pages 76–82). Do you find his reasons persuasive? Why or why not? **3.** Hornberger is a libertarian (see the sidebar on page 464). Identify specific points in his article that reveal his libertarian views. To what extent do you think most Americans would agree with his views? **4.** Hornberger identifies six main arguments against immigration and offers a rebuttal to each one. Do you think this way of addressing the position of those who oppose immigration is an effective one? Why or why not? **5.** Hornberger's essay is an example of an argument based on deductive reasoning (see pages 26–31). What is the fundamental belief or principle on which he bases his argument? How effective do you think this strategy for argumentation is in the case of the issue of immigration?

④ STEVEN CAMAROTA, "Too Many: Looking Today's Immigration in the Face"

Steven Camarota is the director of the Center for Immigration Studies (CIS), a nonprofit organization devoted to analyzing the effects of immigration on the United States and generally favoring greater restrictions on immigration to the United States (see www.cis.org/). He is a well-known voice in public discussions about immigration. The following essay, which first appeared in 2002 in the *National Review*, a respected politically conservative magazine, lays out his position on immigration in detail. In his essay Camarota addresses the main issues that often emerge in debates about immigration: concerns about jobs, schools, taxes, and poverty. But in addressing those issues and providing extensive factual evidence to support his points about each, Camarota is also presenting a view of what he believes America should be. As you read, pay attention to how his vision of America emerges in his essay — and how that vision shapes his argument about U.S. immigration policy.

Too Many: Looking Today's Immigration in the Face
STEVEN CAMAROTA

1 When the history of the 1990s is written, the most important story may not be the GOP takeover of Congress, the boom economy, or the Clinton impeachment. The big story may be the decade's unprecedented level of immigration: a social phenomenon of enormous significance, affecting everything from the nation's schools to the political balance between the two parties.

Newly released census figures show that the foreign-born population reached 31.1 million in 2000 (including some 7 to 8 million here illegally). This is by far the largest immigrant population in U.S. history, and represents a 57 percent increase from 1990. The rate of increase is itself unprecedented: Even during the great wave of immigration from 1900 to 1910, the foreign-born population grew by only about 31 percent (from roughly 10 million to 13.5 million). Over the past 30 years, the number of immigrants in the U.S. has tripled. If current trends are allowed to continue, the foreign-born share of the population will in fact pass the all-time high by the end of this decade. Many defenders of high immigration argue that the current immigration is not really unusual, because although the numbers and growth are without precedent, the total U.S. population was smaller 100 years ago and immigrants constituted a larger share of the total. It is true that the 11.1 percent of the nation's population that is foreign-born today is lower than the all-time high of nearly 15 percent reached in 1910. But one may ask why 1910 should be the benchmark by which to judge today's immigration. In evaluating its effect on modern society, it seems more reasonable to compare today's immigration with that of the more recent past. And in that context, today's figures represent a fundamental break with prior decades: From 1940 to 1990 the foreign-born population averaged less than 7 percent, and as recently as 1970 it was less than 5 percent.

The implications for American society are enormous. For example, a good deal of attention has been given to the fact that the number of people who live in poverty did not decline in the 1990s, despite a strong economy. What has generally not been reported is that new immigrants and their U.S.-born children accounted for the nation's stubborn poverty rate. The primary reason so many immigrant families live in poverty is that a large percentage have very little education. Newly arrived adult immigrants, for example, are more than three times as likely as natives to lack a high-school education.

Immigrants and their children also account for nearly two-thirds of the increase in the population lacking health insurance over the last decade. By dramatically increasing the uninsured population, immigration creates significant costs for taxpayers, and it drives up costs for insured Americans as providers pass along the costs of treating the uninsured to paying customers. The central role immigration has played in creating the nation's health-insurance quandary has largely gone unreported.

5 The impact on public schools is even more significant. In the last 20 years the school-age population has grown by roughly 8 million. Most observers agree that this increase has strained resources in districts across the country. What most media accounts of this growth leave out is that census data indicate that there are about 8 million school-age children from immigrant families — and, because they are much poorer on average than natives, this increase in enrollment has not been accompanied by a corresponding increase in local tax revenue. Moreover, because of language barriers, the children of immigrants often cost significantly more to educate than those of natives. Most news coverage of the issue discusses how to meet the needs of these children, but fails to point out that federal immigra-

COMPLICATION

From *Immigration Policy Reports*, a project of the American Immigration Law Foundation:

With 56 million, or 20 percent of the current U.S. population estimated as foreign-born, the Census Bureau's report claims these numbers are the highest in history. However, past demographic data shows otherwise. For example, at the turn of the century when the total foreign-born percentage was 13, the first and second generation accounted for nearly 35 percent of the U.S. population — much higher than today's 20 percent. In fact, from 1870 through 1930, the combination of these two generations was even larger, totaling 1/3 of the total population.

cally influential ethnic organizations whose leaders often adhere to an anti-assimilation multicultural ideology. Whether the immigrants in question represent 10 percent or 30 percent of a city's population is not so important; it's the raw numbers that count, and the numbers are already well over twice what they were in 1910.

In one sense, today's immigrants are more diverse than ever before, in that significant numbers arrive from all continents and races. But in a more important sense, today's immigration wave is considerably less diverse than those of the past, because Spanish speakers dominate in a way no other group ever did before. While German speakers accounted for a little over a quarter of all immigrants in the late 1800s and Italians for about one-fifth in the first decades of the 1900s, such concentrations were transitory. In contrast, the domination of immigrants from Latin America has grown steadily. In 1970, 19 percent of the foreign-born were from Latin America; by 2000, it was more than half. One ethno-linguistic group can now predominate in schools, neighborhoods, entire metropolitan areas, and even whole states.

One institution that helped immigrants and their children acquire an American identity in the past was public education. Schools brought children from different immigrant backgrounds into contact with natives and helped to forge a common American culture. But today, basic demographics makes this much more difficult. Unlike in the past, immi-

tion policy created the problem in the first place.

Despite the clear implications mass immigration has for the future of American society, many boosters still argue that today's immigration is very much like that of 1910. No doubt, there are similarities, but the differences are profound and striking to even the casual observer. America is a fundamentally different place than it was 100 years ago, and today's immigration is also very different.

As far as assimilation is concerned, numbers matter at least as much as percentages. For example, a quarter of a million immigrants in a metropolitan area are enough to create linguistic isolation: neighborhoods where immigrants can live and work without ever learning much English. Large numbers also create politi-

grants now have many more children on average than natives, which means kids from immigrant families very quickly predominate in public schools. For example, although about a quarter of California's total population is foreign-born, half of the school-age population is from immigrant families. In many districts in high-immigration states, immigrant families now account for more than 80 percent of school kids.

10 Of course, neighborhood schools in 1910 saw heavy immigrant concentrations. But because of the large differences in fertility rates, immigration today creates many more districts in which the cultural norms are set by children from immigrant families, who have relatively little contact with their counterparts from native families.

There is, of course, another problem with expecting public schools to play the role they did in the past of assimilating immigrants: Schools don't want to. A very significant share of the U.S. elite has embraced the anti-assimilation ethos, which regards America as a collection of peoples, each with its own distinct culture, which vie for political power as groups. America's educational establishment has embraced this multicultural vision. This is why history textbooks look as they do, and why bilingual education* remains widely popular among educators. This trend shows no signs of abating; in fact, the growing number of immigrants only feeds the multiculturalist perspective. Immigration provides further justification for it by creating an ever larger aggrieved class, whose cultures must be preserved in the face of an oppressive majority culture.

Of course, some form of assimilation does take place, even in the modern public school. While language acquisition almost certainly has slowed in recent years, most immigrants learn to speak at least some English. But assimilation is much more than learning to speak English, or driving on the right side of the road. It involves what John Fonte of the Hudson Institute calls "patriotic assimilation," the belief that American history is one's own history. A century ago it meant that immigrants and their children came to see America's past as something "we" did, not something "they" — white people of European ancestry — did. To the extent that immigrants are assimilating they are doing so, in many cases, as "multicultural" Americans.

Some conservatives, and even some liberals, have a different conception of assimilation, but it is not at all clear that those who wish to see a more robust love of country inculcated in our children (immigrant or native) are winning the debate. It simply makes no sense, therefore, for a society that cannot agree on its own history or even what it means to be an American to welcome over a million newcomers each year from outside.

Technology is another obstacle to assimilation. It is now possible to call — or even to visit — one's home country with a frequency that was inconceivable even 50 years ago. One can listen to a hometown radio station or read the local newspapers on the Internet. The costs of travel and communication are now so low that many wealthier immigrants can live in two countries at the same time, traveling back and forth with ease. In such a world, it is less likely that immigrants will develop a deep attachment to the U.S.

15 The American economy is also fundamentally different, with serious consequences for the assimilation process. A century ago, manufacturing, mining, and agriculture employed the vast majority of

*In 1998 California voters adopted Proposition 227, which requires all instruction in public schools to be conducted in English, effectively ending bilingual education in California public schools. In 2002 Massachusetts voters approved a similar referendum, ending bilingual education in that state. (For additional resources, see the Web site for the Centre for Studies of Language in Education, www.ntu.edu.au/ education/csle/ issues/prop227.html.)

CONTEXT

In 1995 education scholar Mike Rose reported on the increasing diversity of American public schools. At Pasadena High School in California, for example, more than thirty-eight different languages were spoken by students enrolled there. Source: *Possible Lives* (1995).

See the margin gloss about green cards on page 452. Also see the margin gloss about the Immigration Marriage Fraud Amendment on page 455.

the workforce, creating plentiful work for unskilled immigrants. These jobs eventually led to solid working-class incomes for immigrants and their children. (In fact, most native-born Americans a century ago worked in the same kinds of jobs.) Though most people were poor by today's standards, most historians agree that there was not a very large economic gap between the standard of living of natives and that of immigrants; this was because, on average, immigrants were not that much less skilled than natives. Data are limited, but in terms of years of schooling or literacy, immigrants 100 years ago were roughly equal to natives.

This is no longer the case. While a number of today's immigrants are quite skilled, immigrants overall are significantly less educated than natives. As a result, when it comes to average income, poverty rates, welfare use, and other measures of economic well-being, today's immigrants are much worse off than natives. Unlike that of 1910, today's U.S. economy offers very limited opportunity for those with little education, and this creates a very sizable gap between the two groups.

Another important change since 1910 is the profound expansion in the size and scope of government. Spending on everything from education to infrastructure maintenance is many times greater than it was back then. With federal, state, and local government now eating up roughly one-third of GDP, the average individual must be able to pay a good deal in taxes to cover his use of public services. In practice, the middle and upper classes pay most of the taxes; the poor, immigrant or native, generally consume significantly more in public services than they pay in taxes.

This means that the arrival of large numbers of relatively poor immigrants has a significant negative effect on public coffers in a way that was not the case in the past. In 1997 the National Academy of Sciences estimated that immigrant households consumed between $11 and $20 billion more in public services than they were paying in taxes each year. (Other estimates have found this deficit to be even higher.) A smaller government may well be desirable, but it is politically inconceivable that we would ever return to the situation of 100 years ago, when government accounted for a tiny fraction of the economy. Thus, continually allowing in large numbers of unskilled immigrants has very negative implications for taxpayers.

The situation of today's immigrants is, then, dramatically different from what it was at the turn of the last century. But even if one ignores all these differences, one undeniable fact remains: The last great wave of immigration was stopped, as an act of government policy. World War I, followed by restrictive legislation in the early 1920s, dramatically reduced immigration to about a quarter of what it had been in previous decades. This immigration pause played a critically important role in turning yesterday's immigrants into Americans. So if the past is to be our guide, then we should significantly reduce immigration numbers.

20 If we don't, the assimilation problem will only get worse. We know from experience that it is often the children of immigrants who have the greatest difficulty identifying with America. While their parents at least know how good they have it, the children tend to compare their situation to that of other Americans, instead of that in their parents' homeland. Unless the gap between themselves and other Americans has been closed in just one generation, something few groups have been able to accomplish, this can

be a source of real discontent. Moreover, it is children born in the U.S. to immigrant parents who often feel caught between two worlds and struggle with their identity.

What we should do is call a halt to the current heedless increase in annual immigration, and reduce the numbers to something like their historical average of 300,000 a year. In the mid 1990s, the bipartisan immigration-reform panel headed by the late Barbara Jordan suggested limiting family immigration to the spouses and minor children of U.S. citizens and legal non-citizens, and to the parents of citizens. However, we should probably eliminate the preferences for the spouses and minor children of non-

citizens, since these provisions apply to family members acquired after the alien has received a green card but before he has become a citizen. If we also eliminated the parents of U.S. citizens as a category, family immigration would fall to less than half what it is today. The Jordan panel also wisely suggested eliminating the visa lottery and tightening up the requirements for employment- and humanitarian-based immigration.

These changes would, taken together, reduce legal immigration to roughly 300,000 annually. Only if we get the numbers down to this reasonable level can we begin the long process of assimilating the huge number of immigrants and their children who are already here.

Questions for Discussion

1. Examine the way in which Camarota uses statistical information as evidence to support his argument, especially in paragraph 2. What specific point do these statistics help him make? How effectively do you think he uses these statistics? **2.** Camarota asserts that "America is a fundamentally different place than it was 100 years ago, and today's immigration is also very different." What does he mean? What evidence does he offer to support this assertion? Do you think he is right? Why or why not? **3.** What is Camarota's view of the assimilation of immigrants into U.S. society? What does he mean when he refers to "the assimilation problem"? Why is his view of assimilation important to his overall argument? Do you agree with him about this issue? Why or why not? How might your own views about immigration affect your reaction to Camarota's point about assimilation? **4.** Camarota writes that "in terms of years of schooling or literacy, immigrants 100 years ago were roughly equal to natives." How does he arrive at this conclusion? What evidence does he present? Do you think he make a persuasive case that this point is valid? Explain. **5.** Evaluate the way in which Camarota uses history to make his argument about what should be done about immigration today. What historical events or developments does he cite? How does he use these historical references to build his argument? What do you think is his general view of America's past? How does that view influence his use of historical references in his argument? Identify specific passages in his essay to illustrate your answer. **6.** Several times in his essay Camarota refers to "liberals" and to "boosters" — that is, people who favor immigration. Who exactly are these boosters? Identify places in the essay where they are described or identified. Does Camarota see any common ground between him and boosters of immigration?

NEGOTIATING DIFFERENCES

Each of the authors in this section presents an argument about immigration policy in the United States. But each author also presents a vision of what America is — and what it should be. Part of the challenge in sorting through debates about immigration policy is understanding the way these visions of America inform the views of participants in these debates. Ultimately, decisions about immigration policy reflect some general agree-ment about what America is and who Americans are. In other words, when laws governing immigration are passed by the U.S. Congress, or when policies regarding immigrants are adopted by schools or state agencies, these laws are implicitly saying, "This is the kind nation or society we believe we want to have."

With that in mind, imagine that you are part of a committee created by your state government to examine the impact of immigration on your state. Your committee's task is to draft a report to the governor in which you present and justify a general immigration policy in your state. That task requires you to investigate immigration in your state: who the immigrants in your state are; where they have come from and why; how many there are; and what impact they have on schools, jobs, and social life. It also requires you to consider your own views about what kind of society you believe America should be and who should be allowed to become an American.

Working by yourself or with a group of your classmates, write a report to your governor in which you make an argument for a general immigration policy for your state. In your report, you might draw on the perspectives presented in the four essays in this section and on any other relevant material that is familiar to you.

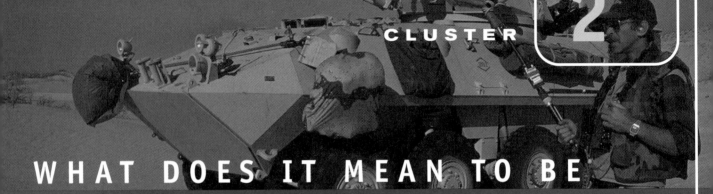

WHAT DOES IT MEAN TO BE
A GOOD AMERICAN CITIZEN?

In a famous line from his inaugural address, President John F. Kennedy challenged Americans: "Ask not what your country can do for you. Ask what you can do for your country." (See Con-Text on page 477.) His challenge implied a sense of duty that he hoped all Americans would feel. It was a time of political uncertainty and tension between the United States and the Soviet Union, both of which possessed nuclear weapons of fearful power — a time that seemed to require Americans to put their own desires aside to help protect their nation. To be a good citizen, Kennedy seemed to be saying, means placing the nation's good before your own. ■ Many Americans have shared Kennedy's belief in this sense of duty, especially in times of war and crisis. But the question of what it means to be an American citizen has never been simple and has at times created great conflict. During the Vietnam War, for example, some Americans believed fervently that it was their patriotic duty to serve their country by fighting with the U.S. armed forces in southeast Asia. Others believed just as fervently that the demands of citizenship required them to oppose their country's involvement in Vietnam through protest and resistance to the draft. Still others supported the American war effort in Vietnam despite genuine misgivings about it. The deep divisions among Americans caused open conflict as well as soul-searching about what it meant to be a good citizen. ■ Of course, debate and conflict about citizenship and patriotism date back to the very beginnings of the United States. During the Revolutionary War many Americans remained loyal to the British Crown as their rightful government. The Civil War highlighted the conflicting loyalties that many Americans felt to their states and to their national government. In our own time a different kind of war — what many call the "war on terror" — has again provoked debate about citizenship, patriotism, and duty in the aftermath of September 11, 2001. As several of the writers in this section demonstrate, those events have prompted Americans to examine not just their opinions about their government's response to terrorism but also their most fundamental beliefs about citizenship, patriotism, and American identity. Once again, young Americans are being asked to risk their own lives for their country. Such great sacrifice inevitably causes Americans to pause and think hard about what they must do — and what they *should* do — as citizens. ■ Although these questions about citizenship might emerge most provocatively during war and crisis, they are not questions *about* war or crisis. Even in peacetime Americans wrestle with the idea of citizenship, which sometimes seems to conflict with beliefs about individual freedom and self-determination that run deep in U.S. culture. As the following essays suggest, the problem of defining what it means to be a good citizen can emerge in such seemingly common activities as voting or expressing political opinions. It might be that these more mundane acts of citizenship can give Americans cause to wonder about the relationship between their duties as citizens and their religious or ethnic loyalties, as Wilfred McClay reminds us in his essay. ■ In the end, the question of what it means to be a good citizen is a complicated and difficult one in part because it can be answered in so many different ways. As you engage the various arguments about citizenship in this section, you might ask yourself how your own view of what it means to be an American shapes your sense of duty as a citizen — and how you would respond to President John F. Kennedy's challenge.

CON-TEXT: President John F. Kennedy's Inaugural Address 1961

1 . . . In your hands, my fellow citizens, more than mine, will rest the final success or failure of our course. Since this country was founded, each generation of Americans has been summoned to give testimony to its national loyalty. The graves of young Americans who answered the call to service surround the globe.

Now the trumpet summons us again — not as a call to bear arms, though arms we need — not as a call to battle, though embattled we are — but a call to bear the burden of a long twilight struggle, year in and year out, "rejoicing in hope, patient in tribulation" — a struggle against the common enemies of man: tyranny, poverty, disease and war itself.

Can we forge against these enemies a grand and global alliance, North and South, East and West, that can assure a more fruitful life for all mankind? Will you join in that historic effort?

In the long history of the world, only a few generations have been granted the role of defending freedom in its hour of maximum danger. I do not shrink from this responsibility — I welcome it. I do not believe that any of us would exchange places with any other people or any other generation. The energy, the faith, the devotion which we bring to this endeavor will light our country and all who serve it — and the glow from that fire can truly light the world.

5 And so, my fellow Americans: ask not what your country can do for you. Ask what you can do for your country.

My fellow citizens of the world: ask not what America will do for you, but what together we can do for the freedom of man.

Finally, whether you are citizens of America or citizens of the world, ask of us here the same high standards of strength and sacrifice which we ask of you. With a good conscience our only sure reward, with history the final judge of our deeds, let us go forth to lead the land we love, asking His blessing and His help, but knowing that here on earth God's work must truly be our own.

① JOHN BALZAR, "Needed: Informed Voters"

The right to vote is a fundamental right guaranteed to Americans by the U.S. Constitution. It is a hallmark of our political system, central to the workings of democracy. But it is a right that has not always been enjoyed by all Americans. Women were not allowed to vote in the United States until 1920, and African Americans were often prevented from voting by local and state restrictions even after Congress passed the Voting Rights Act in 1963. Perhaps Americans take this hard-won right for granted, since only about half of eligible voters usually turn out for presidential elections, and often fewer than half vote in local and state elections. As reporter John Balzar notes in the following essay, political commentators routinely lament these low voter turnouts, suggesting that low participation in American political campaigns ultimately weakens democracy. Balzar has a somewhat different view. He believes not only that voting is a right, but also that it entails responsibility; in his view, it is not enough simply to show up at the polling place to vote. Citizenship requires more than that. As you engage his argument, consider your own views about voting. How important is the right to vote? What responsibilities come with that right? Does being an American *require* you to vote? Or does it mean that you can choose *not* to exercise that right?

John Balzar has covered politics and served as a foreign correspondent for the *Los Angeles Times*. The author of *Yukon Alone* (1999), Balzar has won the Scripps-Howard Foundation Prize for his human interest and adventure stories.

Needed: Informed Voters
JOHN BALZAR

1 More than 150 years ago, the writer James Fenimore Cooper* put it this way: "The man who can right himself by a vote will seldom resort to a musket."

Cooper found agreement on the point even with his old nemesis, Mark Twain, who set aside humor to observe: "Where every man in a state has a vote, brutal laws are impossible."

Ah, voting. When you read through American civics, you find that almost everybody who presumed to comment on our nation had something celebratory to say about the franchise.

The United States, no one should forget, pioneered the idea of self-governance on a grand scale by way of popular elections.

5 Only elections aren't so popular any-more. In the 2002 primaries, 83 percent of eligible Americans exercised their rights as free citizens and chose not to vote. Far more people stake their hopes on playing the Lotto than on participating in democracy. We now bemoan the results: With the onset of autumn, the public begins to lay eyes on the matchups of candidates chosen by tiny fractions of their neighbors.

Yikes.

Our normal suspicions about those who seek political office turn into outright alarm. Consequently, fewer people muster the enthusiasm to drive down the block and cast a vote in the election.

Two truths: I've never met anyone who would forfeit his or her right to vote. Likewise, everyone knows that the United States would be a much different country if everyone availed himself of the opportunity and actually cast an informed vote.

So, do we have a crisis on our hands? Instinctively, we are conditioned to say yes. But I don't think it's quite as simple as that.

10 The hand-wringers have been telling us for decades now that something must be way wrong in the land for participation to be so low. Yet many nonvoters I know are not distraught, but content.

We live in an age of decidedly centrist politics, driven in large measure by personality. Most candidates are foursquare in favor of a full-employment economy, equal opportunity, a healthy environment, good schools and health care. Thus, political differences boil down to the tactics and philosophy of governance, and for a good number of people, it's enough to leave that choice to others.

There's another matter, usually too delicate to be discussed directly. That's the distinction between voting and voting wisely.

For as long as I've covered politics, I've listened to experts say that we need to make registration and voting simpler, easier. In truth, registration has never been simpler in most places, and it's getting more so all the time.

The real difficulty in voting is the preparation involved. To cast an intelligent ballot requires more than casual exposure to TV commercials.

15 Many Americans have lost faith in those who offer considered election guidance, whether political parties, newspaper editorials or interest groups. Thus the rise of the vaunted "independent voter."

Sounds lofty. But in truth, the homework necessary to inform oneself about the issues and candidates in most elections is no less than that faced in an upper-division college class.

From what I can tell, many Americans aren't up to the task. Reading through opinion surveys is always as amusing as it is sobering. Almost half the nation believes that the communist creed "from each according to his abilities, to each according to his needs" is spelled out in the U.S. Constitution. And although 66 percent of adults can identify Regis

*Considered by some critics to be America's first successful novelist, James Fenimore Cooper (1789–1851) is best known today for his novel *The Last of the Mohicans* (1826). But like Mark Twain, author of *The Adventures of Huckleberry Finn* (1884), Cooper was also widely known in his day as a social and political critic whose writings about American democracy were often controversial.

INDEPENDENT VOTERS

When he refers to the "independent voter," John Balzar is invoking the belief that Americans tend to vote for their favored candidates regardless of party affiliation. In other words, especially in presidential elections, voters will vote for the candidate they like best, whether or not that candidate represents their own party. According to the Center for Voting and Democracy, 64 percent of voting-age Americans were registered with a political party in 2002. In the eighteen states that require voters to register with a party to vote, 34.1 percent of voting-age persons were registered as Democrats, 22.6 percent as Republicans, and 17.4 percent as independent or with a third party — an increase from 15.8 percent in 1998. (See www.fairvote.org/turnout/csae2002.htm.)

COMPLICATION

Balzar asserts that being an informed voter requires "homework" equivalent to the work required in "an upper-division college class." Is he right? According to political commentator Thomas Sowell,

Ideally, each citizen should both become informed about issues and candidates and go to the polls on Election Day. But the real question is what to do in a world that is seldom ideal. Even informed voters sometimes have trouble understanding that they can only choose among alternatives actually available. Some voters vote — or don't vote — according to whether their elected officials have lived up to all their hopes. Seldom can any officials in a democracy do that ("High Stakes Elections," 2002).

According to Martin Wattenberg, Americans who choose not to vote tend to have less education than those who do vote. In 1998 U.S. college graduates voted at 36 percent above the national average; those with "some high school" voted at 43 percent below it. (Source: *Where Have All the Voters Gone?* 2002.)

In 1849 Henry David Thoreau wrote in his famous essay "Civil Disobedience,"

All voting is a sort of gaming, like checkers or backgammon, with a slight moral tinge to it, a playing with right and wrong, with moral questions; and betting naturally accompanies it. . . . Even voting *for the right* is *doing* nothing for it. It is only expressing to men feebly your desire that it should prevail. A wise man will not leave the right to the mercy of chance, nor wish it to prevail to the power of the majority.

Philbin as host of a TV game show, only 6 percent can name Dennis Hastert, R-Ill., as speaker of the U.S. House of Representatives.

So, would our democracy be better served if more people voted? As I said, it's not as simple as answering yes.

Questions for Discussion

1. What do you think Balzar accomplishes with his references in paragraphs 1 and 2 to two well-known American writers from the 19th century, James Fenimore Cooper and Mark Twain? How do those references relate to his main argument? **2.** Why does Balzar disagree with political commentators who believe there is a crisis among U.S. voters because of low turnout rates for elections? What support does he offer for his own position on voter turnout rates in the United States? **3.** Balzar states that "we live in an age of decidedly centrist politics." What does he mean? Do you agree with him that politics today are "driven in large measure by personality"? Explain. **4.** What evidence does Balzar offer for his assertion that "many Americans aren't up to the task" of informing themselves on the issues and candidates in most elections? Do you find his evidence convincing? Why or why not? **5.** What do you think are the implications of Balzar's argument? What might his view of U.S. voters say about democracy? What might it suggest about how elections should be run? What response would you offer to his argument?

② RUSS BAKER, "Want to Be a Patriot? Do Your Job"

In January 1991, several months after Iraq invaded Kuwait in the Persian Gulf, the United States and its allies began an intense bombing campaign of Iraq. During the first days of that campaign, Peter Arnett of CNN was one of the few U.S. journalists to report from Baghdad, Iraq's capital city. His reports about the destruction caused by the bombing of Baghdad infuriated many Americans, some of whom accused him of treason for filing reports that they viewed as sympathetic to the enemy. The controversy surrounding Arnett's reporting from Iraq raised larger questions about the responsibilities of journalists to their governments. Was a journalist such as Arnett really an independent reporter whose responsibility was to objectively report the events he was witnessing, whether or not those reports were unflattering to the United States? Or was such a reporter an American first, responsible to his government like any other citizen? In debating such questions, Americans were also asking each other what it means to be patriotic. In the following essay, Russ Baker addresses that same question more than ten years after the Peter Arnett controversy. He believes that U.S. journalists do have a responsibility as citizens. But he defines that responsibility in terms of the Constitutional guarantee of a free press, which he views as fundamental to American democracy. In making his argument, Baker challenges not only journalists but all of us to define what we really mean by the term *patriot*. Baker is a contributing editor to the *Columbia Journalism Review*, in which this essay was published in 2002.

Want to Be a Patriot? Do Your Job
RUSS BAKER

1 In the aftermath of September 11, Dan Rather publicly shed patriotic tears on David Letterman's show, demonstrating that he was in as much pain as any American and as loyal to the national cause. At the same time, TV news programs across the country were wrapping themselves in stars-and-stripes graphics as news outlets of all kinds rushed to associate themselves, in subtle and not-so-subtle ways, with the nation's surge of patriotic emotion

Flag-waving is not surprising in the aftermath of a full-scale attack on American civilians. As individuals, we are all part of a severely traumatized body politic. But it is precisely during the most trying periods that journalists must distance themselves from their emotions if they are to do their best work. And it is also imperative to distinguish between patriotism, love of one's country, and nationalism — the exalting of one's nation and its culture and interests above all others. If patriotism is a kind of affection, nationalism is its dark side. Nationalistic pressure also makes it hard for journalists to do their job. Even today, eight months after the events, many journalists are troubled by a sense that we have failed an important test, that we have allowed certain kinds of honest reporting to be portrayed as somehow disloyal.

Raising questions about the wisdom of government actions in wartime, particularly early in a war, is not easy. For example, early in Operation Desert Storm,* ABC anchor Peter Jennings says he commissioned a piece on the antiwar activist Ramsey Clark. Despite his own sense of urgency, Jennings recalls that it took weeks to get the piece on the air. "It was not quite the right moment," he says. Internally, "people were arguing less about the relationship between the media and the administration than about the media's relationship with its public." To confront a popular government at such a time, he says, is to be "running emotionally upstream."

When war began in Afghanistan, Jennings says, "We decided early on that we would not exploit the violence of all of this without losing sight of how violent it was, and that we would be reluctant to sloganeer." But when Jennings and his people departed from the patriotic consensus they paid a price. Jennings had a howling pack after him, inflamed by Rush Limbaugh's charge that the anchor was disloyal for raising questions about Bush's conduct on September 11, when the presidential

plane zig-zagged across the nation while the World Trade Center and the Pentagon were burning. (ABC eventually was able to get Limbaugh to issue a correction noting that Jennings had merely observed that some presidents are perceived as handling crises better than others.) After a study showed that Jennings paid more attention to civilian casualties in Afghanistan than either his NBC or CBS rivals, he was subject to on-air criticism from Fox News's Brit Hume, while conservative media critics pointed to his Canadian citizenship.

5   Another news program that successfully upheld journalistic principles in the post-9/11 world was Ted Koppel's *Nightline,* which consistently asked pointed questions about the executive branch's newly assumed domestic law-enforcement powers, and insisted on airing cautionary voices. This on a show that, during the Letterman affair, an unnamed ABC executive called irrelevant.

We are, of course, at war. And the public does not have a right to know every-

*"Desert Storm" was the name given to the military operation conducted by the United States and its allies against Iraq in 1991.

†The First Amendment to the U.S. Constitution stipulates that "Congress shall make no law respecting an establishment of religion, or prohibiting the free exercise thereof; or abridging the freedom of speech, or of the press; or the right of the people peaceably to assemble, and to petition the Government for a redress of grievances."

thing. Still, in the post-September 11 world, an official obsession with secrecy has grown out of the war against terrorism, making the job of the journalist even harder. As we know, Americans have been given less information about what is being done in this war than in any prior conflict in U.S. history (see "Access Denied," *Columbia Journalism Review,* January/February). Lack of access to information is not, in itself, a journalistic dereliction of duty. Failing to make a public issue out of it is, however.

"Information is being managed in this war, and frankly, we can't expect a lot of breaks," says Jeffrey Dvorkin, ombudsman at National Public Radio. But why don't we read and see more news about this serious problem? Walter Cronkite, who set the standard for television anchors,

laments that TV no longer has the kind of editorial voice typified by the late Eric Sevareid. Cronkite says if it were up to him, he would be running "opinion of the management" editorials. "Complaining to the Pentagon is not good enough," he says. "We should be letting the public know the restrictions under which we operate."†

The need for tough-minded reporting has never been clearer. When journalists hold themselves back — in deference to their own emotions or to the sensitivities of the audience or through timidity in the face of government pressure — America is weakened. Journalism has no more important service to perform than to ask tough, even unpopular questions when our government wages war.

COMPLICATION

After September 11, 2001, some people criticized the U.S. government for what Baker describes as an "official obsession with secrecy," which they believe is part of the government's efforts to ignore civil liberties in the war against terrorism. Laura Murphy of the American Civil Liberties Union was quoted in the *Washington Post* as saying, "The FBI is now telling the American people, 'You no longer have to do anything unlawful to get that knock on the door. You can be doing a perfectly legal activity like worshiping or talking in a chat room and they can spy on you anyway.'" Others argued that some civil liberties must be curtailed or compromised in times of war. Columnist Michael Kelly, for example, argued that "this war must be successfully prosecuted and success in war pretty much always requires the violation of civil liberties" (See "Liberties Are a Real Casualty of War" on pages 521–523.)

CONTEXT

This essay was first published in the *Columbia Journalism Review (CJR)*, which describes itself as

America's premiere media monitor — a watchdog of the press in all its forms, from newspapers and magazines to radio, television, and cable to the wire services and the Web. Founded in 1961 under the auspices of Columbia University's Graduate School of Journalism, *CJR* examines not only day-to-day press performance but also the many forces — political, economic, technological, social, legal, and more — that affect that performance for better or worse. The magazine, which is edited by a dedicated staff of professional journalists and published six times a year, offers a mix of reporting, analysis, criticism, and commentary, always aimed at its basic goal: the continuing improvement of journalism in the service of a free society.

In what ways does author Russ Baker address the audience for that journal? In what ways does his essay reflect the journal's stated purpose?

Questions for Discussion

1. What distinction does Baker make between patriotism and nationalism? Why is this distinction important, in his view? How does it fit into his main argument in this essay? **2.** What point does Baker make with the examples of criticisms made about ABC television news anchor Peter Jennings and *Nightline* anchor Ted Koppel? Do you think these examples are effective in helping Baker make his point? Explain. **3.** On what grounds does Baker assert that the press should be reporting to the American public about the restrictions that the U.S. government has placed on information? Do you agree with him? Why or why not? Should any event or piece of information be fair game for the press to report? What, if anything, should the press be banned from reporting? **4.** What is the fundamental assumption on which Baker rests his argument about the role of the press? What basic strategy for argumentation does Baker employ in this essay? (You might wish to refer to Chapter 2 in answering this question.) **5.** Given that public opinion polls routinely indicate that Americans are skeptical of journalists, how do you think most Americans might react to Baker's argument, which was originally written for other journalists? In what ways might Baker have made his argument differently if he had been writing for a more general audience?

③ WILFRED M. MCCLAY, "America: Idea or Nation?"

The question that Wilfred M. McClay poses in the title of the following essay is perhaps misleading because it suggests that the answer must be that the United States is *either* an idea *or* a nation. But in his carefully reasoned essay, McClay makes it clear that the issue is much more complicated than that. He makes it clear, too, that because understanding America as an idea *and* a nation can be challenging, patriotism is also a challenging concept. McClay explores what it means to be a patriot in a nation that is a powerful symbol of democracy both for its own citizens and for citizens of other nations. In exploring the symbolic importance of America, McClay refuses to simplify the issue of patriotism. The complexity of his argument might be appropriate, because McClay believes that many Americans have not thought carefully enough about what it means to be a patriotic citizen. His essay challenges us to reflect on our own patriotism and how it relates to our sense of identity. Wilfred M. McClay is the SunTrust Bank Chair of Excellence in Humanities and a professor of history at The University of Tennessee at Chattanooga; he is also the author of *The Masterless: Self and Society in Modern America* (1994) and a contributing editor of *Touchstone: A Journal of Mere Christianity.* The following essay was published in *The Public Interest* in 2001.

America: Idea or Nation?
WILFRED M. MCCLAY

1 At first glance, American patriotism seems a simple matter. But it is simple only until one actually starts to think about it, inquire after its sources, and investigate its manifestations. Consider a small but significant case in point, an observation recently made by a distinguished rabbi who serves a large and prosperous Reform congregation in the New York suburbs. This man takes the business of premarital counseling very seriously, and therefore gets to know many of his congregation's younger members in a fairly intimate way. In the course of interviewing and counseling them over the years, he has discovered an interesting pattern: a high correlation between the level of these young people's patriotic sentiments and the extent of their opposition to intermarriage, meaning marriage to non-Jews. In other words, those with the strongest love of country were also those most firmly committed to marrying only within the Jewish faith. Conversely, those most indifferent or hostile to patriotism were also most likely to have no reservations about intermarriage — and most likely to find fault with those who do.

Loyalties Large and Small

The rabbi's observation rings true to me. And yet if it is true, it would seem to throw much of our conventional wisdom about patriotism into a cocked hat. Don't we generally assume that loyalty to the nation is a form of belonging that tends, as it intensifies, to divert, diminish, or even swallow up lesser loyalties and more particular affiliations? Doesn't the study of European history indicate precisely this, that the modern nation-state* grew in power and prestige at the expense of local and regional identities and affinities, including those of religion? Wouldn't it therefore be more reasonable to predict that observant American Jews would value their nation less, because they value their faith more — particularly when theirs is a faith that sets them apart from the vast majority of Americans? And by the same token, wouldn't it stand to reason that intensely patriotic American Jews would see an act of such primal loyalty to the Jewish community, particularly on a matter as personal and intimate as the question of a marriage partner, as an atavism and a betrayal of the American promise of universal liberty and equality?

Reasonable guesses all, except that they happen not to be borne out by this rabbi's experiences. To be sure, this seeming paradox may have a lot to do with the history and current state of the factions within American Jewry. But it also is wonderfully illustrative of a more general truth, which is this: A considerable part of the genius of American patriotism resides in the fact that being a proud and loyal American does not require one to yield up all of one's identity to the nation. On the contrary, American patriotism has generally affirmed and drawn upon the vibrancy and integrity of other, smaller-scale, and relatively independent loyalties. Far from weakening American national sentiment, or causing it to be half-hearted or anemically "thin," these other traditions have strengthened it immeasurably. Nor is this ideal a recent innovation, brought on by the nation's growing ethnic diversity and the vogue of multiculturalism. Instead, it is an ideal as old as the nation itself, going back to the fundamental concept of a federated republic, which consisted of free and self-governing states, counties, and townships, and which loomed so large in the minds of the nation's Founders.

Needless to say, it has not been an easy ideal to realize or sustain, as recurrent crises in American history from the Whiskey Rebellion to the Civil War to the post–World War II conflicts over school desegregation and voting rights have shown. America's national government has grown steadily in power and influence, and the political, economic, legal, technological, and social forces tending to impose homogeneity upon the national culture are stronger than ever. Yet there is an enduring power in this more diffuse patriotic ideal, which seats the general in the local, and asserts that one does not become more of an American by becoming less of something else — less Southern, less Virginian, less small-town, less black, less Jewish, less whatever.

5 Of course, there will always be instances in which certain profound loyalties come into conflict, in ways that cannot be reconciled. Such is the human condition, and such is the stuff of civil wars, religious martyrdoms, and Sophoclean tragedies. But the American patriotic ideal has generally been wise and generous about granting the widest possible berth to our disparate loyalties and in assuming a certain respect for the multiplicity of the person. Loyalty, like love, is not necessarily a zero-sum game, in which any loyalty accorded to X is

*The Merriam-Webster dictionary defines *nation-state* as "a form of political organization under which a relatively homogeneous people inhabits a sovereign state; especially: a state containing one as opposed to several nationalities."

*French political writer Alexis de Tocqueville (1805–1859) examined the characteristics of the American political system and the American people in his classic book *Democracy in America* (1835). He argued that a crucial component of democracy is "self-interest rightly understood," which refers to a citizen's understanding that acting in ways that society deems good is actually in one's own self-interest.

thought to take away from what Y might have received. A husband does not love his wife less because he also loves his children; if anything, the opposite is the case. And, as Burke and Tocqueville* both well understood, something of the same is true of political and social life. By giving as free a hand as possible to the "little platoons," local institutions, and independent associations in a free society, the nation not only makes it possible for many citizens to be meaningfully involved in the work of public life but also elicits from them a deep, unfeigned, and uncoerced patriotism. In a word, the health of local and particular freedoms strengthens the nation. . . .

The Problems of Commerce

So where will the next generation of American patriots come from? The particulars of the situation are not terribly encouraging. There is no iron-clad guarantee that there will even be such a generation. The heart of the problem is the well-known fact that the cultivation of patriotic virtue does not come naturally to a commercial society such as the United States. When the self-interested pursuit of material well-being, rather than the inculcation of public-spiritedness, has become the glue of social cohesion and the chief engine of social progress, where can such a society catch a glimpse of broader and longer horizons, or find compelling rationales for sacrificial acts devoted to the common good? Tocqueville showed persuasively how far the principle of "self-interest rightly understood" could go in reproducing many of the salutary effects of virtue. Rather than appealing to an obsolete standard of noble thoughts and character, the principle of "self-interest rightly understood" succeeded by persuading citizens that it was both prudent and useful for them to behave in outwardly virtuous

ways. But even that principle has its limits, and it reaches those limits at precisely the moment when the utilitarian payoff for virtuous behavior is no longer so plainly evident.

The martial virtues fall first. How can the principle of self-interest serve to persuade a soldier to lay down his life for his country or to risk life and limb by withholding confidential information when he is held prisoner? Or, on a less heroic level, how does this principle command sufficient loyalty from the general populace to fight an extended, costly war, or form affective bonds that will take precedence over self-interest in moments of national crisis? Even the self-restraints entailed by more commonplace virtues such as thrift, modesty, and marital fidelity are likely to weaken when there is no obvious utility in respecting them, and no obvious risk in disdaining them. In any event, the broad spirit of patriotism, which blends the martial virtues with the commonplace ones, cannot thrive without being nourished by moral sources, ones that the principle of self-interest cannot provide. Finding and sustaining those alternative sources turns out to be one of the perennial problems of American society. It is a problem very much facing us in the prosperous present.

Happily complicating the matter, however, is the undeniable fact that the United States has managed to produce more than its share of genuine patriots — warriors and heroes great and small, gallant and unprepossessing, romantic and gritty, aristocratic and plebeian, all united by a willingness to put their lives on the line for their country. How then, in light of the formidable obstacles mentioned above, has the United States managed to bring forth such patriots? And how can it find the means to honor them properly in the present, and — most important of all — produce more of them in the future? The answers to these questions have never been obvious, either to the generation of the Founders or to our own, but a great deal hangs upon the way they are answered, or not answered. Hence it is a fortunate event that Walter Berns, one of our most thoughtful political philosophers, has come forward with a lucid new book, *Making Patriots,* the fruit of his many years of reflection on the American polity and society, to address precisely these questions. "Designing a public-spirit curriculum for such a people" is, Berns writes, "no easy task." But few are better qualified to help initiate the process.

American Exceptionalism

To begin with, Berns argues, we need to recognize that patriotism in America is an entirely different animal from patriotism in other times and places. The ancient Greek city-state of Sparta, for example, which Berns takes to represent the apex of the classical world's understanding of patriotism, was legendary for its public-spirited citizenry. But it achieved that distinction at far too high a cost, at least according to our standards, by imposing a comprehensive regime of severe, near-totalitarian control upon its people. Every aspect of life, from education to marriage to childrearing to eating, fell under the state's purview. Ruthlessly obliterating any elements of privacy or individuality in its citizen's lives, or any of the institutions that mediated between the state and the individual, Sparta sought to achieve a homogeneous, mobilized, martially virtuous populace, imbued with an overwhelming sense of duty to the collective whole, and rendered invulnerable to the siren songs of self-interest and self-gratification. All private sentiments became displaced onto the state itself, so

> ### *MAKING PATRIOTS,* BY WALTER BERNS
>
> "The Founders . . . knew, and accepted as a fact, that the nation was formed by self-interested men, men, as John Locke puts it, naturally in a 'state of perfect freedom to order their actions and dispose of their possessions and persons as they think fit . . . without asking leave or depending on the will of any other man.' But they also knew, as Locke knew, that these men ceased to be autonomous, or simply self-interested men, when they entered civil society and agreed to be governed. That agreement made them citizens, and a citizen is obliged to think of his fellows and of the whole of which he is a part. This requires that he possess certain qualities of character, or virtues, and, as Madison says in *Federalist* 55, 'republican government presupposes the existence of these qualities in a higher degree than any other form [of government].' Because these qualities cannot be taken for granted, they must somehow be cultivated" Source: *Making Patriots* (2001).

that self-love was sublimated and absorbed entirely into the love of Sparta. Such discipline made for a mighty and disciplined war machine. But it neglected nearly every other aspect of human potentiality and would be entirely inappropriate as a model of patriotism or patriot-formation for the American republic.

10 This is true in part because the American polity would emphasize commerce over warmaking, and protection of men's natural rights over enforcement of their social obligations. But it also is true, Berns points out, because the classical model had long before been shattered by the advent of Christianity, which separated the spiritual duties of men from their political ones and the things of God from the things of Caesar. This decisively changed the nature of patriotism, driving a wedge between the private and public virtues, and demoting the latter to a decisively subordinate role. If Sparta had made the cultivation of public virtue and patriotic sentiment the be-all and end-all of social existence, then Christianity did something like the opposite, downgrading the sentiment of

*Important figures in the founding of the United States as a nation, Thomas Jefferson and Alexander Hamilton held different ideals for American democracy. Jefferson believed that democracy could be fostered through a society of land-owning farmers whose stake in preserving their land and their way of life would ensure good citizenship. Hamilton envisioned a nation built on commerce driven by American entrepreneurship that is regulated by a strong central government.

CONTEXT

To read part of *The Declaration of Independence,* see *Con-Text* on page 507.

patriotism and presenting it with an enduring dilemma. Would patriotism become conflated with religious sentiment, and thereby absorbed into the vision of a crusading worldly theocracy? Or would it remain aloof from religious sentiment, and thereby run the risk of becoming the distant junior partner of a gnostic, otherworldly faith?

The American solution, which could not have been arrived at without the clarifying help of centuries of European religious wars, managed to split the difference, with a decisive move in the direction of separation, though also with a healthy expression of generalized Protestant civil religion undergirding and enlivening the whole. It is a settlement that defies easy formulation and is more fragile than many Americans appreciate. Berns overstates matters a bit in asserting baldly that the Founders "consigned [religion] to the private sphere." In fact, that prospect didn't come fully into view until the century just past, and its effects have always been highly controversial. But Berns is right, in the end, to say that the Constitution the Framers devised did not envision the United States government as the custodian of men's souls. That was to be the task of other entities. Instead, the Constitution was designed to free men to engage in the self-interested pursuits of a bourgeois society.

Which brings us back to the central problem: How does a republic that is based upon cupidity and self-seeking make public-spirited patriots? Thomas Jefferson, like Rousseau before him, was himself dubious about the possibility, which was one reason why he preferred the agrarian ideal of a virtuous landowning yeomanry over the Hamiltonian vision of a restless and inventive commercial class of continental-minded men.* A farmer, after all, lived a settled life and had a citizen's substantial stake

in the land he inhabited and cultivated. But what about the holder of stocks, bonds, and bank notes? He was a man ever on the move, a citizen of no place, a man whose only home was the market.

Yet Jefferson was also principal author of the document that, for Berns, provides the one sure basis for American patriotism: the Declaration of Independence. The key to American patriotism, in Berns's view, is that it is twofold, entailing not only devotion to one's country but also devotion to the principles upon which that country had been founded and to which it was consecrated. These principles are not peculiar to Americans, but are thought to be universal in scope, grounded self-evidently in human nature. First among these principles are the famous assertions that all men are created equal, that they are endowed by their Creator with certain inalienable rights, including life, liberty, and the pursuit of happiness, and that governments derive their legitimacy from the consent of the governed and are instituted for the purpose of securing these rights. From these principles may be derived a more generalized commitment to democratic self-government, which Lincoln called government "of the people, by the people and for the people." This is the creed to which Americans assent, Berns argues, and it is out of admiration for these ideals, and not merely out of filial loyalty to "their" country, that American patriots derive their animating sentiments.

The figure of Abraham Lincoln looms especially large for Berns. He is "patriotism's poet," the uncommon common man whose words and personal example offer eloquent testimony to the possibilities of American democracy. Hence Berns twice cites words from Lincoln's 1852 eulogy to Henry Clay as a definitive statement on the shape of American patriotism. Clay, Lincoln said, "loved his country partly because it was his own

Alexander Hamilton

country, but mostly because it was a free country; and he burned with a zeal for its advancement, because he saw in such, the advancement, prosperity, and glory of human liberty, human right, and human nature." It was this sense of America's mission, as the carrier and leading advocate for universal ideals, and not merely as another nation seeking to preserve its territory or expand its place in the sun, that animated Clay and Lincoln. And, Berns argues, it has animated the generations of American patriots who fought to preserve the Union and to defeat the totalitarian powers of the twentieth century.

15 Berns does not deny the stains on the national record, particularly the institution of slavery and its aftermath. But he is determined that those failures be estimated properly, as the ex-slave Frederick Douglass himself did, as remediable defects in an otherwise admirable and promising structure, rather than be exaggerated and used to denigrate the whole. Berns endorses Lincoln's contention that America represents "the last, best hope of earth," with all the enormous responsibilities that that entails. And he concludes by insisting that it is all-important to defend the legitimacy of America's liberal democracy and the ideal

it embodies against the armies of its postmodernist, relativist, and multiculturalist detractors. For once this legitimacy is damaged, and once the foundational truths are no longer regarded as self-evident by the citizenry, then the American nation will be uprooted and fatally undermined to the detriment not only of America but of all humanity.

Dangerous Abstractions

Berns is himself a member of the generation of patriots, now gradually disappearing from our midst, that fought in the war against Hitler. That poignant fact echoes through his pages, subtly but unmistakably, giving an added measure of

LINCOLN AT GETTYSBURG

authority to his words. He has written a deeply moving book, personal without being the least bit mawkish or confessional and vibrant with the full range of human emotions — pride, reverence, tenderness, and occasional flashes of anger. This is, after all, his country that he is writing about. He manages to convey a keen sense of connection to the American past, a sense that is much more than merely historical. There is a feeling of urgency, too, a concern that the rising generations have not been taught about what they have inherited, about what their inheritance cost — and about those who were willing to pay the price for it. "Ours is not a parochial patriotism," Berns insists, because "it comprises an attachment to principles that are universal." Anything less would be "un-American."

One hopes there will be young readers

of Berns's book who will find themselves stirred by such a full-throated and unabashed endorsement of America's sense of heroic mission. But there will be other readers, even ones as admiring as this reviewer, who may want to pause at such words and the argument they embody. For there is a danger in coming to regard America too exclusively as an idea, the carrier of an idea, or the custodian of a set of principles, rather than as a real nation that exists in a world of other nations, with all the features and limitations of a nation, including its particular history, institutions, and distinctive national character.

To be sure, Berns is right to stress the twofold character of American patriotism: The patriot loves America partly because it is his own country and partly because of his love for the ideals for which the country stands. The two motives are in tension, but they also are inseparable and mutually indispensable. America is not a class-ridden traditional society or a homogeneous blood-and-soil nation-state, but neither is it a universalistic ideological crusade. What is worrisome and lopsided in Berns's account of American patriotism is the near-exclusive weight he gives to the abstract and ideological dimensions of American patriotism, to the virtual exclusion of all other elements.

Indeed, at one point in his book he unfairly ridicules (and misquotes) a famous toast delivered in 1815 by the heroic American naval officer Stephen Decatur, declaring the words to be unpatriotic, even "un-American," because of their failure to endorse abstract universal principles of political right. The toast goes like this: "Our country! In her intercourse with foreign nations may she always be in the right; but our country, right or wrong!" In his rendering, Berns omits the words "In her intercourse with foreign nations," which changes the meaning of the quote rather dramatically. But even in its truncated form, the quote does not deserve the scorn Berns heaps upon it. For patriotism, like any love, withers and dies if it is not accorded some degree of instinctive assent. Berns's position could be interpreted to be that our country deserves our support only when its motives are demonstrably pure and its course of action demonstrably unassailable, that our loyalty to it is always revocable, that the nation stands every day freshly before the bar of judgment, to be assessed solely on the basis of its consonance that day with the universal principles of political right. This is much too brittle and unstable a foundation for any durable patriotism — particularly, one might add, in a nation's intercourse with foreign nations.

20 Berns, of course, is not advocating any such thing. But his words inadvertently point to the problem with interpreting America exclusively as an idea. Obviously, no decent patriotism can ever be completely unconditional, blindly loyal on all occasions, deaf to the claims of morality. That way lies tyranny and human degradation. But compelling reasons of state do not always translate into readily apprehended principles of universal morality, and there are times when being a patriot means being like a soldier, following leaders who have had to make complex judgments beyond the soldier's ken. Even Berns's beloved Lincoln is vulnerable to the charge that the human rights of slaves and such fundamental rights as habeas corpus were less important to him than the preservation of the Union, that the Emancipation Proclamation was primarily a cynical and calculated war measure, and that only the relentless pressure of events and other men led Lincoln to end slavery. If

those charges sound familiar, it is because they are the same charges that two generations of morally indignant historians have hurled at Lincoln, convicting him by reference to a universalistic (and unrealistic and ungenerous) standard very much like the one Berns advocates.

We Are Family?

So how might one arrive at a more complex understanding of the mixed nature of American patriotism? One might find some insight in an analogy to marriage, an institution in which something very much like Berns's twofold division of motives obtains. The parallels are suggestive. A man is devoted to his wife partly because she is admirable — and partly because she is his. And it is easy to see how, in a marriage, one cannot separate these two things in practice. A man may perhaps initially fall in love with a woman because she is admirable and lovely. But it is an entirely different matter to explain why he stays married and faithful to her, even when he knows full well that she is not always admirable and lovely. Should a man continue to love and honor his wife only if she is always admirable? Of course not. We all recognize that only a very shallow and insubstantial love would express itself in this way. Are there not occasions when a good husband honors and defends his wife, even when she may be in the wrong, simply because she is his and he is hers? Is there not a mutual obligation subsisting between them, far more deep-seated than any transient wrong? Obviously. Are there times when the strict pursuit of justice in a marriage takes a back seat to the preservation of the union? Yes. Can a happy and healthy marriage endure when justice is always subordinated to the preservation of the union? No.

In other words, the nature of the commitment made in a good marriage is a

*Poet, novelist, playwright, and journalist G. K. Chesterton (1874–1936) was also a Catholic who unabashedly argued for a moral political philosophy based on Christian values.

complex blend of motives, ideal and primal, extrinsic and intrinsic, practical and impractical. It would be unthinkable, and in fact somewhat ludicrous, to imagine that one set of motives could exist without the counterbalance of the other. There is merit in a love that is directed toward a person who possesses abundant admirable qualities. But there is even more merit in a love that is able, over time, and within the enclosure of a mutual commitment, to acknowledge and accept — up to a point — what is less than fully admirable, what is all-too-human, about the otherwise admirable other. Where that point is located and when it is reached are questions almost impossible to answer in any general way. Tolstoy, wrong in so many other things, was also wrong in proposing that happy families are always the same. General principles may be helpful, but they always have to be weighed against other considerations.

One might also extend the analogy to encompass other relationships within the family. If a country is like a spouse, it is also like a parent, since it constitutes one of the irreducible sources of one's being. One's gratitude to one's forebears is very much like the gratitude a patriot should feel toward those, like Walter Berns, who fought to preserve their nation. So then: Is it a good thing to admire one's father (and to be an admirable father)? Of course. Should one's love for one's father be conditional upon his always having been an admirable person and having always done admirable things? Of course not. Should one love one's father even when he has behaved shamefully, as a criminal or a traitor? That is more difficult. Perhaps even then, though only up to a point. But then, who is to say? The truth of the matter is buried in the particulars.

Like all analogies, these marital and familial ones break down at some point.

Mario Cuomo's famous words notwithstanding, a nation is not a family. Indeed, the analogy becomes problematic when overtaxed precisely because (as Berns points out) Americans have never spoken of their country as a "fatherland," in the way so many Europeans spoke of their own nations in the pre-European Union era. In fact, it might be said that America was the country one came to in order to escape from one's father, both literally and figuratively. It was the country where one put aside the heavy lumber of inherited identity and tradition, and was freed to begin again. Hence Berns much prefers G. K. Chesterton's* notion that America, far from being a fatherland, is "the only nation in the world that is founded on a creed," and is therefore "a nation with the soul of a church." To be an American, in this view, is not a matter of whose child you are but of what principles you accept. It is a nation of the twice-born, politically and culturally, a nation founded not upon descent but consent.

A Creedal Nation?

25 There is profound truth in this, but it is not the whole of the matter. The Chestertonian analogy breaks down too — or more precisely, it tells us more than was intended. Indeed, it goes directly to the heart of what is so troubling about Berns's view of American patriotism. For a church is much more than its creed. The creed is indispensable, as an intellectual guidepost, a check upon heresy, a means of instructing the young, and a handy distillation of church doctrine. Documents like the Westminster Confession are masterpieces of theological clarity and concision. But a church that had only a creed would be no church at all. One need only visit an old churchyard and see the gravestones of several generations of a family clustered together to understand how this is so.

All churches, even the most nouveau-Protestant ones, possess a rich storehouse of conscious and unconscious traditions, liturgies, songs, rituals, and customs. Over time these become inseparable in the minds and hearts of the worshipers from the content of their faith. Creeds are useful, but the Biblical and liturgical texts and the sacraments and rituals are not finally reducible to propositional statements; they are not reducible to anything less than themselves. There is a seamless web that unites every piece of church life with every other, for better or worse. This is why any changes in the pattern of church life become fraught with peril: Such changes may seem to disturb the bones of the dead and tamper with the very structure of the cosmos.

So a creed can be useful to shake up the musty complacency and cultural stasis that can creep into such a hidebound environment. It may also have defensive uses, as a means of keeping the train from going off the tracks. But it is not the soul of a church or a nation. Or, to put it another way, a living creed is a distillation and codification of beliefs that are grounded elsewhere — embodied in the habits and mores and institutions of the people. The words have to be made flesh and dwell among us. Without such quickening, a creed soon becomes a dead letter.

And for the same reasons, indoctrination into the principles of the Declaration of Independence alone will not make our young Americans into patriots. It is a beginning, but only a beginning. As both Thomas Jefferson and John Adams made clear, the Americans of the Revolutionary generation did not need instruction in what their Declaration declared. Their Declaration was mainly a press release to the world which attempted to put into words what most Americans already believed and embodied

in their way of life. For our young people to know about it is, in the end, indispensable. But what is just as needful — perhaps even more so — is a recognition that there can be no meaningful patriotism in a society whose most privileged young people know nothing, remember nothing, respect nothing, cherish nothing, feel responsible for nothing, and are grateful for nothing.

This litany is not meant as a disparagement of the young but of those adults who have abdicated their responsibility for the young's formation, setting them free to be shaped by cable television, shopping malls, Internet chat rooms, and all the other flotsam of our feckless commercial culture. That irresponsibility, I think, is what has produced the conditions that sadden, anger, and worry Walter Berns, as they should all of us. But if no grand national program of ideological revitalization can rebuild what has been eroded, there is still hope for America in the patriotism of those young Jews mentioned earlier who have chosen to swim against the tide by paying homage to their birthright. A second birth does not have to renounce the first, and faithfulness in large things begins with faithfulness in smaller ones. The genius of American patriotism resides here just as much as it does in the Declaration of Independence. And if taken seriously, it will do far more to change the way Americans live.

A final image. When Lincoln wondrously invoked the "mystic chords of memory" in his first inaugural address, he envisioned them as the emanations of musical strings, "stretching from every battlefield and patriot grave to every living heart and hearthstone all over this broad land." It is an amazingly rich and well-considered image. We should not miss the fact that the strings are held in place not only by the deeds of warriors

CONTEXT

This essay was published in the fall 2001 edition of *The Public Interest*, which likely means that it was written before the September 11, 2001, attacks. After those attacks, patriotism became an important topic of discussion among many Americans. How might the September 11th attacks change the way readers respond to McClay's argument about patriotism? Does his argument become stronger or weaker in light of those attacks?

at one end but also by the domestic world, the world of family and home, at the other. Gratitude to one's country, however principled, must also draw upon forms of gratitude that are more primary — upon the things that are personal, particular, and singular. The things, in short, that are one's own. Without them, there can be no music, no memory, and no chorus of the Union.

Questions for Discussion

1. What is the central problem that McClay believes faces the United States when it comes to encouraging a patriotic citizenry? Why, in McClay's view, does the United States face this problem? **2.** McClay devotes much of his essay to discussing the ideas of Walter Berns in the book *Making Patriots* (see the sidebar on page 488). Why does McClay discuss Berns's book at such length? What main points does he use Berns's ideas to make? Do you think this is an effective strategy on McClay's part? What other strategies might be used to make these points? **3.** What is the danger that McClay sees in thinking of the United States as an idea and a set of principles rather than as a real nation that exists in the world? **4.** McClay has divided his essay into six main sections. What point does he make in each of these sections? How does each of these main points fit together to help McClay make his main argument about patriotism? Do you think his way of organizing his argument is effective? Why or why not? **5.** How would you describe the tone and style of this essay? Compare McClay's tone and style to those of the other writers in this section. In what ways do his tone and style contribute to the main argument of this essay? **6.** In his essay McClay makes many references to young Americans as well as to older Americans. How does he characterize young Americans? Do you think his characterization is accurate and fair? Given these references to young Americans, whom do you think McClay imagined as his primary audience for this essay? To whom is his argument primarily addressed? Do you think his argument is effective for that audience? Why or why not? Cite specific passages from his essay to support your answer. **7.** McClay uses several analogies in his essay. For example, he compares patriotism to the loyalty two married people feel toward one another. Evaluate McClay's use of these analogies. What do they contribute to his main argument? How effectively do they help him make his points?

④ MICHAEL KAZIN, "A Patriotic Left"

It is an old practice in American politics for a candidate to question an opponent's patriotism during an election. It is also common for those who question U.S. policies or actions to be called unpatriotic. As Michael Kazin suggests in the following essay, not only do Americans with leftist political views seem to regularly endure the accusation of being unpatriotic, but they also reject patriotism itself as a kind of blind loyalty to the United States. Whether it is true or not that left-leaning Americans are more commonly charged with being unpatriotic than are their fellow citizens with more moderate or conservative views, Kazin believes that patriotism is an important element in political debate. As an avowed leftist, he refuses to accept the criticism that leftists are unpatriotic because of their willingness to question their government. For Kazin, patriotism is something much more complicated than loyalty or love of country. It involves a deep sense of duty founded on the moral and ethical principles implicit in the U.S. Constitution. That duty might sometimes require the true patriot to question or criticize the government, as many important political figures in America's history have done. In making his argument, Kazin looks to those figures in America's past — people such as Frederick Douglass, Mother Jones, and Eugene Debs — to highlight the long tradition in American politics of patriots criticizing the U.S. government in their efforts to create a more just America. You might disagree with Kazin's politics, but consider how his argument can help you to clarify your own sense of what it means to be a patriot. Kazin serves on the editorial board of *Dissent* magazine, in which this essay was published in 2002.

A Patriotic Left
MICHAEL KAZIN

1 I love my country. I love its passionate and endlessly inventive culture, its remarkably diverse landscape, its agonizing and wonderful history. I particularly cherish its civic ideals — social equality, individual liberty, a populist democracy — and the unending struggle to put their laudable, if often contradictory, claims into practice. I realize that patriotism, like any powerful ideology, is a "construction" with multiple uses, some of which I abhor. But I persist in drawing stimulation and pride from my American identity.

*The term *American exceptionalism* refers to the idea that the United States is unique among nations because of the special circumstances of its beginnings as a democracy that was built on the principles of individual liberty and self-determination.

Regrettably, this is not a popular sentiment on the contemporary left. Antiwar activists view patriotism as a smokescreen for U.S. hegemony, while radical academics mock the notion of "American exceptionalism"* as a relic of the cold war, a triumphal myth we should quickly outgrow. All the rallying around the flag after September 11 increased the disdain many leftists feel for the sentiment that lies behind it. "The globe, not the flag, is the symbol that's wanted now," scolded Katha Pollitt in the *Nation*. Noam Chomsky described patriotic blather as simply the governing elite's way of telling its subjects, "You shut up and be obedient, and I'll relentlessly advance my own interests."

Both views betray an ignorance of American history, as well as a quixotic desire to leap from a distasteful present to a gauzy future liberated from the fetters of nationalism. Love of country was a demotic faith long before September 11, a fact that previous lefts understood and attempted to turn to their advantage. In the United States, Karl Marx's dictum that the workers have no country has been refuted time and again. It has been not wage earners but the upper classes — from New England gentry on the Grand Tour a century ago to globe-trotting executives and cybertech professionals today — who view America with an ambivalent shrug, reminiscent of Gertrude Stein's line, "America is my country, Paris is my hometown."

One can, like Pollitt and Chomsky, curse as jingoistic all those "United We Stand" and "God Bless America" signs and hope somehow to transcend patriotism in the name of global harmony. Or one can empathize with the communal spirit that animates them, embracing the ideals of the nation and learning from past efforts to put them into practice in the service of far-reaching reform.

5 An earlier version of American patriotism was a forerunner of the modern genre: pride in the first nation organized around a set of social beliefs rather than a shared geography and history. In its novelty, Americanism gave citizens of the new republic both a way to understand and to stand for purposes that transcended their self-interest. Of course, these purposes were not always noble ones. As historian Gary Gerstle points out in his recent book *American Crucible*, "racial nationalism" dominated much of American life through the nineteenth

century and into the early decades of the twentieth. It led some white Americans to justify exterminating Indians, others to hold slaves, and still others to bar immigrants who did not possess "Anglo-Saxon" genes. But the tolerant alternative, which Gerstle calls "civic nationalism," also inspired many Americans in the modern era to help liberate Europe from fascism and Stalinism and to organize at home for social and economic justice.

For American leftists, patriotism was indispensable. It made their dissent and rebellion intelligible to their fellow citizens — and located them within the national narrative, fighting to shape a common future. Tom Paine praised his adopted homeland as an "asylum for mankind" — which gave him a forum to denounce regressive taxes and propose free public education. Elizabeth Cady Stanton issued a "Woman's Declaration of Rights" on the centennial of the Declaration of Independence and argued that denying the vote to women was a violation of the Fourteenth Amendment. Union activists in the Gilded Age such as Eugene Debs and Mother Jones accused employers of crushing the individuality and self-respect of workers. When Debs became a socialist, he described his new vision in the American idiom, as "the equal rights of all to manage and control" society. Half a century later, Martin Luther King, Jr., told his fellow bus boycotters, "If we are wrong, the Supreme Court of this nation is wrong" and proclaimed that "the great glory of American democracy is the right to protest for right."

One could easily list analogous statements from such pioneering reformers as Jane Addams and Betty Friedan, unionists Sidney Hillman and Cesar Chavez, and the gay liberationist Harvey Milk. Without patriotic appeals, the great social movements that attacked inequalities of class,

THE FOURTEENTH AMENDMENT

Adopted in 1868, the Fourteenth Amendment to the U.S. Constitution addresses issues related to voting, such as the number of congressional representatives each state should have. When Elizabeth Cady Stanton, a 19th century activist who campaigned for women's right to vote, invoked this amendment in her famous "Women's Declaration of Rights," she was referring to Section 1, which states,

All persons born or naturalized in the United States, and subject to the jurisdiction thereof, are citizens of the United States and of the state wherein they reside. No state shall make or enforce any law which shall abridge the privileges or immunities of citizens of the United States; nor shall any state deprive any person of life, liberty, or property, without due process of law; nor deny to any person within its jurisdiction the equal protection of the laws.

gender, and race in the United States — and spread their messianic rhetoric around the world — would never have gotten off the ground.

Even slavery couldn't extinguish the promise radicals found in the American creed. On Independence Day, 1852, Frederick Douglass gave an angry, eloquent address that asked, "What to the slave is the Fourth of July?" Every account quotes the fugitive-turned-abolitionist speaking truth to white power: "Your celebration is a sham; your boasted liberty, an unholy license; your national greatness, swelling vanity; your sounds of rejoicing are empty and heartless; your denunciations of tyrants, brass fronted impudence; your shouts of liberty and equality, hollow mockery." But fewer commentators note that when, at the end of his speech, Douglass predicted slavery's demise, he drew his "encouragement from the Declaration of Independence, the great principles it contains, and the genius of American Institutions," as well as from a spirit of enlightenment that he believed was growing on both sides of the Atlantic. After emancipation, Douglass never stopped condemning the hypocrisy of white Americans — or continuing to base his hopes for equality on traditions he and they held in common.

A self-critical conception of patriotism also led Americans on the left to oppose their leaders' aggressive policies abroad. Anti-imperialists opposed the conquest of the Philippines after the war of 1898 by comparing President William McKinley to King George III. Foes of U.S. intervention in World War I demanded to know why Americans should die to defend European monarchs and their colonies in Africa and Asia. In 1917, a mass movement led by socialists and pacifists called for a popular referendum on the question of going to war. Neither group of resisters succeeded at the time, but each gained a mass hearing and saw its arguments incorporated into future policies. Congress promised independence to the Philippines sooner than colonial officials favored. And, challenged by such antiwar voices as Debs, Robert LaFollette, and William Jennings Bryan, Woodrow Wilson proclaimed national self-determination to be the core principle of a new world order.

10 A good deal that we cherish about contemporary America was thus accomplished by social movements of the left, speaking out for national ideals. It may be, as the idiosyncratic Trotskyist Leon Samson argued in 1935, that Americanism served as a substitute for socialism, an ideology of self-emancipation through equal opportunity that inoculated most citizens against the class-conscious alternative. But leftists made what progress they did by demanding that the nation live up to its stated principles, rather than dismissing them as fatally compromised by the racism of the founders or the abusiveness of flag-waving vigilantes. After all, hope is al-

ways more attractive than cynicism, and the gap between promise and fulfillment is narrower for Americanism than it is for other universalist creeds such as communism, Christianity, and Islam.

It's difficult to think of any radical or reformer who repudiated the national belief system and still had a major impact on U.S. politics and policy. The movement against the Vietnam War did include activists who preferred the Vietcong's flag to the American one. But the antiwar insurgency grew powerful only toward the end of the 1960s, when it drew in people who looked for leadership to liberal patriots such as King, Walter Reuther, and Eugene McCarthy rather than to Abbie Hoffman and the Weathermen.

Perhaps one exception to this rule was Malcolm X, who stated, in 1964, that he was a "victim of Americanism" who could see no "American dream," only "an American nightmare." But Malcolm was primarily a spokesman for black anger and pride, not a builder of movements or a catalyst of reforms to benefit his people.

He was, however, a prophetic figure. Soon after Malcolm's death, many on the left, of all races, began to scorn patriotic talk and, instead, to celebrate ethnic and sexual differences. In 1970, writer Julius Lester observed, "American radicals are perhaps the first radicals anywhere who have sought to make a revolution in a country which they hate." At the time, there were certainly ample reasons to consider Americanism a brutal sham. After World War II, the word itself became the property of the American Legion, the House Un-American Activities Committee, and the FBI. In the 1960s, liberal presidents bullied their way into Indochina in the name of what Lyndon Johnson called "the principle for which our ancestors fought in the valleys of Pennsylvania." Fierce love for one's identity group — whether black, Latino, Asian, Native American, or gay or lesbian — seemed morally superior to the master narrative that had justified war abroad and racial exclusion at home.

Yet the history of the last thirty years has also exposed the outsized flaw in such thinking. Having abandoned patriotism, the left lost the ability to pose convincing alternatives for the nation as a whole. It could take credit for spearheading a multicultural, gender-aware revision of the humanities curriculum, but the right set the political agenda, and it did so in part because its partisans spoke forcefully in the name of American principles that knit together disparate groups — anti-union businesspeople, white evangelicals, Jewish neoconservatives — for mutual ends.

15 In the face of such evidence, many leftists would respond that civic idealism should not be confined within national borders. In a provocative 1994 essay, philosopher Martha Nussbaum argued that patriotism is "morally dangerous" because it encourages Americans to focus on their own concerns and minimize or disregard those of people in other lands. "We should regard our deliberations," she wrote, "as, first and foremost, deliberations about human problems of people in particular concrete situations, not problems growing out of a national identity that is altogether unlike that of others." Echoing her words, activists and intellectuals talk of challenging global exploitation with some form of global citizenship.

As an ethicist, Nussbaum is certainly on solid ground. Americans ought to take a massacre in Africa as seriously as one that takes place in lower Manhattan and demand that their government move rap-

"PATRIOTISM AND COSMOPOLITANISM"

In making his argument, Kazin refers to a well-known essay by legal scholar Martha Nussbaum, stating that Nussbaum sees patriotism as "morally dangerous." However, in her essay Nussbaum does not say that *all* patriotism is morally dangerous, only some types of patriotism, and only insofar as patriotism is incompatible with a decent concern for the rights of people everywhere. She writes, "I believe . . . that this emphasis on patriotic pride is both morally dangerous and, ultimately, subversive of some of the worthy goals patriotism sets out to serve — for example, the goal of national unity in devotion to worthy moral ideals of justice and equality. These goals, I shall argue, would be better served by an ideal that is in any case more adequate to our situation in the contemporary world, namely the very old ideal of the cosmopolitan, the person whose primary allegiance is to the community of human beings in the entire world. . . .

As students here grow up, is it sufficient for them to learn that they are above all citizens of the United States, but that they ought to respect the basic human rights of citizens of India, Bolivia, Nigeria, and Norway? Or should they, as I think — in addition to giving special attention to the history and current situation of their own nation — learn a good deal more than is frequently the case about the rest of the world in which they live, about India and Bolivia and Nigeria and Norway and their histories, problems, and comparative successes? . . . Most important, should they be taught that they are above all citizens of the United States, or should they instead be taught that they are above all citizens of a world of human beings, and that, while they themselves happen to be situated in the United States, they have to share this world of human beings with the citizens of other countries?" (From Martha Nussbaum, "Patriotism and Cosmopolitanism," 1994).

idly to halt it. But she offers no guidance for how global leftists can get the power to achieve their laudable objectives. A planetary government is hardly on the horizon, and rich nations would no doubt hog its agenda if it were.

In the meantime, Americans who want to transform the world have to learn how to persuade the nation. At minimum, this means putting pressure on the national government, organizing coalitions of people from different regions and backgrounds, and debating citizens who think their tax money ought to be spent only at home. Disconnected as they are from any national or local constituency, global leftists now live at risk of being thrust to the margins — abstract sages of equity, operatives of nongovernmental organizations engaged in heroic but Sisyphean tasks, or demonstrators roving from continent to continent in search of bankers to heckle.

In the wake of September 11, the stakes have been raised for the American left. Even if the "war against terrorism" doesn't continue to overshadow all other issues, it will inevitably force activists of every stripe to make clear how they would achieve security for individual citizens and for the nation. How can one seriously engage in this conversation about protecting America if America holds no privileged place in one's heart? Most ordinary citizens understandably distrust a left that condemns military intervention abroad or a crackdown at home but expresses only a pro forma concern for the actual and potential victims of terrorism.

Without empathy for one's neighbors, politics becomes a cold, censorious enterprise indeed.

There's no need to mouth the Pledge of Allegiance or affix a flag pin to your lapel or handbag. But to rail against patriotic symbols is to wage a losing battle — and one that demeans us and sets us against the overwhelming majority of Americans for no worthwhile moral or political purpose.

20 Instead, leftists should again claim, without pretense or apology, an honorable place in the long narrative of those who demanded that American ideals apply to all and opposed the efforts of those who tried to reserve them for favored groups. When John Ashcroft denies the right of counsel to a citizen accused of terrorism or a CEO cooks the books to impress Wall Street, they are soiling the flag and ought to be put on the patriotic defensive. Liberals and radicals are the only people in politics who can insist on

"The protesters object to what they see as unfair IMF policies that benefit wealthier nations at the expense of developing nations. The IMF disagrees, saying it is the poor of the world who are benefited by its policies." (From CNN.com, September 27, 2002.)

closing the gap between America as the apotheosis of democratic strivings and the sordid realities of greed and arrogance that often betray it.

There is really no alternative. In daily life, cultural cosmopolitanism is mostly reserved to the rich and famous. Radical environmentalists and anti-IMF crusaders seek to revive the old dream of internationalism in a version indebted more to John Lennon's "Imagine" than to V. I. Lenin's *Comintern*. But three years after bursting into the headlines from the streets of Seattle, that project seems stalled indefinitely in the Sargasso Sea that lies between rhetorical desire and political exigency.

In hope of a revival, left patriots might draw inspiration from . . . the white, conservative skeptic George Santayana, who observed that "America is the greatest of opportunities and the worst of influences. Our effort must be to resist the influence and improve the opportunity." . . .

Throughout our history, and still today, the most effective way to love the country is to fight like hell to change it.

CONTEXT

According to its Web site, "A magazine of the left, *Dissent* is also a magazine of independent minds. A magazine of strong opinions, *Dissent* is also a magazine that welcomes the clash of strong opinions." Does Michael Kazin's essay, which appeared in *Dissent* in 2002, fit this description?

Questions for Discussion

1. In the opening paragraphs of his essay, Kazin summarizes some of the criticisms of leftists who dismiss American patriotism. On what grounds does Kazin disagree with these leftists? What benefit might there be to debating this issue with others who share your own political views? **2.** Evaluate Kazin's introduction to this essay. What does he accomplish by beginning his argument with the statement that he loves his country? What audience do you think Kazin was primarily addressing with this introduction? **3.** Kazin makes many references in this essay to historical events and people, tracing the history of several important political developments in the United States in the 18th, 19th, and 20th centuries. What role does history play in Kazin's argument? How effectively do you think he uses history to help him make his main argument? (You might compare the way Kazin uses history to Steven Camarota's use of history in his essay on pages 468–474.) **4.** How does Kazin define *patriotism* in this essay? Does his understanding of patriotism differ from the ideas of Wilfred McClay or Russ Baker, whose essays appear earlier in this section? Explain. Do you think most Americans would agree with Kazin about what it means to be patriotic? Do you agree with him? Why or why not? **5.** Kazin is a leftist, but he expresses concern about the views of other leftists about patriotism. He is concerned as well about the way those on the political right understand patriotism. Do you think he offers a compelling alternative to the views of the leftists and rightists he criticizes? On the basis of your answer to that question, how effectively do you think his essay works as an example of a Rogerian argument? (See pages 19–21 for a discussion of Rogerian argument.)

NEGOTIATING DIFFERENCES

In their essays in this section, Russ Baker and Michael Kazin refer explicitly to the events of September 11, 2001, and suggest that those events underscore the importance of examining the question of what it means to be patriotic. They argue that being a patriot requires more than loyalty to America, more than even a willingness to go to war. Wilfred McClay reinforces this idea by asking us to consider how we justify the decision to fight and perhaps even to die for our country. And John Balzar shows that even the act of voting, which Americans may take for granted, places a responsibility on citizens that goes beyond simply expressing an opinion. In short, these essays suggest that citizenship is more than a matter of which country you happen to live in; they challenge us to think about what citizenship requires of each of us.

After September 11, 2001, these questions about citizenship and patriotism have understandably preoccupied many Americans. On many college campuses, controversies have arisen when professors or students have openly criticized the U.S. government's actions in its efforts to fight terrorism. In a few cases faculty members have been sanctioned by their schools for such criticisms. In other cases some courses have been criticized because they seem to be sympathetic to the views of America's enemies.

Imagine that such a controversy has emerged at your own college or university. A professor has been publicly criticized for teaching a course that seems to be sympathetic to the point of view of groups that openly espouse violence against Americans. In response to the controversy your school's administration has decided to address the issue by reexamining the school's curriculum. One proposal that is under consideration would require all students to take a newly designed course in citizenship. In effect, the course would teach students how to be good citizens. Not surprisingly, this proposal has generated further controversy as students, faculty, and community members debate what such a course should include and even whether such a course should be required. In the wake of this controversy, students have been invited to express their views about the proposal in writing.

Write an essay in which you present your own position on the question of whether students should be required to take a course in citizenship. In your essay, define what you believe a good citizen is, and discuss what responsibilities citizens have. Using the essays in this section and any other relevant sources you find, make a case for or against the proposed course in citizenship, or suggest some alternative way of addressing the school's concerns about encouraging students to become good citizens. Keep your audience in mind as you construct your argument: the administrators of your school as well as students who attend the school. Try to construct your argument in a way that might address their concerns and help your school community to find a solution to the controversy about the proposed course.

WHAT KIND OF POWER SHOULD WE GIVE OUR GOVERNMENT?

Americans consider the Declaration of Independence to be a sacred document (see *Con-Text* on page 507). American children learn in school that the Declaration, written mostly by Thomas Jefferson, was a catalyst for the American Revolutionary War. Its presentation to King George III of England made it clear that the American colonists were rejecting the British government that had ruled them. What students often overlook is how radical a step the colonists had taken. In the 18th century the idea that citizens, rather than governments, ultimately hold political power was almost unheard of — an idea that flew in the face of the established order, under which people were viewed as the *subjects* of their rulers. But in the Declaration of Independence, Jefferson and his cosigners stated unequivocally that it should be the other way around: Leaders served at the behest of citizens; if those leaders should compromise the inherent rights of the citizens, then citizens were legally and morally justified in removing those leaders. Power to the people. ■ In this sense the founding of the United States ushered in a new era in which the whole idea of government was redefined, but it also created a new set of questions about the relationship between a government and its citizens. If political power ultimately resides in the people, then what is the role of government? How is that role determined? And how much power should a government have over citizens? These questions are not answered in the Declaration of Independence except in the abstract. Jefferson and his cosigners famously declared that government exists to secure the rights of citizens to "Life, Lliberty, and the pursuit of Happiness," but they left it up to later generations to define exactly what "life, liberty, and the pursuit of happiness" means. And each generation has wrestled with the question of how much power government should have to fulfill that purpose. ■ The essays in this section reveal some of the ways in which Americans have confronted this question. In his famous "Letter from a Birmingham Jail," Martin Luther King, Jr., refers directly to the Declaration of Independence to make his argument that citizens are morally justified — and even obligated — to disobey laws that are unjust. The entire Civil Rights Movement of the 1960s, in which King was such an important figure, rested largely on that very idea. After September 11, 2001, Americans revisited some of the same questions that Civil Rights activists and protesters against the Vietnam War raised about granting government too much power over individual citizens. In the wake of the 9/11 terrorist attacks, the U.S. government took several actions to protect the nation against additional attacks. But many Americans believed that the government overstepped its legal powers and compromised the rights of its own citizens. Fierce debates ensued about how much freedom citizens should give up so that their government could better protect them. The essays in this section reveal the complexity and intensity of those debates. ■ As a group, these essays provide various perspectives on the relationship between a government and its citizens. They also suggest that Americans are still trying to answer the same question about government power that Thomas Jefferson and the cosigners of the Declaration of Independence posed more that 225 years ago.

CON-TEXT: "The Declaration of Independence"

1 When in the Course of human events, it becomes necessary for one people to dissolve the political bands which have connected them with another, and to assume among the powers of the earth, the separate and equal station to which the Laws of Nature and of Nature's God entitle them, a decent respect to the opinions of mankind requires that they should declare the causes which impel them to the separation.

We hold these truths to be self-evident, that all men are created equal, that they are endowed by their Creator with certain unalienable Rights, that among these are Life, Liberty and the pursuit of Happiness. That to secure these rights, Governments are instituted among Men, deriving their just powers from the consent of the governed. That whenever any Form of Government becomes destructive of these ends it is the Right of the People to alter or to abolish it, and to institute new Government, laying its foundation on such principles and organizing its powers in such form, as to them shall seem most likely to effect their Safety and Happiness. Prudence, indeed, will dictate that Governments long established should not be changed for light and transient causes; and accordingly all experience has shown, that mankind are more disposed to suffer, while evils are sufferable, than to right themselves by abolishing the forms to which they are accustomed. But when a long train of abuses and usurpations, pursuing invariably the same Object evinces a design to reduce them under absolute Despotism, it is their right, it is their duty, to throw off such Government, and to provide new Guards for their future security. Such has been the patient sufferance of these Colonies; and such is now the necessity which constrains them to alter their former Systems of Government. . . .

① MARTIN LUTHER KING, JR., "Letter From a Birmingham Jail"

Martin Luther King, Jr. (1929–1968), was the most important leader of the movement to secure civil rights for black Americans during the mid-twentieth century. Ordained a Baptist minister in his father's church in Atlanta, Georgia, King became the founder and director of the Southern Christian Leadership Conference, an organization he continued to lead until his assassination in 1968. He first came to national attention by organizing a boycott of the buses in Montgomery, Alabama (1955–1956) — a campaign that he recounts in *Stride Toward Freedom: The Montgomery Story* (1958). An advocate of nonviolence who was jailed fourteen times in the course of his work for civil rights, King was instrumental in helping to secure the passage of the Civil Rights Bill in 1963. His efforts on behalf of civil rights led to many awards, most notably the Nobel Peace Prize in 1964. "Letter from a Birmingham Jail" was written in 1963, when King was jailed for eight days as the result of his campaign against segregation in Birmingham, Alabama. In the letter, King responds to white clergymen who had criticized his work and blamed him for breaking the law. But "Letter from a Birmingham Jail" is more than a rebuttal of criticism; it is a well-reasoned and carefully argued defense of civil disobedience as a means of securing civil liberties. In justifying his refusal to obey what he believed were unjust laws, King invokes a high moral standard by which to judge a government's actions. His famous essay thus prompts us to consider the limits of governmental power and the responsibilities of citizens in supporting or opposing that power.

Letter From a Birmingham Jail
MARTIN LUTHER KING, JR.

April 16, 1963

My Dear Fellow Clergymen:

1 While confined here in the Birmingham city jail, I came across your recent statement calling my present activities "unwise and untimely." Seldom do I pause to answer criticism of my work and ideas. If I sought to answer all the criticisms that cross my desk, my secretaries would have little time for anything other than such correspondence in the course of the day, and I would have no time for constructive work. But since I feel that you are men of genuine good will and that your criticisms are sincerely put forth, I want to try to answer your

statement in what I hope will be patient and reasonable terms.

I think I should indicate why I am here in Birmingham, since you have been influenced by the view which argues against "outsiders coming in." I have the honor of serving as president of the Southern Christian Leadership Conference, an organization operating in every southern state, with headquarters in Atlanta, Georgia. We have some eighty-five affiliated organizations across the South, and one of them is the Alabama Christian Movement for Human Rights. Frequently we share staff, educational, and financial resources with our affiliates. Several months ago the affiliate here in Birmingham asked us to be on call to engage in a nonviolent direct-action program if such were deemed necessary. We readily consented, and when the hour came we lived up to our promise. So I, along with several members of my staff, am here because I was invited here. I am here because I have organizational ties here.

But more basically, I am in Birmingham because injustice is here. Just as the prophets of the eighth century B.C. left their villages and carried their "thus saith the Lord" far beyond the boundaries of their home towns, and just as the Apostle Paul left his village of Tarsus and carried the gospel of Jesus Christ to the far corners of the Greco-Roman world, so am I compelled to carry the gospel of freedom beyond my own home town. Like Paul, I must constantly respond to the Macedonian call for aid.

Moreover, I am cognizant of the interrelatedness of all communities and states. I cannot sit idly by in Atlanta and not be concerned about what happens in Birmingham. Injustice anywhere is a threat to justice everywhere. We are caught in an inescapable network of mutuality, tied in a single garment of des-

tiny. Whatever affects one directly, affects all indirectly. Never again can we afford to live with the narrow, provincial, "outside agitator" idea. Anyone who lives inside the United States can never be considered an outsider anywhere within its bounds.

5 You deplore the demonstrations taking place in Birmingham. But your statement, I am sorry to say, fails to express a similar concern for the conditions that brought about the demonstrations. I am sure that none of you would want to rest content with the superficial kind of social analysis that deals merely with effects and does not grapple with underlying causes. It is unfortunate that demonstrations are taking place in Birmingham, but it is even more unfortunate that the city's white power structure left the Negro community with no alternative.

In any nonviolent campaign (see "Nonviolence" on page 510), there are four basic steps: collection of the facts

NONVIOLENCE

Inspired by the ideas of Mahatma Gandhi, whose nonviolent movement helped to end the British rule of India, Martin Luther King, Jr., developed a philosophy of nonviolent resistance based on the Christian ideal of brotherly love. In an essay published in 1960, King wrote that "the Christian doctrine of love operating through the Gandhian method of nonviolence was one of the most potent weapons available to oppressed people in their struggle for freedom." In a related essay, King responded to a critique of pacifism by Christian philosopher Reinhard Neibuhr by arguing that "pacifism is not unrealistic submission to evil power, as Niebuhr contends. It is rather a courageous confrontation of evil by the power of love." King's philosophy was put to the test in 1956 during the bus boycott in Montgomery, Alabama, during which Blacks and civil rights activists were harrassed and sometimes physically attacked. In the end, King's nonviolent protest movement resulted in a Supreme Court decision that declared segregation on public buses unconstitutional.

to determine whether injustices exist; negotiation; self-purification; and direct action. We have gone through all these steps in Birmingham. There can be no gainsaying the fact that racial injustice engulfs this community. Birmingham is probably the most thoroughly segregated city in the United States. Its ugly record of brutality is widely known. Negroes have experienced grossly unjust treatment in courts. There have been more unsolved bombings of Negro homes and churches in Birmingham than in any other city in the nation. These are the hard, brutal facts of the case. On the basis of these conditions, Negro leaders sought to negotiate with the city fathers. But the latter consistently refused to engage in good-faith negotiation.

Then, last September, came the opportunity to talk with leaders of Birmingham's economic community. In the course of the negotiations, certain promises were made by the merchants — for example, to remove the stores' humiliating racial signs. On the basis of these promises, the Reverend Fred Shuttlesworth and the leaders of the Alabama Christian Movement for Human Rights agreed to a moratorium on all demonstrations. As the weeks and months went by, we realized that we were the victims of a broken promise. A few signs, briefly removed, returned; the others remained.

As in so many past experiences, our hopes had been blasted, and the shadow of deep disappointment settled upon us. We had no alternative except to prepare for direct action, whereby we would present our very bodies as means of laying our case before the conscience of the local and the national community. Mindful of the difficulties involved, we decided to undertake a process of self-purification. We began a series of workshops on nonviolence, and we repeatedly asked ourselves: "Are you able to accept blows without retaliating?" "Are you able to endure the ordeal of jail?" We decided to schedule our direct-action program for the Easter season, realizing that except for Christmas, this is the main shopping period of the year. Knowing that a strong economic-withdrawal program would be the byproduct of direct action, we felt that this would be the best time to bring pressure to bear on the merchants for the needed change.

Then it occurred to us that Birmingham's mayoral election was coming up in March, and we speedily decided to postpone action until after election day. When we discovered that the Commissioner of Public Safety, Eugene "Bull" Connor, had piled up enough votes to be in the run-off, we decided again to postpone action until the day after the run-off so that the demonstrations could not be used to cloud the issues. Like many others, we waited to see Mr. Connor defeated, and to this end we endured postponement after postponement. Having aided in this community need, we felt that our direct-action program could be delayed no longer.

10 You may well ask, "Why direct action? Why sit-ins, marches, and so forth? Isn't negotiation a better path?" You are quite right in calling for negotiation. Indeed, this is the very purpose of direct action. Nonviolent direct action seeks to create such a crisis and foster such a tension that a community which has constantly refused to negotiate is forced to confront the issue. It seeks so to dramatize the issue that it can no longer be ignored. My citing the creation of tension as part of the work of the nonviolent resister may sound rather shocking. But I must confess that I am not afraid of the word "tension." I have earnestly opposed violent tension, but there is a type of constructive, nonviolent tension which is necessary for growth. Just as Socrates felt that it was necessary to create a tension in the mind so that individuals could rise from the bondage of myths and half-truths to the unfettered realm of creative analysis and objective appraisal, so must we see the need for nonviolent gadflies to create the kind of tension in society that will help men rise from the dark depths of prejudice and racism to the majestic heights of understanding and brotherhood.

The purpose of our direct-action program is to create a situation so crisis-packed that it will inevitably open the door to negotiation. I therefore concur with you in your call for negotiation. Too long has our beloved Southland been bogged down in a tragic effort to live in monologue rather than dialogue.

One of the basic points in your statement is that the action that I and my associates have taken in Birmingham is untimely. Some have asked: "Why didn't you give the new city administration time to act?" The only answer that I can give to this query is that the new Birmingham administration must be prodded about as much as the outgoing one, before it will act. We are sadly mistaken if we feel that the election of Albert Boutwell as mayor will bring the millennium to Birmingham. While Mr. Boutwell is a much more gentle person than Mr. Connor, they are both segregationists, dedicated to maintenance of the status quo. I have hoped that Mr. Boutwell will be reasonable enough to see the futility of massive resistance to desegregation. But he will not see this without pressure from devotees of civil rights. My friends, I must say to you that we have not made a single gain in civil rights without determined legal and nonviolent pressure. Lamentably, it is an historical fact that privileged groups seldom give up their privileges voluntarily. Individuals may see the moral light and voluntarily give up their unjust posture; but, as Reinhold Niebuhr* has reminded us, groups tend to be more immoral than individuals.

We know through painful experience that freedom is never voluntarily given by the oppressor; it must be demanded by the oppressed. Frankly, I have yet to engage in a direct-action campaign that was "well timed" in the view of those who have not suffered unduly from the disease of segregation. For years now I have heard the word "Wait!" It rings in the ear of every Negro with piercing familiarity. This "Wait" has almost always meant "Never." We must come to see, with one of our distinguished jurists, that "justice too long delayed is justice denied."

We have waited for more than 340 years for our constitutional and God-given rights. The nations of Asia and Africa are moving with jetlike speed toward gaining political independence, but we still creep at horse-and-buggy pace toward gaining a cup of coffee at a lunch counter. Perhaps it is easy for those who have never felt the stinging darts of segregation to say, "Wait." But when you have seen vicious mobs lynch your mothers and fathers at will and drown your sisters and brothers at whim; when you

*Reinhold Neibuhr (1892–1971) was a Protestant theologian who explored how Christianity related to modern politics and diplomacy (see www.newgenevacenter.org/biography/niebuhr2.htm).

have seen hate-filled policemen curse, kick, and even kill your black brothers and sisters; when you see the vast majority of your twenty million Negro brothers smothering in an airtight cage of poverty in the midst of an affluent society; when you suddenly find your tongue twisted and your speech stammering as you seek to explain to your six-year-old daughter why she can't go to the public amusement park that has just been advertised on television, and see tears welling up in her eyes when she is told that Funtown is closed to colored children, and see ominous clouds of inferiority beginning to form in her little mental sky, and see her beginning to distort her personality by developing an unconscious bitterness toward white people; when you have to concoct an answer for a five-year-old son who is asking, "Daddy, why do white people treat colored people so mean?"; when you take a cross-country drive and find it necessary to sleep night after night in the uncomfortable corners of your automobile because no motel will accept you; when you are humiliated day in and day out by nagging signs reading "white" and "colored"; when your first name becomes "nigger," your middle name becomes "boy" (however old you are) and your last name becomes "John," and your wife and mother are never given the respected title "Mrs."; when you are harried by day and haunted by night by the fact that you are a Negro, living constantly at tiptoe stance, never quite knowing what to expect next, and are plagued with inner fears and outer resentments; when you are forever fighting a degenerating sense of "nobodiness" — then you will understand why we find it difficult to wait. There comes a time when the cup of endurance runs over, and men are no longer willing to be plunged into the abyss of despair. I hope, sirs, you can understand our legitimate and unavoidable impatience.

15 You express a great deal of anxiety over our willingness to break laws. This is certainly a legitimate concern. Since we so diligently urge people to obey the Supreme Court's decision of 1954 outlawing segregation in the public schools, at first glance it may seem rather paradoxical for us consciously to break laws. One may well ask: "How can you advocate breaking some laws and obeying others?" The answer lies in the fact that there are two types of laws; just and unjust. I would be the first to advocate obeying just laws. One has not only a legal but a moral responsibility to obey just laws. Conversely, one has a moral responsibility to disobey unjust laws. I would agree with St. Augustine that "an unjust law is no law at all."

Now, what is the difference between the two? How does one determine whether a law is just or unjust? A just law is a man-made code that squares with the moral law or the law of God. An unjust law is a code that is out of harmony with the moral law. To put it in the terms of St. Thomas Aquinas: An unjust law is a human law that is not rooted in

eternal law and natural law. Any law that uplifts human personality is just. Any law that degrades human personality is unjust. All segregation statutes are unjust because segregation distorts the soul and damages the personality. It gives the segregator a false sense of superiority and the segregated a false sense of inferiority. Segregation, to use the terminology of the Jewish philosopher Martin Buber, substitutes an "I–it" relationship for an "I–thou" relationship and ends up relegating persons to the status of things. Hence segregation is not only politically, economically, and sociologically unsound, it is morally wrong and sinful. Paul Tillich has said that sin is segregation. Is not segregation an existential expression of man's tragic separation, his awful estrangement, his terrible sinfulness? Thus it is that I can urge men to obey the 1954 decision of the Supreme Court, for it is morally right; and I can urge them to disobey segregation ordinances, for they are morally wrong.

Let us consider a more concrete example of just and unjust laws. An unjust law is a code that a numerical or power majority group compels a minority group to obey but does not make binding on itself. This is *difference* made legal. By the same token, a just law is a code that a majority compels a minority to follow and that it is willing to follow itself. This is *sameness* made legal.

Let me give another explanation. A law is unjust if it is inflicted on a minority that, as a result of being denied the right to vote, had no part in enacting or devising the law. Who can say that the legislature of Alabama which set up that state's segregation laws was democratically elected? Throughout Alabama all sorts of devious methods are used to prevent Negroes from becoming registered voters, and there are some counties in which, even though Negroes constitute a

BROWN V. THE *TOPEKA* BOARD OF EDUCATION

On May 17, 1954, Chief Justice Earl Warren read the decision of the unanimous U.S. Supreme Court in the case of *Brown* v. *The Board of Education of Topeka, Kansas*, which overturned the previous policy of providing "separate but equal" education for Black children:

We come then to the question presented: Does segregation of children in public schools solely on the basis of race, even though the physical facilities and other "tangible" factors may be equal, deprive the children of the minority group of equal educational opportunities? We believe that it does. . . . We conclude that in the field of public education the doctrine of 'separate but equal' has no place. Separate educational facilities are inherently unequal. Therefore, we hold that the plaintiffs and others similarly situated for whom the actions have been brought are, by reason of the segregation complained of, deprived of the equal protection of the laws guaranteed by the Fourteenth Amendment.

(For information about the Fourteenth Amendment, see the sidebar on page 499.)

majority of the population, not a single Negro is registered. Can any law enacted under such circumstances be considered democratically structured?

Sometimes a law is just on its face and unjust in its application. For instance, I have been arrested on a charge of parading without a permit. Now, there is nothing wrong in having an ordinance which requires a permit for a parade. But such an ordinance becomes unjust when it is used to maintain segregation and to deny citizens the First-Amendment privilege of peaceful assembly and protest. 20 I hope you are able to see the distinction I am trying to point out. In no sense do I advocate evading or defying the law, as would the rabid segregationist. That would lead to anarchy. One who breaks an unjust law must do so openly, lovingly, and with a willingness to accept the penalty. I submit that an individual who breaks a law that conscience tells him is unjust, and who willingly accepts the penalty of imprisonment in order to

*Nebuchadnezzar, King of Babylon, destroyed the temple at Jerusalem and brought the Jewish people into captivity. He set up a huge image in gold and commanded all to worship it. Shadrach, Meshach, and Abednego refused and were thrown into a fiery furnace from which they emerged unscathed. (See *Daniel* 3.)

†In 1956 Hungarian citizens temporarily overthrew the communist dictatorship in their country. Unwilling to confront the Soviet Union, Western democracies stood by when the Red Army suppressed the revolt by force.

arouse the conscience of the community over its injustice, is in reality expressing the highest respect for law.

Of course, there is nothing new about this kind of civil disobedience. It was evidenced sublimely in the refusal of Shadrach, Meshach, and Abednego to obey the laws of Nebuchadnezzar,* on the ground that a higher moral law was at stake. It was practiced superbly by the early Christians, who were willing to face hungry lions and the excruciating pain of chopping blocks rather than submit to certain unjust laws of the Roman Empire. To a degree, academic freedom is a reality today because Socrates practiced civil disobedience. In our own nation, the Boston Tea Party represented a massive act of civil disobedience.

We should never forget that everything Adolf Hitler did in Germany was "legal" and everything the Hungarian freedom fighters did in Hungary† was "illegal." It was "illegal" to aid and comfort a Jew in Hitler's Germany. Even so, I am sure that, had I lived in Germany at the time, I would have aided and comforted my Jewish brothers. If today I lived in a Communist country where certain principles dear to the Christian faith are suppressed, I would openly advocate disobeying that country's anti-religious laws.

I must make two honest confessions to you, my Christian and Jewish brothers. First, I must confess that over the past few years I have been gravely disappointed with the white moderate. I have almost reached the regrettable conclusion that the Negro's great stumbling block in his stride toward freedom is not the White Citizen's Counciler or the Ku Klux Klanner, but the white moderate, who is more devoted to "order" than to justice; who prefers a negative peace which is the absence of tension to a positive peace which is the presence of justice;

who constantly says, "I agree with you in the goal you seek, but I cannot agree with your methods of direct action"; who paternalistically believes he can set the timetable for another man's freedom; who lives by a mythical concept of time and who constantly advises the Negro to wait for a "more convenient season." Shallow understanding from people of good will is more frustrating than absolute misunderstanding from people of ill will. Lukewarm acceptance is much more bewildering than outright rejection.

I had hoped that the white moderate would understand that law and order exist for the purpose of establishing justice and that when they fail in this purpose they become the dangerously structured dams that block the flow of social progress. I had hoped that the white moderate would understand that the present tension in the South is a necessary phase of the transition from an obnoxious negative peace, in which the Negro passively accepted his unjust plight, to a substantive and positive peace, in which all men will respect the dignity and worth of human personality. Actually, we who engage in nonviolent direct action are not the creators of tension. We merely bring to the surface the hidden tension that is already alive. We bring it out in the open, where it can be seen and dealt with. Like a boil that can never be cured so long as it is covered up but must be opened with all its ugliness to the natural medicines of air and light, injustice must be exposed, with all the tension its exposure creates, to the light of human conscience and the air of national opinion, before it can be cured. 25 In your statement you assert that our actions, even though peaceful, must be condemned because they precipitate violence. But is this a logical assertion? Isn't this like condemning a robbed man because his possession of money precipitated the evil act of robbery? Isn't this like condemning Socrates because his unswerving commitment to truth and his philosophical inquiries precipitated the act by the misguided populace in which they made him drink hemlock? Isn't this like condemning Jesus because his unique God-consciousness and never-ceasing devotion to God's will precipitated the evil act of crucifixion? We must come to see that, as the federal courts have consistently affirmed, it is wrong to urge an individual to cease his efforts to gain his basic constitutional rights because the quest may precipitate violence. Society must protect the robbed and punish the robber.

I had also hoped that the white moderate would reject the myth concerning time in relation to the struggle for freedom. I have just received a letter from a white brother in Texas. He writes: "All Christians know that the colored people will receive equal rights eventually, but it is possible that you are in too great a religious hurry. It has taken Christianity almost two thousand years to accomplish what it has. The teachings of Christ take time to come to earth." Such an attitude stems from a tragic misconception of time, from the strangely irrational notion that there is something in the very flow of time that will inevitably cure all ills. Actually, time itself is neutral; it can be used either destructively or constructively. More and more I feel that the people of ill will have used time much more effectively than have the people of good will. We will have to repent in this generation not merely for the hateful words and actions of the bad people, but for the appalling silence of the good people. Human progress never rolls in on wheels of inevitability; it comes through the tireless efforts of men willing to be coworkers with God, and without this hard work, time itself becomes an ally of the forces of social stagnation. We must use time creatively, in the knowledge that the time is always ripe to do right. Now is the time to make real the promise of democracy and transform our pending national elegy into a creative psalm of brotherhood. Now is the time to lift our national policy from the quicksand of racial injustice to the solid rock of human dignity.

You speak of our activity in Birmingham as extreme. At first I was rather disappointed that fellow clergymen would see my nonviolent efforts as those of an extremist. I began thinking about the fact that I stand in the middle of two opposing forces in the Negro community. One is a force of complacency, made up in part of Negroes who, as a result of long years of oppression, are so drained of self-respect and a sense of "somebodiness" that they have adjusted to segregation; and in part of a few middle-class Negroes who, because of a degree of academic and economic security and because in some ways they profit by segregation, have become insensitive to the problems of the masses. The other force is one of bitterness and hatred, and it comes perilously close to advocating violence. It is expressed in the various black nationalist groups that are springing up across the nation, the largest and best-known being Elijah Muhammad's Muslim movement. Nourished by the Negro's frustration over the continued existence of racial discrimination, this movement is made up of people who have lost faith in America, who have absolutely repudiated Christianity, and who have concluded that the white man is an incorrigible "devil."

I have tried to stand between these two forces, saying that we need emulate neither the "do-nothingism" of the complacent nor the hatred and despair of the

CONTEXT

Elijah Muhammad was a charismatic leader of the Nation of Islam who advocated an ideology of Black superiority and urged Blacks to reject Christianity, which he described as a tool for the enslavement of Blacks by Whites. Muhammad and his followers criticized Martin Luther King, Jr., for his nonviolent philosophy, arguing that violent resistance is necessary to defeat White racism and achieve freedom for Blacks. King's letter was addressed to White ministers who criticized his Birmingham campaign, but he surely knew that members of the Nation of Islam would read it too.

black nationalist. For there is the more excellent way of love and nonviolent protest. I am grateful to God that, through the influence of the Negro church, the way of nonviolence became an integral part of our struggle.

If this philosophy had not emerged, by now many streets of the South would, I am convinced, be flowing with blood. And I am further convinced that if our white brothers dismiss as "rabble-rousers" and "outside agitators" those of us who employ nonviolent direct action, and if they refuse to support our nonviolent efforts, millions of Negroes will, out of frustration and despair, seek solace and security in black-nationalist ideologies — a development that would inevitably lead to a frightening racial nightmare.

30 Oppressed people cannot remain oppressed forever. The yearning for freedom eventually manifests itself, and that is what has happened to the American Negro. Something within has reminded him of his birthright of freedom, and something without has reminded him that it can be gained. Consciously or unconsciously, he has been caught up by the *Zeitgeist,* and with his black brothers of Africa and his brown and yellow brothers of Asia, South America, and the Caribbean, the United States Negro is moving with a sense of great urgency toward the promised land of racial justice. If one recognizes this vital urge that has engulfed the Negro community, one should readily understand why public demonstrations are taking place. The Negro has many pent-up resentments and latent frustrations, and he must release them. So let him march; let him make prayer pilgrimages to the city hall; let him go on freedom rides — and try to understand why he must do so. If his repressed emotions are not released in nonviolent ways, they will seek expression through violence; this is not a threat but a fact of history. So I have not said to my people, "Get rid of your discontent." Rather, I have tried to say that this normal and healthy discontent can be channeled into the creative outlet of nonviolent direct action. And now this approach is being termed extremist.

But though I was initially disappointed at being categorized as an extremist, as I continued to think about the matter I gradually gained a measure of satisfaction from the label. Was not Jesus an extremist for love: "Love your enemies, bless them that curse you, do good to them that hate you, and pray for them which despitefully use you, and persecute you." Was not Amos an extremist for justice: "Let justice roll down like waters and righteousness like an ever-flowing stream." Was not Paul an extremist for the Christian gospel: "I bear in my body the marks of the Lord Jesus." Was not Martin Luther an extremist: "Here I stand; I cannot do otherwise, so help me God." And John Bunyan: "I will stay in jail to the end of my days before I make a butchery of my conscience." And Abraham Lincoln: "This nation cannot survive half slave and half free." And Thomas Jefferson: "We hold these truths to be self-evident, that all men are created equal. . . ." So the question is not whether we will be extremists, but what kind of extremists we will be. Will we be extremists for hate or for love? Will we be extremists for the preservation of injustice or for the extension of justice? In that dramatic scene on Calvary's hill three men were crucified. We must never

COMPLICATION

King describes a number of revered historical figures, including Thomas Jefferson, Abraham Lincoln, and even Jesus, as "extremists" for love and justice. In 1964, a year after King wrote this letter, Arizona Senator Barry Goldwater, then running for nomination as the Republican Party's candidate for president, said in a speech at the Republican Party's national convention, "Extremism in the defense of liberty is no vice" — a statement for which he was severely criticized by many. In 2001 the men who carried out the attacks on the United States on September 11th were routinely described in the press and by U.S. government officials as "extremists." To what extent are all these uses of the term *extremist* similar? To what extent are they different? To what extent is the effectiveness of King's use of this term dependent on the time in which he wrote his essay?

forget that all three were crucified for the same crime — the crime of extremism. Two were extremists for immorality, and thus fell below their environment. The other, Jesus Christ, was an extremist for love, truth, and goodness, and thereby rose above his environment. Perhaps the South, the nation, and the world are in dire need of creative extremists.

I had hoped that the white moderate would see this need. Perhaps I was too optimistic; perhaps I expected too much. I suppose I should have realized that few members of the oppressor race can understand the deep groans and passionate yearnings of the oppressed race, and still fewer have the vision to see that injustice must be rooted out by strong, persistent, and determined action. I am thankful, however, that some of our white brothers in the South have grasped the meaning of this social revolution and committed themselves to it. They are still all too few in quantity, but they are big in quality. Some — such as Ralph McGill, Lillian Smith, Harry Golden, James McBride Dabbs, Ann Braden, and Sarah Patton Boyle — have written about our struggle in eloquent and prophetic terms. Others have marched with us down nameless streets of the South. They have languished in filthy, roach-infested jails, suffering the abuse and brutality of policemen who view them as "dirty niggerlovers." Unlike so many of their moderate brothers and sisters, they have recognized the urgency of the moment and sensed the need for powerful "action" antidotes to combat the disease of segregation.

Let me take note of my other major disappointment. I have been so greatly disappointed with the white church and its leadership. Of course, there are some notable exceptions. I am not unmindful of the fact that each of you has taken some significant stands on this issue. I commend you, Reverend Stallings, for your Christian stand on this past Sunday, in welcoming Negroes to your worship service on a nonsegregated basis. I commend the Catholic leaders of this state for integrating Spring Hill College several years ago.

But despite these notable exceptions, I must honestly reiterate that I have been disappointed with the church. I do not say this as one of those negative critics who can always find something wrong with the church. I say this as a minister of the gospel, who loves the church; who was nurtured in its bosom; who has been sustained by its spiritual blessings and who will remain true to it as long as the cord of life shall lengthen. 35 When I was suddenly catapulted into the leadership of the bus protest in Montgomery, Alabama, a few years ago, I felt we would be supported by the white church. I felt that the white ministers, priests, and rabbis of the South would be among our strongest allies. Instead, some have been outright opponents, refusing to understand the freedom movement and misrepresenting its leaders; all too many others have been more cautious than courageous and have remained silent behind the anesthetizing security of stained-glass windows.

In spite of my shattered dreams, I came to Birmingham with the hope that the white religious leadership of this community would see the justice of our cause and, with deep moral concern, would serve as the channel through which our just grievances could reach the power structure. I had hoped that each of you would understand. But again I have been disappointed.

There was a time when the church was very powerful — in the time when the early Christians rejoiced at being deemed worthy to suffer for what they believed.

In those days the church was not merely a thermometer that recorded the ideas and principles of popular opinion; it was a thermostat that transformed the mores of society. Whenever the early Christians entered a town, the people in power became disturbed and immediately sought to convict the Christians for being "disturbers of the peace" and "outside agitators." But the Christians pressed on, in the conviction that they were "a colony of heaven," called to obey God rather than man. Small in number, they were big in commitment. They were too God-intoxicated to be "astronomically intimidated." By their effort and example they brought an end to such ancient evils as infanticide and gladiatorial contests.

Things are different now. So often the contemporary church is a weak, ineffectual voice with an uncertain sound. So often it is an archdefender of the status quo. Far from being disturbed by the presence of the church, the power structure of the average community is consoled by the church's silent — and often even vocal — sanction of things as they are.

But the judgment of God is upon the church as never before. If today's church does not recapture the sacrificial spirit of the early church, it will lose its authenticity, forfeit the loyalty of millions, and be dismissed as an irrelevant social club with no meaning for the twentieth century. Every day I meet young people whose disappointment with the church has turned into outright disgust.

40 Perhaps I have once again been too optimistic. Is organized religion too inextricably bound to the status quo to save our nation and the world? Perhaps I must turn my faith to the inner spiritual church, the church within the church, as the true *ekklesia** and the hope of the world. But again I am thankful to God

that some noble souls from the ranks of organized religion have broken loose from the paralyzing chains of conformity and joined us as active partners in the struggle for freedom. They have left their secure congregations and walked the streets of Albany, Georgia, with us. They have gone down the highways of the South on torturous rides for freedom. Yes, they have gone to jail with us. Some have been dismissed from their churches, have lost the support of their bishops and fellow ministers. But they have acted in the faith that right defeated is stronger than evil triumphant. Their witness has been the spiritual salt that has preserved the true meaning of the gospel in these troubled times. They have carved a tunnel of hope through the dark mountain of disappointment.

I hope the church as a whole will meet the challenge of this decisive hour. But even if the church does not come to the aid of justice, I have no despair about the future. I have no fear about the outcome of our struggle in Birmingham, even if our motives are at present misunderstood. We will reach the goal of freedom in Birmingham and all over the nation, because the goal of America is freedom. Abused and scorned though we may be, our destiny is tied up with America's destiny. Before the pilgrims landed at Plymouth, we were here. Before the pen of Jefferson etched the majestic words of the Declaration of Independence across the pages of history, we were here. For more than two centuries our forebears labored in this country without wages; they made cotton king; they built the homes of their masters while suffering gross injustice and shameful humiliation — and yet out of a bottomless vitality they continued to thrive and develop. If the inexpressible cruelties of slavery could not stop us, the

Ekklesia is a Greek word meaning assembly, congregation, or church.

opposition we now face will surely fail. We will win our freedom because the sacred heritage of our nation and the eternal will of God are embodied in our echoing demands.

Before closing I feel impelled to mention one other point in your statement that has troubled me profoundly. You warmly commended the Birmingham police force for keeping "order" and "preventing violence." I doubt that you would have so warmly commended the police force if you had seen its dogs sinking their teeth into unarmed, nonviolent Negroes. I doubt that you would so quickly commend the policemen if you were to observe their ugly and inhumane treatment of Negroes here in the city jail; if you were to watch them push and curse old Negro women and young Negro girls; if you were to see them slap and kick old Negro men and young boys; if you were to observe them, as they did on two occasions, refuse to give us food because we wanted to sing our grace together. I cannot join you in your praise of the Birmingham police department.

It is true that the police have exercised a degree of discipline in handling the demonstrators. In this sense they have conducted themselves rather "nonviolently" in public. But for what purpose? To preserve the evil system of segregation. Over the past few years I have consistently preached that nonviolence demands that the means we use must be as pure as the ends we seek. I have tried to make clear that it is wrong to use immoral means to attain moral ends. But now I must affirm that it is just as wrong, or perhaps even more so, to use moral means to preserve immoral ends. Perhaps Mr. Connor and his policemen have been rather nonviolent in public, as was Chief Pritchett in Albany, Georgia, but they have used the moral means of nonviolence to maintain the immoral end of racial injustice. As T. S. Eliot has said, "The last temptation is the greatest treason: To do the right deed for the wrong reason."

I wish you had commended the Negro sit-inners and demonstrators of Birmingham for their sublime courage, their willingness to suffer, and their amazing discipline in the midst of great provocation. One day the South will recognize its real heroes. They will be the James Merediths,[†] with the noble sense of purpose that enables them to face jeering and hostile mobs, and with the agonizing loneliness that characterizes the life of the pioneer. They will be old, oppressed, battered Negro women, symbolized in a seventy-two-year-old woman in Montgomery, Alabama, who rose up with a sense of dignity and with her people decided not to ride segregated buses, and who responded with ungrammatical profundity to one who inquired about her weariness: "My feets is tired, but my soul is at rest." They will be the young high school and college students, the young ministers of the gospel and a host of their elders, courageously and nonviolently sitting in at lunch counters and willingly going to jail for conscience's sake. One day the South will know that when these disinherited children of God sat down at lunch counters, they were in reality standing up for what is best in the American dream and for the most sacred values in our Judeo-Christian heritage, thereby bringing our nation back to those great wells of democracy which were dug deep by the founding fathers in their formulation of the Constitution and the Declaration of Independence.

45 Never before have I written so long a letter. I'm afraid it is much too long to take your precious time. I can assure you that it would have been much shorter if I

[†]In the fall of 1962 James Meredith became the first black student to enroll at the University of Mississippi. His act, which sparked riots on the university's campus that resulted in two deaths, is widely considered an important event in the Civil Rights Movement.

had been writing from a comfortable desk, but what else can one do when he is alone in a narrow jail cell, other than write long letters, think long thoughts, and pray long prayers?

If I have said anything in this letter that overstates the truth and indicates an unreasonable impatience, I beg you to forgive me. If I have said anything that understates the truth and indicates my having a patience that allows me to settle for anything less than brotherhood, I beg God to forgive me.

I hope this letter finds you strong in the faith. I also hope that circumstances will soon make it possible for me to meet each of you, not as an integrationist or a civil-rights leader but as a fellow clergyman and a Christian brother. Let us all hope that the dark clouds of racial prejudice will soon pass away and the deep fog of misunderstanding will be lifted from our fear-drenched communities, and in some not too distant tomorrow the radiant stars of love and brotherhood will shine over our great nation with all their scintillating beauty.

Yours for the cause of Peace
and Brotherhood,
Martin Luther King, Jr.

Questions for Discussion

1. What reason does King give for writing this letter? What justification does he provide for its length? In what ways might these explanations strengthen his argument? **2.** One of the many charges brought against King at the time of his arrest was that he was an "outsider" who had no business in Birmingham. How does he justify his presence in Birmingham? How convincing do you think his justification is? **3.** What does King mean by nonviolent "direct action"? Why did he believe that such action was necessary in Birmingham? How does he build his case for the nonviolent campaign in Birmingham? Do you think he does so convincingly? Why or why not? **4.** Examine the images that King invokes in paragraph 14. What does he accomplish with these images? How do they contribute to his overall argument? Do you think he is intentionally making an emotional appeal there? **5.** How does King distinguish between a just and an unjust law? Why is this distinction important for his main argument? What evidence does King provide to support his contention that unjust laws must be broken? Do you think King's original audience of White ministers would have found his argument on this issue convincing? Explain. **6.** What specific features of King's letter reveal that it was written originally for an audience of White Christian ministers? What strategies does King employ that might be effective for such an audience? Do you think King intended his letter *only* for that audience? Explain. **7.** At one point in his essay King explains that one purpose of the campaign in Birmingham was "to create a situation so crisis-packed that it will inevitably open the door to negotiation." Do you think King's letter itself is intended to lead to negotiation? Explain, citing specific passages in his letter to support your answer.

8. King had much experience as a preacher when he wrote this famous letter. Is there anything about its style that reminds you of oratory? How effective would this letter be if delivered as a speech?

② MICHAEL KELLY, "Liberties Are a Real Casualty of War"

Americans have long debated the extent to which individual liberties can be compromised when issues of national security or public safety are at stake. After September 11, 2001, those debates were renewed as the U.S. government began to vigorously pursue terrorists and take measures that were intended to prevent new attacks like those that occurred on September 11th. In times of war or crisis Americans are often willing to give up some of the freedoms guaranteed by the Constitution. But some critics caution that allowing government to supercede individual rights is a dangerous path that can even lead to the elimination of Constitutional protections that most Americans take for granted. Indeed, some critics argue that it is precisely in times of crisis that Americans must guard their constitutional rights most jealously, for it is the guarantee of those rights that makes America what it is. In the following essay syndicated columnist Michael Kelly discusses such concerns as they emerged after September 11th. He refers to the case of Abdullah al Muhajir (formerly José Padilla), an American citizen who was held as a terrorist without formal charges, without a lawyer, and without a trial, on the grounds that he was plotting a terrorist attack — a case that, according to critics, illustrated the dangers of too much government power over individual rights. Kelly understands such criticisms. But his priorities are clear: National security sometimes means sacrificing individual liberties. That's fine with him. The question his argument raises for us is whether such a sacrifice is warranted or whether it represents a government overstepping the constitutional limits of its power. Kelly's essay was published in June 2002.

Liberties Are a Real Casualty of War
MICHAEL KELLY

The FBI is now telling the American people, "You no longer have to do anything unlawful to get that knock on the door. You can be doing a perfectly legal activity like worshiping or talking in a chat room and they can spy on you anyway."

— Laura Murphy, of the American Civil Liberties Union, as quoted in *The Washington Post*, May 30, 2002.

1 Murphy was referring specifically to new rules promulgated by the FBI that will give federal investigators far greater latitude than in the past to monitor — oh, all right, spy upon — private conversations in such venues as libraries, Internet sites and religious institutions. But her complaint may be taken beyond

*According to its Web site, "The ACLU's mission is to fight civil liberties violations wherever and whenever they occur. Most of our clients are ordinary people who have experienced an injustice and have decided to fight back. The ACLU is also active in our national and state capitals, fighting to ensure that the Bill of Rights will always be more than a 'parchment barrier' against government oppression and the tyranny of the majority" (See www.aclu.org/about/aboutmain.cfm).

its specifics as a fair example of a rising chorus of worry and woe concerning the threat to civil liberties posed by the increasingly hard-nosed security measures being adopted by a nation at war. We have not heard the last of Murphy on this subject. There is not much in life that is certain, but one thing we can be sure of is that the creation of a $37 billion, 22-agency, super-colossal Department of Homeland Security will not usher in a new era of civil liberties sensitivity, and that the ACLU* will find this objectionable.

As traditional as the cries from the once-again-wounded hearts of once-again-outraged liberals is the governmental response in such circumstances: It isn't so. No liberties are at risk, or not much anyway. All safeguards are being taken. This administration stands second to none in its concern for the sacred rights of all Americans, etc.

The whole thing is ritual. When Attorney Gen. John Ashcroft announced new regulations requiring the fingerprinting and photographing of foreign visitors from all nations deemed to harbor anti-

American terrorism, Sen. Ted Kennedy was, of course, "deeply disappointed" in a plan that would "further stigmatize innocent Arab and Muslim visitors." White House press secretary Ari Fleischer was of course quick to assure that President Bush was acting "fully in accordance with protecting civil rights and civil liberties."

Would it be too much to ask that we cut this out? The United States is at war — its first utterly unavoidable war since World War II and its first war since the Civil War in which the enemy has been able to significantly bring the conflict onto American soil. This war must be successfully prosecuted and success in war pretty much always requires the violation of civil liberties.

5 As a generally liberties-minded friend notes, war in itself constitutes the grossest imaginable violation of liberties. In war, the state may choose to say to its citizens: We are exercising our collective right to deprive you of the most fundamental of your individual rights — your liberty and quite possibly life (don't even mention your pursuit of happiness). We are taking you away, putting you in a uniform, subjecting you to a wholly dictatorial order — and, we are sending you off to very likely die. If you run away, we will ourselves shoot you. The proper response to complaints such as those voiced by Murphy and Kennedy is: Yes, it is true, this action will indeed hurt or at least insult some innocent people, and we are sorry about that. And this action does represent an infringement of the rights and liberties enjoyed not just by Americans but by visitors to America, and we are sorry about that, too. But we must do everything we can to curtail the ability of the enemy to attack us. This is necessary.

Right now, there sits in a jail cell an American citizen named Abdullah al Muhajir, formerly José

ABDULLAH AL MUHAJIR (JOSÉ PADILLA)

Abdullah al Muhajir was taken into custody by the United States on May 8, 2002. U.S. officials claimed that he had connections with Al Qaeda, the terrorist organization that carried out the attacks on the United States on September 11, 2001; they also claimed that he was planning to detonate a "dirty bomb" that would release radiation in the United States. Though an American citizen, al Muhajir was declared an "enemy combatant" by the U.S. government, a status that enabled the government to hold him indefinitely without charge and without access to the legal protections and due process to which American citizens are entitled. His detention sparked controversy. Critics charged that al Muhajir was being held illegally; some argued that the case suggested that the rights of all Americans were being put at risk. In September 2002 the American Civil Liberties Union filed a legal challenge to the U.S. government's detention of al Muhajir, arguing that the government did not have the right to detain an American citizen without formally charging him with a crime.

Padilla. He was arrested at O'Hare International Airport in Chicago on a sealed warrant after arriving on a flight from Zurich on May 8. He is accused, based on what is believed to be credible intelligence, of plotting to explode a radioactive bomb in the United States. He was seized as a material witness and has not been charged with a crime, apparently because the U.S. government does not think it possesses evidence sufficient to charge him. Instead, he is being held as "an enemy combatant," which means that the U.S. military can keep him locked up for as long as it wants, with no jury trial. No one outside the government really knows what the evidence is against al Muhajir. The government didn't even reveal his arrest until a scheduled court hearing forced the revelation.

Now, that is what I call a violation of civil liberties. I am sorry about it, and I will be even sorrier in the unlikely event that al Muhajir is innocent and should not have been locked away. But I wouldn't have it any other way.

Questions for Discussion

1. Note how Kelly refers to liberals in this essay. What do these references reveal about Kelly's own politics? How might your own political views influence your reaction to his argument? **2.** Describe Kelly's style and tone in this essay. Do you think they are appropriate for his argument? Explain. In what ways do you think his style and tone make his argument more or less effective? **3.** Kelly asserts that "success in war pretty much always requires the violation of civil liberties." What evidence does he offer for that assertion? Do you agree with him? Why or why not? **4.** Kelly ends his essay by discussing the case of Abdullah al Muhajir, also known as José Padilla (see the sidebar on page 522), and he raises the possibility that al Muhajir might be innocent and therefore jailed unjustly. How does Kelly's raising this possibility contribute to his argument? Do you think this is an effective strategy on his part? Explain. **5.** We might describe Kelly's argument as one based on deductive reasoning (see pages 26–31). What fundamental principle does he based his argument on? Do you think he builds an effective argument on that principle?

③ **HEATHER GREEN, "Databases and Security vs. Privacy"**

Concerns about threats to their country's — and their personal — security after September 11, 2001, led many Americans to reexamine an idea that has been debated in the United States for many years: the establishment of a national identification card system. Such a system would, in effect, require all Americans to carry an authorized identification card to be used for important but routine transactions, such as withdrawing money from a bank account; paying a bill; visiting a doctor; boarding an airplane or train; entering a government building; and purchasing a variety of items, including medications, alcohol, ammunition, knives, or fertilizer. To an extent, some kind of official identification is already required for many of these activities. For example, when you withdraw money from your bank account, you usually must present a photo ID such as a driver's license. A national ID card system, however, would centralize this process and place it in the hands of the federal government. That worries many critics, including business reporter Heather Green, who sees in such ID cards the potential for the abuse of the privacy of individual Americans. As Green points out in the following essay, which was first published in *Business Week* in 2002, the debate over national ID cards is really a broader debate about the extent to which Americans are willing to sacrifice some of their rights to privacy for greater security in a dangerous world. In this respect, the controversy about ID cards is also part of a debate about how much power the government should have over its citizens.

Databases and Security vs. Privacy
HEATHER GREEN

1 The debate about whether or not the U.S. should or would adopt a national identification-card system has emerged with a jolting intensity. Jolting because even through world wars and a cold war, in which the U.S. feared an enemy within the country as much as the armies outside, Americans resisted the creation of a national ID that they would carry to prove their citizenship. Now, however, public surveys, congressional speeches, and remarks by high-profile CEOs are bringing the issue to the forefront, causing everyone to consider whether America is ready to adopt a card ID system — like those widely used in other countries — at the expense of our privacy.

The problem is, the debate over trading security provided by card IDs for a lower standard of privacy focuses on the wrong issue. The federal government and law enforcement don't need national ID cards. Indeed, the Bush Administration stated publicly last month that it had no intention of pushing for cards. Instead, law-enforcement and intelligence agencies can achieve many of the same goals of an ID card by increasing the collection and sharing of data among federal and state agencies, banks, transportation authorities, and credit-card companies.

People concerned about balancing privacy and security need to focus on this point and not get caught up in the red herring* debate around the ID cards themselves.

Robust Resource: After all, the U.S. already is a database nation. In the corporate world, the push to gather, store, and trade information about individuals' daily lives, habits and tastes, families, purchases, health, and financial standing has steadily increased as database software and hardware, data-mining technology, and computer networks have become cheaper to run and connect.

5 The FBI, Central Intelligence Agency, Federal Aviation Administration, Immigration & Naturalization Service, port authorities, and state motor vehicle departments could possibly take a page from Corporate America. By creating data-gathering systems in the background that pull together information about people — including their travel plans, frequent-flier info, license certification, border crossings, and financial records — law-enforcement and intelligence agencies can run a robust national ID system without the card itself.

Two questions: Would government in the U.S. really be able to implement a system of databases, and why have other countries avoided this path? First, commercial databases are a particularly American heritage. We're concerned about privacy, but not urgently. Most believe that if we personally think it's important, we can set limits on how our information

is used: We can call a number provided by the Direct Marketing Assn., say, to get ourselves off catalog lists. And we accept that some benefits and efficiency come from providing data to companies, including health insurers, credit-card issuers, and airlines. So a huge system of commercial databases has been created.

Highly Protected: Second, Europe has a different, more tragic historical perspective. The Nazis used personal information culled from commercial and government files, including telephone and bank records, to track down Jews, communists, resistance fighters, and the mentally ill. As a direct result of that experience, privacy is very highly protected in countries such as Germany and France.

That doesn't mean these countries aren't interested in protecting security. It simply means that instead of amassing huge amounts of information in databases, these countries favor national ID cards. According to privacy group Privacy International, most of the Western European countries that have strict controls protecting the privacy of personal information — including Germany, France, Belgium, Greece, Luxembourg, Portugal, and Spain — have compulsory national ID systems. (See "ID Cards in Europe" on page 526.)

So, Americans need to get more sophisticated and realize that, in the interest of security, law-enforcement and intelligence agencies are likely to start beefing up their databases on citizens. We need to be on guard and informed about this eventuality. Despite how difficult it might be to make these

*A *red herring* is something that distracts attention from the real issue at hand. The term comes from an old practice of dragging a smoked, or "red," herring across a trail to confuse hunting dogs.

COMPLICATION

Established in 1917, the Direct Marketing Association (DMA) claims to be the oldest and largest trade association for direct marketing. It provides a service by which consumers can ask to have their names removed from the lists used by DMA member businesses to market directly to consumers through telephone calls and mailings. In 1995 DMA was the focus of a lawsuit challenging its practice of distributing names of consumers among its member businesses. Documents filed in that case indicated that as of 1995, DMA had more than 3.2 million names of consumers in its databases. The suit led to several bills in Congress that were intended to protect consumers from direct marketing practices that they believe violate their rights to privacy by sharing information about them without permission.

ID CARDS IN EUROPE

As of 2002, citizens in eleven of the fifteen countries in the European Union were required to carry ID cards issued by their national governments. In some countries these cards are used in addition to other forms of identification, such as drivers' licenses; in other countries national ID cards can be used in place of these other forms of identification. Despite a long tradition of such cards (dating back to 1919), Europeans continue to debate whether these cards unnecessarily violate individual privacy or are essential for security. In 2002 citizens of Great Britain were debating a proposal to establish a national ID card system there. During that same year some polls indicated that 70 percent of Americans favored such ID cards.

databases work effectively, you have to believe that security officials view networked databases as key to their war on terrorism.

10 *Overstepped Boundaries:* Facing this likelihood, citizens need to know and make clear what the rules are under which people land in these databases and are flagged as suspects, who gets to look at the information, and what protections can be established so that information collected for one purpose isn't used for another without some kind of oversight. America needs clear definitions about what terrorism is, so that someone who is protesting against U.S. policies isn't labeled a terrorist out of hand. This is where the true privacy vs. security battlefield will be in the future.

After September 11, it's only natural that the nation would search for ways to increase its security. But law enforcement has overstepped the boundaries of acceptable surveillance of Americans in the past. Widespread wiretapping of civil-rights leaders, including Martin Luther King, as well as Vietnam war dissidents including Jane Fonda and John Lennon during the 1960s and early 1970s led to stricter controls over the kind of information intelligence agencies could gather and the type of broad investigations they could conduct.

Just because we depend on the government to protect us doesn't mean that it will always respect our individual rights. That's the contest that has always been waged in a democracy: the rights of individuals against the safety of the community. Individuals have a duty to be aware of the steps a security-focused government will contemplate and to fight for the protection of rights that they believe are the foundation of a democracy. Privacy is a civil liberty worthy of protection.

Questions for Discussion

1. Why does Green believe that the debate about national ID cards focuses on the wrong issue? On what point, according to Green, should Americans focus instead? **2.** Green calls the United States a "database nation." What does she mean by that phrase? What evidence does she offer to support that statement? Do you agree with her? Why or why not? **3.** What is the main difference between European countries where ID cards are in use and the United States when it comes to information privacy, in Green's view? Why is this difference important to her main argument? **4.** What is Green's primary concern regarding the use of a national ID card in the United States? What evidence does she present that such a concern is justified? Do you find this evidence persuasive? Why or why not? **5.** How does the fact that Heather Green is a business reporter — and that her essay was published in a business journal — affect your reaction to her argument? Do you think her identity as a business reporter enhances her credibility in making this argument? Explain.

④ ALAN M. DERSHOWITZ, "Why Fear National ID Cards?"

The right to individual liberty is guaranteed to U.S. citizens by the Constitution. But that right is more than a legal one; it also reflects a belief in individual freedom that runs deep in American culture. Perhaps that is one reason that the debate about national ID cards has been so intense in the United States. Any proposal that seems to compromise individual rights tends to make Americans suspicious. But balancing the rights of individuals with the well-being of all Americans is a challenge, in part because of the great diversity of the United States and in part because of the enormous difficulties of protecting citizens from harm. If, like Alan M. Dershowitz, you prefer "a system that takes a little bit of freedom from all to one that takes a great deal of freedom and dignity from the few," then perhaps you will agree with him that a national ID card is a worthwhile tradeoff. On the other hand, you might share the concerns of many Americans about the danger of giving up any of your freedoms to your government. As you read the following essay by this well-known lawyer and activist, consider how your own views about individual liberties influence your reaction to his argument. Alan M. Dershowitz is also a columnist and the author of many books on legal issues, including *Why Terrorism Works* (2002).

Why Fear National ID Cards?
ALAN M. DERSHOWITZ

CONTEXT

This essay was originally published in October 2001 on the editorial page of the *New York Times*, which has one of the largest national circulations of any publication in the United States. What audience do you think Dershowitz primarily intended to address with this essay? Do you think he addressed this audience effectively?

1 At many bridges and tunnels across the country, drivers avoid long delays at the toll booths with an unobtrusive device that fits on a car's dashboard. Instead of fumbling for change, they drive right through; the device sends a radio signal that records their passage. They are billed later. It's a tradeoff between privacy and convenience: the tolltakers know more about you — when you entered and left Manhattan, for instance — but you save time and money.

An optional national identity card could be used in a similar way, offering a similar kind of tradeoff: a little less anonymity for a lot more security. Anyone who had the card could be allowed to pass through airports or buildings more expeditiously, and anyone who opted out could be examined much more closely.

As a civil libertarian,* I am instinctively skeptical of such tradeoffs. But I support a national identity card with a chip that can match the holder's fingerprint. It could be an effective tool for preventing terrorism, reducing the need for other law-enforcement mechanisms — especially racial and ethnic profiling — that pose even greater dangers to civil liberties.

I can hear the objections: What about the specter of Big Brother?† What about fears of identity cards leading to more intrusive measures? (The National Rifle Association, for example, worries that a government that registered people might also decide to register guns. See "Complication" on page 530.) What about fears that such cards would lead to increased deportation of illegal immigrants?

5 First, we already require photo ID's for many activities, including flying, driving, drinking and check-cashing. And fingerprints differ from photographs only in that they are harder to fake. The vast majority of Americans routinely carry photo ID's in their wallets and pocketbooks. These ID's are issued by state motor vehicle bureaus and other public and private entities. A national card would be uniform and difficult to forge or alter. It would reduce the likelihood that someone could, intentionally or not, get lost in the cracks of multiple bureaucracies.

The fear of an intrusive government can be addressed by setting criteria for any official who demands to see the card. Even without a national card, people are always being asked to show identification. The existence of a national card need not change the rules about when ID can properly be demanded. It is true that the card would facilitate the deportation of illegal immigrants. But President Bush has proposed giving legal status to many of the illegal immigrants now in this country. And legal immigrants would actually benefit from a national ID card that could demonstrate their status to government officials.

Finally, there is the question of the right to anonymity. I don't believe we can afford to recognize such a right in this age of terrorism. No such right is hinted at in the Constitution. And though the Supreme Court has identified a right to privacy, privacy and anonymity are not the same. American taxpayers, voters and drivers long ago gave up any right of anonymity without loss of our right to engage in lawful conduct within zones of privacy. Rights are a function of experience, and our recent experiences teach that it is far too easy to be anonymous — even to create a false identity — in this large and decentralized country. A national ID card would not prevent all threats of terrorism, but it would make it more difficult for potential terrorists to hide in open view, as many of the Sept. 11 hijackers apparently managed to do.

A national ID card could actually enhance civil liberties by reducing the need for racial and ethnic stereotyping. There would be no excuse for hassling someone merely because he belongs to a particular racial or ethnic group if he presented a card that matched his print and that permitted

*A civil libertarian generally supports individual rights as opposed to state control. In the United States, civil libertarians are usually defenders of the specific rights guaranteed by the U.S. Constitution, including the right to free speech and protection against unreasonable search and seizure. The American Civil Liberties Union, the best known such organization, describes its mission as "fighting to ensure that the Bill of Rights will always be more than a 'parchment barrier' against government oppression and the tyranny of the majority." (See the sidebar on Libertarianism on page 464).

†"Big Brother" refers to the totalitarian government in George Orwell's novel *1984*. The term is generally used to describe an omnipotent and oppressive government or institution.

his name to be checked instantly against the kind of computerized criminal-history retrieval systems that are already in use. (If there is too much personal information in the system, or if the information is being used improperly, that is a separate issue. The only information the card need contain is name, address,

photo and print.) From a civil liberties perspective, I prefer a system that takes a little bit of freedom from all to one that takes a great deal of freedom and dignity from the few — especially since those few are usually from a racially or ethnically disfavored group. A national ID card would be much more effective in preventing terrorism than profiling millions of men simply because of their appearance.

NEGOTIATING DIFFERENCES

In his famous "Letter from a Birmingham Jail," Martin Luther King, Jr., argues on moral grounds that citizens are justified and even obligated to resist their government if that government imposes unjust laws on them. Many people who resisted the military draft during the Vietnam War made the same argument, asserting that their government was forcing them to fight in an unjust war, so they were justified in defying the laws that required them to submit to the military draft. In a sense, the arguments about U.S. government actions in response to the terrorist attacks on September 11, 2001, focus on the same basic question of the moral responsibility of citizens to disobey their government's laws if they determine that those laws are immoral or unjust. For most Americans these arguments about government power and moral responsibility can seem abstract. But they can become real when the government takes action that directly affects the lives of citizens, as the military draft did during the Vietnam War. Americans who have never faced such a situation might wonder, "What would *I* do?"

In 2003 the possibility that some Americans would have to answer that question arose in the form of a war with Iraq. If the United States were to find itself in a protracted war — with Iraq or any other nation — young men and women might eventually be subject to the military draft. They would, in effect, be asked to

Questions for Discussion

1. Notice the images Dershowitz describes in his opening paragraph. How do these images help him to establish his position in the debate about national ID cards? Do you think the use of these images is a good strategy for introducing his argument? Explain. **2.** Dershowitz describes himself as a "civil libertarian." Why do you think he does so? How might describing himself in this way affect his readers' response to his argument? **3.** In his essay Dershowitz addresses several possible objections to his position on ID cards What are those objections? Do you think Dershowitz answers them effectively? Explain. Evaluate the extent to which Dershowitz strengthens or weakens his argument by including these possible objections. **4.** Dershowitz makes a distinction between the right to privacy and the right to anonymity. Why is this distinction important to his argument? **5.** How does Dershowitz support his point that national ID cards could enhance civil liberties? Do you agree with him on this point? Why or why not? What counterarguments might you offer in response to this point?

sacrifice their own safety and liberty for the sake of their government and other citizens.

What would you do in such a case? In an essay in which you draw on the readings in this chapter (and any other appropriate sources), put forth your position on the question of the government's authority to ask you to sacrifice your life for your country. Under what circumstances do you think the government is justified in compelling young men and women to serve in the military and possibly go to war? When is it acceptable for a government to ask you to sacrifice your health and maybe your life? When is it not acceptable? To what extent are you justified in blatantly disobeying the laws that would require you to serve in the military? On what moral or legal or philosophical grounds would you do so? And do Americans have any special obligations to serve their country because of its history? In other words, how does your idea of America figure into your answer to these questions?

These are some of the question you should try to address in your essay. In effect, you are writing a position paper on the military draft in which you make an argument about the extent and the limits of your government's power over you and other citizens.

Alternatively, you may make your argument about the use of national ID cards or other security measures that were proposed after 9/11.

MidAmerica Commodity Exch

12

FREE ENTERPRISE

FREE EN

Cluster 1
WHAT IS A FREE MARKET?

① Barbara Wilder, "Greed Despoils Capitalism"

② Don Mathews, "The True Spirit of Enterprise"

③ Joseph Heath and Andrew Potter, "The Rebel Sell: If We All Hate Consumerism, How Come We Can't Stop Shopping?"

④ David Korten, "Economies of Meaning"

CON-TEXT
The Wealth of Nations

Cluster 2
WHAT DOES IT MEAN TO BE A CONSUMER?

① Ian Frazier, "All-Consuming Patriotism: American Flag: $19.95. New Yacht: $75,000. True Patriotism: Priceless."

② James Deacon, "The Joys of Excess"

③ Norman Solomon, "Mixed Messages Call for Healthy Skepticism"

④ Peter Singer, "The Singer Solution to World Poverty"

CON-TEXT
Conspicuous Consumption

Cluster 3
HOW SHOULD WORKERS BE TREATED?

① Nicholas Kristof, "Let Them Sweat"

② Linda Hales, "Rugmaking, Interwoven with Social Justice"

③ Jim Hightower, "Going Down the Road"

④ Cindy Richards, "Just Another Hollow Day"

CON-TEXT
Industrial Workers of the World

ERPRISE

WHAT IS A

FREE MARKET?

I n 1776 Scottish philosopher Adam Smith published a treatise entitled *An Inquiry Into the Nature and Causes of the Wealth of Nations.* It was a time when much of the attention of Western Europe was focused on the revolution in the British colonies in North America. Smith could not have known the outcome of that revolution as he was completing his groundbreaking book. Nor could he have known that the nation that was to emerge from that revolution would become a symbol for the kind of free market economic system he described in the book. ■ Smith's *The Wealth of Nations* is widely considered "capitalism's founding document," as writer Barbara Wilder puts it (her essay appears on page 536). It describes the principles by which Smith believed a free market system should function. In particular, Smith is credited with developing the idea of the "invisible hand," a term that refers to the natural workings of supply and demand of the marketplace (see *Con-Text* on page 535). According to Smith, this "invisible hand" allows markets to set prices that best serve both buyers and sellers — without the intervention of governments or institutions. This fundamental idea has become the basis for most mainstream economic theory in the West. Even today, many influential economists and government policy makers look to Smith's principles to guide their decisions about such important matters as tax policies, wages, and tariffs. So deeply rooted are Smith's ideas that they have almost become a belief system that transcends the purely economic matters of supply and demand. ■ It is understandable that Smith's free market ideas have taken such deep root in American culture, for economics seem so central to the way we live. Our ideas about "the good life" are intimately connected to our experiences as consumers and workers and to our beliefs about the role of money in our lives. The free market seems to offer the possibility of a better life for those who are willing to work hard and take advantage of economic opportunities. Indeed, Smith himself believed that a sound economic system was a means to a better life for all citizens. In comparing a society based on a free market to the "savage" societies of Native Americans in the New World, Smith wrote that "the produce of the whole labour of the society is so great, that all are often abundantly supplied, and a workman, even of the lowest and poorest order, if he is frugal and industrious, may enjoy a greater share of the necessaries and conveniencies of life than it is possible for any savage to acquire." But as the essays in this section show, the connection between a free market and the good life is not so simple. From the time his book was first published, Smith's ideas have been vigorously debated, even as they became the foundation for the economic systems of many nations, including the United States. Many critics have argued that Smith's principles seem sound in theory but rarely work in practice. In particular, critics have challenged his view that a free market system will ultimately benefit all citizens, whether they are workers, merchants, or the wealthy. In the 19th century German philosopher Karl Marx mounted what was to become the greatest challenge to the free market system. Marx argued that such a system inevitably results in inequalities among the classes and therefore is inherently unfair; according to Marx, there was no possibility of a "free" market, only one that benefited the ruling classes. He believed that this inherent unfairness would eventually lead to capitalism's demise, and in its place he proposed a socialist — or communist — system, in which major industries and services would be owned by the people and the state rather than by individual capitalists. ■ Of course, whatever the merits of Marx's arguments about the unfairness of capitalism, he was wrong about its demise. By the turn of the new millennium in 2000 the major socialist states in the world either had disappeared, like the Soviet Union, or, like the People's Republic of China, had begun to restructure their economies on the basis of free market ideas. Capitalism and the principles of the free market now seem to dominate worldwide thinking about how economies should be run. ■ The global spread of free market ideas has not diminished the intensity of debates about how markets should be managed, however. As the essays in this chapter reveal, free markets do not exist apart from our social, cultural, and political lives, and these aspects of our lives complicate not only how markets work but also how we manage them. As a result, arguments about the moral and ethical aspects of free markets have become ever more complex, as economies grow and evolve and as new technologies create new possibilities and problems. In addition, many people continue to wonder whether free markets, no matter how efficiently they are run, really do make our lives better, as Adam Smith believed. The essays in this chapter will help you to understand the complexity of these debates. They might also encourage you to reexamine your own ideas about free markets and their role in the life you wish to have.

CON-TEXT: The Wealth of Nations

1 There is in every society or neighbourhood an ordinary or average rate both of wages and profit in every different employment of labour and stock. This rate is naturally regulated, as I shall show hereafter, partly by the general circumstances of the society, their riches or poverty, their advancing, stationary, or declining condition; and partly by the particular nature of each employment.

There is likewise in every society or neighbourhood an ordinary or average rate of rent, which is regulated too, as I shall show hereafter, partly by the general circumstances of the society or neighbourhood in which the land is situated, and partly by the natural or improved fertility of the land.

These ordinary or average rates may be called the natural rates of wages, profit, and rent, at the time and place in which they commonly prevail.

When the price of any commodity is neither more nor less than what is sufficient to pay the rent of the land, the wages of the labour, and the profits of the stock employed in raising, preparing, and bringing it to market, according to their natural rates, the commodity is then sold for what may be called its natural price. . . .

The market price of every particular commodity is regulated by the proportion between the quantity which is actually brought to market, and the demand of those who are willing to pay the natural price of the commodity, or the whole value of the rent, labour, and profit, which must be paid in order to bring it thither.

SOURCE: Adam Smith, *An Inquiry into the Nature and Causes of the Wealth of Nations* (1776).

① BARBARA WILDER, "Greed Despoils Capitalism"

In the hit 1980s movie *Wall Street*, Gordon Gecko, an extremely successful and ruthless stock market trader, speaks to a meeting of the stockholders of a company that he has invested in. In effect, Gecko has taken over the company by purchasing a majority of its stock, and he wants to rid the company of most of its managers, who, he claims, have kept it from becoming profitable by honoring old loyalties and playing by old rules. At one point, Gecko famously tells his audience, "Greed is good." That scene caused a stir when the film was first released in 1986, a time when Wall Street traders and investors were making enormous profits while large corporations such as General Motors were closing down factories that had once employed thousands of U.S. workers. It was also a time of scandals involving several well-known stock traders, on whom the character of Gecko seems to have been based. For some critics the film *Wall Street* reflected the reality that a free market system rewards greed. It is an old argument, and it has been heard often in recent years in the wake of several sensational scandals involving large and successful corporations. Barbara Wilder disagrees. In the following essay, which was published in the *Rocky Mountain News* in 2002, she responds to a columnist who believes that capitalism breeds successful businesspeople who have no conscience. Wilder acknowledges that such businesspeople exist, but she argues that capitalism requires not greed but ethical business practices. Otherwise, she believes, we all lose. Wilder is the author of *Money Is Love: Reconnecting to the Sacred Origins of Money* (1998) and *In the Company of Powerful Women: Coming of Age in the Second Half of Life* (2001).

Greed Despoils Capitalism
BARBARA WILDER

Editor's note:
1 On July 13, business editor Rob Reuteman wrote a column titled "Conscience, Capitalism? Coexistence an Anomaly." In part, it read:

"Listening to President Bush's Wall Street speech on Tuesday, I was stunned to hear him say, 'There can be no capitalism without conscience, there is no wealth without character . . .'

"No capitalism without conscience? No wealth without character? In fact, there is — and always has been — plenty of both. From Jay Gould to J.P. Morgan, from Andrew Carnegie to John D. Rockefeller to William Randolph Hearst, you simply cannot write U.S. history without citing the stupendous financial accomplishments of capitalism's ruthless pioneers. Modern-day counterparts abound."

What follows is a rebuttal:

5 I could never be accused of supporting President Bush, but all the same I find merit in his call for conscience and character in capitalism, whether he means it or not.

The idea that conscience, character, and morality are incongruent with capitalism, as Rob Reuteman mentions in his July 13 column, flies in the face of the social contract. In fact, capitalism's origins are deeply rooted in ethics and human dignity. Adam Smith,* the father of western capitalism, wrote, "What improves the circumstances of the greater part can never be regarded as an inconveniency to the whole. No society can surely be flourishing and happy, of which the far greater part of the members are poor and miserable." Smith would turn over in his grave if he could observe the antics of the Enron CEOs and their fellows.

It is no mere coincidence that American democracy and capitalism's founding document, *The Wealth of Nations,* were conceived in the same year. These two philosophies are inextricably interwoven, based as they are on beliefs in the inherent right of the individual to life, liberty and the pursuit of happiness.[†]

Capitalism does not rely on the whims of despots, or even benign governments, for its leadership, but on the genius and talent of the brightest and most visionary citizens. Capitalism is a system of economics guided by the people willing and able to build businesses that create wealth for all. This is done by creating more jobs, which creates more products, which creates more profit, which then is meant to be reinvested to create more jobs, more product, and more profit, ad infinitum. And the system works for everyone — if there is integrity and vision in the people at the top. But when

the people at the top are driven by greed and line their pockets with the profits instead of reinvesting in the production of goods for the benefit of all, the system fails.

And when the system fails it fails for all of us. No human being stands alone. We are all part of the world economy. We all have to take the fall when the guys at the top decide to keep all the marbles. 10 But capitalism, of itself, is not the culprit. Capitalism has the potential to bring the most good to the most people, if it is directed by people of conscience.

What we lost in the '80s and '90s juggernaut of bottom-line profits (see "Context" on page 538) is the understanding that industry is about labor and product and profits and reinvesting those profits in the labor and the production of products. And most importantly, we lost the connection to the human element. We have created a bottom line that does not consider anything but profit for profit's sake, and therefore the bottom line has no substance.

We have created an economy based on fear and greed that is unprecedented, and in so doing we have alienated both our enemies and our friends around the

*The 18th century Scottish philosopher and economist Adam Smith wrote *An Inquiry into the Nature and Causes of the Wealth of Nations* (1776), which many economists consider to be the most important work on free markets ever written. (See *Con-Text* on page 535.)

The famous phrase "life, liberty and the pursuit of happiness" comes from the Declaration of Independence. (See *Con-Text* on page 507.)

CONTEXT

Economists consider the economic expansion of the 1980s and 1990s to be the largest in history. The Center on Budget and Policy Priorities reports that between 1993 and 2000, the Gross Domestic Product, a measure of economic performance, grew 50 percent faster annually than it did from 1973 to 1993. During this same time the stock market soared. The NASDAQ composite index, for example, which includes many high-tech companies, rose from about 800 in 1995 to more than 5000 in the year 2000. (As of mid 2003, the NASDAQ stood at about 1700.)

world. The nation that was created on the most moral foundations of any nation in history has become, or is quickly becoming, the most immoral. And it is all because of greed.

To change this — to turn back to a path toward goodness, prosperity, and peace — we must all make a moral commitment. We must call not only for the punishment of those who have been caught, because there are many who have sinned against the world marketplace who will go unpunished; but we must call for all participants in the market, from corporate leaders to small investors to workers, to realign with a standard of integrity.

We must create a new bottom line. We must move out of an economy based on fear and greed and move into an economy based on integrity and love and caring for our fellow human beings.

Over-the-top market prices may go down as we struggle to give up our fear and greed, but the market will readjust itself as we all begin to invest more of our attention in integrity.

15 Money and the economy are directed by all of the peoples' thoughts and feelings. When love, caring and integrity replace greed, fear, anger and disrespect, the economy will do more than recover, it will transform. But for this to happen we must all begin to believe in a new kind of bottom line.

When we as individuals think in terms of love, caring and integrity, we will expect it of others, and that expectation will demand corporate integrity and the creation of a new bottom line on Wall Street and in the world marketplace. America wasn't founded on greed — it was founded on freedom for all. And that means economic freedom for all.

Questions for Discussion

1. What support does Wilder offer for her assertion that "capitalism's origins are deeply rooted in ethics and human dignity"? How convincing is her support for this assertion? **2.** How would you summarize Wilder's main argument in this essay? Do you think most Americans would agree with her? Explain. **3.** According to Wilder, what are the reasons for the failure of a capitalist system? Do you think she is right? Why or why not? **4.** Wilder proposes that the problems with our capitalist system must be addressed by a "moral commitment." What does she mean by that term? How effective do you think such a step would be in addressing the problems Wilder discusses in this essay?

② DON MATHEWS, "The True Spirit of Enterprise"

The figure of the successful entrepreneur looms large in U.S. history. Indeed, it is hard to imagine the American free market system without such imposing and influential figures as Andrew Carnegie, Henry Ford, or, more recently, Sam Walton and Bill Gates — people whose great success in business helped to shape American society. Henry Ford, for example, developed manufacturing techniques for automobiles that not only became the foundation for an entire industry but also profoundly shaped how Americans live. Similarly, Bill Gates's computer operating system is now a worldwide standard that pervades our work and private lives. Such wildly successful entrepreneurs have sometimes been criticized as ruthless businesspeople whose success results from greed and unethical competitiveness. In the following essay economist Don Mathews dismisses such criticisms, arguing instead that people such as Ford and Carnegie reflect the true spirit of free enterprise. Mathews presents a view of the free market that emphasizes the entrepreneur and the idea of individual initiative. As you read, consider how Mathews's argument also implies a more general view of human nature: To what extent does a free market system depend on a certain idea of human nature? Don Mathews teaches economics at Coastal Georgia Community College.

The True Spirit of Enterprise
DON MATHEWS

CONTEXT

In 2002, as the U.S. stock market continued a downturn that followed a great market expansion in the 1990s, several large U.S. corporations were involved in well-publicized scandals resulting from questionable accounting practices. At some of the corporations involved, such as Enron, a large energy-trading corporation, these accounting practices eventually led to the layoffs of many employees and the loss of employee retirement funds.

1 Does business run on greed?

More than a few commentators are saying so. Reacting to the corporate accounting scandals and the bursting of the Internet stock bubble, some pundits are claiming that recent business events are symptoms of a larger crisis. "Capitalism itself is corrupt," the pundits say. "The spirit of enterprise is nothing more than the spirit of greed."

The charge is not just an overreaction; it's wrong. It needs an antidote. A good, strong, historical antidote, an antidote that reminds at least the pundits what it is that businesses do and where wealth comes from.

Harvard University business historian Richard Tedlow offers such an antidote with his book, *Giants of Enterprise: Seven Business Innovators and the Empires They Built* (see "Giants of Enterprise" on page 540).

5 *Giants,* Tedlow writes in the very first sentence of his book, "is a book about what Americans do best — founding and building new businesses."

That simple sentence reveals what the true spirit of enterprise is all about. It's not about greed. It's about creating. It's about building. It's about discovery. And it's about innovating.

So many critics of capitalism assume

GIANTS OF ENTERPRISE

"Carnegie was ebullient; until the very end of his life he was incurably optimistic; he was by turns genuinely sincere and hypocritical, intensely realistic and grandiose. Slightly manic, he was a man of enthusiasms which could be painlessly transformed into wholly different enthusiasms. He was capable of physical exertion, but he was also a physical coward. He was loyal; he was fickle. He could love; he could betray. There was an unbridgeable gulf between the man he wanted to be and the man the business world rewarded him for being. This is a critical attribute of Carnegie's career, and one which he shares with many another businessperson." Source: Richard Tedlow, *Giants of Enterprise: Seven Business Innovators and the Empires They Built* (2001).

other goods don't automatically appear, nor do the operations that make such goods. There are no historical forces of progress. There is only human action, the action of individuals.

Individuals create wealth. They do so by creating and building enterprises that combine labor, capital, and materials to make things that didn't exist before, things that people value. The consequence of their actions is economic growth and development.

10 That might be lost on the pundits, but it's not lost on Tedlow, and it won't be lost on anyone who reads *Giants of Enterprise*.

Giants describes the careers of seven great American businessmen: Andrew Carnegie, the steel magnate; George Eastman, creator of Eastman Kodak; auto pioneer Henry Ford; Thomas Watson, Sr., IBM's first CEO; Charles Revson, who built

that economic growth and development are inevitable, that economies are somehow impelled to grow by historical forces of progress or some other abstraction.

But growth and development are not inevitable. Food, medicine, houses, and

Andrew Carnegie

Henry Ford

Revlon cosmetics; Wal-Mart's Sam Walton; and Robert Noyce, inventor of the integrated circuit and co-founder of Intel.

These men were quite different from one another. They were from different time periods — Carnegie was born in 1835, Noyce in 1927. They had different backgrounds — Revson's parents were Russian-born Jews, Ford was a Michigan farm boy. And they had different personalities — Eastman was quiet and soft-spoken; Walton, cheerful and gregarious. There was nothing typical about any of them.

But then, there is nothing typical about any of America's business leaders. Such people comprise a heterogeneous group. So don't bother searching for the typical American business executive. "There is no typical American business executive," Tedlow informs us.

Business leaders do have some characteristics in common, however. They are confident and ambitious, and are tireless workers. They are not afraid to take risks, but they are not reckless, either. And they are adept at seizing opportunities that others miss — opportunities to create and to build.

15 Tedlow's seven businessmen were builders and creators of the highest order. They became very wealthy, for which they are disparaged by the critics, who view the economy as a zero-sum world. What the critics neglect is that Tedlow's seven became wealthy by building large pieces of the American economy.

Quite literally, in Carnegie's case.

Railroads were still using cast iron rails in 1875 when Andrew Carnegie began his career in the steel business. Cast iron was brittle and inflexible and cracked all too frequently under great weight. Steel rails were far superior in strength and durability but were prohibitively expensive, even after Henry Bessemer* discovered a better method of producing steel in 1856.

Carnegie made the Bessemer method economical. Fabulously economical. Carnegie was neither a scientist nor a technician. He was a practical businessman who figured out that the Bessemer method could be made economical by producing on a massive scale.

He was also an organization man. To academic economists, economies of scale[†] are datum, but in the real world of business, they must be built and organized — no easy feat. Andrew Carnegie pulled it off in grand fashion.

20 Carnegie opened his famous Edgar Thomson steel mill in 1875. That year, the mill produced 5,840 tons of steel rails. By 1900, it produced 626,900 tons of steel rails. It sold them for $20 a ton. The price in 1856, the year Bessemer made his famous discovery, had been $265 a ton.

Steel was not only used to build the railroads, it was also used to construct large buildings in America's rapidly growing cities. By 1900, steel had become, in Tedlow's words, "the material basis of civilization." It was largely Carnegie's doing.

The other six biographical essays in *Giants* are also remarkable tales of creating and building. And in each case, the creating and building benefited large masses of Americans.

For Eastman, Ford, and Walton, that was the plan from the beginning. Eastman took up photography as a hobby in 1877. Taking pictures back then was an expensive and complicated affair. Eastman paid $50 for his first camera and photographic gear, which included an alarming array of chemicals, and then had to pay $5 for lessons to learn the craft. Still, he became convinced that photography could be made easy and inexpensive, and when it was, people would take to it in droves.

Eastman had difficulty finding investors for such a bold project, but the

*British inventor Henry Bessemer (1813–1989) developed the process by which steel can be inexpensively refined and mass-produced. His process, originally developed to improve artillery shells for the British Army, is the basis for modern steel production.

[†]The term *economies of scale* refers to the principle of reducing production costs by increasing the number of items produced. As the number of products increases, the cost of producing individual products decreases, thereby improving profits.

C O M P L I C A T I O N

Referring to the great figures in U.S. business during the "Gilded Age" of the late 19th and early 20th centuries, such as Carnegie and Rockefeller, Charles Derber writes,

The Gilded Age brought both hope and tragedy. It ushered in the American century, with the United States emerging as the new industrial power that would replace Britain as the guardian of a new world order. Americans — among them millions of immigrants who dreamed of a better future — were never more hopeful about their prospects for prosperity. The booming new industrial economy created by the robber barons — the popular name given to Gilded Age business leaders — allowed many citizens to realize their dreams, and the Gilded Age showed the remarkable potential of American business to harness the resources of the nation.

Yet millions of Gilded Age Americans worked in sweatshops, and the intensity of economic and social exploitation wrought by the robber barons became legendary. The growth of urban slums, the concentration of new monopoly power in the trusts, and the scandalous corruption of politics made many turn-of-the-century Americans feel their nation was losing its democratic promise.

Today's new Gilded Age order stems from an economy fueled by revolutionary advances in market scale and technology. It is dominated by dynamic corporations larger than any in history, and run by men possessed of power, business networks, and personal fortunes far exceeding those of the robber barons. It is defined by a democracy in which popular sovereignty is eroding. And it features a culture in which old-fashioned "virtues" like laissez-faire economies, social Darwinism, and accumulation of wealth are enjoying redoubled popularity. Despite some central differences, the new order and the old reveal parallels at almost every level. Source: Charles Derber, *Corporation Nation*, 1998.

ones he found never had regrets. In 1888, Eastman introduced the first Kodak camera. The price: $25. In 1900, he introduced the Kodak Brownie. Price: $1.

25 What Eastman did for photography, Henry Ford did for the automobile. Ford's stated goal was to improve people's lives by providing inexpensive, quality transportation.

"I will build a car for the great multitude," said Ford, "constructed of the best materials by the best men to be hired after the simplest designs that modern engineering can devise . . . so low in price that no man making a good salary will be unable to own one — and enjoy with his family the blessing of hours of pleasure in God's great open spaces."

This was an audacious statement when Ford made it sometime around 1903. Most everybody in the fledgling automobile industry was convinced that the automobile was and would always be a luxury for the rich man. In 1900, no one even knew whether gasoline, steam, or electricity would emerge as the dominant source of power for the vehicle.

On June 16, 1903, the Ford Motor Company was incorporated. In 1908, Ford rolled out the first Model Ts. The original price of the Model T was $825, and in 1908 the company sold 5,986 units. Eight years later, Ford had driven the price down to $360, and the company sold 575,000 units. This luxury for the rich man had become a staple for the common man.

Sam Walton's market strategy was to cater to people of modest means in more rural, under-served areas. It was a good strategy. Wal-Mart is now the largest corporation in the nation.

30 Tedlow's seven giants of enterprise were not saints, and Tedlow doesn't describe them as such. Each had his quirks and qualms, and some had serious flaws. They were not immune from greed. Nor

were they unmoved by the temptations of power.

But the most valuable lesson of Tedlow's *Giants of Enterprise* is that great businessmen, for all their humanness, are creators and builders and are driven by, above all else, the desire to create and build. And it is the drive to create and build that is the true spirit of enterprise.

Questions for Discussion

1. Who do you think are the "pundits" to whom Mathews refers in the beginning of his essay? What purpose does his references to these pundits serve in Mathews's argument? Do you think his references to pundits is an example of "opposing a straw man" (see page 39 in Chapter 2)? Justify your answer. **2.** According to Mathews, what is the "true spirit of enterprise"? What is Mathews's primary strategy for supporting his claim about the true spirit of enterprise? **3.** On what fundamental belief or principle does Mathews rest his main argument in this essay? Cite specific passages from his essay to support your answer. **4.** Near the end of his essay, Mathews acknowledges that the seven men he discusses in this essay were not "saints" and that "some had serious flaws." In what ways do you think this acknowledgement strengthens Mathews's argument? Do you think this acknowledgement is adequate for anticipating possible objections to his argument? Explain. **5.** As the headnote for this essay indicates (page 539), Mathews is a professor of economics. What indications, if any, can you find in this essay of Mathews's professional expertise? How might the knowledge that Mathews is an economist influence your reaction to his argument?

③ JOSEPH HEATH AND ANDREW POTTER, "The Rebel Sell: If We All Hate Consumerism, How Come We Can't Stop Shopping?"

Americans generally seem to view consumption as a good thing, one of the benefits of a free market system. We can choose to buy one car or piece of clothing instead of another, for example, on the basis of our personal preferences. But Joseph Heath and Andrew Potter believe that there is more to being a consumer than personal choice. They argue that the choices consumers make can have far-reaching consequences; as a result, our choices are much more than a matter of personal preference. For these reasons there has been a backlash against consumerism in recent years, led by advocacy groups that emphasize the damage that a consumer culture can do to society, to the environment, and to our individual lives. But Heath and Potter believe that this backlash misses the point. In their view, consumer culture arises not just from the desire to acquire material goods, as many advocacy groups claim, but also from a deeply rooted desire among Americans to be different, to set themselves apart as individuals. Whether or not Heath and Potter's detailed analysis convinces you, their essay highlights some of the complications of a free market system; it also reveals that our behavior as consumers in a free market system is related to our beliefs about who we are as people. As you read their argument, consider their analysis in light of your own experiences as a consumer. Perhaps they will lead you to think differently about what it means to be a consumer. Andrew Potter is on the editorial board of *This* Magazine, in which the following essay appeared in 2002. Joseph Heath is a professor of philosophy at the University of Montreal and the author of many books and articles, including *Communicative Action and Rational Choice* (2001).

The Rebel Sell: If We All Hate Consumerism, How Come We Can't Stop Shopping?

JOSEPH HEATH AND ANDREW POTTER

Released in 1999, Fight Club was hailed by many critics as an incisive critique of American consumer culture. For some information on American Beauty, see Context on page 413 in Chapter 10.

1 Do you hate consumer culture? Angry about all that packaging? Irritated by all those commercials? Worried about the quality of the "mental environment"? Well, join the club. Anti-consumerism has become one of the most important cultural forces in millennial North American life, across every social class and demographic.

This might seem at odds with the economic facts of the 1990s — a decade that gave us the "extreme shopping" channel, the dot-com bubble, and an absurd orgy of indulgence in ever more luxurious consumer goods. But look at the non-fiction bestseller lists. For years they've been dominated by books that are deeply critical of consumerism: *No*

Logo, Culture Jam, Luxury Fever and *Fast Food Nation*. You can now buy Adbusters at your neighbourhood music or clothing store. Two of the most popular and critically successful films in recent memory were *Fight Club* and *American Beauty*,* which offer almost identical indictments of modern consumer society.

What can we conclude from all this? For one thing, the market obviously does an extremely good job at responding to consumer demand for anti-consumerist products and literature. But isn't that a contradiction? Doesn't it suggest that we are in the grip of some massive, society-wide, bipolar disorder? How can we all denounce consumerism, and yet still find ourselves living in a consumer society?

The answer is simple. What we see in films like *American Beauty* and *Fight Club* is not actually a critique of consumerism; it's merely a restatement of the "critique of mass society" that has been around since the 1950s. The two are not the same. In fact, the critique of mass society has been one of the most powerful forces driving consumerism for more than 40 years.

5 That last sentence is worth reading again. The idea is so foreign, so completely the opposite of what we are used to being told, that many people simply can't get their head around it. It is a position that Thomas Frank, editor of *The Baffler*,[†] has been trying to communicate for years. Strangely, all the authors of anti-consumerism books have read Frank — most even cite him approvingly — and yet not one of them seems to get the point. So here is Frank's claim, simply put: books like *No Logo,* magazines like *Adbusters,* and movies like *American Beauty* do not undermine consumerism; they reinforce it.

This isn't because the authors, directors or editors are hypocrites. It's because they've failed to understand the true nature of consumer society.

One of the most talked-about cinematic set-pieces in recent memory is the scene in *Fight Club* where the nameless narrator (Ed Norton) pans his empty apartment, furnishing it piece by piece with Ikea furniture. The scene shimmers and pulses with prices, model numbers and product names, as if Norton's gaze was drag-and-dropping straight out of a virtual catalogue. It is a great scene, driving the point home: the furniture of his world is mass-produced, branded, sterile. If we are what we buy, then the narrator is an Allen-key-wielding corporate-conformist drone.

In many ways, this scene is just a CGI-driven update of the opening pages of John Updike's *Rabbit, Run*.[‡] After yet another numbing day selling the MagiPeel Kitchen Peeler, Harry Angstrom comes home to his pregnant and half-drank wife whom he no longer loves. Harry takes off in his car, driving aimlessly south. As he tries to sort out his life, the music on the radio, the sports reports, the ads, the billboards, all merge in his consciousness into one monotonous, monolithic brandscape.

It may give us pause to consider that while *Fight Club* was hailed as "edgy" and "subversive" when it appeared in 1999, *Rabbit, Run* enjoyed enormous commercial success when it was first published — in 1960. If social criticism came with a "sell by" date, this one would have been removed from the shelf a long time ago. The fact that it is still around, and still provokes awe and acclaim, makes one wonder if it is really a criticism or, rather, a piece of modern mythology.

10 What *Fight Club* and *Rabbit, Run* present, in a user-friendly fashion, is the critique of mass society, which was developed in the late 1950s in classic works like William Whyte's *The Organization Man* (1956), Vance Packard's *The Status Seekers* (1959) and Paul

[†]**Founded in 1988, *The Baffler* is a magazine that focuses on culture from a leftist perspective. According to its Web site, it sees itself as part of "a long American tradition of dissent, especially the critique of business culture that grew up back in the hopeful days of the teens, twenties, and thirties."**

[‡]**See the margin gloss on John Updike on page 412.**

*In the late 1950s and early 1960s a number of social critics argued that capitalism requires conformity to function effectively. Among the best-known books in which this argument was made were William Whyte's *The Organization Man* (1956), Vance Packard's *The Status Seekers* (1959) and Paul Goodman's *Growing Up Absurd* (1960).

†Progressive British rock band Pink Floyd released several successful records in the 1970s and 1980s that included songs critiquing Western society. One such record was *The Wall*; the title song criticizes formal education as conformist.

‡French philosopher Jean-Jacques Rousseau (1712–1778) became well known in part for his view that humans in their natural, or "savage," state, without the influence of society and culture, are most noble and are superior in character to civilized humanity. His book *The Social Contract* was a major influence on the French Revolution.

Goodman's *Growing Up Absurd* (1960).* The central idea is quite simple. Capitalism requires conformity to function correctly. As a result, the system is based upon a generalized system of repression. Individuals who resist the pressure to conform therefore subvert the system, and aid in its overthrow.

This theory acquired such a powerful grip on the imagination of the left during the 1960s that many people still have difficulty seeing it for what it is — a theory. Here are a few of its central postulates:

1. Capitalism requires conformity in the workers. Capitalism is one big machine; the workers are just parts. These parts need to be as simple, predictable, and interchangeable as possible. One need only look at an assembly line to sec why. Like bees or ants, capitalist workers need to be organized into a limited number of homogeneous castes.

2. Capitalism requires conformity of education. Training these corporate drones begins in the schools, where their independence and creativity is beaten out of them — literally and figuratively. Call this the Pink Floyd† theory of education.

3. Capitalism requires sexual repression. In its drive to stamp out individuality, capitalism denies the full range of human expression, which includes sexual freedom. Because sexuality is erratic and unpredictable, it is a threat to the established order. This is why some people thought the sexual revolution would undermine capitalism.

4. Capitalism requires conformity of consumption. The overriding goal of capitalism is to achieve ever-increasing profits through economies of scale. These are best achieved by having everyone consume the same limited range of standardized goods. Enter advertising, which tries to inculcate false or inauthentic desires. Consumerism is what emerges when we are duped into having desires that we would not normally have.

Both *Fight Club* and *American Beauty* are thoroughly soaked in the critique of mass society. Let's look at *Fight Club*.

Here's the narrator's alter ego, Tyler Durden (Brad Pitt), explaining the third thesis: "We're designed to be hunters and we're in a society of shopping. There's nothing to kill anymore, there's nothing to fight, nothing to overcome, nothing to explore. In that social emasculation this everyman is created." And the fourth: "Advertising has us chasing cars and clothes, working jobs we hate, so we can buy shit we don't need." And here he is giving the narrator a scatological summary of the whole critique: "You're not your job. You're not how much money you have in the bank. You're not the car you drive. You're not the contents of your wallet. You're not your fucking khakis. You're the all-singing, all-dancing crap of the world."

Fight Club is entirely orthodox in its Rousseauian‡ rejection of the modern order. Less orthodox is its proffered solution, which in the middle and final acts moves swiftly from Iron John to the Trenchcoat Mafia.

A more conventional narrative arc, combined with a more didactic presentation of the critique, can be found in *American Beauty*, the Oscar-winning companion piece to *Fight Club*. The two films offer identical takes on the homogenizing and emasculating effects of mass society, though the heroes differ in their strategies of resistance. *Fight Club* suggests

Fight Club

that the only solution is to blow up the whole machine; in *American Beauty,* Lester (Kevin Spacey) decides to subvert it from within.

20 When Lester first starts to rebel against his grey-scale, cookie-cutter life, he begins by mocking his wife's (Annette Bening) Martha Stewart materialism. Here's Lester in a voice-over: "That's my wife, Carolyn. See the way the handle on her pruning shears matches her gardening clogs? That's not an accident."

Later, Carolyn halts Lester's sexual advances in order to prevent him from spilling beer on the couch. They fight. "It's just a couch," Lester says. Carolyn: "This is a $4,000 sofa upholstered in Italian silk. It is not just a couch." Lester: "It's just a couch!" Capitalism offers us consumer goods as a substitute for sexual gratification. Lester strains at the bit.

The relationship between sexual frustration and mass society is a general theme of the movie. Here is Lester giving his family theses one and three over dinner:

Carolyn: Your father and I were just discussing his day at work. Why don't you tell our daughter about it, honey?

Lester: Janie, today I quit my job. And then I told my boss to go fuck himself, and then I blackmailed him for almost $60,000. Pass the asparagus.

Carolyn: Your father seems to think this type of behaviour is something to be proud of.

Lester: And your mother seems to prefer I go through life like a fucking prisoner while she keeps my dick in a mason jar under the sink.

American Beauty

So what does Lester do to reassert his individuality, his masculinity? He takes a new job. He starts working out. He lusts after, then seduces, his daughter's friend. He starts smoking pot in the afternoon. In short, he rejects all of the demands that society makes on a man of his age. But does he stop consuming? Of course not. Consider the scene in which he buys a new car. Carolyn comes home and asks Lester whose car that is in the driveway. Lester: "Mine. 1970 Pontiac Firebird. The car I've always wanted and now I have it. I rule!"

Lester has thrown off the shackles of conformist culture. He's grown a dick, become a man again. All because he bought a car. Carolyn's couch may be "just a couch," but his car is much more than "just a car." Lester has become the ultimate consumer. Like a teenager, he consumes without guilt, without foresight, and without responsibility. Meanwhile, Carolyn's questions about how he intends to make the mortgage payments are dismissed as merely one more symptom of her alienated existence.

*In the popular television sitcom *Frasier*, psychiatrist Frasier Crane and his brother Niles lead an apparently refined life that includes frequent visits to a wine club.

Lester is beyond all that. He is now what Thomas Frank calls "the rebel consumer."

What *American Beauty* illustrates, with extraordinary clarity, is that rebelling against mass society is not the same thing as rebelling against consumer society. Through his rebellion, Lester goes from being right-angle square to dead cool. This is reflected in his consumption choices. Apart from the new car, he develops a taste for very expensive marijuana — $2,000 an ounce, we are told, and very good. "This is all I ever smoke," his teenaged dealer assures him. Welcome to the club, where admission is restricted to clients with the most discriminating taste. How is this any different from Frasier and Niles at their wine club?*

25 What we need to see is that consumption is not about conformity, it's about distinction. People consume in order to set themselves apart from others. To show that they are cooler (Nike shoes), better connected (the latest nightclub), better informed (single-malt Scotch), morally superior (Guatemalan handcrafts), or just plain richer (BMWs).

The problem is that all of these comparative preferences generate competitive consumption. "Keeping up with the Joneses," in today's world, does not always mean buying a tract home in the suburbs. It means buying a loft downtown, eating at the right restaurants, listening to obscure bands, having a pile of Mountain Equipment Co-op gear and vacationing in Thailand. It doesn't matter how much people spend on these things, what matters is the competitive structure of the consumption. Once too many people get on the bandwagon, it forces the early adopters to get off, in order to preserve their distinction. This is what generates the cycles of obsolescence and waste that we condemn as "consumerism."

Many people who are, in their own minds, opposed to consumerism nevertheless actively participate in the sort of behaviour that drives it. Consider Naomi Klein. She starts out *No Logo* by decrying the recent conversion of factory buildings in her Toronto neighbourhood into "loft living" condominiums. She makes it absolutely clear to the reader that her place is the real deal, a genuine factory loft, steeped in working-class authenticity, yet throbbing with urban street culture and a "rock-video aesthetic."

Now of course anyone who has a feel for how social class in this country works knows that, at the time Klein was writing, a genuine factory loft in the King-Spadina area was possibly the single most exclusive and desirable piece of real estate in Canada. Unlike merely expensive neighbourhoods in Toronto, like Rosedale and Forest Hill, where it is possible to buy your way in, genuine lofts could only be acquired by people with superior social connections. This is because they contravened zoning regulations and could not be bought on the open market. Only the most exclusive segment of the cultural elite could get access to them.

Unfortunately for Klein, zoning changes in Toronto (changes that were part of a very enlightened and successful strategy to slow urban sprawl) allowed yuppies to buy their way into her neighbourhood. This led to an erosion of her social status. Her complaints about commercialization are nothing but an expression of this loss of distinction. What she fails to observe is that this distinction is precisely what drives the real estate market, what creates the value in these dwellings. People buy these lofts because they want a piece of Klein's social status. Naturally, she is not amused. They are, after all, her inferiors — an inferiority that they demonstrate through their willingness to accept mass-produced, commercialized facsimiles of the "genuine" article.

NAOMI KLEIN

"The astronomical growth in the wealth and cultural influence of multinational corporations over the last fifteen years can arguably be traced back to a single, seemingly innocuous idea developed by management theorists in the mid-1980s: that successful corporations must primarily produce brands, as opposed to products.

"Until that time, although it was understood in the corporate world that bolstering one's brand name was important, the primary concern of every solid manufacturer was the production of goods. . . .

"And for the longest time, the making of things remained, at least in principle, the heart of all industrialized economies. But by the eighties, . . . [t]he very process of producing — running one's own factories, being responsible for tens of thousands of full-time, permanent employees — began to look less like the route to success and more like a clunky liability.

"At around this same time a new kind of corporation began to rival the traditional all-American manufacturers for market share; these were the Nikes and Microsofts, and later, the Tommy Hilfigers and Intels. These pioneers made the bold claim that producing goods was only an incidental part of their operations, and that thanks to recent victories in trade liberalization and labor-law reform, they were able to have their products made for them by contractors, many of them overseas. What these companies produced primarily were not things, they said, but images of their brands. Their real work lay not in manufacturing but in marketing." Source: Naomi Klein, *No Logo: Taking Aim at the Brand Bullies* (2000).

Klein claims these newcomers bring "a painful new self-consciousness" to the neighbourhood. But as the rest of her introduction demonstrates, she is also conscious — painfully so — of her surroundings. Her neighbourhood is one where "in the twenties and thirties Russian and Polish immigrants darted back and forth on these streets, ducking into delis to argue about Trotsky and the leadership of the international ladies' garment workers' union." Emma Goldman, we are told, "the famed anarchist and labour organizer," lived on her street! How exciting for Klein! What a tremendous source of distinction that must be. 30 Klein suggests that she may be forced to move out of her loft when the landlord decides to convert the building to condominiums. But wait a minute. If that happens, why doesn't she just buy her

*French sociologist Pierre Bourdieu (1930–2002) was best known for his theories about culture, especially as they are described in his book *Reproduction in Education, Society, and Culture* (1970).

loft? The problem, of course, is that a loft-living condominium doesn't have quite the cachet of a "genuine" loft. It becomes, as Klein puts it, merely an apartment with "exceptionally high ceilings." It is not her landlord, but her fear of losing social status that threatens to drive Klein from her neighbourhood.

Here we can see the forces driving competitive consumption in their purest and most unadulterated form.

This ad is 6 years late.

Once we acknowledge the role that distinction plays in structuring consumption, it's easy to see why people care about brands so much. Brands don't bring us together, they set us apart. Of course, most sophisticated people claim that they don't care about brands — a transparent falsehood. Most people who consider themselves "anti-consumerist" are extremely brand-conscious. They are able to fool themselves into believing that they don't care because their preferences are primarily negative. They would never be caught dead driving a Chrysler or listening to Celine Dion. It is precisely by not buying these uncool items that they establish their social superiority. (It is also why, when they do consume "mass society" products, they must do so "ironically — so as to preserve their distinction.)

As Pierre Bourdieu* reminds us, taste is first and foremost distaste — disgust and "visceral intolerance" of the taste of others. This makes it easy to see how the critique of mass society could help drive consumerism. Take, for example, Volkswagen and Volvo advertising from the early 1960s. Both automakers used the critique of "planned obsolescence" quite prominently in their advertising campaigns. The message was clear: buy from the big Detroit automakers and show everyone that you're a dupe, a victim of consumerism; buy our car and show people that you're too smart to be duped by advertising, that you're wise to the game.

This sort of "anti-advertising" was enormously successful in the 1960s, transforming the VW bug from a Nazi car into the symbol of the hippie counterculture and making the Volvo the car of choice for an entire generation of leftist academics. Similar advertising strategies are just as successful today, and are used to sell everything from breakfast cereal to clothing. Thus the kind of ad parodies that we find in *Adbusters,* far from being subversive, are indistinguishable from many genuine ad campaigns. Flipping through the magazine, one cannot avoid thinking back to Frank's observation that "business is amassing great sums by charging admission to the ritual simulation of its own lynching."

35 We find ourselves in an untenable situation. On the one hand, we criticize conformity and encourage individuality and rebellion. On the other hand, we lament the fact that our ever-increasing standard of material consumption is failing to generate any lasting increase in happiness. This is because it is rebellion, not conformity, that generates the competitive structure that drives the wedge between consumption and happiness. As long as we continue to prize individuality, and as long as we express that individuality through what we own and where we live, we can expect to live in a consumerist society.

It is tempting to think that we could just drop out of the race, become what Harvard professor Juliet Schor calls "down-shifters." That way we could avoid competitive consumption entirely. Unfortunately, this is wishful thinking. We can walk away from some competitions, take steps to mitigate the effects of others, but many more simply cannot be avoided.

In many cases, competition is an intrinsic feature of the goods that we consume. Economists call these "positional goods" — goods that one person can have only if many others do not. Examples include not only penthouse apartments, but also wilderness hikes and underground music. It is often claimed that a growing economy is like the rising tide that lifts all boats. But a growing economy does not create more antiques, more rare art, or more downtown real estate, it just makes them more expensive. Many of us fail to recognize how much of our consumption is devoted to these positional goods.

Furthermore, we are often forced into competitive consumption, just to defend ourselves against the nuisances generated by other people's consumption. It is unreasonable, for example, for anyone living in a Canadian city to own anything other than a small, fuel-efficient car. At the same time, in many parts of the North America, the number of big SUVs on the road has reached the point where people are forced to think twice before buying a small car. The suvs make the roads so dangerous for other drivers that everyone has to consider buying a larger car just to protect themselves.

This is why expecting people to opt out is often unrealistic; the cost to the individual is just too high. It's all well and good to say that SUVs are a danger and shouldn't be on the road. But saying so doesn't change anything. The fact is that SUVs are on the road, and they're not about to disappear anytime soon. So are you willing to endanger your children's lives by buying a subcompact?

40 Because so much of our competitive consumption is defensive in nature, people feel justified in their choices. Unfortunately, everyone who participates contributes just as much to the problem, regardless of his or her intentions. It doesn't matter that you bought the SUV to protect yourself and your children, you still bought it, and you still made it harder for other drivers to opt out of the automotive arms race. When it comes to consumerism, intentions are irrelevant. It is only consequences that count.

This is why a society-wide solution to the problem of consumerism is not going to occur through personal or cultural politics. At this stage of late consumerism, our best bet is legislative action. If we were really worried about advertising, for example, it would be easy to strike a devastating blow against the "brand bullies" with a simple change in the tax code. The government could stop treating advertising expenditures as a fully tax-deductible business expense (much as it did with entertainment expenses several years ago). Advertising is already a separately itemized expense category, so the change wouldn't even generate any additional paperwork. But this little tweak to the tax code would have a greater impact than all of the culture jamming in the world.

Of course, tweaking the tax code is not quite as exciting as dropping a "meme bomb" into the world of advertising or heading off to the latest riot in all that cool MEC gear. It may, however, prove to be a lot more useful. What we need to realize is that consumerism is not an ideology. It is not something that people get tricked into. Consumerism is something that we actively do to one another, and that we will continue to do as long as we have no incentive to stop. Rather than just posturing, we should start thinking a bit more carefully about how we're going to provide those incentives.

Questions for Discussion

1. What problems do Potter and Heath see with consumer culture? How do they establish the point that these problems exist and are worth addressing? **2.** What is the main argument that Potter and Heath make about consumer culture in this essay? Cite passages from their essay to support your answer. **3.** Early in their essay Potter and Heath write that "the critique of mass society has been one of the most powerful forces driving consumerism for more than 40 years." What do they mean by this statement? How does this statement relate to the main argument of their essay? **4.** Potter and Heath devote much of their essay to an analysis of the films *Fight Club* and *American Beauty*. What do they believe each of these films reveals about consumer culture? How does their analysis of each film contribute to their main argument about consumer culture? How convincing do you find their analyses of these films? How effectively do their analyses help them to support their main argument? **5.** What point do Potter and Heath make through the use of the example of author Naomi Klein? Why is this example important to their main argument? Do you think they use this example effectively? Why or why not? **6.** What support do Potter and Heath offer for their assertion that "most people who consider themselves 'anti-consumerist' are extremely brand-conscious"? How convincing do you find this assertion? **7.** Near the end of their essay, Potter and Heath write, "When it comes to consumerism, intentions are irrelevant. It is only consequences that count." How would you react to this statement? What counterarguments can you offer to this statement? **8.** What solution to the problems of consumerism do Potter and Heath offer? How feasible do you find their solution? What alternatives can you identify to the solution they propose? **9.** Potter and Heath are Canadian writers, and their essay was first published in a Canadian magazine (see Context on this page). Do you think their argument would be persuasive for U.S. readers? Why or why not?

④ **DAVID KORTEN, "Economies of Meaning"**

The belief that a free market system and "the good life" go hand in hand runs deep in American culture. But not everyone shares that belief. Economist and activist David Korten is one influential voice in a growing chorus that questions the belief in the free market as a means to a better society for all. In the following essay, Korten looks carefully at the values that seem to drive the development of a global free market, and he argues that those values are not consistent with the good life that so many people hope for. In particular, Korten examines what he believes are myths about free markets — myths that lead to policies and business practices that undermine rather than foster justice and economic stability for the majority of people worldwide. In considering Korten's argument, you might compare the fundamental values that he seems to hold about how we should live together to the values of the other writers in this section — and to your own. David Korten is the founder and president of the People-Centered Development Forum, an advocacy group for just and sustainable economic development; he is also the author of *The Post-Corporate World: Life After Capitalism* (1999) and of the best-selling *When Corporations Rule the World* (1995), from which the following essay is drawn.

Economies of Meaning
DAVID KORTEN

1 The politics of meaning poses a challenging question: What would be the characteristics of an economy that both meets our material needs and serves to create the ethos of caring relationships and of ethical, spiritual, and ecological sensitivity essential to life in a good society? If we take this to be a two-fold performance test of the good economy, then it is evident that our existing economy is serving us poorly.

There is little room for ethical, spiritual, and ecological sensitivity in a global economy that defines success purely in terms of the financial bottom line, creates a growing gap between its winners and losers, and provides fabulous financial rewards to those willing to sacrifice long-term human and environmental interests for short-term financial gain.

Leading proponents of the new global economy such as Rosabeth Kanter, Harvard Business School professor and author of the business best-seller, *World Class,* counsel that in the global economy financial success belongs to those who are willing to sacrifice loyalty to community and nation in the pursuit of personal economic opportunity (see "World Class" on page 554). The

*Neoliberal economic policy is based on the belief that laws and policies should foster free markets within which businesses can function unfettered so that market forces can lead to social benefits for most people.

†See the sidebar on libertarianism on page 464 in Chapter 11.

March 25, 1995 issue of *Fortune* advises young graduates to approach every job as though they are self-employed, because success will come to those who look out for number one, always using one's present job to open better opportunities with other employers.

It is abundantly clear: In the global free-market economy, caring, loyalty, and moderation are out. Individual self-interest, materialism, and opportunism are in. **5** Since the disintegration of the Soviet Empire in 1989, countries nearly everywhere have joined in an uncritical embrace of market-driven economic growth based on deregulating markets, privatizing public assets, scaling back social programs, and removing barriers to the free international flow of goods and finance. Political parties from across the political spectrum have converged on a commitment to variations of this agenda, leaving those who question the underlying assumptions or the moral implications with few political alternatives.

In spite of its claims to firm theoretical and empirical foundations, the neoliberal economic policy agenda* is best described as an ideology of corporate libertarianism† based on the perpetuation of myths deeply embedded in our political culture and an embrace of social dysfunction as the foundation of a perverse moral philosophy. It is useful to examine a few of the more central of these myths. For example:

The myth that growth in aggregate economic output‡ is a valid measure of human well-being and progress.

To the contrary, the indicators of aggregate economic output by which economic policy managers evaluate their performance tell us nothing about the social utility of that output. Expanded use of cigarettes and alcohol increases economic output both as a direct consequence of their consumption and because of the related increase in health-care needs. The need to clean up oil spills increases economic activity. Gun sales to minors generate economic activity. A divorce generates both lawyers fees and the need to buy or rent and outfit a new home, increasing real estate brokerage fees and retail sales. It is now well documented that in the United States and a number of other countries the quality of living of ordinary people has been declining as aggregate economic output increases.

The myth that technology frees us from environmental restraints on economic growth.

‡Economists use the term *aggregate economic output* to refer to a variety of economic statistics related to productivity in specific sectors of the economy. It is generally seen as a measure of the strength or weakness of the economy in general.

Market economies are highly responsive to the wants of those who have money. They are blind to the needs of those who have no money. In contrast to political democracy, which is based on one person, one vote, economic democracy is about one dollar, one vote. Under conditions of relative economic equality, the market mechanism has an important role in the fair, efficient, and democratic allocation of resources. Under the conditions of extreme inequality that presently prevail, an unfettered market allocates resources in ways that are grossly unfair, inefficient, and undemocratic. Contrary to the rhetoric of ideologues from both Right and Left, markets are neither inherently good nor inherently bad. It is a question of the conditions under which a particular market functions.

The myth that the only alternative to a free market economy is a state-planned, command economy.

Our own history is one of many sources of alternative examples. During the post–World War II period, in which a large and prosperous middle class was a defining feature of the Western industrial nations, the market functioned within a framework of rules set through a democratic public process. The institutions of government, market, and civil society functioned in a reasonable pluralistic balance. A combination of deregulation and globalization have freed the market and destroyed this balance, rapidly eroding the conditions on which efficient market function depends. For example, in the absence of government intervention, successful competitors gain ever greater monopolistic advantage through their accumulation of economic and political power. Now the competitive market economy is being steadily replaced by a centrally planned global economy managed by an ever more tightly integrated alliance of global corporations.

10 While technology in some instances allows us to use ecosystem resources more efficiently, there is a strong historical relationship between growth in economic output and growing human demands on the earth's finite ecosystem. Furthermore, a five-fold increase in the world's economic output since 1950 has now pushed the human burden on the planet's regenerative systems, its soils, air, water, fisheries, and forestry systems beyond what the planet can sustain. Continuing to press for economic growth beyond the planet's sustainable limits accelerates the rate of breakdown of those systems, as we see so dramatically demonstrated in the case of many ocean fisheries, and intensifies the competition between rich and poor for the earth's remaining output of life-sustaining resources.

The myth that an open and unregulated "free" market is the fairest and most efficient way to allocate society's resources and is the foundation of human freedom and democratic citizen sovereignty.

*The North American Free Trade Agreement (NAFTA), the General Agreement on Trade and Tariffs (GATT), and the Maastricht Treaty are separate international agreements signed during the 1990s governing international trade. In general, these agreements weakened laws on trade between nations, thereby making it easier for businesses to operate across international borders.

15 The related myths that trade agreements are about trade, that open economic borders are universally beneficial, and that economic globalization is a consequence of immutable historical forces.

The truth is that most trade agreements — such as NAFTA, GATT, and the European Maastricht Treaty* — are really economic integration agreements intended to guarantee the rights of global corporations to move both goods and investments wherever they wish, free from public interference and accountability. Greater rights for global corporations inevitably mean fewer rights for ordinary citizens to set the rules by which their own local and national economies will function. The trend toward ever greater global economic integration is inevitable only so long as we allow the world's largest corporations to buy our politicians and write our laws.

The myth that global corporations are benevolent institutions that, once freed from governmental interference, will provide local prosperity, jobs, and a clean environment for all.

In reality, the institution of the corporation was invented to concentrate control over economic resources while shielding those who hold the resulting power from personal accountability for the public consequences of its use. In a globalized, deregulated market, the only legal public accountability of corporate management in the use of their power is to a global financial market that has one incessant demand: Maximize short-term returns to shareholders. This puts enormous pressures on management to take advantage of every available opportunity to pass the costs of production onto the community by lowering wages and working conditions, obtaining government subsidies and tax breaks, and cutting corners on environmental protection. Gains are privatized to the benefit of the

power-holders. Costs are socialized by passing them to those who have no political or economic voice.

These myths of our political culture are buttressed by a number of moral premises embedded in the corporate libertarian ideology that serves as the foundation for most neoliberal economic theory. These moral premises may be summarized as follows:

- People are by nature motivated primarily by greed.
- The drive to acquire material wealth is the highest expression of what it means to be human.
- The relentless pursuit of greed and acquisition leads to socially optimal outcomes.
- It is in the best interest of human societies to encourage, honor, and reward these values.

20 While most economists would not state these premises in such stark terms, this is the essence of the value assumptions underlying most contemporary market theory. Unfortunately, economic policies driven by these deeply flawed moral premises create a self-fulfilling prophecy by rewarding dysfunctional behaviors deeply detrimental to the healthy function of human societies, as we now see demonstrated all around us.

Our development models — and their underlying myths and values — are artifacts of the ideas and institutions of the industrial era. The corporation and the modern state have been cornerstones of that era, concentrating massive economic resources in a small number of centrally controlled institutions. They have brought the full power of capital-intensive technologies to bear in exploiting the world's natural and human resources so that a small minority of the world's people could consume far more than their rightful share of the world's real wealth.

Economic globalization has served to advance this exploitation of the earth's social and environmental systems beyond their limits of tolerance, by freeing errant corporations from restraints to their growth, their ability to monopolize ever larger markets, and the use of their economic power to win political concessions that allow them to pass on to the community ever more of the costs of their production. It has delinked corporations and financial markets from accountability to any public jurisdiction or interest, contributed to a massive concentration of financial power, and richly rewarded those who place the values of acquisition, competition, and self-interest ahead of values of simplicity, cooperation, and sharing.

We are not limited to choosing between markets or governments as the instruments of our exploitation. Nor is there need to eliminate markets, trade, private ownership, the state, or even the institution of the corporation. Rather, it is a matter of creating a new architecture for each of these institutions appropriate to the values we believe a good society should embody and nurture. This creative task belongs neither to corporations nor to states, which are incapable of questioning the assumptions on which the legitimacy of their present institutional form is based. It belongs to citizens — to the people whose interests and values the new architecture is intended to serve. It is people rather than corporations or other big-money interests that appropriately set the terms of the economic and political agenda.

Citizen groups throughout the world are already actively engaged in the experimental creation of economies of meaning aligned with life-affirming values. Powerful formative ideas are emerging from these initiatives. For example, millions of people in the voluntary simplicity movement are dis-

VOLUNTARY SIMPLICITY

Popularized by author Duane Elgin and often seen as a reaction to consumerism, the term *voluntary simplicity* refers generally to a philosophy and lifestyle based on understanding our connections to each other and to the earth and living in a way that acknowledges one's responsibility to others and to the environment. In the 1980s and 1990s a number of organizations and advocacy groups were formed to promote a lifestyle based on these ideas, in part out of concerns for the environment. In his book *Voluntary Simplicity* (1981), Elgin describes voluntary simplicity as

a manner of living that is outwardly more simple and inwardly more rich, a way of being in which our most authentic and alive self is brought into direct and conscious contact with living. This way of life is not a static condition to be achieved, but an ever-changing balance that must be continuously and consciously made real. Simplicity in this sense is not simple. To maintain a skillful balance between the inner and outer aspects of our lives is an enormously challenging and continuously changing process. the objective is not dogmatically to live with less, but is a more demanding intention of living with balance in order to find a life of greater purpose, fulfillment, and satisfaction.

covering that good living is more fulfilling than endless accumulation and consumption. In a healthy society, a life of material sufficiency and social, cultural, intellectual, and spiritual abundance can readily be sustained in balance with the environment.

25 Others are learning that there are alternatives to a global economy that inherently fosters inequality and global competition among local people and communities. They are demonstrating such possibilities by building strong, self-reliant, local economies that root resource management and ownership in democratically governed communities and recognize that all people have an inherent right of access to a basic means of creating a livelihood. Such economies are an essential foundation of healthy societies able to engage in cooperative and caring exchanges with their neighbors.

These are lessons with profound implications for a politics of meaning. In large

CONTEXT

For another perspective on promoting local economies, see Vandana Shiva's essay in Chapter 13 (page 619.).

measure, societies express and sustain their cultural values through their choice of economic structures. The fact that our present economic system values and rewards greed, gluttony, and disregard for the needs of others didn't just happen. It is a consequence of conscious acts of choice — poorly informed though they may be. It is equally within our means to create a globalized system of localized economies that thrive on life-affirming values of sufficiency, caring, cooperation, and reverence for life. It is a matter of adequately informed collective political choice.

Yet our existing political formations, no matter where they are positioned on the traditional Left-Right spectrum, reveal no awareness of even the possibility of replacing an economy of meanness with economies of meaning. That is one of many compelling reasons why we need a new political movement in the United States that is not defined by traditional Left-Right values and agendas. The politics of meaning movement is engaging this task. I believe that building public awareness of the potential to create economies of meaning and putting forward a policy agenda that advances this outcome must receive high priority on the movement's agenda.

NEGOTIATING DIFFERENCES

The essays in this cluster are as much about values as they are about free markets. Each author makes an argument about free markets on the basis of values regarding how we should live together. In this sense, our views about free markets and economic policy are intimately connected to our hopes and beliefs about how we should live together.

Imagine that you have been asked to write a statement in which you present your own position on free markets and the economic policies by which we live. Using the four essays in this cluster as a starting point, write such a position paper, directed at your classmates as your primary audience. In your position paper, identify your fundamental values regarding the kind of life you believe we should have the opportunity to live. Make a case for the kind of economic market you believe we should have to create the kind of life you seek. Try to be specific about the policies you would advocate or oppose. For example, do you believe that government should closely regulate businesses

Questions for Discussion

1. On what basis does Korten make the claim that "there is little room for ethical, spiritual, and ecological sensitivity" in our growing global economy? What kinds of evidence does he present to support this claim? Do you think he is right? What might your answer to that question suggest about your own values?

2. Korten structures much of this essay around discussion of what he calls central myths that are "deeply embedded in our political culture." Evaluate Korten's discussion of these "myths." To what extent is his discussion of these myths an attempt to address objections to his own position? How effectively does he debunk these myths, in your view? How effective do you find his discussion of these myths in supporting his main argument about free markets? **3.** On the basis of this essay, what values do you think Korten holds most dear? Do you think most Americans would agree with him about those values? **4.** Examine the moral premises that Korten states are embedded in the corporate ideology (paragraph 19). Do you agree that these moral premises are embedded in corporate culture? Why or why not? **5.** What is the "new architecture" that Korten believes is needed to counteract what he sees as the dangers of global markets? How feasible is this "new architecture" as an alternative to global capitalism? What evidence does Korten provide that such a new architecture can be created? **6.** What does Korten mean by the term *politics of meaning*? In what sense is that term important to his main argument? **7.** This essay is taken from *When Corporations Rule the World*. On the basis of this essay, who do you think is the audience Korten imagined for his book? How effectively do you think he addresses that audience with his argument? Cite passages from his essay to support your answer.

and industries in the interest of the public good? Do you believe that government should generally allow businesses and industries to operate without restriction? Should local governments have the authority to control economic matters in the interests of local communities? Or is it the job of the federal government to ensure that there are fair economic policies for all communities? Try to identify and discuss the implications of your position statement. For instance, if you advocate minimal taxes so that markets can function more freely, consider how governments might pay for the services they provide if they cannot rely on taxes.

Above all, try to address the question "What role should free markets play in our lives as citizens?"

Alternatively, create a Web site in which you present your position on free markets and economic policy. Be sure to consider design in creating your site (see Chapter 4, pages 82–96).

WHAT DOES IT MEAN
TO BE A CONSUMER?

I n the 1980s a popular television show called *Lifestyles of the Rich and Famous* featured celebrities in their spectacular homes or in other locations such as their yachts or vacation homes. In the 1990s a similar show on the MTV network called *Cribs* focused on the expensive homes of well-known musicians, actors, and athletes. The astronomically expensive homes featured on these shows are out of reach of the vast majority of Americans, but perhaps the popularity of the shows reflects the dreams and desires of that majority. If so, then we might think of "conspicuous consumption" as a good thing. ■ *Conspicuous consumption* is a term coined in 1899 by American economist and social critic Thorstein Veblen (1857–1929) to describe the spending of money as a way to display wealth (see *Con-Text* on page 561). In other words, a person spends conspicuously, so that others can see his or her wealth. Veblen originally used the term in reference to what he called "the leisure class," which was made up of well-to-do businesspeople, property owners, professionals, and others in "non-industrial" occupations. But in the decades since Veblen first published his theory, the term *conspicuous consumption* has taken on a larger meaning. Today we tend to use it to refer to anyone's "conspicuous" spending, especially if that spending can be considered unnecessary. For example, someone of very modest means who buys an extremely expensive sports car can be said to be engaged in conspicuous consumption. Just as the celebrities in *Lifestyles of the Rich and Famous* or *Cribs* do not really need such enormous and expensive homes for their basic shelter, neither does the person who bought the expensive sports car truly need such a vehicle for basic transportation. Yet many people would defend that person's right to buy such a car, whether or not it is necessary — and whether or not that person can afford it. ■ Conspicuous consumption of this kind raises questions about the decisions individuals make in spending their money. Do we really have the right to spend our money in any way we please, without regard to possible consequences? Is the kind of excessive consumption featured on television shows such as *Cribs* something that people should aspire to in a society that includes some people who are desperately poor? In other words, what responsibilities, if any, do consumers have in deciding how to spend their money? ■ The essays in this cluster reveal that there are many different answers to such questions. A few of these authors argue that consumers do not make their decisions in isolation and therefore must sometimes face ethical considerations when deciding how to spend their money. Such arguments seem to fly in the face of mainstream American attitudes about individual choice and free markets. Indeed, some critics argue that it is patriotic to be a consumer, since consumption can contribute to a strong U.S. economy. Yet other critics offer warnings about how consumers can fall prey to business practices that seek to maximize profits at the expense of individual consumers. ■ All these arguments suggest that buying things as consumers might not be as straightforward as we might think. The essays in this cluster might therefore deepen your appreciation for the ways in which our choices as consumers — conspicuous or not — are connected to many other aspects of our lives.

CON-TEXT: "Conspicuous Consumption"

1 Conspicuous consumption of valuable goods is a means of reputability to the gentleman of leisure. As wealth accumulates on his hands, his own unaided effort will not avail to sufficiently put his opulence in evidence by this method. The aid of friends and competitors is therefore brought in by resorting to the giving of valuable presents and expensive feasts and entertainments. Presents and feasts had probably another origin than that of naive ostentation, but they required their utility for this purpose very early, and they have retained that character to the present; so that their utility in this respect has now long been the substantial ground on which these usages rest. Costly entertainments, such as the potlatch or the ball, are peculiarly adapted to serve this end. The competitor with whom the entertainer wishes to institute a comparison is, by this method, made to serve as a means to the end. He consumes vicariously for his host at the same time that he is witness to the consumption of that excess of good things which his host is unable to dispose of single-handed, and he is also made to witness his host's facility in etiquette.

SOURCE: Thorstein Veblen, *Theory of the Leisure Class* (1899).

① IAN FRAZIER, "All-Consuming Patriotism: American Flag: $19.95. New Yacht: $75,000. True Patriotism? Priceless"

Shortly after the terrorist attacks of September 11, 2001, fears about the potential damage of those attacks to the U.S. economy prompted President George W. Bush to urge Americans to carry on as usual. In particular, President Bush suggested, Americans should patronize businesses as they normally would, and maybe even take their families on vacation. The idea was that spending money was good for the economy and therefore good for the country. In other words, it would be patriotic to be a consumer. Some critics scoffed at President Bush's comments, but the idea that it is patriotic to consume is not far-fetched for many Americans. In the 1980s, as some U.S. industries seemed to be losing ground in the marketplace to expanding Japanese companies, there were calls for American consumers to "buy American" as a way to keep the U.S. economy strong in the face of foreign competition. And during the economic downturn in the first few years of the 21st century, some economists indicated that the buying habits of Americans were keeping the economy from an even more serious recession. Such news prompted some political leaders to suggest that consumers were actually doing their patriotic duty by buying goods at a time when the U.S. economy was weak. In the following essay, writer Ian Frazier examines this connection between consumption and patriotism. Although he pokes fun at the idea that consumption is patriotic, Frazier is making a serious point about what it means to be a consumer and a patriot. As you read his essay, which was published in 2002 in *Mother Jones* magazine, consider what it might say about the role of consumers in American society.

All-Consuming Patriotism: American Flag: $19.95. New Yacht: $75,000. True Patriotism? Priceless.

IAN FRAZIER

1 I think of myself as a good American. I follow current events, come to a complete stop at stop signs, show up for jury duty, vote. When the government tells me to shop, as it's been doing recently, I shop. Over the last few months, patriotically, I've bought all kinds of stuff I have no use for. Lack of money has been no obstacle; years ago I could never get a credit card, due to low income and lack of a regular job, and then one day for no reason credit cards began tumbling on me out of the mail. I now owe more to credit card companies than the average family of four earns in a year. So when buying something I don't want or need, I simply take out my credit card. That part's been easy; for me, it's the shop-

FRAZIER 563

ALL-CONSUMING PATRIOTISM: AMERICAN FLAG: $19.95. NEW YACHT: $75,000. TRUE PATRIOTISM? PRICELESS.

ping itself that's hard. I happen to be a bad shopper — nervous, uninformed, prone to grab the first product I see on the shelf and pay any amount for it and run out the door. Frequently, trips I make to the supermarket end with my wife shouting in disbelief as she goes through the grocery bags and immediately transfers one wrongly purchased item after another directly into the garbage can.

It's been hard, as I say, but I've done my duty — I've shopped and then shopped some more. Certain sacrifices are called for. Out of concern for the economy after the terror attacks, the president said that he wanted us to go about our business, and not stop shopping. On a TV commercial sponsored by the travel industry, he exhorted us to take the family for a vacation. The treasury secretary, financial commentators, leaders of industry — all told us not to be afraid to spend. So I've gone out of my comfort zone, even expanded my purchasing patterns. Not long ago I detected a look of respect in the eye of a young salesman with many piercings at the music store as he took in my heavy middle-aged girth and then the rap music CD featuring songs of murder and gangsterism that I had selflessly decided to buy. My life is usually devoid of great excitement or difficulty, knock wood and thank God, and I have nothing to cry about, but I've also noticed in the media recently a strong approval for uninhibited public crying. So now, along with the shopping, I've been crying a lot, too. Sometimes I cry and shop at the same time.

As I'm pushing my overfull shopping cart down the aisle, sobbing quietly, moving a bit more slowly because of the extra weight I've lately put on, a couple of troubling questions cross my mind. First, I start to worry about the real depth of my shopping capabilities. So far I have more or less been able to keep up

with what the government expects of me. I'm at a level of shopping that I can stand. But what if, God forbid, events take a bad turn and the national crisis worsens, and more shopping is required? Can I shop with greater intensity than I am shopping now? I suppose I could eat even more than I've been eating, and order additional products in the mail, and go on costlier trips, and so on. But I'm not eager, frankly, to enter that "code red" shopping mode. I try

to tell myself that I'd be equal to it, that in a real crisis I might be surprised by how much I could buy. But I don't know.

My other worry is a vague one, more in the area of atmospherics, intangibles. I feel kind of wrong even mentioning it in this time of trial. How can I admit that I am worried about my aura? I worry that my aura is not . . . well, that it's not what I had once hoped it would be. I can explain this only by comparison, obliquely. On the top shelf of my bookcase, among the works vital to me, is a book called *Trials and Triumphs: The Record of the Fifty-Fifth Ohio Volunteer Infantry,* by Captain Hartwell Osborn. I've read this book many times and studied it to the smallest detail, because I think the people in it are brave and cool and admirable in every way.

5 The Fifty-Fifth was a Union Army regiment, formed in the Ohio town of Norwalk, that fought throughout the Civil War. My great-great-grandfather served in the regiment, as did other relatives. The book lists every mile the regiment marched and every casualty it suffered. I like reading about the soldiering, but I can't really identify with it, having never been in the service myself. I identify more with the soldiers' wives and mothers and daughters, whose home-front struggles I can better imagine, *Trials and Triumphs* devotes a chapter to them, and to an organization they set up called the Soldiers' Aid Society.

The ladies of the Soldiers' Aid Society worked for the regiment almost constantly from the day it began. They sewed uniforms, made pillows, held ice-cream sociables to raise money, scraped lint for bandages, emptied their wedding chests of their best linen and donated it all. To provide the men with antiscorbutics* while on campaign, they pickled everything that would pickle, from onions to potatoes to artichokes. Every other

day they were shipping out a new order of homemade supplies. Some of the women spent so much time stooped over while packing goods in barrels that they believed they had permanently affected their postures. When the war ended the ladies of the Soldiers' Aid said that for the first time in their lives they understood what united womanhood could accomplish. The movements for prohibition and women's suffrage that grew powerful in the early 1900s got their start among those who'd worked in similar home-front organizations during the war.

I don't envy my forebears, or wish I'd lived back then. I prefer the greater speed and uncertainty and complicatedness of now. But I can't help thinking that in terms of aura, the Norwalk ladies have it all over me. I study the pages with their photographs, and admire the plainness of their dresses, the set of their jaws, the expression in their eyes. Next to them my credit card and I seem a sorry spectacle indeed. Their sense of purpose shames me. What the country needed from those ladies it asked for, and they provided, straightforwardly; what it wants from me it somehow can't come out and ask. I'm asked to shop more, which really means to spend more, which eventually must mean to work more than I was working before. In previous wars, harder work was a civilian sacrifice that the government didn't hesitate to ask. Nowadays it's apparently unwilling to ask for any sacrifice that might appear to be too painful, too real.

But I want it to be real. I think a lot of us do. I feel like an idiot with my tears and shopping cart. I want to participate, to do something — and shopping isn't it. Many of the donors who contributed more than half a billion dollars to a Red Cross fund for the families of terror attack victims became angry when they learned that much of the

*The term *antiscorbutics* refers to herbal medicines that provide vitamin C.

money would end up not where they had intended but in the Red Cross bureaucracy. People want to express themselves with action. In New York City so many have been showing up recently for jury duty that the courts have had to turn hundreds away; officials said a new surplus of civic consciousness was responsible for the upsurge. I'd be glad if I were asked to — I don't know — drive less or turn the thermostat down or send in seldom-used items of clothing or collect rubber bands or plant a victory garden or join a civilian patrol or use fewer disposable paper products at children's birthday parties. I'd be willing, if asked, just to sit still for a day and meditate on the situation, much in the way that Lincoln used to call for national days of prayer.

A great, shared desire to do something is lying around mostly untapped. The best we can manage, it seems, is to show our U.S.A. brand loyalty by putting American flags on our houses and cars. Some businesses across the country even display in their windows a poster on which the American flag appears as a shopping bag, with two handles at the top. Above the flag-bag are the words "America: Open for Business." Money and the economy have gotten so tangled up in our politics that we forget we're citizens of our government, not its consumers. And the leaders we elect, who got where they are by selling themselves to us with television ads, and who often are only on short loan from the corporate world anyway, think of us as customers who must be kept happy. There's a scarcity of ideas about how to direct all this patriotic feeling because usually the market, not the country, occupies our minds. I'm sure it's possible to transform oneself from salesman to leader, just as it is to go from consumer to citizen. But the shift of identity is awkward, without

> ### THE RED CROSS AND 9-11
>
> "In the hours after the Sept. 11 attacks, a record-breaking amount of donations started pouring into more than 1,000 local American Red Cross chapters.
>
> "What donors didn't know was that some of the chapters entrusted with all that money had been identified by Red Cross headquarters just a few weeks before for having poor accounting procedures, inaccurate financial reports and for keeping national disaster contributions that should have been sent to headquarters in Washington. That according to internal documents obtained by CBS news. . . .
>
> "According to documents obtained by CBS News, a dozen of the Red Cross chapters audited were marking, or 'coding', donations as local funds. This means chapters like San Diego, Southwest Florida, and Gateway Area, Iowa would keep the money instead of sending it in for Sept. 11 victims." Source: Sharyl Attkisson, "Red Faces at the Red Cross." CBSNews.com (July 2002).

many precedents, not easily done. In between the two — between selling and leading, between consuming and being citizens — is where our leaders and the rest of us are now.

10 We see the world beyond our immediate surroundings mostly through televi-

sion, whose view is not much wider than that of a security peephole in a door. We hear over and over that our lives have forever changed, but the details right in front of us don't look very different, for all that. The forces fighting in Afghanistan are in more danger than we are back home, but perhaps not so much more; everybody knows that when catastrophe comes it could hit anywhere, most likely someplace it isn't expected. Strong patriotic feelings stir us, fill us, but have few means of expressing themselves. We want to be a country, but where do you go to do that? Surely not the mall. When Mayor Giuliani left office at the end of 2001, he said he was giving up the honorable title of mayor for the more honorable title of citizen. He got that right. Citizen is honorable; shopper is not.

Questions for Discussion

1. How would you summarize Frazier's main argument in this essay? Identify the passage or passages in the essay that you think most clearly state his main point. **2.** According to Frazier, why is it difficult for Americans to determine how to express their patriotic feelings? Do you agree with him? Why or why not? **3.** The tone of Frazier's essay might be described as tongue-in-cheek — an attempt to poke fun at the idea that it is patriotic for Americans to spend money on consumer goods. What features of his writing style create this tongue-in-cheek approach to his subject? Cite specific passages from the essay to support your answer. **4.** Frazier devotes considerable space in his essay to discussing *Trials and Triumphs*, a book about a Civil War infantry unit, and the men and women described in that book. What purpose does this discussion serve in Frazier's essay? How does this discussion relate to his main argument about consumption? Do you find this discussion effective? Explain. **5.** This essay was originally published in *Mother Jones* magazine, which generally reflects a left-leaning political viewpoint that is often critical of the U.S. government. In what ways does Frazier's essay reflect the editorial viewpoint of *Mother Jones*? Do you think Frazier's argument would be effective for a wider audience than readers of *Mother Jones*? Explain, citing specific passages from the essay to support your answer.

② JAMES DEACON, "The Joys of Excess"

Americans are sometimes criticized for excessive buying habits as consumers. But as James Deacon makes clear in the following essay, Americans are not the only people who might be guilty of conspicuous consumption. (For a discussion of conspicuous consumption, see the introduction to this cluster on page 560; see also *Con-Text* on page 561.) Deacon describes some of the spending habits of wealthier citizens of his own country, Canada, a nation whose economy and culture are in many ways similar to those of the United States. But although Deacon is critical of what he believes is excessive spending on consumer goods by many Canadians, he avoids simply judging consumers; rather, he is interested in understanding why consumers engage in conspicuous consumption. His essay raises questions about the implications of such consumption — especially when it involves items that can obviously damage the environment, such as fuel-inefficient SUVs. In asking why such consumption occurs, Deacon helps us to explore the complicated issue of what it means to be a consumer. His essay was published in 2002 in *MacLean's* magazine.

The Joys of Excess
JAMES DEACON

*Canadian lawyer J.J. Robinette is well known throughout Canada for having argued a number of high-profile cases before the Canadian Supreme Court. *Barrister* is another term for lawyer.

1 Back in 1904, a banker named James Breckenridge moved his family into a gorgeous new red-brick home on one of the most sought-after streets in Rosedale, a leafy enclave in the centre of Toronto. Over the years, the rambling, three-story classic was home to a couple of other families, including famed barrister J.J. Robinette,* his wife and their three children. But the home isn't there anymore. The next-door neighbours bought it and tore it down so they could put an addition on their already substantial home. They also bought and demolished two even bigger houses immediately behind them for yet more additions that are currently under construction.

As conspicuous consumption goes, that's tough to beat. But nowadays, even with the uncertainties of the stock market, the competition is fierce. Just two blocks away, someone bought a pair of century-old homes on vast, side-by-side lots, ripped them down and is erecting what, at a projected 7,500 square feet, can only loosely be termed a single-family dwelling. It will not only be the biggest house on the block; it will tower over the elementary school directly across the street. Still, that place is puny compared to the $16-million, 48,500-

C O N T E X T

According to the U.S. Census Bureau, the relative share of income declined for 80 percent of all Americans between 1970 and 1998; in that same time period the wealthiest 20 percent of Americans saw their share of income increase from 43 percent to 49 percent. In other words, as of 1998, nearly half of total wealth in the United States was owned by the richest 20 percent of the population. More recent census data indicate little change in those figures.

The relative distribution of incomes in Canada has changed less noticeably. For example, in 1980 the wealthiest 20 percent of Canadians accounted for 42 percent of total income; in 1996 that figure increased to 44 percent.

square-foot lakeside home that a businessman has planned for himself, his wife and their one child in suburban Oakville. And so on — in Calgary, Montreal, Vancouver, wherever, the stories are the same. Bigger is better, and spare no expense. Heck, someone recently paid $10 million for a lakeside chalet in Whistler, B.C., which begs the question: how many hot tubs do you get for 10 million bucks?

And it's not just monster homes. It's monster cars, too. One-upmanship in the sports-utility market has prompted automotive companies to produce vehicles with the square footage and creature comforts of two-storey condos. Luxury car manufacturers such as Mercedes-Benz Canada, BMW Canada and Infiniti have all reported record sales in the first months of 2002. There's hot demand for mega-yachts and money's-no-object holiday packages, and there seems no limit on what people will spend for big-screen home-entertainment units. You've got to fill those vast basements with something.

Have the rich gone mad? The numbers shout yes, but the experts who track such things say no. In the last two decades, while low- and middle-income paycheques remained static or declined, the country's top earners saw their incomes more than double. (That was partly due to companies' generous outlay of stock options, a practice that, in the post-Enron world, is in retreat). At any rate, all they're doing now is spending at comparably lavish levels. And if you believe Adam Smith, the noted 18th-century Scottish economist, the ravenous craving for ultra-luxurious goods is actually a good thing. It was Smith 200-odd years ago who suggested that the pursuit of individual self-interest would ultimately produce gains for society as a whole. Free markets create wealthier economies, he argued, and free-spending puts more cash in more pockets.

5 Many wealthy people are discreet about it, but there have always been those who are willing to throw money around like confetti. The term "conspicuous consumption,"* in fact, was coined more than a century ago by an eccentric University of Chicago economist named Thorstein Veblen, and the practice has likely been going on forever. And as in the past, the current luxury-goods craze has boosted, as Smith promised, the fortunes of countless car dealers and retailers and tradesmen and architects.

But others argue that there are costs that don't get paid by the conspicuous consumers, and that undercut whatever benefits free-spending offers. Humongous boats and SUVs are fearsome gas-guzzlers that deplete resources and release far more pollutants into waterways and the atmosphere than do smaller cars and boats. There is enormous waste when one monster home replaces two, three or even four pre-existing houses: in many cases, more people are forced to commute, and a street loses some diversity. And that kind of creeping neighbourhood imperialism can tear at local heritage and destroy historically significant architecture. More practically for people nearby, demolition and construction projects produce months and sometimes years of aggravating noise, dirt and disruption.

Look-at-me displays of wealth may seem vulgar to some, but for those in the dough, it's all relative. For example, Bill Gates' 65,000-square-foot home sounds positively Versailles-like, but it's still smaller (by nearly 10,000 square feet) than the behemoth built for another Microsoft exec, Paul Allen. Perhaps Mr. Allen was thinking of having his football team, the Seattle Seahawks, play their home games at, well, home. Anyway, from that perspective, your neighbour's renovation suddenly appears restrained.

All of the excess would be less problematic if it weren't for the desire of others to keep up. Not everyone is driven by the consumer urge, but there's still a ton of house envy (or car or boat or you-name-it) out there, and that's the insidious downside of conspicuous consumption, says Robert Frank, a Cornell University economics professor and author of *Luxury Fever: Money and Happiness in an Era of Excess.* As the luxury bar gets set so much higher, he says, it tends to make less affluent people feel that they're falling behind — their circumstances may not have declined, but the gap between them and the rich is greater.

And while baby-boomers may once have seen themselves as anti-consumerism Woodstockers, they got over it while watching *Dynasty* and *Lifestyles of the Rich and Famous.* Most can't compete with the big-mansion set, but they're doing their best to transform their 25-foot lots. The average square footage of a North American home has increased by more than 50 per cent in the last 30 years. That means more expensive mortgages and property taxes, and higher costs for everything from utilities to yard care. And you're supporting a life that's in keeping with others nearby — the car, the schools, the built-in fridge. "How do you afford it?" Frank asks. "Well, you have both parents working, you commute longer distances, you work longer hours, you save less and you borrow more." And that's led mainly by the spending at the top. "When everyone else builds bigger," he adds, "the main effect of that is to make you feel that you need to build bigger, too."

10 And for what? It bears asking because while conspicuous consumption may well enhance the economy, it's of no use to the people doing the spending if they're working too hard to enjoy the bigger houses and cars and TVs. And the money that's being spent keeping up could be used in other ways — everything from longer family holidays to charitable contributions — that enhance both domestic and community affairs. "The resources that it takes to build bigger," Frank says, "could be used for other things that, on objective grounds, would make more of a difference." Less of the good life to make a better life? It's a lovely concept, but not everyone's buying it.

*See *Con-Text* on page 561.

CONTEXT

Figures from the U.S. Environmental Protection Agency from 2000 indicate that average fuel economy for all vehicles (various passenger cars, vans, light trucks, SUVs) was 23.6 miles per gallon. For vehicles classified as SUVs, vans, and pickup trucks, the figure was 18 miles per gallon. The five models with the lowest fuel economy were all SUVs. A report by the National Research Council indicates that increasing fuel efficiency results in lower consumption of oil and decreases emissions that contribute to greenhouse gases.

LUXURY FEVER

"[T]he spending of the superrich, though sharply higher than in decades past, still constitutes just a small fraction of total spending. Yet their purchases are far more significant than might appear, for they have been the leading edge of pervasive changes in spending patterns of middle- and even low-income families. The runaway spending at the top has been a virus, one that's spawned a luxury fever that, to one degree or another, has all of us in its grip." Source: Robert H. Frank, *Luxury Fever: Money and Happiness in an Era of Excess* (2000).

Questions for Discussion

1. Deacon discusses both benefits and drawbacks of conspicuous consumption. What are some of these benefits and drawbacks? Do you think Deacon presents a fair picture of conspicuous consumption? Why or why not? **2.** According to Deacon, what is the effect of the excessive consumption of the wealthy on less affluent people? What evidence does he provide to support this claim about the effect of such consumption? How persuasive do you find this evidence? **3.** On the basis of this essay, what do you think is Deacon's idea of "the good life"? What role should consumption play in that life, in Frank's view? Do you think Frank expects that most readers will agree with him on this point? Explain, citing specific passages from the essay to support your answer. **4.** This essay might be considered an example of an argument based on inductive reasoning (see pages 25–26). How effectively do you think Deacon leads us to his conclusion about conspicuous consumption?

③ NORMAN SOLOMON, "Mixed Messages Call for Healthy Skepticism"

Writer Norman Solomon has a very specific answer to the question of what it means to be a consumer: It means being skeptical. In the following essay Solomon examines what he sees as the contradictory messages conveyed by the news media, especially when it comes to issues such as health. For Solomon, who writes a syndicated column on media and politics, these contradictory messages are not just a reason for consumers to be skeptical of media reports; these contradictory messages also reflect a more fundamental problem in the media industry. As Solomon sees it, the media help to create the very health problems they report on, in large part because they support products that are unhealthy and environmentally destructive. In making his argument, Solomon encourages us to cast a skeptical eye on the news media. But perhaps more important, he may prompt us to reexamine our own habits and our beliefs about what it means to be a consumer. Solomon is coauthor (with Reese Erlich) of *Target Iraq: What the News Media Didn't Tell You* (2003). The following essay appeared in his syndicated column in 2003.

Mixed Messages Call for Healthy Skepticism
NORMAN SOLOMON

1 A special issue of *Time*, the nation's biggest newsmagazine, was filled with health information in mid-January, offering plenty of encouragement under the rubric of medical science with an ethereal twist: "How Your Mind Can Heal Your Body."

The spread on "The Power of Mood" begins with this teaser: "Lifting your spirits can be potent medicine. How to make it work for you." An article about "Mother Nature's Little Helpers" is a discussion of alternative remedies. Other pieces probe techniques of psychotherapy, investigate high-tech ways of scanning the brain, and ponder "Are Your Genes to Blame?"

Of course, more than altruism is at work here. While the Jan. 20 issue of *Time* contains page after page of informative journalism, it also includes dozens of lucrative full-color ads pegged to the theme of health. There are elaborate pitches for laxative capsules, a purple pill for heartburn, over-the-counter sinus medication, and prescription drugs for allergies and Alzheimer's. On a preventative note, there's even a full-page ad for an inhaler that "helps you beat cigarette cravings one at a time" and another for a "stop smoking lozenge."

While all this was going on inside *Time* magazine, the same kind of advertising appeared in *Newsweek* to harmonize with its cover's keynote: "What Science Tells Us About Food and Health."

5 We may feel that it's nice of America's largest-circulation news weeklies to print so much healthful information. But if you picked up the previous week's *Time* and turned past the cover, the first thing you saw was a two-page layout for Camels, with the heading "Pleasure to Burn." Like the multi-entendre slogan, the ad's graphic is inviting; a handsome guy, presumably quite debonaire as he stands next to a liquor shelf, lights up a cigarette as he eyes the camera.

And so it goes. Many big media outlets tell us how to make ourselves healthy while encouraging us to make ourselves sick. They offer us tips and new scientific data on how to maximize longevity. But overall complicity with the lethal cigarette industry — whether through glamorization or silence — is widespread and ongoing.

The media's mixed messages about health are unabashedly self-contradictory, but they're also customary to such an extent that they're integral to a media cycle that never quits. The same news organizations that produce innumerable downbeat stories about obesity in America are beholden to huge quantities of ad revenue from fast food — and usually wink at the most popular artery-clogging chains. If most people are ignorant of the deep-fried dangers posed by McDonald's and Burger King, they can thank the news media for dodging the matter.

With television, radio and print media now devoting plenty of coverage to health concerns, and with aging baby boomers serving as a massive demographic target, the media emphasis is tilted toward high-end health expectations. But we need much more than news about the latest theories and scientific findings on preventative measures, palliatives and cures.

FAST FOOD ADVERTISING

"White Castle is credited with being the first fast-food chain, opening the doors to its first restaurant in 1921. Eleven years later, the home of the square, steamed hamburger inaugurated another lasting trend — fast-food advertising — placing coupons in local newspapers.

"Columbus, Ohio–based White Castle has grown to 327 restaurants and $418 million in sales. Restaurant advertising has had its own, even more remarkable growth, topping $3 billion last year. Though the White Castle concept has changed little since 1932, restaurant advertising has become an increasingly sophisticated and high-stakes game.

"Oak Brook, Ill.–based McDonald's Corp. was the single most heavily advertised brand — in any product category — in 1998, according to Competitive Media Reporting, New York, even though the chain's total spending declined 1.2% to $569.2 million. The second most heavily advertised single brand last year also was a fast-food chain, Miami-based Burger King Corp. It, too, cut spending in 1998, reporting a 4.4% drop to $404.6 million.

"In third place was Taco Bell ($202.8 million), followed by Wendy's ($187.3 million) and KFC ($161.6 million).

"Together, these five restaurant chains accounted for nearly 2% of the $79.3 billion in consumer ad spending logged by all U.S. companies in all media, according to CMR data." Source: Paul O'Connor, "Getting the Message," *Restaurants and Institutions* magazine (1999).

Until news outlets shift their commitments, they will continue to undermine
public health as well as promote it. The
present-day contradictions are severe:
Journalists do not equivocate about cancer; we all understand that there's nothing good about the disease. Yet
journalists routinely go easy on proven
causes of cancer, such as cigarettes and
an array of commercially promoted chemicals with carcinogenic effects.
10 Air pollution from gas-guzzling vehicles certainly qualifies as cancer-causing.
But for every drop of ink that explores
such causality, countless gallons are devoted to convincing Americans that they
should own air-fouling trucks or SUVs.
While the health-oriented front covers of
Time and *Newsweek* now on the stands
are similar, the back covers are identical

— an advertisement for Chevy's Silverado diesel truck. The headline trumpets the appeal: "A Sledgehammer in a Ballpeen World."

In a 1986 essay, the American writer Wallace Stegner wrote: "Neither the country nor the society we built out of it can be healthy until we stop raiding and running, and learn to be quiet part of the time, and acquire the sense not of ownership but of belonging."

Such outlooks are antithetical to the functional precepts of the media industry. It is largely dedicated to "raiding and running." It perceives quiet as dead air and squandered space. It portrays ownership as the essence of success and human worth. How healthy can such operative values be?

CONTEXT

This essay appeared in 2003 on the Web site for Fairness and Accuracy in Reporting (FAIR), a national media watch group that describes itself as an anticensorship and progressive organization that "believes that structural reform is ultimately needed to break up the dominant media conglomerates, establish independent public broadcasting and promote strong non-profit sources of information. . . . We maintain a regular dialogue with reporters at news outlets across the country, providing constructive critiques when called for and applauding exceptional, hard-hitting journalism. We also encourage the public to contact media with their concerns, to become media activists rather than passive consumers of news." Consider the extent to which Solomon's essay is consistent with the purpose and perspective of FAIR.

Questions for Discussion

1. Solomon opens this essay with descriptions of the contents and advertising of two issues of *Time* and *Newsweek*, two large and well-known newsmagazines. How effectively do you think these examples illustrate Solomon's claim that "the media's mixed messages about health are unabashedly self-contradictory"?

2. What does Solomon mean by his assertion that the media's mixed messages about health are "integral to a media cycle that never quits"? What exactly is the media cycle to which he refers? Why does it concern Solomon? Do you think his concern is justified? Explain. **3.** On the basis of this essay, identify what you think are Solomon's own views about a healthy lifestyle. Cite specific passages from his essay to support your answer. **4.** This essay originally appeared on a Web site maintained by Fairness and Accuracy in Reporting, a media watch group (see Context above). In what ways do you think this essay is addressed to the kind of readers who might visit the FAIR Web site? Do you think the essay makes an effective argument for a more general audience as well? Why or why not?

④ PETER SINGER, "The Singer Solution to World Poverty"

Do relatively comfortable consumers have any responsibility for people living in poverty? If so, what exactly is that responsibility? Well-known ethicist and philosopher Peter Singer has a very specific and provocative answer to those questions: Singer believes that people who are economically comfortable do indeed have a responsibility for the economic plight of others who may be less fortunate; moreover, he has calculated exactly what that responsibility is in dollar figures. He does so by examining how much money an average person in the United States must have to provide for basic needs. Any additional money, he asserts, is unnecessary and should be used to alleviate the pressing problem of world poverty. Singer's argument will no doubt raise a few eyebrows — especially among readers in the United States, where the consumption of goods is viewed almost as a fundamental right of all Americans. But although you might find Singer's views too extreme or idealistic, his essay challenges us to think about the responsibilities consumers have for others who share our planet. Singer addresses the matter of consumption as an overtly ethical issue. He surely knows that most consumers don't see it that way, and he understands that few Americans will take his advice and willingly give up such a substantial portion of their money to the poor. But he also believes that we must all accept our responsibility for each other. As you read, consider how far you believe that responsibility extends. Peter Singer is the Ira. W. DeCamp Professor of Bioethics at Princeton University and the author of many books about ethics, including *Animal Rights* (1975), *Practical Ethics* (1979), and *One World: The Ethics of Globalization* (2002). The following essay was published in the *New York Times Sunday Magazine* in 1999.

The Singer Solution to World Poverty
PETER SINGER

1 In the Brazilian film *Central Station,* Dora is a retired schoolteacher who makes ends meet by sitting at the station writing letters for illiterate people. Suddenly she has an opportunity to pocket $1,000. All she has to do is persuade a homeless 9-year-old boy to follow her to an address she has been given. (She is told he will be adopted by wealthy foreigners.) She delivers the boy,

gets the money, spends some of it on a television set and settles down to enjoy her new acquisition. Her neighbor spoils the fun, however, by telling her that the boy was too old to be adopted — he will be killed and his organs sold for transplantation. Perhaps Dora knew this all along, but after her neighbor's plain speaking, she spends a troubled night. In the morning Dora resolves to take the boy back.

Suppose Dora had told her neighbor that it is a tough world, other people have nice new TV's too, and if selling the kid is the only way she can get one, well, he was only a street kid. She would then have become, in the eyes of the audience, a monster. She redeems herself only by being prepared to bear considerable risks to save the boy.

At the end of the movie, in cinemas in the affluent nations of the world, people who would have been quick to condemn Dora if she had not rescued the boy go home to places far more comfortable than her apartment. In fact, the average family in the United States spends almost one-third of its income on things that are no more necessary to them than Dora's new TV was to her. Going out to nice restaurants, buying new clothes because the old ones are no longer stylish, vacationing at beach resorts — so much of our income is spent on things not essential to the preservation of our lives and health. Donated to one of a number of charitable agencies, that money could mean the difference between life and death for children in need.

All of which raises a question: In the end, what is the ethical distinction between a Brazilian who sells a homeless child to organ peddlers and an American who already has a TV and upgrades to a better one — knowing that the money could be donated to an organization that

would use it to save the lives of kids in need?

5 Of course, there are several differences between the two situations that could support different moral judgments about them. For one thing, to be able to consign a child to death when he is standing right in front of you takes a chilling kind of heartlessness; it is much easier to ignore an appeal for money to help children you will never meet. Yet for a utilitarian philosopher* like myself — that is, one who judges whether acts are right or wrong by their consequences — if the upshot of the American's failure to donate the money is that one more kid dies on the streets of a Brazilian city, then it is, in some sense, just as bad as selling the kid to the organ peddlers. But one doesn't need to embrace my utilitarian ethic to see that, at the very least, there is a troubling incongruity in being so quick to condemn Dora for taking the child to the organ peddlers while, at the

*Utilitarianism is a school of philosophy that is concerned with identifying the values and actions that will result in the greatest benefit for the most people.

CONTEXT

Originally organized in 1946 as the United Nations International Children's Emergency Fund to aid children who had been affected by World War II, UNICEF became a permanent part of the United Nations in 1953. Its primary mission is to work with governments and non-governmental organizations to address the plight of children living in poverty worldwide. Oxfam America offers financial and technical aid to grassroots organizations around the world in an effort to alleviate poverty, hunger, and injustice.

same time, not regarding the American consumer's behavior as raising a serious moral issue.

In his 1996 book, *Living High and Letting Die,* the New York University philosopher Peter Unger presented an ingenious series of imaginary examples designed to probe our intuitions about whether it is wrong to live well without giving substantial amounts of money to help people who are hungry, malnourished or dying from easily treatable illnesses like diarrhea. Here's my paraphrase of one of these examples:

Bob is close to retirement. He has invested most of his savings in a very rare and valuable old car, a Bugatti, which he has not been able to insure. The Bugatti is his pride and joy. In addition to the pleasure he gets from driving and caring for his car, Bob knows that its rising market value means that he will always be able to sell it and live comfortably after retirement. One day when Bob is out for a drive, he parks the Bugatti near the end of a railway siding and goes for a walk up the track. As he does so, he sees that a runaway train, with no one aboard, is running down the railway track. Looking farther down the track, he sees the small figure of a child very likely to be killed by the runaway train. He can't stop the train and the child is too far away to warn of the danger, but he can throw a switch that will divert the train down the siding where his Bugatti is parked. Then nobody will be killed — but the train will destroy his Bugatti. Thinking of his joy in owning the car and the financial security it represents, Bob decides not to throw the switch. The child is killed. For many years to come, Bob enjoys owning his Bugatti and the financial security it represents.

Bob's conduct, most of us will immediately respond, was gravely wrong.

Unger agrees. But then he reminds us that we, too, have opportunities to save the lives of children. We can give to organizations like UNICEF or Oxfam America. How much would we have to give one of these organizations to have a high probability of saving the life of a child threatened by easily preventable diseases? (I do not believe that children are more worth saving than adults, but since no one can argue that children have brought their poverty on themselves, focusing on them simplifies the issues.) Unger called up some experts and used the information they provided to offer some plausible estimates that include the cost of raising money, administrative expenses and the cost of delivering aid where it is most needed. By his calculation, $200 in donations would help a sickly 2-year-old transform into a healthy 6-year-old — offering safe passage through childhood's most dangerous years. To show how practical philosophical argument can be, Unger even tells his readers that they can easily donate funds by using their credit card and calling one of these toll-free numbers: (800) 367-5437 for Unicef; (800) 693-2687 for Oxfam America.

Now you, too, have the information you need to save a child's life. How should you judge yourself if you don't do it? Think again about Bob and his Bugatti. Unlike Dora, Bob did not have to look into the eyes of the child he was sacrificing for his own material comfort. The child was a complete stranger to him and too far away to relate to in an intimate, personal way. Unlike Dora, too, he did not mislead the child or initiate the chain of events imperiling him. In all these respects, Bob's situation resembles that of people able but unwilling to donate to overseas aid and differs from Dora's situation.

10 If you still think that it was very wrong of Bob not to throw the switch that would have diverted the train and saved the child's life, then it is hard to see how you could deny that it is also very wrong not to send money to one of the organizations listed above. Unless, that is, there is some morally important difference between the two situations that I have overlooked.

Is it the practical uncertainties about whether aid will really reach the people who need it? Nobody who knows the world of overseas aid can doubt that such uncertainties exist. But Unger's figure of $200 to save a child's life was reached after he had made conservative assumptions about the proportion of the money donated that will actually reach its target.

One genuine difference between Bob and those who can afford to donate to overseas aid organizations but don't is that only Bob can save the child on the tracks, whereas there are hundreds of millions of people who can give $200 to overseas aid organizations. The problem is that most of them aren't doing it. Does this mean that it is all right for you not to do it?

Suppose that there were more owners of priceless vintage cars — Carol, Dave, Emma, Fred and so on, down to Ziggy — all in exactly the same situation as Bob, with their own siding and their own switch, all sacrificing the child in order to preserve their own cherished car. Would that make it all right for Bob to do the same? To answer this question affirmatively is to endorse follow-the-crowd ethics — the kind of ethics that led many Germans to look away when the Nazi atrocities were being committed. We do not excuse them because others were behaving no better.

We seem to lack a sound basis for drawing a clear moral line between Bob's situation and that of any reader of this article with $200 to spare who does not donate it to an overseas aid agency. These readers seem to be acting at least as badly as Bob was acting when he chose to let the runaway train hurtle toward the unsuspecting child. In the light of this conclusion, I trust that many readers will reach for the phone and donate that $200. Perhaps you should do it before reading further.

15 Now that you have distinguished yourself morally from people who put their vintage cars ahead of a child's life, how about treating yourself and your partner to dinner at your favorite restaurant? But wait. The money you will spend at the restaurant could also help save the lives of children overseas! True, you weren't planning to blow $200 tonight, but if you were to give up dining out just for one month, you would easily save that amount. And what is one month's dining out, compared to a child's life? There's the rub. Since there are a lot of desperately needy children in the world, there will always be another child whose life you could save for another $200. Are you therefore obliged to keep giving until you have nothing left? At what point can you stop?

Hypothetical examples can easily become farcical. Consider Bob. How far past losing the Bugatti should he go? Imagine that Bob had got his foot stuck in the track of the siding, and if he diverted the train, then before it rammed the car it would also amputate his big toe. Should he still throw the switch? What if it would amputate his foot? His entire leg?

As absurd as the Bugatti scenario gets when pushed to extremes, the point it

*Although there is no universally accepted definition of *middle class,* many economists use income figures to define the term, grouping the middle class around the national income average. For example, one measure sets middle-class annual income in the United States as ranging from about $25,000 to $65,000 per household, which would account for about 70 percent of all Americans. Another measure sets the range as $25,000 to $45,000, which would include about 25 percent of the U.S. population. Some economists and scholars define middle class by using other criteria, such as educational level and the kind of job a person holds or by setting a ratio of income to needs.

raises is a serious one: only when the sacrifices become very significant indeed would most people be prepared to say that Bob does nothing wrong when he decides not to throw the switch. Of course, most people could be wrong; we can't decide moral issues by taking opinion polls. But consider for yourself the level of sacrifice that you would demand of Bob, and then think about how much money you would have to give away in order to make a sacrifice that is roughly equal to that. It's almost certainly much, much more than $200. For most middle-class Americans,* it could easily be more like $200,000.

Isn't it counterproductive to ask people to do so much? Don't we run the risk that many will shrug their shoulders and say that morality, so conceived, is fine for saints but not for them? I accept that we are unlikely to see, in the near or even medium-term future, a world in which it is normal for wealthy Americans to give the bulk of their wealth to strangers. When it comes to praising or blaming people for what they do, we tend to use a standard that is relative to some conception of normal behavior. Comfortably off Americans who give, say, 10 percent of their income to overseas aid organizations are so far ahead of most of their equally comfortable fellow citizens that I wouldn't go out of my way to chastise them for not doing more. Nevertheless, they should be doing much more, and they are in no position to criticize Bob for failing to make the much greater sacrifice of his Bugatti.

At this point various objections may crop up. Someone may say: "If every citizen living in the affluent nations contributed his or her share I wouldn't have to make such a drastic sacrifice, because long before such levels were reached, the resources would have been there to save

the lives of all those children dying from lack of food or medical care. So why should I give more than my fair share?" Another, related, objection is that the Government ought to increase its overseas aid allocations, since that would spread the burden more equitably across all taxpayers.

20 Yet the question of how much we ought to give is a matter to be decided in the real world — and that, sadly, is a world in which we know that most people do not, and in the immediate future will not, give substantial amounts to overseas aid agencies. We know, too, that at least in the next year, the United States Government is not going to meet even the very modest United Nations–recommended target of 0.7 percent of gross national product; at the moment it lags far below that, at 0.09 percent, not even half of Japan's 0.22 percent or a tenth of Denmark's 0.97 percent. Thus, we know that the money we can give beyond that theoretical "fair share" is still going to save lives that would otherwise be lost. While the idea that no one need do more than his or her fair share is a powerful one, should it prevail if we know that others are not doing their fair share and that children will die preventable deaths unless we do more than our fair share? That would be taking fairness too far.

Thus, this ground for limiting how much we ought to give also fails. In the world as it is now, I can see no escape from the conclusion that each one of us with wealth surplus to his or her essential needs should be giving most of it to help people suffering from poverty so dire as to be life-threatening. That's right: I'm saying that you shouldn't buy that new car, take that cruise, redecorate the house or get that pricey new suit.

After all, a $1,000 suit could save five children's lives.

So how does my philosophy break down in dollars and cents? An American household with an income of $50,000 spends around $30,000 annually on necessities, according to the Conference Board, a nonprofit economic research organization. Therefore, for a household bringing in $50,000 a year, donations to help the world's poor should be as close as possible to $20,000. The $30,000 required for necessities holds for higher incomes as well. So a household making $100,000 could cut a yearly check for $70,000. Again, the formula is simple: whatever money you're spending on luxuries, not necessities, should be given away.

Now, evolutionary psychologists tell us that human nature just isn't sufficiently altruistic to make it plausible that many people will sacrifice so much for strangers. On the facts of human nature, they might be right, but they would be wrong to draw a moral conclusion from those facts. If it is the case that we ought to do things that, predictably, most of us won't do, then let's face that fact head-on. Then, if we value the life of a child more than going to fancy restaurants, the next time we dine out we will know that we could have done something better with our money. If that makes living a morally decent life extremely arduous, well, then that is the way things are. If we don't do it, then we should at least know that we are failing to live a morally decent life — not because it is good to wallow in guilt but because knowing where we should be going is the first step toward heading in that direction.

When Bob first grasped the dilemma that faced him as he stood by that railway switch, he must have thought how extraordinarily unlucky he was to be placed in a situation in which he must choose between the life of an innocent child and the sacrifice of most of his savings. But he was not unlucky at all. We are all in that situation.

Questions for Discussion

1. Singer opens this essay with a summary of a Brazilian film entitled *Central Station.* How effectively do you think this summary introduces the issue of poverty that Singer wishes to address? In what ways do you think the example of the film *Central Station* is appropriate for Singer's main argument? Does it matter whether you have seen the film? Explain. **2.** Examine the kinds of items and activities that Singer describes as unnecessary in this essay. What does his description of such things as unnecessary indicate about his values? Do you think most American readers would share those values? Do you think Singer expects that most of his readers would share his values? Explain, citing specific passages from his essay to support your answer. **3.** At one point in his essay, Singer poses the question, "What is the ethical distinction between a Brazilian who sells a homeless child to organ peddlers and an American who already has a TV and upgrades to a better one — knowing that the money could be donated to an organization that would use it to save the lives of kids in need?" How does he answer that question? How would you answer it? **4.** What issues does Singer use the hypothetical example of "Bob" to raise (see paragraphs 7–9)? How effective do you find this

NEGOTIATING DIFFERENCES

As a group, the essays in this cluster raise several complicated questions about what it means to be a consumer. To a degree, though, all of these essays ask you to consider the implications of the choices you make as a consumer in a free market economy. This assignment asks you to explore the implications of your specific decisions as a consumer.

In an essay intended for an audience made up primarily of people who live in your region of the country, examine the effects of a decision to buy a specific item that is commonly available to consumers. For example, in their essays, James Deacon and Peter Singer mention SUVs as questionable choices for consumers who are buying an automobile. You might consider other common items: entertainment equipment such as a television, certain kinds of clothing, services such as wireless telephone service, transportation such as airline travel. Once you have selected the item you wish to focus on, closely examine the reasons that you — or any consumer — might choose to buy that item. Look at the specific choices available for that item — for example, the different kinds of cars you could choose from if you were going to buy a car. Examine as well the possible effects that purchasing that item might have on the local economy, the environ-

example in raising these issues and in supporting Singer's main argument? Would some other kind of example be more effective, in your view? Explain. **5.** Singer addresses his readers directly as "you" throughout this essay, posing ethical dilemmas for his readers to consider. Evaluate the effectiveness of this strategy in helping Singer make his argument. What does he accomplish by addressing readers in this way? What potential drawbacks do you see in this strategy? Do you think Singer intends to make his readers uncomfortable by addressing them in this way? Explain, citing passages from his essay to support your answer. **6.** How does Singer arrive at the specific amount of money that he believes middle-class Americans should contribute to the poor? What purposes do you think his numerical calculations serve in supporting his argument? Do you think Singer is serious about the specific amount of money he believes Americans should give to the poor? Cites specific passages in the essay to support your answer. **7.** What counterarguments could you offer to Singer's proposal?

ment, your health, and the well-being of your neighbors or community. You might have to do some research to learn about such effects, and you might consider interviewing people who have made such a purchase. Once you have explored these matters, write an essay in which you make an argument about your responsibilities as a consumer. Use the item you have selected as an example to help make your argument.

Alternatively, select one of the essays in this cluster and write an argument in response to it. In your response, summarize the main argument of the essay you are responding to, identify the central issue that is being ad-

dressed in that essay, and explain why you think that the essay does not adequately address that issue. Offer an alternative approach to addressing the issue. For example, you might disagree with Peter Singer that contributing a significant portion of your income to the poor is an adequate way to address poverty. In responding to Singer, identify what you see as the central problem to be solved, and offer an alternative to his proposal. Be sure to justify your alternative on practical and ethical grounds.

CLUSTER **3**

HOW SHOULD WORKERS
BE TREATED?

In 1905 several American labor activists, frustrated by the fragmented nature of the labor movement in the United States, organized a convention in Chicago in the hope of creating a new, more powerful and effective union representing all workers. Out of that convention was born the Industrial Workers of the World (IWW), which held a radical, anticapitalist view of labor and advocated a socialist system of worker-owned businesses. The radical perspective of the IWW was evident in the Manifesto on Organizing the Industrial Workers of the World, which was adopted at the 1905 convention and which called for "resistance to capitalist tyranny" by workers. (See *Con-Text* on page 585.) Members of the IWW, who came to be known as "the Wobblies," were active participants in the labor struggles of the early 20th century, which sometimes turned violent. However, the IWW never achieved the widespread membership it sought, and by the second half of the 20th century, other unions, such as United Auto Workers and the Teamsters, had acquired much greater power and influence. ■ The labor movement in the United States has steadily declined in membership and influence since the turbulent early days of the IWW. Nevertheless, as the free market economic system has become established worldwide since the 1980s, some of the concerns of the Wobblies about the conditions of workers and their diminishing control over their working lives are as valid as ever. Those concerns have taken on new forms, notably in sweatshops in which workers, many of whom are children, make expensive consumer goods, such as trendy clothing and athletic shoes, for wages that are sometimes as low as pennies a day. In the late 1990s activists called attention to the conditions of these workers by publicizing the fact that several very successful companies, such as Nike, were contracting with such sweatshops to produce their popular and pricey products. These activists called for consumers to boycott companies whose products were manufactured in sweatshops. In some cases, as a result of these boycotts, embarrassed corporate executives discontinued contracts with sweatshops. ■ These recent efforts to bring attention to the plight of workers recall the struggles of the Wobblies and other labor activists in the early 20th century. But as several of the essays in this cluster reveal, the problems associated with sweatshops — and issues related to labor conditions in general — are not always straightforward. In some cases the wages that are paid to factory workers in developing nations, which seem pitifully low by U.S. standards, are actually lucrative in comparison with the wages of other workers in those nations. Moreover, in some regions child labor is not looked on as exploitation in the same way that it is in the United States. These issues highlight the complexities of questions about fair wages and ethical labor practices. What exactly is a "fair wage"? How do we decide? *Who* decides? In some ways the answers to these questions are no easier to find today than they were when the Wobblies formed their union in the early 20th century. ■ As you read the essays in this cluster, consider how the definition of *worker* relates to specific historical and cultural contexts. Consider, too, how our values regarding work and fairness might be related to those historical and cultural contexts. Understanding these complex relationships could be essential if we are to negotiate the differences we have regarding work, which is so central to the lives of so many people.

CON-TEXT: "Industrial Workers of the World"

1 The worker, wholly separated from the land and the tools, with his skill of craftsmanship rendered useless, is sunk in the uniform mass of wage slaves. He sees his power of resistance broken by craft divisions, perpetuated from outgrown industrial stages. His wages constantly grow less as his hours grow longer and monopolized prices grow higher. Shifted hither and thither by the demands of profit-takers, the laborer's home no longer exists. In this hopeless condition he is forced to accept whatever humiliating conditions his master may impose. He is subjected to a physical and intellectual examination more searching than was the chattel slave when sold upon the auction block. Laborers are no longer classified by differences in trade skill, but the employer assigns them according to the machines to which they are attached. These divisions, far from representing differences in skill or interests among the laborers, are imposed by the employers so that the workers may be pitted against one another and spurred to greater exertion in the shop, and that all resistance to capitalist tyranny may be weakened by artificial distinctions.

SOURCE: *Manifesto on Organizing the Industrial Workers of the World* (1905).

① NICHOLAS KRISTOF, "Let Them Sweat"

In the 1990s activist groups began to call attention to the fact that several high-profile U.S. companies were manufacturing their products in factories located in developing nations where wages paid to workers seemed abysmally low and working conditions were sometimes terrible. In some cases efforts to boycott these products resulted in decisions by American companies to stop manufacturing their products in these "sweatshops," both in the United States and abroad. At first glance, such decisions seem to represent progress in international efforts to improve working conditions for all workers. After all, sweatshops seem to exploit workers, and closing them down or reforming them should lead to better wages and conditions for workers. But columnist Nicholas Kristof offers a different view. He argues that sweatshops, which have become a dirty word in many Western nations, can actually benefit the very same workers that advocacy groups describe as "exploited." Writing in the summer of 2002, when representatives of the world's leading economic powers — the so-called G-8 — were preparing to meet in Canada, Kristof cites examples of individual workers to illustrate the potential benefits of factories that are called "sweatshops." He urges the G-8 leaders to look carefully at such examples, and he accuses anti-sweatshop activists of ignoring the realities of the lives of the people they claim to be helping. In doing so, he reminds us that when it comes to working conditions and fair wages, what might be exploitation in one context could be something very different in another. This essay was originally published in the *New York Times*.

Let Them Sweat
NICHOLAS KRISTOF

*The United Nations Population Fund is a U.N. education and aid initiative focused on family planning and reproductive health. Because its efforts include contraception, it has been controversial in the United States, and in 2002 the U.S. government withheld monies that were appropriated for the fund.

1 When the G-8 leaders meet this week, cowering in a Canadian mountain resort beyond the reach of organized anarchists, here's a way for them to bolster terror-infested third world countries like Pakistan.

They should start an international campaign to promote imports from sweatshops, perhaps with bold labels depicting an unrecognizable flag and the words "Proudly Made in a Third World Sweatshop!"

The Gentle Reader will think I've been smoking Pakistani opium. But the fact is that sweatshops are the only hope of kids like Ahmed Zia, a 14-year-old boy here in Attock, a gritty center for carpet weaving.

Ahmed, who dropped out of school in the second grade, earns $2 a day hunched over the loom, laboring over a rug that will adorn some American's living room. It is a pittance, but the American campaign against sweatshops could make his life much more wretched by inadvertently encouraging mechanization that could cost him his job.

5 "Carpet-making is much better than farm work," Ahmed said, mulling alternatives if he loses his job as hundreds of others have over the last year. "This makes much more money and is more comfortable."

Indeed, talk to third world factory workers and the whole idea of "sweat-shops" seems a misnomer. It is farmers and brick-makers who really sweat under the broiling sun, while sweatshop workers merely glow.

The third world is already battered by heartless conservatives in the West who peddle arms and cigarettes or who (like the Bushies) block $34 million desperately needed for maternal and infant health by the United Nations Population Fund.* So it's catastrophic for muddle-minded liberals to join in and cudgel impoverished workers for whom a sweatshop job is the first step on life's escalator.

By this point, I've offended every possible reader. But before you spurn a shirt made by someone like 8-year-old Kamis Saboor, an Afghan refugee whose father is dead and who is the sole breadwinner in the family, answer this question: How does shunning sweatshop products help Kamis? All the alternatives for him are worse.

"I dream of a job in a factory," said Noroz Khan, who lives on a garbage dump and spends his days searching for metal that he can sell to recyclers. He earns about $1.40 a day, and children earn just 30 cents a day for scrounging barefoot in the filth — a few feet away from us, birds were pecking at the bloated carcass of a cow, its feet in the air.

10 Of course, Western anti-sweatshop activists mean well and aim only for improved conditions and a "living wage" (see "Complication" on page 588). But the reality is that the bad publicity becomes one more headache for companies considering operating in international hellholes (where the only lure is wages so low that it would be embarrassing if

journalists started asking questions about them), and so manufacturers opt to mechanize their operations and operate in somewhat more developed countries.

For example, Nike has 35 contract factories in Taiwan, 49 in South Korea, only 3 in Pakistan and none at all in Afghanistan — if it did, critics would immediately fulminate about low wages, glue vapors, the mistreatment of women.

But the losers are the Afghans, and especially Afghan women. The country is full of starving widows who can find no jobs. If Nike hired them at 10 cents an hour to fill all-female sweatshops, they and their country would be hugely better off.

Nike used to have two contract factories in impoverished Cambodia, among the neediest countries in the world. Then there was an outcry after BBC reported that three girls in one factory were under 15 years old. So Nike fled controversy by ceasing production in Cambodia.

CONTEXT

Originally formed in the late 1970s as the Group of Seven, the Group of Eight (G-8) is composed of the original G-7 members — Canada, France, Germany, Italy, Japan, the United Kingdom, and the United States — and Russia, which joined the group in 1997. Excluding Russia, these countries account for about two thirds of the world's economic output. Representatives from these nations have met annually since 1976 to discuss global economic and social issues. In June 2002, G-8 representatives met in the western Canadian province of Alberta. The meetings became the focus of large protests by various advocacy groups and nongovernmental organizations (NGOs) that are opposed to many of the economic and trade policies adopted by the G-8. Anti-sweatshop advocacy groups were among those protesting G-8 policies on trade and labor.

C O M P L I C A T I O N

In 2002 the Global Exchange, an advocacy group for workers' rights and social justice, released a report on conditions in Asian factories where Nike shoes are made. That report concluded that "although some improvements have been made in working conditions in sport shoe factories producing for Nike and Adidas Salomon in Indonesia, the measures taken fall well short of ensuring that workers are able to live with dignity." According to the report, these workers earn about $2 per day working full time and are unable to support their families without incurring debt. In addition, workers report being threatened and even assaulted if they speak with labor organizers. Source: Timothy Connor, "We Are Not Machines" Global Exchange, www. globalexchange.org/campaigns/sweatshops/nike/machines. (2002).

The result was that some of the 2,000 Cambodians (90 percent of them young women) who worked in those factories faced layoffs. Some who lost their jobs probably were ensnared in Cambodia's huge sex slave industry — which leaves many girls dead of AIDS by the end of their teenage years.

15 The G-8 leaders will never dare, of course, begin a pro-sweatshop campaign. But at a summit that will discuss how to bring stability and economic growth to some of the world's poorest nations, it would be a start if Westerners who denounce sweatshops would think less of feel-good measures for themselves and more about how any of this helps people like Ahmed and Kamis.

Questions for Discussion

1. In his third paragraph Kristof refers to his audience as "Gentle Reader." Why do you think he does so? How does that phrase relate to the overall tone of this essay? What effect do you think Kristof intends to have on readers with such a phrase? What effect did that phrase have on you? What might your answer to that question indicate about you as a reader? **2.** In paragraph 8 Kristof writes that he has "offended every possible reader." What does he mean by that statement? Do you think he intends his readers to take it literally? In what ways might he have offended readers? Did he offend you in any way? Explain, citing specific passages from his essay to support your answer. **3.** Examine the way Kristof uses the examples of Ahmed Zia and Kamis Saboor. What information does he provide about these two children? What specific details about their lives does he include in his descriptions of them? What effect do you think these details might have on American readers? What effect did they have on you? Do you think Kristof intended such effects on his readers? Explain. What kind of appeal is he making here? (To answer this question, you might refer to the discussion of different kinds of argument strategies in Chapter 2.) **4.** Kristof describes the anti-sweatshop measures proposed by activists as "feel-good measures." What evidence does he provide to support this claim? Do you think he is right? Explain. How does this claim fit into his main argument about sweatshops? **5.** Kristof wrote this essay in the summer of 2002, when the G-8 leaders (see Context on page 587) were meeting to discuss global economic issues and were facing protests about policies related to sweatshops and working conditions in developing nations. Examine the influence of that historical context on his argument. In what ways is his argument connected specifically to that context? In what ways is his argument related to more general issues that go beyond the G-8 meetings in 2002?

② LINDA HALES, "Rugmaking, Interwoven with Social Justice"

When you buy something, do you think about where and by whom it was made? If your answer is no, then you are in good company. As journalist Linda Hales points out in the following essay, the vast majority of consumers admit that they wouldn't change their decisions about buying an item even if they knew the item was produced in a sweatshop or by child labor. But Hales doesn't want to leave the issue there. Her essay examines some efforts to encourage companies to buy products that are certified to have been made by workers who have not been exploited. Such efforts, especially by a nonprofit organization called Rugmark, are an attempt to use the free market to foster social change. Organizations such as Rugmark hope to improve the lives of workers at the same time that companies can realize profits from their sales and consumers can buy what they want. It is an ambitious goal. As Hales writes at the end of her essay, "In an imperfect world, there are no easy answers, only questions waiting be asked." Her essay raises some of those questions. And it might help you to begin to answer them as well. Linda Hales is a staff writer for the *Washington Post,* in which this essay appeared in 2002.

Rugmaking, Interwoven with Social Justice
LINDA HALES

CONTEXT

In the late 1990s, as activists called attention to poor conditions in factories that produce goods for large clothing corporations, several advocacy groups focused their publicity efforts on the Gap, one of the world's largest clothing manufacturers. One group, Behind the Label, accused the Gap of "creating a global sweatshop system" by having its products manufactured in hundreds of factories where workers are low paid and often claim to be mistreated. For information on the sweatshop controversy involving Nike, a large athletic shoe company, see Complication on page 588.

1 Interior design makes an unlikely companion for social activism. But the era of globalization has linked the two with tiny hand-tied knots. A rug cannot be beautiful if you know it was made with a child's forced labor. Unless, of course, you don't mind leaving your footprints in an innocent's sweat and blood.

As First World prosperity collides with Third World poverty, fashion brands such as Nike and the Gap have been blistered by controversies over foreign sweatshops. Now, it's the turn of the age-old rug-making business. Demand for beauty on our floors provides des-

perately needed employment in rural villages in India, Pakistan and Nepal. No one doubts that Afghanistan's revival will prove challenging. But who is tending the looms, under what conditions, and how will you know? And if you know, how much will you care?

At the Phillips Collection, art patrons can peer guilt-free at the paintings. That's because the pale green or gold or apricot rugs underfoot have been certified by their maker to be slave labor-free.

The Phillips, like the J. Paul Getty Museum* in Los Angeles, chose its carpets from the company founded by Stephanie Odegard (see gloss on page 590). The former Peace Corps worker and World Bank consultant has devoted the

*Located in Washington, D.C., the Phillips Collection is the oldest museum of modern art in the United States. The J. Paul Getty Museum in Los Angeles holds one of the country's foremost art collections.

†For more information about Rugmark, visit www.rugmark.org.

past 15 years to socially conscious rugmaking. Luxurious Himalayan and New Zealand wool and silk are colored with vegetable dyes in a range of 900 hues, then knotted by skilled artisans Odegard encountered as a consultant in Nepal. The finished works are subtle, stunningly beautiful and politically correct. A percentage of sales is directed back to Nepal to rehabilitate children rescued from illegal situations.

5 Odegard is a member of the nonprofit Rugmark Foundation,† created eight years ago by Indian activist Kailash Satyarthi to exert consumer pressure on the rug industry in India, Pakistan and Nepal. The extent of the problem is hard to quantify, whether trying to document children in bondage or under legal working age. But suffice to say that some companies have agreed to independent inspection of looms in return for a label that identifies their goods to customers.

I met Satyarthi and Odegard a few days apart. He blitzed through between human rights meetings in Brazil and appearances in New York, but posed a provocative question relevant to interior design: "Why can't you think about designing the future of a child?"

Odegard spoke at the Washington Design Center, where her company has a showroom. She would be the first to agree that in much of the world, life is not as soft as lamb's wool. And yet, she makes no apology for the price of rugs that may cost $14,000 apiece.

"I think we're very privileged to live in a time when we can make some impact by what we buy," she says.

In other words, put your money where your heart is. Rugmark's poster shows a Nepalese schoolgirl named Laxmi Shresta, who was found rolling wool for her mother at the age of 6. She was rescued and now attends a Rugmark-funded school.

10 Against this emotional backdrop, rational counterarguments pale. Conscientious American importers such as Chris Walter of Yayla Tribal Rugs in Cambridge, Mass., take pains to explain that child labor is a fact of life. Walter has founded his own project, Cultural Survival, to help Tibetan refugees. He says he has never encountered children in bondage but has heard such conditions exist. More often, families work together at the loom. If children weren't working on rugs, they could fall into worse pursuits.

Carol Bier, a research associate at the Textile Museum, argues persuasively that carpet weaving, which relies on numerical combinations to achieve patterns, has untapped potential to teach geometry and algebra — in other words, propel Third World children into the digital age. She points out that loom technology led "directly and incontrovertibly" to the development of computers. "The issue, the way it's being treated by Rugmark people," she says, "is completely not cognizant of this other end of the spectrum."

Rugmark deserves credit for generating concern in the first place. In Nepal, 70 percent of the carpetmaking industry is said to be enrolled in Rugmark. In India and Pakistan the percentage is far lower, but competing programs and labels have materialized. Mass-market importers such as Ikea and Pottery Barn take the issue seriously. Williams-Sonoma, parent company of Pottery Barn, insists that vendors and suppliers abide by "a prohibition against, among other things, hiring underage workers directly or through middlemen or agents, prison or forced labor, manufacturing conditions that expose workers to immediate risk of injury, or payment of below-minimum wage."

Underlying any labeling system is the belief that if consumers only knew, they would act. Marsha Dickson, an associate professor of apparel, textiles and interior design at Kansas State University, isn't so sure. After a Senate debate over clothing sweatshops raised the question, she conducted a survey to find out how much impact a "No Sweat" label would have on the purchase of a shirt. A paltry 16 percent of respondents said that knowledge

of working conditions would outweigh issues of color, fabric or price.

"When you had to decide between something really dear to you, working conditions was not up there," she says. 15 Dickson points out, "Children work for a reason.

"Certainly we have a right to ask, but if we ask, we have a responsibility to understand that whole picture. The root problem is poverty. What do you do about poverty?"

Perhaps the worst thing a caring consumer could do would be to deprive families of income by not buying a handmade rug.

In an imperfect world, there are no easy answers, only questions waiting to be asked.

COMPLICATION

"Thus far Rugmark is a success story. But new challenges are inevitably already emerging. A sizeable number of carpet manufacturers, for example, are stealthily shifting their weaving operations into the neighbouring state of Bihar [where Rugmark does not carry out factory inspections]. . . .

"'Since I was seven years of age,' says 13-year-old Ansari of Garhwa, 'I have been working on the loom owned by my maternal uncle. Then his manufacturer asked him to shift the loom to a safer place where there were no raids or surprise checks by child-rights activists. I am paid 1,000 rupees ($28) for one *gaheha* (carpet), which normally takes three to four months to weave, and for it I have to work 12 to 16 hours a day on the loom.' . . .

"Rugmark needs to broaden its areas of operation. Otherwise looms will continue to shift to alternative 'catchment areas' where child labour is in abundance." Source: Mukul Sharma, "Marked for Life" *New Internationalist* (1997).

Questions for Discussion

1. How would you summarize Hales's main argument in this essay? What primary strategy does she use to make this argument? **2.** Describe Hales's writing style, identifying specific words and phrases that you think illustrate her style. How does her style contribute to her main argument? How effective do you find her writing style? **3.** At one point in her essay, Hales writes that against the emotional backdrop of stories like that of Nepalese schoolgirl Laxmi Shresta, "rational counterarguments pale." What specific counterarguments does Hales present in this essay? Do you think she presents these counterarguments fairly? Explain. Do you think she is right that these counterarguments "pale" when situations like that of Laxmi Shreta are considered? Why or why not? **4.** At the end of her essay, Hales writes that "there are no easy answers, only questions waiting to be asked." To what extent do you think her essay supports that statement? **5.** Do you think this essay might be described as an example of a Rogerian argument? Explain, citing specific passages from the essay to support your answer. (In answering this question, you might wish to refer to the discussion of Rogerian argument on page 19–21.)

③ JIM HIGHTOWER, "Going Down the Road"

If we accept the idea that all workers should be paid adequately and treated fairly, then it is easy to con-clude that sweatshops — factories where workers labor under poor and even abusive conditions for very low pay — should somehow be eliminated. But how? That question is a complicated one, especially in a free market, in which companies work for profits partly by keeping their labor costs low. In other words, paying workers less money might be good for companies. That is one reason that political observer Jim Hightower believes that the problem of sweatshops will not be addressed by government regulations intended to force businesses to treat workers better. In the following essay, Hightower proposes an alternative approach: us-ing the free market itself to create demand for goods that are produced in socially responsible ways. Using the example of a company called SweatX, Hightower argues that companies can compensate workers ade-quately and still realize profits. In effect, Hightower suggests that business success and social improvement can go hand in hand. Whether or not you agree with him, his essay might challenge you to think about the responsibilities of employers as well as consumers for the fair treatment of workers. A former Commissioner of Agriculture in Texas, Jim Hightower writes essays about social and political issues for radio and print. This essay appeared in *The Nation* in 2002.

Going Down the Road
JIM HIGHTOWER

CONTEXT

The minimum wage in the United States in 2002 was set at $5.15 per hour, al-though that figure was higher in some states. According to the U.S. Department of Labor, the average hourly wage for all workers in the U.S. in 2003 was about $15.

1 A couple of years ago, Susan DeMarco and I were doing our radio talk show, Chat & Chew, on the topic of sweatshop goods. A lady from Jackson, Mississippi, called to say that whenever she goes into a store to shop for clothing, she always tries to find a manager and asks, "Can you tell me where your made-in-the-USA section is?" Good question. Go into any clothing department and everything in there — from overcoats to undies, hats to shoes — bears labels that shout: made in China, Bangladesh, El Salvador, the Philippines . . . everywhere but the US of A. This is not only in the Wal-Marts and Targets but also in the upscale Talbotses and Abercrombie & Fitches.

It's not that Americans are unable to make quality stuff, but the ugly fact is that corporations have abandoned US workers and communities in hot pursuit of ever-fatter profits, rushing off to the lowest-wage hellholes they can find to cut and sew their garments. Instead of paying even a minimum wage of $5.15 an hour here, they can get wage slaves at 13 cents an hour in China — then ship the goods back here without lowering the price they charge us. The corporations gleefully pocket the difference in labor costs — and claim that this is the "magic" of the new global market at work. It is certainly magic for them.

For us it is globaloney — just the same old greed. But what's a consumer to do? Even if a garment is made in the United States, some companies also run sweatshops here, with workers, usually recent immigrants, crammed into basement "contract shops," making less than minimum wage. How can we combat the scourge of sweatshops everywhere? Government could take action, but even under Bill Clinton, it was Nike, Gap, Ralph Lauren and other bigwigs that dominated the discussion, so Washington did nothing but dabble and dawdle. Of course, under King George the W, even discussion has stopped.

SweatX Is Chic

The good news is that people themselves — especially children and young people — see sweatshops as a moral abomination, putting them (yet again) well ahead of officialdom. Major groups like United Students Against Sweatshops, the National Labor Committee, Global Exchange and the garment union UNITE have been aggressively exposing, agitating and organizing against sweatshop labor. As this political organizing expands, an important assault on sweatshops has come from the one place the multibillion-dollar industry least expects: The marketplace itself.

5 SweatX is a new brand of garment in every sense of the word. The Hot Fudge Social Venture Fund,* set up by Ben Cohen, the puckish entrepreneur and social activist of Ben & Jerry's ice cream fame, has invested $1 million to date in a brand-new garment business

*For information on SweatX and the Hot Fudge Social Venture Fund, visit www.sweatx.net.

in Los Angeles. The business, called teamX, is based on a thoroughly radical principle: "Garment workers don't have to be exploited in order to operate a financially successful apparel factory." Imagine. Inspired and informed by Spain's Mondragon Industrial Cooperatives (a fifty-year-old network of successful employee-owned businesses: www.mcc.es), teamX is organized as a worker-owned co-op that (1) is a union shop organized by UNITE; (2) pays a living wage starting at $8.50 an hour; (3) provides good healthcare, a pension and a share of profits through co-op ownership; (4) practices the "solidarity ratio," in which no executive is paid more than eight times what the lowest-paid worker gets; and (5) intends to make a profit, grow and spread its progressive seed.

This is no touchie-feelie, froufrou social exercise but a bottom-line business initiative to show that doing well can also mean doing good. Pierre Ferrari's twenty-five years in the corporate world ranges from being VP of Coca-Cola to being director of Ben & Jerry's . . . to now being CEO of teamX. These entrepreneurial folks believed that there had to be a better way than sweatshops. Ferrari immersed himself in the economics of garment production. His most shocking (and enlightening) discovery was that a sweatshop worker in the United States gets about 25 cents to make a T-shirt that retails for as much as 18 bucks. Let's say that a worker grosses about $9,000 a year. Poverty. What if you doubled the wage — to 50 cents per shirt? The increase would not affect the buyer, but that worker would suddenly be getting $18,000 a year. Not exactly a fortune, but a livable wage. "Come on," says Ferrari, "they're exploiting people for a lousy 25 cents?"

Building the Brand

This March, twenty teamX employee-owners, many of whom previously had been sweatshop workers, began production in Los Angeles on their company's first line of stylish shirts, shorts, caps and other casual wear, working with state-of-the-art equipment in a brand-new factory. "I've been working in clothing for twenty years, and I never had a paid holiday before this," one of the employees told the *Los Angeles Times*. A small, experienced team of managers has been assembled, drawing especially on some older managers who are not merely chasing bucks but looking to add a moral dimension to their work lives.

To build the brand identity, teamX is initially targeting the activist community — campuses, unions, churches, local governments, nonprofits, etc. (The T-shirts for my Rolling Thunder Downhome Democracy Tour[†] proudly bear the SweatX label.) This "market of conscience" alone has a huge and virtually untapped potential — as Ferrari discovered, for example, unions buy a lot of T-shirts for rallies, organizing drives and such. After Oprah recently featured teamX on her show, the phones began ringing off the hook with orders, and Ferrari now expects this upstart startup to break even by July — an investment miracle by anyone's standards.

By tapping this growing market of conscience, SweatX not only can be successful but will put the lie to the garment industry's cynical assertion that low wages are an inevitable component of globalization. We can help by talking to our local organizations, clothing store managers, school board members and others, introducing them to the SweatX possibility (www.sweatx.net), showing with our dollars that commerce and conscience can cohabitate.

[†]Begun in 2002, the Rolling Thunder Down-Home Democracy Tour is a series of festivals around the United States featuring music and speeches by well-known progressive political activists about current social and political issues (see www. rollingthundertour.org).

Questions for Discussion

1. What is Hightower's view of American corporations and of business in general? How does that view fit into his main argument about the problem of sweatshops? How do you think American readers would react to his view of business? How did you react? **2.** What sets SweatX apart from other clothing manufacturers, according to Hightower? Why are these differences important? **3.** Hightower rests his main argument on the example of SweatX. How effective is this example in illustrating Hightower's argument? What disadvantages can you see in using this example as Hightower does? What counterarguments can you offer to his argument about SweatX? **4.** What fundamental principles do you think Hightower holds when it comes to work? How do these principles shape his main argument? Do you think most American readers share these principles? Explain, citing specific passages from his text in your answer. **5.** This essay was published in *The Nation*, a political affairs magazine that is known for its liberal viewpoint. Citing specific passages from his essay, identify some ways in which Hightower's essay reflects *The Nation's* editorial slant. Do you think Hightower wrote this essay specifically for an audience with liberal political views? Why or why not?

④ CINDY RICHARDS, **"Just Another Hollow Day"**

Many Americans associate Labor Day with the end of summer and the beginning of the new school year. Since its establishment as a national holiday in 1894, Labor Day has come to mean backyard barbeques, small-town parades, and baseball games. But writer Cindy Richards reminds us that Labor Day originated as a celebration of workers and the labor movement, and she laments what she believes is the loss of that meaning. Richards uses the occasion of the Labor Day holiday to examine the condition of working Americans in the first few years of the 21st century. She is concerned that as membership in labor unions has declined since the middle of the 20th century, so have the fortunes of the average worker. For Richards, Labor Day is a sad reminder of the influence that labor unions once had – but no longer do – to improve the working lives of Americans. Not all Americans would lament the decline of labor unions; indeed, many believe that Americans are better off without powerful unions. But Richards' essay encourages us to consider the history of labor in the United States in order to assess our present circumstances. Her essay was published in the *Chicago Sun-Times* in 2002.

Just Another Hollow Day
CINDY RICHARDS

*In July 2002, nine miners were trapped in a coal mine in western Pennsylvania after an explosion flooded the shaft they were working in, cutting off their escape route. They waited for 77 hours in a cramped, cold, and wet mineshaft as rescuers dug a tunnel to free them. Extensive media coverage brought the ultimately successful rescue efforts to American households.

1 Perhaps it is time we stopped celebrating Labor Day. I'm not saying we should give up a holiday. Never. We still should take off on the first Monday of September. But we should give it a new name and celebrate something really important to America. Perhaps we could celebrate Shareholders' Day. Or honor investors. Or commemorate capital gains.

But using that day as a pretense to honor working people seems so out of touch with American realities. A country that has so little regard for workers, and even less for unions, should give up Labor Day.

This holiday, which traditionally marks the end of summer, has its roots as a celebration of unionization, of the power of workers who band together to give themselves a stronger voice (see "Context" on page 598).

Oh, we Americans continue to pay lip service to the hardworking tradition of working people.

5 We admire the nine Pennsylvania miners for their grit and determination to survive as the waters in the collapsed mine crept ever higher.*

We sing the praises of the struggling single mom who got herself off welfare and still keeps her kids on the straight and narrow.

and importance by taking our cell phones, pagers and laptops with us wherever we go so we can always be on call and in touch.

What we don't do often enough is ask: Why?

Why were those miners trapped in a collapsed mine? Why was the map they were using so tragically wrong? Why, in the 21st century, do some people still have to risk their lives to make a decent living for their families?

10 Why do we force single welfare moms to put their kids in day care so they can spend eight hours a day working at some dead-end, minimum-wage job? If those women were middle class and chose to put their children in high-quality day care while they worked at good jobs, we would scorn them as bad moms.

And why, after everything we have seen in the last two decades, do we continue to delude ourselves into believing that we are indispensable to our employers?

And we fool ourselves into thinking that we are vital to the future of our employers, demonstrating our commitment

When the economy is booming, the bosses are writing themselves multimillion dollar checks while doling out 2 per-

---

CONTEXT

The U.S. Department of Labor describes Labor Day as "a creation of the labor movement . . . dedicated to the social and economic achievements of American workers." However, its origins lie in labor unrest and conflict between workers and the U.S. government. The first Labor Day celebration, which was held in New York City on September 5, 1882, was organized by the Central Labor Union. Over the next decade, other cities organized similar celebrations, and many states began to recognize Labor Day as an official holiday. By the early 1890s, labor unions were pushing for a national holiday. But those years were also marked by labor unrest as unions vied with companies to improve working conditions and wages for workers. In 1894, the infamous Pullman strike in Pullman, Illinois erupted into violence, and President Grover Cleveland ordered 12,000 U.S. troops to the town. Eventually the strike was broken, but not before several workers were killed when U.S. marshals fired into a crowd of protesters. Later that year, during which Grover Cleveland sought re-election, the U.S. Congress passed a law establishing Labor Day as a national legal holiday. Many believed that the law was passed to appease angry workers in the wake of the Pullman strike.

cent and 3 percent raises to the workers. When the economy is crashing, the bosses are writing themselves multi-million dollar checks while doling out pink slips to workers and canceling health insurance coverage for retirees.

Yet we maintain this ruse of honoring workers on Labor Day. This holiday was founded in 1882 as a way to celebrate American labor unions. But interest in honoring labor organizations has declined along with labor organizing.

These days, only 9 percent of workers at private employers are members of labor unions. Add to that the 37.4 percent of government workers who are union

EXECUTIVE COMPENSATION

In the 1990s, as the stock market soared, executives at many large corporations received lucrative compensation packages. But during the economic downturn in the first few years of the 21st century, many critics complained that executives continued to receive lavish compensation while their companies lost money and their workers suffered. According to the American Federation of Labor, in 2002 median pay for chief executive officers (CEOs) increased by 6 percent, which was more than twice the growth in workers' wages for that year. According to the advocacy group United for a Fair Economy (see www.ufenet.org), in 2001 the average CEO was paid 411 times what that average worker earned; in 1982, that figure was 42-to-1.

COMPLICATION

Although Richards laments the decline in union membership over the past two decades, some scholars see this decline as an inevitable result of the evolving global economy. For example, Michael Goldfeld suggests that as the economy has developed into a technology-driven, service-oriented economy, workers' situations have changed and working conditions have improved, thus lessening the need for labor unions. He describes these changes as "part of the natural development of capitalism" (*The Decline of Organized Labor in the United States*, 1987).

*In the 19th century, various labor unions in the United States advocated limiting the workday to eight hours, and several regional and national movements attempted to persuade Congress and state governments to pass laws to establish an eight-hour workday. In the 1880s the Knights of Labor was instrumental in organizing a national campaign to establish an eight-hour workday. During the following decades, various states implemented laws limiting the length of the workday, but Congress didn't establish a national standard until 1938, when it passed the Fair Labor Standards Act, which limited the work week to 44 hours. An amendment to that act in 1940 set the federal work week at 40 hours.

members (that number is so much higher because of the high unionization rates among police officers, firefighters and teachers), and you get an overall American unionization rate of a dismal 13.5 percent. That is down from a high of just over 20 percent in 1983.

15 As unions have fallen out of favor, the meaning of Labor Day has shifted. Rather than celebrate the gains of labor unions — big, important gains such as the eight-hour workday,* paid vacation and employer-provided health insurance — the holiday now focuses on the glorification of work itself and the individuals who work so hard and risk so much and too often get so little in return.

Some people see this shift in the meaning of Labor Day as the embodiment of American individualism. I see it as proof that as the power of Big Labor has declined, so have the fortunes of average Americans. And that is nothing to celebrate.

NEGOTIATING DIFFERENCES

The essays in this cluster suggest that arguments about issues related to work are really about fundamental questions about how we want to live together. For example, controversies about sweatshops often revolve around questions about the right of individual workers to be treated fairly and compensated adequately for their labor. But determining what it is fair or adequate can be difficult indeed. The challenge in such controversies is to find agreement about these complicated questions of fairness. This assignment asks you to take up that challenge.

Identify a current controversy related to work that you think is important. You might choose an issue from one of the readings in this cluster — for example, the controversy surrounding sweatshop labor. Or you might choose a similar issue related to work and the conditions of workers' lives. For example, recently there have been controversies about increasing the minimum wage for workers, establishing a living wage for all workers, and providing universal health care for all workers. Each of these controversies raises difficult questions about what is fair for workers but

Questions for Discussion

1. Why does Richards call the celebration of the Labor Day holiday a "ruse"? What evidence does she offer to support the use of that term to describe this holiday? How convincing do you find her evidence? **2.** At the beginning of her essay, Richards proposes that we stop celebrating Labor Day. Do you think she is serious about this proposal? Why or why not? How does this proposal fit into her main argument in this essay? How would you summarize her main argument? **3.** What shift in the meaning of the Labor Day holiday does Richards see? How does this shift relate to her main argument? **4.** How would you describe Richards' tone in this essay? How does she create this tone? Do you think her tone is appropriate for her argument? Explain, citing specific words and phrases from her essay to support your answers. **5.** What do you think this essay reveals about Richards' views regarding work? Do you think Richards believes that most Americans share her views? Why or why not?

also reasonable and beneficial for companies and communities. Very often, proposals that seem beneficial for one group can harm another. To find a solution to such a controversy requires taking these potential consequences into account.

Once you have selected a controversy, examine that controversy so that you can understand the issues involved. Write an essay in which you offer a proposal for solving the controversy in a way that addresses the concerns of the people involved. In your essay, explain the controversy as fully as you can, identifying the key issues and points of contention. Then describe and justify your proposal for solving the problem in a way that you believe is fair for all. Be sure to offer support for your proposal, and try to account for the potential consequences of your proposal for those involved.

13

GLOBALIZATION

GLOBAL

Z A T I O N

IS GLOBALIZATION

PROGRESS?

I n 1947, as the world was recovering from the appalling devastation of World War II, U.S. Secretary of State George C. Marshall outlined an expansive economic initiative to help Europe recover from the war. In a commencement speech at Harvard University, Marshall identified the need for nations to work together to rebuild the ruined European economies, and he claimed a leading role for the United States in doing so. (See *Con-Text* on page 605.) This initiative, which became known as the Marshall Plan, pumped millions of dollars of economic aid into Europe — money that was essential for those nations to return to economic health. But the Marshall Plan did more than help Europe rebuild its economy; it also reshaped the world economic map. Even as the Cold War that pitted the United States and its allies against the Soviet Union was starting up, the Marshall Plan was laying the foundation for a new global economy that would emerge decades later in the late 1980s when the Soviet Union broke apart. In this sense we can think of the Marshall Plan as an important step in the process that we now call globalization. ■ Globalization is a tricky term to define, but it refers to a general trend toward more numerous and intimate connections among nations around the world. For many, globalization is primarily an economic phenomenon. Since the 1980s the economies of individual nations have become more integrated, as developments such as the North America Free Trade Agreement (NAFTA) or the General Agreement of Trade and Tariffs (GATT) have facilitated international trade. But although globalization might be fueled by economic developments, it is not exclusively an economic phenomenon. Globalization also refers to the rapid increase of cross-cultural exchange, driven in part by powerful new communications technologies and media, including the Internet, and by increased international travel made possible by cheaper and more accessible transportation. With these new technologies both time and space become lesser obstacles to social and cultural interactions. The kind of exchange that was once rare, if not impossible — between, say, an American engineer from Seattle and a village leader in a remote region in Nepal — can now occur quite easily via the Internet. The frequency of such interactions, together with the expansion of broadcast media into previously isolated regions, have made the world a smaller place. In the process, the boundaries between cultures have become blurred, and some critics now describe a global consumer culture that is replacing what was once an extensive network of distinct and diverse cultures. (See Chapter 12 for readings on consumer culture and international trade.) American travelers might no longer be surprised to see a resident of a tiny village in Central Asia wearing Nike running shoes or a T-shirt emblazoned with the New York Yankees baseball team logo. It is perhaps more surprising to realize how much larger and separate the world seemed when George C. Marshall gave his famous commencement address in 1947. His statement that "the people of this country are distant from the troubled areas of the earth" no longer seems true. ■ For many globalization represents great opportunity and progress. It means that the villager in Nepal can have access to the same consumer goods as a shopper in New York City. It means that an immigrant from Ukraine living in Fort Worth, Texas, can read the news of his homeland in his native language by buying a Ukrainian newspaper at his local newsstand or by visiting a Ukrainian Web site. But globalization has a growing number of critics. In the early years of tthe 21st century, as world economies became more integrated, large-scale protests against globalization became common at meetings of international organizations such as the World Bank and the World Trade Organization. For some critics globalization represents not opportunity but the growing power of multinational corporations and the dominance of American consumer culture at the expense of local cultures. It means that people have less control as more and more aspects of their lives seem to be determined by distant economic and cultural forces. ■ The essays in this cluster highlight these complexities. Each one makes an argument about some aspect of globalization: economic, cultural, political, social. In the process, these essays remind us why globalization can be so difficult to define and understand. They also remind us that this process that we now call globalization is perhaps the most important development of our time — perhaps even more important than the Marshall Plan proved to be in post–World War II Europe. For that reason alone, arguments about globalization are increasingly important.

CON-TEXT: The Marshall Plan

1 I need not tell you gentlemen that the world situation is very serious. That must be apparent to all intelligent people. I think one difficulty is that the problem is one of such enormous complexity that the very mass of facts presented to the public by press and radio make it exceedingly difficult for the man in the street to reach a clear appraisement of the situation. Furthermore, the people of this country are distant from the troubled areas of the earth and it is hard for them to comprehend the plight and consequent reactions of the long-suffering peoples, and the effect of those reactions on their governments in connection with our efforts to promote peace in the world. . . .

There is a phase of this matter which is both interesting and serious. The farmer has always produced the foodstuffs to exchange with the city dweller for the other necessities of life. This division of labor is the basis of modern civilization. At the present time it is threatened with

breakdown. The town and city industries are not producing adequate goods to exchange with the food-producing farmer. Raw materials and fuel are in short supply. Machinery is lacking or worn out. The farmer or the peasant cannot find the goods for sale which he desires to purchase. So the sale of his farm produce for money which he cannot use seems to him an unprofitable transaction. He, therefore, has withdrawn many fields from crop cultivation and is using them for grazing. He feeds more grain to stock and finds for himself and his family an ample supply of food, however short he may be on clothing and the other ordinary gadgets of civilization. Meanwhile people in the cities are short of food and fuel. So the governments are forced to use their foreign money and credits to procure these necessities abroad. This process exhausts funds which are urgently needed for reconstruction. Thus a very serious situation is rapidly developing which bodes no good

for the world. The modern system of the division of labor upon which the exchange of products is based is in danger of breaking down.

The truth of the matter is that Europe's requirements for the next three or four years of foreign food and other essential products — principally from America — are so much greater than her present ability to pay that she must have substantial additional help or face economic, social, and political deterioration of a very grave character.

The remedy lies in breaking the vicious circle and restoring the confidence of the European people in the economic future of their own countries and of Europe as a whole. The manufacturer and the farmer throughout wide areas must be able and willing to exchange their products for currencies the continuing value of which is not open to question.

SOURCE: George C. Marshall, U.S. Secretary of State, Commencement Address, Harvard University, June 5, 1947.

① DANIEL YERGIN, "Giving Aid to World Trade"

One of the most persistent criticisms of economic globalization is that it contributes to poverty, particularly in developing nations whose populations are already poor. Some critics point out that as multinational corporations take advantage of relaxed international trade policies to increase their business in developing nations, they exploit resources at the expense of local populations. Daniel Yergin, a leading proponent of globalization, argues that such criticisms miss the point. In the following essay, which appeared in the summer of 2002 as members of the Group of Eight, a powerful international trade organization, were meeting in Canada, he maintains that globalization offers opportunities for poorer nations to reap the same benefits that wealthier nations enjoy. The key, according to Yergin, is greater access to international trade, so that developing nations can become successful participants in the world marketplace. Their success, in turn, will lead to prosperity for their citizens. In acknowledging that this process is not necessarily easy, Yergin implicitly reminds us that economic progress, which we tend to think of as a good thing, is never simple and can sometimes result in losers as well as winners in the marketplace. His essay might encourage you to examine some of the tradeoffs we may all face as global markets evolve. Daniel Yergin is coauthor of *The Commanding Heights: The Battle for the World Economy* (1998) and the author of *The Prize: The Epic Quest for Oil, Money and Power* (1991), for which he received the Pulitzer Prize. This essay was first published in the *New York Times*.

Giving Aid to World Trade
DANIEL YERGIN

1 By meeting in an idyllic retreat in the Canadian Rockies, leaders of the Group of 8,* a conference of the leading industrial powers plus Russia, may succeed in avoiding the critics of globalization. But they will hardly be getting away from the question of global poverty. Confronting Africa's appalling economic distress is at the top of their agenda.

One of the great tests for globalization will be its inclusiveness — what it does to improve the plight of the terribly poor in developing countries. Sept. 11 has pushed the question even more to the fore, as is evident in the 50 percent increase in foreign aid — reaching a level of $15 billion in three years — proposed by the Bush administration in March.

But the debate is often upside down, with critics of globalization contending that it causes poverty. On the contrary,

*For information on the Group of Eight, also known as G-8, see Context on page 587 in Chapter 12.

globalization — in the form of expanded trade and investment — offers the most significant means for reducing poverty. Foreign aid can play a very important role in relieving hardship and helping poor countries improve health, education and national infrastructure. It can also help build legal and lending institutions, making it possible for the poor to participate in market economies and poor countries to participate in the global economy. Such improvements can attract long-term foreign investment that creates jobs and encourages transfers of technologies to poorer nations.

It is trade, however, that is the primary engine for economic development. The best proof is from some nations in Asia. Four decades ago, Asian countries were among the poorest in the world. They varied widely in their political systems, but the common theme among the economically successful countries was their engagement with the world trading system. The results have been extraordinary. In 1960 South Korea was as poor as India. Today its per capita income is 20 times higher than India's.

5 In the last decade, India has also moved to participate more actively in the world economy through trade. Within India, this engagement has stimulated growth rates, and now India is on its way to becoming a force in the world economy. It's hard to imagine the Internet as we know it without India and Indian technologists.

Singapore provides an even more dramatic example. In the late 1960's, it was so poor that its very survival was problematic. Today its per capita income is higher than Britain's.

For developing countries to benefit from trade, the first requirement is better access to markets in developed countries and increased flows of investment. That was the message of the developing countries that was lost in the din of the

*In 1999 the meeting of the World Trade Organization (WTO) in Seattle was the focus of large protests by a number of advocacy groups and nongovernmental organizations opposed to the policies of the WTO. Thousands of protesters gathered in the streets of Seattle during the WTO meetings, sometimes clashing with police. The event became known as the "Battle in Seattle."

World Trade Organization meeting in Seattle in 1999.*

What would expanding trade mean for poorer nations? Sub-Saharan Africa, hit by falling commodity prices, poorly governed and unable to attract even much domestic investment, missed out on the manufacturing-led trade boom of the late 20th century. But if it were simply to regain the share of the world's non-oil exports that it held in 1980, it would have earned $161 billion in 2000 — not the $69 billion it actually earned.

Developing countries need to work to make themselves, as Singapore's senior minister, Lee Kuan Yew, has put it, "relevant" to the world economy in terms of education, skills, legal systems and economic culture.

10 At the same time, industrialized countries need to reduce barriers to imports from the poorest countries, a principle that has been increasingly recognized by the United States and the European Union. But it's a principle that needs to be put into practice.

For expanded market access to work, it must be accompanied by adjustment mechanisms in the industrial countries for workers that are adversely affected. But it would be a great error to think that giving poorer countries a share of global trade means a loss for the industrial countries.

In the 1990's, world trade, American imports and American exports all doubled. In that same decade, 17 million new jobs, on a net basis, were created in the United States. By any calculation, that's a pretty good deal, and one well worth remembering in these troubled economic times.

COMPLICATION

"As Yergin noted, expanded trade has indeed fueled startling economic development in Asia over the past four decades. What he didn't mention was that the three countries he cited as examples — South Korea, India, and Singapore — have been among the world's worst mercantilists and interventionists. Does Yergin really want the rest of the third world to follow this example? Could global economic stability possibly tolerate this?" Source: Alan Tonelson, "Follies: Yergin-Nonsense, Not Yergin-omics," TradeAlert.org (2002).

COMPLICATION

Arguments about trade and globalization often involve statistical information, such as Daniel Yergin uses in this essay. But there is often disagreement about how to measure such things as income and economic output; moreover, economists often disagree on what these figures mean. In this paragraph Yergin states that Singapore had a higher per capita income than Britain's in 2002. However, according to the World Bank, per capita income in Britain in 2001 was $24,230 (U.S. dollars). At the same time the government of Singapore reported that per capita income in that country was approximately $23,000. It is possible that Singapore's per capita income surpassed Britain's in 2002. It is also possible that Yergin used different figures, which might have reflected different formulas for calculating per capita income. Such subtle differences in statistics like these underscore the need to examine statistical evidence carefully in an argument. (See also the discussion of evidence on pages 76–81.)

Questions for Discussion

1. On what basis does Yergin make his claim that trade is the primary engine for the economic development of poor nations? How effective is Yergin's evidence for this claim? **2.** Much of Yergin's essay is devoted to discussion of examples of countries that he believes have evolved from poverty into economic successes. How convincing do you think these specific examples are in helping Yergin make his argument? Do you think these examples will make sense to most readers? Explain. (Keep in mind that Yergin's essay was originally published in the *New York Times*, which has a large national and international readership.) **3.** Examine Yergin's use of statistical information in this essay. What kinds of statistics does he provide? How relevant are these statistics to his claims? Do you think most readers would find these statistics to be persuasive? Why or why not? (See Complication on page 608.) **4.** Yergin wrote this essay just as representatives from the Group of Eight (see Context on page 587) were meeting in western Canada to discuss trade-related issues, including poverty in developing nations. In what ways is Yergin's argument specifically connected to this event? Do you think his main argument would be relevant even if it were not connected to the G-8 meeting? Explain. **5.** Yergin's essay might be considered an example of an essay based on inductive reasoning. How effectively do you think his approach helps him make his argument? (In answering this question, you might wish to refer to the discussion of arguments based on inductive reasoning on pages 25–26.)

② HELENA NORBERG-HODGE, "The March of the Monoculture"

As Helena Norberg-Hodge points out in the following essay, globalization not only results in economic change, but can also have a profound and devastating impact on local cultures. Where many advocates of globalization see great benefits in the increased availability of consumer goods in remote places, Norberg-Hodge sees the loss of distinctive and vibrant ways of life. In this sense, she suggests, the costs of globalization might far outweigh its benefits. Moreover, she argues that the ideal of the "global village" might reflect Western values that are not shared by other cultures. But what is most troubling to Norberg-Hodge is that although the global consumer culture that is replacing many local cultures might bring more material goods for consumers, it might not result in greater well-being for individuals. In other words, this emerging global monoculture could make our lives less happy, less satisfying, less fulfilling. This is a disconcerting view of globalization. Even if you do not share her view, Norberg-Hodge's essay might prompt you to consider the implications of globalization for the kind of life you hope to have. Helena Norberg-Hodge is the director of the International Society for Ecology and Culture, a nonprofit organization promoting local culture and biodiversity.

The March of the Monoculture
HELENA NORBERG-HODGE

1 Around the world, the pressure to conform to the expectations of the spreading, consumer monoculture is destroying cultural identity, eliminating local economies and erasing regional differences. As a consequence the global economy is leading to uncertainty, ethnic friction, and collapse, where previously there had been relative security and stability.

For many, the rise of the global economy marks the final fulfillment of the great dream of a 'Global Village'. Almost everywhere you travel today you will find multi-lane highways, concrete cities and a cultural landscape featuring grey business suits, fast-food chains, Hollywood films and cellular phones. In the remotest corners of the planet, Barbie, Madonna and the Marlboro Man are familiar icons. From Cleveland to Cairo to Caracas, Baywatch is entertainment and CNN news.

The world, we are told, is being united by virtue of the fact that everyone will soon be able to indulge their innate human desire for a Westernised, urbanised consumer lifestyle. West is best, and joining the bandwagon brings closer a harmonious union of peaceable, rational, democratic consumers 'like us'.

This world-view assumes that it was the chaotic diversity of cultures, values and beliefs that lay behind the chaos and conflicts of the past: that as these differences are removed, so the differences between us will be resolved.

5 As a result, all around the world, villages, rural communities and their cultural traditions, are being destroyed on an unprecedented scale by the impact of globalising market forces. Communities that have sustained themselves for hundreds of years are simply disintegrating. The spread of the consumer culture seems virtually unstoppable.

Consumers R Us: The Development of the Global Monoculture

Historically, the erosion of cultural integrity was a conscious goal of colonial developers. As applied anthropologist Goodenough explained: "The problem is one of creating in another a sufficient dissatisfaction with his present condition of self so that he wants to change it. This calls for some kind of experience that leads him to reappraise his self-image and re-evaluate his self-esteem."[1] Towards this end, colonial officers were advised that they should:

"1: Involve traditional leaders in their programmes.

2: Work through bilingual, acculturated individuals who have some knowledge of both the dominant and the target culture.

3: Modify circumstances or deliberately tamper with the equilibrium of the traditional culture so that change will become imperative.

4: Attempt to change underlying core values before attacking superficial customs."[2]

It is instructive to consider the actual effect of these strategies on the well-being of individual peoples in the South. For example, the Toradja tribes of the Poso district in central Celebes (now Sulawesi, Indonesia) were initially deemed completely incapable of 'development' without drastic intervention. Writing in 1929, A.C. Kruyt reported that the happiness and stability of Toradja society was such that "development and progress were impossible" and that they were "bound to remain at the same level".[3]

Toradja society was cashless and there was neither a desire for money nor the extra goods that might be purchased with it. In the face of such contentment, mission work proved an abject failure as the Toradjas had no interest in converting to a new religion, sending their children to school or growing cash crops. So, in 1905 the Dutch East Indies government decided to bring the Poso region under firm control, using armed force to crush all resistance. As a result of relocation and continual government harassment, mortality rates soared among the Toradjas. Turning to the missionaries for help, they were "converted" and began sending their children to school. Eventually they began cultivating coconut and coffee plantations and began to acquire new needs for oil lamps, sewing machines, and 'better' clothes. The self-sufficient tribal economy had been superseded, as a result of deliberate government action.

In many countries, schooling was the prime coercive instrument for changing "underlying core values" and proved to be a highly effective means of destroying self-esteem, fostering new 'needs', creating dissatisfactions, and generally disrupting traditional cultures. An excerpt from a French reader designed in 1919 for use by French West African schoolchildren gives a flavour of the kinds of pressure that were imposed on children:

"It is . . . an advantage for a native to work for a white man, because the

Whites are better educated, more advanced in civilisation than the natives. . . . You who are intelligent and industrious, my children, always help the Whites in their task. That is a duty."[4]

The Situation Today: Cultural Erosion

10 Today, as wealth is transferred away from nation states into the rootless casino of the money markets, the destruction of cultural integrity is far subtler than before. Corporate and government executives no longer consciously plan the destruction they wreak — indeed they are often unaware of the

consequences of their decisions on real people on the other side of the world. This lack of awareness is fostered by the cult of specialisation and speed that pervades our society — the job of a public relations executive is confined to producing business-friendly soundbites — time pressures and a narrow focus prevent a questioning of the overall impact of corporate activity. The tendency to undermine cultural diversity proceeds, as it were, on 'automatic pilot' as an inevitable consequence of the spreading global economy.

But although the methods employed by the masters of the 'Global Village', are less brutal than in colonial times, the scale and effects are often even more devastating. The computer and telecommunications revolutions have helped to speed up and strengthen the forces behind the march of a global monoculture, which is now able to disrupt traditional cultures with a shocking speed and finality which surpasses anything the world has witnessed before.

Preying on the Young

Today, the Western consumer conformity is descending on the less industrialised parts of the world like an avalanche. 'Development' brings tourism, Western films and products and, more recently, satellite television to the remotest corners of the Earth. All provide overwhelming images of luxury and power. Adverts and action films give the impression that everyone in the West is rich, beautiful and brave, and leads a life filled with excitement and glamour.

In the commercial mass culture which fuels this illusion, advertisers make it clear that Westernised fashion accessories equal sophistication and 'cool'. In diverse 'developing' nations around the world, people are induced to meet their needs not through their community or local economy, but by trying to 'buy in' to the global market. People are made to believe that, in the words of one US advertising executive in China, "imported equals good, local equals crap".

Even more alarmingly, people end up rejecting their own ethnic and racial characteristics — to feel shame at being who they are. Around the world, blonde-haired blue-eyed Barbie dolls and thin-as-a-rake 'cover girls' set the standard for women. Already now, seven-year-old girls in Singapore are suffering from eating disorders. It is not unusual to find east Asian women with eyes surgically altered to look more European, dark-haired southern European women dying their hair blonde, and Africans with blue- or green-coloured contact lenses aimed at 'correcting' dark eyes.

15 The one-dimensional, fantasy view of modern life promoted by the Western media, television and business becomes a slap in the face for young people in the 'Third World'. Teenagers, in particular, come to feel stupid and ashamed of their traditions and their origins. The people they learn to admire and respect on television are all 'sophisticated' city dwellers with fast cars, designer clothes, spotlessly clean hands and shiny white teeth. Yet they find their parents asking them to choose a way of life that involves working in the fields and getting their hands dirty for little or no money, and certainly no glamour. It is hardly surprising, then, that many choose to abandon the old ways of their parents for the siren song of a Western material paradise.

For millions of young people in rural areas of the world, modern Western culture appears vastly superior to their own. They see incoming tourists spending as much as $1,000 a day — the equivalent of a visitor to the US spending about $50,000 a day. Besides promoting the il-lusion that all Westerners are multi-millionaires, tourism and media images also give the impression that we never work — since for many people in 'developing' countries, sitting at a desk or behind the wheel of a car does not constitute work.

People are not aware of the negative social or psychological aspects of Western life so familiar to us: the stress, the loneliness and isolation, the fear of growing old alone, the rise in clinical depression and other 'industrial diseases' like cancer, stroke, diabetes and heart problems. Nor do they see the environmental decay, rising crime, poverty, homelessness and unemployment. While they know their own culture inside out, including all of its limitations and imperfections, they only see a glossy, exaggerated side of life in the West.

Ladakh: The Pressure to Consume

My own experience among the people of Ladakh or 'Little Tibet', in the trans-Himalayan region of Kashmir, is a clear, if painful, example of this destruction of traditional cultures by the faceless consumer monoculture. When I first arrived in the area 23 years ago, the vast majority of Ladakhis were self-supporting farmers, living in small scattered settlements in the high desert. Though natural resources were scarce and hard to obtain, the Ladakhis had a remarkably high standard of living — with beautiful art, architecture and jewellery. Life moved at a gentle pace and people enjoyed a degree of leisure unknown to most of us in the West. Most Ladakhis only really worked for four months of the year, and poverty, pollution and unemployment were alien concepts, ln 1975, I remember being shown around the remote village of Hemis Shukpachan by a young Ladakhi called Tsewang. It seemed to me, a newcomer, that all the

CONTEXT

Situated in mountainous northern India, Ladakh is part of the arid Tibetan plateau. Once nearly isolated from outside societies, Ladakh remains remote and sparsely populated, though it has seen Western-style economic development in the form of tourism and trade in locally made arts and crafts. In recent years, as travel and communication have connected it more intimately with the rest of India, Ladakh has been affected by the sometimes violent tensions among Muslims, Hindus, and Buddhists in the Indian state of Kashmir, of which Ladakh is part.

houses I saw were especially large and beautiful, and I asked Tsewang to show me the houses where the poor lived. He looked perplexed for a moment, then replied, "We don't have any poor people here."

In recent years external forces have caused massive and rapid disruption in Ladakh. Contact with the modern world has debilitated and demoralised a once-proud and self-sufficient people, who today are suffering from what can best be described as a cultural inferiority complex. When tourism descended on Ladakh some years ago, I began to realise how, looked at from a Ladakhi perspective, our modern, Western culture appears much more successful, fulfilled and sophisticated than we find it to be from the inside.

20 In traditional Ladkhi culture, virtually all basic needs — food, clothing and shelter, were provided without money. Labour was free of charge, part of an intricate and long-established web of hu-

man relationships. Because Ladakhis had no need for money, they had little or none. So when they saw outsiders — tourists and visitors — coming in, spending what was to them vast amounts of cash on inessential luxuries, they suddenly felt poor. Not realising that money was essential in the West — that without it, people often go homeless or even starve — they didn't realise its true value. They began to feel inadequate and backward. Eight years after Tsewang had told me that Ladakhis had no poverty, I overheard him talking to some tourists. "If you could only help us Ladakhis," he was saying, "we're so poor."

Tourism is part of the overall development which the Indian government is promoting in Ladakh. The area is being integrated into the Indian, and hence the global, economy. Subsidised food is imported from the outside, while local farmers who had previously grown a variety of crops and kept a few animals to provide for themselves have been encouraged to grow cash crops. In this way they are becoming dependent on forces beyond their control huge transportation networks, oil prices, and the fluctuations of international finance. Over the course of time, financial inflation obliges them to produce more and more, so as to secure the income that they now need in order to buy what they used to grow themselves. In political terms, each Ladakhi is now one individual in a national economy of 800 million, and, as part of a global economy, one of about six billion.

As a result of external investments, the local economy is crumbling. For generation after generation Ladakhis grew up learning how to provide themselves with clothing and shelter; how to make shoes out of yak skin and robes from the wool of sheep; how to build houses out of mud and stone. As these building traditions give way to 'modern' methods, the plentiful local materials are left unused, while competition for a narrow range of modern materials — concrete, steel and plastic — skyrockets. The same thing happens when people begin eating identical staple foods, wearing the same clothes and relying on the same finite energy sources. Making everyone dependent on the same resources creates efficiency for global corporations, but it also creates an artificial scarcity for consumers, which heightens competitive pressures.

As they lose the sense of security and identity that springs from deep, long-lasting connections to people and place, the Ladakhis are starting to develop doubts about who they are. The images they get from outside tell them to be different, to own more, to buy more and to thus be 'better' than they are. The previously strong, outgoing women of Ladakh have been replaced by a new generation — unsure of themselves and desperately concerned with their appearance. And as their desire to be 'modern' grows, Ladakhis are turning their backs on their traditional culture. I have seen Ladakhis wearing wristwatches they cannot read, and heard them apologising for the lack of electric lighting in their homes — electric lighting which, in 1975, when it first appeared, most villagers laughed at as an unnecessary gimmick. Even traditional foods are no longer a source of pride; now, when I'm a guest in a Ladakhi village, people apologise if they serve the traditional roasted barley, ngamphe, instead of instant noodles.

Ironically, then, modernisation — so often associated with the triumph of individualism — has produced a loss of individuality and a growing sense of personal insecurity. As people become self-conscious and insecure, they feel pressured to conform, and to live up to an idealised image. By contrast, in the traditional village, where everyone wore essentially the same clothes and looked the same to the casual observer, there was more freedom to relax. As part of a close-knit community, people felt secure enough to be themselves.

25 In Ladakh, as elsewhere, the breaking of local cultural, economic and political ties isolates people from their locality and from each other. At the same time, life speeds up and mobility increases — making even familiar relationships more superficial and brief. Competition for scarce jobs and political representation within the new centralised structures increasingly divides people. Ethnic and religious differences began to take on a political dimension, causing bitterness and enmity on a scale hitherto unknown. With a desperate irony, the monoculture — instead of bringing people together, creates divisions that previously did not exist.

As the fabric of local interdependence fragments, so do traditional levels of tolerance and co-operation. In villages near the capital, Leh, disputes and acrimony within previously close-knit communities, and even within families, are increasing. I have even seen heated arguments over the allocation of irrigation water, a procedure that had previously been managed smoothly within a co-operative framework. The rise in this kind of new rivalry is one of the most painful divisions that I have seen in Ladakh. Within a few years, growing competition has actually culminated in violence (see "Complication" on page 616) — and this in a place where, previously, there had been no group conflict in living memory.

Deadly Divisions
The rise of divisions, violence and civil disorder around the world are the consequence of attempts to incorporate di-

TENSIONS IN LADAKH

Norberg-Hodge refers to political and ethnic tensions that have emerged in recent years in Ladakh. Those tensions relate to longstanding religious and ethnic conflicts in India, of which Ladakh is part. In 2001 *The Indian Express* reported on one Ladakhi leader, Lama Lobzang, who attempted to find solutions to these conflicts, which had worsened in nearby regions of Kashmir. Here is part of that report:

A key campaigner for separate Union Territory status for Ladakh region, Lama Lobzang, has said that autonomy for Jammu and Kashmir could be the best solution possible for the state's problems, if it is coupled with trifurcation of the state. The Lama, also a member of the Scheduled Castes and Scheduled Tribes Commission, said trifurcation was the only realistic solution to the Kashmir tangle within the ambit of the Constitution. Speaking to *The Indian Express*, the Lama said Ladakhis were "disturbed with the hobnobbing between the Centre and the J-K government over autonomy package." Ladakhis, he said, foresaw a bleak future for themselves if more political powers were given to Jammu and Kashmir without giving cognisance to the feelings of the people of the other two regions. . . . Ladakh's problem, the Lama said, was a gradual encroachment upon their land and political powers by the Kashmiri-speaking people. He alleged it was being done under a design and with the blessings from the National Conference government. Moreover, the state was communalising the situation in the border region by brazenly favouring Muslims in admissions to professional colleges and jobs against Buddhists. Source: Aasha Khosa, "Autonomy with trifurcation is the answer: Ladakh leader."

verse cultures and peoples into the global monoculture. These divisions often deepen enough to result in fundamentalist reaction and ethnic conflict. Ladakh is by no means an isolated example.

In Bhutan, where different ethnic groups had also lived peaceably together for hundreds of years, two decades of economic development have resulted in the widespread destruction of decentralised livelihoods and communities — unemployment, once completely unknown, has reached crisis levels. Just like in Ladakh, these pressures have created intense competition between individuals and groups for places in schools, for jobs, for resources. As a result, tensions between Buddhists and Bhutanese Hindus of Nepalese origin have led to an eruption of violence and even a type of 'ethnic cleansing'.

Elsewhere, Nicholas Hildyard has written of how, when confronted with the horrors of ethnic cleansing in Yugoslavia or Rwanda, it is often taken for granted that the cause must lie in ingrained and ancient antagonisms. The reality, however, as Hildyard notes, is different: 30 "Scratch below the surface of inter-ethnic civil conflict, and the shallowness and deceptiveness of 'blood' or 'culture' explanations are soon revealed. 'Tribal hatred' (though a real and genuine emotion for some) emerges as the product not of 'nature' or of a primordial 'culture', but of a complex web of politics, economics, history, psychology and a struggle for identity."[5]

In a similar vein, Michel Chossudovsky, Professor of Economics at the University of Ottawa, argues that the current Kosovo crisis has its roots at least partly in the macro-economic reforms imposed by Belgrade's external creditors such as the International Monetary Fund (IMF). Multi-ethnic Yugoslavia was a regional industrial power with relative economic success. But after a decade of Western economic ministrations and five years of disintegration, war, boycott, and embargo, the economies of the former Yugoslavia are in ruins. Chossudovsky writes:

"In Kosovo, the economic reforms were conducive to the concurrent impoverishment of both the Albanian and Serbian populations contributing to fuelling ethnic tensions. The deliberate manipulation of market forces destroyed economic activity and people's livelihood creating a situation of despair."[6]

It is sometimes assumed that ethnic and religious strife is increasing because modern democracy liberates people, allowing old, previously suppressed, prejudices and hatreds to be expressed. If there was peace earlier, it is thought it was the result of oppression. But after more than twenty years of first-hand experience on the Indian subcontinent, I am convinced that economic 'development' not only exacerbates existing tensions but in many cases actually creates them. It breaks down human-scale structures, it destroys bonds of reciprocity and mutual dependence, while encouraging people to substitute their own culture and values with those of the media. In effect this means rejecting one's own identity — rejecting one's self.

Ultimately, while the myth makers of the 'Global Village' celebrate values of togetherness, the disparity in wealth between the world's upper income brackets and the 90 per cent of people in the poor countries represents a polarisation far more extreme than existed in the 19th century. Use of the word 'village' — intended to suggest relative equality, belonging and harmony — obscures a reality of high-tech islands of privilege and wealth towering above oceans of impoverished humanity struggling to survive. The global monoculture is a dealer in illusions — while it destroys traditions, local economies and sustainable ways of living, it can never provide the majority

CONTEXT

Helena Norberg-Hodge directs the International Society for Ecology and Culture (ISEC). According to its Web site, ISEC promotes "locally based alternatives to global consumer culture." Based in Great Britain, ISEC is "a non-profit organisation concerned with the protection of both biological and cultural diversity. Our emphasis is on *education for action*: moving beyond single issues to look at the more fundamental influences that shape our lives." Norberg-Hodge was involved in an ISEC project in Ladakh that began the 1970s. Consider the extent to which her long experience in that region might influence her credibility as author of this essay.

with the glittering, wealthy lifestyle it promised them. For what it destroys, it provides no replacement but a fractured, isolated, competitive and unhappy society.

References:

1. Quoted, John Bodley, Victims of Progress, Mayfield Publishing, 1982, pp. 111–112.
2. Ibid., p. 112.
3. Ibid., p. 129.
4. Ibid., p. 11.
5. N. Hildyard, Briefing 11 — Blood and Culture: Ethnic Conflict and the Authoritarian Right, The Cornerhouse, 1999.
6. M. Chossudovsky, Dismantling Yugoslavia, Colonising Bosnia, Ottawa, 1996, p. 1.

Questions for Discussion

1. Near the beginning of her essay, Norberg-Hodge asserts that "we are told" that the world is being united in a global, Western-style consumer culture. Who is the "we" to whom she refers here? Why do you think Norberg-Hodge begins her essay in this fashion? What advantages do you see to such a beginning? What disadvantages? **2.** Early in her essay Norberg-Hodge refers to the ideas of an anthropologist about the impact of colonial power on local culture. What point does she use these ideas to make? How is this point related to her main argument about globalization? **3.** Norberg-Hodge cites several historical examples of non-Western societies becoming "converted" to Western values and economic practices. What do these examples illustrate, in her view? Do you find these examples persuasive? Why or why not? Do you think they strengthen or weaken her argument? Explain. **4.** According to Norberg-Hodge, what are the differences between the destruction of local cultures by the current process of globalization and the destruction caused by colonialization in previous eras? Why is this difference important to her main argument? **5.** Evaluate Norberg-Hodge's use of the example of Ladakh to help her make her main argument. What points does she use this example to make? What specific details about Ladakh does she include in making these points? How effective do you think this example is in supporting her main argument? **6.** Throughout her essay Norberg-Hodge challenges the view that a Western-style consumer culture is good for all people. She claims that such a consumer culture reflects values that not all cultures share. On the basis of your reading of this essay, what values regarding lifestyle and community do you think Norberg-Hodge holds? Do you think most Western readers share these values? Cite specific passages from her essay to support your answer. **7.** How does Norberg-Hodge support her claim that consumer culture does not lead to a better life? What specific kinds of evidence does she cite? How convincing is this evidence, in your view? Do you think she presents a fair picture of consumer culture and its possible benefits and disadvantages? Why or why not?
8. How would you describe the tone of this essay? Do you think the tone is appropriate to the subject matter? Explain. In what ways might the tone enhance or weaken the main argument?

③ VANDANA SHIVA, "The Living Democracy Movement: Alternatives to the Bankruptcy of Globalisation"

In 1999, when thousands of anti-globalization activists gathered in Seattle to protest the policies of the World Trade Organization (WTO), the press labeled the event "The Battle in Seattle." Press reports during the protests sometimes focused on the unusually diverse nature of the protesters: environmentalists, animal rights activists, trade unionists and advocates for workers rights, civil libertarians, even anarchists. Many very different people, it seemed, had a wide range of concerns that were somehow connected to the process of globalization. Some critics suggested that this diversity of concerns indicated a lack of a clear purpose to the antiglobalization movement; according to such critics, that was why so many different interests were represented among the protesters. But the following essay by human rights and environmental activist Vandana Shiva suggests another explanation: So many different concerns were expressed by the protesters because globalization involves so much more than economic policy. Shiva, a physicist who has become one of the world's foremost critics of globalization, argues that the policies of international organizations such as the WTO are not only economic measures, but also reflect philosophical, political, and ecological beliefs that are not shared by the world population. For Shiva the process of globalization that is fueled by such policies is bankrupt because it reduces the complex needs of human beings to commodities. In rejecting globalization, Shiva transforms the issue from an economic one to a human one. Her argument is challenging, but it reminds us that the growing debates about globalization are intense precisely because the stakes are so high. Vandana Shiva founded the Research Foundation for Science, Ecology, and Technology, which supports biodiversity and indigenous foods and local cultures. The following essay was originally delivered as an address to the World Social Forum in 2002.

The Living Democracy Movement: Alternatives to the Bankruptcy of Globalisation
VANDANA SHIVA

The Bankruptcy of Globalisation

1 Globalisation was projected as the next great leap of human evolution in a linear forward march from tribes to nations to global markets. Our identities and context were to move from the national to the global, just as in the earlier phase of state driven globalisation, it was supposed to have moved from the local to the global.

Deregulated commerce and corporate

5 The dominant political and economic order has a number of features that are new, which increase injustice and non-sustainability on scales and at rates that the earth and human community have not experienced.

1. It is based on enclosures of the remaining ecological commons* — biodiversity, water and air, and the destruction of local economies on which people's livelihoods and economic security depends.
2. The commodification of water and biodiversity is ensured through new property rights built into trade agreements like the WTO which are transforming people's resources into corporate monopolies viz. TRIPs and trade in environmental goods and services.
3. The transformation of commons to commodities is ensured through shifts in governance with decisions moving from communities and countries to global institutions, and rights moving from people to corporations through increasingly centralised and unaccountable states acting on the principle of eminent domain[†] — the absolute sovereignty of the ruler.

*For other perspectives on the idea of the commons, see the essays by Radha D'Souza (page 370) and David Bollier (page 374).

[†]Eminent domain is a principle by which a government can acquire private property for public use, such as parks, public transportation, or defense. Usually, laws require governments to compensate private citizens or businesses that lose property to eminent domain.

rule was offered as the alternative to the centralised bureaucratic control under communist regimes and state dominated economies. Markets were offered as an alternative to states for regulating our lives, not just our economies.

As the globalisation project has unfolded, it has exposed its bankruptcy at the philosophical, political, ecological and economic levels. The bankruptcy of the dominant world order is leading to social, ecological, political and economic non-sustainability, with societies, ecosystems, and economies disintegrating and breaking down.

The philosophical and ethical bankruptcy of globalisation was based on reducing every aspect of our lives to commodities and reducing our identities to merely that of consumers on the global market place. Our capacities as producers, our identity as members of communities, our role as custodians of our natural and cultural heritage were all to disappear or be destroyed. Markets and consumerism expanded. Our capacity to give and share were to shrink. But the human spirit refuses to be subjugated by a world view based on the dispensability of our humanity.

This in turn led to political bankruptcy and anti-democratic formations and constellations. Instead of acting on the public trust doctrine and principles of democratic accountability and subsidiarity, globalisation led to governments usurping power from parliaments, regional and local governments, and local communities.

For example the TRIPs agreement was based on central governments hijacking the rights to biodiversity and knowledge from communities and assigning them as exclusive, monopolistic rights to corporations.

The Agreement on Agriculture was based on taking decisions away from farming communities and regional governments.

The General Agreement on Trade in Services (GATS) takes decisions and ownership over water from the local and public domain to the privatised, global domain. This undemocratic process of privatisation and deregulation led to increased political bankruptcy and corruption and economic bankruptcy.

A decade of corporate globalisation has led to major disillusionment and discontentment. Democracy has been eroded, livelihoods have been destroyed. Small farmers and businesses are going bankrupt everywhere. Even the promise of economic growth has not been delivered. Economic slow down has been the outcome of liberalising trade. Ironically some corporations that led the process of trade liberalisation and globalisation have themselves collapsed.

10 Enron[‡] which came to India as the "Flagship" project of globalisation with the full force of backing and blackmail by the U.S. Trade Representative has gone bankrupt and is steeped in scandals of corruption. Chiquita, which forced the banana wars on Europe through a U.S./Europe W.T.O. dispute has also declared bankruptcy.

First South East Asia, now Argentina have exposed how vulnerable and volatile current economic arrangements are.

The non-sustainability and bankruptcy of the ruling world order is fully evident. The need for alternatives has never been stronger.

Creating Alternatives to Corporate Globalisation

During the last decade of the 20th century, corporate driven globalisation shook up the world and the economic and political structures that we have shaped to govern us.

In December 1999, citizens of the world rebelled against the economic totalitarianism of corporate globalisation. Social and economic justice and ecological sustainability became the rallying call for new movements for citizen freedoms and liberation from corporate control. **15** September 11th 2001 shut down the spaces that people's movements had opened up. It also brought back the focus on the intimate connection between violence, inequality and non-sustainability and the indivisibility of peace, justice and sustainability. Doha[§] was rushed through in the shadow of global militarisation in response to the terror attacks.

As we face the double closure of spaces by corporate globalisation and militarised police states, by economic facism aided by political facism, our challenge is to reclaim our freedoms and the freedoms of our fellow beings. Reclaiming and recreating the indivisible freedom of all species is the aim of the Living Democracy Movement. The living democracy movement embodies two indivisibilities and continuums. The first is the continuum of freedom for all life on earth, and all humans without discrimination on the basis on gender, race, religion, class and species. The second is the continuum between and indivisibility of justice, peace and sustainability — without sustainability and just share of the earth's bounties there is no justice, and without justice three can be no peace.

Corporate globalisation ruptures these continuities. It establishes corporate rule through a divide and rule policy, and creates competition and conflict between different species and peoples and between different aims. It transforms diversity and multiplicity into oppositional differences both by breeding fundamentalisms through spreading insecurity and

[‡]A large U.S. energy-trading corporation, Enron was beset by accounting scandals in 2002.

[§]Doha, Qatar, was the site of the Fourth World Trade Organization Ministerial Conference, in November 2001.

CONTEXT

TRIPs, GATS, and the Agreement on Agriculture, international agreements negotiated by the World Trade Organization, all relax barriers to various kinds of trade and thus contribute to economic globalization. TRIPs, the Agreement On Trade-Related Aspects of Intellectual Property Rights, governs international copyright and related issues. GATS, the General Agreement on Trade in Services, sets international trade policies on such services as telecommunications and transportation. The Agreement on Agriculture is intended to open national agricultural markets to international competition by reducing agricultural subsidies that governments often provide for their farmers. These three agreements, along with the General Agreement on Trade and Tariffs, form the foundation of the international economic policies of the WTO and are often the focus of protest and criticism.

then using these fundamentalisms to shift humanities focus and preoccupation from sustainability and justice and peace to ethnic and religious conflict and violence.

We need a new paradigm to respond to the fragmentation caused by various forms of fundamentalism. We need a new movement which allows us to move from the dominant and pervasive culture of violence, destruction and death to a culture of non-violence, creative peace and life. That is why in India we started the living democracy movement.

Creative Resistance
Seattle was a watershed for citizens movements.* People brought an international trade agreement and W.T.O. the institution that enforces it to a halt by mobilising globally against corporate globalisation. Seattle was the success of a strategy focussing on the global level and on protest. It articulated at the international level what citizens do not want. Corporations and governments responded quickly to Seattle's success. They killed protest possibilities by moving to venues like Doha where thousands could not gather. And they started to label protest and dissent of any kind as "terrorism".

20 The Biotech industry (*Economist,* Jan 12th, 18th, p. 62) has called on governments to use anti-terror laws against groups like Greenpeace and Friends of the Earth and groups critical of the industry. Mr. Zoellick, the US Trade Representative has called the anti-globalisation movement terrorist.

A different strategy is needed post September 11/post Doha. Massive protests at global meetings can no longer be the focus on citizen mobilisation. We need international solidarity and autonomous organising. Our politics needs

to reflect the principle of subsidiarity. Our global presence cannot be a shadow of the power of corporations and Bretton Woods institutions.[†] We need stronger movements at local and national levels, movements that combine resistance and constructive action, protests and building of alternatives non-cooperation with unjust rule and cooperation within society. The global, for us, must strengthen the local and national, not undermine it. The two tendencies that we demand of the economic system needs to be central to people's politics — localisation and al-

*Seattle was the site of meetings of the World Trade Organization in 1999 that drew thousands of protestors. See the margin gloss on page 608 in this cluster.

†In July 1944, representatives of nations from around the world met at a resort called Bretton Woods in New Hampshire to discussion international economic and monetary policy. The agreement that was adopted at Bretton Woods established the International Bank for Reconstruction and Development, a precursor to the World Bank.

COMPLICATION

Robert Zoellick, the U.S. Trade Representative, spoke out about the importance of economic globalization in the wake of the terrorist attacks of September 11, 2001. According to a press release by the U.S. Department of State in September, 2001,

The U.S. trade representative also challenged the anti-globalization movement. "We will not be intimidated by those who have taken to the streets to blame trade — and America — for the world's ills," he said. Erecting new barriers to trade won't help the poor, but open markets will, he said. Zoellick noted that per capita income for globalizing developing countries has grown at more than 5 percent annually compared to 1 percent a year for non-globalizing countries. The absolute poverty rates for globalizing developing countries, he added, have fallen sharply over the past 20 years.

Zoellick further argued that trade liberalization will add stability to skittish global financial markets by providing important stimulus for global economic recovery.

ternatives. Both are not just economic alternatives they are democratic alternatives. Without them forces for change cannot be mobilised in the new context.

At the heart of building alternatives and localising economic and political systems is the recovery of the commons and the reclaiming of community. The living democracy movement is reclaiming people's sovereignty and community rights to natural resources.

Rights to natural resources are natural rights. They are not given by States, nor can they be extinguished by States, the W.T.O, or by corporations, even though under globalisation, attempts are being made to alienate people's rights to vital resources of land water and biodiversity.

25 Globalisation has relocated sovereignty from people to corporations, through centralising, militarising States. Rights of people are being appropriated by States to carve out monopoly rights of corporations over our land, our water, our biodiversity, our air. States acting on the principle of eminent domain or absolute sovereignty of the State are undermining people's sovereign rights and their role as trustees of people's resources on the public trust doctrine. State sovereignty, by itself, is therefore not enough to generate countervailing forces and processes to corporate globalisation.

The reinvention of sovereignty has to be based on the reinvention of the state so that the state is made accountable to the people. Sovereignty cannot reside only in centralised state structures, nor does it disappear when the protective functions of the state with respect to its people start to wither away. The new partnership of national sovereignty needs empowered communities which assign functions to the state for their protec-

tion. Communities defending themselves always demand such duties and obligations from state structures. On the other hand, TNCs and international agencies promote the separation of the community interests from state interests and the fragmentation and divisiveness of communities.

The Living Democracy Movement

We started the living democracy movement to respond to the enclosures of the commons that is at the core of economic globalisation. The living democracy movement is simultaneously an ecology movement, an anti-poverty movement, a recovery of the commons movement, a deepening of democracy movement, a peace movement. It builds on decades of movements defending people's rights to resources, the movements for local, direct democracy, our freedom movements gifts of Swadeshi (economic sovereignty),

Swaraj (self-rule) and Satyagraha (non-cooperation with unjust rule). It seeks to strengthen rights enshrined in our Constitution.

The living democracy movement in India is a movement to rejuvenate resources, reclaim the commons and deepen democracy. It relates to the democracy of life in three dimensions.

Living democracy refers to the democracy of all life, not just human life. It is about earth democracy not just human democracy.

30 Living democracy is about life, at the vital everyday level, and decisions and freedoms related to everyday living — the food we eat the clothes we wear, the water we drink. It is not just about elections and casting votes once in 3 or 4 or 5 years. It is a permanently vibrant democracy. It combines economic democracy with political democracy.

Living democracy is not dead, it is alive. Under globalisation, democracy even of the shallow representative kind is dying. Governments everywhere are betraying the mandates that brought them to power. They are centralising authority and power, both by subverting democratic structures of constitutions and by promulgating ordinances that stifle civil liberties. The September 11 tragedy has become a convenient excuse for anti-people legislation worldwide. Politicians everywhere are turning to xenophophic and fundamentalist agendas to get votes in a period when economic agenda have been taken away from national levels and are being set by World Bank, IMF, W.T.O. and global corporations.

The living democracy movement is about living rather that dead democracy. Democracy is dead when governments no longer reflect the will of the people but are reduced to anti-democratic unaccountable instruments of corporate rule under the constellation of corporate globalisation as the Enron and Chiquita case make so evident. Corporate globalisation is centered on corporate profits.

Living democracy is based on maintaining life on earth and freedom for all species and people.

Corporate globalisation operates to create rules for the global, national and local markets which privilege global corporations and threaten diverse species, the livelihoods of the poor and small, local producers and businesses.

35 Living democracy operates according to the ecological laws of nature, and limits commercial activity to prevent harm to other species and to people.

Corporate globalisation is exercised through centralising, destructive power.

Living democracy is exercised through decentralised power and peaceful coexistence.

CHIQUITA BANANA DISPUTE

In 1993 the European Union (EU) imposed stiff new tariffs on bananas imported to Europe from countries that were not members of the EU or territories of EU nations. Chiquita Brands International, Inc., a U.S. company, challenged the EU policy, charging that it discriminated against bananas produced in Latin American nations, where Chiquita operated. The dispute continued throughout the 1990s, during which time the World Trade Organization (WTO) issued several rulings on the case. In 1999 the United States, frustrated by developments in the case, retaliated by imposing new tariffs on several kinds of imports from European nations. In 2001 the EU agreed to a new policy, to be implemented by 2006, that would effectively open European markets to banana imports from countries that have been subject to its high tariffs. This agreement between the European Union and the United States generally conformed to WTO rulings on the issue. Although some criticized the ruling, it was generally seen as the end of the dispute.

Corporate globalisation globalises greed and consumerism. Living democracy globalises compassion, caring and sharing.

Democracy emptied of economic freedom and ecological freedom becomes a potent breeding ground for fundamentalism and terrorism.

40 Over the past two decades, I have witnessed conflicts over development and conflicts over natural resources mutate into communal conflicts, culminating in extremism and terrorism. My book *Violence of the Green Revolution* was an attempt to understand the ecology of terrorism. The lessons I have drawn from the growing but diverse expressions of fundamentalism and terrorism are the following:

Nondemocratic economic systems that centralize control over decision making and resources and displace people from productive employment and livelihoods create a culture of insecurity. Every policy decision is translated into the politics of "we" and "they." "We" have been unjustly treated, while "they" have gained privileges.

Destruction of resource rights and erosion of democratic control of natural resources, the economy, and means of production undermine cultural identity. With identity no longer coming from the positive experience of being a farmer, a craftsperson, a teacher, or a nurse, culture is reduced to a negative shell where one identity is in competition with the "other" over scarce resources that define economic and political power.

Centralized economic systems also erode the democratic base of politics. In a democracy, the economic agenda is the political agenda. When the former is hijacked by the World Bank, the IMF, or the WTO, democracy is decimated. The only cards left in the hands of politicians eager to garner votes are those of race, religion, and ethnicity, which subsequently give rise to fundamentalism. And fundamentalism effectively fills the vacuum left by a decaying democracy. Economic globalisation is fueling economic insecurity, eroding cultural diversity and identity, and assaulting the political freedoms of citizens. It is providing fertile ground for the cultivation of fundamentalism and terrorism. Instead of integrating people, corporate globalization is tearing apart communities.

The survival of people and democracy are contingent on a response to the double facism of globalization — the economic facism that destroys people's rights to resources and the fundamentalist facism that feeds on people's displacement, dispossession, economic insecurities, and fears. On September 11, 2001, the tragic terrorist attacks on the World Trade Center and at the Pentagon unleashed a "war against terrorism" promulgated by the US government under George W. Bush. Despite the rhetoric, this war will not contain terrorism because it fails to address the roots of terrorism — economic insecurity, cultural subordination, and ecological dispossession. The new war is in fact creating a chain reaction of violence and spreading the virus of hate. And the magnitude of the damage to the earth caused by "smart" bombs and carpet bombing remains to be seen.

45 Living Democracy is true freedom of all life forms to exist on this earth.

Living Democracy is true respect for life, through equitable sharing of the earth's resources with all those who live on the planet.

Living Democracy is the strong and continual articulation of such democratic principles in everyday life and activity.

The constellation of living democracy is people's control over natural resources, and a just and sustainable utilisation of land, water, biodiversity, communities having the highest sovereignty and delegating power to the state in its role as trustee. The shift from the principle of eminent domain to the public trust doctrine for functions of the State is key to localisation, to recovery of the commons and the fight against privatisation and corporate take over of land, water and biodiversity.

This shift is also an ecological imperative. As members of the earth family, Vasudhaiva Kutumbhakam, we have a share in the earth's resources. Rights to natural resources for needs of sustenance are natural rights. They are not given or assigned. They are recognised or ignored. The eminent domain principle inevitably leads to the situation of "all for some" — corporate monopolies over biodiversity through patents, corporate monopolies on water through privatisation and corporate monopolies over food through free trade.

50 The most basic right we have as a species is survival, the right to life. Survival requires guaranteed access to resources. Commons provide that guarantee. Privatisation and enclosures destroy it. Localisation is necessary for recovery of the commons. And living democracy is the movement to relocate our minds, our production systems and consumption patterns from the poverty creating global markets to the sustainability and sharing of the earth community. This shift from global markets to earth citizenship is a shift of focus from globalisation to localisation of power from corporations to citizens. The living democracy movement is a movement to establish that a better world is not just possible, it is necessary.

Questions for Discussion

1. What specifically does Shiva mean by "the bankruptcy of globalisation"? How does she establish that globalization is "bankrupt"? Cite specific passages from her essay to support your answer. **2.** According to Shiva, what do we lose when markets and consumerism grow? Do you think she is right? Why or why not? **3.** What is the "dominant political and economic order," as Shiva sees it? What features of this dominant order does she identify? Why are these features important, in her view? How does her discussion of these features fit into her main argument? **4.** How would you describe the style and tone of this essay? Identify specific words and phrases that you think contribute to this style. In what ways do you think the style and tone are appropriate for the argument Shiva makes in this essay? **5.** At one point in her essay Shiva writes, "The non-sustainability and bankruptcy of the ruling world order is fully evident. The need for alternatives has never been stronger." What evidence does Shiva offer for this claim? What kinds of evidence does she offer for her claims about globalization in general? Do you think her use of evidence strengthens or weakens her essay? Explain. **6.** As an alternative to globalization, Shiva proposes what she calls the Living Democracy Movement. What exactly is this movement, as Shiva describes it? What are its primary characteristics and goals? In what specific ways does it differ from globalization? Do you think the goals and principles of this movement are widely shared? Explain. **7.** On what fundamental rights or beliefs does Shiva base her argument? To what extent do you think these rights or beliefs strengthen or weaken her argument?

④ BJORN SKORPEN CLAESON, **"Singing for the Global Community"**

In the late 1990s and the first years of the 21st century, large-scale protests against globalization became almost commonplace. Each meeting of the World Trade Organization or the World Bank seemed to attract thousands of protesters followed by hundreds of journalists, whose articles and television reports often focused on the number of protesters and sometimes on clashes between protesters and security forces. The irony of such large-scale events is that they seemed to obscure the very same individuals whom the protesters claimed are most negatively affected by globalization. In the following essay, Bjorn Skorpen Claeson tries to keep those individuals in view by putting a human face on the concerns that are so often heard in protests against globalization. He describes a different kind of event that occurred in Bangor, Maine, in the summer of 2002: a concert and fair that were intended not only to publicize the plight of the workers whose lives have been harmed by globalization, but also to celebrate these same workers and the global community we are all part of. In comparison to the weighty and sometimes angry arguments that focus on the political and economic aspects of globalization, Claeson's essay might strike you as idealistic and perhaps even romantic. But his argument about what it means to be part of a world that is increasingly interdependent is not so easy to dismiss. As you read, consider the values that lie at the heart of Claeson's concerns for the people he describes. To what extent might his values represent a realistic vision for the global community to which we all contribute in some way? Bjorn Skorpen Claeson is an organizer with Peace through Interamerican Community Action (PICA). This essay was published in the Bangor (Maine) *Daily News* in 2002.

Singing for the Global Community
BJORN SKORPEN CLAESON

*Well-known folk singer Pete Seeger (b. 1919) has also been a political activist whose views made him a target during the anticommunist campaigns of the 1950s. Among the many songs he composed are "If I Had a Hammer" and "Where Have All the Flowers Gone."

1 Imagine 50 children from across the globe, arm in arm, singing out: "Drop the gun! Drop the gun!" That promises to be a highlight of the Concert for Our Future, Thursday, July 11, at the Bangor City Waterfront Park.

Eleven-year-olds from Brazil, Chile, El Salvador, Mexico, the United States, Canada, Norway, Sweden, Finland, Germany, Italy and India living together in an international month-long children's summer village in Old Town will join members of the St. Mary's youth choir to open the concert with Pete Seeger's* latest song, "Take It From Doctor King." Written in response to Sept. 11 and intended for children to teach adults, the song carries an important message: Let's expand our sense of community across boundaries of nation, language, race and class for, surely, a semi-permanent state of war is not a solution with which most people can live.

We hard-to-convince hardened adults might do well to memorize the song's refrain: "Don't say it can't be done. The battle's just begun. Take it from Doctor King. You too can learn to sing!"

The children, the concert and the immediately preceding Clean Clothes Fair speak to us of international community, a notion that is increasingly rare in the versions of the globalization story that most of us today are living to some extent.

5 In one such version there are two main sorts of characters. First there are the consumers who are painted as passive, atomized and disengaged from workers by complicated corporate chains of production. They are more or less economically secure but feel powerless to make change since the market, rather than human beings, is in control. Confined into an artificially safe and insulated universe, consumers' ability to do good rests on their ability to buy. According to this version of globalization, consumers might even be called upon to make a sacrifice by buying products made in poor countries: the more we buy, the better for them.

The other main set of characters are the disposables: the anonymous, the nobodies, the forgotten, the excluded. They are not only in the Southern Hemisphere, or in poor, developing countries. In Bangor, they are, for example, laid-off shoe workers who receive a fraction of what they need to survive in unemployment insurance, while the companies that once employed them now make the very same shoes in China for a fraction of Maine wages and higher profits. "To be considered disposable by the country we so dearly love is intolerable," says one.

In China, they are, for example, the shoe workers who toil 14 to 16 hours a day, seven days a week, in an environment of intense heat and stinging odor.

They are an expendable, short-term source of labor to be used until worn out. These are the people whom Thomas Friedman, in his celebrated telling of this story of globalization, "The Lexus and the Olive Tree," calls "turtles" (see page 630): They simply don't run fast enough in the fast world and are desperately trying to avoid becoming road kill. In this fashion the gap between the consumers and the disposables grows ever wider.

In another now often-told version of this globalization story this gap has become charged with hostility and danger. It's a world of "us and them," people lumped into mutually exclusive categories who are for or against, good or evil, black or white.

Differences, middle grounds and alternatives have gone the way of dialogue, diplomacy and understanding. Believing "it can't be done," we suspend ourselves in a state of "yellow alert," a never-ending conflict without borders.
10 The Concert for Our Future and the Clean Clothes Fair help us break the artificial isolation imposed by consumerism and the new go-at-it-alone mentality. At the fair the workers behind the labels are real human beings whose lives are woven into the very clothes we wear. Come and meet Hathaway shirt workers from Waterville selling the

CONTEXT

The Clean Clothes Fair is part of the Clean Clothes Campaign, which is an effort to publicize the poor conditions of workers in the garment industry. According to the Web site for the Campaign, "the purchasing power of consumers is being mobilized on the issue of working conditions in the garment industry." Through publications, rallies, and the Internet the Campaign tries to educate consumers, particularly young people, about the origins of the clothes they buy. (See www. cleanclothes.org/campaign.htm.)

THE LEXUS AND THE OLIVE TREE

"The defining economists of the globalization system are Joseph Schumpeter and former Intel CEO Andy Grove, who prefer to unleash capitalism. Schumpeter, a former Austrian Minister of Finance and Harvard Business School professor, expressed the view in his classic work, *Capitalism, Socialism and Democracy*, that the essence of capitalism is the process of "creative destruction" — the perpetual cycle of destroying the old and less efficient product or service and replacing it with new, more efficient ones. Andy Grove took Schumpeter's insight that "only the paranoid survive" . . . and made it in many ways the business model of globalization capitalism. Grove helped to popularize the view that dramatic, industry-transforming innovations are taking place today faster and faster. Thanks to these technological breakthroughs, the speed by which your latest invention can be made obsolete or turned into a commodity is now lightning quick. Therefore, only the paranoid, only those who are constantly looking over their shoulders to see who is creating something new that will destroy them and then staying just one step ahead of them, will survive. Those countries that are most willing to let capitalism quickly destroy inefficient companies, so that money can be freed up and directed to more innovative ones, will thrive in the era of globalization. Those which rely on their governments to protect them from such creative destruction will fall behind in this era." Source: Thomas L. Friedman, *The Lexus and the Olive Tree* (1999).

products they make. Come and hear the stories of immigrant Mexican workers in Los Angeles who have found respect and dignity as union workers making the new SweatX label.* Learn about artisans in West Africa, Nepal, Thailand, El Salvador and Peru from local small businesses committed to fair trade without middle-men. Meet local Native American artisans who tell the stories of their lives and histories in their crafts. Hear music from West Africa, the Andes and local indigenous people. The people without voice will be speaking loud and clear.

Perhaps because either-or choices don't come naturally to children, or because their curiosity and imagination defy the artificial limits of consumerism, our children can teach us a story of globalization where our sense of community is as global as our economy. We should be all ears.

*For more information about SweatX, see the essay by Jim Hightower on page 593.

NEGOTIATING DIFFERENCES

Part of the challenge of negotiating the debates about globalization is understanding just what is meant by the term *globalization*. As the essays in this cluster suggest, participants in these debates define the term in different ways and focus on different aspects of globalization: social, cultural, economic, political, and philosophical. If we are to make arguments that can lead to viable solutions to the problems associated with globalization, then we must understand just what globalization is. This assignment encourages you to do so.

Imagine that you are participating in an international conference of college students who are concerned about globalization. Your task is to write a position statement on globalization for the conference. If your teacher allows it, consider working with a group of your classmates to complete this assignment.

To accomplish this task will require two steps. First, you will need to do some research on globalization to gain an understanding of what people mean by that term and what the most important concerns about globalization are. You might start with the four essays in this cluster, but you might also wish to consult additional sources. There are many very good sources, and part of your challenge will be

Questions for Discussion

1. What are the two versions of the "globalization story" that Claeson describes in his essay? What is his purpose in describing these two versions? How do they contribute to his main argument? **2.** What is the vision of a global community that Claeson offers? On what values or beliefs is his vision based? Do you think most people would share his vision? **3.** Examine Claeson's descriptions of the workers who he claims are most directly affected by globalization. What specific details does he provide about these workers? What kind of picture do these details paint? How effectively does this picture contribute to his main argument? **4.** Claeson claims that globalization has been framed in public discussion as a debate about how "the consumers" can deal with "the disposables." He asserts that the children's concert addresses globalization in a way that avoids such "either-or" thinking. Examine the articles in this cluster and determine whether you see this kind of either-or thinking. Visit the Clean Clothes Campaign, Rugmark and SweatX Web sites. Do these organizations provide the kind of exploration of "differences" and "middle ground" that Claeson believes is important? **5.** Claeson's essay is connected to a specific event that occurred in Maine in 2002. In what ways does that specific context influence his argument? In what ways might his description of that event enhance or weaken his main argument about globalization? **6.** Claeson's appeal in this essay is both an announcement for an event and an argument about workers' rights. After reading this article, would you be inclined to attend the event he is announcing?

sorting through the wide range of available sources. You might begin by visiting this Web site: www.globalisationguide.org/01.html.

Once you have gained a better understanding of globalization, draft your position statement. Your statement should clearly define the issues associated with globalization that you (and your classmates) consider to be most important. These issues can be related to jobs, poverty, the environment, politics, or any other concerns you see as important. Your statement should also present a position on these issues and justify that position. Ideally, your position should address the concerns of many other people about globalization. In other words, your position statement can make an argument that is a step toward solving the problems associated with globalization.

Alternatively, consider organizing a student forum to address the issues that you and your classmates have identified as important. This forum can be limited to members of your class, but you might also consider a larger forum involving students and faculty at your school as well as community members. In organizing this forum, develop a flyer that explains the purpose of the forum and its intended outcome.

WHAT IS FAIR TRADE?

In the early 20th century many Americans had grave concerns about the rapid growth of large corporations. One concern was that smaller businesses could not survive in competition with such corporations, which could use their size to set lower prices and drive smaller companies out of business. In the late 19th and early 20th centuries Congress had passed several antitrust laws to prevent large corporations from engaging in such practices, including the Sherman Anti-Trust Law of 1890. Ironically, however, that law also prohibited smaller businesses from engaging in certain practices to protect themselves from large corporations. One such practice was *retail price maintenance*, which was also called *fair trade*, by which manufacturers would set minimum, or "fair," retail prices for their goods. This practice was intended to counteract the ability of very large companies to set extremely low retail prices for products — lower than their smaller competitors could match. It was also a reaction to the growing influence of chain stores, which sold products at very low prices that cut into manufacturers' profits. With fair trade, smaller manufacturers could still realize a profit, even in the face of competition from larger companies; they could also protect themselves from the effects of chain stores. The problem was that fair trade was illegal under the Sherman Act. ■ As a result, Congress passed the Miller-Tydings Act in 1937, which allowed fair trade practices. But there was strong resistance to this new law from the beginning, especially from consumer groups, which feared that the law would mean higher prices for consumers. And the law did not always result in the kind of fair trade it was intended to foster. For some products, minimum prices were maintained among all manufacturers, thus protecting manufacturers from price competition. But in other cases individual manufacturers set their own prices and policies, undercutting the intent of the law. Fair trade agreements began to decrease in number as large chain stores such as Macy's gained influence and market share. In addition, several Supreme Court rulings held that fair trade agreements were violations of antitrust laws. In 1952 Congress passed yet another law that exempted fair trade agreements from antitrust violations, a measure that President Harry S. Truman reluctantly supported (see *Con-Text* on page 633). Truman's ambivalence about fair trade seemed to reflect the general view of the nation as a whole, for there was deep disagreement among Americans about fair trade. ■ That disagreement remains today, as the essays in this cluster clearly reveal. But today the issue of fair trade might be even more complicated than it was when President Truman expressed his views in 1952, for today trade is rarely contained within national borders. The arguments in this cluster about fair trade in coffee, for example, suggest that the impact of globalization on trade is not always easy to identify. In some cases measures that were intended to protect growers and help them improve their working conditions seem to harm consumers. On the other hand, lower prices and business practices that seem to benefit consumers can result in the exploitation of workers. And when trade involves goods such as coffee that cross international borders, many different laws and policies can come into play. Solutions are never easy to find. ■ But solutions will need to be found, because the question of what constitutes fair trade is a vitally important one. It relates not only to the prices we pay for goods but also to the responsibilities we all have as consumers. In that respect, fair trade is of concern to all of us.

CON-TEXT: **Harry Truman and Fair Trade**

1 This act has to do with the so-called fair-trade laws of 45 States. Under these State fair-trade laws, a manufacturer of a trademark or brand name product can, if he wishes, fix the price at which his product may be sold. . . . This means that every retailer in a given State may be required to sell "fair-traded" products at the same price, and no retailer may attempt to attract customers by reducing his prices on any such product. . . .

The central question posed by this act, therefore, is whether the limitations on competition that are established under the State fair-trade laws should be given the sanction of Federal law.

The main reason given for enacting the State fair-trade laws is to prevent some merchants from selling branded items at very low prices (often below cost) in order to drive other merchants out of business, or in order to attract customers who are then sold other items on which high prices are charged. There is no doubt that such practices exist, and that the fair-trade laws prevent them to some extent. . . .

At the same time, there is no doubt that the fair-trade laws also have the effect of removing some competitive forces which otherwise would operate to help keep prices down. Under the fair-trade laws, retailers cannot compete with each other by reducing the price of branded products, even where such reductions may reflect greater efficiency by one retailer as compared to another. . . .

5 I do not believe that the fair-trade laws are as harmful to competition as some have asserted. There are and will be strong competitive forces among manufacturers, wholesalers, and retailers even with the fair-trade laws in effect.

At the same time, it is clear that fair-trade laws are no cure-all for the problems of small retailers. While the fair-trade laws protect him against some types of cutthroat competition, the local independent merchant will continue to have to offer better and more convenient service, and to sell at reasonable prices, if he is to survive against the legitimate and keen competition of such modern advances in the retail field as the supermarket, the mail-order house, and the branch department store.

I have signed this act because it does have value in eliminating certain unfair competitive practices, and thereby will help small businessmen to stay in business — which I believe is a healthy thing for our economy and our society.

At the same time, I believe the fair-trade laws do remove some competitive forces which should be retained in our progressive free enterprise economy.

SOURCE: Statement by President Harry S. Truman on Signing "Fair Trade" Law, July 14, 1952.

① PATRICIA HEWITT, "Free Trade for a Fair, Prosperous World"

Free trade and fair trade are not the same thing. In fact, many critics of globalization and of the economic policies of large capitalist nations such as the United States argue that truly free trade can never be fair because free trade ultimately means that some people will suffer. As corporations try to maximize their profits, some critics say, they inevitably make decisions that harm some people, usually low-paid workers. For example, when U.S. automakers moved factories from Michigan to Mexico to reduce labor costs, they left many American autoworkers jobless and avoided giving Mexican workers the benefits that had once been provided to Americans. Good business practices can thus lead to bad outcomes for some people. Patricia Hewitt does not believe that such tradeoffs are inevitable. She is a proponent of free trade because she believes that it will lead to fair and prosperous conditions for workers, provided that it is conducted ethically. In the following essay, which was originally delivered as a speech in 2001 to the European Institute, a public policy organization in Washington, D.C., Hewitt lays out her vision for ethical free trade. In the process, she offers a vision of fairness in trade as well, and she challenges businesspeople — especially those who support globalization — to accept their responsibilities for fostering fairness in the marketplace. Patricia Hewitt is the British Secretary of State for Trade and Industry.

Free Trade for a Fair, Prosperous World
PATRICIA HEWITT

*The World Trade Round to which Hewitt refers is a round of trade negotiations facilitated by the World Trade Organization, which describes itself as "the only global international organization dealing with the rules of trade between nations."

1 I'm delighted to be here today.

I am here in Washington to demonstrate that we can work together to advance those principles, to boost free trade and economic growth through a new World Trade Round.*

But the backdrop for our discussion today is Genoa, and the appalling violence that marked the G8 summit last weekend. The Plan for Africa lost in media coverage of the protests. A beautiful city devastated. Hundreds of police officers and protesters injured [around 500 people injured, more than 70 police]. And a young man dead.

Many of those protesters came from the United Kingdom. A few from the United States. If you read the eyewitness accounts of the journalists who traveled with them to Genoa, I think you will be struck by two things. First, that many of the protesters — although a minority — had no interest whatsoever in peaceful protest. They wanted violence — and they got it. As Tony Blair said last weekend, protesters have learned that if they make their point peacefully, the media aren't interested. Trash a city, and you are seen on every TV in the world.

5 But you would have to be struck, too, by how varied the protesters were. The middle-aged priest. The elderly woman. The retired sub-postmaster. The retired vicar and his daughter. A software engineer from IBM. The middle-aged community nurse.

I see similar groups in my own Parliamentary constituency — churchgoers, active supporters of development charities, who truly believe that world trade is a disaster for the world's poor. They may disapprove of the violent methods of the anarchists and the extremists — but they are united in their hatred of globalisation.

This is the challenge to all of us. We must make the case for globalisation. We must show that free and fair trade is the only answer. And we must create the institutions that will make globalisation work for the poor as well as the rich.

The question is not whether we should be for or against globalisation, but — in the words of Kofi Annan[†] — "how to ensure that globalisation becomes a positive force for all the world's people, instead of leaving billions of them behind in squalor."

The arguments for globalisation are, in essence, quite simple. On the one hand, the threat of protectionism. On the other, the hope of prosperity.

The Threat of Protectionism

10 When the economic cycle turns down, when people are losing jobs, it is the easiest time to argue against global trade. But history shows that protectionism[‡] always and everywhere damages the interests of working people.

That was the painful lesson of the 1930s, when raising tariffs to their highest level in US history simply intensified the Depression, compounding the misery for businesses and working people.

My father grew up in Australia in the great depression. He never forgot it — and as a young public servant with the Australian government after the war, he helped write GATT, the General Agreement on Tariffs and Trade[§] — the great contribution of his generation to promoting prosperity.

NAFTA and the last World Trade Round, the Uruguay Round, built on GATT and — over the last ten years — contributed to the longest period of economic growth in US history.

As we now experience a slowdown we must not repeat the mistakes of the past.

15 Those who stand in the way of world trade make the threat of a global recession more real.

If we in the West retreat to protectionism now, it will be damaging for us . . . but disastrous for the poor.

The Hope of Prosperity

That is, if you like, the negative argument for world trade. But look too at its flip side: the hope of prosperity.

Look at South Korea. In 1970, their economy was hidden behind protection-

> CONTEXT
>
> In 2001 representatives of the Group of Eight, or G-8 (see Context on page 587 in Chapter 12), met in Genoa, Italy, to discuss issues of world poverty, health, and debt relief. At the summit G-8 leaders agreed to adopt an extensive plan for economic development in Africa, addressing such issues as democratization, health, education, technology, corruption, and trade. The summit was marked by protests, some of which turned violent, leaving one man dead.

[†]A native of Ghana, Kofi Annan is the Secretary-General of the United Nations. He was appointed to the post in 1997.

[‡]Protectionism refers to a nation's efforts to protect its agriculture and industry from international competition. It usually involves tariffs on imported goods and subsidies to support its own industries.

[§]The General Agreement on Trade and Tariffs (GATT) and the North American Free Trade Agreement (NAFTA) are intended to foster international trade. See the margin gloss on NAFTA, GATT, and Maastricht on page 555 in Chapter 12.

COMPLICATION

For another view of Korea's economic success, see Complication on page 608 of this chapter.

*Everything But Arms is an initiative of the European Union (EU), begun in 2001, to open access to markets for developing nations. Everything But Arms grants duty-free and quota-free access to exports from developing nation to the EU.

ist walls. They were poorer than Nigeria. Today, South Korea is six times richer than Nigeria — and the opening up of the country to world trade is one of the reasons why.

Developing countries — like Bangladesh, China, India, Ghana, Nepal, Uganda and Vietnam — that became much more open to trade in the 1980s and 90s, have experienced growth rates above, in some cases well above, the global average.

20 As George Bush said in his address to the Organisation of American States here in Washington in April: "Open trade fuels the engines of economic growth that creates new jobs and new income. It applies the power of markets to the needs of the poor. It spurs the process of economic and legal reform' [and] reinforces the habits of liberty that sustain democracy over the long term."

We cannot stand by when 1.2 billion people — a fifth of the world's population — are living on less than $1 a day.

The answer is not a global minimum wage. The answer is capacity building — to help them build their economies, build their societies, so that they can earn a living.

As the old development movement proverb puts it: "Give a man a fish, and he'll eat for a day. Teach him how to fish and he'll eat forever".

The 49 least developed countries account for nearly 11% of the world's population, but only 0.4% of the world's exports — and that small percentage has been falling. They have suffered from the 30% fall in world commodity prices over the last 20 years. But that is not the sole reason for their marginalisation in the world trading system. These countries — that most need trade to raise them out of poverty — face significant trade barriers. Barriers we must remove.

25 We're starting to make progress.

In the European Union, with the Everything But Arms agreement,* we are giving the Least Developed Countries duty and quota free access for all products except arms.

And last year the United States increased duty free access for countries in sub-Saharan Africa. In the first three months of this year these countries increased their exports to the United States by 24% compared to the same period in 2000.

Nor has that hurt American industries — as some opponents claimed it would. In the same period, US exports of products such as machinery, automobiles and wheat to sub-Saharan Africa were up 23%.

So we need to build on these initiatives.

Fair Rules for World Trade
30 We must deliver an international, rules-based framework for fair trade which provides poor countries with a pathway out of poverty.

We know the poorest countries haven't always benefited from the trading system. It is essential they do so this time. One of the lessons we learnt in Seattle, when we failed to launch a new round, was that a new world trade round will only happen if it benefits the developing countries.

That in turn benefits the West too. We want to open up protected markets in developing countries. Over the next twenty years India and China will emerge as amongst the biggest economies in the world — we must be in there.

And we must be in the next generation of growing economies. We cannot predict which countries or regions of the world economy will grow fastest over the coming decades.

A WTO Round, involving more than

140 member nations, is the best way of ensuring that our businesses can benefit from — and contribute to — future economic growth anywhere in the world.

35 It is estimated that a comprehensive new world trade round could boost the world economy by more than $400 billion annually, and US prosperity by around $45 billion a year.

So the successful launch of a new WTO round is perhaps the single biggest thing we can do to boost confidence in the world economy.

Transcontinental Trade

We also need to work together to extend trade between Europe and America. In the United Kingdom, our businesses and consumers are benefiting from the single European market. Here you are seeing the same benefits from NAFTA. We now need to think transcontinentally as well as continentally.

In the 1980s, at the start of the move towards creating a single European market, we commissioned a serious economic study — the Cecchini report[†] — to quantify the economic gains which it could bring. The figures were so impressive that they convinced European leaders to move forward quickly and enabled them to explain to the people of Europe what this would mean in terms of jobs and prosperity.

We now need to consider a similar report that looks at the potential benefits for businesses and our people on both sides of the Atlantic if we remove the remaining barriers to a fully open trading and commercial relationship between Europe and America. This would be a useful complement to add to the main trade policy task of bold liberalisation in a multilateral trade round.

40 I believe the benefits could be significant. Take one example. In the European Union businesses benefit from mutual recognition of standards — a product which is approved for sale in one country can be put on the market across the European Union without further testing or approval. This saves businesses time and money.

Imagine the benefits if we extended this between Europe and America. Once a company got approval for its home market it could then sell straight into the combined EU and American markets. Increasing trade, cutting costs for business, reducing prices for consumers. The same case can be made for mutual recognition of professional qualifications.

E-commerce is already enabling even the smallest businesses to reach customers around the world; removing nontariff barriers to trade would provide a further boost.

The Challenge to Business

Making globalisation work for all our people is a challenge to governments. But there is also a big challenge to business.

Global businesses have to help win the arguments for globalisation. But win-

[†]Written in 1988 by Paolo Cecchini, a special adviser to the European Commission, "The Cost of Non-Europe," which became known as the Cecchini Report, was a study of the implications of creating a single economic market that included all the nations of Europe. It became the foundation for the Single European Act in 1992, which established the European Union — in effect, a common market encompassing all member nations in Europe.

ning the argument will take deeds as well as words.

45 It is not acceptable for a company to make highly priced clothes for highly paid consumers in the developed world, by ruining the health of women and children in the sweatshops of the developing world.

It is not acceptable for a company to make beautiful furniture for the homes of rich families in the west, but leave a devastated forest landscape in Brazil.

Sooner or later, companies like that will be found out. Their customers will walk away. They will lose their moral licence to operate. And they will lose the argument for globalisation — not only for themselves, but for everyone else as well.

We need global companies that don't just talk the talk, but walk the walk as well.

The companies that do so are seeing the benefits. The other week I went to an awards ceremony in London for businesses who take their social responsibility seriously. I presented one award — to a bank [the Co-operative bank] which estimate that over 15% of their profits come from the fact that they operate a comprehensive ethical policy, using their investment to support human rights and encourage fair trade for developing countries.

50 And we need more companies like the leading home improvement store in Britain (B&Q) which takes seriously its responsibility to reduce the environmental impact of its business on global trading partners. Its environmental strategy includes a strict purchasing policy only to use properly managed timber sources.

And some businesses have found from experience the cost of getting a bad reputation for their activities in developing countries. Nike and GAP have learnt from this experience and now both companies

sponsor an independent NGO, the Global Workers Alliance,* to review their operations.

Shell encountered enormous public concern over its activities in Nigeria, regarding the Ogoni people, and the death of Ken Sarawiwa.† Shell too has made huge efforts to learn from the experience. It has put in place a real campaign to change company culture right from the top. So the businesses that will help to win the argument for globalisation are those that understand that corporate social and environmental responsibility isn't just a nice-to-have. In the global economy, it is a must-have.

Responsible corporate behaviour wins employee loyalty and consumer trust — at a time when more and more citizens are questioning the whole moral basis of the global economy.

Responsible corporate behaviour wins support in the developing world — at a time when many developing countries are reluctant to engage in world trade talks.

Conclusion

55 Responsible corporate behaviour offers an opportunity to improve everyone's quality of life — in developing and developed countries alike.

Opening up markets creates new opportunities for prosperity for people and businesses across the world.

We need a new Trade Round which will benefit our businesses and citizens here, in Europe and in the developing world. Failure risks depriving the slowing global economy of the stimulus it needs and which previous rounds have provided. It risks depriving the world's poorer countries of the opportunities they need to lift themselves out of poverty.

To achieve a new Round we need to work together, to provide leadership and build consensus. The prize is great. We should not let it slip from our grasp.

*Founded in 1999, the Global Workers Alliance is a partnership of foundations, companies, and international institutions devoted to improving the workplace conditions and well-being of workers in developing countries. (See www. globalalliance.org.)

†Nigerian activist and writer Ken Sarawiwa (also spelled Sarowiwa) was opposed to what he believed was the exploitation of Africa by multinational corporations. An internationally known voice for the rights of African peoples, he was frequently jailed for his criticisms of the Nigerian government. In 1994 he was charged with murder as a result of an incident related to ongoing protests against Shell Oil, which had contracts with the Nigerian government that he believed were detrimental to the people of Nigeria. He was convicted and executed in 1995 in what many critics called a gross miscarriage of justice.

Questions for Discussion

1. How does Hewitt set the stage for her argument? What events and developments does she refer to? Why are these events and developments important to her main argument about free and fair trade? Do you think her argument would be less effective without the references to these events and developments? Explain.

2. Hewitt asserts that the arguments for globalization are simple. What are these arguments? Do you agree with her that these arguments are simple? Why or why not? **3.** What evidence does Hewitt present for her claims in support of globalization? How convincing do you find this evidence? What counterarguments can you present to her claims? **4.** In what ways will globalization help the poor, according to Hewitt? How does she support her claim that globalization will lead to prosperity for the poor? **5.** According to your reading of this essay, what are Hewitt's fundamental beliefs about trade and about how a society should function? In what ways do her beliefs influence her main argument? Do you think that most people would share these beliefs? Explain. **6.** What is the challenge facing businesses when it comes to globalization, according to Hewitt? Why is this challenge so important, in her view? What might her discussion of this challenge indicate about her purposes in making this argument? **7.** Hewitt made this argument to an audience at a Washington-based policy organization devoted to issues of cooperation between North American and Europe. In what ways is her argument appropriate for such an audience? Do you think her argument would be persuasive to a broader, more general audience? Why or why not?

② DAVID RANSOM, "Fair Trade: Small Change, Big Difference"

Fair trade is usually understood as a business arrangement whereby the producer of something is fairly paid for a product. On the surface, it is straightforward idea: Workers are fairly compensated for what they produce, and the prices consumers pay for products enable those workers to enjoy a comfortable life. But as David Ransom shows in the following essay, fair trade is no simple matter. Ransom is a vigorous opponent of globalization and an advocate of fair trade. He argues that fair trade can be an important element in the growing effort to counteract globalization, and he describes many of the benefits of fair trade. But he acknowledges the drawbacks of fair trade as well, not the least of which is the small impact it has made so far in the global marketplace. In doing so, Ransom helps us understand the daunting complexities of issues related to globalization and fair trade. He might therefore help you to negotiate arguments about these issues, whether or not you agree with his staunch position. David Ransom writes for the *New Internationalist,* in which this essay appeared in 2000.

Fair Trade: Small Change, Big Difference
DAVID RANSOM

*For information on the anti-globalization protests in Seattle, see the margin gloss on the World Trade Organization meeting in Seattle in 1999 on page 608 of this chapter.

1 Last December *The Economist,* the in-house journal of big business, featured a front-cover picture of a malnourished child crouching under the headline: 'The real losers from Seattle.'[1*] The World Trade Organization (WTO) had just been stopped in its tracks by an unlikely alliance of environmentalists, trade unionists, Southern governments and official bungling. Big business was displeased — it hadn't got the cosy deal it expects from all such occasions.

Now, *The Economist* rarely enlists the 'the poor' to its cause. It may seem churlish to suggest that something must be amiss when it does. But precious little evidence is produced here to support its humanitarian thesis. The editorial just burbles away: India, 'home of our cover child', is poor because 'for four decades it pursued policies of socialist anti-globalization'. Now it has come to its senses and 'begun to embrace globalization, gradually opening itself up to the world. Finally, its economic growth rate, and with it the welfare and prospects of the poor, has begun to pick up. The process has barely begun, but hopes are high.'

So it all boils down to yet more jam tomorrow. No attempt here to explain that India suffered relatively less from the Asian economic crash precisely because its economy was more closed and thus better protected than 'open' economies like Indonesia or Brazil. Nothing to contradict the forecast made by Oxfam — among many others — when the WTO was set up back in 1995, that by 2002 the European Union would have gained $80 billion from trade liberalization while Africa would have lost $2.6 billion.[2] Nothing to deny the hard evidence of history that the 'freer' trade is, the wider the gap between rich and poor invariably becomes. Two hundred years ago, an equivalent headline might well have read: 'Slaves — the real losers from abolition.'

Free trade may have its virtues, but fairness is certainly not one of them. The way it works is quite simple. The awesome forces of globalization are in truth nothing of the kind, merely the result of mundane trade 'deregulation' — in other words, the removal of any democratic control. Transnational corporations, inanimate beings that lay legal claim to human rights and immortality as well, like world trade to be 'free' because they control two-thirds of it, and most of the governments they want to control us.

5 Big business aims to buy cheap from producers and sell dear to consumers, enhancing its profit margins and 'shareholder value' as it goes. Nothing unusual about that, you might think. But 80 per cent of the world's resources are consumed by the richest 20 per cent of the world's population, most of whom live in the North. An increasing proportion of the world's resources, on the other hand, is produced by the 80 per cent of its population who live mostly in the South. That means making monarchs of Northern consumers and wage slaves of Southern producers — hence the notion of 'consumer capitalism'.

World trade was ever thus, from the earliest days of European imperialism, through industrialization to the post-industrial corporate empire of 'information' and consumer capitalism today. There's no obvious reason why it should ever be otherwise. Unless, that is, 80 per cent of the world's population should ever decide to restore some sanity to the situation and take democratic control.

The cure for an illness depends on the diagnosis. In real people the terrible affliction of schizophrenia bears little resemblance to the 'split personality' associated with the label. In consumer capitalism, however — which makes labels and 'brands' the most valuable things on earth — everything is split in two: image and reality, supply and demand, producers and consumers. Real people are never entirely consumers or entirely producers, always both at the same time — and a great deal more besides. We have just one life to live, and one shrinking planet on which to live it. If we are ever to live at peace with ourselves, let alone with one another and the planet, the two halves made by consumer capitalism have to be put back together again.

How can this be done? Revolution, marching in the rain dressed as a turtle, pulling up plants, even writing a letter to your local bigwig are not everyone's cup of tea. So how about this instead? Go shopping! Keep your eyes open for 'Fair Trade' labels on your local supermarket shelves, be prepared to pay a little extra, and it's sorted! This might eventually be everyone's cup of fairly traded tea.

Of course no fair traders ever make such a claim. There are, nonetheless, widely differing claims they do make. Some say that traditional products like handicrafts, made in the South for a fair price and sold in the North by alternative trading organizations (ATOs), help to overcome 'exclusion' from the benefits of conventional trade. Others say that selling Southern products like coffee,

CONTEXT

One of the world's most respected weekly publications, *The Economist* reports on political and economic issues. It openly supports free trade and free markets, and it describes its political viewpoint as "the extreme centre." *The Economist* "considers itself the enemy of privilege, pomposity and predictability. It has backed conservatives such as Ronald Reagan and Margaret Thatcher. It has supported the Americans in Vietnam. But it has also endorsed Harold Wilson and Bill Clinton, and espoused a variety of liberal causes: opposing capital punishment from its earliest days, while favouring penal reform and decolonisation, as well as — more recently — gun control and gay marriage."

CHIQUITA AND FAIR TRADE

In 2001, after years of labor conflicts, Chiquita Brands International, Inc., the largest employer of unionized banana workers in Latin America, signed an agreement on "Freedom of Association, Minimum Labour Standards and Employment in Latin American Banana Operations" with several unions representing banana workers. The agreement requires Chiquita to collaborate with international labor unions to address health and safety concerns at its workplaces. Ron Oswald, General Secretary of the International Union of Food, Agricultural, Hotel, Restaurant, Catering, Tobacco and Allied Workers' Associations (IUF), called the agreement "historic in the truest sense, meaning that it offers the possibility for workers and employers to seek a new basis for the resolution of problems in an industry which has throughout its history been highly confrontational." In 1998 Chiquita had become the focus of controversy after an investigative report about its questionable business practices was published in the *Cincinnati Enquirer*. Among those practices were sustained efforts to oppose labor organizing on its banana plantations and to intimidate workers sympathetic to unions.

*See the margin gloss on Anita Boddick and the Body Shop on page 671 later in this chapter.

chocolate and tea in supermarkets, with a fair-trade label that guarantees a better deal for the producers, not only helps more people but challenges orthodox trading relationships. Still others believe that even more people will benefit if big business is made socially responsible and signs up to codes of conduct. Yet more combine various elements of all three. **10** There are, inevitably, snags with them all. Not every ATO is content with the charitable overtones of a steadily shrinking niche market. Fair-trade labellers have to make unholy alliances with giant retail corporations. Some people think we'd be better off with no world trade at all. Social responsibility, meanwhile, can be an optional extra. Since 1982 Levi Strauss, originally a pioneer in the field, has laid off almost 30,000 largely unionized employees in the US and shifted its garment factories to wage-slave locations in the South — the process continues today.[3] Marks and Spencer is doing much

the same thing in Britain. Market forces trump social responsibility every time.

Besides, there are just 2,000 self-styled 'socially responsible' businesses — like Ben and Jerry's ice cream or The Body Shop* — in the world with an annual turnover of about $2 billion between them. That may sound like a lot, but it is a mere one-hundredth of one per cent of the $20 trillion in sales from 80–100 million enterprises worldwide. Simple maths suggests that we're more likely to experience global boiling than to live in a socially responsible world. As one respected observer, Paul Hawken, has commented: 'What we have is not a management problem but a design problem.'[4]

So what's fair, how do we know and who decides? Is it unfair to a Chiquita banana if a fair-trade banana sits right next to it on a supermarket shelf? Would fair-trade heaven have descended to earth if, say, fair-trade Nescafé were sold by a socially responsible Wal-Mart? Heaven only knows.

Nonetheless, the first and most important task is to get such questions asked at all — and it's because of fair trade that they are. Most fair traders are keenly aware of the compromises they make with survival 'in and against the market' — as most of us do in our everyday lives. All pioneers tend to get lost before they arrive.

Fair trade has now grown up into a venerable middle age. Why, it even has its own veterans. Roy Scott set off into a wilderness 35 years ago and is still going strong from his One Village shop in Woodstock, Britain.[5] Way back in 1972 Richard and Vi Cottrell returned to Aotearoa/New Zealand from India, where they had been working with Tibetan refugees. Determined not to break the connection, they started importing Tibetan crafts at fairer prices — and Trade Aid in Christchurch got going. This year Traidcraft in Gateshead — another pioneer in Britain — celebrates its twenty-first birthday.[6]

15 In the Netherlands and Germany fairly traded coffee now accounts for roughly two per cent of all coffee sales — perhaps $100 million in annual turnover. Fairly traded products reach the public through some 45,000 different points of sale across Europe. Annual ATO sales worldwide exceed $200 million.[3]

I first stumbled across the other end of fair trade late in 1993, while I was researching a magazine about Mexico. I was travelling through the southern state of Chiapas just before the uprising — which, incidentally, coincided with the signing of the North American Free Trade Agreement (NAFTA) on 1 January 1994. In the village of Las Margaritas I found a group of coffee farmers who seemed to believe quite firmly in fair trade and were beginning to receive real benefits from it — better prices, more reliable markets and equal trading partnerships in place of predatory coyotes (intermediaries). Fair trade worked for them, free trade worked against them, and it wasn't hard to tell the difference.

So I decided to look into it a little more closely. I went to Peru in 1995 to talk to coffee farmers on the Andean escarpment of the Amazon rainforest. This time I followed the coffee bean back to Britain with Gregorio Gomez, one of the farmers, finding out along the way exactly how the rip-off gets passed down the free-trade chain to the first and 'weakest' link, coffee farmers like him. Gregorio had only a few reservations about the alternative. What he wanted was more of it.

Last June I was in the Dominican Republic looking at bananas. The growers I met at Finca 6, near the border with Haiti, had achieved something quite remarkable: a fairly traded and organic

fruit. They were delighted with the results, and the reasons were plain enough to see — decent working conditions, decent houses, decent water, kids in college, plump cheeks. . . .

The fact remains that fair trade really does work. There is an alternative. Many thousands of people in the South who would otherwise be living in much more

desperate conditions really do benefit. People who buy fairly traded products in the North really do make a difference. **20** Like any adult, however, fair trade has to take its share of responsibility for the big bad world it inhabits. Why just two per cent of coffee sales and only a tiny proportion of the 20 million lives that depend on farming coffee? The banana growers of Finca 6 seemed so prosperous precisely because their neighbours — that is, virtually everyone else — were anything but. No-one can feel satisfied until fair trade benefits everyone, otherwise it's not fair at all. For that to happen, political change is essential.

Most of the products involved in fair trade are still traditional commodities produced by small farmers or crafts people. Some of them can, and do, take control over what they produce and the land from which they produce it — a basic requirement of fair trade. ATOs in the North can, and do, form partnerships of equals with them. The International Federation

for Alternative Trade (IFAT) is controlled by its members, most of whom represent Southern producers. AgroFair in the Netherlands and the Day Chocolate Company in Britain share ownership with Southern producers.

The vast majority of them, however, work as wage slaves on plantations and in factories, making potato chips and computer chips consumed in the North. 'Fairness' for them hinges on the health or otherwise of the labour movement, part of a Southern civil society — distinct from government and crucial to the development of democracy — that is rapidly emerging. Fair trade and the international labour movement will eventually have to come to terms with each other.

Otherwise the dangers are real. In Seattle, environmental and social clauses were rejected by the opposition to the WTO for the sake of its own unity and on the grounds that the WTO has done quite enough damage already — which is perfectly true. But conceding that the environmental and social agendas belong to Northern, corporate, free-trade interests is quite another matter. Unless the Southern voice of the labour movement is heard loud and clear at the WTO, that is the way it will stay — leaving the opposition without a principle to stand on.

The Canadian journalist Naomi Klein* has just published a brilliant assault on consumer capitalism. She argues at one point that fair trade privatizes what are essentially public issues of democratic accountability. She goes on to suggest that the worst problems of labour exploitation could be overcome almost straight away if the International Labour Organization (ILO) were able to implement its basic standards worldwide.[7] **25** But it can't, because the ILO is part of the UN system and therefore has no teeth. The WTO is not part of the UN system and therefore has a fearsome array

*See the sidebar on Naomi Klein on page 549 in Chapter 12.

of trade penalties it can sink into anyone who steps out of line. Eventually this could affect all public services like health, education and transport. It claims to be democratic because it is supposed to be run by virtually all the world's governments, North and South. But in Seattle the rich countries repaired to the Green Room and cut deals on their own. Market forces prevailed again. What is needed, of course, is a fearsome World Fair Trade Organization run by the UN and accountable to the majority of the world's people who need it, not to the corporations that can fend for themselves all too well.

Trade is the jugular of consumer capitalism, and fair trade in its broadest sense is a very useful weapon, another link in a dynamic new network that has grown from the 1992 Earth Summit and now has to fill the space it created for itself in Seattle. Michael Barratt Brown describes wonderfully well how such networks of people, which fair trade mimics in material form, grow out of localities and regions across national, cultural and geographical boundaries.[8]

My nagging worry is that fair-trade products still cost more to buy and so are apparently aimed at people like me who can just about afford them. In the article that follows ("Dream Scheme," *New Internationalist* 322), Mari Marcel Thekaekara mentions the direct links that her project in India has made with Matson, a neighbourhood of Gloucester. That's not far from where I live, and I decided to pay them a visit.

Matson is a pretty bleak area of public housing where 8,000 tenants got together some ten years ago to stop their homes being sold from under their feet. They won. They also set up the Matson Neighbourhood Project[9] which runs the only shop in one corner of the estate. It's been ram-raided (smashed into by a stolen car and looted) twice and the windows are still boarded up. No place for fancy fair trade, you might think.

Far from it. They've been exploring the scope for Matson Tea, imported directly from the growers in India and sold to local authorities, employers, co-op retailers and anyone else who's interested. True, as yet they don't actually have the tea. True, not everyone in Matson likes the taste of it. True, ram-raiding doesn't help. These things take time.

So I asked one of the more sceptical women if she thought she'd been wasting her time with fair trade. She was indignant. 'Good lord, no!' she said. 'We've had great fun!'

Up to that point no-one had suggested to me that fair trade, with or without the tea, could ever be fun. The very best motive there could possibly be, I reckon.

1. *The Economist,* 11–17 December 1999.
2. See *New Internationalist* 271, September 1995, keynote. Available at www.newint.org/issue271/intro.html.
3. Information from Fuerza Unida: chisme@igc.apc.org
4. I'm indebted to Bob Thomson for this information — more is available on www.fairtrade.org/fairtrade or www.transfair.ca
5. Contact progress@onevillage.co.uk
6. Contact details in 'Action' section. Available at www.newint.org/issue322/action.htm.
7. Naomi Klein, *No Logo,* Flamingo, London, 2000.
8. Michael Barratt Brown, *Fair Trade,* Zed Books, London and New Jersey, 1993.
9. Contact andy.jarrett@talk21.com

COMPLICATION

According to its Web site, the World Trade Organization is not an undemocratic organization, as its critics often claim. It asserts that its decisions are made generally by consensus and states, "It would be wrong to suggest that every country has the same bargaining power. Nevertheless, the consensus rule means every country has a voice, and every country has to be convinced before it joins a consensus. Quite often reluctant countries are persuaded by being offered something in return."

CONTEXT

Based in Oxford, the *New Internationalist* claims to "report on issues of world poverty and inequality; to focus attention on the unjust relationship between the powerful and the powerless in both rich and poor nations; to debate and campaign for the radical changes necessary if the basic material and spiritual needs of all are to be met." It is published by the New Internationalist Cooperative, which "opposes all forms of oppression and campaigns for social justice worldwide, acting as a vehicle for unheard voices from the South and elsewhere."

Questions for Discussion

1. What are Ransom's central complaints about globalization? How does he establish the problems that he sees with globalization? **2.** Ransom never explicitly defines what he means by *fair trade* in this essay. But he describes several examples of fair trade and discusses what he believes are the benefits and drawbacks of fair trade. On the basis of these discussions in his essay, define *fair trade* as Ransom seems to understand it. **3.** What kinds of facts and figures does Ransom use to support his claims about the effects of globalization? Do you find these facts and figures credible? Explain. In what ways do you think they strengthen his argument? **4.** What solution to the problems of globalization does Ransom propose? What benefits does he claim his solution would have? What drawbacks to his solution does he acknowledge? How realistic do you think his solution is, in view of the problems with globalization that he describes? **5.** Ransom offers two primary examples of fairly traded goods: coffee and bananas. How effectively do these examples illustrate his claims about fair trade as a solution to the problems of globalization? What do these two examples suggest about the potential benefits and limitations of fair trade as a solution to the problems Ransom describes? **6.** How would you characterize Ransom's tone in this essay? Do you think his tone is appropriate for his argument? Does it strengthen or weaken his argument, in your view? Explain, citing specific passages from his essay to support your answer. **7.** Ransom's essay was published in the *New Internationalist,* which reflects a progressive anticapitalist editorial viewpoint (see Context on page 645). In what ways does his essay address the kind of audience that is likely to read this journal? How effective do you think his argument would be for readers of *The Economist,* a pro–free trade magazine that Ransom criticizes in his essay?

③ **BIANCA JAGGER, "Squeezed to the Last Drop"**

The simple pleasure of a cup of coffee seems to obscure the importance of coffee in the complicated debates about fair trade. As a product with worldwide appeal, coffee was traded actively in international markets long before globalization became a controversial issue. But as globalization reshaped international markets, the coffee industry began to experience changes that led to labor conflicts as well as environmental controversies. Coffee suppliers began to buy large quantities of coffee from growers in Central and South America, which led to changes in growing and labor practices — changes that many critics claimed were unfair to workers and damaging to the environment. Meanwhile, the popularity of coffee continued to increase, particularly in the United States, where specialty coffees claimed a growing share of the market. But despite its popularity, coffee decreased in price, and the industry as a whole suffered. As human rights activist Bianca Jagger reports in the following essay, no one has suffered more than the small coffee growers. She describes the plight of such growers in her native Nicaragua and elsewhere in Central America, an important coffee-producing region. She traces the problem to the practices of large corporations involved in the coffee trade, and she calls for support of fair trade coffee as a solution. In doing so, Jagger helps us to see the role that coffee plays in the complicated relationship between free trade and fair trade. Her essay was published in the *Washington Post* in 2002.

Squeezed to the Last Drop
BIANCA JAGGER

*Founded in 1942, Oxfam is one of the world's leading nongovernmental relief organizations. Its programs focus on alleviating poverty throughout the world.

1　When I was growing up in Nicaragua, I used to spend my summer vacations in the beautiful mountains of Matagalpa and Jinotega, an area with some of the best coffee plantations in the country. My father would say with pride, "Coffee produced in this region is among the finest in the world."

　　Today the mountains remain as beautiful as ever, and Nicaraguans continue to rely on coffee as one of the country's main sources of income. But coffee growers, who have faced difficult conditions throughout Nicaragua's tumultuous history, are coping with an unprecedented disaster. The development and relief organization Oxfam* has documented in its new report "Mugged: Poverty in Your Coffee Cup" how a nearly 50 percent drop in the world coffee price in the past three years has left 25 million small-scale coffee producers in abject poverty around the world.

　　In Central America alone, some 600,000 coffee workers have been left unemployed in the past two years,

according to a recent World Bank report. The plantations on which they work are being shut down as prices have plummeted to their lowest levels in a century. In Nicaragua, already the second-poorest nation in the hemisphere, thousands of coffee farm workers are without food, land or hope.

The current coffee crisis must be placed in a historical perspective. The coffee exporting and importing countries created the International Coffee Agreement (ICA) in 1962 to manage supply and demand on the world market, and as a result prices remained relatively high and stable. The United States played a lead role in establishing the ICA because it recognized that coffee is

CONTEXT

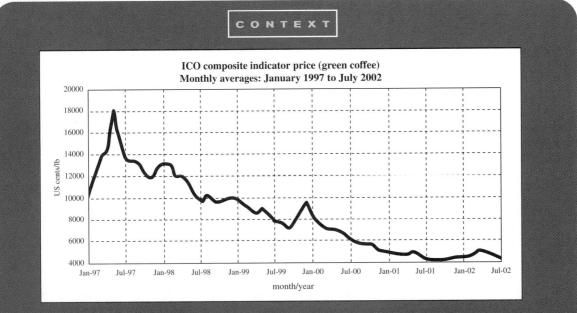

ICO composite indicator price (green coffee)
Monthly averages: January 1997 to July 2002

Established to implement the International Coffee Agreement, the International Coffee Organization (ICO) monitors the coffee industry and serves as an advocate for those involved in the industry. It estimates that more than 125 million people worldwide depend upon coffee for their livelihood, but the continued drop in world coffee prices since the 1990s has caused hardship among coffee growers, especially in countries where coffee is a primary source of revenue (see chart). The ICO asserts that the current crisis "is caused by the current imbalance between supply and demand for coffee. . . . Coffee production has been rising at an average annual rate of 3.6%, but demand has been increasing by only 1.5%. At the origin of this coffee glut lies the rapid expansion of production in Vietnam and new plantations in Brazil, which is harvesting a record crop in the current season."

critical to maintaining political and economic stability in dozens of developing countries.

5 In 1989 the agreement collapsed, in part because the U.S. government no longer viewed a managed coffee market as vital to national security. Instead it championed the ideology of free trade, coupled with "structural adjustment" policies imposed on developing countries by the International Monetary Fund and the World Bank. These institutions promoted a general model of export-led growth tied to developing countries' "comparative advantage." This strategy often encouraged poor nations to increase production of green coffee and other raw materials, thereby deepening their dependence on primary commodities whose value has plummeted in the global marketplace. Not surprisingly, these large production increases have resulted in a global oversupply of coffee that has depressed prices to record lows.

Little more than a decade ago, coffee-producing countries were receiving about $10 billion of a $30 billion annual retail market. At present exporting countries' share has shrunk to less than $6 billion, while the value of the annual coffee retail market has nearly doubled, to $55 billion.

And who is getting ever-larger portions of the coffee bounty while everyone else is going hungry? The world's biggest coffee companies: Procter & Gamble, Kraft, Sara Lee and Nestle. Meanwhile, millions of poor coffee growers have been left in economic ruin.

The system must be changed. I urge coffee companies, governments, international institutions and consumers to join me in supporting Oxfam's campaign to alleviate this humanitarian crisis. The campaign calls for the following actions:

■ The "Big Four" coffee companies should demonstrate their commitment to addressing the crisis by paying farmers a decent price. Companies should review and overhaul their core sourcing practices and, as a down payment, immediately commit to buying at least 2 percent of their coffee on Fair Trade terms. Fair Trade Certification guarantees that farmers receive a minimum price of $1.26 per pound ($1.41 for organic beans) — a far cry from the meager 20 to 30 cents per pound they are now generally receiving.

■ The United States and other coffee-consuming countries should provide political and financial support to resolve the oversupply problem, including monitoring coffee quality and destroying lowest-quality coffee stocks. The United States should rejoin the International Coffee Organization to contribute to multilateral efforts to address this global crisis.

I applaud the House of Representatives — led by Reps. Sam Farr (D-Calif.), Benjamin A. Gilman (R-N.Y.) and Cass Ballenger (R-N.C.) — and the Senate — led by Sens. Patrick J. Leahy (D-Vt.), Christopher J. Dodd (D-Conn.) and Arlen Specter (R-Pa.) — for recently passing resolutions that call on the United States to "adopt a global strategy to respond to the current coffee crisis." Now that this legislation has passed unanimously in both chambers, Congress must take

COMPLICATION

"Bianca Jagger writes that governments and companies must 'support Oxfam's campaign' to help the world's poor coffee farmers, who are experiencing prices at a 30-year low. Unfortunately, Ms. Jagger's proposal will only harm poor farmers and consumers.

"Jagger calls for multinational companies to pay farmers a 'decent' price. But driving this proposal is small coffee companies who want to use the International Coffee Organization to drive up production prices for multinational companies (and consumers). This will harm farmers who produce cheaply, such as those in Vietnam, who will likely be forced back into the poverty of subsistence agriculture. Oxfam has also recommended that governments spend $100 million of aid money to destroy surplus coffee, but this will simply encourage more farmers to produce coffee, sowing more trouble down the road.

"The real perpetrators of the problem are the vested interests who benefit from economic protectionism provided by agricultural subsidies in the US and Europe, which distort prices against goods produced by poor farmers and prevent them from diversifying into other, highly valued agricultural products. Likewise, high tariffs on finished goods (such as processed, 'instant' coffee) mean that companies do not invest in processing technologies in poor countries, again to the detriment of poor farmers." Source: Kendra Okonski, International Policy Network (2002).

concrete and meaningful action in the next session to support a sustainable solution to this crisis.

■ International institutions such as the World Bank and the United Nations should develop a long-term integrated strategy to tackle the problem of commodities pricing, provide additional debt relief and support a major international stakeholders' conference on the coffee crisis next spring.

The price of coffee is a matter of life or death to millions of small-scale producers throughout the developing world. Free trade has left them in economic ruin. **10** The time has come to make the coffee trade fair.

Questions for Discussion

1. Jagger begins her essay with a reference to her childhood in a coffee-growing region of Nicaragua. What effect do you think her reference to her childhood in Nicaragua might have on readers? What effect did it have on you? What kind of appeal do you think Jagger is making with this reference? (You might refer to Chapter 2 in answering this question.) **2.** How does Jagger establish the crisis in the coffee industry? What evidence does she offer to support her claims about this crisis? How persuasive do you find this evidence? **3.** As a solution to the coffee crisis, Jagger calls for support of a fair trade campaign by the international relief organization Oxfam. What justification does she offer for such a solution? How convincing do you think her argument is in support of this solution? **4.** In addition to being a well-known human rights activist, Bianca Jagger is famous for having been married to Mick Jagger, the lead singer of the rock band the Rolling Stones. Do you think her celebrity status in any way influences her credibility as an advocate for fair trade in coffee? Explain.

④ **RODNEY NORTH, "Finding Meaning in a Cup of Coffee"**

Like Bianca Jagger, whose essay appears in this cluster (page 647), Rodney North advocates fair trade as a way to address the serious economic and environmental problems in the coffee industry. But unlike Jagger, North makes his argument from the perspective of a businessperson. He works for Equal Exchange, a business organization that promotes fair trade in coffee. His perspective is important in part because debates about the coffee crisis and about fair trade in general often fall along predictable lines: businesspeople versus environmentalists, workers' rights advocates versus corporations. When debates about issues as complicated as fair trade are reduced to such either-or positions, common ground can be difficult to find, but North offers common ground in his essay. He argues that business success and the principles of fair trade can be achieved at the same time. Given the complexity of the issues he addresses (a complexity that is shown in the other essays in this cluster), you might find North's argument idealistic. On the other hand, his argument might be a step toward a solution that all parties in the debates about fair trade can live with. His essay was published in 2001 as a syndicated column by the Center for a New American Dream.

Finding Meaning in a Cup of Coffee
RODNEY NORTH

1 Imagine this. I'm a businessman. But I'm also an environmentalist. And I worry whether our suppliers in poor countries are paid enough. Is all that at odds? Can such a mix of values — profit, nature, fairness — really be reconciled? Or does progress in one area always mean falling short in another? Not necessarily. I know firsthand that companies can do this, and that mindful consumers help make it happen.

My example comes from the specialty coffee industry, a $3 billion sector that is taking small, but critical steps towards tackling entrenched social and ecological problems involved in coffee production.

Coffee is big business. Americans alone drink over 400,000,000 cups every day. 20 million people around the world make their living growing, harvesting and supplying the rest of us with all that coffee. Most of those people are laborers or farmers with small plots of land. Some are both. Normally it's a hard life, but these days it's even worse. Coffee prices for farmers are at an eight-year low, around 62 cents a pound. Your coffee's the same as always; so is the farmer's work. But their "paycheck" has been cut in half. Few farmers get even 62 cents per pound. After the exporter, the processor and others take their cuts, a

COFFEE GROWING AND THE ENVIRONMENT

"Traditionally coffee had been shade grown, cultivated on small family farms beneath forest canopies often as richly biodiverse as tropical rain forests. Came, then, an economic move to growing coffee as a mono-crop, based on newly-developed seed strains and agro-chemicals. To facilitate these changes forest canopies were thinned; sometimes stripped completely.

"The changeover to sun grown coffee was massive, a conversion of nearly 40% of coffee growing land in Latin America and the Caribbean during the early Nineties. In the short term the benefits of intensification to small growers have been significant. However, little time passed before a down side began to emerge. . . .

"Sun coffee farming has also been demonstrated to impact negatively on the environment in several ways. Studies in Colombia and Mexico indicated 90% fewer bird species than in canopied farm land. This suggests insects and other species have also diminished, gone as quickly as the habitat that had sustained them. Gone too are their ecological benefits.

"Agro-chemical inputs — fertilizers, pesticides, and herbicides — have been shown to damage water quality. In some documented cases, hundreds of local people have fallen ill due to pollution." Source: Arthur Montague, "Organic Coffee by Default," INeedCoffee.com (2002).

small farmer might not get even 30 cents a pound.

A Fair Price for the Farmer

Some farmers will give up, and look for work on the plantations or in the overcrowded cities. Others will try to hold on to their family's land and probably go into debt. They will hope for better prices at the next harvest, as they and their ancestors have done for generations.

5 Fortunately there's another option. It's called "fair trade." Think of it as a minimum wage safety net for small farmers. When coffee is fairly traded, importers like us buy directly from co-ops of small farmers, not the elites who normally control coffee exports. And the farmers will always get at least a fair price (currently $1.26 a pound), or the market price, whichever is higher.

But how can paying extra work as a profitable business? First, because we have different goals — and maximizing our profits isn't one of them. By accepting smaller profits, and recruiting investors who share our values, we have more money available to pay the farmers. Second, it works because consumers go for it. We have found that many people care where their shopping dollars go, and when they know they have an alternative like fair trade, at a fair price, they buy it — literally.

Farming with Nature

Coffee production and consumption also offer some important ecological choices. Since an area the size of Ohio is used to grow the world's coffee it matters how that land is farmed. Much of the world's crop is grown in what some call "green deserts." These are places where the native forest has been replaced with endless rows of short coffee trees, dependent upon a toxic cocktail of chemical fertilizers, pesticides, and herbicides. Loss of

CONTEXT

This essay originally appeared as a column on the Web site for the Center for a New American Dream, an organization that "helps Americans consume responsibly to protect the environment, enhance quality of life and promote social justice." The center supports a variety of education and advocacy initiatives focused on environmental protection and community revitalization. Consider the extent to which North's essay reflects the mission of the center.

wildlife habitat, contamination of streams, and pesticide poisonings are all common problems. However, most of the best coffee can grow well without chemicals, especially when planted in a mixed ecosystem that resembles the original forest. The yield per acre from such organic farming is lower, but so are the costs to the farmer. Meanwhile, the coffee trees live longer, soil erosion is less, and the farmer gets a better price thanks to the growing popularity of organic foods. That strong consumer demand in turn allows our company to be both profitable and gentle on the earth.

Just One Example

Organic coffee and fair trade coffee are just two examples of how commerce can be combined with a concern for the earth and for fairness. In Europe they have extended fair trade to cocoa, bananas, and sugar. Here at home Americans already buy over seven billions dollars of organic food annually.

In the end I choose to view business as a tool, and not just for the so-called fat cats and old style capitalists. All of us, whether as consumers, investors, or entrepreneurs, can help decide how this tool is used and to what end.

10 And while the old definition of success may have centered on money and status, a new definition of success can mean that everyone — not just the business owner — has enough, and that our work today leaves the earth undiminished for future generations.

Questions for Discussion

1. North uses the example of the coffee industry to make his main argument about fair trade. Summarize that main argument. How effective is his use of the example of coffee in making that argument? What advantages and disadvantages do you see to his using the example of coffee in this way? **2.** North claims that maximizing profits is not one of his goals as a businessperson. What are his goals? Given that maximizing profits is usually considered the primary goal of a business, how do you think other businesspeople might react to North's claim? How might such a reaction affect his main argument? **3.** What are the main reasons that North offers in support of his claim that fair trade in coffee will help both coffee growers and businesspeople? How persuasive is his support for this claim? **4.** How would you describe North's tone and style in this essay? In what ways are his tone and style appropriate to his argument? What effect do you think they have on his credibility? Do you think they enhance or weaken his argument in any way? Explain. **5.** Using the Toulmin Model of Argumentation (see pages 31–35), identify North's central claim in this essay. Also identify his main warrant (or warrants) for that claim. Do you think most readers would accept his warrant? Explain. Does North justify that warrant in any way? Does he need to?

NEGOTIATING DIFFERENCES

Because globalization tends to be defined in economic terms, fair trade has become an increasingly important part of the ongoing debates about globalization. Moreover, as the essays in this section indicate, fair trade is not just about economic issues but also about questions of lifestyle, ethics, and culture. These essays also show that such issues are not abstract but can affect us directly in the form of such seemingly simple things as coffee or bananas. For this assignment you will examine one such "sim-

ple" product in your life to explore the implications of fair trade.

First, identify a product that you use regularly. The essays in this section mention several products — coffee, bananas, and chocolate, to name a few. Each of these products is traded internationally, and the consumers of these products generally live far from where the products themselves are produced. Try to identify a product with such characteristics. You might choose to focus on one of the products mentioned in these essays, or you might wish to identify a different product.

Once you have identified the product, examine how it is used by you and by others in your community. How important is this product? What role does it play in your life and in your community? Find out how it is produced and marketed. Try to learn the kinds of things about this product that David Ransom, Bianca Jagger, and Rodney North tell us about coffee in their essays.

Now write an essay in which you make an argument about fair trade, using your selected product as an example of what fair trade means from the point of view of a consumer in your community. What are the effects of fair trade on you and other consumers of this product? Are these effects good or bad? What changes should be made? Try to support your position with specific facts and information about the product you have identified, and try to base your argument on your own beliefs about how fair trade should contribute to our collective well-being.

HOW SHOULD WE SHARE THE EARTH?

I n 1997 the United Nations organized an international conference in Kyoto, Japan, to address the problem of climate change. The conference grew out of increasing concerns that the earth's atmosphere is growing warmer. Scientific studies seemed to provide evidence that changes in the earth's atmosphere, brought on in part by human activity, especially the burning of fossil fuels, would have potentially catastrophic results, including extreme droughts, rising tides, and altered growing seasons in the world's agricultural regions. In the face of such concerns, representatives of 124 nations gathered in Kyoto, hoping to reach an agreement that would lead to a reduction in the greenhouse gases believed to cause global warming. The conference was marked by controversy, in part because of disagreements among some nations about whether global warming was in fact happening and whether humans were causing it. Despite the controversy, an agreement was reached. It came to be known as the Kyoto Protocol (see *Con-Text* on page 657). ■ The Kyoto agreement called for nations to take steps to reduce the production of greenhouse gases significantly by the year 2010. These steps would emphasize efforts to reduce carbon dioxide emissions as well as other gases from power plants and automobiles. The goal was to slow, if not reverse, the addition of these gases to the atmosphere and thereby slow the rate at which the atmosphere is warming. But achieving that goal would mean significant changes in the way human beings produced electricity and power; it could also affect automobile and air travel and other forms of transportation. In other words, the Kyoto Protocol had the potential to profoundly change how human beings live and work. Largely for this reason, many people in the United States opposed the agreement. Business leaders, for example, argued that the agreement would lead to economic hardship in many industries and perhaps even provoke a recession that would have consequences around the world. Some critics argued that the agreement was based on poor scientific evidence and that more time was needed to determine whether global warming was a result of human activity. Despite these intensifying debates, 105 nations had ratified the agreement as of early 2003. The United States was not among them. ■ In late 2002 President George W. Bush's declaration that the United States would not ratify the agreement provoked severe criticism from many world leaders. They worried that without the participation of the United States, the world's leading economic power — and a leading producer of greenhouse gases — the Kyoto Protocol could not achieve its goals. The ongoing controversy underscores the challenge of addressing serious environmental problems. ■ Global warming is only one such problem. The essays in this cluster address two others: the depletion of fish populations in the world's oceans and the environmental destruction caused by energy use, especially fossil fuels. But the list of such problems is a long one, including

- the scarcity of water resources in many parts of the world;
- the disappearance of hundreds of species of plants and animals;
- the loss of biodiversity as rain forests are destroyed for logging, farming, and ranching;
- and the environmental destruction caused by acid rain.

Such problems are not contained within national borders. They are global problems that affect all the earth's residents. That fact makes them extremely pressing problems. It also makes them extremely difficult to solve. ■ As the continuing controversy about the Kyoto Protocol suggests — and as the essays in this cluster also indicate — environmental problems like global warming are much more than scientific or ecological challenges. They are also social, cultural, and ethical challenges, and to address these challenges requires us to confront the question, How should we share our earth? These essays might help you begin to find answers to that question.

CON-TEXT: The Kyoto Protocol

Article 1

1. Each Party included in Annex I, in achieving its quantified emission limitation and reduction commitments under Article 3, in order to promote sustainable development, shall:

(a) Implement and/or further elaborate policies and measures in accordance with its national circumstances, such as:

(i) Enhancement of energy efficiency in relevant sectors of the national economy;

(ii) Protection and enhancement of sinks and reservoirs of greenhouse gases not controlled by the Montreal Protocol, taking into account its commitments under relevant international environmental agreements; promotion of sustainable forest management practices, afforestation and reforestation;

(iii) Promotion of sustainable forms of agriculture in light of climate change considerations;

(iv) Research on, and promotion, development and increased use of, new and renewable forms of energy, of carbon dioxide sequestration technologies and of advanced and innovative environmentally sound technologies;

(v) Progressive reduction or phasing out of market imperfections, fiscal incentives, tax and duty exemptions and subsidies in all greenhouse gas emitting sectors that run counter to the objective of the Convention and application of market instruments;

(vi) Encouragement of appropriate reforms in relevant sectors aimed at promoting policies and measures which limit or reduce emissions of greenhouse gases not controlled by the Montreal Protocol;

(vii) Measures to limit and/or reduce emissions of greenhouse gases not controlled by the Montreal Protocol in the transport sector;

(viii) Limitation and/or reduction of methane emissions through recovery and use in waste management, as well as in the production, transport and distribution of energy; . . .

Article 2

1. The Parties included in Annex I shall, individually or jointly, ensure that their aggregate anthropogenic carbon dioxide equivalent emissions of the greenhouse gases listed in Annex A do not exceed their assigned amounts, calculated pursuant to their quantified emission limitation and reduction commitments inscribed in Annex B and in accordance with the provisions of this Article, with a view to reducing their overall emissions of such gases by at least 5 percent below 1990 levels in the commitment period 2008 to 2012.

SOURCE: The Kyoto Protocol to the United Nations Framework Convention on Climate Change, 1997.

① BOB HERBERT, "No Margin for Error"

The intense debates about global warming often focus on scientific evidence. Those concerned about global warming point to numerous studies that seem to provide overwhelming evidence that the earth's temperature is indeed rising. But even if there were agreement about rising global temperatures (and there isn't), there remain questions about whether the warming is caused by humans and, perhaps more important, what the consequences of rising global temperatures will be. Columnist Bob Herbert is chiefly concerned with this last question. In the following essay he describes the apparent effects of global warming on one crucial ecosystem: the earth's oceans. Herbert knows that scientists and policy makers disagree about the extent of global warming and its impact. But he argues that the potential for catastrophic environmental damage is so great that we cannot waste time debating any longer. His essay underscores the sense of urgency that many people feel about problems like global warming. Bob Herbert is an award-winning columnist for the *New York Times,* in which this essay was published in 2002.

No Margin for Error
BOB HERBERT

1 Global warming is already attacking the world's coral reefs and, if nothing is done soon, could begin a long-term assault on the vast West Antarctic Ice Sheet. If the ice sheet begins to disintegrate, the worldwide consequences over the next several centuries could well be disastrous.

Coral reefs are sometimes called the rain forests of the oceans because of the tremendous variety of animal and plant life that they support.

"They're the richest ocean ecosystem, and if they are destroyed or severely damaged, a lot of the biological diversity simply goes away," said Dr. Michael Oppenheimer, a professor of geosciences and international affairs at Princeton who is an expert on climate change.

Dr. Oppenheimer and Brian C. O'Neill, a professor at Brown, have an article in the current issue of *Science* magazine that addresses some of the long-term dangers that could result if nothing is done about global warming.

5 One of the things that is not widely understood about the greenhouse gases that are contributing to the warming of the planet is that once they are spewed into the atmosphere, they stay there for centuries, and in some cases, millenniums. So a delay of even a decade or so in reducing those emissions can make it much more difficult — and costly — to slow the momentum of the warming and avert the more extreme consequences.

In their article, Dr. Oppenheimer and Dr. O'Neill suggest that public officials and others trying to determine what levels of global warming would actually be dangerous could use the destruction of the world's coral reefs as one of their guides.

Coral reefs, which are breathtakingly beautiful natural phenomena, tend to thrive in water temperatures that are only slightly below the maximum temperature at which they can survive. There is not much margin for error. Even allowing for some genetic adaptation, a sustained increase in water temperatures of as little as a couple of degrees Fahrenheit can result in widespread coral reef destruction in just a few years.

A number of factors are already contributing to the destruction of coral reefs, and global warming is one of them. As the earth's temperature continues to rise, global warming will most likely become the chief enemy of what Dr. Oppenheimer calls "these wonderful sources of biological diversity."

The threat to coral reefs is clear and indisputable. Much less clear is the danger that global warming presents to the West Antarctic Ice Sheet (see "Polar Ice Melt" on page 660).

10 "We really don't know with any level of certainty what amount of warming would destroy the ice sheet or how quickly that would happen," said Dr. Oppenheimer. He and Dr. O'Neill wrote, "In general, the probability is thought

CONTEXT

According to a 2001 study of the effects of global warming by the Intergovernmental Panel on Climate Change (IPCC),

Impacts on highly diverse and productive coastal ecosystems such as coral reefs, atolls and reef islands, salt marshes and mangrove forests will depend upon the rate of sea-level rise relative to growth rates and sediment supply, space for and obstacles to horizontal migration, changes in the climate-ocean environment such as sea surface temperatures and storminess, and pressures from human activities in coastal zones. Episodes of coral bleaching over the past 20 years have been associated with several causes, including increased ocean temperatures. Future sea surface warming would increase stress on coral reefs and result in increased frequency of marine diseases.

New analyses of proxy data for the Northern Hemisphere indicate that the increase in temperature in the 20th century is likely to have been the largest of any century during the past 1,000 years.

POLAR ICE MELT

Scientists have no clear evidence that melting of the Antarctic ice sheet is occurring. However, some recent studies have documented melting of the Arctic ice sheet. In 2002 researchers from the University of Colorado reported that the surface melt on the Greenland ice sheet was the greatest on record. According to a press release from the National Snow and Ice Data Center,

Preliminary measurements from the Greenland Ice Sheet show the melt extent of 265,000 square miles, a new record, underscoring the unusual warming there and surpassing the maximum melt extent from the past 24 years by more than 9 percent, said climatologist Konrad Steffen, a professor in geography and in the Program in Atmospheric and Oceanic Sciences at the University of Colorado. . . .

CU scientists estimate that a change in the Greenland climate toward warmer conditions would lead to an increase in the rate of sea-level rise mainly due to the dynamic response of the large ice sheet and not so much to the surface melting.

For every degree (F) increase in the mean annual temperature near Greenland, the rate of sea level rise increases by about 10 percent," Steffen said. Currently the oceans are rising by a little more than half an inch per decade. In addition, melt water has been shown to directly affect the rate of ice flow off Greenland, penetrating the ice sheet and causing the glaciers to accelerate in speed as they slide over a thin film of melt water.

to be low during this century, increasing gradually thereafter."

There is not even agreement among scientists on the amount of warming necessary to begin the destruction. But what is clear is that if the ice sheet were to disintegrate, the consequences would be profound. So you don't want to play

around with this. You want to make sure it doesn't happen.

"We know," said Dr. Oppenheimer, "that if the ice sheet were destroyed, sea levels would rise about five meters, which would be catastrophic for coastal regions. That would submerge much of Manhattan below Greenwich Village, for instance. It would drown the southern third of Florida, an area inhabited by about four million people."

Five meters is approximately 16 feet. Tremendous amounts of housing, wetlands and farming areas around the world would vanish. Large portions of a country like Bangladesh, on the Bay of Bengal, would disappear.

So what could actually set this potential catastrophe in motion? Dr. Oppenheimer has looked back at past geological epochs. "There is some evidence," he said, "that when the global temperature was warmer by about four degrees Fahrenheit than it is today the ice sheet disintegrated."

15 It is now estimated that if we do nothing to stem the rise of global warming, the increase in the earth's temperature over the course of this century will be between 3 and 10.5 degrees Fahrenheit. That is a level of warming that could initiate the disintegration of the ice sheet. And stopping that disintegration, once the planet gets that warm, may be impossible.

COMPLICATION

In the 1990s, as various studies suggested that the earth's atmosphere was warming, disagreement about the scientific evidence was widespread among scientists as well as policy makers. For example, in 1996, after the widely respected Intergovernmental Panel on Climate Change (IPCC) released a major report concluding that the earth is getting warmer, Frederick Seitz, President Emeritus of Rockefeller University and former president of the National Academy of Sciences, criticized the report as a "deception." He wrote in the *Wall Street Journal*, "this report is not what it appears to be — it is not the version that was approved by the contributing scientists listed on the title page." And he urged policy makers to reject the report's recommendation ("A Major Deception on Global Warming," *Wall Street Journal*, 1996).

In 1997 David Ridenour, vice president of the National Center for Public Policy Research, reviewed several surveys of scientists about their opinions of the evidence for global warming. He concluded that there is "no scientific consensus on global warming" and that available scientific evidence does not support global warming ("The Myth of Scientific Consensus on Global Warming," *National Policy Analysis* #177, 1997). Such disagreements continue today. (For more information on the Intergovernmental Panel on Climate Change, see the margin gloss on the Intergovernmental Panel on Climate Change on page 663 of this chapter.)

Questions for Discussion

1. Why are coral reefs important in the debates about global warming, according to Herbert? What evidence does he provide to support this claim? **2.** How does Herbert establish that global warming is a pressing problem that must be addressed immediately? How convincing do you think his case is that we must act now? **3.** In making his argument, Herbert relies heavily on a study done by scientists Michael Oppenheimer and Brian O'Neill. How might this focus on a single study affect your reaction to Herbert's argument?

4. What counterarguments can you make to Herbert's position on global warming? What factors related to global warming and its impact do you think Herbert fails to account for in his argument? **5.** Evaluate Herbert's use of the example of coral reefs as a strategy for his argument about global warming. In what ways might this example strengthen his argument? Would any other examples have worked better for this purpose?

② R O B E R T C . B A L L I N G , J R . , "The Global Warming Scapegoat"

The sometimes confusing nature of debates about climate change might be related to the complexity of the issue itself. Despite a great deal of scientific research, global warming is not well understood, and scientists continue to disagree about its extent, its causes, its impact, and even whether it is occurring. Moreover, the potential implications of climate change involve extremely complicated social, economic, and environmental effects that no one can really anticipate. No wonder that debates about global warming can be difficult to sort out. But Robert C. Balling, Jr., an expert on climate and geology, believes that the debates themselves are part of the problem. In the following essay, Balling examines how misconceptions about the relationship between climate change and recent weather events, such as hurricanes and tornadoes, leads to misleading press reports about global warming. He argues that the scientific evidence does not support what is often reported in the press. Although he does not dismiss the possibility that the earth's atmosphere is indeed warming, he urges caution in how we make sense of the available scientific data. In this way, his essay might help us to understand better *how* arguments are made when it comes to the issues like global warming. Dr. Robert C. Balling, Jr., is the director of the Office of Climatology and associate professor of geology at Arizona State University (USA). His essay was published by the Policy Network in 2002.

The Global Warming Scapegoat
R O B E R T C . B A L L I N G , J R .

1 Floods in Europe! Hurricanes in the US! Droughts in India! The scapegoat: Global warming, an irrefutable fact which remains unchallenged by any reputable scientist. Governments, bureaucrats and non-governmental organizations recently convened in New Delhi, India, to attempt to stave off these looming environmental catastrophes with discussions and resolutions.

They'll be meeting at the 8th Conference of Parties (COP-8) to the United Nations Framework Convention on Climate Change. A discussion of how countries can deal with an increase in severe weather events due to global warming is on the agenda.

Climate crusaders have utilized individual weather events to buttress their argument that nations must act quickly to prevent death and destruction caused by human-induced global warming. The news media are quick to lap up this claim, treating any extreme weather event — be it hurricane, blizzard, drought or tornado — as more evidence of impending environmental doom.

A 1999 study by Sheldon Ungar of the University of Toronto confirms this phenomenon, indicating that American television viewers are substantially more likely to see coverage of disasters than their counterparts thirty years ago. Such increased coverage leads the viewer to perceive an overall increase in severe storm activity. However, the empirical evidence on actual trends tells a different story.

5 Most scientific analyses of historical severe storm records — including thunderstorms, hail events, intense precipitation, tornadoes, hurricanes, and winter storm activity — show no overall upward trend in severe weather over the past half century. The trends are downward in other severe storm categories, although well within the natural variability of the climate system. In other words, there is a severe mismatch between perception and reality.

Let's look at some examples. First, scientists have examined available tornado data, and have been unable to identify any realistic upward trend in tornado activity. Using historical data collected from 1950 to 2000, no observable trend in severe tornado occurrence is seen over the last fifty years. Tom Grazulis, head of The Tornado Project, notes that "any link of tornado activity with climatic change of any kind should be treated with the greatest skepticism. The ingredients that go into the creation of a tornado are so varied and complex that they could never be an accurate indicator of climate change."

Scientists with the United Nations Intergovernmental Panel on Climate

Change (IPCC)* concurred, saying "No systematic changes in the frequency of tornadoes, thunder days, or hail events are evident in the limited areas analysed."

Another popular misconception relates to the frequency of hurricanes. Media reports often claim that climate scientists believe hurricanes and tropical storms will increase in frequency and intensity as the planet warms in response to elevated concentrations of greenhouse gases.

Yet the many scientists who have examined selected hurricane records over the past century have found no upward trend. Some found declining levels of tropical storm frequency and intensity in the specific types of tropical cyclones they examined. Robert M. Wilson, a research scientist at the National Atmospheric and Space Agency in Alabama, examined intense hurricanes in the Atlantic Basin over the period 1950

*Established by the United Nations in 1988, the Intergovernmental Panel on Climate Change (IPCC) evaluates scientific, technical, and socioeconomic information in order to understand human-induced climate change. The IPCC does not conduct research; rather, it reviews and synthesizes existing research for its reports. While it is respected as an important source of information about climate change, it has been subject to controversy as well. (See Complication on page 660 in this chapter.)

CONTEXT

Balling's essay was published by the International Policy Network, which describes itself as

a non-profit, non-governmental organisation whose mission is to encourage the sharing of ideas by intellectuals and others interested in public policy issues, especially those having international implications. . . . The mission of International Policy Network is to "share ideas that free people". We believe that people around the world would be better off if they were governed not by overbearing autocrats or unaccountable bureaucrats, but by the institutions of the free society — property rights, the rule of law, free markets and free speech. (Where regulations are necessary, we believe they should be based on sound science and good economics.)

To what extent is Balling's argument consistent with this mission?

to 1998, and found a decreasing trend, with fewer intense hurricanes during warmer periods.

10 The IPCC's view on tropical storms was that "Changes globally in tropical and extra-tropical storm intensity and frequency are dominated by inter-decadal and multi-decadal variations, with no significant trends evident over the 20th century."

The same applies to blizzards, extra-tropical cyclones, and winter storms: overall, there appears to be no upward trend in severe weather over the past half century. Many scientists have identified an increase in heavy precipitation, but this observation is consistent with models that show an invigorated hydrological cycle in a world warmed by greenhouse gas buildup. What may be observed in coming years is an increase in absolute damage caused by such events, because people are living closer to areas that are more prone to storm activity.

There is considerable concern about future climate change and potential impacts on severe storms. General circulation model simulations do exist that suggest an increase in greenhouse gas concentration could significantly warm the planet and create an environment more favorable for severe storms over mid-latitude continental areas.

Nonetheless, the typical doomsday presentation regarding global warming often ignores or distorts crucial facts found in reports of the UN's Intergovernmental Panel on Climate Change.

Most scientists would agree that present-day numerical climate models (because of their low spatial resolution and poor quality of input data) have substantial limitations with regard to predicting future changes in severe weather events in any specific region of the planet, and their results should be interpreted with caution. Ultimately, weather patterns are only one part of a very complicated debate about the potential effects of higher greenhouse gas concentrations.

Woven together with increased news coverage of disasters, and a public audience prone to pay attention to bad news, the models and empirical data are often manipulated to rally support for misguided policies that would have little impact on greenhouse gas concentrations, and whose climate impact would be undetectable for many decades to come.

15 Though climate crusaders during COP-8 in New Delhi are likely to argue otherwise, uncertainty and disagreement still characterize the climate change debate. Many scientists agree that current proposed policies would actually have little impact, even if the public believes otherwise.

Questions for Discussion

1. Evaluate the effectiveness of Balling's introduction to his argument. How well do you think his opening paragraph introduces his subject? In what ways does it set the tone for his argument? Do you think his introduction enhances or weakens his argument? Explain. **2.** Balling claims that recent weather events, such as severe tropical storms or tornadoes, do not by themselves indicate the existence of global climate change. What evidence does he present to support that claim? How convincing is this evidence? **3.** Does Balling completely reject the view that global climate change might be occurring? If not, what is his primary concern in this essay when it comes to debates about climate change? Support your answer by citing specific passages from his essay. **4.** Examine Balling's use of language in this essay. How does his language contribute to his tone? In what ways do you think his use of language strengthens or weakens his argument? Cite specific passages from his essay to support your answer. **5.** How does Balling portray the public in this essay? Do you think his portrayal is accurate? Why or why not? How might his portrayal of the public enhance or weaken his argument? **6.** In a sense, Balling's essay can be described as an argument about arguments about global climate change. In what ways do you think his essay can contribute to public debates about climate change?

③ KWEGSI, "Injustice? Duress and the Burnt Church First National Fisheries Agreement with Canada"

In the latter part of the 20th century the stocks of many species of fish were found to have declined dramatically as a result of overfishing. During that same period international pressure effectively ended whaling, which had depleted whale populations worldwide. But as governments signed agreements with each other that were intended to protect the world's natural resources and wildlife, the rights of native peoples were often overlooked. Some Native American tribes in Alaska, Minnesota, and Washington, for example, found themselves unable to engage in traditional whaling or other fishing practices because of international environmental agreements or because of national laws. In some cases native peoples sought help through the court systems of the same governments that had taken away their rights in the first place. One such case emerged in Canada, which, like the United States, has long experienced conflict between its government and its native peoples, who are usually referred to as First Nations. In the 1990s the Esgenoôpetitj, or Burnt Church, First Nation of Nova Scotia found themselves fighting to retain their traditional fishing and lobstering rights in the face of confusing legal decisions and violent attacks by nonnative residents. In the following essay Kwegsi, a leader of the Burnt Church First Nation, discusses this conflict, arguing that it is another instance of a longstanding effort by the Canadian government to deny First Nation peoples their rights. His essay, which was published in the *Turtle Island Native Network News* in 2002, reminds us of how difficult it can be to determine how to share the earth among so many diverse peoples.

Injustice? Duress and the Burnt Church First National Fisheries Agreement with Canada
KWEGSI

1 Merriam-Webster's Collegiate Dictionary defines Duress as forcible restraint or restriction, compulsion by threat; specifically: unlawful constraint or coercion.

I am a Hereditary Chief of the Mi'kmaq Grand Council. I am also a member of Esgenoôpetitj community. Non-natives know us as Burnt Church First Nation. There was recently an agreement signed concerning lobster fishing between the federal government of Canada and the Band Council appointed under the Indian Act to act as Indian Agents on our reserve.

The Mi'kmaq have been exercising the

right to fish, hunt, gather and harvest since time immemorial. What the Euro-Canadians have failed to see is that these rights were not based on the covenant chain of treaties that were made between the crown, Mi'kmaq, and other nations, but rather the peace and friendship treaties. These treaties identified the inherent right to fish, gather, and harvest. They identified and clarified boundaries for the foreigners specifically their involvement with Indians, in order to maintain peace. The Crown and its subjects were forbidden to interfere with Indians in their natural habitat. Belchers Proclamation on May 4, 1762 and the Royal Proclamation of 1763 restated this fact.*

Before the ink dried, the crown started violating these treaties. The Mi'kmaq continued to honor the treaties that were made in the name of peace, and at no time surrendered or ceded territory, government, or the inherent right to sustain themselves. However, the occupiers/squatters have done nothing but to try to starve the Indian out of his existence by denying him what is rightfully his.

5 To keep peace, when denied our inherent right, we took it to Euro-Canadian

---

CONTEXT

In 1993 Donald Marshall of the Burnt Church First Nation in Nova Scotia was arrested for violating fishing laws. He argued in court that treaties signed between his people and the British Crown in the 18th century entitled him to practice traditional fishing. The Supreme Court of Canada eventually ruled in his favor in 1999, a decision that provoked protest among nonnative fishers and eventually led to violence. Subsequently, the Canadian Department of Fisheries and Oceans (DFO) implemented several policies that intensified the controversy. In 2000 the DFO tried to reach a sweeping agreement on fishing rights with thirty-four First Nation bands. However, five of those bands, including Kwegsi's Burnt Church band, refused to sign the agreement, claiming that it compromised their rights as Native peoples. Despite not having signed the agreement, Burnt Church First Nation members continued to set lobster traps and fish, claiming that right under older treaties. As a result, they continued to suffer DFO sanctions. As of 2002 the Burnt Church band still had not signed the agreement.

---

courts to find a solution. This turned out to be one of the biggest mistakes my people ever made. For those making the judgments were more than willing to change the laws and turn them against my people.

One example is the Donald Marshall ruling which was made by the Supreme Court of Canada in 1999. This ruling affirmed the Mi'kmaq right to fish, hunt, gather, and harvest. The judgment came down as if it were a treaty right when in all reality; it was and is an inherent right. After the court had made the ruling, we once again came under attack when we tried to exercise our rights. The first assault by non-native fishermen and then by the government agents themselves under the Department of Fisheries and Oceans.[†] As the pressure began mounting from these attacks, Mi'kmaq and Maliseet communities started signing agreements with the government. These agreements deny the Mi'kmaq the right to make a living, or provide for their families.

My community of Burnt Church felt that this right was meant not just for the individual, but for the entire Mi'kmaq Nation and especially for our community. We decided to develop our own commu-

---

*The Belchers Proclamation and the Royal Proclamation were signed in 1762 and 1763, respectively, by the British Crown, which at the time controlled all of what is now Canada and the eastern United States, and by several Native American tribes living in those regions. These treaties guaranteed that the Native peoples would retain control of lands they claimed as traditionally theirs.

†The Canadian Department of Fisheries and Oceans (DFO) regulates fishing in Canadian waters.

nity-based management plan in harvesting fish. This plan was reviewed and highly supported by conservation and environmentalist groups.

Violence began as soon as we decided not to sign away our rights. Our gear was cut out in the waters, costing my community over $200,000. The government began seizing traps, ramming our boats, and assaulting my people in the waters. Charges were brought up against my people for obstruction, assault, and once again illegal fishing. No charges were ever laid against those who destroyed and seized our traps, assaulted our people, and rammed our boats.

The government utilized an addendum to the ruling by doing a study on what might threaten conservation. They went to the courts and lied, stating that according to their study any additional fishing would jeopardize the stock. Thus, conservation became a just cause to stop Indians from exercising the right to fish. What they deliberately failed to mention to the courts was that within our management plan we would have only had 2% of what the non-natives were already currently fishing. They also didn't mention that the Indian fishery did not cause some of the increase in the lobster fishery, but rather non-natives poaching the lobster with no regard for undersized or berried lobster.

10 The DFO started buying out licenses from the non-native fishermen to make room for the Indians. A specified amount was set aside for my community. We declined these licenses and went with our plan, a plan based on conservation to protect the species for the seventh generation of yet unborn. We refused to subject ourselves to a fisheries act with a bad conservation track record. For example, depletion of the cod and salmon industry and placing over 300 other species

at risk. Since we did not accept the licenses, they sat idle, so in no way did lobster fishery increase. With our management plan we realized that with what had been allotted to our community, only 75% would have been utilized. Instead of going with the maximum usage the way the DFO proposed, we would have conserved 25%.

The government's approach, as before, has been to "negotiate" agreements with poverty stricken Indian communities and by carefully wording the agreements and offering monies, they devised a way to deceitfully take away the rights of the Mi'kmaq people. The latest agreement was signed by a small number of Band Council people, its Indian Agents, in a room without even a lawyer present to advise them. This new fishery agreement is already being represented as a historic breakthrough.

The agreement was entered into under duress. The government of Canada used our hunger and poverty, violence against us, our vulnerable position, the threats of the Crown, the charges against all of our people who were defending our rights, as coercion against us. All this was used to get our people to "agree" to a fishery agreement that the community did not want.

The United Nations Human Rights Committee* has ruled that the extinguishment of our aboriginal and treaty rights is violation of fundamental human rights. History will show this present injustice and it will be said that the Mi'kmaq people signed under great duress. Peace cannot arise out of injustice and no "certainty" can result from the imposing of an unequal agreement. The Crown, and Canadians, will get no lasting benefit from these "deals" involving the annihilation of our rights, except the despair and resentment of generations of our children and people.

*Since 1995 the United Nations Human Rights Committee has overseen a special initiative intended to monitor the well-being of indigenous peoples around the world. It offers several programs to aid such peoples in their efforts to preserve their cultural heritage.

Questions for Discussion

1. Why does Kwegsi distinguish among the various treaties between his people, the Canadians, and the British Crown? How does this distinction contribute to his main argument? **2.** Kwegsi argues that the Canadian courts did not protect the rights of his people in their fishing dispute. How does he support this claim? **3.** How did concerns about the environment and the local fishing stocks become a weapon against the Burnt Church people, according to Kwegsi? What might this development suggest about the relationship among the environment, the law, and cultural diversity? **4.** This essay was published in the *Turtle Island Native Network News,* a publication that is intended primarily for native peoples. In what ways do you think this essay is appropriate for such an audience? Do you think Kwegsi's argument would be effective for a broader Canadian audience? Do you think he intended it to be? Explain, citing passages from his essay to support your answer. **5.** In what ways do you think Kwegsi's strategies for argument in this essay might reflect his cultural heritage? (In answering this question, you might refer to the discussion of cultural context in Chapter 3 on pages 58–64.)

④ BARUN MITRA, "Stop Energy Eco-Imperialism"

In many ways the following essay by Indian writer and free market advocate Barun Mitra brings together several of the themes addressed in this chapter and elsewhere in this book: free trade, environmental protection, the idea of the commons, and globalization. Like many of the other writers in this chapter, Mitra is concerned about the effects of globalization on the health of the environment, especially in his native India. But he is convinced that what is good for the economy is also good for the environment, and he argues vigorously in favor of free market policies that, he believes, will lead to economic growth in developing nations such as India. Mitra rejects the efforts of Western activists who claim to support environmental protection in developing nations, calling such activism "eco-imperialism." In his view, people in developing nations such as India should have access to the same economic benefits that are available to industrialized nations such as the United States. His essay reminds us of the diversity of interests that must be accommodated when we are trying to decide how to share the earth. A former engineer, Barun Mitra is the president of the Liberty Institute, a think tank that advocates free market policies, in New Delhi, India. This essay was published in *Policy Analysis* in November 2002.

Stop Energy Eco-Imperialism
BARUN MITRA

1 Does Anita Roddick* warm her home with cow or buffalo manure? No? Then why is the Body Shop owner telling poor rural Indians that they should choose outdated and dangerous energy sources instead of the modern electricity that she and many of her do-gooder counterparts in organisations like Greenpeace use?

Though British consumers have yet to make dung warming stoves the "must have" heating source this season, Greenpeace and The Body Shop's

Choose Positive Energy campaign, urges developing countries to "Choose Positive Energy" since "Oil, coal and gas cannot meet the needs of the poorest, but 'positive' or renewable energy can. Renewable energy technologies are the most appropriate, affordable, reliable and environmentally friendly."

European governments, third-world bureaucrats, businesses such as The Body Shop and the European Wind Energy Association, and NGOs such as

Greenpeace, have decided that 'renewable energy' and 'clean development' are the future for third world countries. At the World Summit on Sustainable Development,[†] this coalition lobbied for renewable energy targets. These same groups will also be attending this week's United Nations Framework Convention on Climate Change[‡] meetings in Delhi, to discuss actions by governments to avoid the risk of a warmer climate in about 100 years.

But while the coalition focuses on preventing the hypothetical, long-run risk of climate change, they have conspicuously ignored the real risks that poor people face today. The immediate need of poor people in India and other poor countries is to consume more energy, in any form. Likewise, India's economy needs reliable, cheap energy of any kind to fuel economic growth and improved quality of life.

5 It is estimated that about 95 percent of India's rural population already relies on one form of renewable energy: biomass. Firewood, agricultural residues, or cow and buffalo manure which is made into pats, dried, and stored — all are burned inside homes in inefficient, poorly-flued stoves called chulhas, which have inadequate ventilation. Around the world, about 2 billion people rely on such fuels.

The human health, economic, and environmental impact of burning these 'renewable' fuels is immense. Young children and women spend hours each day in the drudgery of collecting firewood or collecting, drying, and storing manure for use in cooking, heat, or light

> **CONTEXT**
>
> A joint effort of the environmental advocacy group Greenpeace and the Body Shop, the Choose Positive Energy Campaign has two primary goals: to encourage world leaders to support the development of renewable energy for the world's poor and to encourage all people to use renewable energy in their homes and workplaces. (See www.choose-positive-energy.org.)

— rather than attending school or engaging in more satisfying or productive economic activity. Most homes in rural villages are not connected to an electrical grid and remain dark at night. The refrigerators, televisions, and computers that environmentalists take for granted are not to be seen here.

While environmentalists fret about the effects of air pollution caused by the burning of fossil fuels, the risk that poor people face is indoor air pollution. The World Health Organization says that indoor air pollution is linked to 4.3 million childhood deaths worldwide each year — primarily from respiratory illnesses such as pneumonia. Burning biomass also contributes to asthma and lung cancer, particularly in women.

Likewise, the unsustainable cutting of firewood on marginal lands leads to erosion and environmental degradation. The burning of wood in urban areas contributes to air pollution. If biomass were to be used for major energy production, many millions of acres of vegetation and trees would be cleared.

Energy poverty is directly related to economic poverty, and India's national and state governments have engaged in prolonging both types by inhibiting development of new energy sources, over-regulating existing energy supplies, and unnecessarily intervening in energy markets.

10 At the same time, they have focused on promoting renewable energy, rather than cleaner forms of energy, including gas, coal, hydro, oil and nuclear. These forms of energy are far cheaper than so-

[*]A British entrepreneur, human rights activist, and environmentalist, Anita Roddick founded The Body Shop, which produces a line of popular cosmetics products. She is perhaps as well known in Great Britain for her antiglobalization activism as for her successful business, which, according to its mission statement, dedicates itself "to the pursuit of social and environmental change."

[†]Organized by the United Nations in Johannesburg, South Africa in 2002, the World Summit on Sustainable Development brought together political and business leaders as well as representatives from nongovernmental organizations to discuss environmental and economic issues and to examine the challenges of sustainable development in the coming decades.

[‡]For more information on the U.N. Framework Convention on Climate Change, see the introduction to this cluster on page 656.

IS RENEWABLE ENERGY VIABLE?

"The price at which an electric power plant can supply electricity depends principally on two factors: the capital costs of the plant (including investments in land, machinery and civil works) and running or operational costs (including salaries and raw material costs). Needless to say, the higher the two cost elements, the less competitive, the source will be. Renewable sources take a beating on both fronts. More than eighteen thousand villages in India still need to be electrified, many of them in remote areas far from the grid. Save a few demonstration projects entirely bankrolled by the government, why have rural communities not installed renewable energy projects which could light up these villages? The capital costs are too high, way beyond the capacity of even small businessmen to finance, forget about impoverished rural communities. Renewable energy sources usually fail to deliver economies of scale, resulting in high capital costs. Except wind energy, capital costs of all other renewables are far higher than fossil fuels." Source: Satanu Guru, "Renewable Energy Sources in India: Is It Viable?" Julian Simon Centre for Policy Research (2002).

lar and wind power in nearly all contexts and become cheaper as demand increases which would happen as India's economy develops, and as companies take advantage of economies of scale. So far, this has not happened in India.

The indirect effect of other regulations and restrictions has also impacted energy development in India. Foreign investment regulations have discouraged companies from bringing new technologies and capital to India. The legal system provides no clear enforcement of contracts, leading companies to engage in shady deals with government. The Enron scandal in Maharashtra, India, was one such example — the pure product of a company cavorting with government, characterized by a lack of transparency.

In a new working paper published the Liberty Institute, Sutanu Guru shows that government's failure to allow a free energy market means that industries install their own generating capacity because they cannot get enough energy to run their plants and factories — "power cuts, load shedding and grid failures are common occurrences all over India." While wealthier consumers are able to insulate themselves from erratic electricity with diesel generators, and inverters, poorer consumers simply go without electricity.

At the behest of green NGOs and international pressure, India's government and bureaucrats have decided that renewable energy is deserving of subsidies, grants, international aid money, and tax breaks. Companies that invest in 'renewable' energy sources such as windmills get a 100 percent, one-year depreciation scheme from the Indian government, and a five-year income tax holiday. In Tamil Nadu during 1995–96, dozens of companies used this income tax break and accelerated depreciation to avoid paying any tax on income derived from other sources entirely.

Guru's research indicates that "Government largesse to renewable energy is comprehensive, widespread, and highly attractive. . . . A majority of wind energy projects in India have come up mainly to cash in on these tax breaks. Electric power generation is a secondary — and often neglected — priority." **15** Reduced economic productivity, increased human suffering and loss of life, and negative environmental consequences all result from current reliance on 'renewable' energy. For India's poor rural people, efficient, reliable energy remains a dream rather than a reality.

Sadly, they will probably continue to suffer because of market interventions by the Indian government, and at the hands of environmental elitists from wealthy countries who believe that poor people must not have the same opportunities to grow and develop as the first world did.

This week in Delhi, third world governments should reject eco-imperialism from NGOs, first world governments, and international agencies. The poor citizens of the world have everything to gain from more energy consumption, and nothing to lose but their poverty.

Questions for Discussion

1. Mitra begins his essay with a reference to Anita Roddick, a well-known anti-globalization activist in Great Britain (see the margin gloss on Anita Roddick and the Body Shop on page 671). What does this reference tell you about Mitra's intended audience? Do you think his argument would be less effective for readers who are unfamiliar with Roddick? Explain. **2.** What specific concerns does Mitra have about renewable energy sources for the world's poor, especially the use of biomass as a fuel? What evidence does he supply to support these concerns? How convincing do you think his evidence is? How does his use of evidence compare to that of the other writers in this cluster? **3.** In what ways would a free energy market help address the problem of poverty in developing nations such as India, according to Mitra? On what fundamental principles does he base these claims? Do you think most people who would be affected by his proposals would share Mitra's belief in these principles? Explain. **4.** How does Mitra refer to environmental activists? What does his references to such activists reveal about his own views regarding environmental protection? In what ways do you think his references to environmental activists might strengthen or weaken his argument?

5. Mitra's essay was published in *Policy Analysis*, which is published by an organization that advocates free markets (see Context on page 673 in this chapter). What characteristics of Mitra's essay indicate that he was making his argument for readers who share this free market perspective? Do you think Mitra hoped to persuade readers who might oppose such a free market view? Explain.

NEGOTIATING DIFFERENCES

The essays in this cluster suggest that the question of how we should share the earth is a global one. But these essays also reveal that global environmental problems are also local ones. Kwegsi's essay focuses on how the need to share fishing resources can lead to difficulties in a specific local context — with its particular characteristics and challenges. Similarly, Barun Mitra's argument is really about how people in the rural villages of India will meet the challenge of finding energy sources. If the old saying that "all politics is local" is true, it might also be true that all environmental problems are local.

With that in mind, identify what you think is the most pressing environmental problem facing your community. You can define *community* in a variety of ways for this assignment: your neighborhood or town, the region of the country where you live, your college campus, even your dormitory or apartment. However you define the community of interest to you, you should identify an environmental issue that affects it in some significant way. Explore that issue, trying to learn what you can about it. Then write an essay in which you make an argument that is intended to offer what you believe is a viable solution to that problem. Direct your essay at an audience of people in your community (perhaps as an editorial for your local newspaper). In your essay, be sure to define the problem clearly and explain why it is a significant one. Support your proposed solution as effectively as you can, drawing on your research and relying on what you see as the fundamental principles related to the question of how we should share the earth. (For one kind of model for this assignment, read Kristen Brubaker's essay about a factory hog farm in her community on page 140.)

TEXT CREDITS

PHOTO
CREDITS

Cover: Mario Tama/Getty Images

Inside Front Cover: UN/DPI Photo

Chapter 1: p. 8: AFP/Corbis; **p. 13:** Bryan Mitchell/Getty Images; **p. 19:** Carl Rogers Memorial Library; **p. 20:** John Li/Getty Images

Chapter 2: p. 22: Jeff Cadge/Image Bank/Getty Images; **p. 48:** Ezra Shaw/Getty Images

Chapter 3: p. 52: AFP/Corbis

Chapter 4: p. 68: Brendan Smialowski/Getty Images; **p. 71:** Bettmann Archive/Corbis; **p. 83:** Ken Lambert/AP Wide World; **p. 84:** Evan Agostini/Getty Images; **p. 89: top right:** Archivo Iconografico, S.A./CORBIS; **p. 89:** Tyler Hicks/New York Times; **p. 90:** Copyright Ball State University Museum of Art, Muncie, Indiana. Used with permission. Thomas Cole, American, born England (1801-1848), Storm King of the Hudson, circa 1825-1827, oil on linen canvas, 23 in. x 32 in. Ball State University Museum of Art, Muncie, Indiana, Frank C. Ball Collection, partial gift and promised gift of the Ball Brothers Foundation, 1995.035.055; **p. 91:** Minneapolis Institute of Arts, The Modernism Collection, gift of Norwest Bank Minnesota; **p. 96:** Maurice Hornocker/Hornocker Wildlife Institute;

Chapter 5: p. 112: Robert King/Getty Images;

Chapter 6: p. 150: Yellow Dog Productions/The Image Bank/Getty Images;

Chapter 7: p. 178: 2003 John Coletti Photography

Chapter 8: p. 210: Justin Sullivan/Getty Images; **p. 215:** Bill Bachmann/PhotoEdit; **p. 216:** Tom Stewart/Corbis; **p. 220:** Najlah Feanny-Hicks/Corbis; **p. 224:** Warner Brothers/The Kobal Collection; **p. 226:** Jose Fuste Raga/Corbis; **p. 236:** Robert Brenner/PhotoEdit; **p. 238:** Michael Newman/PhotoEdit; **p. 241:** Lester Lefkositz/Corbis; **p. 243:** Ariel Skelly/Corbis; **p. 247:** Najlah Feanny-Hicks/Corbis; **p. 251:** Reuters NewMedia Inc./Corbis; **p. 258:** top, Bonnie Kamin/PhotoEdit; bottom, Scott Gries/Getty Images; **p. 263:** AP Photo/Amir Shah; **p. 265:** Tony Freeman/PhotoEdit; **p. 270:** Scott Gries/Getty Images; **p. 271:** Michael Newman/PhotoEdit; **p. 275:** Richard Hutchings/PhotoEdit

Chapter 9: p. 280: Kim Kulish/SABA/Corbis; **p. 285:** Royalty-Free/Corbis; **p. 291:** Michael Pole/Corbis; **p. 297:** Spencer Grant/PhotoEdit; **p. 302:** Cindy Charles/PhotoEdit; **p. 310:** Bryn Colton/Assignments Photographers/Corbis; **p. 313:** Tony Freeman/PhotoEdit; **p. 314:** Eric Fowke/PhotoEdit; **p. 318:** Jose Luis Pelaez, Inc./Corbis; **p. 320:** Spencer Grant/PhotoEdit; **p. 330:** Dennis Brack/IPN/Aurora; **p. 333:** Rob Lewine/Corbis; **p. 340:** Gallo Images/Corbis; **p. 343:** Lee Snider/Corbis; **p. 344:** Richard T. Nowitz/Corbis; **p. 350:** Charles Gupton/Corbis; **p. 358:** Bill Pugliano/Getty Images

Chapter 10: p. 362: Taxi/Getty Images; **p. 367:** Bettmann/Corbis; **p. 369:** Reuters NewMedia Inc./Corbis; **p. 372:** Roger Lemoyne/Getty Images; **p. 376:** Lester Lefkowitz/Corbis; **p. 377:** Lee Snider/Corbis; **p. 385:** Royalty-Free/Corbis; **p. 399:** Mark E. Gibson/Corbis; **p. 403:** Royalty-Free/Corbis; **p. 404:** Andrew Lichtenstein/Aurora; **p. 407:** Royalty-Free/Corbis; **p. 408:** Royalty-Free/Corbis; **p. 414:** Hulton/Archive/Getty Images; **p. 415:** Wes Thompson/Corbis; **p. 422:** Justin Sullivan/Getty Images; **p. 423:** James Shaffer/PhotoEdit; **p. 425:** Bettmann/Corbis; **p. 429:** Cary Anderson/Aurora; **p. 434:** Peter Essick/Aurora; **p. 438:** Layne Kennedy/Corbis; **p. 445:** Robin Prange/Corbis; **p. 446:** Terry W. Eggers/Corbis

Chapter 11: p. 448: AFP/Scott Olson/Corbis; **p. 451:** PhotoDisc/Getty Images; **p. 454:** AFP/Scott Olson/Corbis; **p. 460:** Robert Essel NYC/Corbis; **p. 461:** Davis Barber/PhotoEdit; **p. 465:** David McNew/Getty Images; **p. 466:** A. Ramey/PhotoEdit; **p. 469:** Bettmann/Corbis; **p. 470:** Will Hart/PhotoEdit; **p. 483:** Peter Turnley/Corbis; **p. 484:** Reuters NewMedia Inc./Corbis; **p. 491:** left, Archivo Iconografico, S.A./CORBIS; right, Bettman Archive/Corbis; **p. 492:** Painting by Fletcher C. Ransom/Hulton Archive/Getty Images; **p. 498:** Amy Etra/PhotoEdit; **p. 502:** Reuters NewMedia Inc./Gregg Newton/Corbis; **p. 509:** Bettman/Corbis; **p. 512:** Bettman/Corbis; **p. 523:** Reuters NewMedia Inc./Rickey Rogers/Corbis; **p. 529:** AFP/Mark Leffingwell/Corbis

Chapter 12: p. 532: David Turnley/Corbis; **p. 537:** Powerstock/Index Stock; **p. 540:** left, Hulton Archive/Getty Images; right, Hulton Archive/Getty Images; **p. 542:** Hulton Archive/Getty Images; **p. 547:** top, Kobal Collection/20th Century Fox/Morton, Merrick; bottom, Kobal Collection/Dreamworks/Jinks/Cohen/Sebastian,Lorey; **p. 548:** Digital Vision/Getty Images; **p. 554:** Johnathan Nourok/PhotoEdit; **p. 563:** Mark Richards/PhotoEdit; **p. 565:** Eric Sander/Getty Images; **p. 568:** David Young-Wolff/PhotoEdit; **p. 570:** Cathy Melloan Resources/PhotoEdit; **p. 573:** Michael Newman/PhotoEdit; **p. 574:** Getty Images; **p. 577:** Tony Freeman/PhotoEdit; **p. 590:** Mark Richards/PhotoEdit; **p. 591:** Per-Anders Pettersson/Getty Images; **p. 598:** Gene J. Puskar-Pool/Getty Images; **p. 599:** Robert Brenner/PhotoEdit

Chapter 13: p. 607: David McNew/Getty Images; **p. 612:** David Young-Wolff; **p. 614:** Rick Ergenbright/Corbis; **p. 621:** Bonnie Kamin/PhotoEdit; **p. 623:** Richard Lord/PhotoEdit; **p. 629:** James Keivom/Newsmakers/Getty Images; **p. 637:** Paul Conklin/PhotoEdit; **p. 643:** Spencer Grant/PhotoEdit; **p. 644:** Paul Conklin/PhotoEdit; **p. 648:** Cathy Melloan Resources/PhotoEdit; **p. 652:** Cindy Charles/PhotoEdit; **p. 653:** John Hoagland/Liaison/Getty Images; **p. 658:** Stephen Frink/Corbis; **p. 659:** Anna Zukerman-Vdovenko/PhotoEdit; **p. 663:** Photodisc/Getty; **p. 672:** Doug Plummer/SuperStock; **p.** Adrian Arbib/Corbis

INDEX

A

C